Virgil, Robert C. Singleton

Virgil in English Rhythm

With Illustrations from the British Poets, from Chaucer to Cowper. Second Edition

Virgil, Robert C. Singleton

Virgil in English Rhythm
With Illustrations from the British Poets, from Chaucer to Cowper. Second Edition

ISBN/EAN: 9783337179236

Printed in Europe, USA, Canada, Australia, Japan

Cover: Foto ©Thomas Meinert / pixelio.de

More available books at **www.hansebooks.com**

VIRGIL

IN

ENGLISH RHYTHM.

WITH ILLUSTRATIONS FROM THE BRITISH POETS, FROM CHAUCER TO COWPER.

BY THE

REV. ROBERT CORBET SINGLETON, M.A.,
FIRST WARDEN OF ST. PETER'S COLLEGE, RADLEY.

A MANUAL FOR MASTER AND SCHOLAR.

"Hic illa ducis Melibœi
Parva Philoctetæ subnixa Petelia muro."—Æn. III., 401, 2.

"Sweet Poetry's
A flow'r, where men, like bees and spiders, may
Bear poison, or else sweets and wax, away:
Be venom-drawing spiders they that will,
I'll be the bee, and suck the honey still."
BEAUMONT AND FLETCHER, *Four Plays in One.*

SECOND EDITION,
RE-WRITTEN AND ENLARGED.

LONDON:
BELL AND DALDY, YORK STREET, COVENT GARDEN.
1871.

LONDON:
PRINTED BY WILLIAM CLOWES AND SONS, STAMFORD STREET
AND CHARING CROSS.

PREFATORY REMARKS.

IT would scarcely seem to need any proof that, when the work of a Poet is to be translated from one language into another, the poetic character should still be observed; nor is it less obvious that, if the object of the undertaking is the benefit of the youthful scholar, the strictest regard should be had to accuracy in the process. Further, it would appear to be quite indispensable that, whatever may be the design of the operation, easy numbers in the original should be represented by harmonious arrangement in the version.

How far any free Translation can be of real service in the case of the more advanced student, is a question with which the Author of the following attempt has no present concern, as he designs his book for the advantage of those to whom such freedom would, in his opinion, be a positive injury; for his object has been to afford assistance to the classical Teacher in the instruction of his young disciples, and to these latter all such laxness would surely be a serious evil. It is for this reason that, in producing VIRGIL in a new English dress for their benefit, he has endeavored to combine the three great requisites already alluded to—rigid exactness, poetic diction, and rhythmical flow.

In carrying out this design, the Author has thought it necessary to submit to certain restrictions, from which had he relieved himself, his work would have lost in usefulness, though he would have gained by increased facility in the execution of it. For instance, among other reasons, with a view to facilitate the process of construing, the Latin words have been rendered according to the order in which they appear in the original, so far at least as seemed consistent with a necessary regard to the English idiom, and the reasonable requirements of the rhythm. Then, again, no single word in the Latin has ever been consciously passed over without the supply of its English equivalent. Further, it has often happened that a passage might have been rendered much more effective by the employment of words different from those which have been used; yet, notwithstanding the temptation to introduce them, they have been rejected, simply because fidelity to the Latin demanded others.

Were it not, indeed, for such ties as these, the present work, instead of being a close Translation for the schoolboy, might with much less of trouble have been turned into a Poem for the general reader. Still, though it is not intended for the latter class, it is only fair to observe that any one who desires to see in English what VIRGIL says in his own tongue, will probably find him presented here in as agreeable a form as that of any prose version, which should aim at equal faithfulness, and be fettered by the same restrictions.

The Translation is accompanied by copious extracts from the British Poets from an early date down to the beginning of the present century. This has been done, not only to meet the tastes of those for whom parallelisms have a great attraction, but also to impart to the young student a love for English poetry itself, by introducing him to its greatest masters, whose remains are conspicuous for their genius, beauty, and power.

YORK, *June* 1. 1871.

THE ECLOGUES.

Eclogue I. TITYRUS.

MELIBŒUS. TITYRUS.

Melibœus. Thou, Tityrus, reclining underneath
A canopy of widely-spreading beech,
Thy woodland song upon the slender pipe
Dost practise; we our patrimony's bourns,
And charming fields, are leaving; native land
We fly: thou, Tit'rus, easy in the shade,
Dost teach the woods with Amaryll the fair
To ring.
    Tityrus.   O, Melibœus, 'tis a god
These restful hours for us hath gained.
    For he
Shall ever be a god to me: his altar oft 10
A tender lambkin from our folds shall steep.
He hath allowed my kine to rove at large—
As thou perceivest—and myself to play
What [airs] I list upon my rural reed.
    Mel. In sooth I envy not; I marvel more:

Through the whole country round to such extent
Confusion reigns. Lo! I [these] female goats
Myself am driving onward, sick at heart;
This, too, with effort, Tityrus, I lead.
For here, among the clustered hazel-shrubs,
Twins having yeaned but now, my hope of flock, 21
Alas! she left them on the naked flint.
Oft this mischance to us—had not my wit
Been stupid—I remember that the oaks,
Blasted from heav'n, foretold; [this] oft foretold
The luckless crow from out the hollow holm.
But ne'ertheless, that deity of thine
Who may he be, impart, O Tityrus,
To us.
    Tit. The city which they title "Rome,"
O Melibœus, I, a simpleton, 30
Deemed like to this of ours, whither oft
We shepherds are accustomed down to drive
The ewes' soft offspring. So I knew that whelps
Were like to dogs, so kidlings to their dams;
So with the petty to compare the great
Was I accustomed. But as high hath this
'Mong other cities lifted up her head,

Line 3-5. The complaint of Melibœus somewhat resembles that of Colin in Spenser's *Shepheard's Calender*, June 13-16:
"Thy lovely layes here maist thou freely boste;
But I, unhappie man! whom cruell Fate
And angrie gods pursue from coste to coste,
Can no where finde to shroude my luckless pate."
Elsewhere Colin follows the example of Tityrus, but surpasses his prototype; *Colin Clout*, 636:
"The speaking woods, and murmuring waters fall,
Her name I'll teach in known termes to frame;
And eke my lambs, when for their dams they call,
I'll teach to call for Cynthia by name."
Shakespeare, with great beauty:
"Holla your name to the reverberate hills,
And make the babbling gossip of the air
Cry out, 'Olivia!'" *Twelfth Night*, i. 5.
Elsewhere, somewhat differently:
"Bondage is hoarse, and may not speak aloud;
Else would I tear the cave where Echo lies,
And make her airy tongue more hoarse than mine,
With repetition of my Romeo's name."
Romeo and Juliet, ii. 2.
7. J. Fletcher has "Amaryll" for "Amaryllis," where the metre required it; e. g., *The Faithful Shepherdess*, v. 3.

24. "As when Heaven's fire
Hath scath'd the forest oaks, or mountain pines;
With singèd top their stately growth, though bare,
Stands on the blasted heath." Milton, *P. L.*, i.
"My piteous plight in yonder naked tree,
Which bears the thunder-scar, too plain I see;
Quite destitute it stands of shelter kind,
The mark of storms, and sport of every wind."
A. Philips, *Past.* 2.
26. "For did you ever hear the dusky raven
Chide blackness?"
John Webster, *Vittoria Corombona*, v. 1.
36. "Look down, Drusilla, on these lofty towers,
These spacious streets, where every private house
Appears a palace to receive a king:
The site, the wealth, the beauty of the place,
Will soon inform thee 'tis imperious Rome:
Rome, the great mistress of the conquered world."
J. Fletcher, *The Prophetess*, ii. 3.

ECLOGUE I.

v. 26—36.

As cypresses are wont among the lithe
Wayfaring bushes,
  Mel. Pray, what proved to thee
So grave a reason for thy seeing Rome? 40
  Tit. 'Twas Freedom, which, [though]
    late, yet cast a look
Upon an idle man, when once his beard
More silv'ry to the shaver 'gan to fall.
Yet did she look, and after length of time
She came, since us doth Amaryllis own,
[Us] Galatee hath left. For—seeing I
Will it avow—so long as Galatee
Enthralled us, there was neither hope
Of freedom, nor for perquisite concern.
Though many a victim issued from my folds,
And for the thankless city oily cheese 51
Was pressed, ne'er laden with a coin for me,
Did [this] my right hand to my home return.

---

43. *Tendenti,* the "barber," should the reader prefer it: but it may be supposed that a slave would shave his own beard when cash was scarce. A barber would find some difficulty in giving such a spendthrift as Tityrus any credit.

45. Tityrus seems to have been somewhat in the condition of Cowley, if we may judge from his ballad of infinite playfulness, the *Chronicle*; e. g.:
"Mary then, and gentle Anne,
  Both to reign at once began:
Alternately they sway'd;
  And sometimes Mary was the fair,
And sometimes Anne the crown did wear,
  And sometimes both I obeyed."

46. Perhaps it was his own fault, like Thenot's in Fletcher's *Faithful Shepherdess*, iv. 5:
"Oh, hapless love, which, being answered, ends!
And, as a little infant cries and bends
His tender brows, when, rolling of his eye,
He hath espied something that glisters nigh,
Which he would have; yet, give it him, away
He throws it straight, and cries afresh to play
With something else: such my affection, set
On that which I should loathe if I could get."

Perhaps it was Galatea's:
"Go, false one! now I see the cheat:
Your love was all a counterfeit,
And I was galled to think that you,
Or any she, could long be true.
How could you once so kind appear,
To kiss, to sigh, to shed a tear,
To cherish and caress me so,
And now not let, but bid, me go?"
          Charles Cotton, *Sonnet*.

48. "For such a foole I doe him firmly hold,
That loves his fetters, though they were of gold."
          Spenser, *F. Q.*, iii. 9, 8.

51. Tityrus would probably have been dissatisfied with Cicero:
"Should Rome, for whom you've done the happy service,
Turn most ingrate, yet were your virtue paid
In conscience of the fact: so much good deeds
Reward themselves!"
          Ben Jonson, *Catiline*, iii. 2.

52. The cause of Tityrus coming home with empty purse was the same that enriched Autolycus, at the Clown's expense, in Shakespeare's *Winter's Tale*, iv. 3:

---

v. 37—55.

  Mel. I used to marvel, Amaryllis, why,
In sorrow, on the gods thou wouldest call;
For whom thou would'st allow the fruits to hang
Upon their native tree: 'twas Tityrus
Was absent hence. The very pines on thee,
O Tityrus, on thee the very springs,
These very copses called.
  Tit.   What could I do? 60
I neither from my bondage could escape,
Nor elsewhere come to know such kindly gods.
Here I that youth, O Melibœus, saw,
T' whom yearly twice six days our altars smoke;
'Twas here to me, his suppliant, he first
Vouchsafed the answer, "Feed, as hitherto,
Your oxen, O my swains, break in your bulls."
  Mel. O blest old man, then thine thy fields shall bide!
Yea, large enough for thee, though naked stone
May [cover] all, and fen with oozy rush 70
The pastures overlay. No wontless food
Shall harm the breeding females great with young,
Nor scathful contact with a neighbor flock
Shall damage them. O blest old man, thou here,
Amid familiar streams and hallowed springs,
Shalt snatch the shady cool. On hither side,
The hedge, which at th' adjoining boundary
Hath aye its willow-blossom made a feast
By bees of Hybla, oft shall thee entice

"If I were not in love with Mopsa, thou shouldst take no money of me; but being enthralled as I am, it will also be the bondage of certain ribands and gloves."

67. "You virgins, that did late despair
To keep your wealth from cruel men,
Tie up in silk your careless hair,
  Soft peace is come again.
Now lovers' eyes may gently shoot
  A flame that will not kill;
The drum was angry, but the lute
  Shall whisper what you will.
Sing Io, Io! for his sake,
  Who hath restored your drooping heads;
With choice of sweetest flowers, make
  A garden where he treads:
Whilst we whole groves of laurel bring,
  A petty triumph to his brow,
Who is the master of our spring,
  And all the bloom we owe."
          Shirley, *The Imposture*, i. 2.

76. Or— "Shalt shady cool enjoy."
          See Ecl. ii. *l.* 12.

79. "There flowery hill Hymettus, with the sound
Of bees' industrious murmur, oft invites
To studious musing." Milton, *P. R.* b. iv.

By gentle murmuring to drop to sleep. 80
On th' other side, beneath the lofty rock,
The pruner shall be warbling to the gales;
Nor yet, meanwhile, hoarse culvers, thy delight,
Nor turtle, cease from tow'ring elm to coo.
⸺ it. Then sooner nimble harts shall feed in air,
And seas leave fishes bare upon the strand;
Sooner,—both countries' frontiers traversed o'er,—
Or Parthian exile shall the Arar drink,
Or Germany the Tigris, than *his* looks
Can from my bosom fade away.
    Mel.   But we,   90
Some hence shall pass to Afric's thirsty sons;
At Scythia others of us shall arrive,

84. " Making that murm'ring noise that cooing doves
Use in the soft expression of their loves."
            Dryden, *The Indian Queen,* iii. i.
" No more shall meads be decked with flowers,
Nor sweetness dwell in rosy bowers;
Nor greenest buds on branches spring,
Nor warbling birds delight to sing;
Nor April violets paint the grove,
Ere I forget my Celia's love."
            Carew, *The Protestation.*
Shakespeare uses the powerful aid of impossibilities for a different purpose; *Merchant of Venice,* iv. 1:
" You may as well go stand upon the beach,
And bid the main flood bate his usual height;
You may as well use question with the wolf,
Why he hath made the ewe bleat for the lamb;
You may as well forbid the mountain pines
To wag their high tops, and to make no noise,
When they are fretted with the gusts of heaven,
As seek to soften that, his Jewish heart."
And again, in *Coriolanus,* v. 3:
" Then let the pebbles on the hungry beach
Fillip the stars; then let the mutinous winds
Strike the proud cedars 'gainst the fiery sun,
Murdering impossibility, to make
What cannot be, slight work."
91. " But poorer now than poverty itself;"
" Now, like a sea-tost navy in a storm,
Must we be severed unto divers shores?"
Webster, *The Weakest goeth to the Wall,* ii. 3.
            " Thou hast forced
My heart to sigh, my hands to beat my breast,
My feet to travel, and my eyes to weep." iii. 1.
Goldsmith feelingly alludes to the miseries of exile:
" Have we not seen, at pleasure's lordly call,
The smiling, long-frequented village fall?
Beheld the duteous son, the sire decay'd,
The modest matron, and the blushing maid,
Forced from their homes, a melancholy train,
To traverse climes beyond the western main;
Where wild Oswego spreads her swamps around,
And Niagara stuns with thundering sound?"
                                    Traveller.
Again in the *Deserted Village:*
" Ah, no! To distant climes, a dreary scene,
Where half the convex world intrudes between,
Through torrid tracts with fainting steps they go,
Where wild Altama murmurs to their woe."

And Crete's swift Axus; at the Britons, too,
Cut off completely by the whole of earth.
Lo! shall I ever, [though] a long time hence,
My native bourns, and humble cabin's roof,
Uppiled with turf, some beards of corn—my realm—
Hereafter viewing, be in wonder held?
Shall these fresh-broken lands, so finely tilled,
A godless soldier hold? a foreigner   100
These crops of corn? Behold! to what a pass
Disunion us poor citizens hath brought!
Behold! for whom we've sown the fields!
    Graft now
Thy pear-trees, Melibœus, range arow
Thy vines. Away! my goats, once happy flock,
Away! You nevermore shall I, [while] stretched
Within the verdant grot, see hanging far
Adown the braky cliff; no carols I
Shall sing; with me to feed you, O my goats,
No [more] upon the cytisus in bloom, 110
And bitter sprays of willow, shall you browse.
Tit. Yet here this night hadst thou along with me

" Far different these from every former scene,—
The cooling brook, the grassy-vested green,
The breezy covert of the warbling grove,
That only shelter'd thefts of harmless love."

94. So Ambrose Philips, with a pleasing variety;
Past. 2:
" Sweet are thy banks! Oh, when shall I once more
With ravish'd eyes review thine smell'd shore?
When in the crystal of thy waters scan
Each feature faded, and my colour wan?
When shall I see my hut, the small abode
Myself did raise, and cover o'er with sod?
Small though it be, a mean and humble cell,
Yet is there room for peace and me to dwell."
100. " His stubborn hands my net hath broken quite;
My fish, the guerdon of my toil and pain,
He causeless seized, and, with ungrateful spite,
Bestowed upon a less deserving swain:
The cost and labour mine, his all the gain."
                        P. Fletcher, *Ecl.* ii. 7.
" So many new-born flies his light gave life to,
Buzz in his beams, flesh-flies and butterflies,
Hornets, and humming scarabs, that not one honey-bee,
That's loaden with true labour, and brings home
Increase and credit, can 'scape rifling;
And what she sucks for sweet, they turn to bitterness."
        J. Fletcher, *The Loyal Subject,* ii. 5.
112. So Spenser's *Shepheards Calender,* September, 254:
" But if to my cotage thou wilt resort,
So as I can I will thee comfort;
There mayst thou ligge in a vetchy bed,
Till fairer Fortune shew forth his head."

| v. 81—83. | ECLOGUE II. | v. 84. |

Been able on the leaf of green to rest. With us are mellow apples, chestnuts soft, And store of curded milk; and now afar The roof-tops of the rural houses smoke,	And longer fall from lofty mounts the shades.
113. The young student may be referred to *Ec.* ix. 50, where he will see that *poma* is used of pears.	Collins, with a further variety; *Ec.* iii.: "While evening dews enrich the glittering glade, And the tall forests cast a longer shade."
116. Milton treats the idea in the closing line differently: "And now the sun had stretched out all the hills." *Lycidas.*	Dryden applies the idea figuratively to the declining age of David, king of Israel: "Behold him setting in the western skies, The shadows lengthening as the vapours rise." *Absalom and Achitophel*, 268, 9.

Eclogue II.   Alexis.

The shepherd Corydon with fervor loved
The fair Alexis, darling of his lord;
Nor had he aught to hope: only among
The clustered beeches, shade-abounding crests,
He used unceasingly to come: he there
Would these unstudied [verses], all alone,
To mounts and forests fling with idle zeal.
  O barbarous Alexis, reckest thou
Naught of my lays? no pity hast for me?
Thou in the end wilt goad me on to die.   10
Now e'en the cattle snatch the shades and cool;
Now e'en the thorny brakes green lizards shroud;
And Thestylis for reapers, faint with raging heat,
Together bruises garlic and wild thyme,
Herbs strong of odor: but along with me,

Line 6, 7. "Give sorrow words: the grief, that does not speak,
Whispers the o'er fraught heart, and bids it break."
  Macbeth, iv. 3.
"Unkindness, do thy office! poor heart, break!
Those are the killing griefs, which dare not speak." Webster, *Vittoria Corombona,* ii. 1.
9. "Mercy hangs upon your brow, like a precious jewel,
  O let not then,
Most lovely maid, best to be loved of men,
Marble lie upon your heart, that will make you cruel!
  Pity, pity, pity!
  Pity, pity, pity!
That word begins that ends a true-love ditty."
  T. Middleton, *Blurt,* iii. 1.
13. Milton makes *his* Thestylis assist the reapers in a different way, assigning the culinary department to Phillis:
"Hard by, a cottage-chimney smokes,
From betwixt two aged oaks,
Where Corydon and Thyrsis met,
Are at their savoury dinner set
Of herbs and other country messes,
Which the neat-handed Phyllis dresses;
And then in haste her bower she leaves,
With Thestylis to bind the sheaves."
  L'Allegro.

Thy footsteps while I trace, ring out the trees
With hoarse cicadas 'neath a blazing sun.
Was it not better brook the rueful wrath
Of Amaryllis, and her haughty scorn?
Not [better brook] Menalcas? e'en though he 20
Were swarthy, e'en though thou wert fair.
O lovely boy, trust not too much thy hue:
White privets drop, dark martagons are culled.
By thee am I disdained; nor who I am
Dost thou, Alexis, ask; how rich in flock,
How full to overflow in snowy milk.
A thousand lambs of mine upon the mounts
Of Sic'ly wander; new milk fails me not
In summer-tide, nor in the [wintry] cold.
I chant [the lays] which used—if e'er his droves   30
He called—Amphion, of Dircæan [birth],
On Attic Aracynth.   Nor am I so
Uncomely.   Late I viewed me on the shore,

21. "Why, sir? black
(For 'tis the colour that offends your eyesight,)
Is not within my reading, any blemish:
Sables are no disgrace in heraldry."
  Shirley, *Lady of Pleasure,* ii. 1.
27. "Two thousand sheep have I as white as milk,
Though not so sweet as is thy lovely face;
The pasture rich, the wool as soft as silk:
All this I give, let me possess thy grace."
  Sir Philip Sidney, *The Lady of May.*
"'An hundred udders for the pail I have,
That give me milk and curds, that make me cheese
To cloy the markets; twenty swarm of bees,
Whilk all the summer hum about the hive,
And bring me wax and honey in *bilive."
  B. Jonson, *Sad Shepherd,* ii. 1.
33. This may call to mind the language of Eve:
"And laid me down . . . . to look into the clear
Smooth lake, that to me seemed another sky.
As I bent down to look, just opposite
A shape within the watery gleam appeared,
Bending to look on me: I started back,
It started back; but pleased, I soon returned."
  Milton, *P. L.,* iv.

* "Bilive," with life, quickly.

When quiet through the breezes stood the
   sea :
I should not Daphnis fear, thyself the judge,
Since never doth reflection's form beguile.
Oh ! could it but thy pleasure be with me
The paltry farms, and unobtrusive cots,
To haunt, and pierce the harts; and drive
   in group
The flock of kidlings to the mallow green !
With me together in the forests thou   41
Shalt copy Pan in singing. Pan first taught
To brace together divers reeds with wax ;
Pan guards the sheep and keepers of the
   sheep.
Nor let it irk thee with a reed to chafe
Thy tiny lip : that he these very [strains]
Might master, what did not Amyntas do ?
I have, with seven unequal hemlock-reeds
Close set, a pipe, which for a gift to me
Damœtas whilom gave, and, dying, said, 50
"Thee now doth this its second master
   own."
Damœtas spoke ; the fool Amyntas grudged.
Moreo'er, two roes, discovered by myself
In no safe glen, their coats e'en still be-
   sprent
With white, a ewe's twain udders daily
   drain :
Which I for thee reserve. This long time
   past,

That she might carry them away from me,
Hath Thestylis been craving, and her end
   will gain,
Since paltry are my presents in thine eyes.
Come hither, O thou beauteous boy ! For
   thee   60
Their lilies, lo ! in baskets full, the Nymphs
Are carrying ; for thee a Naiad fair,
Her sallow gillyflowers and the heads
Of poppies gath'ring, doth narcissus add,
And blossom of the sweetly-smelling dill :
Then, interlacing them with widow-waile,
And other fragrant plants, soft martagons
Betrims with yellowing caltha. I myself
Will cull thee quinces hoar with velvet
   down,
And chestnuts, which my Amaryllis loved.
I waxy plums will add : to this fruit, too,
Shall dignity be [deigned] : and you, O
   bays,   72
I'll cull, and thee, O myrtle-plant, the next,
Since ye, so placed, your musky perfumes
   blend.
A boor thou art, O Corydon, nor recks
Alexis of thy gifts ; nor, if in gifts
Should'st thou vie with him, would Iollas
   yield.
Alas ! alas ! what is it I have willed
For my unhappy self ? Upon my flowers
The southern blast, and on my crystal
   springs   80

33. Carew gives another turn to the idea :
  "Stand still, you floods ! do not deface
      That image which you bear :
  So votaries, from every place,
      To you shall altars rear.
  No winds but lovers' sighs blow here,
      To trouble these glad streams,
  On which no star from any sphere
      Did ever dart such beams.
  To crystal, then, in haste congeal,
      Lest you should lose your bliss ;
  And to my cruel fair reveal
      How cold, how hard she is."
Sight of a Gentlewoman's face in the Water.
" And fair my flock, nor yet uncomely I,
If liquid fountains flatter not :—and why
Should liquid fountains flatter us, yet show
The bordering flowers less beauteous than they
  grow ?"   A. Philips, *Past.* 1.
38. See C. Cotton's "*Invitation to Phillis.*" Also
Note on *Æn.* vi. *l.* 248.
        " I must have you
To my country villa : rise before the sun,
Then make a breakfast of the morning dew,
Served up by Nature on some grassy hill :
You'll find it nectar."
        Philip Massinger, *The Guardian*, i. 1.
44. "Sing his praises, that doth keep
     Our flocks from harm,
  Pan, the father of our sheep ;
     And arm in arm
  Tread we softly in a round,
  Whilst the hollow neighbouring ground
  Fills the music with her sound."
     J. Fletcher, *Faithful Shepherdess*, i. 2.

58.   "And she will do so," is very tame.
  61. So "Sensuality" in Nabbes' *Microcosmus*, iv.
      "Gather all the flowers
  Tempe is painted with, and strew his way.
  Translate my bower to Turia's rosy banks ;
  There, with a chorus of sweet nightingales,
  Make it perpetual spring."
Similarly Venus engages to Paris :
" The laurel and the myrtle shall compose
  Thy arbours, interwoven with the rose,
  And honey-dropping woodbine ; on the ground
  The flowers ambitiously shall crowd themselves
  Into love-knots and coronets, to entangle
  Thy feet, that they may kiss them as they tread,
  And keep them prisoners in their amorous stalks."
        Shirley, *Triumph of Beauty*.
69.   "I pr'ythee let me bring thee where crabs
    grow ;
  And I with my long nails will dig thee pig-nuts ;
  Show thee a jay's nest, and instruct thee how
  To snare the nimble marmoset : I'll bring thee
  To clustering filberds, and sometimes I'll get
    thee
  Young scamels from the rock : wilt thou go with
    me ?"   Shakespeare, *Tempest*, ii. 2.
75 Spenser imitates Virgil here ; *Shepheard's
Calender*, January. 55 :
" It is not Hobbinol wherefore I plaine,
  Albee my love hee seeke with dayly suit ;
  His clownish gifts and curtsies I disdaine,
  His kids, his cracknelles, and his early fruit."
80. "I am no prophet, nor do wish to see
  Upon your spring another wind, than what

Wild boars have I, [to reason] lost, let in.
Whom art thou flying, ah! thou witless one?
Even the gods have tenanted the woods,
And Dardan Paris. Pallas by herself
Let haunt the fortresses, which she hath built;
Us above all things let the woods delight.
The grisly lioness pursues the wolf;
The wolf himself the goat; the cytisus
In blossom doth the wanton goat pursue;
Thee, O Alexis, Corydon: draws each 90
His proper fancy. See, the ploughs upraised
The bullocks by the yoke are bearing home;
The sun, too, doubles, as he draws away,
The lengthening shades: me, ne'ertheless, is love
Consuming; for what bound can there be set

The wings of pregnant western gales do enrich
The air withal, which, gliding as you walk,
May kiss the teeming flowers, and with soft breath
Open the buds, to welcome their preserver."
  Shirley, *The Imposture*, iii. 3.

90. "And every humour hath its adjunct pleasure,
Wherein it finds a joy above the rest."
  Shakespeare, *Sonnet* 91.
The force of *ipse*, in verse 63 of the original, would be best brought out by "in turn."

To love? Ah! Corydon, [ah!] Corydon,
What frenzy thee hath seized! Halfpruned for thee
Thy vine is [lying] on the leafy elm.
Why rather dost thou not some [share], at least,
Of what thy service needs, prepare thee to weave off 100.
Of withes and pliant rush? If this doth thee
Disdain, another Alexis thou shalt find.

100. How clearly the poet saw that useful employment was a cure for irregular desires!
  "Wherefore if thou, I say,
    Dost covet to avoid
  That Bedlam Boy's deceitful bow,
    That others hath annoyed:
  Eschew the idle life!
    Flee! flee from doing naught:
  For never was there idle brain
    But bred an idle thought."
    Turberville, *The Lover to Cupid*.
Philosophy, religious solitude
And labour wait on temperance. In these
Desire is bounded; they instruct the mind's
And body's actions. 'Tis lascivious ease,
That gives the first beginning to all ills.
The thoughts being busied on good objects, sin
Can never find a way to enter in."
  Nabbes, *Microcosmus*, iv.

Eclogue III. PALÆMON.

MENALCAS. DAMŒTAS. PALÆMON.

Menalcas. Inform me, O Damœtas! whose the flock?
Is't that of Melibœus?
  Damœtas.   It is not,
But Ægon's; Ægon lately it consigned
To me.
  Men. O sheep, ye ever luckless flock!
While he himself Neæra fonds, and dreads
Lest she should me prefer to him, his ewes
This caitiff keeper milketh twice an hour,
And from the flock the sap is filched away,
And from the lambs the milk.
  Dam.   Still bear in mind

Line 7. It is very doubtful that *alienus* means "hireling;" for Damœtas *may* have been in too comfortable a position to accept of formal pay. He paid himself, however, unless Menalcas was untruthful,—which he may very well have been, and his companion with him. The character of each depends on the testimony of the other; and all that is certain is, that they had both very abusive tongues. The probability is, that Damœtas was a thief, at all events; and so he *need* not have sought a remuneration for his trouble in honest cash. Vide v. 16 of the Latin text.

That these [misdoings] should with more reserve 10
Be charged on those who 're men. We know both who
'Twas . . . thee,—the he-goats eyeing it askance,—
And in what holy grot;—but laughed the easy Nymphs.
  Men. 'Twas then, I fancy, when they me espied
With scathful bill-hook hacking Mycon's grove,
And infant vines.
  Dam.   Or here by th' agèd beech,
When you the bow and shafts of Daphnis broke;
Which when, O curst Menalcas, you beheld
Bestowed upon the lad, you were not only vexed,

15. *Malè* may either be referred to *falce*, as in the translation; or to Damœtas, when it should be rendered "spiteful."

ECLOGUE III.

But, if you had not somehow done him harm, 20
You would have died.
Men. What *can* flock-owners do,
When venture knaves the like? Did I not see
You, villain, Damon's he-goat catch by craft,
Lycisca in full bark? And when I cried,
"Now whither doth yon fellow hie him off?
O Tityrus, collect thy flock,"—you skulked
Behind the rush-plats.
Dam. Should he not, when beat
In playing, give the he-goat up to me,
Which my reed-pipe had by its warblings won?
Should you not know it, that he-goat was mine, 30
And Damon did himself acknowledge it
To me, but said he could not give it up.
Men. In playing *you* beat *him*? Or hath a pipe,
With wax cemented, e'er belonged to *you*?
Were you not in the crossways, dunderhead,
Customed to murder some unhappy tune
Upon your squeaking straw?
Dam. Do you, then, wish
We should between us try what each can do
By turns? I this young cow (lest you perchance
Decline, twice comes she to the pail, twin calves 40
She suckles at her udder;) stake: do you

Say with what bet you will with me compete.
Men. Aught from the herd I could not dare to stake
With you : for I a father have at home,
A harsh step-dame I have: and twice a day
They reckon over, *both* of them the flock,
And *one* the kids. But that which you, e'en you,
Yourself, by far more costly will admit—
Seeing it is your fancy to be mad—
My beechen cups I'll pledge, the gravenwork 50
Of heav'n-inspired Alcimedon, whereon,
Embossed upon them with an easy tool,
A limber vine attires the berry tufts,
Profusely scattered by the ivy wan.

---

44. Spenser has imitated this passage ; *Sh. Cal.*, March, 40:
" For, alas ! at home I have a syre,
A stepdame eke, as hote as fyre,
That dewly adayes counts mine."
So the unfortunate Imogen complains of
" A father cruel, and a stepdame false."
Shakespeare, *Cymbeline*, i. 7.
" A father? No !
In kinde a father, not in kindlinesse."
Thomas Sackville, *Ferrex and Porrex*, i. 1.
46. " His corn and cattle served the neighbour towns
With plentiful provision, yet his thrift
Could miss one beast among the herd."
J. Fletcher, *The Noble Gentleman*, ii. 1.
52. On a comparison of v. 38 of the Latin with *Ec.* v. 42, it seems doubtful that Salmasius and La Cerda are right in taking *torno* to mean a " lathe," and *superaddita*, " superadded." This latter word there plainly means " inscribed ;" and so here it appears to have the force of " embossed over."
53. So Spenser, in his 8th Æglogue, which is amœbæan, in imitation of his predecessors, Theocritus and Virgil :
" And over them spred a goodly wilde vine,
Entrailed with a wanton yvy twine."
Sh. Cal., Aug. 29.
And again, he ornaments the porch of the Castle of Temperance with the ivy and vine ; *Faerie Queene*, ii. 9, 24 :
" Of hewen stone the porch was fayrely wrought,
Stone more of valew, and more smooth and fine,
Then iett or marble far from Ireland brought :
Over the which was cast a wandring vine,
Enchaced with a wanton yvie twine."
The same image of trailing ivy is reproduced in an exquisite passage in the description of a fountain in the " Bower of Bliss ;" *F. Q.*, ii. 12, 61 :
" And over all of purest gold was spred
A trayle of yvie in his native hew ;
For the rich metall was so coloured,
That wight, who did not well avis'd it vew,
Would surely deeme it to bee yvie trew :
Low his lascivious armes adown did creepe,
That themselves dipping in the silver dew
Their fleecy flowres they fearfully did steepe,
Which drops of christall seemd for wantones to weep."

---

20. Anthon, in referring *nocuisses* to the bow and arrows, seems to be singular.
21. " You are a rascal ! he that dares be false
To a master, though unjust, will ne'er be true
To any other."
P. Massinger, *A New Way to Pay Old Debts*, v. 1.
25. " Soft ! Whither away so fast ?
A true man, or a thief, that gallops so ?"
Shakespeare, *Love's Labour's Lost*, iv. 3.
26. " Contemned of all ! and kicked too ! Now I find it :
My valour's fled, too, with mine honesty ;
For since I would be knave I must be coward."
Beaumont and Fletcher, *The False One*, iii. 2.
36. " *Gracculo.* Our most humble suit is,
We may not twice be executed.
Timoleon. Twice ! How meanest thou ?
Grac. At the gallows first, and after in a ballad
Sung to some villainous tune."
Massinger, *Bondman*, v. 3.
" You shall scrape, and I will sing
A scurvy ditty to a scurvy tune."
Duke of Milan, ii. 1.
See Milton's *Lycidas* :
" And when they list, their lean and flashy songs
Grate on their scrannel pipes of wretched straw."

[Stand] in the midst two figures—Conon, and—
Who was the other one, that with his wand
Mapped out for earth the universal sphere;
The seasons which the sickleman, those which
The stooping ploughman should observe?
My lips
I have not hitherto to them approached, 60
But keep them up in store.
Dam. For us as well
The same Alcimedon two cups hath made,
And with the soft acanthus wreathed around
Their handles, and an Orpheus in the midst
Hath set, and forests following him. My lips
I have not hitherto to them approached,
But keep them up in store. If you give heed
To my young cow, there is no ground for you
To praise your cups.
Men. You never shall escape
This day; I'll come where'er you've called.
Let but—

---

56. As Virgil did not want to make Menalcas too learned, so Spenser makes Thomalin (*Sh. Cal.*, July, 161), after mentioning Moses, forget Aaron's name:
" This had a brother (his name I knew)," &c.
Gay is more true to pastoral life than any of his predecessors; his swains have not even heard of philosophers. See the *Shepherd's Week*, Monday, 20–30.

64. Shakespeare's song in *Henry the Eighth* will readily occur to the reader; iii. 1:
" Orpheus with his lute made trees,
And the mountain-tops that freeze,
Bend themselves when he did sing:
To his music plants and flowers
Ever sprung; as sun and showers,
There had been a lasting spring.
" Every thing that heard him play,
Even the billows of the sea,
Hung their heads, and then lay by:
In sweet music is such art—
Killing care and grief of heart
Fall asleep, or, hearing, die."

Dryden puts the immortal Purcell before Orpheus:
" We beg not hell our Orpheus to restore;
Had he been there,
Their sovereign's fear
Had sent him back before.
The power of harmony too well they knew:
He long ere this had tuned their jarring sphere,
And left no hell below."
Elegy on the Death of Mr. Purcell.
" Music has charms to soothe a savage breast,
To soften rocks, or bend a knotted oak.
I've read that things inanimate have moved,
And, as with living souls, have been informed
By magic numbers and persuasive sound."
Congreve, *The Mourning Bride*, I. i. 1–5.

Hear these, or let Palæmon, who, behold,
Is coming. I shall manage that henceforth
You do not challenge any man at song.
Dam. Come, then, if aught thou hast; in me delay
There shall be none, nor any man I fly;
Only, Palæmon neighbor, these store up
Within thy deepest thoughts—the matter is
No trifle.
Palæmon. Sing ye on, since we our seats
Have ta'en together on the velvet turf; 79
And now teems every field, now every tree,
Now leaf the woods, now fairest is the year.
Begin, Damœtas; thou shalt follow then,
Menalcas: in alternate strains ye'll sing:
Camenian [maidens] love alternate strains.
Dam. From Jove, ye muses, is my spring [of song];
Of Jove are all things full; he tends the lands;
For him my lays an interest possess.
Men. And me doth Phœbus love; his rightful gifts
For Phœbus are for ever [found] with me—
His bays, and sweetly-blushing martagon. 90
Dam. Me with an apple Galatæa pelts—
The wanton maid—and towards the willow trees
She hies, and longs that she may first be seen.
Men. Aye, but to me presents himself unasked
My flame Amyntas, so that Delia is
No longer more familiar to our dogs.
Dam. For my own Venus presents are procured;
For I myself marked out the spot, whereon
The airy culvers have amassed [their nest].
Men. That which I could, ten golden apples culled, 100

---

72. " I loathe to brawl with such a blast as thou,
Who art nought but a valiant voice; but if
Thou shalt provoke me further, men shall say,
' Thou wert,' and not lament it."
Beaumont and Fletcher, *Philaster*, i. 2.

73. *Lacessas* (v. 51) would seem to mean "challenge," and not "provoke," for the reasons which are given by Dr. Trapp.

78. Palæmon might have replied:
" Why, look you, sir! I can be as calm as silence
All the while music plays. Strike on, sweet friend,
As mild and merry as the heart of innocence."
T. Middleton, *The Mayor of Queenborough*, iii. 1.

93. " He kissed her, and breathed life into her lips,
Wherewith, as one displeased, away she trips;
Yet, as she went, full often looked behind."
C. Marlowe, *Hero and Leander*, Sestiad iii. 3–6.

" A brisk Arabian girl came tripping by;
Passing she cast at him a side-long glance,
And looked behind in hopes to be pursued."
J. Dryden, *Don Sebastian*, iv. 1.

From off a wild-wood tree, I to my hoy
Have sent; to-morrow other [ten] I'll send.
Dam. Oh ! times how many, and what
 [honied words],
To us hath Galatæa said ! Some part,
O breezes, waft ye to the ears of gods.
Men. What boots it that, Amyntas, thou
 dost not
Disdain me in thy very soul, if whilst
The boars thou huntest, I watch o'er
 the nets ?
Dam. Send Phyllis to me ; 'tis my
 natal-day,
Iollas : when I for the crops shall make
An off'ring with a heifer, come thyself.
Men. I Phyllis love 'fore other maids ;
 for she   112
At my departure wept, and long she cried,
"Handsome Iollas, fare thee well, fare-
 well."
Dam. The wolf is ruefulness to folds,
To ripened fruit are showers, to the trees
Are storms, to us is Amaryllis' wrath.
Men. To seeded crops is moisture a
 delight,
To weaned kids the arbute, willow lithe
To teeming flock, Amyntas is alone to me.
Dam. Our Muse doth Pollio affect,
 although   121
It is agrestic : O Pierian dames,
Do ye a heifer for your reader feed.
Men. Yea, Pollio doth e'en himself com-
 pose

---

101. " Here be grapes, whose lusty blood
  Is the learnèd poet's good ;
  Sweeter yet did never crown
  The head of Bacchus ; nuts more brown
  Than the squirrel's teeth that crack them :
  Deign, O fairest fair, to take them.
  For these black-eyèd Dryope
  Hath oftentimes commanded me
  With my claspèd knee to climb."
   J. Fletcher, *Faithful Shepherdess*, i. 1.
 A Philips gracefully expands the idea : *Past.* 1 :
" How would I wander every day to find
 The choice of wildings, blushing through the
  rind !
 For glossy plums how lightsome climb the tree !
 How risk the vengeance of the thrifty bee ?"
103. ' His lip is softer, sweeter than the rose ;
  His mouth, and tongue, with dropping honey
   flows."   Ben Johnson, *Sad Shepherd*, ii. 2.
" Oh ! Charm me with the music of thy tongue !
  I'm ne'er so blest, as when I hear thy vows,
  And listen to the language of thy heart."
       Otway, *The Orphan*, ii. end.
108. "We prune the orchards, and you cranch the
  fruit."
      Massinger, *The Emperor of the East*, iv. 2.
113. "When I was absent then her ga'lèd eyes
  Would have shed April showers, and outwept
  The clouds in that same o'er-passionate moode,
  When they drowned all the world."
       Marston, *Insatiate Countesse*, ii. 2.

Rare poems : feed a bull that with his horn
Now butts, and tosses with his hoof the
 sand.
Dam. Who loves thee, Pollio, may he
 come where'er
He joys that thou art too ! May honies
 stream
For him, and prickly brier spikenard
 yield !
Men. Who Bavius hateth not—that he
 may love   130
Thy verses, Mævius ! and may he, the
 same,
Put foxes in the yoke, and milk he-goats !
Dam. Ye, who cull flow'rs, and straw-
 berries, that grow
Along the ground, O swains, escape ye
 hence ;
A chilly snake is lurking in the grass.
Men. O sheep, forbear ye to advance too
 far ;
There's no safe trusting to the bank ; the
 ram
Himself his fleece is drying even still.
Dam. O Tit'rus, from the river force
 thou back
Thy browsing she-goats ; when there shall
 be time,   140
Myself will in spring-water wash them all.
Men. Drive on the sheep, ye striplings :
 if the heat
Shall have forestalled the milk, as lately, we
In vain shall squeeze their udders in our
 hands.
Dam. Alas ! alas ! how meagre is my
 bull
Amid the fatt'ning vetch ! The selfsame
 love
Is bane to flock and master of the flock.
Men. In these, sure, love is not at all
 the cause :
Scarce hold they by the bones together : I
Know not what eye doth witch my tender
 lambs.   150

---

126. " Roscommon writes: to that auspicious hand,
 Muse, feed the bull that spurns the yellow sand."
     Dryden, *Ep. to Lord Roscommon*, 66, 7.
137. This form of expression is used by Shake-
 speare :
   " For 'tis no trusting to yon foolish lowt."
        Two Gentlemen of Verona, iv. 4.
150. Or, perhaps, viewing *nescio quis* as an
 idiom :
   They scarcely hold together by the bones :
   Some eye or other witches my soft lambs.
" Yet pity me, Leneothoe, over the wound
  Thine eyes have made ; pity a begging king :
  Uncharm the charms of thy bewitching face,
  Or thou wilt leave me dead."
       T. May, *The Heir*, iv.

Dam. Inform me in what lands—and thou shalt be
My great Apollo—may the range of heaven
Expand itself no further than three ells.
Men. Inform me in what lands may flowers grow,
O'erwritten with the names of kings, and thou
Possess my Phillis to thyself alone.
Pal. It is not in my power to adjust
Disputes between you of such high concern :
Both you are worthy of the cow, and he ;
And whosoe'er may either dread the sweets,

" My venom eyes
Strike innocency dead at such a distance."
Beaumont and Fletcher, *The Coxcomb*, v. 2.
" His eyes shoot poison at me ; ha ! he has Bewitched me, sure."
Shirley, *The Brothers*, iv. 1.
" You leer upon me, do you ? There's an eye Wounds like a leaden sword."
Shakespeare, *Love's Labour's Lost*, v. 2.
155. To this Milton seems to allude in *Lycidas*, where he speaks of Cam "footing slow," with
" his bonnet-sedge,
Inwrought with figures dim, and on the edge
Like to that sanguine flower, inscribed with woe."
And Young more directly, *Night* iii. 271, 2 :
" As poets feign'd from Ajax' streaming blood
Arose, with grief inscribed, a mournful flower."
160, 161. Or, if this be considered too free a version, the passage may be more literally rendered thus :
And whosoe'er may either dread sweet loves,
Or may the bitter prove.
But what these lines have to do with the matter in dispute nobody apparently can tell. According to the received text, they seem to furnish simple nonsense, from which no unauthorised supply of imaginary ellipses appears to relieve them. Heyne would cut the matter very short by evicting them at once, though all the manuscripts agree in conferring a legal title on these very troublesome tenants. Anthon alters the text without improving the sense. The emendation proposed by Wagner is extremely slight, and hardly unwarrantable. He prefixes an " H ", before the first " aut ;" and so the passage assumes this form :
" Et quisquis amores
Haut metuet dulces, aut experietur amaros ;"
which, paraphrased, yields the following meaning :
And (this appears from the experience of you both, that) whosoever is not afraid of love, (and therefore admits it into his heart,) will find it (one or other of two very opposite things, either) sweet or (else) bitter. (He clearly runs a great risk, and therefore perhaps he had better have nothing to do with it.)
Yet does not this come in very awkwardly, as part of a solemn judgment upon the relative merits

Or prove the gall, of love. Now shut ye up
The rills, my swains ; the meads have drunk enough.

---

of two aspirants for poetic fame, who, however coarse, or worse than coarse, either or both may have been, were plainly very accomplished composers ? But even if it were not awkward, surely it is commonplace and weak. After such a trial of extreme skill, it was unsatisfactory enough to be told that the issue of it was a drawn battle ; but to receive the further announcement, that love was either honey or gall, must have seemed to them very like trifling with their disappointment.
Perhaps the explanation of Ruæus is as good as any : " Whoever is able to express, in the masterly way that you have done, the various effects of love."
Spenser makes Sir Scudamore agree with Palæmon's premises, though not in the implied advice which the above interpretation attributes to him : *Faerie Queene*, iv. 10, 1 :

" True he it sayd, whatever man it sayd,
That love with gall and hony doth abound ;
But if the one be with the other wayd,
For every dram of hony, therein found,
A pound of gall doth over it redound :
That I too true by triall have approved ;
For since the day that first with deadly wound
My heart was launcht, and learned to have loved,
I never ioyed howre, but still with care was moved."

Shakespeare, too, introduces Venus predicting this heavy curse upon Love for the death of her lover :

" Since thou art dead, lo ! here I prophesy,
Sorrow on love hereafter shall attend :
It shall be waited on by jealousy,
Find sweet beginning, but unsavoury end.
Ne'er settled equally, but high and low ;
That all love's pleasure shall not match her woe."
Venus and Adonis.

" Love is sweet :
Wherein sweet ?
In fading pleasures that do pain ;
Beauty sweet :
Is that sweet,
That yieldeth sorrow for a gain ?
If Love's sweet,
Herein sweet
That minutes' joys are monthly woes :
'Tis not sweet,
That is sweet
Nowhere but where repentance grows.'
Robert Greene, *Menaphon's Song.*
" Love is my bliss, and love is now my bale.'
R. Greene, *Friar Bacon.*

" An undigested heap of mixed extremes,
Whose pangs are wakings, and whose pleasures dreams."
Beaumont and Fletcher, *Triumph of Love*, i.
" Such is the posie Love composes ;
A stinging nettle, mixt with roses."
Browne, *Brit. Past.* b, i. song 3.

Eclogue IV. Pollio.

Sicilian muses, somewhat grander strains
Sing we! Not all do vineyards charm
And lowly tam'risks: if we sing the woods,
May woods deserving of a Consul prove!
  The latest era of Cumæan song
Hath now arrived; afresh the mighty
  round
Of ages is begun. And now returns the
  Virgin,
Returns the dynasty of Saturn. Now
A new succession is from heav'n on high
Let fall. Do thou but at his birth the boy,
'Neath whom the [race] of iron first shall
  cease, 11
And rise throughout the world the race of
  gold,
Lucina chaste, befriend: now thine Apollo
  reigns.
And thou, too, Pollio, the consul thou—
This glorious age shall enter [on its course]
And mighty months begin to roll. With
  thee
Our chief, if any traces of our guilt
Continue, cancelled they shall free the
  lands
From endless terror. He shall share the
  life
Of gods, and heroes with divinities 20

Lines 6, 7. Derrick tells us that a new star was said to have been seen in the open day about the time of Charles the Second's birth. To this Dryden thus alludes:
" Or one, that bright companion of the sun,
  Whose glorious aspect seal'd our new-born king;
And now, a round of greater years begun,
  New influence from his walks of light did bring." *Annus Mirabilis*, st. xviii.

8. " That was the righteous Virgin, which of old
Liv'd here on earth, and plenty made abound;
But after Wrong was lov'd, and Justice solde,
She left th' unrighteous world, and was to heaven extold." Spenser, *F. Q.* vii. 7, 37.

12. " And with iron sceptre rule
Us here, as with his golden those in heaven."
Milton, *P. L.* ii.

13. So Pericles: Shakespeare, *Pericles*, iii. 1:
" Lucina, O
Divinest patroness and midwife, gentle
To those that cry by night, convey thy deity
Aboard our dancing boat: make swift the pangs
Of my queen's travails!"

15. Strictly, " this pride of time;" for to make the expression refer to *puer* makes verse 12 come in very awkwardly.

16. " Henceforth a series of new time began,
The mighty years in long procession ran."
Dryden, *Abs. and Achit.* 1028, 29.

See intermingled, and himself be seen of
  them;
And with ancestral virtues shall he rule
A world at peace. But unto thee, O boy,
Her earliest tiny gifts with tillage none,
Her gadding ivies at each step, with bac-
  caris,
Shall earth unbosom, and Egyptian beans,
With the acacia smiling interspersed.
The she-goats of themselves shall carry
  home
Their udders swoln with milk; nor shall
  the herds
Huge lions fear. The cradle's self for thee
Shall pour forth charming flowers, and the
  snake 31
Shall die, and guileful plant of bane shall
  die;
At large Assyrian spikenard grow. But
  soon
As th' heroes' praises, and a father's deeds,

26. Spenser makes the earth equally obsequious to Dame Nature:
" But th' Earth herself of her owne motion,
Out of her fruitful bosom made to growe
Most dainty trees, that, shooting up anon,
Did seem to bow their bloss'ming heads full lowe
For homage unto her, and like a throne did shew.
And all the Earth far underneath her feete
Was dight with flowers, that voluntary grew
Out of the ground, and sent forth odours sweet;
Tenne thousand more of sundry sent and hew,
That might delight the smell, or please the view,
The which the nymphes from all the brooks thereby
Had gathered, they at her footstoole threw;
That richer seem'd than any tapestry
That princes bowres adorne with painted imagery."
Faerie Queene, vii. 7, 8, 10.

28. Such a primeval state as Milton finely describes: *P. L.* iv.:
" About them frisking play'd
All beasts of the earth, since wild, and of all chase
In wood or wilderness, forest or den.
Sporting the lion ramp'd, and in his paw
Dandled the kid; bears, tigers, ounces, pards,
Gamboll'd before them; the unwieldy elephant,
To make them mirth, used all his might, and wreathed
His lithe proboscis: close the serpent sly,
Insinuating, wove with Gordian twine
His braided train, and of his fatal guile
Gave proof unheeded."

34. Now is he apt for knowledge: therefore know
It is a more direct and even way,
To train to virtue those of princely blood
By examples than by precepts: if by examples
Whom should he rather strive to imitate
Than his own father?"
Webster, *Vittoria Corombona*, ii.

Thou shalt be able now to read, and learn
What be their worth, the plain shall by
degrees
With downy ear wax yellow, and the bunch
Shall dangle blushing from untutored thorns,
And churlish oaks their dewy honies still.
Yet some few footsteps of the ancient
crime   40
Shall steal behind, to bid [men] Thetis
tempt
In ships, and girdle round with walls the
towns,
And cleave-in furrows into earth. Another
Tiphys then
Shall be, another Argo, too, to waft
Choice heroes; there shall e'en be other
wars ;
Aye, and again to Troy a great Achilles
Shall be despatched. Thereafter, when
shall now
Established age have fashioned thee a
man,
Yea, of himself shall from the main with-
draw
The voyager, nor naval pine its wares 50
Shall barter : every produce every land
Shall yield. The ground shall not the
harrows brook,
Nor shall the vine the pruning-knife. Now,
too,
The stalwart ploughman shall from off his
bulls
Their yokes unloosen. Neither shall the
wool
Learn motley hues to feign ; but of himself
The ram shall in the meadows change his
fleece
With now sweet-blushing purple dye, with
now
The weed of saffron ; of its own accord,

Vermilion, as they graze, shall drape the
lambs.   60
"Through ages such as these, career ye
on !"
The Destinies have to their spindles said,
In union with the steadfast will of Fates.
Advance on thy grand dignities—the time
Will presently arrive,—O darling child
Of gods, the mighty foster-son of Jove !
Behold with spherick mass a nodding
world,
E'en lands, and ocean-paths, and sky
sublime !
Behold how at the age, decreed to come,
All things rejoice ! Oh ! that to me might
last   70
The latest stage of such a lengthful life,
And inspiration, far as it shall prove
Sufficient thy achievements to proclaim !
No, nor shall Thracian Orpheus me surpass
In songs, nor Linus; though a mother
that—
And *this* a father aid—Calliope
Orpheus; the fair Apollo Linus. E'en if
Pan,
Arcadia umpire, should with me compete,
E'en Pan, Arcadia umpire, would avow
Himself surpassed. Begin, O infant boy, 80
To recognise thy mother with a smile ;.
Ten months have brought thy mother long-
some qualms.
Begin, O infant boy : [that babe,] on whom
His parents have not smiled, nor god of
board,
Nor goddess hath deemed worthy of her
bed.

---

37. Or : "waving ear."

39. Query ? " the dews of honey."

"The earth unploughed shall yield her crop,
Pure honey from the oak shall drop,
The fountain shall run milk ;
The thistle shall the lily bear,
And every bramble roses wear,
And every worm make silk."
Ben Jonson, *The Golden Age Restored.*

56. Or perhaps *mentiri* might be rendered " to
forge," as Spenser says of Duessa :

"So could she forge all colours save the trew."

60. Or : "Shall scarlet, as they feed, array the lambs."

63. Spenser finely describes the offices of the Parcæ: *Faerie Queene*, iv. 2, 48 :
" There she them found all sitting round about
The direfull Distaffe standing in the mid,
And with unwearied fingers drawing out
The lines of life, from living knowledge hid.
Sad Clotho held the rocke, the whiles the thrid
By griesly Lachesis was spun with paine,
That cruel Atropos eftsoones undid,
With cursed knife cutting the twist in twaine :
Most wretched men, whose dayes depend on thrids
so vaine !"

70. So Eve dreams that Adam says to her :
" Heaven wakes with all his eyes,
Whom to behold but thee, Nature's desire ?
In whose sight all things joy."
Milton, *P. L.* v.

Eclogue V. DAPHNIS.

MENALCAS. MOPSUS.

Menalcas. Why not, O Mopsus, seeing we have met,
Both skilful,—thou in breathing into slender reeds,
In singing verses I,—here seat us down
Among the elms, with hazels interspersed?
Mopsus. The elder thou : to thee 'tis fair that I
Give way, Menalcas, whether underneath
The fitful shades — the zephyrs fanning them—
Or rather 'neath the grot we go. Behold,
How hath the wild-wood vine the grot o'erspread
With scattered bunches!
Men. In our mounts with thee 10
Amyntas only vies.
Mop. What if the same
Should strive in singing Phœbus to surpass?

Men. Do thou begin, O Mopsus, first, if thou
Or any flames of Phyllis, or the lauds
Of Alcon hast, or Codrus' brawls : begin ;
The kids, while feeding, Tityrus will watch.
Mop. Nay rather I those verses, which of late
Upon a beech's verdant bark I scored,
And sang and marked them down by turns, will try :
Do thou bid then Amyntas to compete. 20
Men. As much as doth the supple willow yield
To olive wan, as much as lowly nard
To beds of crimson roses, in our mind
So much Amyntas yieldeth unto thee.
Mop. But cease thou more, O swain ;
we've reached the grot.
Quenched by fell death, the Nymphs did Daphnis weep.

Line 3. It is evident from this whole Eclogue, and especially from comparing vv. 51, 55 of Ecl. III., that *dicere versus* means to sing songs, not to rehearse or indite them.
See also Ecl. IX., and compare v. 35 with v. 36.

7. " My lovely Aaron, wherefore look'st thou sad,
When every thing doth make a gleeful boast?
The birds chaunt melody on every bush ;
The snake lies rolled in the cheerful sun :
The green leaves quiver with the cooling wind,
And make a chequer'd shadow on the ground :
Under their sweet shade, Aaron, let us sit."
Shakespeare, *Tit. And.* ii. 3.
" How sweet these solitary places are! how wantonly
The wind blows through the leaves, and courts and plays with 'em!
Will you sit down and sleep? The heat invites you.
Hark, how yond purling stream dances and murmurs!
The birds sing softly too: pray, take some rest, sir."
J. Fletcher, *The Pilgrim,* v. 4.

9. " So fashioned a porch with rare device,
Archt over head with an embracing vine,
Whose bounches hanging downe seemd to entice
All passers by to taste their lushious wine."
Spenser, *F. Q.* ii. 12, 54.
Another side, umbrageous grots and caves
Of cool recess, o'er which the mantling vine
Lays forth her purple grape, and gently creeps
Luxuriant." Milton, *P. L.* iv.
' Deep in the gloomy glade a grotto bends,
Wide through the craggy rock an arch extends ;
The rugged stone is clothed with mantling vines,
And round the cave the creeping woodbine twines."
Gay, *The Fan,* i. 99-102.

12. *Certat* seems to have better authority than *certet,* and is certainly a more graphic reading.

15, 16. So Spenser, *Sh. Cal.* May, 172 :
" Now, Piers, of fellowship, tell us that saying ;
For the lad can keep both our flockes from straying."
A. Philips varies the idea : *Past.* 4 :
" And since our ewes have grazed, what harm if they
Lie round and listen, while the lambkins play?"
20. " Shall the queen of the inhabitants of the air,
The eagle, that bears thunder on her wings,
In her angry mood destroy her hopeful young,
For suffering a wren to perch too near them?
Such is our disproportion."
P. Massinger, *The Great Duke of Florence,* iv. 2.

26. See Milton's *Lycidas* :
" But oh ! the heavy change, now thou art gone,
Now thou art gone, and never must return !
Thee, shepherd, thee the woods and desert caves,
With wild thyme and the gadding vine o'ergrown,
And all their echoes mourn :
The willows and the hazel-copses green
Shall now no more be seen
Fanning their joyous leaves to thy soft lays."
The same miseries Spenser makes the consequence of Colin Clout's absence. Hobbinol tells him : *Colin Clout,* xxii. :
" Whilst thou wast hence, all dead in dole did lie :
The woods were heard to waile full many a sythe,
And all their birds with silence to complaine :
The fields with faded flowers did seem to mourne,
And all their flocks from feeding to refraine :
The running waters wept for thy returne,
And all their fish with languour did lament."
26-29. So Alexander on the death of Clytus :
" Here I will lie
Close to his bleeding side, thus kissing him ;

Ye [stood] the witnesses, O hazel-shrubs
And rivers, for the Nymphs, when, clasping round
The pitiable body of her son,
The mother cruel calls both gods and stars.
None in those days their pastured oxen drove, 31
O Daphnis, to the chilly streams ; no quadruped
Or sipped the brook, or touched a blade of grass.
O Daphnis, that e'en Afric lions wailed
Thy death, both mountains wild and forests tell,
Yea, Daphnis to the chariot taught to yoke
Armenian tigresses ; 'twas Daphnis [taught]
Processionals of Bacchus t'introduce,
And wreathe with velvet leaves the limber spears.
As is the vine the grace to trees, as grapes
To vines, as bulls to herds, as standing corn 41
To teemful fields—all grace art thou to thine.
When once the Weirds reft thee away, the fields
E'en Pales, and Apollo e'en, forsook.
Upon the furrows, whereunto we oft
Plump grains of barley have consigned, there grow
The fruitless darnel and the barren oats ;
For violet soft, for purple daffodil,
Thistle, and paliure with pointed thorns
Spring up. Bestrew the ground with leaves, draw shades 50

Upon the springs, O shepherds : such behests
Daphnis enjoins to be for him observed.
Do ye both form a tomb, and on the tomb
The lay inscribe : "I, Daphnis, in the woods,
Hence even to the constellations famed,
Of a fair flock the guard, more fair myself."
Men. Thy song is such to us, O heav'nly bard,
As slumber to the weary on the grass ;

54. Instead of an inscription on Albino's tomb, Philips introduces Angelot praying :
"Oh ! peaceful may thy gentle spirit rest !
 The flowery turf be light upon thy breast ;
 Nor shrieking owl nor bat thy tomb fly round,
 Nor midnight goblins revel o'er the ground."
            Past. 3.
" But since that I shal die her slauve,
  Her slauve, and eke her thrall :
  Write you, my frendes, upon my grauve
  This chaunce that is befall :
 ' Here lieth unhappy Harpalus,
  By cruell louve now slaine ;,
  Whom Phylida vnjustly thus
  Hath murdred with disdaine.' "
These are the concluding verses of a beautiful composition, probably the earliest Pastoral poem in the language. It will be found among "Poems of Vncertaine Auctors" in Chalmers' "English Poets," vol. ii.
It is impossible here to withhold Ben Jonson's masterly Epitaph on the Countess of Pembroke :
" Underneath this sable herse
  Lies the subject of all verse,
  Sidney's sister, Pembroke's mother :
  Death ! ere thou hast slain another,
  Learned, and fair, and good as she,
  Time shall throw a dart at thee."
            Underwoods, xv.
"As soon as I am dead,
 Come all and watch about my hearse ;
 Bring each a mournful story and a tear,
 To offer at it when I go to earth :
 With fluttering ivy'clasp my coffin round ;
 Write on my brow my fortune ; let my bier
 Be borne by virgins, that shall sing by course
 The truth of maids and perjuries of men."
Beaumont and Fletcher, *The Maid's Tragedy*, ii. 1.
57. "For, while I sit with thee, I seem in Heaven
 And sweeter thy discourse is to my ear
 Than fruits of palm-tree, pleasantest to thirst
 And hunger both, from labour at the hour
 Of sweet repast : they satiate, and soon fill,
 Though pleasant ; but thy words, with grace divine
 Imbued, bring to their sweetness no satiety."
            Milton, *P.L.* viii.
58. *Sopor* strictly means "deep sleep," but the Latin poets use it for "sleep" in general. In the same lax way, "slumber" is used by English poets to represent "sleep," though strictly it means "light sleep." Still, though there is so marked a difference between *sopor* and " slumber," yet as the poet does not seem to use the word here in the accurate signification attached to it in *Æn.* iii. 173, " slumber " may well be admitted, being far more harmonious in this passage than " sleep." The same liberty is taken in rendering *Æn.* iv. 522.
V. 45-47 are amplified by Spenser in his exquisite

These pale dead lips that have so oft advised me ;
Thus bathing o'er his reverend face with tears :
Thus clasping his cold body in my arms,
Till Death, like him, has made me stiff and horrid."
            Lee, *Rival Queens*, iv. end.
A. Philips happily imitates this passage :
" The pious mother comes, with grief oppress'd ;
  Ye trees and conscious fountains can attest
  With what sad accents, and what piercing cries,
  She fill'd the grove, and importuned the skies,
  And every star upbraided with his death,
  When, in her widow'd arms, devoid of breath,
  She clasp'd her son."   *Past.* 3.
33. So Spenser says of Dido's death : *Sh. Cal.* Nov. 133 :
" The feeble flockes in field refuse their former foode,
  And hang their heades as they would learne to weepe."
39. Velvet, or, "waving," "pliant."
50. That is, plant flowers to grace the ground, and trees to shade the founts.
" This rosemary is withered ; pray get fresh !
  I would have these herbs grow up in his grave,
  When I am dead and rotten. Reach the bays ;
  I'll tie a garland here about his head :
  'Twill keep my boy from lightning."
            Webster, *Vittoria Corombona*, v. 1.

v. 47—63.   ECLOGUE V.   v. 64—82.   15

As in the summer-tide to slake the thirst
By some delicious water's skipping rill.   60
Nor is't alone on reeds, but in thy voice,
Thou rivallest thy master : happy swain !
Thou now shalt be the second after him.
Still we will these of ours, howe'er [we may],
To thee in turn recite, and Daphnis thine
Raise to the stars ; we Daphnis to the stars
Will bear away : us, too, did Daphnis love.
Mop. Can aught to us of higher value be
Than such a favor ? Both the swain himself
Was worthy to be sung, and those thy lays
Now long since Stimicon hath praised to us.
Men. Bright Daphnis marvels at th' unwonted gate   72
Of th' Empyrean, and beneath his feet
Beholds the clouds and stars. Hence lively joy
Absorbs the woods, and other rural scenes,
And Pan, and shepherds, and the Dryad maids.
Nor doth the wolf an ambush for the flock,
Nor any toils their craft for harts, devise :
Benignant Daphnis loves repose. The mounts
Themselves, unshorn, in gladness to the stars   80
Fling forth their voices ; now the very cliffs,

The very trees, ring out the lays : " A god,
A god is he, Menalcas !" O be kind
And gracious to thine own ! Lo ! altars four !
Behold, O Daphnis, twain of them for thee ;
Twain altars high for Phœbus. Drinking-cups,
A couple frothing with new milk, each year,
And craters twain of unctuous oil, I'll set
For thee ; and specially with copious wine
Enlivening the feast—before the hearth,   90
If it shall winter be ; if harvest [tide],
Within the shade—the Ariusian wines,
A novel nectar, from the tankards I
Will pour. To me shall [both] Damætas sing,
And Lyctian Ægon ; frisking Satyrs ape
Alphesibœus. These shall aye be thine,
Alike what time our yearly off'rings we
Shall pay the Nymphs, and when we shall perform
The circuit of the fields. While mountain-brows
The boar [shall love], while fish shall love the floods,   100
And while upon the thyme the bees shall feed,
While cicads on the dew, [thy] glory aye,
And thy renown, and praises shall endure.
As unto Bacchus and to Ceres, so to thee
Their vows each year shall husbandmen perform :
Thou also shalt oblige them to their vows.
Mop. What [boons] to thee, what boons can I return
For such a song ? For neither me delight

---

description of the "Bower of Bliss :" *Faerie Queene*, ii. 5, 30 :

" And fast beside there trickled softly downe
  A gentle streame, whose murmuring wave did play
Emongst the pumy stones, and made a sowne,
  To lull him soft asleepe that by it lay :
The wearie traveiler, wandring that way,
  Therein did often quench his thristy heat,
And then by it his wearie limbes display,
  (Whiles creeping slomber made him to forget
His former payne,) and wypt away his toilsom sweat."

72. So Spenser of Dido, in *Sh. Cal.* Nov. 175 ; see also 195, &c. :

" She raignes a goddess now emong the saintes,
That whilome was the saynt of shepheards light,
And is enstalled nowe in heavens night."

   " Now, free from earth, thy disencumber'd soul
Mounts up, and leaves behind the clouds and starry pole."   Dryden, *Abs. and Achit.* 850, 1.

More directly imitated in *Amyntas*, 66-73.

" Damon, behold yon breaking purple cloud ;
Hear'st thou not hymns and songs divinely loud ?
There mounts Amyntas ; the young cherubs play
About their godlike mate, and sing him on his way.
He cleaves the liquid air, behold, he flies,
And every moment gains upon the skies.
The new-come guest admires the etherial state,
The sapphire portal, and the golden gate."

74. Or : " lively," or " active."

82.   " If, like a statue,
Cold and unglorified by art, you call
Our sense to wonder, where shall we find eyes
To stand the brightness, when you're turned a shrine,
Embellished with the burning light of diamonds,
And other gifts, that dwell, like stars about you !"
               Shirley, *The Imposture,* ii. 3.

84. *Ara* and *altare* are used of the same altar in *Æn.* ii. 514, 515, xii. 171, 174.

107. Milton similarly in *Par. Lost,* viii. 5 :

" What thanks sufficient, or what recompense
Equal, have I to render to thee, divine Historian ?"

108. " Colin, to heare thy rymes and roundelayes,
Which thou were wont on wastefull hilles to sing,
I more delight then larke in sommer dayes,
Whose echo made the neighbour groves to ring."
               Spenser, *Sh. Cal.* June, 49.
                     " O happy fair !
Your eyes are lodestars, and your tongue sweet air,
More tuneable than lark to shepherd's ear,
When wheat is green, and hawthorn buds appear."
       Shakespeare, *Midsummer Night's Dream,* i. 1.

A. Philips happily imitates verses 45-47, 81-84 : *Past.* 4 :

So much the rising Auster's whisp'ring sound,
Nor shores by billow buffeted, nor brooks,
Which rill adown among the rocky glens.

" Oh, Colinet ! how sweet thy grief to hear !
How does thy verse subdue the listening ear !
Soft falling as the still, refreshing dew,
To slake the drought, and herbage to renew ;
Not half so sweet the midnight winds, which move
In drowsy murmurs o'er the waving grove ;
Nor valley brook, that, hid by alders, speeds
O'er pebbles warbling, and through whispering reeds ;
Nor dropping waters, which from rocks distil,
And welly grots with tinkling echoes fill."

111. " For first she springs out of two marble rocks,
On which a grove of oakes high-mounted growes,
That as a girlond seemes to deck the locks
Of some faire bride, brought forth with pompous showes

Men. We'll first present thee with this brittle reed.   112
This taught us, " Corydon with fervor loved
The fair Alexis ;" this the same, " Whose flock ?
Is't that of Melibœus ?"
Mop.   But do thou
Accept this crook, which, though he begged me oft,
Antigenes hath never borne away—
He, too, was worthy then of being loved—
With even knobs and bronze, Menalcas, fair.

Out of her bowre, that many flowers strowes :
So through the flowry dales she tumbling downe
Through many woods and shady coverts flowes,
That on each side her silver channell crowne."
               Spenser, Canto vi. of *Mutabilitie.*

118. Or : " Though he."

Eclogue VI. SILENUS.

The first that in the Syracusan strain
Deigned to disport, nor blushed to haunt the woods,
Was our Thalia. When I would of kings
And battles sing, the Cynthian twitched mine ear,
And warned : "A shepherd, Tit'rus, it becomes
To feed fat sheep, recite a flimsy lay."
Now I—for thou shalt have full many [a bard]
Who may thy praises, Varus, yearn to tell,
And thy grim wars record—will practise o'er
The rural song upon my slender reed.   10
Unbidden [strains] I do not sing. Yet still,
If any one, if any one e'en these,

Line 6. Does any classical British author apply the literal meaning of *deductum*, " thin-spun," to compositions of any kind ? Milton uses it of life, but evidently with reference to the trite idea of life's thread. If the metaphor must be abandoned in the translation, many words offer themselves for acceptance, of which perhaps " homely" is as good as any.
     Addison, in speaking of Spenser, whom he had not enough of poetic taste to admire, says :
" The long-spun allegories fulsome grow."
Pope employs the word which is used in the version :
" Proud of a vast extent of flimsy lines."
             Prologue to Satires.
" His breeding,
It was not spun the finest ; but his wealth,
Able to gild deformity, and make
Even want of wit a virtue."
       Shirley, *The Constant Maid,* i. 1.

By fancy charmed, shall read, O Varus, thee
Our tam'risks, thee shall all the woodland sing ;
Nor any page to Phœbus sweeter is
Than that which hath the name of Varus traced
Upon its front. Proceed, Pierian maids.
The striplings Chromis and Mnasylos spied
Silenus lying in a cave asleep,
With yestern Bacchus swollen through his veins,   20
As ever. Garlands just outside him lay,
But merely fallen off his head, and hung
His heavy beaker by its handle worn.
Assailing him—for oft the agèd man
Had, with the expectation of a song,
Played false with both of them—they fetters throw
Upon him, from the very garlands [forged].
As their companion, Ægle joins herself,
And sudden comes upon them in their fear,
Ægle, the fairest of the water Nymphs. 30
And now, as up he looks, with mulberries
Blood-red his forehead and his brows she stains.
He, laughing at the trick,—" Why fetters tie ?"
Exclaims : " Release me, lads ; it is enough
That it is seen that you have had the power.

20. " Help, Virtue ! these are sponges and not men !
Bottles ! mere vessels !"
       Ben Jonson, *Pleasure reconciled to Virtue.*

The songs, which wish ye, hear: the songs
   for *you*;
For *her* shall be another kind of fee."
At once begins he of his own accord.
Then, sooth, both Fauns and savage beasts
   to rhythm
You might see frolic, then stiff oaks to wave
Their crests. Nor doth so much in Phœbus
   joy   41
Parnassus' crag, nor Rhodope and Ismarus
So much at Orpheus marvel. For he sang
How through the vasty void had been com-
   bined
The seeds alike of lands, and air, and sea,
And at the same time those of flowing fire;
How all beginnings from these rudiments,
And e'en the yielding ball of th' atmosphere
Together grew; then how the ground began
To harden, and within the deep apart   50
To shut the ocean up, and by degrees
To take the shapes of things; and [how] anon
The lands at glimm'ring of a new-born sun
Are in amaze, and from a greater height
From clouds uplifted do the showers fall;
When forests first begin to spring, and when
Are straying through the mounts, that know
   them not,
The scattered forms of life. He next relates
The stones by Pyrrha cast, the Saturn reign,
And birds of Caucase, and Prometheus'
   rape.   60
To these he adds, how, quitted at the spring,
The seamen had on Hylas called aloud,
That all the strand with "Hylas! Hylas!"
   rang.

And, blessèd if there never had been herds,
Pasiphaë he comforts in her love
For the young snowy bull. "Ah! hapless
   dame!
What frenzy thee hath seized! The Prœtides
With their fantastic lowings filled the fields;
But, ne'ertheless, not one of them pursued
So scandalous embracements of the beasts,
Though for her neck she'd feared the plough,
   and oft   71
Upon her glossy forehead sought for horns.
Ah! hapless dame! You now on moun-
   tains rove;
He, cushioned on his side of snowy white
With downy martagon, beneath a dun
Holm-oak, on yellowing grasses chews the
   cud,
Or courts some female in the mighty herd."
"Shut, nymphs, Dictæan nymphs, now shut
The forest-passes, if by any chance
The truant footsteps of the bull may come
Across mine eyes. Him, haply, either
   charmed   81
By grass of green, or following the droves,
Some cows may lure away to Gortyn's
   stalls."
He next the damsel chants, who in amaze
Beheld the apples of th' Hesperides.
He next the sister-train of Phaeton
Encircles with the moss of bitter bark,
And rears them tow'ring alders from the
   ground.
Then sings he how, while straying by the
   streams
Of the Permessus, to Aonian mounts   90
One of the sisters Gallus led; and how
The choir of Phœbus to the hero all
In homage rose; how Linus these to him—
The shepherd of a heav'nly lay; with flowers

39. So Piers says of Cuddie: Spenser, *Sh. Cal.*
Oct. 25:
" Soone as thou gynst to sette thy notes in frame,
O how the rural routes to thee do cleave!"

" For we will have the wanton Fauns,
   That frisking skip about the lawns,
   The Panisks, and the Sylvans rude,
   Satyrs, and all that multitude,
   To dance their wilder rounds about
   And cleave the air with many a shout
   As they would hunt poor Echo out."
               Ben Jonson, *The Penates*.

A different effect of the voice is seen in Shirley:
" The tongue that's able to rock heaven asleep,
And make the music of the spheres stand still,
To listen to the happier airs it makes,
And mend their tunes by it." *Love Tricks*, iv. 2.
So in Shakespeare, quoted by Gifford:
" And when Love speaks the voice of all the gods
Makes heaven drowsy with the harmony."

46. But whether *liquidus* means here " flowing,"
or " transparent," or " unmingled," it is not easy to
: ee.

63. " Or that same daintie lad, which was so deare
   To great Alcides, that, whenas he dyde,
   He wailed womanlike with many a teare,
   And every wood and every valley wyde
He filld with Hylas name: the nymphes eke Hylas
   cryde." Spenser, *Faerie Queene*, iii. 12, 7.

75. It may as well be remarked here that in this
work there is no preteusion of determining what is
meant by the terms which stand for plants. "*Hyacinthus*" is usually rendered "martagon," only
because the learned and careful Martyn is so positive that this is the flower intended: and to call it
"hyacinth" would be simply to mislead. Whatever *hyacinthus* meant, it is certain that it did *not*
mean " hyacinth." But, it must be confessed, that
the "imperial martagon" would not form exactly
the sort of bed that a sensible bull would be likely
to choose. In autumn, at least, he might nearly as
well select a couch of sticks.

86. Spenser thus finely alludes to the story of
Phaeton:
" As when the firie-mouthed steedes, which drew
   The Sunne's bright wayne to Phaeton's decay,
   Soone as they did the monstrous Scorpion vew,
   With ugly craples crawling in their way,
   The dreadful sight did them so sore affray,
   That their well-knowen courses they forwent ;
   And, leading th' ever burning lampe astray,
   This lower world nigh all to ashes brent,
And left their scorched path yet in the firmament."
                                   F. Q. v. 8, 40.
                                                   C

And bitter parsley on his tresses crowned—
Pronounced : "These reeds to thee the Muses grant—
Lo, take them !—which to Ascra's agèd [bard
They granted] erst ; wherewith in playing he
Was wont to trail stiff ashes from the mounts.
Thereon by thee the birth of Grynium's glade 100
Be chanted, lest there should be any grove,
Wherein Apollo more may boast himself."
Why should I tell how [he] of Scylla [sang, Daughter] of Nisus, whom hath rumor traced :

95. So Gray makes Nature address Shakespeare:
"What time, where lucid Avon stray'd
 To him the mighty mother did unveil
 Her awful face: the dauntless child
 Stretch'd forth his little arms and smil'd :
'This pencil take,' she said, 'whose colours clear
 Richly paint the vernal year.
Thine, too, these golden keys, immortal Boy !
 This can unlock the gates of Joy ;
 Of Horror that, and thrilling Fears,
Or ope the sacred source of sympathetic tears.'"
                              Progress of Poesy.

104. Catrou's and Doering's reading of *aut* before *quam* would relieve this passage of much of its difficulty : but there is so little manuscript authority

That she, beneath her snowy waist begirt
With baying monsters, plagued Dulichia's ships,
And in the deepsome gulf, ah ! piecemeal rent
The frighted mariners with her sea-dogs ?
Or how he told of Tereus' limbs trans-shaped ;
What cates for him, what presents Philomel
Prepared ; with what career the wastes she sought, 111
And with what pinions first, unhappy [bird] !
She o'er her own abode flew to and fro.
[The lays], all which, as Phœbus played them erst,
The blest Eurotas heard, and bade his bays
By aid of memory to learn, he sings :
The stricken vales return them to the stars ;
Until to gather in the cotes the sheep,
And count their tale, did Vesper give command,
And issue forth upon unwilling heaven. 120

for it, that, with Heyne, Forbiger, Wagner, and Weise, it is better to leave the difficulty as it is, than to tamper with the text.

118. "By this the moystie Night approaching fast, Her deawy humour 'gan on th' earth to shed, That warn'd the shepheards to their home to hast Their tender flocks, now being fully fed."
                    Spenser, *Faerie Queene,* vi. 9, 13.

Eclogue VII. MELIBŒUS.

MELIBŒUS. CORYDON. THYRSIS.

Melibœus. By hazard underneath a whisp'ring holm
Had Daphnis sat him down, and Corydon
And Thyrsis had together driv'n their flocks
Into one spot—sheep Thyrsis, Corydon
His she-goats swollen out with milk :
Both blooming in their age, Arcadians both,
And matched in song, and ready at reply.
Hither from me, while I bescreen from cold
The tender myrtle-shrubs, the goat himself,
The husband of my flock, had strayed away ; 10
And Daphnis I espy. When he sees me
On th' other hand, he cries : "Quick, hither come,
O Melibœus ; safe for thee thy goat
And kids : and if thou canst delay awhile,
Beneath the shade repose thee ! hither of themselves

The steers will come along the leas to drink:
Here lines his em'rald banks with tender reed
The Mincius, and from out the holy oak
The swarms are humming. What was I to do ?
I nor Alcippe, nor a Phyllis had, 20
The lambkins, banished from the milk, to pen
At home ; a match, there was, too—Corydon
With Thyrsis ;—['twas] a mighty [match]. Still I
Postponed my grave pursuits to their disport.
They, therefore, in alternate verses both
Began to strive : the Muses willed that they
Alternate [verses] should recite. These Corydon,
Those Thyrsis, [each] repeated in his turn.
Cor. Libethran Nymphs, our charm, or deign to me

A sonnet, such as ye to Codrus mine ;— 30
To lays of Phœbus he the nearest makes ;—
Or, if we have not all the pow'r, my pipe
Here tuneful from the holy pine shall hang.
Thy. Arcadian shepherds, with the ivy
    deck
Your rising poet, that may Codrus' sides
Be burst with envy ; or, if he have praised
Beyond his will, with baccar bind my brow,
Lest tongue of mischief harm your future
    bard.
Cor. This bristly boar's head, Delia,
    [gives] to thee
The little Mycon, and the branching horns
Of long-lived hart. If lasting this should
    prove,   41
Of polished marble thou full-length shalt
    stand,
With scarlet buskin booted on thy legs.
Thy. A bowl of milk, Priapus, and these
    cakes,
Each year for thee to look for is enough :
Thou 'rt keeper of a wretched garden.
    Now
Of marble, suited to our present means,
We've made thee ; but do thou, if teemful-
    ness
Our flock shall have recruited, be of gold.
Cor. O Nerean Galatee, to me more
    sweet   50
Than Hybla's thyme, more bright than
    swans, more fair
Than blanching ivy—soon as shall the bulls,
Full-fed, reseek their cribs, if any care
For thy own Corydon possess thee, come.
Thy. Nay, may I seem more bitter unto
    thee
Than Sardon herbs, more rough than
    butcher's-broom,
Than stranded sea-weed baser, if this light
Is not already longer unto me

Than a whole year. Go home, full-fed ;
    if [you
Have] any modesty, begone, ye steers. 60
Cor. Ye mossy springs, and grass more
    soft than sleep,
And verdant arbute, which is screening
    you
With scattered shade, the solstice from the
    flock
Ward off ; now comes the scorching sum-
    mer, now,
Upon the merry vine-spray swell the buds.
Thy. Here hearth and oily pines, here
    plenteous fire
Aye be, and lintels black with ceaseless
    soot :
Here we as much for chills of Boreas care
As either for the number [of the sheep]
The wolf, or boiling rivers for their banks.
Cor. Both junipers and prickly chestnut
    trees   71
Stand bristling ; strewed in every quarter
    lie
Its fruits beneath each tree ; now all things
    smile :
But if the fair Alexis from these mounts
Depart, you e'en would see the rivers dry.
Thy. The field is parched ; through
    tainture of the air
The dying herbage thirsts ; his viny shades,
Hath Liber grudged the hills : at the
    approach
Of our own Phyllis all the grove will
    bloom,

"For dayes, but houres ; for moneths that passed
    were,
She told but weeks, to make them seeme more
    few :
Yet, when she reckned them still drawing neare,
Each hour did seem a moneth, and every moneth a
    yeare."
" The art of numbers cannot count the hours
    Thou hast been absent."
        Middleton, *The Family of Love*, v. 2.
" *Marian.* Could you so long be absent?
Robin. What, a week ! Was that so long ?
Marian. How long are lovers' weeks,
Do you think, Robin, when they are asunder ?
Are they not prisoners' years ?"
        B. Jonson, *Sad Shepherd*, i. 2.
" Still, when we expect
Our bliss, time creeps ; but when the happier things
Call to enjoy, each saucy hour hath wings."
        Shirley, *The Traitor*, i. 2.
74. " But neither breath of Morn, when she ascends
With charm of earliest birds ; nor rising sun
On this delightful land ; nor herb, fruit, flower,
Glistening with dew ; nor fragrance after showers ;
Nor grateful evening mild ; nor silent Night,
With this her solemn bird ; nor walk by moon,
Or glittering star-light, without thee is sweet."
        Milton, *P. L.* iv.
79. Cowley gives a different turn to the idea :
speaking of spring, he says :

Line 35. Strictly, *frontem* should be rendered by
"his brow," not " my brow," referring to *poeta* ;
but the confusion between Codrus and Thyrsis
would thus become inextricable.
" *Cæsar.* Cato, you will undo him with your
praise.
Cato. Cæsar will hurt himself with his own envy.
People. The voice of Cato is the voice of Rome.
Cato. The voice of Rome is the consent of
heaven."   Ben Jonson, *Catiline*, iii. 1.
49.   " What is't ? but effect it,
And thou shalt be my Æsculapius :
Thy image shall be set up in pure gold,
To which I will fall down, and worship it."
Beaumont and Fletcher, *Thierry and Theodoret*,
ii. 1.
58. Much the same were the feelings of Britomart
at the absence of Artegal : Spenser, *F. Q.* v. 6, 5 :
" And then, her griefe with errour to beguyle,
She fayn'd to count the time againe anew,
As if before she had not counted trew :

And Jove drop plenteous down in joyful rain. 80
Cor. T' Alcides poplar dearest is, the vine
To Bacchus, to the lovely Venus plant
Of myrtle, unto Phœbus his own bay ;
Loves Phyllis hazel-shrubs : so long as these
Shall Phyllis love, nor myrtle-plant, nor bay
Of Phœbus, shall the hazel-shrubs surpass.

" How could it be so fair, and you away?
How could the trees be beauteous, flowers so gay?
Could they remember but last year,
How you did them, they you delight,
The sprouting leaves which saw you here,
And call'd their fellows to the sight,
Would, looking round for the same sight in vain,
Creep back into their silent barks again."
The Mistress : Spring.

Thy. The ash-tree in the woods is loveliest,
The pine in gardens, poplar by the floods,
The silver-fir upon the lofty mounts :
But if thou oft'ner would'st revisit me, 90
Fair Lycidas, the ash-tree in the woods,
The pine in gardens should make way for thee.
Mel. I these remember, and that all in vain
Competed conquered Thyrsis. From that time
Is Corydon the Corydon for us.

---

93. Is it quite certain that " Corydon for ever," (which is, after all that has been written about it, the meaning of the last line in the Latin,) is exactly a judicious cheer ?

Eclogue VIII. PHARMACEUTRIA.

DAMON. ALPHESIBŒUS.

THE shepherds Damon and Alphesibœus' song,
Whom, mindless of her browse, the heifer viewed
In wonder, while contending ; at whose lay
The pards were with amazement struck, and, changed
In their careerings, rivers came to rest :—
We Damon's and Alphesibœus' song will chant.
Whether thou dost for me now overpass
The rocks of great Timavus, or dost cruise
Along the margin of Illyria's sea ;
Lo ! will that day be ever [here], when I 10
May be allowed to celebrate thy deeds ?
Lo ! will it [come],that I may be allowed
To bear throughout the universe thy lays,
Alone for Sophoclean buskin meet ?
My spring [of song] from thee on thee shall end :

Line 5. The active use of *requiesco* seems to rest on slender foundation. The passage from *Ciris* proves nothing ; and that from Propertius, ii. 22, 25, little more. However, there is one from the latter author much more to the point: ii. 34, 75: " Quamvis ille suam lassus requievit avenam." Able authors take both views of the matter ; and this is certain, that no one can say that the word is *not* used actively here, though such a use is extremely rare.
The skill of Damon and Alphesibœus is attributed to Thyrsis by Milton in his *Comus:*
" Thyrsis? whose artful strains have oft delayed
The huddling brook to hear his madrigal."
15. " Then ever, beauteous Contemplation, hail !
From thee began, auspicious maid, my song ;
With thee shall end."
Warton, *Pleasures of Melancholy.*

Receive the lays, commenced at thy commands,
And suffer thou this ivy round thy brows
To creep along among thy conqu'ring bays.
The chilly shadow of the night had scarce
Departed from the sky, what time the dew
Upon the tender herbage to the flock 21
Is welcomest ;—upon his rounded crook
Of olive leaning, Damon thus began :
Damon. Arise, and usher in the bounteous day,
Forestalling it, O Lucifer ; while I,
By Nisa my betrothed's unworthy love
Beguiled, am plaining, and the deities,
(Though by their being witnesses [thereto]
No vantage have I gained, yet) as I die,
Am I addressing at my latest hour. 30
Begin with me, my pipe, Mænalian strains.
Mænalus both a tuneful wood, and pines
That speak, hath ever ; ever doth he hear
The shepherds' loves, and Pan, who was the first,
Who suffered not that reeds should idle [rest].
Begin with me, my pipe, Mænalian strains.

18. " Laurel is a victor's due !
I give it you,
I give it you ;
Thy name with praise,
Thy brow with bays
We circle round :
All men rejoice
With cheerful voice,
To see there like a conqueror crowned.
Middleton, *More Dissemblers besides Women*, i. 3.

To Mopsus is my Nisa given: what
May not we lovers look for? Griffins now
With horses shall be yoked, and in the age
Ensuing shall the fearful fallow-deer   40
With stag-hounds to the drinking-troughs
   repair.
Fresh torches, Mopsus, cut: for thee a bride
Is being escorted [home]: O bridegroom,
   strew
The nuts: for thee doth Hesper Œta quit.
Begin with me, my pipe, Mænalian strains.
O mated to a worthy spouse! Whilst
   thou
Look'st down on every man, and while my
   pipe
Is thy abhorrence, while my she-goats, too,
And shaggy eye-brow, and my dangling
   beard;
Nor deem'st thou any god minds human
   things.   50
Begin with me, my pipe, Mænalian strains.
   In our enclosures thee, a tiny [maid]—
Your guide was I—I with thy mother saw
The dewy apples culling: then the year,
Next from th' eleventh, just had me em-
   braced;
I just was able from the ground to reach
The brittle branches. When I looked, how
   I was lost!

37. "If his possessing her your rage does move,
   'Tis jealousy, the avarice of love."
               Dryden, *The Maiden Queen*, iii. 1.
"Then, when our eager wishes soared the highest,
Ready to stoop and grasp the lovely game,
A haggard owl, a worthless kite of prey,
With his foul wings, sailed in, and spoiled my
   quarry."   Otway, *Venice Preserved*, i. 1.
39. Such anomalies are graphically paralleled by
Pope in the 3rd Book of the *Dunciad*:
"Thence a new world, to Nature's laws unknown,
Breaks out refulgent, with a heaven its own:
Another Cynthia her new journey runs,
And other planets circle other suns.
The forests dance, the rivers upward rise,
Whales sport in woods, and dolphins in the
   skies."
57. "Why, Philocles, what lost already, man!
Struck dead with one poor glance!"
                           May, *The Heir*, ii.
                  "I tell you what she is,
What she expects, and what she will effect,
Unless you be the miracle of men,
That come with a purpose to behold,
And go away yourself."
Beaumont and Fletcher, *The Laws of Candy*, ii. 1.
"How art thou lost! How on a sudden lost!"
                           Milton, *P. L.* b. ix.
Similarly Marcus, of the sight of Lucia, in
Addison's *Cato*, iii. 1:
"And yet, when I behold the charming maid,
I'm ten times more undone."
And Cowley:
"I came, I saw, and was undone."
               Mistress: The Thraldom.

How fell distraction hurried me away!
Begin with me, my pipe, Mænalian strains.
Now know I what is Love: to him
   among   60
The rugged rocks doth either Tomarus,
Or Rhodope, or utmost Garamants,
An imp nor of our breed, nor blood, give
   birth.
Begin with me, my pipe, Mænalian strains.
Fell Love hath taught a mother to distain
Her hands all over with her children's
   blood:
O mother, also barbarous wert thou!
More barbarous the mother, or that boy
More impious? More barbarous that boy;
O mother, also barbarous wert thou!   70
Begin with me, my pipe, Mænalian strains.
Now even let the wolf unbidden fly
The sheep; let churlish oaks gold apples
   bear;
With daffodilly let the alder bloom;
Let tam'risks drop rich ambers from their
   rinds;
E'en owlets vie with swans; let Tityrus

63. "For such a warped slip of wilderness
     Ne'er issued from his blood."
   Shakespeare, *Measure for Measure*, iii. 4.

65. The unprejudiced reader, who is not absurdly
wedded to Virgil, as Dr. Trapp and others, can
hardly help going along with Heyne in his caustic
remarks on verses 49, 50. However, he seems too
hasty in expunging them from the text. Why may
not Virgil have written bad lines as well as any
other poet? Milton, who was vastly his superior in
genius, has written scores of them.
   In the 49th verse, instead of the awkward supply
of *magis* before *improbus*, may not *puer improbus
ille* be one phrase? Vide *Geo.* iii. 431, *Hic improbus*; *Æn.* v. 397, *Improbus iste*. So that the
meaning would be: Fell Love taught, &c. You,
mother, were barbarous as well as he (Love). Was
the mother the more barbarous, or that wicked boy?
That wicked boy was (more barbarous); you,
mother, were barbarous too (though he more so).

66. "Oh, mother, do not lose your name! forget
   not
The touch of nature in you, tenderness!
'Tis all the soul of woman, all the sweetness!
Forget not, I beseech you, what are children,
Nor how you have groaned for them; to what
   love
They are born inheritors, with what care kept;
And, as they rise to ripeness, still remember
How they imp out your age! and when time
   calls you,
That as an autumn flower you fall, forget not
How round about your hearse they hang like
   pennons."
Beaumont and Fletcher, *Thierry and Theodoret*,
v. 2.

67.   "This is the very top,
The height, the crest, or crest unto the crest
Of murder's arms: this is the bloodiest shame,
The wildest savagery, the vilest stroke,
That ever wall-eyed wrath, or staring rage,
Presented to the tears of soft remorse."
           Shakespeare, *King John*, iv. 3.

Become an Orpheus, Orpheus in the woods,
Among the dolphins an Arion [be].
Begin with me, my pipe, Mænalian strains.
Let all things even to mid sea be turned.
Ye forests, fare ye well.   Headforemost I
Shall from a skyey mountain's watching-
post   82
Upon the waves be borne adown: this gift,
The latest of a dying man, retain.
Cease thou, now cease, my pipe, Mænalian
strains.
  These Damon [sang] : do ye, Pierian
maids,
What [strains] Alphesibœus in reply
Returned declare : we cannot all do all.
Alphesibœus. Bring water forth, and with
a downy wreath
Festoon these altars, and rich vervains
burn,   90
And the male frankincense : that I may
try
My paramour's sound senses to derange
With sorc'rous rites : naught here, but
spells, there lacks.
Bring home from town, my spells, bring
Daphnis [home].

---

82. " Still fate is in my reach : from mountains
high,
Deep in whose shadow craggy ruins lie,
Can I not headlong fling this weight of woe,
And dash out life against the flints below ?
Are there not streams, and lakes, and rivers wide,
Where my last breath may bubble on the tide ?"
                                      Gay, *Dione*, v. 2.

90. " Black spirits and white, red spirits and gray,
Mingle, mingle, mingle, you that mingle may !
    Titty, Tiffin, keep it stiff in !
    Firedrake, Puckey, make it lucky !
    Liard, Robin, you must bob in !
Round, around, around, about, about !
All ill come running in, all good keep out !
                    Middleton, *The Witch*, v. 2.

93. The power of magic is described with infinite
beauty by Shakespeare in his *Tempest*, v. 1:
" Ye elves of hills, brooks, standing lakes, and
groves ;
 And ye, that on the sands with printless foot,
Do chase the ebbing Neptune, and do fly him,
When he comes back ; you demy-puppets, that
By moonshine do the green-sour ringlets make,
Whereof the ewe not bites ; and you, whose
pastime
Is to make midnight mushrooms : that rejoice
To hear the solemn curfew ; by whose aid
(Weak masters though ye be) I have bedimm'd
 The noontide sun, call'd forth the mutinous winds,
And 'twixt the green sea and the azur'd vault
Set roaring war ; to the dread rattling thunder
Have I given fire, and rifted Jove's stout oak
With his own bolt ; the strong-bas'd promontory
Have I made shake, and by the spurs pluck'd up
The pine and cedar ; graves, at my command,
Have wak'd their sleepers ; oped, and let them
forth
By my so potent art."

94. Or :   " my Daphnis bring."

Spells even can from heav'n unsphere
the moon ;
By spells did Circe change Ulysses' mates ;
Cold in the meads through charming bursts
the snake.
Bring home from town, my spells, bring
  . Daphnis [home].
I first around thee twine these triple
threads,
With threefold color chequered, and three
times   100
This image round the altars do I lead :
In number odd the deity delights.
Bring home from town, my spells, bring
Daphnis [home].
Twine thou, O Amaryllis, in three knots
Three colors ; twine them, Amaryllis, now,
And say : "The chains of Venus do I
twine."
Bring home from town, my spells, bring
Daphnis [home].
As doth this clay grow hard, and as this
wax
Grows fluid at the one and selfsame fire—

---

95.   " Can you doubt me, then, daughter,
That can make mountains tremble, miles of
woods walk,
Whole earth's foundation bellow, and the spirits
Of the entombed to burst out from their marbles ;
Nay, draw yond moon to my involved designs ?"
                          Middleton, *The Witch*, v. 2.

99. There is a marked allusion to these magical
rites in Spenser's account of Glauce's efforts in
behalf of Britomart, though her object was the
exact reverse of Virgil's witch :—" to undoe her
daughter's love :"
" Then, taking thrise three heares from off her
head,
Them trebly breaded in a threefold lace,
And round about the pots mouth bound the
 . thread ;
And, after having whispered a space
Certein sad words with hollow voice and bace,
Shee to the virgin sayd, thrise sayd she itt :
' Come, daughter, come ; come, spit upon my
face ;
Spitt thrise upon me, thrise upon me spitt :
Th' uneven nomber for this business is most fitt.' "
                                      F. Q. iii. 2, 50.

100. So Dame Partlett to Chanticleer: Dryden,
Cock and Fox, 187, 8 :
" Take just three worms, nor under nor above,
Because the gods unequal numbers love."

109. " His picture made in wax, and gently molten
By a blue fire, kindled with dead men's eyes,
Will waste him by degrees."
                          Middleton, *The Witch*, v. 2.

" As thus I stab his picture, and stare on it,
Methinks the duke should feel me now : is not
His soul acquainted ? Can he less than tremble,
When I lift up my arm to wound his counterfeit ?
Witches can persecute the lives of whom
They hate, when they torment their senseless
figures,
And stick the waxen model full of pins."
                          Shirley, *The Traitor*, v. 2.

So Daphnis by our love. Strew salted meal, 110
And with bitumen light the crackling bays.
Me felon Daphnis burns, in Daphnis I this bay.
Bring home from town, my spells, bring Daphnis [home].
May such a passion Daphnis [seize], as when,
Worn out in seeking for the youthful bull
Through lawns and lofty groves, a heifer sinks
Down by a water-rill on verdant sedge,
Distracted, nor remembers to withdraw
From night's late [hour.] Him such a passion seize,
Nor let his curing be a care to me ! 120
Bring home from town, my spells, bring Daphnis [home].
This cast-apparel erst th' arch-traitor left
For me, dear pledges of himself, which now
I at the very entrance, earth, consign
To you; these pledges Daphnis owe [to me].
Bring home from town, my spells, bring Daphnis [home].
These herbs and poisons these, in Pontus culled,
Mœris himself gave me : full many grow
In Pontus. Oft with these I've Mœris seen
Become a wolf, and hide him in the woods; 130
Oft spirits summon from their lowest graves,
And seeded crops transport to other ground.

111. The bay was probably put inside the image, being hollow.

132. " Or dost thou envy
The fat prosperity of any neighbour ?
I'll call forth Hoppo, and her incantation
Can straight destroy the young of all his cattle ;

Bring home from town, my spells, bring Daphnis [home].
The ashes, Amaryllis, bear abroad,
And throw them in a running brook, and o'er
Thy head ; nor should'st thou cast a look behind.
With these I Daphnis will assail : naught he
Of deities, naught recks he of my spells.
Bring home from town, my spells, bring Daphnis [home].
Behold ! while I delay to bear them forth, 140
The very ashes of their own accord
Have on the altars seized with bick'ring flames.
Auspicious may it prove ! I know not what,
[But something] 'tis for certain ; Hylax, too,
Is barking in the sill. Do we believe
[The omen] ? Or do they, who are in love,
Themselves to their own selves imagine dreams ?
Spare, spells, now spare him ! Daphnis comes from town.

Blast vineyards, orchards, meadows ; or in one night
Transport his dung, hay, corn, by reeks, whole stacks,
Into thine own ground."
                Middleton, *The Witch*, i. 2.
144. This expression is used by Milton in *Comus* :
    " For certain
Either some like us night-foundered here."
And by Shakespeare, *Merchant of Venice*, v. 1 :
  " For here I read for certain that my ships
  Are safely come to road."
147. " Am I awake, or dream I ? Is it true,
Or does my flattering fancy but suggest
What I most covet ?" May, *The Heir*, ii.

Eclogue IX. MŒRIS.

LYCIDAS. MŒRIS.

Lycidas. Whither, O Mœris, do thy feet [bear] thee ?
Is't to the city, whither leads the way ?
Mœris. O Lycidas, we've reached [the day] alive,
When a strange owner of our little farm,
(Which ne'er we feared,) should tell us, " These are mine ;
Old tenants, move away." Now overborne,

Line 6. " Greedy of gain, either by fraud or stealth ;
And whilst one toils, another gets the wealth."
Middleton, *More Dissemblers besides Women*, iii. 2.

In woe, since chance is shifting all, do we
These kids to him—no luck go with them ! —send.
Ly. I sooth had surely heard, that where the hills
Begin to slope them off, and sink their ridge,
With gentle dip, as far as to the stream, 11
And antiquated beech, now shivered tops,
All by his lays had your Menalcas saved.
Mœ. Hear it thou didst ; a rumor e'en it was ;
But lays of ours as much, O Lycidas,
Avail 'mid warlike weapons, as they say
Do Chaon pigeons when the eagle swoops.

But save a crow upon the left, from out
A hollow ilex, had forewarnèd me
By any means whatever to cut short   20
The fresh disputes, nor would thy Mœris
here,
Nor would Menalcas even, be alive.
Ly. Alas! occurs to any guilt so deep?
Alas! were consolations thine from us,
Well nigh along with thee, Menalcas,
reft?
Who could the Nymphets sing? Who strew
the ground
With blooming plants, or mantle o'er the
springs
With emerald shade? Or [who could sing]
the lays
Which I caught up by stealth from thee of
late,
When thou to Amaryllis, our delight,   30
Would'st take thee :—"Tityrus, till I re-
turn—
The journey is but short—feed thou my
goats,
And drive them on to drink when they are
fed,
O Tityrus; and, in thy driving them,
Of going in the way of my he-goat—
That fellow butteth with his horn—be-
ware!"
Mœ. Nay, rather those,— nor they yet
finished off,—
Which he to Varus sang : "Varus, thy
name,
Let only Mantua for us survive—
Ah! Mantua, a neighbor, too, too near   40
The evil-starred Cremona—as they chant,
The swans on high shall carry to the stars."

26. "Strew, strew the glad and smiling ground,
   With every flower, yet not confound
The primrose drop, the spring's own spouse,
Bright day's-eyes, and the lips of cows,
The garden-star, the queen of May,
The rose, to crown the holyday."
                Ben Jonson, *Pan's Anniversary.*
"Whose name shall now make ring
The echoes? Of whom shall the nymphets sing?"
"Blush no more, rose, nor lily pale remain,
Dead is that beauty which yours late did stain."
            Drummond, *Sonnets*, P. ii. 13, 10.
41. Shakespeare thus alludes to the warbling of
the swan :
"Let music sound while he doth make his choice;
Then, if he lose, he makes a swan-like end,
Fading in music." *Merchant of Venice*, iii. 2.
And again, in *King John*, v. 7 :
        " 'Tis strange that death should sing.
I am the cygnet to this pale faint swan,
Who chaunts a doleful hymn to his own death,
And from the organ-pipe of frailty sings
His soul and body to their lasting rest."
"Thus on Mæander's flowery margin lies .
The expiring swan, and as he sings he dies."
                Pope, *Rape of the Lock*, canto v.

Ly. So may thy swarms escape Cyrnean
yews!
So may, upon the cytisus full-fed,
Thy kine swell out their teats! Begin, if
aught
Thou hast. Me also have a poet made
Pieria's ladies; I have verses too;
Me likewise do the shepherds call a bard :
But not in them a weak believer I.
For [lays] I seem to warble, neither yet   50
Of Varus nor of Cinna worthy, but a goose
To cackle in the midst of tuneful swans.
Mœ. That sooth am I about, and silently,
O Lycid, with myself I turn it o'er,
If I could recollect it; nor is mean
The sonnet : "Hither come, O Galatee;
For what is thy diversion in the waves?
Here spring all bright; here, round the
rills,
The earth unbosoms her enamelled flowers;
The silver poplar here o'erhangs the grot,   60
And limber vines pleach bowers. Hither
come;
The frantic waves allow to lash the shores."
Ly. What those, which I had heard thee
when alone
Warbling beneath the cloudless night? The
air
I recollect, if I could catch the words.
Mœ. "O Daphnis, wherefore art thou
gazing up
Upon the constellations' rise of old?
Lo! hath the Dionæan Cæsar's star
Advanced; the star, whereby might fields
of corn
Delight them in their produce, and whereby
The bunch might draw its hue on sunny
hills.   71
Engraft the pear-trees, Daphnis; sons of sons

Garth, still more musically :
"The tuneful swans on gliding rivers float,
And warbling dirges die on every note."
                Dispensary, canto iv.
51. "At last, whenas our quire wants breath,
        Our bodies being blest,
We'll sing, like swans, to welcome death,
        And die in love and rest."
            Webster, *The Duchess of Malfi*, iv. 2.
"Who hath his flock of cackling geese compared
With thy tuned quire of swans?"
            Carew, *To Ben Jonson.*
59. "Shepherd, I pray thee stay. Where hast
thou been?
Or whither goest thou? Here be woods as green
As any; air likewise as fresh and sweet
As where smooth Zephyrus plays on the fleet
Face of the curlèd streams; with flowers as many
As the young spring gives, and as choice as any;
Here be all new delights, cool streams and wells,
Arbours o'ergrown with woodbines, caves, and
dells."
    J. Fletcher, *The Faithful Shepherdess*, i. 3.

Shall cull thy fruits." Age all things sweeps away,
The mem'ry too. I recollect that oft, a boy,
The ling'ring suns I buried as I sang :
So many songs are now by me forgot.
Now very voice, too, Mœris flies ; the wolves
Have first seen Mœris. But, however, these
Full oft to thee Menalcas will recite.
Ly. By pleading pretexts our enjoyments thou 80
Deferr'st for long. And now, all lulled for thee,

The surface [of the lake] is still ; and, look! Hath ev'ry breath of breezy whisper fallen.
From this we have exactly half the way ;
For 'gins Bianor's burial-place to show.
Here, where the farmers strip the clustered leaves,
Here, Mœris, sing we ; here do thou the kids
Set down : we still shall to the city come.
Or, if we fear lest night may gather rain
Before, we may—the road will irk the less—
Go singing still ; that singing we may go, 91
I'll disencumber thee of this thy load.
Mœ. Cease more, O swain ; and that which presses now
Let us discharge : the songs we then shall sing
The better, when he shall have come himself.

---

73. This idea is beautifully expressed by Dryden :
" O'er whom Time gently shakes his wings of down,
Till with his silent sickle they are mown."
Astræa Redux, 109.
" The end crowns all ;
And that old common arbitrator, Time,
Will one day end it."
Shakespeare, *Troilus and Cressida,* iv. 5.
75. " How oft in pleasing tasks we wear the day,
While summer suns roll unperceived away!"
Pope, *Ep. to Mr. Jervas.*
A. Philips, somewhat differently from Virgil :
" For many songs and tales of mirth had I
To chase the loit'ring sun adowne the sky."
Past. 1.
78. To this notion Dryden alludes ; *Hind and Panther,* 551, 2 :
" The surly Wolf, with secret envy burst,
Yet could not howl : the Hind had seen him first."

82. So Parnell in his beautiful *Night-piece on Death* :
" The slumb'ring breeze forgets to breathe ;
The lake is smooth and clear beneath."
84. *Medius* seems not to be used by classical writers strictly in the sense of "half;" but it is hard to make decent English of the sense "middle," without an objectionable paraphrase.
" Discourse hath made the way less tedious :
We have reached the cell already."
Shirley, *St. Patrick for Ireland,* v. 3.
90. Or, if *tædit* be read with Wagner: "the journey irketh less."

Eclogue X. GALLUS.

This latest effort, Arethuse, do thou
Vouchsafe me : lays a few to Gallus mine,
But which Lycoris may herself peruse,
Must be recited : who will lays deny
To Gallus ? So along with thee, when thou
Shalt underneath Sicilian surges glide,
May not salt Doris blend her wave ! Begin :
Let us the restless loves of Gallus tell,
While flat-nosed she-goats nibble tender shrubs.
We sing not to the deaf : woods echo all. 10
What lawns, or woodlands what, held you, O Naiad maids,

When Gallus with unworthy passion pined?
For neither unto you Parnassus' brows,
For neither any [brows] of Pindus caused
Delay, nor Aon Aganippe. Him
E'en bay-trees, even tamarisks bewept ;
Him, lying underneath a lonely cliff,
E'en piny Mæn'lus and the rocks of cold
Lycæus wept. The sheep, too, stand around ;—

Line 11. There is a marked resemblance between this Eclogue and Milton's *Lycidas* ; but how immeasurably the English has distanced the Latin poet, must be obvious to any one who can divest himself of prejudice :
" Where were ye, nymphs, when the remorseless deep
Closed o'er the head of your loved Lycidas ?
For neither were ye playing on the steep,
Where your old bards, the famous Druids, lie,
Nor on the shaggy top of Mona high," &c.

19. So Pope, *Past.* 2 :
" Soft as he mourn'd the streams forgot to flow,
The flocks around a dumb compassion show."
" There was speech in their dumbness, language in their very gesture."—Shakespeare, *Winter's Tale,* v. 2.
This whole account of Gallus brings to mind the melancholy youth in Gray's *Elegy* :
" There at the foot of yonder nodding beech,
That wreathes its old fantastic roots so high,
His listless length at noontide would he stretch,
And pore upon the brook that babbles by.
Hard by yon wood, now smiling as in scorn,
Mutt'ring his wayward fancies, would he rove ;
Now drooping, woful, wan, like one forlorn,
Or craz'd with care, or cross'd in hopeless love."

They neither are ashamed of us, nor thou 20
Be of the flock ashamed, O heav'nly bard:
Yea, sheep by rivers fair Adonis fed ;—
And came the shepherd ; plodding swine-
   herds came ;
The drenched Menalcas came from wintry
   mast.
All ask, " Whence [comes] this passion
   unto thee ?"
Apollo came : " Why, Gallus, rave ?" he
   cries ;
" Thy care, Lycoris, hath another tracked
Alike through snows, and through dread
   camps." Came, too,
Silvanus, with a [crown of] rural grace
Upon his head, his blooming fennel plants,
And monster lilies tossing to and fro. 31
Pan came, the god of Arcady, whom we
Ourselves beheld with berries bloody-red
Of danewort, and with cinnabar, aglow.
" Will there be any bound [to this] ?" saith
   he ;
" Love recks not of the like. Nor felon
   Love
By tears, nor grasses by the rills, nor bees
By cytisus are cloyed, nor by the leaf
She-goats." But sad the other saith :
   " Still ye
Shall sing of these, Arcadians, to your
   mounts ;— 40
In singing ye, Arcadians, skilled alone.
Oh ! then how softly might my bones re-
   pose,
Should your reed-pipe hereafter tell my
   loves !
And would to heav'n that I were one of
   you,

42.   " Farewell for evermore !
If you shall hear that sorrow struck me dead,
And after find me loyal, let there be
A tear shed from you in my memory,
And I shall rest in peace."
      Beaumont and Fletcher, *Philaster*, iii. 1.
" Lie lightly on my ashes, gentle earth !"
                J. Fletcher, *Bonduca*, iv. 3.
44. " Oh, that I had been nourished in these woods
With milk of goats and acorns, and not known
The right of crowns, nor the dissembling trains
Of women's looks ; but digged myself a cave,
Where I, my fire, my cattle, and my bed,
Might have been shut together in one shed ;
And then had taken me some mountain girl,
Beaten with winds, chaste as the hardened rocks,
Whereon she dwelt, that might have strewed my bed
With leaves and reeds, and with the skins of beasts,
Our neighbours."
      Beaumont and Fletcher, *Philaster*, iv. 2.
                   " Take again
Your ill-timed honours ; take 'em, gods !
And change me to some humble villager,
If so at last for toils at scorching noon,
In mowing meadows, and in reaping fields,
At night she will but crown me with a smile."
                Lee, *Theodosius*, i. 1.

And had been either guardian of your flock,
Or vintager of your enripened bunch !
Of surety, had or Phyllis been my rage,
Or had Amyntas, or whoever else—
What then, if swart Amyntas were ? E'en
   dark
Are violets, and martagons are dark— 50
With me among the willows, underneath
The limber vine, he might lie down ; her
   wreaths
For me would Phyllis cull, Amyntas, [he]
Would sing. Here icy springs, here velvet
   meads,
Lycoris, here the woodland ; here could I
Be worn away with thee through very age.
Now madding love of callous Mars in arms,
Among mid weapons and confronted foes,
Detains me : thou far off thy native land,—
Ne'er may it be my fortune to believe 60
[A truth] so grievous !—dost the snows of
   Alps,
Ah ! heartless ! and the chills of Rhine,
   apart
From me, alone behold. Ah ! let the chills
Not harm thee ! Ah ! let rugged ice not
   gash
Thy tender foot-soles ! I will go, and lays,
Which in Chalcidian strain by me were
   framed,
On the Sicilian shepherd's reed will play.
'Tis fixed that I within the woods, among
The dens of savage beasts would liefer bear,
And carve my loves upon the tender trees :—

54. " Fly to the arbours, grots, and flowery meads,
    And in soft murmurs interchange our souls ;
    Together drink the crystal of the stream,
    Or taste the yellow fruit which autumn yields,
    And when the golden evening calls us home,
    Wing to our downy nest, and sleep till morn."
                Lee, *Theodosius*, ii. 1.
56.   " My all that Heaven can give !
Death's life with you ; without you, Death to live."
              Dryden, *Aurungzebe*, iv. 1.
64. " But oh ! that hapless virgin, our lost sister !
Where may she wander now, whither betake her
From the chill dew, among rude burs and thistles !
Perhaps some cold bank is her bolster now,
Or 'gainst the rugged bark of some broad elm
Leans her unpillowed head." Milton, *Comus*.

    70. When Prince Arthure discovers the " gentle
squire," he finds that he had followed the example
of Gallus, in making the trees the monuments of his
affection :

" And eke by that he saw on every tree
   How he the name of one engraven had
   Which likely was his liefest love to be."
              Spenser, *F. Q.* iv. 7, 46.

And so also Colin : *Colin Clout*, 632 :
" Her name in every tree I will endosse,
That, as the trees do grow, her name may grow."
We find Orlando doing the same in *As You Like
It*, iii. 2 :

Grow they will, ye will grow, my loves.
  Meanwhile   71
O'er Mœn'lus will I range with mingled
  Nymphs,
Or hunt the hot wild boars; no chills shall
  bar
My compassing with hounds Parthenian
  glades.
Meseems that now through rocks and ring-
  ing groves
I'm roaming; 'tis my joy from Parthian bow
To shoot Cydonian arrows; as if this
Were healing for my frenzy, or *that* god
May learn to soften at the ills of men.
Now neither Hamadryads any more, 80
Nor songs themselves charm us; ye very
  woods,

"Hang there, my verse, in witness of my love:
  And thou, thrice crowned queen of night, survey
With thy chaste eye, from thy pale sphere above,
  Thy huntress' name, that my full life doth sway.
O Rosalind! these trees shall be my books,
  And in their barks my thoughts I'll character;
That every eye, which in this forest looks,
  Shall see thy virtue witness'd everywhere.
Run, run, Orlando; carve on every tree
The fair, the chaste, and unexpressive she."

Drayton varies the idea in *Quest of Cynthia*,
5, 6:
  "At length upon a lofty fir
    It was my chance to find
  Where that dear name, most due to her,
    Was carved upon the rind.
  Which whilst with wonder I beheld,
    The bees their honey brought,
  And up the carvèd letters filled,
    As they with gold were wrought."

Shirley uses tears instead of wood-cuts:
  "That every tear could fall
Into some character, which you might read,
  That so I might dispense with my sad tongue,
And leave my sorrows legible."
                                The Imposture, iv. 5.

Cowley makes such carvings fatal to the tree:
  "I cut my love into his gentle bark,
    And in three days, behold! 'tis dead."

"Pardon, ye birds and nymphs, who loved this
    shade;
  And pardon me, thou gentle tree;
I thought her name would thee have happy made,
  And blessèd omens hoped from thee:
'Notes of my love, thrive here,' said I, 'and
    grow;
  And with ye let my love do so.'"
                                The Mistress: The Tree.

  "Oh! might I here
In solitude live savage: in some glade
Obscured, where highest woods, impenetrable
To star or sunlight, spread their umbrage broad
And brown as evening: cover me, ye pines,
Ye cedars; with innumerable boughs
Hide me."   Milton, *P. L.*, b. ix.

Once more give way. Our woes cannot
  change him,
Nor if we in the midst of frosts were both
To drink the Hebrus, and Sithonian snows
Of wat'ry winter-tide to undergo;
Nor if, when dying on the lofty elm,
The bark is shriv'ling, we should shift the
  sheep
Of Æthiopians under Cancer's star.
Love conquers all: let us too yield to Love."
'Twill be enough, Pierian maids divine, 90
That these your bard hath chanted, while
  he sits,
And weaves with mallow slim his slender
  frail.
Ye these of deepest interest will make
To Gallus: [yea] to Gallus, love of whom
As fast is growing on me every hour,
As in the infant spring the alder green
Uprears her. Let us rise; the shade is wont
To prove calamitous to those who sing;
Calamitous the shade of juniper;
The shades, too, harm the crops. Go, full-
  fed, home,—   100
The star of Eve is rising;—go, she-goats.

82. "Nothing rocks love asleep but death."
                    J. Fletcher, *The Pilgrim*, v. 4.

89. "Love is your master, for he masters you;
And he that is so yoked by a fool,
Methinks, should not be chronicled for wise."
    Shakespeare, *Two Gentlemen of Verona*, i. 1.

94. Cardinal Wolsey speaks similarly of his de-
votion to the king: Shakespeare, *Hen. VIII.* iii. 2:
                              "My loyalty,
  Which ever has, and ever shall be growing,
  Till death, that winter, kill it."

99. Cowley says the same of the yew:
  "Beneath a bower for sorrow made,
    Th' uncomfortable shade
  Of the black yew's unlucky green,
  Mixed with the mourning willow's careful grey."
                                The Complaint.

100. "Shepherds all and maidens fair,
  Fold your flocks up, for the air
  'Gins to thicken, and the sun
  Already his great course hath run.
  See the dewdrops, how they kiss,
  Every little flower that is,
  Hanging on their velvet heads,
  Like a rope of crystal beads:
  See the heavy clouds are falling,
  And bright Hesperus down calling,
  The dead night from under ground;
  At whose rising mists unsound,
  Damps and vapours fly apace,
  Hovering o'er the wanton face
  Of these pastures, where they come,
  Striking dead both bud and bloom."
    J. Fletcher, *The Faithful Shepherdess*, ii. 1.

THE GEORGICS.

BOOK I.

WHAT makes gay crops, beneath what star the earth
To turn, Mæcenas, and to elms to wed
The vines, 'tis meet; what be the care of beeves,
What management in keeping of the flock;
How vast the knowledge for the thrifty bees :—
I hence will undertake to sing. O ye,
All-brilliant luminaries of the world,
Who lead the year, as through the heav'n it glides ;
O Liber and boon Ceres, since the earth
Hath through your gift Chaonian mast exchanged   10
For the rich ear, and Acheloan cups
Hath blent with [new] discovered grapes ;
and ye,
The rustics' fav'ring Pow'rs, O Fauns—advance
Your foot in time, both Fauns and Dryad maids :—

Your gifts I sing. And thou, O [thou], for whom
The earth, by thy majestic trident struck,
Unbosomed first the snorting courser, Neptune !
And patron [thou] of lawns, through whom three hundred steers,
Snow-white, are browsing Cea's juicy brakes ;
E'en thou, too, quitting thy paternal lawn,
And woodlands of Lycæus, Pan ! of sheep
The guardian, if thy Mænalus to thee   22
Is of concern, be kindly present here,
O [god] of Tegea ! Minerva, too,
Creatress of the olive ; and thou youth,
Discloser of the crooked plough; and [thou,]
Silvanus, bearing, from its root [uptorn],
A tender cypress ; and ye gods and goddesses,
All, whose delight it be to guard the fields,
Both ye, who rear from no [implanted] seed   30
The infant fruits, and who on seeded crops
Drop down the plenteous show'r from heav'n ; and thou,
In chief, whom what assemblies of the gods
Hereafter shall enjoy is unresolved :
Whether to visit cities, Cæsar, and the charge
Of countries mayest thou desire, and thee
The vasty globe, as parent of its fruits,
And of its weather-changes lord, may hail,
Environing thy brows with myrtle-plant
Of thy own mother ;—or thou mayest come
The god of the immeasurable sea,   41
And mariners thy deity alone
Adore, the farmost Thule be thy serf,

Line 3. "Two rows of elms ran with proportioned grace,
Like Nature's arras, to adorn the sides ;
The friendly vines their lovèd barks embrace,
With folding tops the checkered ground-work hides."
    Shirley, *Narcissus,* st. 13.
"Or they led the vine
To wed her elm : she, spoused, about him twines
Her marriageable arms, and with him brings
Her dower, the adopted clusters, to adorn
His barren leaves."   Milton, *Par. Lost,* b. v.
Shakespeare makes Titania say beautifully of the ivy :
"Sleep thou, and I will wind thee in my arms :
Fairies, begone ; and be all ways away.
So doth the woodbine, the sweet honeysuckle,
Gently entwist,—the female ivy so
Enrings the barky fingers of the elm."
    Midsummer Night's Dream, iv. 1.
"Thou art an elm, my husband, I a vine,
Whose weakness, married to thy stronger state,
Makes me with thy strength to communicate."
    Shakespeare, *Comedy of Errors,* ii. 2.
"Everlasting hate
The vine to ivy bears, nor less abhors
The colewort's rankness, but with amorous twine
Clasps the tall elm."   J. Philips, *Cider,* b. i.
11. Or, "draughts."
14. Or, "at once."

16. See the fabled dispute between Neptune and Minerva, treated by Spenser in his beautiful poem, *Muiopotmos.*
"Percussa" is rather "thrilled," or "shocked."
18. Or, "Tenant," "haunter."
25. *Inventrix,* creatress ; so *repertor,* creator : Æn. xii. 829.
34. That is, though it might be known in heaven, it is a question on earth.

And Tethys buy thee for her son-in-law
With all her waves ;—or whether thou a star,
New [-born], annex thee to the lazy months,
There where a space between Erigone
And the pursuing Claws is opened out :—
The fiery Scorpion of himself for thee
E'en now draws in his arms, and hath resigned   50
A more than due proportion of the sky :—
Whate'er thou'lt be—for let nor Tartarus
Expect thee for its monarch, nor on thee
Let so accurst a lust of ruling come,
Though Greece may her Elysian plains admire,
Nor Proserpine recovered feel concern
T' attend her mother:—grant an easy course,
And nod [thy sanction] to my bold emprize :
And pitying with me the rural [swains],
Unknowing of the path, advance, and now,
Inure thee now to be invoked with vows. 61
In early spring, when rimy moisture thaws
On hoary mountains, and the crumbling clod
Unbinds itself before the western breeze,
Let now at once the bull begin for me
Beneath the deeply sunken plough to groan,
And, by the furrow worn, the share to flash.
That corny seedland answers at the last
The greedy tiller's prayers, which twice the sun,
Twice frosts hath felt : its harvests passing bound   70
Have burst his garners. But ere we with steel
An unknown surface cleave, be it our task
The winds, and changeful habit of the clime,

---

51. " But this fair gem, sweet in the loss alone,
When you fleet hence, can be bequeathed to none ;
Or, if it could, down from th' enamelled sky
All heaven would come to claim this legacy."
     Marlowe, *Hero and Leander*, Sestiad 1.

" Thou shalt
Be drawn with horses, white as Venus' doves,
Till heaven itself, in envy of our bliss,
Snatch thee from earth, to place thee in his orb,
The brightest constellation."
     Shirley, *The Politician*, ii. 1.

62. " And made the downy Zephyr, as he flew,
Still to be followed by the Spring's best hue."
B. Jonson, *The Vision of Delight*. See note on *Geo.* ii. *l.* 449.

But he introduces a harbinger, still more charming :

" I grant the linnet, lark, and bullfinch sing,
But best the dear good angel of the spring,
The Nightingale."
     The Sad Shepherd, ii. 2.

To learn before, and both the native tilths
And dispositions of the spots, and what
Each district may produce, and what may each
Refuse. Here cereal crops, there clusters come
More happily ; the fruits of trees elsewhere ;
And uncommanded wax the grasses green.
Dost thou not see how Tmolus saffron scents,   80
Ind iv'ry sendeth, Saba's tender sons
The frankincense their own ; but naked Chalybs,
Their iron ; Pontus, too, rank castory,
Epirus palm-wreaths of Elean mares ?
From first these laws and everlasting terms
Upon established spots hath Nature laid,
What time at first Deucalion tossed the stones
Upon an empty globe, whence men were born,
A flinty race. Then come, the soil of earth
That's rich, let straightway from the year's first months   90
Thy sturdy bulls upturn, and as they lie,
Let dusty-mantled summer bake the clods
With rip'ning suns. But should the land not prove
Prolific, towards Arcturus' very [rise],
Sufficient will it be to hang it up,
With a diminished furrow : *there*—lest weeds
May harass the delighted produce ; *here*—
Lest scanty moisture quit the barren sand.
In every other year shalt thou, the same,
Allow thy fallow-lands, that have been reaped,   100
To idle, and the listless plain to cake
With rust ; or there shalt sow the golden spelts
Beneath a constellation changed, whence thou
Shalt first the merry pulse with rattling pod,
Or tiny seeds of vetch, and brittle haulm
Of bitter lupin, and its rustling grove,
Have carried off. For burneth up the plain
The crop of flax, the oat [-crop] burns it up,
Burn it up poppies, soaked in Lethe's sleep.
But still in every other year the toil   110
Is easy : only be thou not ashamed
To glut the sapless mould with ordure rich,
Nor over thy exhausted grounds to toss
The ash unclean. Thus, too, by change of crops

---

114. Ben Jonson has " ash " in the singular :
     " Put it out rather, all out, to an ash."
          D. is an Ass, ii. 1.

The fields repose; nor meanwhile no return
Ariseth from the earth unploughed. Oft, too,
It hath bestead to fire the barren fields,
And burn light stubble in the crackling flames:
Whether thereby the lands secreted powers
And juicy food conceive; or every fault 120
Is melted out of them by fire, and forth
The baneful moisture oozes; or that heat
More passages, and darksome breathing-pores
Unloosens, where to th' infant blades the sap
May come; or hardens more, and braces close
The gaping arteries, lest filmy rains,
Or too fierce power of the raging sun,
Or piercing cold of Boreas sear them up.
Much, too, doth he, who breaks the lazy clods
With rakes, and hurdles of the osier trails,
Bestead the fields; nor him in vain regards
The golden Ceres from Olympus high: 132
And who the ridges, which upon the plain,
When broken up, he rears, once more breaks through
With plough transversely turned, and works his ground
Incessantly, and lords it o'er his lays.
For dropping summers and for winters fair
Entreat, O swains: through wintry dust the spelts
Are blithest, blithe the field. In tillage none
Doth Mysia vaunt herself so much, and e'en 140
At their own harvests marvel Gargar's [heights].
Why sing of him, who, when the seed is cast,
In close encounter presses on his fields,
And quells the piles of no rich land? Then brings he o'er
His seeded grounds a flood and following rills;
And when the seared ground is withering up

With dying herbage, lo! adown the brow
Of some hill-channel he the brook allures.
It, tumbling o'er the glossy shingle, wakes
A noisy brawl, and with its bubbling streams 150
Relieves the parching fields. Why [sing of him],
Who, lest the straw should lodge through loaded ears,
His crops' rank humor in the tender blade
Feeds down, when first the seedlings level make
His furrows; and who through the spongy sand
Drains off the gathered moisture of the pool?
In chief if in unsettled months a stream,
O'erflowing, bursts abroad, and far and near
Encases all with crusted slime, whence reek
The hollow channels with the moisture warm. 160
Nor still, when these have travails both of men
And beeves, in turning up the earth, essayed,
Naught do the graceless goose, and Strymon's cranes,

161. See note on l. 115, where examples are quoted of Milton's imitation of such constructions as those in verses 118-120.

163. *Improbus* has a variety of meanings, whether applied to persons, qualities, or things; all of which arise from the radical signification of "improper," and hence "immoderate." In the present instance, the great mass of commentators refer the expression more to the physical desires of the goose than to his (poetically) moral turpitude; that is, the goose was rather a glutton than a rogue. Now the fact is, that he was both,—and a mischievous bird besides; an exact parallel to his brother in crime, the *anguis*, in the third Book. The following remarks may serve as a help to ascertain its sense in the present case.

The word in question is employed sixteen times by Virgil; and after a careful analysis of its signification in these different instances, which it would be too long to detail, these conclusions would seem to result:

It is applied eleven times to persons, and five times to qualities or things.

Of the eleven times used of persons, in seven cases it is used in the strongest sense, implying moral guilt. Twice it is doubtful, leaving the application to *anser* and *anguis* to be determined.

Of the five occasions on which it is used in connection with qualities or things, thrice it bears a bad, and twice a harmless, sense.

Upon the whole, then, considering the immense mischief perpetrated by the wild goose, joined to his extraordinary appetite; (for he eats hugely, and tramples and scalds what he does not eat:) considering also the plain predominance of the bad sense in Virgil, "graceless" would seem to meet the necessities of the case, or the excellent term employed by Dr. Kennedy, "felon."

If the more usual view be taken, "glutton" is

---

115. The construction in verse 83 is imitated by Milton in several places: e. g. *Par. Lost*, b. i.:
"Nor did they not perceive the evil plight
In which they were."
"Nor doth the moon no nourishment exhale."
Ib., b. v.

134. *Proscindo* is technically to "break up," *i.e.* lay-ground; for *arva* here obviously means this.

140. That is, "in such a climate as this."

And succory with bitter roots, obstruct,
Or shade molest. The Father hath himself
Decreed that easy should not be the path
Of tilth, and he first roused the lands by skill,
Whetting with cares the hearts of human kind;
Nor suffered he his realms to lie benumbed
In leaden torpor. Ere [the reign of] Jove
No swains reduced the fields: not e'en to mark, 171
Or parcel off the champaign by a bourn,
Was lawful. For the common stock they sought,
And of her own accord the earth her all
More freely, at demand of none, produced.
He baleful venom to the sable snakes
Imparted, and commanded wolves to prowl,
And ocean to be roused; and from the leaves
Shook honies down, and he sequestered fire,
And, everywhere in rills careering, wines
He stayed; that practice, by the dint of thought, 181
The various crafts might slowly hammer out,

And in the furrows seek the blade of corn;
That from the veins of flint it forth might strike
The hidden fire. Then first the rivers felt
The hollowed alders; then the mariner
Numbers and names invented for the stars,
The Pleiads, Hyads, and Lycaon's sheeny Bear.
In nooses then wild creatures to entrap,
And dupe them with the lime, it was devised, 190
And mighty glades to girdle round with dogs.
And one now lashes with his casting-net
The spacious river, searching for its depths;
And through the main another trails along
His dripping lines. Then stiffness of the steel,
And blade of grating saw; for primal men
With wedges used to cleave the splitting wood.
Then divers crafts came in: unsparing Toil
Prov'd conq'ror over all, and Indigence,
That spurs [men] on in their distressed estate. 200
'Twas Ceres first instructed mortal kind
With iron to upturn the earth, when now
The mast and arbutes of the holy wood
Were failing, and Dodone refusing food.
Soon, too, was travail to the corn annexed,

---

an effective rendering: which word is surely an adjective, though Johnson and Webster do not recognise it as such. Richardson differs from them, as well he may; for it is too constantly joined by the poets to nouns substantive to admit of "apposition;" e. g. Spenser, *Muiopotmos*, 179, "glutton sense;" Shakespeare, 2 *Hen. IV.* i. 3, "glutton-bosom;" and again, "glutton eye;" Dryden, *Rel. Lai.* 33, "glutton souls;" *Hind and P.* 2275, "glutton kind;" &c.

166. "For sloth, the nurse of vices,
And rust of action, is a stranger to him."
Massinger, *The Great Duke of Florence*, i. 1.
"The fort, that's yielded at the first assault,
Is hardly worth the taking." ii. 3.
"The thrifty heavens mingle our sweets with gall,
Least, being glutted with excess of good,
We should forget the giver."
Rawlins, *The Rebellion*, v. end.

174. "Covered with grass more soft than any silk,
The trees dropt honey, and the springs gushed milk;
The flower-fleeced meadow, and the gorgeous grove,
Which should smell sweetest in their bravery strove;"
"Whilst to the little birds' melodious strains
The trembling rivers tripped along the plains;"
"The battening earth all plenty did afford,
And without tilling, of her own accord."
Drayton, *Noah's Flood*.

176. Or, perhaps: "He wicked venom to the baleful snakes."

182. How poor are they, that have not patience!"
Shakespeare, *Othello*, iii. 3.

183. Or, "through," "by."

185. "These earthly godfathers of heaven's lights
That give a name to every fix'd star."
Shakespeare, *Love's Labour's Lost*, i. 1.

186. Or: "Then the sailor coined
Numbers and names for stars, the Pleiad-train,
The Hyads," &c.

192. With the great weight of commentators, it is better to make *alta* refer to *amnem*. Notwithstanding Forbiger's steadiness, and Wagner's change of mind, does there seem to be sufficient warrant for the awkwardness which their view involves? Does it not impose an unfair duty upon the conjunction *que*?

198. "Impossible! Nothing's impossible!
We know our strength only by being tried.
If you object the mountains, rivers, woods
Impassable, that lie before our march:—
Woods we can set on fire: we swim by nature:
What can oppose us then but we may tame?
All things submit to virtuous industry:
That we can carry with us; that is ours."
Southern, *Oroonoko*, iii. 4.

205. This primitive condition of the earth, prior to culture, is realised by the loss of Peace; which miserable state of things is feelingly described by the Duke of Burgundy in *King Henry V.* v. 2:

"Alas! she hath from France too long been chas'd,
And all her husbandry doth lie on heaps,
Corrupting in its own fertility.
Her vine, the merry cheerer of the heart,
Unpruned dies; her hedges even-pleached,
Like prisoners wildly overgrown with hair,

That scathful blight should prey upon the
    stalks,
And in his laziness might bristle up
The thistle in the fields. Crops go to
    wrack ;
Succeeds a prickly forest, even burrs
And caltrops ; and amid the shiny tilths 210
Curst darnel and the barren oats bear rule.
Wherefore, unless with unremitting rakes
Thou both shalt worry weed, and with a din
Alarm the birds, and with thy pruning-
    hook
The shadow of the darkling country check,
And in thy prayers shalt have invoked the
    shower ;—
Alas ! upon another's massy pile
Thou bootlessly shalt gaze, and in the
    woods
Thy hunger comfort through the shaken oak.
Sung, too, must be what are the imple-
    ments   220
Of hardy rustics, without which their crops
Nor could be sown, nor spring. The share
    in chief,
And heavy timber of the bended plough,
And waggons of the Eleusinian Dame,
That lazy troll ; the sledges, too, and drags,
And harrows of unrighteous weight ; more-
    o'er,
The furniture of Celeus, wrought of twig,
And cheap, and hurdles of the arbutus,
And mystic fan of Bacchus : all the which,
Long previously foreseen, in thoughtful
    mood,   230
Shalt thou lay by in store, if thee awaits
The honor, to the heav'n-born country due.
First, in the forests bowed with mighty
    force,
Into a plough-tail is an elm reduced,
And [this] the figure of a crooked plough
Receives. Thereto from out the base a
    pole,
Stretched forward to eight feet, twain
    moulding-boards,
Share-beams with double back, are fitted
    on.
Felled, too, there is beforehand for the
    yoke
A lightsome linden, and a lofty beech 240
For staff, which from the rear may wheel
    around

Put forth disorder'd twigs ; her fallow leas
The darnel, hemlock, and rank fumitory
Doth root upon ; while that the coulter rusts,
That should deracinate such savagery :
The even mead, that erst brought sweetly forth
The freckled cowslip, burnet, and green clover,
Wanting the scythe, all uncorrected, rank,
Conceives by idleness ; and nothing teems,
But hateful docks, rough thistles, kecksies, burs,
Losing both beauty and utility."

The bottom of the carriage ; and the smoke
Searches the timber hung above the hearths.
    Pow'r have I many a rule of them of yore
To cite to thee, unless thou dost recoil,
And slender interests it irks to learn.
    The floor, among the chief, with roller huge
Must levelled be, and kneaded with the
    hand,
And rendered firm with binding Cretan
    earth,
Lest weeds work up, or, overcome by dust,
It gape, and divers plagues at thee should
    mock.   251
Oft hath the tiny mouse beneath thy lands
Both placed her homestead, and her garners
    built ;
Or, cheated of their eyes, the moles have
    delved
Their chambers ; and, in hollows found,
    the toad :
And vermin, which, full many, breed thy
    grounds ;
Both weevil wastes a vasty pile of corn,
And ant, in terror at a helpless eld.
    Mark also, when the almond in the
    woods
Shall throw her into rich array of bloom, 260
And arch her scented boughs, if embryoes
Abound, in equal sort will corn ensue,
And mighty threshing come with mighty
    heat ;
But if through rampancy of leafage shade
    exceeds,
Stalks, rank in chaff, thy floor will vainly
    bruise.

242. Every editor seems to read *currus* instead of *cursus*, which is substituted by Wagner and For-biger, though, as it would seem, with small manuscript authority. The difficulty in the common text to them was this : 1st, that *currus* implies wheels, and that no Roman plough had such an appendage ; and 2nd, that it must be capable of carrying somebody, which the plough was not. To the first objection the reply is, that their authority, Schulz, was mistaken in saying that no Roman plough had wheels, as an antique has been discovered which represents one with them. To the second, that a machine drawn by brutes, and guided by a human being, may, in poetic language, fairly claim the name : a consideration which is strengthened by a remark of Holdsworth, that the *stiva* was actually a foot-board, on which the ploughman stood.
243. *Focis* is not rendered by "flues" or "chimneys," as it is a disputed point whether the Romans had any special aperture for the escape of smoke.
254. " As the blind mole, the properest son of earth, Who, in the casting his ambitious hills up, Is often taken and destroyed i' the midst Of his advanced work."
    Middleton, *A Game at Chess*, iv. 4.
265. "The careful ploughman doubting stands, Lest on the threshing-floor his hopeless sheaves Prove chaff." Milton, *P. L.* iv.

Their seeds have I, in sooth, seen many drug
When sowing, and in natron steep them first,
And murky olive-lees, that there might prove
A fuller produce in the guileful pods.
And though they, quickened o'er a scanty fire, 270
Were moistened, have I seen them,— gathered long,
And tested with a world of travail,—yet
Deteriorate, unless the energy of man
Year after year each largest with the hand
Should cull. So all things by the Destinies
Are hasting to decay, and, sinking down,
Are backward borne: not otherwise than he
Who up the breasting river scarce his skiff
With oarage forces on, if he his arms
Hath haply slacked, and down the swift descent 280
The channel sweeps him with its giddy tide.
Moreo'er, as much are to be watched by us
Arcturus' constellation, and the days
Of Kids, and sheeny Dragon, as by those
By whom, when wafted towards their native land

Across the gusty waters, are essayed
Pontus and oyster-full Abydos' straits.
When Libra even shall have made the hours
Of day and sleep, and midway now disparts
The globe to light and shades, my masters, work 290
Your bulls, sow barleys in the plains, e'en close
To th' eve of latest show'r of brumal-tide,
Impracticable. Yea, a flax-crop, too,
And Cereal poppy is it time in earth
To hide, and now at once to bend to ploughs;
While, dry the ground, we may, while hang the clouds.
In spring time is for beans the sowing; then
Thee likewise, O thou Median [plant], receive
The crumbling furrows, and for millet comes
The yearly care, when, bright with gilded horns, 300
The Bull unlocks the year, and, slinking off
Before the star his foeman, sets the Dog.
But if for wheaten crop, and hardy spelts,
Thou'lt work thy ground, and press for ears alone,
First let th' Atlantic maidens at the Dawn
To thee be hidden, and the Gnosian star
Of blazing Diadem withdraw, ere thou
Consign to furrows seeds their due, and ere
Thou haste to trust the promise of the year
To earth unwilling. Many have commenced
Before the set of Maia; but those [swains] 311
The hoped-for crop with empty ears hath duped.
But if both vetch and paltry kidney-bean
Thou'lt sow, nor the Pelusian lentil's care
Shalt spurn away, no darkling signs to thee
Bootes, as he sinks, will send: begin,
And stretch thy sowing to mid [-winter] frosts.
For this, in settled portions meted out,
The golden Sun directs the sphere along
The constellations of the world in twelves.
Five zones embrace the heav'n; whereof is one 321
For ever crimsoned with the flashing Sun,
And scorched for ever by its fire; round which
The outermost upon the right and left
Are drawn, with azure ice and murky showers
Congealed. 'Tween these and that in centre, twain
To sickly mortals by the boon of gods

---

271. It is hard to acquiesce in the view which puts a period after *maderent*, instead of *esset*. This arrangement displaces *quamvis* from its natural relation to *tamen*, in order to set it in a weak connection with *exiguo*; it assigns to *maderent* a meaning which it is doubtful that it ever bore; and gives an abruptness to the commencement of a new sentence, which is thus made to begin at *vidi*. The objections to the opposite view are not fatal, and do not seem to be strong. However, if the more modern interpretation be preferred, the translation will run thus:
  that there might prove
A fuller produce in the guileful pods,
And they might o'er a fire, however small,
Be softened quick. I've seen those gathered long, &c.

276. So several translators; but, if deemed a little too free, it is easy to substitute:
  "Are hurrying to worse."
So thought Thenot in Spenser's *Sh. Cal.* Feb. 12:
"Must not the worlde wende in his common course
From good to bad, and from bad to worse,
From worst unto that is worst of all,
And then returne to his former fall?"
  "These our actors,
As I foretold you, were all spirits, and
Are melted into air, into thin air:
And like the baseless fabric of this vision,
The cloud-capped towers, the gorgeous palaces,
The solemn temples, the great globe itself,
Yea, all which it inherit, shall dissolve,
And, like this insubstantial pageant faded,
Leave not a rack behind."
    Shakespeare, *Tempest*, iv. 1.

280. *Atque* certainly does sometimes mean "immediately," but not in classical times. A good sense can be obtained by the ordinary use, and therefore it is to be preferred.

309. "With conscious certainty the swain
Gives to the ground his trusted grain,
With eager hope the reddening harvest eyes
And claims the ripe autumnal gold,
The meed of toil, of industry the prize."
    T. Warton, *Ode* xvi.

D

Are granted; and a path is scored thro' both,
Whereon aslant the cycle of the signs
Might wheel itself. The world, as e'en aloft
To Scythia and Rhipæan heights it towers,
Is sunk aslope to Lybia's southern gales. 332
This pole to us is ever reared on high;
But *that* beneath our feet the pitchy Styx
Beholdeth, and the Manes deep adown.
The monster Dragon here with coiling fold
Glides off around and midst of the two Bears,
After the fashion of a flood,—the Bears,
In ocean's surface fearing to be dipped.
There, as they tell, or hushes dead of night,
And ever by a pall of night the dark   341
Is thickened; or returns from us the Dawn,
And takes them back the day; and when
  on us
The Sun at rising earliest hath breathed
With puffing coursers, purpling Eve lights
  up
Her backward fires.   From this can we
  forelearn
The weather in the changeful sky; from this
Both harvest day and sowing tide, and when
The traitor face of sea with oars to force
Is fitting; when to launch the furnished
  fleets,   350
Or pine in season in the woods to fell.
Nor is it to no purpose that we watch
The settings and the risings of the signs,
And, even with its seasons four distinct,
The year.   If e'er a chilly show'r confines
The farmer, many a labor, which would
  needs
Be hurried over at a future hour
Beneath a sky unclouded,—to advance
Is giv'n. The ploughman forges to a point
His blunted ploughshare's churlish fang;
  he scoops   360

Troughs from the tree; or on his flock the
  brand
Hath he enstamped, or tallies on his heaps.
Stakes others point, or forks of double prong,
And ties Amerian for the limber vine
Prepare. Let now the pliant frail be plight
Of bramble twig; now roast upon the fire
Thy grains, now bray them in the quern.
  Nay e'en
On days of jubilee some tasks to ply
The law divine and human laws allow.
The rills to drain no scruple hath forbid; 370
Before the corn to stretch a fence; for birds
To plan an ambush; thorns to fire; and
  plunge
The flock of bleaters in the wholesome flood.
Ofttimes the plodding ass's ribs with oil,
Or with cheap apples, doth its driver lade,
And, trudging back, a dented stone, or lump
Of jetty pitch, he brings him home from
  town.
The Moon herself hath granted various
  days
In various rank, auspicious to your toils.
The fifth do thou avoid: [upon that day] 380
Were ghastly Orcus and the Furies born;
Then Terra in an execrable birth
Both Cœus and Iapetus brings forth,
And fell Typhœus, and the brotherhood,
Banded by oath to tear the heavens down.
They thrice attempted Ossa to implant
On Pelion; aye, on Ossa, too, to roll
Leaf-fraught Olympus; thrice the up-piled
  mounts
The Father laid in ruins with his bolt.
The seventh, [coming] next upon the tenth,

---

340. *Tempestivus* means "timeful," "timely," "timous:" that is, "in the proper time," with a tendency to the signification of "earlier than *need* be." So *intempestivus, intempestus,* means "untimeful," "untimely," "timeless," with a tendency to the signification of "earlier than *ought* to be." Now it is plain, that *intempesta* here must have an import different from those borne by the last three terms. It would seem, then, that it takes its force from the primitive meaning of "unbroken into periods." The night is practically unbroken into periods, when people cease to work, and retire to rest: thus, *intempesta nox* comes to signify "dead of night." Further, if they lie awake, or have to keep watch during the hours of darkness, these seem so long, that it is *as if* there were no periods, no end: hence the idea of "dreary." Either of these terms would appear to satisfy the expression.

344. "But look! the morn, in russet mantle clad,
  Walks o'er the dew of yond' high eastern hill."
              Shakespeare, *Hamlet,* i. 1.
"The blushing childhood of the cheerful morn
  Is almost grown a youth, and over-climbs
  Yonder gilt eastern hills."
              Brewer, *Lingua,* i. 5.

362. Or, perhaps: "sacks."
367. If "quern" be thought a little too free a version of *saxo,* a dull substitute is easily found, without damage to the rhythm.
380. "A wicked day, and not a holy day: . . .
Nay, rather, turn this day out of the week;
This day of shame, oppression, perjury:
Or, if it must stand still, let wives with child
Pray that their burdens may not fall this day,
Lest that their hopes prodigiously be cross'd:
But on this day let seamen fear no wreck;
No bargains break that are not this day made:
This day, all things begun come to ill end;
Yea, faith itself to hollow falsehood change."
              Shakespeare, *King John,* iii. 1.

381. To quote Milton on the subject of the evil angels would be trite, as his sublime descriptions are familiar to every one; but his great predecessor says finely:
"Th' Almighty, seeing their so bold assay,
Kindled the flame of His consuming yre,
And with His onely breath them blew away
From heavens hight, to which they did aspyre,
To deepest hell and lake of damned fyre,
Where they in darkness and dread horror dwell,
Hating the happie light from which they fell."
              Spenser, *Hymne of Heavenly Love,* 85.

Auspicious is, as well to plant the vine, 391
As captured beeves to tame, and to attach
The leashes to the warp; the ninth for flight
More favorable, enemy to thefts.
Sooth many [tasks] have 'neath the chilly night
Presented them more fitly, or what time,—
The Sun new [-ris'n],—the lands is Lucifer
Bedewing. In the night the stubbles light
More fitly, in the night dry meads are mown;
The ropy moisture faileth not the nights. 400
E'en one there is, who by the lasting fires
Of winter light keeps up his watch, and points
His torches with the sharpened steel. Meanwhile,
Her tedious travail cheering with a song,
With shrilly reed his partner threads the warp;
Or through [the aid of] Vulcan simmers down
The liquor of the nectared must, and skims
With leaves the palpitating cauldron's wave.
But ruddy Ceres in the midst of heat
Is cut, and in the midst of heat the floor 410
The [sun-] dried harvest bruises. Robeless plough,
Sow robeless. Winter to the husbandman
Is idle [time]. In frosts the farmers chief
Their store enjoy, and, blithe among themselves,
Reciprocal carousals make their care:
Lures jolly winter, and unbinds their woes.
As when the heavy-freighted vessels now
Have touched the haven, and upon the sterns
The happy sailors ranged their wreaths. But still
Both oaken mast 'tis then the time to strip,
And berries of the bay, and olive, too, 421
And blood-red myrtle-fruits; then gins for cranes,
And toils for harts to set, and long-eared hares

---

394. " He works by glow-worm light; the moon's too open.", Ben Jonson, *Time Vindicated*.

409. " Have we been tilling, sowing, labouring, With pain and charge, a long and tedious winter, And when we see the corn above the ground, Youthful as is the morn, and the full ear, That promises to stuff our spacious garners, Shall we then let it rot, and never reap it ?"
J. Fletcher, *The Noble Gentleman*, ii. 1.

423. " Yet if for silvan sports thy bosom glow, Let thy fleet greyhound urge his flying foe. . . . He snaps deceitful air with empty jaws, The subtle hare darts swift beneath his paws: She flies, he stretches: now with nimble bound Eager he presses on, but overshoots the ground: She turns, he winds, and soon regains the way, Then tears with gory mouth the screaming prey."
Gay, *Rural Sports*, ii. 289.
See also Somerville, *The Chase*, b. ii.

To course; 'tis then [for him] the fallow-deer
To pierce, who whirls around the hempen thongs
Of Balearic sling, when deep the snow
Is lying, when the floods drive down the ice.
Why should I sing of Autumn's storms and stars?
Aye, and, when now both shorter is the day,
And gentler is the heat, what watchful arts
Must be employed by men; or when down falls 431
Spring rife in rain, now when hath on the plains
The bearded harvest bristled up, and when
The milky grains upon their stalk of green
Are swelling? Frequently have I, what time
Upon his golden fields the husbandman
Would introduce the sickler, and would now
Reap off his barleys with their bitter haulm,
The battles of the winds all clashing seen,
Which far and near the burdened standing corn 440
Would, from their deepest roots shot forth aloft,
Upwrench:—so in some pitchy hurricane
Would winter carry off both airy straw
And stubbles on the wing. Oft, too, there swoops
A boundless host of waters from the sky,
And, mustered from the height [of heav'n], the clouds
A grim tornado coil with sable showers;
The lofty firmament comes sluicing down,
And with stupendous rain the merry crops
And travails of the oxen washes off; 450
The dykes are brimmed, and hollow rivers swell
With roaring, and with panting waters seethes
The ocean-plain. The Sire himself, amidst
A night of clouds, with gleaming right hand hurls
His levin-fires, at which commotion quakes

---

435. There is a fine description of a storm by Milton, *P. R.* iv.:
" And either tropic now
'Gan thunder, and both ends of heaven; the clouds,
From many a horrid rift, abortive pour'd
Fierce rain with lightning mix'd, water with fire
In ruin reconciled: nor slept the winds
Within their stony caves, but rush'd abroad
From the four hinges of the world, and fell
On the vex'd wilderness, whose tallest pines,
Though rooted deep as high, and sturdiest oaks
Bow'd their stiff necks, loaden with stormy blasts,
Or torn up sheer."
Thomson also (*Autumn*, 311-343) finely imitates this and other of Virgil's descriptions of storms. He has many other successful passages on the like subject: see *Summer*, 1103-1168.

D 2

The vasty earth; wild beasts have fled away,
And through the nations crouching dread
   dismayed
The hearts of men. He with his blazing bolt
Or felleth Athos down, or Rhodope,
Or the Ceraunian heights; the southern
   blasts   460
Redouble and the thickest rain; now woods,
Now shores, beneath the mighty tempest
   wail.
In dread of this, the months and stars of
   heaven
Watch thou: whereto may Saturn's chilly
   star
Withdraw him; to what circuits through
   the sky
The fire Cyllenian strays. In special wise
Adore the gods, and yearly rites repeat
To mighty Ceres, on the merry turf
Performing, just at latest winter's fall,
Now in the cloudless spring. Then fat are
   lambs,   470
And then most mellow wines; then slum-
   bers sweet,
And thick upon the mounts the shades.
   For thee
Let worship Ceres all the rural youth,
For whom do thou thy honeycombs with
   milk
And Bacchus mild dilute; and thrice around
The infant produce let the victim pass
Auspicious, which let all thy choir and mates
Escort in glee, and Ceres with a shout
Woo to their homesteads. Nor let any first
The sickle lay beneath his ripened ears, 480
Before to Ceres, with the twisted oak
Encircled on his temples, he presents
Ungainly gambols, and his carols sings.
And these that we may have it in our
   power
By symptoms sure to learn, the Sire himself
Hath fixed what warning should the monthly
   Moon
Afford; with what foretoken should subside
The southern blasts; what viewing many a
   time,
The husbandmen the nearer to the sheds
Their cattle might confine. Forthwith,
   when winds   490
Are rising, either ocean's friths begin

Betossed to swell, and on the lofty mounts
Dry crashing to be heard; or, booming
   far,
The shores to be in turmoil, and the growl
Of woods to freshen. Even then the surge
Can ill refrain itself from bending keels,
When from mid ocean fleet wing home
   their way
The divers, and a screaming waft to shore,
And when sea-coots upon dry land disport,
And fens well known the heron quits, and
   soars   500
Above the lofty cloud. Oft, too, the stars,
When wind is hanging over, thou wilt see
Glide headlong from the sky, and through
   the shade
Of night long trains of blazes in the rear
Gleam white: oft airy chaff and fallen
   leaves
A-flutt'ring, or upon the water's face

Rolls o'er the muttering earth, disturbs the flood,
And shakes the forest-leaf without a breath."
        Summer, 1116.

Does Virgil anywhere, in his descriptions of a gale of wind, introduce this sublime element of stillness? Dryden is a little too bold:

" Thus when black clouds draw down the labouring skies,
Ere yet abroad the wingèd thunder flies,
An horrid stillness first invades the ear,
And in that silence we the tempest fear."
        Astræa Redux, 5-8.

"We often see, against some storm,
A silence in the heavens, the rack stand still,
The bold winds speechless, and the orb below
As hush as death, anon the dreadful thunder
Doth rend the region."
        Shakespeare, *Hamlet*, ii. 2.

It is doubtful whether *freta* here means more than "waters:" which secondary meaning, if it be insisted on, may be adopted by substituting "floods" for "friths" in the translation. However, as a general rule, it is safer, where there is no strong reason to the contrary, to take a word in its primary rather than in a derived signification. See v. 386. The poet probably alludes here to what is technically called the "swell" of the sea, which, it is well known, often reaches a lee-shore in advance of the wind which has raised it. This phenomenon Shakespeare seems to have had in view in *Richard III.*, ii. 3:

"By a divine instinct men's minds mistrust
Ensuing danger; as, by proof, we see
The water swell before a boist'rous storm."

498. One cannot pretend always to render correctly the terms which stand for birds, any more than those which mean plants or colours. All the translators here render *mergi* by "cormorants;" but it is uncertain that this is the import of the word, though it doubtless means "divers" of some sort or other. Ruæus, who is particular in such matters, says that it means the bird so called. However, if the common rendering is insisted on, there seems to be no means of proving it wrong; and so the line may be read:

The cormorants, and waft their scream to shore.

506. The poet does not mean to imply by *impru-*

---

457. Some say that *humilis pavor* implies a feeling of cowardice; if so, it should be rendered by "base alarm." But would not this weaken the poet's meaning? If the fear were unwarrantable, it would detract from the greatness of the display.

484. See this fine passage finely imitated by Thomson, *Winter*, 118-147.

491.   "A boding stillness reigns
Dread through the dun expanse, save the dull
   sound
That from the mountain, previous to the storm

The swimming feathers in a frolic join.
But from the quarter of the grisly North
What time it lightens, and what time the dome
Alike of East and West is thund'ring, all
With brimming dykes the rural regions swim,   511
And every seaman on the ocean furls
His dripping canvas. Never storm of rain
To inadvertent [swains] hath proved of harm :
Or, at its rising, in the valley-depths
Therefrom the skyish cranes have fled away ;
Or heifer, as she gazes up to heaven,
With widely-spreading nostrils snuffed the gales ;
Or twitt'ring swallow flitted round the meres,
And frogs in ooze croaked forth their old complaint.   520
The oftener, too, from out her inner cells,
Fretting a narrow path, the ant her eggs
Hath carried : and the giant bow hath drunk ;
And, from their feed withdrawing in a train
Immense, the host of rooks with serried wings
Hath whizzed. Now divers ocean-birds, and those,
Which rummage round the Asian meads, among
Sweet plashes of Cayster, may you see
In rivalry upon their shoulders shed
The plenteous dews, now run upon the waves,
And joy with zeal of washing all in vain.   531
Then with full voice the saucy crow invokes

The rain, and solitary, by herself,
She struts along upon the thirsty sand.
Nor even, as they card their nightly tasks,
Have maidens been unconscious of a storm,
When they within their blazing lamp of earth
Should see the oil its sparkles sputter off,
And mould'ring mushroom-forms in clusters rise.
Nor less, ensuing on a gush of rain,   540
Suns and clear open weather to foresee,
And learn by settled marks, shalt thou have power.
For neither then their margin in the stars
Looks blunt, nor, debted to a brother's beams,
The moon to rise, nor filmy flakes of wool
Throughout the welkin to be borne along.
Outspread not to the soft-warm sun their wings
Upon the beach the halcyons, beloved
Of Thetis ; frowzy swine bethink them not
To toss about the bundles from their mouth,
Unloosened ; but the vapors rather seek 551

---

dentibus that rain cannot damage those who do not foresee it; for they are just the persons to *be* damaged ;—but, that the signs of it are so plain, that, popularly speaking, no one can be said to be "inadvertent," who thus, popularly, having no existence, cannot be damaged.

526. Weise, and most other editors, if not all but Wagner and Forbiger, have *varias*, a much better reading than *variæ*.

532. "Saucy," either from the impudence of her demeanour, or the impertinence of her act; for what business has she to call for rain, when her betters would rather be without it?

If this word of multifarious meaning, *improbus*, (see note on l. 163,) be considered, with Ruæus, to have the force of *importunus* here, the line will run thus:

Then with full voice the crow invokes the rain,
Importunate, and lonely by herself.

In the first edition of this work the passage appeared thus :

Then doth the saucy crow with husky voice,
The rain invoke, and on the thirsty sand
[All] solitary saunter by herself.

This noisiness before wet is attributed by Shakespeare to a different bird. Rosalind, in bantering

Orlando, says that she will be "more clamorous than a parrot against rain."
                       As You Like It, iv. 1.

The different effect that can be produced by an alliteration of the letter "S" may be seen in Collins' *Ode to Evening*:

" Now air is hush'd, save where the weak-eyed bat,
With short shrill shriek, flits by on leathern wing."

But a softer combination appears immediately after :

" May not unseemly with its stillness suit."

A more pointed effect than that in the Latin text is produced by Pope, *Windsor Forest*:

" She said, and melting as in tears she lay,
In a soft silver strain dissolved away."

Alliterations, when sparingly used, are at times very effective. For instance, in Dryden's line, *Cock and the Fox*, 411:

" I fear not death, nor dangers, nor disgrace,"
the sense would be just the same if "perils" were substituted for "dangers ;" but few would say that the change entailed no detriment. The same is true of a preceding line, 406. Speaking of doctors, Chanticleer says :

" Their tribe, trade, trinkets, I defy them all."
Shakespeare also: *Two Gentlemen of Verona*, i. 3.:
" Sweet love, sweet lines, sweet life !
Here is her hand, the agent of her heart."
Churchill, in his *Prophecy of Famine*, says :

" Who often, but without success, have prayed
For apt alliteration's artful aid."

534. Or, " stalks."

544. " How she conveyed him softly in a sleep,
His temples bound with poppy, to the steep
Head of old Latmus, where she stoops each night,
Gilding the mountain with her brother's light,
To kiss her sweetest."   [*The allusion is to the Moon and Endymion.*]

J. Fletcher, *The Faithful Shepherdess*, L 3.

The lowest [grounds], and brood upon the
    plain ;
And, sunset watching from a gable-top
To idle purpose plies the bird of night
Late hootings. Nisus looms in view, aloft
In limpid air, and for the purple lock
The forfeit Scylla pays. What way soe'er
She flying cleaves light ether with her wings,
Lo ! hostile, murderous, with mighty whirr,
Along the breezes Nisus hunts her close ;
Where Nisus to the breezes wafts him on,
She flying cleaves light ether with her
    wings   562
In hurried snatches. Then their brilliant
    notes
The rooks, with straitened throat, three
    times or four,
Redouble ; oft, too, in their roosts on high,
I know not with what charm, past custom,
    blithe,
Among themselves they rustle in the leaves.
It joys them, when the show'rs are chased
    away,
Their tiny offspring, and their darling nests,
Again to visit : not, I sooth believe,   570
Because a god-born intellect is theirs,
Or deeper insight into things by fate ;
But when the storm, and shifting damp of
    heaven,
Have changed their paths, and Jove, with
    Austers dank,
Condenses what but now was rarefied,
And what was dense relaxes, altered be
The pictures of their spirits, and their
    breasts
Now different emotions—different,
So long as wind was driving on the clouds—
Conceive : hence [springs] that symphony
    of birds   580

Throughout the fields, and cattle in delight,
And ravens croaking triumph from their
    throats.
But if to the swift-speeding Sun, and
    moons,
That follow in their cycle, thou shalt look,
Ne'er thee to-morrow's hour shall lead
    astray,
Nor by the crafts of cloudless night shalt
    thou
Be tricked. What time the Moon first
    gathers in
Returning fires, if she shall have embraced
The sable ether with a darkling horn,
Immense for tillers, and the deep, will rain
Be brewing. But if she a maiden red   591
Have o'er her visage poured, there will be
    wind :
At wind doth ever golden Phœbe flush.
But if at her fourth rise—for that [will
    prove]
The most unerring counsellor—undimmed,
Nor with blunt horns, through heav'n shall
    she career,
Both all that day, and those which shall
    arise
Therefrom, to the completion of the month,
From rain and tempests will be free ; and
    vows
The rescued mariners upon the shore   600
Shall pay to Glaucus, and to Panope,
And Melicerta [of] Inoan [birth].
    The Sun, too, both as he is rising forth,
And when he hides him in the waves,
    will signs

---

554. In his magnificent description of the Cave of Despair, Spenser finely introduces the owl:
    " On top whereof ay dwelt the ghastly owle,
    Shrieking his balefull note."
        Faerie Queene, l. 9, 33.
" And when the bleating lamb doth bld good night
Unto the closing day, then tears begin
To keep quick time unto the owl, whose voice
Shrieks like the belman in the lover's ears."
            Middleton, *Blurt,* iii. 1.
" It was the owl that shrieked, the fatal belman,
Which gives the stern'st good night."
        Shakespeare, *Macbeth,* ii. 2.

571. Dryden applies the idea to the emigrating swallow :
    " From hence she has been held of heavenly line,
    Endued with particles of soul divine."
        Hind and Panther, 1727, 8.

580. " Therein the mery birdes of every sorte
    Chaunted alowd their chearefull harmonee,
    And made emongst themselves a sweete consort."
        Spenser, *F. Q.* ii. 5, 31.

" Here is melody,
A charm of birds."
    G. Peele, *The Arraignment of Paris,* i. 1.
" With charm of earliest birds."
        Milton, *P. L.* iv. 641.
" The warblers lively tunes essay,
The lark on wing, the linnet on the 'spray ;
While music trembles in their songful throats,
The bullfinch whistles soft his flute-like notes.
The bolder blackbird swells sonorous lays ;
The varying thrush commands a tuneful maze ;
Each a wild length of melody pursues ;
While the soft-murmuring, amorous wood-dove
    cooes ;
And when in spring these melting mixtures flow,
The cuckoo sends her unison of woe."
        Savage, *Wanderer,* c. 5.

582. *Corvus* seems properly to mean the "raven;" but in v. 382 it most certainly stands for the "rook," which probably is its signification in v. 410. Here it may represent the same bird ; in which case the line should run :
    And rooks a triumph cawing from their throat.

604. Gay thus beautifully describes the sun setting in the sea :
    " Engag'd in thought, to Neptune's bounds I stray,
    To take my farewell of the parting day.
    Far in the deep the sun his glory hides,
    A streak of gold the sea and sky divides ;

Afford : the sun the surest signs attend,
Both those which in the morning he restores,
And those which at the rising of the stars.
When he with blotches shall have chequered o'er
His infant dawning, buried in a cloud,
And from his central disk shall have re-recoiled, 610
Be show'rs mistrusted by thee ; for there swoops
From [heav'n] on high a southern blast, alike
To trees, and crops, and cattle, fraught with woe.
Or when towards dawn among the huddled clouds
His scatt'ring beams shall shoot them forth, or when
Aurora wan shall rise, the saffron couch
Of Tithon leaving—welaway !—ill then
The vine-leaf shall bescreen the mellow grapes,
In such profusion, patt'ring on the roofs,
Leaps bristling hail. This, too, what time he now 620
Departs from spanned Olympus, 'twill be stead
The more to bear in mind. For oft we see
Upon his visage straying fitful hues :
The dun speaks rain, the fiery, eastern gales.
But if the blotches with a crimson glare
Shall 'gin to be commixed, all [nature] then
Alike with storm and torrents thou shalt view
In ferment. Let not any in that night
Encourage me to voyage through the deep,
Nor wrest away my cable from the land.
But if when he shall both restore the day,
And bury it restored, all-bright his disk 632
Shall prove, thou needlessly wilt be appalled

The purple clouds their amber linings show,
And edg'd with flames rolls every wave below ;
Here pensive I behold the fading light,
And o'er the distant billow lose my sight."
Rural Sports, i. 99-106.
612. So Shakespeare, *Venus and Adonis:*
" Like a red moon, that ever yet betoken'd
Wreck to the seaman, tempest to the field,
Sorrow to shepherds, woe unto the birds,
Gusts and foul flaws to herdsmen and to herds."
616. " Oh, lend me all thy red,
Thou shame-faced Morning, when from Tithon's bed
Thou risest ever-maiden !"
J. Fletcher, *The Faithful Shepherdess*, i. 3.
" Is not yon gleame, the shuddering morne that flakes,
With silver tinctur, the east vierge of heaven ?"
Marston, *Antonio and Mellida*, 1st P., iii.

By showers, and with bright'ning Aquilo
Thou shalt behold the forests waved. In fine,
What evening late may bring, wherefrom the wind
May chase the calmy clouds, what Auster dank
May hatch, the Sun to thee will signs afford.
The Sun to call a traitor who may dare ?
He e'en that dark convulsions are at hand
Oft gives us warning, and that treachery
And shrouded wars begin to swell. He e'en 642
[When] Cæsar ['s light was] quenched compassioned Rome,
What time his lustrous head he curtained o'er
With rusted iron's darkling hue, and feared
Ungodly ages everlasting night.
Though at that hour e'en earth, and ocean-plains,
And dogs ill-omened, and ill-boding birds,
Afforded presages. How oft we saw,

643. Shakespeare thus finely describes the death of Cæsar, *J. C.* iii. 2 :
" For when the noble Cæsar saw him stab,
Ingratitude, more strong than traitor's arms,
Quite vanquish'd him : then burst his mighty heart ;
And, in his mantle muffling up his face,
Even at the base of Pompey's statue,
Which all the while ran blood, great Cæsar fell.
Oh ! what a fall was there, my countrymen !"
" But sneaking Brutus,
Whom none but cowards and white-livered knaves,
Would dare commend, lagging behind his fellows,
His dagger in his bosom, stabbed his father."
Dryden, *The Duke of Guise*, ii. 1.
645. " So, when the sun in bed,
Curtain'd with cloudy red,
Pillows his chin upon an orient wave."
Milton, *Ode on Nativity*, 26.
" 'Twas such a night involv'd thy towers, O Rome,
The dire presage of mighty Cæsar's doom,
When the sun veil'd in rust his mourning head,
And frightful prodigies the skies o'erspread."
Gay, *Trivia*, iii. 377.
648. Is attention to gender to be insisted on, in spite of the claims of refinement ?
649. Like those that Shakespeare makes presage the death of Duncan :
" The night has been unruly. Where we lay
Our chimneys were blown down, and, as they say,
Lamentings heard i' the air : strange screams of death ;
And prophesying, with accents terrible,
Of dire combustion, and confus'd events
New hatch'd to the woeful time. The obscure bird
Clamour'd the livelong night ; some say the earth
Was feverous and did shake." *Macbeth*, ii. 3
And more directly of Cæsar's death itself, Casca says, *J. C.* i. 3 :
" O Cicero,
I have seen tempests, when the scolding winds
Have riv'd the knotty oaks ; and I have seen

Forth surging from her bursten furnaces,
Ætna boil over on the Cyclops' fields, 651
And roll her balls of flames and molten
    rocks !
The din of weapons through the breadth of
    heaven
Germania heard ; Alps thrilled with wont-
    less quakes.
A voice was also heard by all the world
Throughout the stilly groves—a mighty
    [voice]—
And spectres wan in wond'rous shapes were
    seen
Towards dusk of night ; the brutes, too,
    uttered speech ;
Accursed thought ! the rivers pause, and
    lands
Yawn wide ; and iv'ry, struck with grief,
Weeps o'er the fanes, and bronzes sweat
    distil.   661
Whirling them round within his frantic gulf,
The monarch of the floods, Eridanus,
Washed off the forests, and through all the
    plains
The cattle with their cotes he swept away.
Nor, at the selfsame hour, or did the veins
In dismal entrails threatful cease to look,
Or from the wells the stream of blood to
    flow,
And stately towns to echo through the night
With howling wolves. At no time else
    there fell   670

The ambitious ocean swell, and rage, and foam,
To be exalted with the threat'ning clouds ;
But never till to-night, never till now,
Did I go through a tempest dropping fire.
Either there is a civil strife in heaven,
Or else the world, too saucy with the gods,
Incenses them to send destruction."
" In the most high and palmy state of Rome,
A little ere the mightiest Julius fell,
The graves stood tenantless, and the sheeted dead
Did squeal and gibber in the Roman streets.
As, stars with train of fire and dews of blood,
Disasters in the sun ; and the moist star,
Upon whose influence Neptune's empire stands,
Was sick almost to doomsday with eclipse."
                                    Hamlet, i, 1.
" Why all this noise because a king must die ?
Or does heaven fear because he swayed the earth,
His ghost will war with the high Thunderer ?
Curse on the babbling fates, that cannot see
A great man tumble, but they must be talking !"
                            Lee, *Rival Queens*, ii. 1.
660. *Illacrimo* usually signifies to "weep for, or
over " a thing. If this meaning, which is adopted
in the translation, be accepted, the import of the
passage will be,—that the statues of the gods were
alarmed for the safety of the temples and of religion,
and so wept at the sad prospect of what might
happen : those of ivory weep, those of bronze per-
spire, with the agitation of grief. This is the more
beautiful view, though not therefore necessarily
the right one : yet *mæstum* seems to render it
imperative.

More levin-flashes from a cloudless sky,
Nor have so oft disastrous comets blazed.
Therefore a second time Philippi saw
Rome's marshalled lines in mutual fight
    engage,
With balanced arms ; nor was it [deemed]
    unmeet
By gods above that twice with blood ot
    ours
Emathia fat should wax, and spacious
    plains
Of Hæmus. Aye, in sooth, the time will
    come,
When in those bourns the husbandman, as
    he
The ground is working with his bended
    plough,   680
On javelins, gnawed away with rugged rust,

---

672. " Woe to the hand that shed this costly blood !
Over thy wounds now do I prophesy,—
Which, like dumb mouths, do ope their ruby lips,
To beg the voice and utterance of my tongue ;—
A curse shall light upon the limbs of men ;
Domestic fury, and fierce civil strife,
Shall cumber all the parts of Italy ;
Blood and destruction shall be so in use,
And dreadful objects so familiar,
That mothers shall but smile when they behold
Their infants quarter'd with the hands of war ;
All pity chok'd with custom of fell deeds ;
And Cæsar's spirit, ranging for revenge,
With Atè by his side, come hot from hell,
Shall in these confines, with a monarch's voice,
Cry, "Havock !" and let slip the dogs of war ;
That this foul deed shall smell above the earth,
With carrion men groaning for burial."
    Mark Antony's Soliloquy over Cæsar's Corpse:
                            J. C. iii. 1.
" O thou soft natural death, thou art joint twin
To sweetest slumber ! No rough-bearded comet
Stares on thy mild departure ; the dull owl
Beats not against thy casement ; the hoarse wolf
Scents not thy carrion : pity winds thy corse,
Whilst horror waits on princes."
                Webster, *Vittoria Corombona*, v. 1.
674. " The jars of brothers, two such mighty ones,
Are like a small stone thrown into a river,
The breach scarce heard ; but view the beaten
    current,
And you shall see a thousand angry rings
Rise in his face, still swelling and still growing."
                J. Fletcher, *The Bloody Brother*, ii. 1.
680. Perhaps it may be necessary to remark on
molitus, v. 494, that it has been rendered "working," although a past participle. This proceeds
upon the assumption that Virgil here has followed
the principle, so common with the poets, of using
the past participle of deponent verbs in a present
sense, though they have a participle present. The
reason of the license may be seen in Wagner, *Quæs.
Virg.* xxix. 3. In the present instance it is plain
that it is during the *act* of working the earth that
the ploughman makes his strange discovery. Forbiger, indeed, observes that, strictly speaking, it is
after the operation that the wonder appears ; but
perhaps it is truer to say that the operation and the
wonder are contemporaneous. The past sense would
seem to separate the one from the other by too wide
an interval.

Shall light, or with his weighty harrows strike
On helmets empty, and gigantic bones
Behold with wonder in their graves unearthed.
Gods of my ancestors! my country's gods!
And Romulus, and matron Vesta, who
The Tuscan Tiber, and Palatial heights
Of Roma dost protect, this youth, at least,
Forbid ye not to help a ruined age!
Enough now long time past by blood of ours 690
Laomedontian Troja's broken oaths
We've expiated. Now this long time past
Heav'n's royal court begrudges thee to us,
O Cæsar, and complains of thy concern
For triumphs of [a world] of men, as where
Reversed are right and wrong; so many wars

Throughout the globe; so many shapes of crimes;
Not any worthy homage to the plough;
The fields lie waste, the tillers drafted off,
And bending sickles into yieldless sword [s]
Are forged. Euphrates here, Germania there, 701
Is rousing war; the leagues between them burst,
The cities that are neighbors bear their arms;
Ungodly Mars fumes all throughout the globe:—
As when from forth the barriers four-horse cars
Have flung them, on the courses do they spring,
And, idly straining thongs, the charioteer
Is hurried by his steeds, nor heeds the car the reins.

---

683. The same wonder is excited, according to Collins, by an opposite cause. Speaking of one of the Hebrides, he says:
"To that hoar pile, which still its ruins shows:
In whose small vaults a pigmy folk is found,
Whose bones the delver with his spade upthrows,
And culls them, wondering, from the hallowed ground."
Ode on the Superstitions of the Highlands.
692. Dryden makes the tears of England equally effective in a graver case:
"So tears of joy, for your returning spilt,
Work out and expiate our former guilt."
Astræa Redux, 274, 5.
696. "We shall have other liberal sciences
Taught us too soon; lying and flattering,
Those are the studies now; and murder shortly
I know will be humanity."
Beaumont and Fletcher, *Cupid's Revenge*, iii. 3.

"So our most just decrees,
Dead to infliction, to themselves are dead,
And liberty plucks justice by the nose;
The baby beats the nurse, and quite athwart
Goes all decorum."
Shakespeare, *Measure for Measure*, i. 4.

699. Pope finely describes the evils of tyranny:
"The fields are ravish'd from the industrious swains,
From men their cities, and from gods their fanes;
The levelled towns with weeds lie covered o'er;
The hollow winds through naked temples roar;
Round broken columns clasping ivy twined;
O'er heaps of ruin stalk'd the stately hind;
The fox obscene to gaping tombs retires,
And savage howlings fill the sacred quires."
Windsor Forest.

BOOK II.

Thus far the tilth of fields and stars of heaven:
Now thee, O Bacchus, will I chant, and e'en
Along with thee the saplings of the wood,
And brood of olive, of a lazy growth.
Hither, O thou Lenæan father—here
Are all things with thy bounties full; for thee
With vine-leafed Autumn laden, blooms the field,
Froths up the vintage with its brimming vats;
Hither, O thou Lenæan father, come,
And thy uncovered legs, their buskins doffed, 10
In must new [-made] along with me distain.
In the first place, in giving birth to trees
Diversified is Nature ['s plan]. For some,
No sons of men compelling, of themselves,

Of their unfettered will, appear, and plains,
And winding rivers, far and wide possess;
As downy osier, and elastic brooms,
Poplar, and groves of willow, silv'ring o'er
With blue-gray leaf. But some from planted seed
Arise, as stately chestnuts, and [the tree,] 20
Which leafs for Jove the chiefest of the woods,
The Æsculus; and, counted oracles by Greeks,

Line 21. Or, "Monarch," or "Giant."
22. Dryden takes an ingenious advantage of the legend in his *Panegyrick of Charles II.*, 129:
"Thus, from your royal oak, like Jove's of old,
Are answers sought, and destinies foretold:
Propitious oracles are begg'd with vows,
And crowns that grow upon the sacred boughs."

The oaks. Sprouts up in others from the root
The closest thicket, as in cherry-trees,
And elms: aye, even the Parnasian bay,
An infant 'neath a mother's vasty shade,
Uprears itself. These methods Nature first
Vouchsafed: by these springs verdant every race
Of forests, and of shrubs, and holy groves.
Others there are, the which along its path   30
Mere practice hath discovered for itself.
One,—suckers from the mothers' tender frame
Dissund'ring, hath in furrows laid them down ;
Another—plunges settings in the field,
And four-cleft stakes, and poles with pointed wood;
And of the [members of the] forest some
The lowered arches of the layer wait,
And nurseries alive in soil their own.
No root need others, and the topmost shoot
The pruner scruples not to earth to trust, 40
Restoring it. Nay e'en, when cut the trunks—
A marvel to be told !—there is a root
Of olive thrust from out the sapless wood.
And many a time the branches of one [tree]
Undamaged to another's see we turn ;—
And, changed, the pear engrafted apples yield,
And stony cornels blush upon the plums.

32. In v. 23 Manso reads *teneras* instead of *tenero*, on slender manuscript authority. Virgil perhaps consulted the sound somewhat to the prejudice of the sense, thinking that the ear would be more offended by the close proximity of such definite syllables as *as*, than the mind would be by the transference of tenderness from the offspring to the mother. Perhaps, too, he thought that the unmerciful tearing of suckers from her frame might reduce her to a condition which, in poetry at least, might warrant the soft epithet.

47. It seems much better to render v. 34 thus, rather than according to the other view, which would compel a change to
    And stony cornels purple o'er with plums.
For, 1st. It makes *corna* the tree instead of the fruit, which ought not to be done except in case of necessity. 2nd. It is far-fetched to call any tree *lapidosa*, however suitable the term may be to its produce. The objection to the other view is, that no one would think of engrafting an inferior fruit, like the cornelian cherry, on its superior, the plum. But to this it may be answered, that the matter is one of taste. Some people might prefer cornels to plums, especially to bad plums, which the Romans doubtless had as well as ourselves.
Cowley has a graceful passage upon the subject itself:
" We nowhere Art do so triumphant see,
    As when it grafts or buds the tree :
In other things we count it to excel,
If it a docile scholar can appear
To Nature, and but imitate her well ;

Wherefore arise ! O learn their special tilths,
According to their kind, ye husbandmen,
And their wild fruits by culture soften down ;   50
Nor let your lands lie idle. 'Tis a joy
The heights of Ismarus with Bacchus thick to plant,
And with the olive to array
The great Taburnus. And be thou at hand,
And launch with me upon our task commenced,
O [thou] our pride ! O justly of our fame
The noblest share,—Mæcenas ! and on wing
Vouchsafe the canvas to the opening sea.
I list not every [subject] in my lays
To compass, no, not even though I had 60
A hundred tongues, and hundred mouths, a voice
Of iron :—be at hand, and coast along
The margin of the nearest shore : the lands
[Are lying] within grasp. I will not here
With fabled verse, and thro' digressive rounds
And prefaces protracted thee detain.
[The trees,] which lift them of their free accord
Up to the climes of light, unfruitful sooth,
But blithe and brave, arise ; because there lives,
In secret in the soil, conceptive power. 70
Still these, too, if should any graft, or trust,
Transferred, to trenches deeply worked, will doff
Their savage nature, and by constant tilth,
To whatsoe'er expedients you invite,
Not slow will follow. Yea moreo'er, the stem,
Which barren issues from the lowest roots,
Will do the same, if it be ranged apart

It overrules, and is her master, here.
It imitates her Maker's power divine,
And changes her sometimes, and sometimes does refine :
It does, like grace, the fallen tree restore
To its bless'd state of Paradise before :
Who would not joy to see his conquering hand
O'er all the vegetable world command ?
And the wild giants of the wood receive
    What law he's pleased to give ?
He bids th' ill-natured crab produce
The gentler apple's winy juice ;
    The golden fruit, that worthy is
    Of Galatea's purple kiss :
He does the savage hawthorn teach
To bear the medlar and the pear :
He bids the rustic plum to rear
A noble trunk, and be a peach.
Even Daphne's coyness he does mock,
And weds the cherry to her stock,
    Though she refused Apollo's suit ;
    Even she, that chaste and virgin tree,
    Now wonders at herself, to see
That she's a mother made, and blushes in her fruit."
                                               The Garden.

Through fields unplanted: now the lofty leaves
And branches of the mother shade it o'er,
And rob it, growing, of its fructive powers,
And parch it when it bears. Again, the tree, 81
Which rears her up from scattered seeds, slow comes,
For late descendants doomed to form a shade;
And fruits degen'rate, in forgetfulness
Of former juices; and the grape sends forth
Unseemly clusters, booty for the birds.
 In sooth on all is travail to be spent,
And all into a furrow forced, and tamed
At heavy cost. But olives give return
From truncheons better, from a layer vines,
The Paphian myrtle from the solid wood. 91
From sets both hardy hazels take their rise,
And ash gigantic, and the shady tree
Of coronal Herculean, and the mast
Of the Chaonian sire; moreover, [thus]
Takes stately palm its rise, and silver-fir
The haps of ocean doomed to see. Yea, too,
Is grafted on the offspring of the nut
The bristly arbutus, and barren planes
Have borne stout apple-stems; with chest-nut's [bloom] 100
Hath beech, and mountain-ash hath silvered o'er
With snowy blossom of the pear, and swine
Have craunched the acorn underneath the elms.
 Nor single is the way to graft, and eyes

Insert. For where the buds thrust forth themselves
From 'mid the bark, and burst its filmy coats,
A slight incision in the knot itself
Is made; therein from out another tree
A bud they womb, and with the sappy bark
They teach it to incorp'rate. Or again, 110
Stocks clear of knot are open cut, and deep
Into the solid [wood] a path is split
With wedges; then are bearing stems let in:
Nor long the time, and vast hath shot to heaven
A tree with teemful boughs, and in amaze
It views strange leaves, and fruitage not its own.
 Moreover, single is not [found] the race,
Nor in the gallant elms, nor willow-tree
And lotus, neither in the cypresses
Of Ida; neither do the olives rich 120
Into one fashion grow,—the Orchades,
And Radii, Pausia, too, with berry harsh;
And apples, and Alcinous's groves.
Nor is the shoot the same in Crustuman,
And Syrian, and the weighty Voleme pears;
Hangs not the same the vintage from our trees,
That Lesbos gathers from Methymna's spray.
 There be the vines of Thasos, and there be
The Mareotic whites;—for unctuous lands
These fit, for lighter those; the Psithian, too, 130
More serviceable for a raisin wine;
And thin Lageos, [that is] doomed anon
To try the feet, and tie the tongue; the reds,

 " You see, sweet maid, we marry
 A gentler scion to the wildest stock,
 And make conceive a bark of baser kind
 By bud of nobler race : this is an art
 Which does mend nature."
  Winter's Tale, iv. 3.

J. Philips also; *Cider*, b. i.:
" Wouldst thou thy vats with generous juice should froth?
Respect thy orchats: think not that the trees
Spontaneous will produce a wholesome draught.
Let art correct thy breed; from parent bough
A scion meetly sever; after, force
A way into the crab-stick's close-wrought grain
By wedges, and within the living wound
Enclose the foster twig; nor over nice
Refuse with thy own hands around to spread
The binding clay: ere long their differing veins
Unite, and kindly nourishment convey
To the new pupil: now he shoots his arms
With quickest growth; now shake the teeming trunk:
Down rain the impurpled balls, ambrosial fruit!"

133. Thomson, in a graphic but coarse description of a drunken bout, alludes to the effect of excessive liquor on the feet and tongue: *Autumn*, 535, 552:

---

81. *Uruntque ferentem*: i. e. should the *ademptio* not be so complete as absolutely to deprive it of *fetus*. *Uruntve* would make the passage much more intelligible; but there does not appear to be any authority for the reading; while nothing should be more strenuously resisted than amending an author's text in the absence of any evidence that it is corrupt.

92. "Sets" for *plantis* seems the only term which will apply to all the trees named. It would appear that rooted plants are intended, which are struck or reared in a nursery, and then removed to the grove. If this be not the meaning of this difficult passage, it is hard to say what is. Perhaps Virgil may here be more of a poet than a planter; or trees may be propagated in a different way now from the modes current in his time. One thing is certain, that what he says in vv. 69-72 is utterly at variance with the experience and philosophy of modern days. Botanists affirm, that it not only never was done, but that it is impossible.

104. The translations generally understand by *simplex* "identical;" i. e. that the mode of grafting and inoculating were not the same. Is it likely that people would think they were? Is it not more natural to suppose, with Heyne, that the poet means that there were different methods of conducting both these operations, though he gives but one example of each?

Shakespeare thus alludes to them:

And early-ripe. And with what verse shall I
Sing thee, O Rhœtic? Nor for this do thou
With bins Falernian vie. Vines, too, there be
Of Amineum, soundest-bodied wines,
In whose respect the Tmolian rises up,
And Phanæ's king himself; Argitis, too,
The less, with whom no other could have
vied   140
Or in so full a flow, or lasting on
Throughout so many years. I could not
thee,
O welcomed of the gods and second boards,
Thou Rhodian, have passed by; Bumastus,
too,
With swollen clusters. But no reckoning is
How many be the kinds, nor what their
names;
Nor sooth in reckoning to embrace them
doth it boot;
Which he who fain would know, the self-
same would
Fain learn how many sands on Lybia's plain
By Zephyr are turmoiled; or, when on
barks   150
More furious swoops the eastern blast, [fain]
know
How many Ionian surges reach the shores.

Nor, sooth, can every soil bear every
[sort].
By rivers willows, and by miry tarns
Grow alders; barren on the craggy mounts
The mountain ashes; shores in myrtle-
groves
Are most delighted; lastly, Bacchus loves
The open hills, yews Aquilo and frosts.
See, too, the world by farthest tillers tamed,
And eastern homes of Arabs; and tattooed
Geloni. Unto trees are portioned out 161
Their countries: Ind alone black ebony
Brings forth; to Saba's sons alone belongs
The sprig of incense. Why to thee re-
hearse
Both balsams oozing from the musky wood,
And berries of Acanthus aye in leaf?
Why woods of Æthiopians, silv'ring o'er
With velvet wool, and how the Chinamen
Comb down the filmy fleeces from the
leaves?
Or groves, which nearer to the ocean, Ind
Doth bear, the corner of the farthest globe,
Where to out-top the tree's aerial crest 172
Not any arrows have at [one] discharge
Had power;—and that nation is, in sooth,
Not slack, when donned their quivers.
Media yields
The rueful juices and the ling'ring taste
Of blessèd citron, than the which more
prompt—
If felon stepdames e'er have tainted draughts,
And mingled drugs and not unharmful
spells,—
No antidote arrives, and from the limbs 180
Expels the sable bane. The tree itself
Gigantic is, and likest in its guise
The bay; and were it not it flings far-wide
A different perfume, it a bay would be:

" But earnest, brimming bowls
Lave every soul, the table floating round,
And pavement faithless to the fuddled foot. . . .
       Their feeble tongues,
Unable to take up the cumbrous word,
Lie quite dissolved."

J. Philips, too, in *Cider*, b. i.; which whole
poem is a happy imitation of the *Georgics*:
" But, farmer, look where full-ear'd sheaves of rye
Grow wavy on the tilth; that soil select
For apples; thence thy industry shall gain
Tenfold reward; thy garners thence with store
Surcharged shall burst; thy press with purest
juice
Shall flow, which in revolving years may try
Thy feeble feet, and bind thy faltering tongue."

Yet this is not always the effect:
      " When we get a cup, sir,
We old men prate apace."
      J. Fletcher, *The Loyal Subject*, iv. 5.

138. To make *Tmolius* and *Phanæus* refer immediately to wine, would seem too gross a Græcism
even for Virgil.

149. " The which more eath it were for mortall
wight
To tell the sands, or count the starres on hye."
      Spenser, *F. Q.* iv. 11, 53.

Addison introduces the Libyan whirlwind in a
noble simile, foreshadowing the death of Cato:
Cato, end of 2nd Act:
" So, where our wide Numidian wastes extend,
Sudden, the impetuous hurricanes descend,
Wheel through the air, in circling eddies play,
Tear up the sands, and sweep whole plains away.
The helpless traveller, with wild surprise,
Sees the dry desert all around him rise,
And smothered in the dusty whirlwind dies."

166. Milton uses an equivalent for *semper fron-
dentis*:
" With myrtle brown, and ivy never-sere."
                           Lycidas.

171. It is not easy to see the exact meaning of
sinus here. Voss thinks it signifies the swelling
out of the world's extremity; in which case it
should be rendered " bosom."

174. So Dryden of the height of Arcite's pyre:
" So lofty was the pile, a Parthian bow,
With vigour drawn, must send the shaft below."
      Palamon and Arcite, 2229, 30.

179. " For the maid servants and the girls of the
house,
I spiced them lately with a drowsy posset:
They will not hear in haste."
      Middleton, *The Witch*, iv. 3.
" The surfeited grooms
Do mock their charge with snores: I have drugged
their possets,
That death and nature do contend about them,
Whether they live or die."
      Shakespeare, *Macbeth*, ii. 2.

The leaves not falling off at any winds ;
The bloom retentive e'en among the chief ;
Their breaths and fetid mouths the Medes
 therewith
Foment, and old asthmatic folk they cure.
But neither let the country of the Medes,
Thrice rich in forest, nor let Ganges fair, 190
Aye even Hermus, muddy with its gold,
With eulogies of Italy compete ;
Not Bactra, nor the Indians, and entire
Panchaia, rich with incense-bearing sands.
These spots no bulls, from nostrils breathing
 fire,
Have ploughed for monster dragon's seeded
 teeth ;
Nor hath with helmets, and with serried
 spears,
A springing crop of heroes bristled up ;
But teemful corn, and Bacchus' Massic juice,
Have filled them, olives tenant them and
 fruitful herds.   '   200
'Tis hence forth flings him tow'ring on the
 plain,
The warrior horse ; 'tis hence thy snowy
 droves,
Clitumnus, and that proudest sacrifice,
The bull, oft bathed in thy religious flood,
Rome's triumphs to the fanes of gods have
 led.
Here spring unceasing, and in stranger
 months
A summer-tide ; twice pregnant are the
 flocks,
Twice serviceable for its fruits the tree.

But ravening tigresses are far aloof,
And lions' raging brood ; nor aconites 210
Unhappy [mortals] as they cull betray ;
Nor shoots unmeasured folds along the
 ground
The scaly snake, nor with so huge a trail
Into a coil contracts him. Do thou add
So many peerless cities, and their toil
Of works ; so many towns, up-piled by hand
Upon the craggy cliffs ; the rivers, too,
That glide beneath their agèd walls. Should
 I
The sea describe, which washes her above,
And which below ? Or such her spacious
 lakes ?   220
Thee, Larius, vastest, and Benacus, thee,
With waves and roar of ocean tow'ring
 high ?
Should I describe her havens, and the mole,
Piled on the Lucrine, and the sea in wrath
With thundering hissings, where the Julian
 wave
Booms from afar, as back the deep is poured,
And the Tyrrhenian tide is sluiced within

183. "With laurels evergreen were shaded o'er,
Or oak, or other leaves of lasting kind,
Tenacious of the stem, and firm against the
wind." Dryden, *Flower and Leaf*, 278–80.

188.   "The Britons squeeze the works
Of sedulous bees ; and, mixing odorous herbs,
Prepare balsamic cups, to weezing lungs
Medicinal, and short-breath'd ancient sires."
       J. Philips, *Cider*, b. ii.

189. Thomson has a successful imitation of this fine passage in *Liberty*, v. 32–82, in which he makes Britain take the place of Italy.

204. Garth is very happy in his description of the *Fortunate Islands*, where he dilates upon such a scene as this line suggests :
"Eternal spring with smiling verdure here
Warms the mild air, and crowns the youthful year.
From crystal rocks transparent rivulets flow ;
The tuberose ever breathes, and violets blow.
The vine undress'd her swelling clusters bears,
The labouring hind the mellow olive cheers ;
Blossom and fruit at once the citron shows,
And as she pays discovers still she owes.
The orange to her sun her pride displays,
And gilds her fragrant apples with his rays :
No blasts e'er discompose the peaceful sky,
The springs but murmur, and the winds but sigh.
The tuneful swans on gliding rivers float,
And warbling dirges die on every note."
       Dispensary, c. 4.

211. "The seas in tumbling mountains did not
 roar,
But like moist crystal whispered on the shore ;
No snake did trace her meads, nor, ambushed,
 lower
In azure curls beneath the sweet spring flower ;
The nightshade, henbane, napel, aconite,
Her bowels then not bare, with death to smite
Her guiltless brood."
   Drummond, *Flowers of Sion, Fairest Fair*.

212.   "Here thou shalt rest
Upon this holy bank : no deadly snake
Upon this turf herself in folds doth make ;
Here is no poison for the toad to feed ;
Here boldly spread thy hands : no venomed weed
Dares blister them ; no slimy snail dare creep
Over thy face when thou art fast asleep ;
Here never durst the babbling cuckoo spit ;
No slough of falling star did ever hit
Upon this bank."
   J. Fletcher, *The Faithful Shepherdess*, iii. 1.

"These, as a line, their long dimensions drew,
Streaking the ground with sinuous trace."
       Milton, *P. L.*, b. 7.

223. Thomson, alluding to the public works of Britain :
"And, by the broad imperious mole repell'd,
Hark how the baffled storm indignant roars !"
       Liberty, v. 715.

Goldsmith happily describes similar efforts in Holland :
"Methinks her patient sons before me stand,
Where the broad ocean leans against the land,
And, sedulous to stop the coming tide,
Lift the tall rampire's artificial pride.
Onward methinks, and diligently slow,
The firm, connected bulwark seems to grow :
Spreads its long arms amidst the watery roar,
Scoops out an empire, and usurps the shore ;
While the pent ocean, rising o'er the pile,
Sees an amphibious world beneath him smile."
       Traveller.

The narrows of Avernus? She, the same,
Her rills of silver, and her mines of bronze,
Hath in her veins unveiled to view, and
    flowed   230
With gold full plenteous. She a mettled
    race
Of heroes,—Marsi, and Sabellian youth,
And Ligur, to calamity inured,
And Volsci, armed with javelins, hath pro-
    duced ;
The Decii she, the Marii, and the great
Camilli, Scipio's offspring, steeled in war ;
And thee, O Cæsar, mightiest [of all],
Who at this hour in Asia's farthest coasts,
E'en now a conqueror, art warding off
The craven Indian from the Roman towers.
All hail! great nurse of fruits, Saturnian
    land,   241
Great [nurse] of heroes! For thy sake on
    themes
Of ancient praise and skill do I advance,
The hallowed springs emboldened to un-
    lock,
And Ascra's lay I sing through towns of
    Rome.
There now is place for innate characters
Of soils ; what pow'rs to each, what hue,
    and what,
In yielding produce, be their native force.
First, churlish lands and stingy hills,
    where light
The clay, and shingle on the braky fields,
[Is found], delight in the Palladian grove 251
Of long-lived olive. For a sign there stands
Wild-olive, in profusion springing up
In the same territory, and the fields
Bestrewed with wild-wood berries. But the
    soil,
That greasy is, and in delicious ooze

---

240. Shakespeare makes John of Gaunt say finely :
" This royal throne of kings, this sceptr'd isle,
This earth of majesty, this seat of Mars,
This other Eden, demi-paradise,
This fortress, built by nature for herself
Against infection and the hand of war ;
This happy breed of men, this little world ;
This precious stone set in the silver sea,
Which serves in it the office of a wall,
Or as a moat defensive to a house,
Against the envy of less happier lands ;
This blessed plot, this earth, this realm, this England,
This nurse; this teeming womb of royal kings,
Fear'd by their breed, and famous by their
birth."   *King Richard II.*, ii. 1.

249. Perhaps Collins would furnish a better word, as a version of *maligni*, in his *Ode on Poetic Character* :
" Where, tangled round the jealous steep,
Strange shades o'erbrow the valleys deep."
Milton, in *P. L.*, b. xi. 15, speaks of " envious winds."

Is blithesome, and the plain that thick [is
    stocked]
With grass, and is prolific in its breast,—
Such as within a mountain's hollow vale
Ofttimes to look adown on we are wont ;—
Stream hither from the summits of the cliffs
The brooks, and trail along enriching
    slime :—   262
And that which to the southern gale is
    reared,
And feeds the fern abhorred by crooked
    ploughs :
This will to thee one day right hardy vines,
And with abundant Bacchus rilling forth,
Supply ; this is prolific of the grape ;
This—of the liquor, such as we outpour
From saucers and from gold, what time his
    [horn
Of] iv'ry hath the bloated Tuscan blown 270
Hard by the altars, and we offer up
From bending chargers entrails in a steam.
But if thy fancy rather be to tend
The herds, and calves, and younglings of
    the ewes,
Or goats that sear the tilths, do thou seek
    out
The gorged Tarentum's glades and distant
    [leas],
And,—such as hapless Mantua hath lost,—
A plain, that feeds upon its grassy flood
The snowy swans. Thy flocks no crystal
    springs,
No grass shall fail ; and howsoever much 280
Thy cattle in the lengthful days shall browse,
The icy dew shall in the scanty night
So much replace. Lands, well nigh black,
    and fat
Beneath the sunken ploughshare, and whose
    mould
Is crimp (for we in ploughing copy this),
Is best for corn : from no plain wilt thou
    see
More wains departing home with plodding
    steers ;
Or [that] wherefrom the plougher in his
    wrath
Hath carried off a wood, and overturned
The groves [that] idle [stood] through many
    a year,   290
And the time-honored homesteads of the
    birds

---

272. Or :
The steaming entrails from the bending trays.
291. So Dryden, of the destruction of timber for Arcite's funeral pile :
" Nor how the Dryads, or the woodland train,
Disherited, ran howling o'er the plain :
Nor how the birds to foreign seats repair'd,
Or beasts that bolted out, and saw the forest
bared ;

Hath he uprooted with their deepest stocks;
High [heav'n] have they, their nests forsaken, sought;
But the raw plain hath glistened forth beneath
The ploughshare driven in. For, of a truth,
The hungry gravel of the hilly ground
Scarce caters lowly casia-plants for bees
And rosemary; and tufa rough, and clay
Of Crete, by dun chelydri channelled out,
Deny that other soils alike for snakes   300
Sweet cates purvey, and winding shrouds afford.
That which breathes out thin mist and flitting steam,
And drinks the moisture in, and when it lists
Itself returns it from itself; that, too,
Which robes it aye in emerald turf its own,
Nor iron scathes with scurf and briny rust—
That soil will pleach thee elms with jovial vines;
That teemful is in oil; that thou wilt find
In tilling both indulgent to the flock,
And tol'rant of the crooked share. Such [land]   310
The wealthy Capua ploughteth, and the coasts
Bord'ring Vesuvius' ridge, the Clanius, too,
Not to the tenantless Acerræ just.
  Now, by what method each thou may'st have power
To know, will I declare. If it be thin,
Or past the customary manner close,
Should'st thou demand, (since one befriends thy corn,
The other, wine,—the close doth rather Ceres,
Lyæus all the loosest,—) first a spot
Shalt thou select by sight, and bid a pit 320
Be deeply sunken in the solid [soil],
And all the earth shalt thou replace again,
And level with thy feet the surface sands.
Shall they be lacking, thin, and for the flock
And bounteous vines more fit, its breast will prove.

Nor how the ground, now clear'd, with ghastly fright
Beheld the sudden sun, a stranger to the light."
                          Palamon and Arcite, 2243–8.

299. In rendering *exesa,* commentators differ. One takes it in its simple sense of "eating away;" another in the dependent sense of "making cavities." If the former required justification, *cibum* would furnish more than enough; while *latebras* would at least excuse the latter, which is less commonplace, and more pleasing.

305. Wagner and others read *viridis,* instead of *viridi,* but it would seem with slender authority from manuscripts.

But if they shall deny that they can pass
Into their proper beds, and when the dykes
Are filled, shall earth abound, the field is dense;
For sullen clods and heavy ridges look,
And with thy sturdy steers break up the land.   330
But briny ground, and what is "bitter" called,
For grain unblest,— *that* neither mellow grows
By ploughing, nor doth it preserve his race
For Bacchus, nor for fruits their rightful names:—
Such sample will afford : do thou thy frails
Of matted osier, and the colanders
Of thy wine-presses from the smoky roofs
Pull down. Therein let that malignant soil,
And from the springs sweet waters, to the brim
Be trampled : all the fluid, sooth, will struggle forth,   340
And drops enormous issue through the twigs;
But clear the flavor will a proof betray,
And by a sense of bitterness distort
The miserable mouths of those that try.
So, too, the land which unctuous is, in fine,
By this means learn we: never in the hands
When tossed it crumbles, but in guise of pitch
In handling to the fingers clings. [The soil,]
That moisty is, the nobler grasses feeds,
And of itself is ranker than is right.   350
Ah! be not mine that too prolific ground,
Nor show itself too strong with infant ears!
That which is heavy by its very weight
Its silent self bewrays,—and what is light.
Ready it is beforehand by the eyes
To learn the black, and what to each the hue;
But to search out the cursèd cold is hard:
Pitch-pine trees only, and the harmful yews,
Or ivies dun at times disclose its tracks.
  These things observed, the earth remember thou   360
Long first to throughly melt, and thickly score
Great mounts with trenches, first—the clods outstretched
Upon their back to Aquilo to shew,
Ere thou dig in the vine's rejoicing race.
Most excellent the fields with crumbling mould:

---

358. "Death does delight in yew, and I have robbed a church-yard for him."
                          Shirley, *Cupid and Death,* l. 12.

That [task] the winds and icy hoar-frosts
    make
Their care, and stalwart delver stirring up
His loosened acres. But if any swains
No watchfulness hath 'scaped, first search
    they out
A spot alike, where first may be prepared
A nurs'ry for the trees, and [one,] whereto
Hereafter, ranged abroad, it may be borne,
Lest the young scions should decline to
    know   372
A mother, on a sudden changed. Yea, too,
The quarter of the sky upon the rind
They mark, that in what fashion each hath
    stood,
Upon what side the heats of Auster borne,
What rear it hath directed to the Pole,
They may replace it : 'tis of such avail
To mould their habits in their tender
    [forms.]
Whether on hills or plains it better be
To set the vine, seek first. Should'st thou
    lay out   381
Fields of the fertile champaign, plant them
    close :
In a close [rank] not slower in his yield
Is Bacchus ; but—if soil upraised in knolls,
And hills aslope, be tender to your rows,
Nor less let every alley to a nail—
The trees in posture—with the avenue,
Cut through them, square. As oft in
    mighty war,
What time a lengthful legion has deployed
Its squadrons, and upon the open plain 390
The host hath halted, and the lines are
    ranged,
And all the earth is waving far and near
With flashing bronze, nor yet the grisly
    frays
Do they commingle, but irresolute
Mars wanders in the midst of arms. Let
    all
Be meted out in even ranks of paths ;
Not only that the view the vacant mind
May feed, but since not otherwise will earth
Vouchsafe to all like vigor, nor the boughs
Have pow'r to stretch them into empty
    [space.]   400
    Perchance, too, thou may'st ask what be
    the depths

---

379. Or, if taken more generally :
    To form their habits during tender [years].
396. Similarly Chaucer, *Flower and Leaf*, st. 5 :
" In which were okes great, streight as a line,
Under the which the grass, so fresh of hew,
Was newly sprong, and an eight foot or nine
Every tree well fro his fellow grew,
With branches brode, laden with leves new,
That sprongen out ayen the sunne-shene,
Some very red, and some a glad light grene."

For trenches. I would dare to trust my vine
E'en to a shallow drill. At greater depth,
And far adown in earth the tree is firmed :
The Æsculus among the first, which, high
As with its summit to the gales of heaven,
So deep it stretches with its roots to hell.
Hence this nor storms, nor gusts, nor
    show'rs uptear ;
Unstirred it bides, and many sons of sons,
While rolling [o'er it] many an age of
    men,   410
In lasting it survives. Then far and near
As forth it spreads its gallant boughs and
    arms
On this side and on that, it by itself
Upholdeth in the midst a mighty shade.
    Nor let thy vineyards to the setting
    sun
Incline ; nor hazel plant among the vines ;
Nor seek the topmost scions, or strip down
Thy settings from the summit of the tree ;—
So mighty is their love of earth ! nor harm
The shoots with blunted iron ; nor do thou
Among them sets of wild-wood olive plant.
For oft from heedless shepherds fire hath
    dropped,   422
Which thievishly beneath the oily bark
At first concealed, hath on the timbers
    seized,
And, stealing forth upon the leaves aloft,
A mighty crackling to the welkin raised.
Thence coursing on in conquest through
    the boughs,
And through the lofty crests, it rules, and
    wraps
In blazes all the grove, and gross with
    gloom
Of pitch, shoots forth to heav'n a murky
    cloud ;   430
In chief if some tornado from the height

---

404. But the season may be wrong for removal :
" Thus in the summer a tall flourishing tree,
Transplanted by strong hand, with all her leaves
And blooming pride upon her, makes a show
Of spring, tempting the eye with wanton blossom ;
But not the sun, with all his amorous smiles,
The dews of morning, or the tears of night,
Can root her fibres in the earth again,
Or make her bosom kind to growth and bearing,
But the tree withers."   Shirley, *Chabot*, v. 3.

407. " Observe the forest oak, the mountain pine,
The towering cedar, and the humble vine,
The bending willow that o'ershades the flood,
And each spontaneous offspring of the wood.
The oak and pine, which high from earth arise,
And wave their lofty heads amidst the skies,
Their parent earth in like proportion wound,
And through crude metals penetrate the ground ;
Their strong and ample roots descend so deep,
That fix'd and firm they may their station keep
And the fierce shocks of furious winds defy,
With all the outrage of inclement sky."
        Sir R. Blackmore, *Creation*, b. ii.

Hath tilted on the forests, and the blast
Rolls round the burnings as it hunts them on.
When this [occurs], no vigor from the root
Have they, nor when cut down have pow'r
   to rise
Anew, and like themselves to spring afresh
In verdure from the deep of earth : unblest,
Wild olive lords it with his bitter leaves.
Nor thee let any counsellor so sage
Induce, when Boreas breathes, stiff earth to
   stir :   440
Then winter prisons in the fields with ice,
Nor, when the seed is cast, doth it allow
The frozen root to grapple to the earth.
For vineyards is the planting best, what
   time
In blushing spring the bird of white hath
   come,
Loathed by long snakes : or towards the
   earliest chills
Of autumn, when the speeding Sun not yet
Is touching on the winter with his steeds,
Now slips the summer by. Yea spring
   to leaves
Of groves, to woods is spring a boon ;
   in spring   450
The lands are swelling, and their genial
   seeds

Demand. Then Æther, the almighty sire,
With fertilizing showers droppeth down
Upon the lap of his rejoicing bride,
And all her embryoes he, mighty, feeds,
Blent with her mighty frame. Then echo
   forth
The wayless thickets with the warbling
   birds,
And Venus herds reseek on days decreed ;
The bounteous field is in the throes of birth ;
And to the Zephyr's breezes softly-warm 460
The fields unlock their breasts. Abounds
   in all
A gentle moisture ; and to stranger suns
The buds in safety dare themselves to trust.
Nor fears the viny spray the rising gales
Of south, or shower, hunted through the
   heaven
By mighty northern blasts, but pushes forth
Its buds, and all its leafage it unfolds.
That days none other at the infant birth
Of the arising world had o'er it dawned,
Or held another course, could I have
   deemed.   470
That [tide] was spring ; the mighty globe
   kept spring,
And eastern gales forebore their wintry
   gusts,
What time primeval flocks drank in the
   light,
And men's earth-gendered race its head
   upraised
From flinty fields, and savage beasts were
   loosed
Upon the woods, and stars upon the sky.
Nor would soft things be able to endure
This travail, were not such profound re-
   pose
To intervene betwixt both cold and heat,
And Heav'n's indulgence to relieve the
   lands.   480
For what remains, what shoots soever
   thou
Shalt plunge throughout thy fields, with
   rich manure
Bestrew, and mindful hide with plenteous
   soil ;
Or delve in spongy stone, or rugged
   shells :
For 'tween them will the waters trickle
   through,

---

434. Forbiger thinks, and not without reason, that v. 312 should be punctuated as Wakefield recommends : *Hoc, ubi non a stirpe valent*, &c., making v. 314 the consequence implied by *hoc*. In this case the translation of v. 312 must be varied thus :
" Thus, since they have no vigor from the root,
Nor, when cut down, have pow'r to rise anew,
And, copies of themselves, to spring afresh," &c.
438. Perhaps some may prefer :
" Survives wild olive," &c.
449. Spenser has a beautiful passage on this subject, embodied in an address to Venus, *Faerie Queene*, iv. 10, 45 :
" Then doth the dædale earth throw forth to thee
Out of her fruitfull lap abundant flowres ;
And then all living wights, soone as they see
The Spring breake forth out of his lusty bowres,
They all doe learne to play the paramours :
First doe the merry birds, thy prety pages,
Privily pricked with thy lustfull powres,
Chirpe loud to thee out of their leavy cages,
And thee their mother call to coole their kindly rages."
449. " Wonder must speak or break ! What is this ? grows
The wealth of Nature here, or Art ? it shows
As if Favonius, father of the Spring,
Who in the verdant meads doth reign sole king,
Had roused him here, and shook his feathers, wet
With purple swelling nectar ; and had let
The sweet and fruitful dew fall on the ground,
To force out all the flowers that might be found ;
Or a Minerva with her needle had
The enamoured earth with all her riches clad,
And made the downy Zephyr, as he flew,
Still to be followed with the Spring's best hue."
   Ben Jonson, *Vision of Delight*.

452. " Ethereal Jove then glads with genial showers
Earth's mighty womb, and strews her lap with flowers ;
Hence juices mount, and buds embolden'd try
More kindly breezes, and a softer sky.
Kind Venus revels. Hark ! on every bough
In lulling strains the feather'd warblers woo ;
Fell tigers soften in th' infectious flames,
And lions, fawning, court their brinded dames."
   Tickell, *Fragment on Hunting*.

THE GEORGICS.

And subtile breath [of heav'n] will work below,
Aye, and their spirits will the plants up-raise.
Ere now, too, have been found, who with a stone
At top, and with the burden of a sherd
Enormous, would depress them: this, a shield 490
'Gainst sluicy showers; this, what time with drought
The Dog, heat-bringing, splits the yawning fields.
When planted be the scions, it remains
The soil to crumble oftener at the roots,
And ply remorseless drags, or work the ground
Beneath the sunken share, and wheel about
Among the very vine-rows straining steers.
Then glossy canes, and shafts of rod unbarked,
And ashen stakes to fit, and sturdy prongs,
By strength whereof they may themselves inure 500
To struggle upward, and to scorn the winds,
And track the stages through the heights of elms.
And while their infant age with new [-born] leaves
Is rip'ning, thou must spare the tender [plants];
And while the tendril shoots it to the gales
In joyance, through the cloudless [air] let loose
With slackened reins, it must not yet be tried
With edge of knife, but with the hands inbent
The leaves be nipped, and gathered here and there.
Thereafter, when they now with lusty stems
Their elms infolding, shall have mounted up,
Then strip their locks, then lop their arms:
—ere this 512
They dread the iron:—then at last exert
A heartless sway, and curb the gadding boughs.

Pleached, too, must hedges be, and every flock
Restrained; in chief while delicate the leaf,
And unaware of toils, to which, beyond
The ruffian winters, and the tyrant Sun,
Wild bulls unceasingly and pestering roes,
Do wanton harm; [upon it] browse the sheep 520
And greedy heifers. Nor so much the chills,
All curdled with the silv'ry rime, or heat,
Down bearing scathful on the parching cliffs,
Have worked it mischief, as those flocks [have caused];
The poison, too, of their remorseless fang,
And scar imprinted on the nibbled stem.
For fault none else to Bacchus is the goat
On every altar slain, and olden plays
The stages enter, and rewards for wit,
Hamlets and crossways round, have Theseus' sons 530
Proposed, and 'mid the goblets jovial danced
In downy meadows on the smeary skins.
Yea, Auson boors, a Troy-sprung race, disport
With doggrel ditties and unbridled mirth,
And don the ghastly masks of hollowed bark:
And upon thee, O Bacchus, do they call
In hymns of gladness, and to thee uphang
The swinging visors from the lofty pine.
Hence every vineyard with a plenteous crop
Is rip'ning, and the hollow vales are filled,
And deepsome glades, and every spot, whereto 541
The god hath veered about his comely head.
To Bacchus, therefore, will we duly chant
His rightful honor in our country's songs,
And chargers and the holy cakes present;
And, led by horn, the consecrated goat
Shall at the altar stand, and we will roast
His oily entrails upon hazel-spits.
There is, moreo'er, in tending vines, that second toil,
Which of exhaustion never hath enough. 550
For all the ground from year to year both thrice
And four times must be cloven, and the clod
For ever broken by inverted drags;

---

512. " Go thou, and, like an executioner,
Cut off the heads of too-fast growing sprays."
" All superfluous branches
We lop away, that bearing boughs may live."
Shakespeare, *King Richard II.*, iii. 4.
Spenser uses "locks" of trees, as Virgil *Comæ: F. Q.*, ii. 11, 19:
" As withered leaves drop from their dryed stockes,
When the wroth western wind does reave their locks."
Milton, also, *P. L.*, b. x.:
" While the winds
Blow moist and keen, shattering the grateful locks
Of these fair spreading trees."

525. " So may thy tender blossoms fear no blight,
Nor goats with venom'd teeth thy tendrils bite."
Dryden, *Palamon and Arcite*, 669, 70.
531. " Ful red cheekt Bacchus, let Lyeus flote
In burnisht gobblets. Force the plump lipt god
Skip light lavoltaes in your full sapt vaines."
Marston, *Antony and Mellida*, P. 2, v. 4.
538. Or, perhaps: "gentle visors."

The grove must all be lightened of the leaf.
Returns in cycle to the husbandmen
Past toil, and on itself the year is wheeled
Along through its own tracks. And now at length,
When its late leafage hath the vineyard dropped,
And chilly Aquilo hath shaken down
From woods their pride—e'en then the hind, alert, 560
His pains outstretches to the coming year,
And with hooked fang of Saturn he pursues
His vine forsaken, as he clips it close,
And by his pruning moulds it into shape.
Be first thy ground to dig, be first to burn
The brush-wood borne away, and be the first
The stakes to carry back beneath thy roof;
Be last to reap. Shade twice assails the vines;
Twice overrun the crop with matted thorns
The weeds: sore either toil. Praise spacious farms; 570
A small one cultivate. Moreover, too,
Sharp twigs of butcher-broom throughout the wood,
And by the banks the river-reed is cut,
And care of willow-grove untilled employs.
Now fettered are the vines; now trees lay down
The pruning-blade; now sings his farthest rows
The worn-out vintager: natheless the earth
Is to be worried, and the mould stirred up;
And now must Jove be feared for ripened grapes.
On th' other hand, no tilth is [requisite]
For olives; nor the fore-crooked knife do they 581
Await, and griping harrows, when they once
Have fastened to the earth and borne the gales.
To the young plantings of herself the earth,
When by the hookèd fang she is unlocked,
Purveys her moisture, and her weighty fruits,
When by the share. On this account do thou
The olive foster, rich, and dear to Peace.
The fruit-trees, also, soon as they their stems
Have felt in vigor, and their rightful strength 590
Have gained, in snatches struggle to the stars
By energy their own, and needing naught
Of our assistance. Nor the less, meanwhile,
With produce heavy waxes every grove,
And flush with berries of a bloody hue
The wild resorts of birds. The cytisi
Are cropped, the stately forest brands supplies,
And nightly fires are fed, and pour their rays.
And scruple men to plant and pains bestow?
Why greater [themes] pursue? The sallow-shrubs 600
And lowly brooms,—or they to flock the leaf,
Or shades to shepherds furnish, and a fence
For seeded grounds, and food for honey [-bees].
And 'tis a joy Cytorus to behold,
Waving with box, and groves of Naryx' pitch;
It joys the fields to witness, nor to rakes
Beholden, nor to any pains of men.
The very forests, barren on the crest
Of Caucasus, which gusty eastern blasts
Unceasingly both break and bear away, 610
Grant each their various produce; grant they pines,
A wood for ships of service, for our houses
Both juniper and cypresses. Hence spokes
Have farmers turned for wheels, hence drums for wains,
And bending keels for barks laid down. In twigs
Are willow-trees prolific, elms in leaves;

588. " Then as the olive
Is the meek ensign of fair fruitful peace,
So is this kiss of yours."
Middleton, *The Witch*, iv. 1.

612. Verses 442-453 will bring to the recollection of the readers of Spenser, *Faerie Queene*, i. 1, 8, 9:
" Much can they praise the trees so straight and hy:
The sayling pine; the cedar proud and tall;
The vine-propp elme; the poplar never dry;
The builder oake, sole king of forrests all;
The aspine, good for staves; the cypresse funerall;
The laurell, meed of mightie conquerours
And poets sage; the firre that weepeth still;
The willow, worne of forlorne paramours;
The eugh, obedient to the benders will;
The birch, for shaftes; the sallow for the mill;
The mirrhe sweete-bleeding in the bitter wound;
The warlike beech; the ash for nothing ill;
The fruitfull olive; and the platane round;
The carver holme; the maple, seeldom inward sound."

560. Pope says very beautifully in his 4th Pastoral, 31:
" Now hung with pearls the dropping trees appear,
Their faded honours scatter'd on her bier.
See, where on earth the flowery glories lie,—
With her they flourish'd, and with her they die."

Collins, too, applies " honour " to express leaves; Eclogue iv.:
" Yon citron grove, whence first in fear we came,
Droops its fair honours to the conquering flame."

563. Or: " His widowed vine, close cl'pping it."

E 2

But myrtle for stout spears, and, good for
  war,
The cornel ; into Iturean bows
The yews are bent. Nor do the glossy limes,
Or box that takes a polish in the lathe, 620
No shape receive, or by the sharpened tool
Are grooved. Nor less, too, swims the
  seething wave
The buoyant alder, launched upon the Po;
Nor less, too, do the bees their swarms
  ensconce
As well within the vaulted [hives of] bark,
As in the hollow of the cankered holm.
What to be named alike have Bacchus' gifts
Bestowed ? E'en Bacchus hath for crime
  supplied
Occasions. He the Centaurs in their rage
With death o'erpowered,—Rhœtus both,
  and Pholus, 630
Hylæus, too, with mighty wassail-bowl
Against the Lapithæ denouncing threats.
  O happy, too, too [happy] if they knew
The blessings that are theirs,—the swains,
  to whom,
Of her own self, afar from wrangling arms,
Most righteous earth unbosoms from the soil

621. See note on *Geo.* i. 115.
628. Spenser thus alludes to the fight :
  " And there the relicks of the drunken fray,
  The which amongst the Lapithees befell ;
  And of the bloodie feast, which sent away
  So many Centaures drunken soules to hell,
  That under great Alcides furie fell."
  Faerie Queene, iv. 1, 23.
  " All now was turned to jollity and game,
  To luxury and riot, feast and dance ;
  . . . . . thence from cups to civil broils."
  Milton, *P. L.*, b. xi.
Milton also makes Samson say :
  " Nor envied them the grape,
  Whose heads that turbulent liquor fills with fumes."
  " Nor the Centaurs' tale
Be here repeated, how with lust and wine
Inflamed they fought, and spill'd their drunken souls
At feasting hour." J. Philips, *Cider,* b. ii.
  Gay, however, is rather jealous of the reputation
of Bacchus :
  " Drive hence the rude and barbarous dissonance
  Of savage Thracians and Croatian boors :
  The loud Centaurian broils with Lapithæ
  Sound harsh and grating to Lenæan god."
  Poem on Wine.
  It may be bad enough, even without hostilities :
  " He that lives within a mile of this place
  Had as good sleep in the perpetual
  Noise of an iron mill. There's a dead sea
  Of drink i' the cellar, in which goodly vessels
  Lie wrecked ; and in the middle of this deluge
  Appear the tops of flaggons and black-jacks,
  Like churches drowned i' the marshes."
  Beaumont, *The Scornful Lady,* ii. 2.

633. Thomson finely imitates this whole passage,
verses 458-540, in his *Autumn,* 1235-1373 ; but it
is too long to quote.

A ready diet ! If no mighty tide
Of morning greeters, through its haughty
  doors,
A stately mansion forth from all its halls
Disgorges ; neither do they stare agape 640
On gates enamelled with the lovely shell,
And garments made the sport of gold, and
  forms
In Ephyr's bronze ; nor is their snowy wool
Dyed in Assyria's poison, nor is marred
With casia service of the crystal oil :
Yet careless rest, and life that knows not
  guile,
Rich in a varied wealth ; yet hours of ease
In fields extended, grots, and living meres ;
Yet Tempe cool, and lowings of the kine,
And balmy slumbers underneath the tree,—
Keep not aloof. There woodlands and the
  lairs 651
Of savage beasts, and youth enduring toils,
And used to scantness ; holy rites of gods,

638. " Hast thou not seen my morning chambers
  filled
  With sceptred slaves, who waited to salute me ?"
  Dryden, *All for Love,* iii. 1.
644. " Shall we seek Virtue in a satin gown,
  Embroidered Virtue ? Faith in a well-curled
  feather ?"
  J. Fletcher, *The Loyal Subject,* iii. 2.
  " I want the trick of flattery, my lord ;
  I cannot bow to scarlet and gold lace ;
  Embroidery is not an idol for my worship."
  Shirley, *The Duke's Mistress,* i. 1.
646.   " But carelesse Quiet lyes."
  Spenser, *F. Q.*, i. 1, 41.
  " There in close covert by some brook,
  Where no profaner eye may look,
  Hide me from day's gairish eye,
  While the bee with honied thigh,
  That at her flowery work doth sing,
  And the waters murmuring,
  With such consort as they keep,
  Entice the dewy-feathered sleep."
  Milton, *Il Penseroso.*
  See T. Warton's elegant poem, *The Hamlet.*
 . 652. Shakespeare makes Henry the Sixth agree
with the poet ; the king says, 3 *Hen. VI.*, ii. 5 :
  " Ah, what a life were this ; how sweet ! how
    lovely !
  Gives not the hawthorn bush a sweeter shade
  To shepherds, looking on their silly sheep,
  Than doth a rich embroider'd canopy
  To kings, that fear their subjects' treachery?
  O, yes, it doth ; a thousandfold it doth.
  And to conclude,—the shepherd's homely curds,
  His cold thin drink out of his leather bottle,
  His wonted sleep under a fresh tree's shade,
  All which secure and sweetly he enjoys,
  Is far beyond a prince's delicates,
  His viands sparkling in a golden cup,
  His body couched in a curious bed,
  When care, mistrust, and treason wait on him."
653. " The use of things is all, and not the store :
Surfeit and fullness have killed more than Famine."
  Ben Jonson, *The Staple of News,* end.
  " Upon those lips, the sweet fresh buds of youth,
  The holy dew of prayer lies, like pearl

And worshipped sires : 'mong them her latest tracks
Did Justice, from the earth withdrawing, print.
But me the chiefest, may the Muses, sweet
'Bove all [attractions], whose religious [gifts]
I bear, deep smitten with a mighty love,
Embrace, and shew the pathways and the stars
Of heav'n, the changeful fadings of the sun,
And travails of the moon ; whence [comes] the quake   661
To earth ; beneath what pow'r deep seas upheave,
When burst their barriers, and again sink back
Themselves upon themselves ; why speed so fast
To dip them in the ocean wintry suns,
Or what delay withstands the laggard nights.
But if, lest I be able to approach
These parts of Nature, chill around my heart
My blood have proved a hindrance, may the fields
Charm me, and streamlets rilling in the dales ;   670
The floods and forests may I love, unfamed !
Oh ! [could I live] where [lie] the plains, Sperchæus too,
And, wildly revelled o'er by Spartan maids,
The ridges of Taÿget. Oh ! [for one]
To set me down in Hæmus' icy glens,
And curtain me with vasty shade of boughs !
Happy [the man] who hath availed to learn
The springs of Nature, and all fears, and fate,
Deaf to appeal, hath flung beneath his feet,

And greedy Acheron's roar ! Blest, too, is he,   680
Who knows the rural deities, both Pan,
And old Silvanus, and the sister Nymphs !
Him have no fasces of the populace,
Nor monarchs' purple warped ; nor civil feud,
The traitor brothers goading, or the Dace,
Down swooping from the Danube oath-colleagued ;
Not Roman fortunes and expiring realms :
Nor has he either, in compassion, mourned
The destitute, or envied him that hath.
What fruits the boughs, what willing fields themselves,   690
Of free accord, have yielded, he hath culled ;
Nor laws of iron and the frantic bar,
Nor people's archive-halls, hath he beheld.
Some fret with oarage hidden seas, and rush
On steel ; they pierce the courts and gates of kings.
One with extermination makes assault
Upon his city, and Penates sad,
That he may from a jewel quaff, and sleep

"Dropt from the opening eyelids of the morn
Upon the bashful rose."
    Middleton, *A Game at Chess*, i. 1.
    "The immortal gods
Accept the meanest altars, that are raised
By pure devotion ; and sometimes prefer
An ounce of frankincense, honey or milk,
Before whole hecatombs, or Sabæan gums,
Offered in ostentation."
    Massinger, *The Bondman*, iv. 3.
653. "Or wert thou that just Maid, who once before
Forsook the hated earth ?"
    Milton, *Ode on the Death of an Infant*.
661.   "To dance
With Lapland witches, while the labouring moon
Eclipses at their charms." Milton, *P. L.*, b. ii.
669.   "Nor ask I from you
Your learning and deep knowledge ; though I am not
A scholar, as you are, I know them diamonds,
By your sole industry, patience, and labour,
Forced from steep rocks, and with much toil attained." J. Fletcher, *The Elder Brother*, v. 1.

683. "A wise man never goes the people's way :
But as the planets still move contrary
To the world's motion, so doth he to opinion."
    Ben Jonson, *The New Inn*, iv. 3.
688. That is, in his happy neighborhood there is no poverty to be seen : it does not mean to deny that
"The poor man's cry he thought a holy knell :
No sooner gan their suits to pierce his ears,
But fair-eyed pity in his heart did dwell ;
And like a father that affection bears
So tendered he the poor with inward tears,
And did redress their wrongs when they did call ;
But, poor or rich, he still was just to all."
    Robert Greene, *A Maiden's Dream*.
692. "To drown the tempest of a pleader's tongue."
    Massinger, *The Fatal Dowry*, i. 1.
695. The kings were courted because they lacked either the sense or honesty to say :
    "Wherefore pay you
This adoration to a sinful creature?
I'm flesh and blood, as you are, sensible
Of heat and cold, as much a slave unto
The tyranny of my passions, as the meanest
Of my poor subjects. The proud attributes,
By oil-tongued flattery imposed upon us,
Coined to abuse our frailty, though compounded,
And by the breath of sycophants applied,
Cure not the least fit of an ague in us.
We may give poor men riches, confer honours
On undeservers, raise or ruin such
As are beneath us, and, with this puffed up,
Ambition would persuade us to forget
That we are men : but he that sits above us,
And to whom, at our utmost rate, we are
But pageant properties, derides our weakness."
    Massinger, *The Emperor of the East*, v. 2.
698.   "Instead of gold
And cups of hollowed pearl, in which I used
To quaff deep healths of rich pomegranate wine,
This scallop shall be now my drinking cup
To sip cold water."
    Webster, *The Thracian Wonder*, iii. 2.

On Sarra's purple ; wealth another hoards,
And o'er his deeply-buried gold he broods.
One, awe-struck at the Rostra, stands
  amazed ;   701
Another, staring on with mouth agape,
The clapping through the seats, yea doubly
  pealed,
Of commons both and sires hath held enchained.
They joy, bespattered with their brothers'
  blood,
For exile, too, their homes and thresholds
  dear
Do they exchange, and seek a land that lies
Beneath another sun.   The husbandman
The earth hath sundered with his crooked
  plough :
Hence the year's travail ; hence his native
  land   710
And children's infant children he supports ;
Hence droves of oxen and deserving steers.
Nor is there rest ; but either with its fruits
The year o'erflows, or in the birth of flocks,
Or sheaf of Cereal stalk, and with its yield
The furrows lades, and vanquishes the
  barns.

" Their sumptuous gluttonies, and gorgeous feasts
On citron tables or Atlantic stone ; ....
Their wines of Setia, Cales, and Falerne,
Chios, and Crete ; and how they quaff in gold,
Crystal, and myrrhine cups, emboss'd with gems
And studs of pearl."   Milton, *P. R.*, b. iv.
        " I, that forgot
I was made of flesh and blood, and thought the
  silk,
Spun by the diligent worms out of their entrails,
Too coarse to clothe me, and the softest down
Too hard to sleep on."
        Massinger, *The Bondman*, iii. 3.
700. " You swear, forswear, and all to compass
  wealth :
Your money is your god, your hoard your heaven."
        Robert Greene, *James the Fourth*, v. 4.
" No ! I'll not lessen my dear golden heap,
Which, every hour increasing, does renew
My youth and vigour ; but, if lessened,—then,
Then my poor heart-strings crack ! Let me enjoy
  it,
And brood o'er 't, while I live, it being my life,
My soul, my all."
        Massinger, *The Roman Actor*, ii. 1.
" But the base miser starves amidst his store,
Broods on his gold, and, griping still at more,
Sits sadly pining, and believes he's poor."
        Dryden, *Wife of Bath's Tale*, 468-70.
" As some lone miser, visiting his store,
Bends at his treasure, counts, recounts it o'er ;
Hoards after hoards his rising raptures fill,
Yet still he sighs, for hoards are wanting still."
        Goldsmith, *Traveller.*
703.   " This applause,
Confirmed in your allowance, joys me more
Than if a thousand full-crammed theatres
Should clap their eager hands, to witness that
The scene I act did please, and they admire it."
        Massinger, *The Renegade*, iv. 3.

Winter is come : in olive-mills is brayed
The Sicyon berry ; with the acorn blithe,
The swine return ; their arbutes give the
  woods,
And autumn in variety lays down   720
Its produce, and the mellow vintage high
Is ripened on the sunny rocks. Meanwhile
His darling boys around his kisses hang ;
The taintless house its chastity preserves ;
Their udders do the kine drop milky down,
And plump upon the merry green the kids
Between them struggle with confronted
  horns.
Himself the days of feast observes, and,
  stretched
Along the turf, where in the midst the fire
Is burning, and his comrades wreathe the
  bowl,   730
Thee, pouring, O Lenæan, he invokes ;
And for the masters of the flock appoints
The games of flying javelin on the elm ;
And stalwart frames they strip for rural list.
This life of yore the olden Sabines led ;
This Remus and his brother ; thus in sooth
Etruria brave hath waxed, and Rome become
The loveliest of things, and for herself
Seven heights hath singly girdled with a
  wall.
Ere, too, the sceptre of the Cretan king,
And ere a godless nation banqueted   741
On butchered steers, the golden Saturn led
This life on earth. Nor had they, too,

---

723. The cessation of such tendernesses is sadly
described by Gray in his *Elegy*:
" No children run to lisp their sire's return,
Or climb his knees the envied kiss to share."
Thomson has a tender touch of nature, taken,
like this of Virgil, from home life. In a very successful description of a father lost in a snow-storm,
he says :
" In vain his little children, peeping out
Into the mingling storm, demand their sire
With tears of artless innocence."
        Winter, 313-315.
730.   " The woods, or some near town
That is a neighbour to the bordering down,
Hath drawn them thither 'bout some lusty sport,
Or spiced wassail-bowl, to which resort
All the young men and maids of many a cote,
Whilst the trim minstrel strikes his merry note."
        J. Fletcher, *The Faithful Shepherdess*, v. 1.
743. So Milton describes mankind after the
Flood ; *P. L.*, b. xii. :
" With some regard to what is just and right
Shall lead their lives, and multiply apace,
Labouring the soil, and reaping plenteous crop,
Corn, wine, and oil ; and, from the herd or flock,
Oft sacrificing bullock, lamb, or kid,
With large wine-offerings pour'd, and sacred feast,
Shall spend their days in joy unblamed."
And Thomson, of the reign of Peace ; *Britannia*,
113, &c.:
" Pure is thy reign, when, unaccursed by blood,
Nought save the sweetness of indulgent showers

Yet heard the trumpets blasted, nor as yet,
On hardy stithies laid, the falcions clang.

Trickling distils into the vernant glebe,
Instead of mangled carcases, sad-seen,
When the blithe sheaves lie scattered o'er the field;
When only shares, the crooked knife,

But we have an interminable plain
Accomplished in our circuits, and it now
Is time our coursers' smoking necks to free.

And hooks imprint the vegetable wound;
When the land blushes with the rose alone,
The falling fruitage and the bleeding vine."

BOOK III.

THEE likewise, mighty Pales, also thee,
O worthy of remembrance, will we sing,
Thou shepherd from Amphrysus; you, ye woods,
And rivers of Lycæus. Other [themes],
The which might idle spirits have enchained
With minstrelsy, all now world-wide are spread.
Who either stern Eurystheus doth not know,
Or altars of Busiris, the unpraised?
By whom hath stripling Hylas not been sung,
And Lato's Delos, and Hippodame,   10
And Pelops, with an ivory shoulder badged,
Keen on his steeds? A path must be essayed,
Whereby myself too I may lift from earth,
And float triumphant thro' the mouths of men.
I, foremost, to my native land with me,
(Let only life survive,) as I return
From Aon peak will lead the Muses down;
I, foremost, Mantua, to thee will bring
The palms of Idumea, and a fane
Upon the verdant plain will I uprear   20
Of marble, by the water, where, immense
With lazy windings, Mincius strays away,
And fringes o'er his banks with tender reed.
For me shall Cæsar in the centre stand,
And hold the fane. For him a conq'ror I,
In Tyrian purple, too, observed of all,

A hundred four-yoked chariots will impel
Along the floods. The whole of Greece for me,
Alpheus leaving and Molorchus' groves,
In races and the cestus raw shall strive.   30
Myself, upon my head bedecked with leaves
Of shaven olive, will my gifts present.
E'en now the grave processions to the shrines
It joys to lead, and view the butchered steers;
Or how the scene with shifted fronts withdraws,
And how the intertissued Britons raise
The purple curtains. On the folding-doors
The battle of the Gangarids will I
Of gold and massive ivory portray,
And conquering Quirinus' arms; and here,
Surging with war, and flushing huge, the Nile,   41
And pillars, tow'ring up with naval bronze.
I Asia's humbled cities will subjoin,
And chased Niphates, and the Parth, that trusts
In flight, and in his rear-directed shafts;
Twain trophies, also, from a severed foe
By prowess reft, and, triumphed over twice,
Nations from either shore. And there shall stand
The stones of Paros, effigies that breathe,

Line 15. Gray thus finely alludes to the decay of poetry in Greece, and its translation to Rome; *Progress of Poesy*:
"Where each old poetic mountain
  Inspiration breath'd around;
Ev'ry shade and hallow'd fountain
  Murmur'd deep a solemn sound:
Till the sad Nine, in Greece's evil hour,
Left their Parnassus for the Latian plains."

22. So Milton, in *Lycidas*:
"O fountain Arethuse, and thou honour'd flood,
Smooth sliding Mincius, crown'd with vocal reeds."

26. Ophelia, mourning over Hamlet's insanity, speaks of him as
"The expectancy and rose of the fair state,
The glass of fashion, and the mould of form,
The observ'd of all observers." *Hamlet*, iii. 1.

44. "Oh! let us gain a Parthian victory:
The only way to conquer is to fly."
    Dryden, *Love Triumphant*, ii. 1.

49. "I am but dead, stone looking upon stone:
What was he that did make it? See, my lord,
Would you not deem it breathed, and that those veins
Did verily bear blood?"
    Shakespeare, *The Winter's Tale*, v. 3.
"Some carve the trunks, and breathing shapes bestow,
Giving the trees more life than when they grow."
    Cowley, *Davideis*, b. ii.
"The fairest, softest, sweetest frame beneath,
Now made to seem, and more than seem, to breathe."
    Parnell, *Hesiod*.
"And breathing forms from the rude marble start."
    T. Warton, *Sonnet* v.
"Heroes in animated marble frown,
And legislators seem to think in stone."
    Pope, *Temple of Fame*.

The lineage of Assaracus, and names   50
Of the Jove-issued race, both father Tros,
And Troja's Cynthian founder.   Envy curst
Shall dread the Furies, and the rigid tide
Of Cocyt, and Ixion's twisted snakes,
And monster wheel, and the unconquerable
   stone.
Meanwhile the Dryads' woods and glades
   untouched
Track we, Mæcenas, thy no soft behests :
My soul without thee nothing lofty founds.
Lo! come, burst slow delays! with loud
   halloo
Cithæron calls us, and Tayget's hounds, 60
And Epidaurus, breaker-in of steeds :
The cry, too, doubled by the lawns' ap-
   proof,
Comes thund'ring back.   Soon ne'ertheless
   shall I
Be girt to celebrate the burning fights
Of Cæsar, and his name in fame to waft
Throughout as many years, as Cæsar stands
In distance from Tithonus' earliest source.
   If either any, stricken with amaze
At prizes of Olympic palm, feeds steeds ;
Or any—bullocks, sturdy for the ploughs;—
Chief let him choose the bodies of the
   dams.
Best is the figure of the grim-eyed cow, 72
In whom uncomely is the head, in whom
Abundant is the neck, and from her chin
As far as to her legs the dewlap hangs.
Then to her lengthful side there is no bound:
All is enormous, e'en the foot; and th' ears
Are shaggy underneath the crumpled horns.
Nor would distasteful be to me one badged
With spots and white, or that declines the
   yoke,   80
And is at times uncivil with her horn,
And in her guise [comes] nearer to a bull,
And who all tow'ring [stands], and as she
   walks
Brushes her footsteps with her tip of tail.
The age, Lucina and due marriage-rites
To suffer, ceases before ten, begins
After four years ; the rest is neither meet
For breeding, nor robust for ploughs.
   Meantime,
While to thy flocks survives a merry youth,
Let loose the males ; to Venus be the first
To send thy cattle-droves, and race from
   race   91
Supply by breeding.   Each best day of life
From wretched mortals is the first to fly :
Steal on diseases, and a crabbed eld,

94.   "Who would live long?
Who would be old? 'tis such a weariness,
Such a disease, that hangs like lead upon us.
As it increases, so vexations,

And toil, and ruthlessness of rigid death
Sweeps them away.   There aye will be,
   whose frames
Thou wouldest liefer should be changed :
   then aye
Do thou recruit them ; and lest thou again
Should seek them lost, forestall, and for
   thy herd
A youthful offspring year by year allot. 100
Nor less, too, is the choice the same for
   brood
Of horses.   Do but thou on those, which
   thou
Shalt settle for the nation's hope to raise,
Especial pains now straight from tender
   [years]
Bestow.   From first the colt of noble strain
In statelier fashion paces in the fields,
And plants and plants again his supple
   legs ;
And in the van to enter on the path,

Griefs of the mind, pains of the feeble body,
Rheums, coughs, catarrhs: we are but our living
coffins."
    J. Fletcher, *A Wife for a Month*, ii. 5.
          "Time is the moth
Of Nature, devours all beauty."
    Shirley, *The Humorous Courtier*, i. 1.
" A flower that does with opening morn arise,
And, flourishing the day, at evening dies;
A winged eastern blast, just skimming o'er
The ocean's brow, and sinking on the shore;
A fire, whose flames through crackling stubble
   fly;
A meteor, shooting from the summer sky ;
A bowl adown the bending mountain roll'd ;
A bubble breaking, and a fable told ;
A noontide shadow, and a midnight dream,—
Are emblems which, with semblance apt, proclaim
Our earthly course."   Prior, *Solomon*, b. iii.
99.   "Scions such as these
Must become new stocks, for us to glory
In their fruitful issue: so we are made
Immortal one by other."
           Middleton, *A Fair Quarrel*, iii. 2.
   108. On the impatience of the horse Pope is very
happy :
" The impatient courser pants in every vein,
And, pawing, seems to beat the distant plain :
Hills, vales, and floods appear already cross'd,
And ere he starts a thousand steps are lost."
                                        Windsor Forest.
108-125. "Oft in this season too the horse, provoked,
While his big sinews fill with spirits swell,
Trembling with vigour, in the heat of blood,
Springs the high fence : and, o'er the field effused,
Darts on the gloomy flood, with steadfast eye,
And heart estranged to fear : his nervous chest,
Luxuriant and erect, the seat of strength,
Bears down th' opposing stream : quenchless his
   thirst ;
He takes the river at redoubled draughts,
And with wide nostrils snorting, skims the wave."
       Thomson, *Summer*, 506-515.
" Survey the warlike horse !   Didst thou invest
With thunder his robust distended chest?
No sense of fear his dauntless soul allays :
T'is dreadful to behold his nostrils blaze :

And threatful rivers to essay he dares,
And venture him upon the unknown bridge;
Nor starts at idle noises. High his neck,
And finely shaped his head, his barrel
   short, 112
And plump his back, and rampant swells
   with thews
His mettled chest. [The steeds of] gener-
   ous [stamp]
Are brownish chestnuts, and the iron-greys:
The sorriest hue is of the white and dun.
Then if a clang from far have any arms
Sent forth, he knows not in his place to
   stand;
He quivers with his ears, and in his joints
He quakes, and, snorting, rolls the gathered
   fire 120
Beneath his nostrils. Thick his mane, and
   tost
On the right shoulder down it sinks to rest.
But through the loins a double spine is
   traced;
And earth he scoops, and with its massive
   horn
His hoof deep echoes. Such like, tamed
   by reins
Of Amyclæan Pollux—Cyllarus;
And they, whose story Grecian bards have
   told,
Mars' twain-yoked steeds, and great
   Achilles' car.
And such like did Saturnus e'en himself
Shed forth a mane along a courser's neck,

"To paw the vale he proudly takes delight,
And triumphs in the fulness of his might.
High-raised, he snuffs the battle from afar,
And burns to plunge amid the raging war:
And mocks at death, and throws his foam around,
And in a storm of fury shakes the ground.
How does his firm, his rising heart advance
Full on the brandish'd sword and shaken lance,
While his fix'd eye-balls meet the dazzling shield,
Gaze, and return the lightning of the field!
He sinks the sense of pain in generous pride,
Nor feels the shaft that trembles in his side;
But neighs to the shrill trumpet's dreadful blast
Till death; and when he groans, he groans his
   last."   Dr. Young, *Paraphrase on Job.*

118. Shakespeare gives a different turn to the effect of music on the colt:

"For do but note a wild and wanton herd,
Or race of youthful and unhandled colts,
Fetching mad bounds, bellowing and neighing
   loud,
Which is the hot condition of their blood;
If they but hear perchance a trumpet sound,
Or any air of music touch their ears,
You shall perceive them make a mutual stand,
Their savage eyes turn'd to a modest gaze,
By the sweet power of music."
               Merchant of Venice, v. 1.

What this great poet here says is an accurate picture of the fact, as any one who has been much accustomed to the country must have observed.

Fleet on his wife's approach, and, as he
   fled, 131
Filled lofty Pelion with a shrilly neigh.
Him likewise, when, or burdened with
   disease,
Or now, too languid from his years, he fails,
Conceal at home, nor his unnoble eld
Forgive. The older is for Venus chill,
And vainly his unwelcome task he drags;
And, if it ever to engagement comes,—
As sometimes in the stubbles without
   strength
A mighty fire,—he impotently fumes. 140
Their mettle, therefore, and their age shalt
   thou
Mark chiefly; next, their other qualities,
And parents' race, and what in each the pain
When conquered, what their triumph in
   the palm.
Dost thou not see, when in the headlong
   strife
The cars have seized the plain, and dash
   away,
Forth bursten from the goal; when hopes
   of youths
Are lifted high, and drains a beating throb
Their palpitating hearts? Upon [their
   steeds]
They press with twisted lash, and stooping
   forward give 150
The reins: the axle hot with fury flies;
And crouching now, and now erect, they
   seem
Aloft through empty ether to be swept,
And soaring to the gales. Nor pause, nor rest;
But high is raised a cloud of yellow sand;
They're moist with the pursuers' foam and
   breath:
So deep the love of praises, of so deep
Concern is conquest. Ericthonius first
Adventured cars and coursers four to yoke,
And, fleet, in triumph o'er the wheels to
   stand. 160
Reins gave the Pelethronian Lapithæ,
And the ring-courses, mounted on their
   back,
And taught the rider under arms to prance
Upon the ground, and his disdainful steps
To curve. Alike is either toil; alike
Seek out the masters both the young, and
   hot
In mettle, and in races keen; though oft
In flight the other may his routed foes
Have chased, and as his native land allege
Epirus and Mycenæ brave, and fetch 170
His lineage drawn from Neptune's very
   stock.
These [rules] observed, they're zealous
   towards the time,

And all their pains bestow, with solid fat
To plump out him, whom they have chosen chief,
And have pronounced the husband of the herd;
And downy herbs they cut, and streams purvey
And spelt; lest he should fail to over-match
The charming toil, and puny sons announce
Their fathers' leanness. But the herds themselves
With meagreness do they, resolved of will,
Reduce; and when the now well-known delight   181
First dalliance stimulates, they both with-hold
Their browse, and bar them from the springs. Oft, too,
They shake them in the race, and tire them out
Beneath the sun, when heavily the floor
Is groaning with the beaten grains, and when
To rising Zephyr empty chaff is tossed.
This do they, lest, through pamp'ring in excess,
Too blunt the service for the genial field
Should prove, and sluggish furrows it might coat   190
With fat; but that [the field] athirst may seize
On Venus, and the deeper veil her [form].
Again the care of sires begin to wane,
And that of dams to take its place. What time,—
The months completed,—pregnant do they stray,
Let no one suffer them to draw the yokes
With heavy wains, nor with a leap to clear
The road, and scour the leas in mettled flight,
And swim the ravening floods. In open lawns
They feed, and hard by brimming brooks, where moss   200
[Is found], and bank of brightest green with grass;
And grots may shelter them, and rocky shade
Extend along. There is around the groves
Of Silarus, and, blooming with its holms,
Alburnus, an abundant wingèd thing,
For which *Asilus* is the Latin name ;—
The Greeks have turned it *Æstros* in their tongue ;—

Fierce, buzzing shrill; whereat all panic-struck
Throughout the woods in every quarter fly
The herds: storms ether, with their roars convulsed,   210
And dry Tanager's woods and banks. Erst-while
With this monstrosity did Juno wreak
Her fearful wrath, what time she planned a plague
For the Inachian heifer. This, too, thou
(For fiercer it assails in noon-day heats,)
Shalt from the pregnant herd ward off, and feed
Thy cattle at the newly-risen sun,
Or when the stars are ush'ring in the night.
After the birth, attention to the calves
Is all transferred; and from the first the marks
And titles of the breed on them they brand,
And [sever] those, which either they prefer
To rear for preservation of the herd,   223
Or hallowed for the altars to reserve,
Or earth to sunder, and upturn the plain,
Bristling with broken clods. The other droves
Are fed through emerald herbage. Those which thou
For task and service of the field shalt mould,
Now spur [when] calves, and enter on a course
Of taming, while the spirits of the young
Are flexible, while pliant is their age.   231
And first, loose hoops of slender withy bind
Below the neck; thereon, what time their necks,
Unshackled, they to thraldom shall have used,
Tied from the very collars, fellows yoke,
And force the steers to move their step in time.
And now by them unfreighted wheels be oft
Drawn o'er the ground, and on the surface-dust
Their traces let them print. Next, strain-ing 'neath
A lusty load, let beechen axle creak,   240
And pole of bronze drag on the wedded orbs.
Meanwhile, not grasses only for the young,
Unbroken, neither willows' slender leaves,
And oozy sedge, but seedling corn shalt thou

---

221. The branding of sheep, Thomson, in dig-nified terms, thus describes ; *Summer*, 406:
" Some mingling stir the melted tar, and some,
Deep on the new-shorn vagrants' heaving side
To stamp his master's cypher, ready stand."

---

176. " Downy ;" or, " full-grown."

Crop with thy hand. Nor shall for thee
  thy kine,
That have brought forth, (in fashion of
  our sires,)
Brim up the snowy milk-pails, but dispend
Their udders wholly on their darling brood.
But if thy fancy rather [lead] to wars
And furious brigades, or to scud along 250
Alphenn floods of Pisa on thy wheels,
And in the wood of Jove the flying cars
To drive ; the steed's first task it is to view
The mettle and the arms of warriors, and
  to stand
The trumps, and brook the wheel, as with
  the draught
It groans ; and in his stall the jingling
  curbs
To hear ; then more and more to take
  delight
In the caressing praises of his lord,
And love the sounding of a patted neck.
And these now let him from the first, when
  weaned   260
From his dam's breast, adventure, and in
  turn
To gentle muzzles lend his mouth, [still]
  weak,
Aye, quaking e'en, e'en artless from his age.
But, three completed, when fourth summer-
  tide
Shall have approached, at once let him
  begin
To run the ring, and sound with measured
  steps,
And arch th' alternate foldings of his legs,
And be like one that toils; then to the race,
Then let him dare the winds, and while he
  flies
Throughout the open plains, as one by reins
Untrammelled, let him scarce his footmarks
  plant   271
Upon the surface of the sand. As when
From Hyperborean coasts hath Aquilo
Full swooped, and Scythia's storms and
  droughty clouds
Disperses : then the lofty fields of corn,

And champaigns, waving, with the gentle
  puffs
Wax crisp, and crests of forests raise a roar,
And distant billows hurry to the strands :
It flies, at once the fields in its career,
At once the waters, sweeping. [Such as]
  this   280
Or at the winning-posts and courses vast
Of Elis' plain will reek, and from his mouth
Dash forth the gory foam, and better bear
The Belgic war-cars on his supple neck.
Then at the last with thickened mash allow
Their bulky frame to swell, now broken in ;
For ere their breaking in, they high will
  raise
Their mettle, and when caught refuse to
  brook
The limber thongs, and galling curbs obey.
But no pains-taking braces more their
  powers   290
Than Venus, and the stings of hidden love,
To keep aloof, whether to any [swain],
More pleasing be the use of beeves or
  steeds.
And hence the bulls they banish far away,
And into lonely feeding-grounds, behind
A barrier mount, and over spacious floods ;
Or keep them jailed within at glutted cribs.
For step by step the female saps their
  powers,
And burns them by their gazing, nor allows
The mem'ry of their lawns or grass. She,
  sooth,   300
By her enchanting charms e'en oft compels
Her haughty paramours to wage a war
Between them with their horns. In Sila
  vast
A lovely heifer feeds : they, turn by turn,
With giant vigor intermingle frays
With wounds repeated ; bathes the jetty
  gore
Their frames ; and, turned against the
  struggling [foes],
Their horns are tilted with a thund'ring
  groan,
And forests peal again, and distant heaven.
'Tis not the custom for the combatants 310

---

258. " Nearer and nearer now he stands,
        To feel the praise of patting hands."
                            Gay, F., i. 13.
" The bounding steed, you pompously bestride,
  Shares with his lord the pleasure and the pride."
            Pope, Essay on Man, Ep. iii. 35, 6.
269. " I am of Pliny's opinion, I think he was begot
  by the wind ;
He runs as if he were ballassed with quicksilver."
            Webster, The Duchess of Malfi, i. 2.
" And in that haste, too, madam, I was told
  The speed of wings was slow ; their fiery horse,
  Bathing in foam, yet fled, as if they meant
  To leave the wind and clouds behind them."
            Shirley, The Doubtful Heir, v. 4.

290.   " Bulls and rams will fight
  To keep their females, stand'ng in their sight ;
  But take 'em from them, and you take at once
  Their spleens away : and they will fall again
  Unto their pastures, growing fresh and fat ;
  And taste the waters of the springs as sweet
  As 'twas before."
        Beaumont and Fletcher, Philaster, iii. 1.

300. " Tell her thy brother languishes to death,
  And fades away, and withers in his bloom ;
  That he forgets his sleep, and loathes his food."
        Marcus to Portius, in Addison's Cato, iii. 1.

310. So Octavian addresses Antony :

To stall together; but the vanquished one
Retires, and lives an exile far away
In bourns unknown; sore moaning his disgrace,
And the haught conqu'ror's blows; then o'er the loves
Which he unvenged hath lost; and towards the stalls
Oft casting wistful looks, he hath withdrawn
From his ancestral kingdoms. So his pow'rs
With all concern he practises, and lies
The livelong night, among the galling stones,
On couch unlittered, fed on prickly leaves
And pointed rush; and brings him to the test,   321
And learns his wrath to centre in his horns,
Against a tree-bole butting, and the winds
Provokes with thrusts, and with the scattered sand
Plays prelude to the fight. Thereon, what time
His strength is mustered, and his pow'rs repaired,
He moves his standards, and is headlong borne
On his forgetful foeman: as a surge,
When it begins to whiten 'mid the sea,
Afar and from the deep its bosom draws;
And as, when rolled along to land, all wild   331
It booms among the rocks, nor less than e'en
A mount it topples down; but from its base
The water seethes in whirlpools, and aloft
The sable sand it tosses from below.
Yea, every race on earth, alike of men
And savage beasts, and race of ocean, flocks,
And birds enamelled, rush to rage and fire:
To all is love the same. At no time else,
Forgetful of her cubs, the lioness   340
Hath more ferocious ranged about the plains;
Nor shapeless bears have dealt on every side

So many deaths and havoc through the woods;
Then the wild boar is truculent, then worst
The tigress. Ah! it then is ill to stray
In Libya's lonely fields. Dost thou not see
How thrills a quiv'ring all throughout the frames
Of steeds, if but the scent hath wafted home
The well-known airs. And neither stay them now
The reins of men, nor lashes fell, not cliffs
And vaulted rocks, and floods a barrier set,
And whirling in their wave the mounts engrasped.   352
E'en tilts and whets his tusks the Sabine boar,
And with his hoof the earth before him tears,
And chafes his ribs against a tree, and this
And that side steels his shoulders for the wounds.
What [feat performs] the stripling, in whose bones
Fell passion circulates its mighty fire?
Forsooth, the friths, by bursten storms turmoiled,
Late swims he in the blinded night, o'er whom   360
Is thund'ring heav'n's colossal gate, and dashed
Against the cliffs, the seas return a din;
Nor can his wretched parents call him back,
Nor [yet] the maiden, doomed thereon to die
By felon death. What—Bacchus' spotty pards,
And offspring keen of wolves and dogs? Why [tell]
What battles wage the dastard harts? In sooth,
Before them all is marked the rage of mares;
And Venus e'en herself the soul inspired
That time, wherein his Potnian mares four-yoked   370
Devoured the limbs of Glaucus with their jaws.

" I must perforce
Have shown to thee such a declining day,
Or look on thine; we could not stall together
In the whole world."
Shakespeare, *Antony and Cleopatra*, v. 1.

339. See among Cowley's Poems that on *The Force of Love*, which begins:

" Throw an apple up an hill,
Down the apple tumbles still;
Roll it down, it never stops
Till within the vale it drops:
So are all things prone to love,
All below, and all above."

353. " Or, as two boars, whom love to battle draws,
With rising bristles and with frothy jaws,
Their adverse breasts with tusks oblique they wound;
With grunts and groans the forest rings around."
Dryden, *Palamon and Arcite*, 814-17.

354.   " Speake, fate-crosse lord!
If life retaine his seat within you, speake!
Else like that Sestian dame, that saw her love
Cast by the frowning billowes on the sands,
And leane death, swolne big with the Hellespont,
In bleake Leander's body,—like his love,
Come I to thee: one grave shall serve us both."
Marston, *Insatiate Countesse*, iii. 3.

These passion lures across Gargarean
    heights,
And cross Ascanius booming ; mountains
    they
O'erpass, and over rivers swim. And
    straight,
When 'neath their eager marrows is applied
The flame—in spring the rather, since in
    spring
The ardor to their bones returns—they all,
With face turned toward the Zephyr, take
    their stand,
On lofty crags, and snuff the subtile gales ;
And oft, without embracements any, by
    the wind
Impregnate—wondrous to be told—thro'
    rocks,   381
And cliffs, and sunken dales, they scattered
    fly ;
Not, Eurus, to thy risings, nor the sun's,—
Towards Boreas and Caurus, or [the clime],
Whence Auster is in deepest sable born,
And glooms the welkin with his rainy chill.
Hereon at length, what by a truthful name
" Hippomanes " the shepherds call, drips
    down
A clammy poison from the groin—hippo-
    manes—
Which many a time have felon step-dames
    culled,
And mingled drugs, and not unharmful
    spells.   390
But flies meanwhile, flies past recovery,
    time,
While round each [theme], by love [there-
    of] entranced,
We sail along. Be this enough for herds :
Remains the second portion of our task—
To treat of woolly flocks and shaggy goats.
Be this your toil ; hence hope ye for renown,
Brave swains. Nor am I doubtful in my
    mind,
How vast it is to master these with words,
And add this dignity to petty [themes]. 400

But me along Parnassus' lonely heights
Sweet love transports : it joys to pace its
    peaks,
Where not a path of former [bards] is turned
Adown to Castalie with gentle slope.
Now, Pales worshipful, I now must sound
With lofty lip. Commencing, I decree
That sheep in downy cotes their grass should
    crop,
Till leafy summer is anon restored ;
And that the flinty ground with plenteous
    straw,
And bundles of the ferns, ye strew beneath,
Lest ice in chillness harm the tender flock,
And bring upon them mange, and foot-rot
    foul.   412
Then, deviating hence, I you enjoin
To cater leafy arbutes for the goats,
And runnels fresh supply, and post their
    sheds
Aloof from winds, afront the winter's sun,
Turned towards meridian day, what time
    at length
Now chill Aquarius sets, and drops his dew
At the year's close. These also must by us
Be tended with no lighter pains ; nor less
Will prove their service ; tho' Milesian
    wools   421
Are bartered at a heavy cost, when grained
With Tyrian crimsons. Hence [in] closer
    [rank]
Their offspring, hence a store of plenteous
    milk.
The more,—when drained the udder,—shall
    have frothed
The milk-pail, merry rills the more shall
    stream
From their squeezed paps. Nor less, mean-
    while, the beards,
And chins befrosted, and the flaunting shag
Of the Cinyphian he-goat do they shear
For service of the camps, and covertures
For miserable seamen. But they feed 431
Upon the forests and Lycæus' crests,
And bristly brambles and height-loving
    brakes ;
And of themselves they mindful to the sheds
Return, and lead along their [kids], and
    scarce
With weighty udder overpass the sill.
So with all zeal the frost and squalls of snow,
(The less they have the need of human care,)

---

385. "While through the damp air scowls the lour-
    ing South,
Blackening the landscape's face, that grove and
    hill
In formless vapours undistinguished swim."
                T. Warton, *Pleasures of Melancholy.*

Armstrong, speaking of the climate of England
(*Health*, b. i.), says:
" Steep'd in continual rains, or with raw fogs
Bedew'd, our seasons droop : incumbent still
A ponderous heaven o'erwhelms the sinking soul.
Labouring with storms, in heapy mountains rise
Th' embattled clouds, as if the Stygian shades
Had left the dungeon of eternal night,
Till black with thunder all the South descends."

391. "When we have chid the hasty-footed time."
    Shakespeare, *Midsummer Night's Dream*, iii. 2.

430. " Beasts have more courtesy : they live about
    me,
Offering their warm wool to the shearer's hand
To clothe me with." . . . . " Birds bow to me,
Striking their downy sails to do me service,
Their sweet airs ever echoing to mine honour,
And to my rest their plumy softs they send me."
    F. Beaumont, *The Triumph of Time*, i.

Shalt thou ward off, and gladly bring their food,
And provender of twig; nor shalt thou shut
Thy hay-lofts all throughout the wintertide. 441
But still, at Zephyr's call, when gladsome warmth
To glades and feeding-grounds shall either flock
Despatch, with earliest star of Lucifer
The chilly paddocks let us tread, while morn
Is fresh, while silv'ry are the blades, and dew
Upon the tender herbage to the flock
Is sweetest. Then, when hour the fourth the drought
Of heav'n hath gathered up, and with their chirp
The plaintful cicads shall the vine-trees rend, 450
At wells, or deepsome pools, bid thou thy flocks
To drink the water, as it scampers on
In oaken conduits. But in noon-day heats
Seek out a shady dell, if anywhere
The mighty oak of Jove with agèd wood
Spread giant branches, or if anywhere,
In gloom with clust'ring holms, a grove lies near
With holy shade: then [bid] to give again
The subtile waters, and again to feed
At setting of the sun, when chilly eve 460
Cools down the air, and now the dewy moon
The glades recruits, and shores are echoing back
The halcyon, the thistle-finch the brakes.
Why Libya's shepherds, why their feeding-grounds,
Should I to thee in song describe at large,
Their kraals, too, peopled, with their scattered roofs?
Oft day and night, and for a month entire
In order, feeds the herd, and wends its way
To distant deserts with no hostry-homes ;
So vast a stretch of plain there lies. His all
The Afric herdsman with him drives,—both tent, 471
And Lar, and arms, and Amyclæan hound,
And Cretan quiver; no wise else than doth
The mettled Roman in his father's arms,
When under his unrighteous burden he

463. Dryden, elegantly translating Chaucer, says of the goldfinch :
" A goldfinch there I saw with gaudy pride
Of painted plumes, that hopped from side to side,
Still pecking as she passed, and still she drew
The sweets from every flower, and sucked the dew ;
Sufficed at length, she warbled in her throat,
And tuned her voice to many a merry note."
Flower and Leaf, 106-111.

Pursues the route, and in the foeman's face,
Ere he is looked for, while the camp is pitched,
Stands in battalion. But not so, where [lie]
The hordes of Scythia, and Mæotis' wave,
And muddy Ister, whirling round its sands
Of amber, and where Rhodope returns, 481
Outstretched beneath the centre of the pole.
There, prisoned in the stalls they keep the herds ;
Nor any grass or on the field appears,
Or leaves upon the tree ; but shapeless lies
In snow-drifts, and in ice profound, the earth
Far-wide,. and towers up to seven ells :
Aye winter, aye the Cauri blasting chills.
Then ne'er the Sun disperses blanching shades,
Nor when, upon his coursers borne, he mounts 490
The lofty firmament, nor when he bathes
His headlong car in Ocean's ruddy plain.
Its [icy] casings curdle in a trice
Upon the running stream, and now the wave
Upon its chine upholds the ironed wheels,

489. This is, of course, not true. Dryden beautifully describes the joy felt by the natives of these northerly regions at the approach of their summer, such as it is:
" In those cold regions where no summers cheer,
Where brooding darkness covers half the year,
To hollow caves the shivering natives go ;
Bears range abroad, and hunt in tracks of snow :
But when the tedious twilight wears away,
And stars grow paler at the approach of day,
The longing crowds to frozen mountains run ;
Happy who first can see the glimmering sun."
Prologue to his Royal Highness.

495. " When hoary Thames, with frosted osiers crown'd,
Was three long years in icy fetters bound,
The waterman, forlorn along the shore,
Pensive reclines upon his useless oar,
Sees harness'd steeds desert the stony town,
And wander roads unstable, not their own ;
Wheels o'er the harden'd waters smoothly glide,
And rase with whiten'd tracks the slippery tide."
Gay, *Trivia*, ii. 359-66.

Thomson has a fine description of Frost in his *Winter*, 713, &c. :
" What art thou, Frost? And whence are thy keen stores
Derived, thou secret, all-invading power,
Whom even th' illusive fluid cannot fly?
Is not thy potent energy, unseen,
Myriads of little salts,·or hook'd, or shaped
Like double wedges, and diffused immense
Through water, earth, and ether? Hence at eve
Steam'd eager from the red horizon round,
With the fierce rage of Winter deep-suffused
An icy gale, oft shifting, o'er the pool
Breathes a blue film, and in its mid career
Arrests the bickering stream. The loosen'd ice,
Let down the flood and half dissolved by day,
Rustles no more ; but to the sedgy bank

That [wave] to vessels *crst*, to spreading wains
Now hostess; and the bronzes through the land
Asunder start, and stiffen garbs when donned,
And with their hatchets hew they fluid wines,
And throughly into massive ice the pools
Have turned, and ice-drop on their beards untrimmed   501
Hath grisly caked. Meanwhile throughout the air
No otherwise it snows; die cattle; stand
Enveloped in the rime the bulky frames
Of oxen, and in huddled troop the harts
Are palsied in the new [ly fallen] mass,
And scarce with antler tips above it rise.
These not with hounds slipped on, nor any toils,
Or frighted by the cord of crimson plume,
They chase; but while to purpose none they push   510
The mountain, set a barrier, with their chest,
In conflict close they stab them with the steel,
And kill them as they deeply bray, and blithe
With lusty shouting bring them home. Themselves
In low-delved caverns fleet away their hours
Of leisure underneath the depth of earth,
And piles of oak, and elms entire, have rolled
Upon their hearths, and giv'n them to the flame.
Here night they spend in frolic, and in glee

The viny goblets with fermented wort, 520
And service-berries tart, they copy. Such
A reinless race of mortals, laid beneath
The Hyperborean Wain, is buffeted
By the Rhipæan eastern blast, and wrapt
With tawny shag of cattle o'er their frames.
If wool should be of interest to thee,
First let the prickly thicket, and the burs,
And caltrops be away; shun pastures rank;
And from the very first do thou cull out
The flocks, with wools of velvet white.
    But him,   530
Though he may be a ram e'en lustrous-fair,
Beneath whose palate moist a sable tongue
But lurks, refuse, lest he with dingy spots
Should dusk the fleeces of the [newly] born;
And in the circuit of the teemful plain
Look out another. Thus, with snowy boon
Of wool (if it be worthy of belief)
Did Pan, the god of Arcady, beguile
Thee, duped, O Luna; to the deepsome groves
Thee wooing; nor didst thou the wooer scorn.   540
But let [the swain] whose passion is for milk,
The cytisus, and plenteous melilot,
And salted herbs, himself, with his own hand,
Bear to the cribs. Hence both they love the more
The rivers, and the more their udders stretch,
And in the milk the covert taste of salt
Repeat they. Many [farmers] keep aloof

Fast grows, or gathers round the pointed stone,
A crystal pavement, by the breath of heaven
Cemented firm; till, seized from shore to shore,
The whole imprison'd river growls below." &c.

502. Does not Virgil seem to be describing the *usual* state of things in these northern regions? And if so, can Heyne's rendering of *novd* by *insolente* be sustained? It seems far better, with the learned critic quoted by Wagner, to refer it to a sudden, heavy fall of snow,—perhaps the first in the season.

517. "'Tis late and cold; stir up the fire;
Sit close and draw the table nigher;
Be merry, and drink wine that's old,
A hearty medicine 'gainst a cold;
Your beds of wanton down the best,
Where you shall tumble to your rest."
    J. Fletcher, *The Lover's Progress*, iii. 5.

519. *Ducunt*, they spend; or, eke. The whole passage is imitated happily, yet not without ideas of his own, by Thomson, *Winter*, 809, &c.:
    "Yet there life glows;
Yet cherish'd there, beneath the shining waste,
The furry nations harbour: tipp'd with jet,
Fair ermines, spotless as the snows they press;

Sables, of glossy black; and, dark-embrown'd,
Or beauteous freak'd with many a mingled hue,
Thousands besides, the costly pride of courts.
There, warm together press'd, the trooping deer
Sleep on the new-fall'n snows; and, scarce his head
Raised o'er the heapy wreath, the branching elk
Lies slumbering sullen in the deep abyss.
The ruthless hunter wants nor dogs nor toils,
Nor with the dread of sounding bows he drives
The fearful flying race; with ponderous clubs,
As weak against the mountain-heaps they push
Their beating breast in vain, and piteous bray,
He lays them quivering on th' ensanguined snows,
And with loud shouts rejoicing bears them home."

Their wintry life he describes differently; *Liberty*, iii. 523-32:

"But, cold-compress'd, when the whole loaded heaven
Descends in snow, lost in one white abrupt,
Lies undistinguish'd earth; and, seized by frost,
Lakes, headlong streams, and floods, and oceans sleep.
Yet there life glows: the furry millions there
Deep dig their dens beneath the sheltering snows;
And there a race of men prolific swarms,
To various pain, to little pleasure, used;
On whom, keen-parching, beat Rhipæan winds;
Hard like their soil, and like their climate fierce."

THE GEORGICS.

The kidlings, from their mothers now divorced,
And fasten in the front their infant mouths
With muzzles spiked with steel. What
  they have milked   550
At rising day, and in the daily hours,
At night they press; what now at shades
  [of eve],
And as the sun is setting, towards the dawn
They carry forth in baskets,—to the towns
The shepherd trudges,—or with scanty salt
They season, and for winter store it up.
  Nor should with thee the care of dogs be
  last,
But with [the others] Sparta's nimble pups,
And mettled [mastiff] of Molossus, feed
On fatt'ning whey. Ne'er, — these thy
  sentinels,—   560
Shalt thou the nightly robber for thy stalls,
And inroads of the wolves, or from the rear
Unquieted Iberians, dread. Oft, too,
The shy wild asses thou in chase shalt drive,
And hunt with hounds the hare, with hounds
  the deer.
Oft, routed from their forest wallowing-
  haunts,
Wild boars, pursuing with their bay, shalt
  thou
Discomfit, and thro' lofty mountains force
The giant hart with shouting to the toils.
  Learn also scented cedar in the stalls 570
To burn, and with galbanean fume to chase
The fell chelydri. Many a time beneath
The cribs unstirred, or, baleful to be
  touched,   •
Hath adder skulked, and fled alarmed from
  heaven;
Or snake, beneath the shelter and the shade
Inured to creep, — the bitter plague of
  kine,—
And on the cattle to bespirt his bane,
Hath hugged the ground. Take stones in
  hand, take clubs,
O shepherd, and as he uplifts his crests,
And hissing necks is swelling, strike him
  down.   580
And now in flight his craven head he deep
Hath buried, when his central folds, and
  train

Of his remotest tail are paralysed,
And trails its flagging coils the farthest ring.
There is, moreover, in Calabrian lawns
That baleful serpent, rolling up his chine,
Scale-clad, with chest uplifted, and with
  spots
Enormous speckled o'er his lengthful
  paunch;
Who, while are gushing any streams from
  founts,
And while the lands are dank with moisty
  spring   590
And rainy Austers, haunts the standing
  pools;
And, chamb'ring by the banks, here gluts
  the felon
His jetty maw with fish and croaking frogs.
When once dried up the fen, and with the
  heat
The lands are yawning wide, he sallies
  forth
Upon dry ground, and, rolling eyes ablaze,
He rages through the fields, both fierce
  from thirst,
And frenzied by the heat. May it not prove
My pleasure then beneath the cope of heaven
To snatch soft slumbers, nor upon a ridge
Of woodland to have lain along the grass,
When fresh from casted slough, and bright
  with youth,   602
He rolls, forsaking either young or eggs
Within his shroud, uplifted to the sun,
And quivers in his mouth with trifid tongue.
  Of their diseases, also, I will thee
The springs and symptoms teach. Offensive
  mange
Assails the sheep, what time the chilly
  shower
Hath settled to the quick too deeply down,
And winter, crispy with its silver ice; 610

But when by genial rays of summer sun
Purged of his slough, he nimbler thrids the brake,
Whetting his sting, his crested head he rears
Terrific, from each eye retort he shoots
Ensanguined rays, the distant swains admire
His various neck and spires bedropp'd with gold."
  Cerealia.

585. See a grand paraphrase on the description of Leviathan by Dr. Young, which is too long to quote.

602. " Casted;" or, if Shakespeare's grammar is at fault:
  " When fresh from his cast slough."
So Spenser, *Faerie Queene,* iv. 3, 23:
" Some new-borne wight ye would him surely
    weene:
So fresh he seemed and so fierce in sight;
Like as a snake, whom wearie winters teene
Hath worne to nought, now feeling sommers
    might
Casts off his ragged skin, and freshly doth him
    dight."

---

582.   " On his rear,
Circular base of rising folds, that tower'd
Fold above fold, a surging maze! His head
Crested aloft, and carbuncle his eyes;
With burnish'd neck of verdant gold, erect
Amid his circling spires, that on the grass
Floated redundant."
                    Milton, *Par. Lost,* b. ix.
And J. Philips, in imitation of Milton:
" And as a snake, when first the rosy hours
Shed vernal sweets o'er every vale and mead,
Rolls tardy from his cell obscure and dank;

Or when, on being sheared, unwashed hath
  clung
The sweat, and prickly briers gashed their
  frames.
In the sweet rivers, therefore, all the flock
The masters drench, and with a reeking
  fleece
The ram is in the eddy plunged, and,
  launched
Upon the fav'ring current, down he floats ;
Or, [when 'tis] shorn, with bitter olive-lees
They smear the frame, and scum of silver
  blend,
And living sulphurs, and Idæan pitch,
And bees-wax rich in oiliness, and squill,
And noisome hellebore, and black asphalt.
No happy turn, however, to their woes 622
Comes more immediate than if any [swain]
With which could open lay the ulcer-head.
The plague is fostered, and by being veiled
It thrives, the while the shepherd to the
  wounds
His healing hands refuses to apply,
Or sits him down, demanding of the gods
More favorable omens. Further, too,
When, stealing to the bleaters' inmost
  bones,   630
The anguish rages, and upon their limbs
The parching fever preys, it hath bestead
The kindled inflammations to expel,
And 'tween the lowest [surfaces] of hoof
To stab the vein that pulses with the blood :
In fashion wherewithal Bisalts are wont,
And mettlesome Gelonian, when he hies
To Rhodope and to the Getæ's wastes,
And curded milk with horse's blood he
  swills.
[The ewe,] which far thou mayest have
  remarked,   640
Or ofter 'neath the mellow shade to creep,
Or nibbling tips of grass more listlessly,
And last to follow, or amid the plain
To lay her down when grazing, and alone
Yielding to night advanced, at once with
  knife
The plague arrest, ere dread contagion steal
Among the wareless crowd. Not, bringing
  storm,
So frequent swoops the whirlwind from the
  main,
As many be the maladies of flocks.
Nor single subjects do diseases clutch ; 650
But summer-pastures, wholly, in a trice,
Both hope and herd at once, ay, all the race
From its beginning. [This,] then, might
  he know,
If any one the welkin-mounting Alps,
And Norian fortresses upon the hills,
And Iapydian Timavus' fields,

Now e'en thereafter in so long a time
Should witness, and the shepherds realms
  forlorn,
And lawns unpeopled in their length and
  breadth.
Here erst from [some] distemper of the
  air   660
A piteous season rose, and with full heat
Of autumn glowed, and all the race of flocks
To death delivered over, all [the race]
Of savage beasts ; and lakes it putrified ;
The feeding-grounds with pestilence it
  baned.
Nor single was the path of death ; but when
The fiery thirst, thro' all the arteries forced,
Had shrivelled up their wretched limbs,
  again
O'erflowed a liquid gleet, and all the bones,
Little by little sinking thro' the plague 670
In ruins, to its substance it reduced.
Ofttimes, amid the worship of the gods,
The victim, standing at the altar, whilst
The woollen fillet with the snowy band
Is twined, among the falt'ring ministers
Sank dying down. Or if the priest had first
Slain any with the steel, thence neither
  blaze
The altars with the entrails laid thereon,
Nor answers can the questioned seer return ;
And scarce the knives, beneath [the gullet]
  plunged,   680

---

660. " Thirst, giddiness, faintness, and putrid
  heats,
  And pining pains, and shivering sweats,
On all the cattle, all the beasts did fall ;
With deform'd death the country's cover'd all.
The labouring ox drops down before the plough ;
The crowned victims, to the altar led,
Sink, and prevent the lifted blow ;
The generous horse from the full manger turns his
  head,
Does his loved floods and pastures scorn,
Hates the shrill trumpet and the horn ; . . .
The starving sheep refuse to feed,
They bleat the r innocent souls out into air ;
The faithful dogs he gasping by them there ;
The astonished shepherd weeps, and breaks his
  tuneful reed."   Cowley, *Plagues of Egypt.*
663. " The plague, that in some folded cloud
  remains,
The bright sun soon disperseth ; but observe,
When black infection in some dunghill lies,
There's work for bells and graves, if it do rise."
           Webster, *Appius and Virginia,* iii. 2.

676. Though under very different circumstances,
Spenser finely describes the fall of the victim ;
Faerie Queene, iii. 4, 17 :
" Like as the sacred oxe that carelesse stands
With gilden hornes, and flowry girlonds crownd,
Proud of his dying honor and deare bandes,
Whiles th' altars fume with frankincense arownd
All suddeinly with mortall stroke astownd
Doth groveling fall, and with his streaming gore
Distaines the pillours and the holy grownd,
And the faire flowres that decked him afore."

F

Are dyed with blood, and with a meagre gore
The surface-sand bedarkened. Hence the calves
In every quarter die 'mid fertile grass,
And cherished lives at brimful cribs resign.
Hence on caressing dogs a madness comes,
And shatters sickly swine a wheezing cough,
And suffocates them with their quinzied jaws.
Down falls, no harvest reaping of his tasks,
And mindless of his browse, the conq'ring steed,
And at the springs recoils, and with his hoof
Stamps earth in frequent blows; his ears are sunk;   691
There, too, an intermittent sweat, and that,
In sooth, to those in death's embrace dead-cold;
The skin is parched, and at the touch [the palm]
That handles callous it withstands. These marks
In the first days ere death do they present.
But if, while in its progress, the disease
Begins to rankle, then in sooth the eyes
Are in a blaze, and from a depth is heaved
The breath, at times encumbered by a groan;   700
And stretch with long [-drawn] sob their lowest flanks,
And presses leaguered jaws a furry tongue.
Through horn inserted 'twas of some avail
To pour Lenæan drenches in: that seemed
The only safety for the dying [steeds].
Anon this very [act] their ruin proved,
And, reinforced, with madness did they burn,
And e'en themselves, now just in throes of death,
(The gods vouchsafe the holy better [fates],
And to their foes that frenzy!) piecemeal rent   710
Their mangled members with their naked teeth.
But lo! while smoking 'neath the galling share,
Down sinks the bull, and gore commixed with froth
Spews from his mouth, and heaves his latest groans.
Sad goes the ploughman, loosing from the yoke
The bullock mourning at a brother's death,
And in the middle of his toil deep-firmed
He leaves the ploughs. No shades of stately groves,
No velvet meads, are able to arouse

His soul; not stream, which, tumbled o'er the rocks,   720
More crystalline than amber seeks the plain;
But flaggy have become his deepest flanks,
And dulness whelms his listless eyes, and droops
To earth with downward load his neck.
What boot
His travail or his deeds of kindness? What
With share to have upturned the heavy lands?
And yet to them not Bacchus' Massic gifts,
Nor banquets in removes have proved of harm.
On leaves and diet of the simple grass
They feed; their draughts are crystal springs, and rills   730
Chafed in their flow; nor doth unrest break off

720. "The bubbling spring which trips upon the stones."   Drayton, *Rosamond to Henry.*
731. The idea in *exercita cursu* is beautifully handled by Addison in his *Cato*, end of 1st Act:
" So the pure limpid stream, when foul with stains
Of rushing torrents and descending rains,
Works itself clear, and as it runs, refines;
Till, by degrees, the floating mirror shines,
Reflects each flower that on the border grows,
And a new heaven in its fair bosom shows."
Dryden applies it figuratively, to illustrate the purification of the heart:
" And that so little, that the river ran
More clear than the corrupted fount began.
Nothing remain'd of the first muddy clay;
The length of course had wash'd it in its way:
So deep, and yet so clear, we might behold
The gravel bottom, and that gravel gold."
Elegy on the Death of a very young Gentleman.
Pocula sunt fontes liquidi; so Milton makes the chorus say of Samson:
" Whose drink was only from the liquid brook."
Sir R. Blackmore says the same of the shepherd; *Creation,* b. iv.:
" Behold the shepherd, see th' industrious swain,
Who ploughs the field, or reaps the ripen'd grain,
How mean, and yet how tasteful is their fare!
How sweet their sleep! their souls how free from care!
They drink the streaming crystal, and escape
Th' inflaming juices of the purple grape."
Shakespeare represents Brutus saying to his servant:
" Boy! Lucius! Fast asleep? It is no matter;
Enjoy the honey-heavy dew of slumber:
Thou hast no figures, nor no fantasies,
Which busy care draws in the brains of men:
Therefore thou sleep'st so sound."
Julius Cæsar, ii. 1.
And more at large in *2 Henry IV.,* iii. 1, where the King says:
" How many thousands of my poorest subjects
Are at this hour asleep!—Sleep, gentle sleep!
Nature's soft nurse! how have I frighted thee,
That thou no more wilt weigh my eye-lids down,
And steep my senses in forgetfulness?
Why rather, sleep, liest thou in smoky cribs,
Upon uneasy pallets stretching thee,

Their healthful slumbers. At no other time
They tell that in those districts kine were
sought
For Juno's holy rites, and by wild beeves,
Ill-fellowed, to her stately treasure-domes
The chariots were conveyed. For this it is
With much ado with hoes they chink the
earth,
And with their very nails dig in the corn,
And thro' the lofty mounts with strainèd
neck
The creaking waggons drag. No wolf seeks
out   740

> And hush'd with buzzing night-flies to thy slumber;
> Than in the perfum'd chambers of the great,
> Under the canopies of costly state,
> And lull'd with sounds of sweetest melody?
> O thou dull god, why leav'st thou with the vile
> In loathsome beds; and leav'st the kingly couch,
> A watch-case, or a common 'larum-bell?
> Wilt thou upon the high and giddy mast
> Seal up the ship-boy's eyes, and rock his brains
> In cradle of the rude imperious surge,
> And in the visitation of the winds,
> Who take the ruffian billows by the top,
> Curling their monstrous heads, and hanging them
> With deaf'ning clamours in the slippery clouds,
> That, with the hurly, death itself awakes—
> Can'st thou, O partial sleep! give thy repose
> To the wet sea-boy in an hour so rude;
> And, in the calmest and most stillest night,
> With all appliances and means to boot,
> Deny it to a king? Then, happy low, lie down!
> Uneasy lies the head that wears a crown."

Yet he does sleep; and as the Prince watches by him, the latter exclaims:

> "Why doth the crown lie there upon his pillow,
> Being so troublesome a bedfellow?
> O polished perturbation! golden care!
> That keep'st the ports of slumber open wide
> To many a watchful night!—sleep with it now!
> Yet not so sound, and half so deeply sweet,
> As he, whose brow, with homely biggin bound,
> Snores out the watch of night." Act iv. 4.

Sir Richard Blackmore, too; *Creation*, b. iv.:

> "Familiar horrors haunt the monarch's head,
> And thoughts, ill-boding, from the downy bed
> Chase gentle sleep; black cares the soul infest,
> And broider'd stars adorn a troubled breast."

> "Morpheus! the humble god that dwells
> In cottages and smoky cells,
> Hates gilded roofs and beds of down,
> And, though he fears no prince's frown,
> Flies from the circle of a crown."
>   Sir John Denham, *Song*.

Young's lines are well known:

> "Tired Nature's sweet restorer, balmy Sleep!
> He like the world, his ready visit pays
> Where Fortune smiles; the wretched he forsakes;
> Swift on his downy pinion flies from woe,
> And lights on lids unsullied with a tear."
>   *The Complaint*, Night i. 1-5.

> "No frowning care yon bless'd apartment sees,
> There sleep retires, and finds a couch of ease.
> Kind dreams, that fly remorse, and pamper'd wealth,
> There shed the smiles of innocence and health."
>   Savage, *Wanderer*, c. 1.

A place of ambushment around the folds,
Nor does he prowl about the herds by night:
A fiercer pang subdues him. Craven deer
And flying harts now both among the
hounds,
And round the homesteads wander. Now
the brood
Of the illimitable sea, and all the tribe
Of swimming [creatures] on the farthest
strand,
Like shipwrecked corses, washes up the
wave;
Against their wont to rivers fly the seals;
And dies, within his winding-shroud ensconced   750
In vain, the adder, and with scales erect
The thunder-stricken hydri. E'en to birds
Unrighteous is the air, and, headlong fallen,
Beneath the lofty cloud their life they leave.
Moreo'er, nor now avails it that their food
Is changed, and sought prescriptions harm:
the chiefs
Have yielded,—Chiron son of Phillyra,
Melampus, too, of Amythaon sprung.
Storms wan Tisiphone, and, into light
Let loose from Stygian murk, before her
drives   760
Diseases and Affright; and, day by day
Uprising higher, she her rav'nous head
Advances. With the bleating of the flocks,
And frequent bellowings, streams, and
withered banks,
And sloping hills, resound. And now by
troops
She havoc deals, and in the very stalls
Piles corses, melted with the loathsome
bane;
Till in the earth to hide them, and in pits
To hearse, they learn. For neither in the
hides
Was service, nor the flesh can any [swain]
Or cleanse in waters, or with flame o'ercome.   771
Nor e'en to shear the fleeces, cankered
through
With pestilence and foulness, nor to touch

---

754. J. Philips uses similar expressions in describing the death of birds from a different cause:

> "Sulphureous death
> Checks their mid flight, and heedless while they strain
> Their tuneful throats, the towering heavy lead
> O'ertakes their speed: they leave their little lives
> Above the clouds, precipitant to earth."
>   *Cider*, b. ii.

771. "With flame o'ercome," *i. e.*, cook them. For, upon the whole, the view presented in the version seems to be the most consistent. They burned the carcases entire; as there was no worth in their hides, their flesh, or their fleece.

The mould'ring woof, have they the pow'r.
Nay e'en
If any had the loathsome garbs essayed,
Inflammatory blains and filthy sweat
His fetid limbs pursued ; nor was the time

Thereafter long, when, as he pauses still,
His tainted joints the sacred fire would eat.

778. " As he pauses ;" *i. e.*, to throw off the infected dress.

BOOK IV.

NEXT the ethereal honey's heav'nly boons
Will I pursue : this portion, too, do thou
Regard, Mæcenas. Shows of pigmy things,
That claim thy wonder,—both the high-souled chiefs,
And habits, and pursuits, and clans, and wars,
Of a whole nation will I duly sing.
Upon a petty [theme] the travail, yet
Not petty the renown, if adverse gods
Permit one, and invoked Apollo hears.
 In the first place, a resting-spot and post
Must for thy bees be sought, whereto may lie   11
Nor inlet for the winds, (for winds prevent
Their bringing home their forage,) nor may sheep
And butting kidlings trample on the flowers,
Nor heifer, as she wanders thro' the plain,
Shake down the dew, and bruise the springing blades.
And, speckled o'er their scale-encrusted backs,
Be lizards far aloof from thy rich cotes,
And Meropes, and other birds, and Procne,
Upon her bosom scored with hands of blood.   20

For all they widely waste, and e'en [the bees],
While flying, in their mouth they bear away,
Delicious diet for their ruthless nests.
But crystal springs, and plashes green with moss,
Be nigh at hand, and, scamp'ring thro' the grass,
A shallow rivulet ; and let the palm,
Or oleaster huge, the outer court
O'ershade, that, when the new [ly-issued] kings
Shall lead the earliest swarms in spring their own,
And, sallied from the combs, the youth disport,   30
A neighb'ring bank may woo them to give way
Before the heat, and in their path a tree
Harbor them 'neath its hostelries of leaf.
Into the middle, whether still shall stand
The water, or it shall career along,
Fling willows slant and bulky stones, that they
On frequent bridges may have pow'r to light,
And spread their pinions to the summer sun,
If haply headlong Eurus shall have sprent
The loiterers, or plunged them in the flood.
Round these let em'rald casias, and wild thymes,   41
Their perfume shedding far and near, and store
Of savory, [its scent] strong breathing, bloom,
And beds of violet drink the wat'ring spring.
But let the hives themselves, should they for thee
Or of the hollow bark be stitched, or plight
Of limber twig, have narrow avenues ;
For winter candies honey with its cold,

Line 1.   "But when
He does describe the commonwealth of bees,
Their industry, and knowledge of the herbs
From which they gather honey, with their care
To place it with decorum in the hive,
Their government among themselves, their order
In going forth and coming loaden home,
Their obedience to their king, and his rewards
To such as labour, with his punishments,
Only inflicted on the slothful drone :—
I'm ravished with it."
         J. Fletcher, *The Elder Brother*, l. 2.

3. Or, perhaps :
 "The drama of a pigmy commonwealth."

7. Verses 6 and 7 are imitated by Pope in the opening of his inimitable mock heroic, the *Rape of the Lock*:
 "What dire offence from amorous causes springs,
 What mighty contests rise from trivial things,
 I sing.—This verse to Caryl, Muse ! is due :
 This, even Belinda, may vouchsafe to view ;
 Slight is the subject, but not so the praise,
 If she inspire, and he approve my lays."

22. So Thomson, *Spring*, 675 :
                     " Away they fly,
 Affectionate, and undesiring bear
 The most delicious morsel to their young."
33. More literally : "leafy hostelries."

And heat dissolves the same, to fluid turned:
Each force for bees alike is to be feared. 50
Nor in their homes in vain with rivalry
The narrow vents with wax do they besmear,
And close the rims with fucus and with flowers,
And, gathered for these very services,
A cement keep, more glutinous than e'en
The birdlime and the Phrygian Ida's pitch.
Yea oftentimes in excavated shrouds,
(If true is rumor,) underneath the earth
Their household have they hugged, and deep
Been found both in the vaulted pumicerocks, 60
And grot of [some] heart-eaten tree. Do thou,
However, both with glossy mud anoint
Their chinky chambers, warming them around,
And throw across them thin [supplies of] leaves.
Nor overnear their homes the yew allow,
Nor burn thy coral crabs upon the hearth,
Nor place reliance on the fen profound,
Or where the smell of mire is rank, or where
The vaulted rocks with verberation ring,
And echo of the voice impinged rebounds.
   For what remains, what time the golden Sun 71
Hath chased the routed winter from the lands,
And heav'n uncurtained with his summerlight,
They straight the lawns and forests range, and reap
Gay flow'rs, and sip the surface of the brooks,
Light [-poised]. Hence, with what charm I know not blithe,
Their offspring and their nests they cherish; hence
With skill fresh wax elaborate, and mould
Their gluey honeys. Hence when now discharged

From out their caverns to the stars of heaven, 80
A swarm above thee thou shalt have espied,
Floating throughout the crystal summer-air,
And shalt in wonderment a darkling cloud
See warping on the wind,—observe them close;
Sweet streams and leafy bow'rs they ever seek.
Hither do thou the scents commanded strew,
Bruised balm, and honeywort's unnoble herb;
And tingling sounds awake, and rattle round
The cymbals of the Mother. Of themselves
They on the seats bedrugged will settle down; 90
They of themselves within their inmost cots
Will bury them, in fashion [all] their own.
   But if they shall have issued to the fight,

" Here their delicious task the fervent bees,
  In swarming millions, tend: around, athwart,
Through the soft air, the busy nations fly,
Cling to the bud, and, with inserted tube,
Suck its pure essence, its ethereal soul;
And oft, with bolder wing, they soaring dare
The purple heath, or where the wild thyme grows,
And yellow load them with the luscious spoil."

" Yet hark, how through the peopled air
    The busy murmur glows!
  The insect youth are on the wing,
  Eager to taste the honied spring,
    And float amid the liquid noon:
Some lightly o'er the current skim,
Some show their gayly-gilded trim,
    Quick-glancing to the sun."
                    Gray, *Ode to Spring.*

" Thick as the bees, that with the spring renew
  Their flowery toils, and sip the fragrant dew,
When the wing'd colonies first tempt the sky,
O'er dusky fields and shaded waters fly,
Or, settling, seize the sweets the blossoms yield,
And a low murmur runs along the field."
                    Pope, *Temple of Fame.*

This and other passages in Virgil call to mind Pope's beautiful description of the Sylphs in the *Rape of the Lock*, c. ii.:
" Some to the sun their insect wings unfold,
Waft on the breeze, or sink in clouds of gold;
Transparent forms, too fine for mortal sight,
Their fluid bodies half dissolved in light,
Loose to the wind their airy garments flew,
Thin glittering textures of the filmy dew,
Dipt in the richest tincture of the skies,
Where light disports in ever-mingling dyes;
While every beam new transient colours flings,
Colours that change whene'er they wave their wings."

92. " So swarming bees that, on a summer's day
In airy rings and wild meanders play,
Charm'd with the brazen sound, their wanderings end,
And, gently circling, on a bough descend."
            Dr. Young, *The Last Day*, b. ii.

93. Among the different modes of punctuating this fine, but irregularly constructed, passage,

---

53. " Fucus;" *i. e.*, " propolis."

79. Milton has a very beautiful simile of bees issuing from the hive on a fine day; *P. L.*, b. i.:
              " As bees
In spring-time, when the Sun with Taurus rides,
Pour forth their populous youth about the hive
In clusters: they among fresh dews and flowers
Fly to and fro, or on the smoothed plank,
The suburb of their straw-built citadel,
New rubb'd with balm, expatiate and confer
Their state affairs."

Thomson is also highly successful; *Spring*, 508:

(For many a time on monarchs twain a feud
Hath stalked with mighty hubbub, and
 forthwith
The spirits of the commons and their hearts
Throbbing for war, we may afar foreknow ;
For those that loiter does the warlike bray
Of grating bronze upbraid, and there is
 heard
A sound, that apes the trumpet's broken
 blasts :)   100
Then in commotion they together flock,
And sparkle with their pinions, and their
 stings
Point sharp upon their beaks, and fit their
 thews,
And round the king, and at the very tent
Of their commander, muster they in crowds,
And challenge with their lusty cries the foe.
So, when they have secured a cloudless
 spring,
And open plains, they sally from the gates ;
In heav'n on high 'tis battle ; booms a din ;
Huddled they cluster in a mighty ball 110
And headlong drop :—no thicker in the air
The hail, nor from the shaken holm pours
 down
So thick [a show'r] of mast. [The kings]
 themselves
Throughout the central ranks, with noted
 wings,
Wield giant spirits in a puny breast ;
E'en for so long determined not to yield,
Until the overwhelming conqueror
Or these, or those, hath forced to show
 their backs,

---

none seems satisfactory, and therefore a different
view of the part which is to be considered elliptical,
is here taken. According to this, the embarass-
ment attending *que* in *contivuoque* appears to be
removed ; while the objection, fairly raised by
Wagner against the views of Heyne and Voss, is in
a great measure avoided.

115. " But, boy, fear not ; I will outstretch them
 all :
 My mind's a giant, though my bulk be small."
 Anonymous, *The first part of Jeronimo.*
115. So Milton, *P. L.*, vii., of the ant :
 " In a small room large heart enclosed."
And Shakespeare, *K. H. V.*, ii. Chorus :
" O England !—model to thy inward greatness,
 Like little body with a mighty heart."
And again :   " I never saw
 Such noble fury in so poor a thing."
                                   Cymbeline, v. 5.
Milton in the same way, in *Samson Agonistes* :
" Go, baffled coward ! lest I run upon thee,
 Though in these chains, bulk without spirit vast."
 Dryden, in speaking of the dismay of the Dutch
fleet, inverts the idea :
" Faint sweats all down their mighty members run ;
 Vast bulks which little souls but ill supply."
             Annus Mirabilis, 70.

Reversed in flight. These tumults of their
 souls,
And these encounters so severe, when
 checked   120
By tossing of a little dust, subside.
But when both gen'rals from the battle thou
Shalt have recalled, the one, who meaner
 seems,
(Lest in his waste he mischief thee,) consign
To death ; allow the nobler in the court,
Untenanted, to reign. The one will prove
With gold-encrusted spangles in a blaze.
For twain the species be : this nobler [king]
Both in his guise distinguished, brilliant,
 too,
With ruddy scales ; that other, grim with
 sloth,   130
And trailing, base, a breadth of paunch.
 As twain
The monarchs' figures, so the commons'
 frames.
For some in hideousness are rough ; as
 when
From dust aloft the thirsty traveller comes,
And sputters from his droughty mouth the
 earth.
Others shine forth, and with a glitter flash,
Ablaze upon their bodies, dashed with
 gold
And even drops. This proves the worthier
 breed :
Therefrom in heav'n's appointed season
 thou
Shalt squeeze thy luscious honeys ;—neither
 [yet]   140
So luscious, as both crystal-bright, and
 taste
Austere of Bacchus ready to subdue.
But when the swarms unsettled fly
 abroad,
And in the welkin sport, and scorn the
 combs,
And quit their chilly homesteads, thou
 shalt bar
Their restless spirits from their idle play.
Nor is to bar them a gigantic toil.
Do thou from off the kings their pinions
 pluck :
Not any [bee], while they delay, will dare
To wend his route aloft, or from the camp
To tear the standards up. Let gardens
 woo,   151
That breathe [a perfume] from their saffron
 flowers,
And, sentry 'gainst the robbers and the
 birds,
Be their protection with his willow scythe,
The Hellespontiac Priapus' guard.
Let him to whom such [tasks] of int'rest be,

From lofty mountains bringing thyme and pines,
Plant them himself far-wide around their homes ;
Himself let chafe his hand with galling toil;
Himself set fruiting saplings in the ground,
And loving waters o'er them draw in rills.
And truly, towards my travail's farthest bound   162
Were I not now my canvas drawing in,
And hasting on to veer my prow to land,
I peradventure, too, might sing what pains
Of cultivation gardens rich would deck,
And doubly-blooming Pæstum's beds of rose ;
And how the endive-plants in runnels quaffed
Might take delight, and banks with parsley green ;
And, writhing through the grass, the cucumber   170
Swell out into a paunch. Nor daffodil,
Late-flow'ring, or the lithe acanthus' stalk,
Could I have passed unsung, and ivies wan,
And myrtle-shrubs enamored of the shores.
For I recall to mind, that I beneath
The stately towers of Œbalia, where
The dark Galesus dews the golden tilths,
An agèd swain of Corycus had seen,
To whom few acres of abandoned ground
Belonged ; nor fruitful was that [soil] thro' steers,   180
Nor fit for cattle, nor for Bacchus meet.
Yet even here his potherbs, thin [in row],
Among the brakes and snowy lilies round,
And vervains, planting, fine-grained poppy, too,
The wealth of monarchs in his mind he matched ;
And, late at night returning to his home,
His boards he cumbered with unpurchased cates.
The first was he in spring to cull the rose,

161. Or, if *irriget* be taken in its secondary, and *imbres* in its primary sense :
"And sprinkle over them the loving showers."

185. "My mind's a kingdom." Ben Jonson.
" For 'tis the mind that makes the body rich."
        Shakespeare, *Taming of the Shrew*, iv. 3.
" I want not, for my mind affordeth wealth."
        Robert Greene, *The Hermit's Verses*.
        " No, Lucio, he's a king,
A true right king, that dares doe aught, save wrong,
Feares nothing mortall but to be unjust,
Who is not blowne up with the flattering puffes
Of spungy sycophants, who stands unmoved,
Despite the justling of opinion."
        "This, Lucio, is a king,
And of this empire every man's possest,
That's worth his soule."
        Marston, *Antonio and Mellida*, P. 1, iv. 4.

And in the autumn fruits ; and when e'en still
Drear winter with its cold would brast the rocks,   190
And with its ice the race of waters rein,
He tresses of the downy martagon
E'en now was clipping, chiding summer late,
And lagging Zephyrs. Therefore he, the same,
With pregnant bees, and many a swarm, was first
To overflow; and from squeezed combs to force
The frothing honeys. He had limes and pine
Of fullest yield ; and with as many fruits
In infant blossom as the teemful tree
Had robed itself, so many it retained   200
In autumn ripe. He also into rows
Transplanted far-grown elms, and flinty pear,
And black-thorn stocks, already bearing plums,
And plane, to topers now affording shade.
But these, in sooth, do I, shut out by bounds
Too strict, pass over, and to other [hards]
To be recorded after me I leave.
    Now come, what instincts Jove himself to bees
Assigned, will I unfold ; for what reward
The Curets' tuneful sounds and clanking bronze   210
They, tracing, fed the monarch of the sky
Beneath the grot of Dicte. They alone
Have sons in common, city-mansions shared

192. See note on *Geo.* ii. v. 368.
201. " The teeming autumn, big with rich increase,
Bearing the wanton burden of the prime."
        Shakespeare, *Sonnet* 97.
213, &c.   " For so work the honey bees ;
Creatures that, by a rule of nature, teach
The act of order to a people's kingdom.
They have a king and officers of sorts :
Where some, like magistrates, correct at home ;
Others, like merchants, venture trade abroad ;
Others, like soldiers, armed in their stings,
Make boot upon the summer's velvet buds :
Which pillage they with merry march bring home
To the tent royal of their emperor :
Who, busied in his majesty, surveys
The singing masons building roofs of gold ;
The civil citizens kneading up the honey ;
The poor mechanic porters crouding in
Their heavy burdens at his narrow gate ;
The sad-ey'd justice, with his surly hum,
Delivering o'er to executors pale
The lazy yawning drone."
        Shakespeare, *K. H. V.*, i. 2.
" The careful insect midst his works I view,
Now from the flowers exhaust the fragrant dew ;
With golden treasures load his little thighs,

In partnership, and under noble laws
They pass existence, and a native land,
And settled household-gods alone they
   know ;
And mindful of the coming winter, toil
In summer ply, and for the common stock
Store up their gains. For some watch o'er
   the food,
And by fixed pact are in the fields em-
   ployed.   220
A part within th' inclosures of their homes
Narcissus' tear, and, clammy, [tapped]
   from bark,
A gum, the first foundations for the combs,
Lay down ; then hang they up the gluey
   wax.
Others, the nation's hope, the full-grown
   young,
Lead forth ; thrice limpid honeys others
   pack,
And with the crystal nectar puff the cells.
There are, to whom hath fallen out by lot,
The sentry at the gates, and in their turn
They scan the waters and the clouds of
   heaven ;   230
Or burdens of the [workers] coming in
Receive, or, in battalion formed, the drones,
A lazy cattle, banish from the cribs :
Work glows, and scented honeys smell of
   thyme.
And as when Cyclops haste the thunder-
   bolts

And steer his distant journey through the skies ;
Some against hostile drones the hive defend,
Others with sweets the waxen cells distend ;
Each in his toil his destin'd office bears,
And in the little bulk a mighty soul appears."
                 Gay, *Rural Sports*, i. 83–90.

222. This use of *lacrima*, v. 160, is imitated by Sir Richard Blackmore in one of his beautiful passages in *Creation*, b. ii. :
" The fragrant trees, which grow by Indian floods,
And in Arabia's aromatic woods,
Owe all their spices to the summer's heat,
Their gummy tears, and odoriferous sweat."

235. The same operation is described as going on in Mammon's cave, by Spenser, *Faerie Queene*, ii. 7, 36:
" One with great bellowes gathered filling ayre,
And with forst wind the fewell did inflame ;
Another did the dying bronds repayre
With yron tongs, and sprinckled ofte the same
With liquid waves, fiers Vulcans rage to tame,
Who, maystring them, renew'd his former heat :
Some scumd the drosse that from the metall came ;
Some stird the molten owre with ladles great :" &c.
Milton similarly :
" In other part stood one who, at the forge
Labouring, two massy clods of iron and brass
Had melted ; (whether found where casual fire
Had wasted woods on mountain or in vale,
Down to the veins of earth ; thence gliding hot
To some cave's mouth ; or whether wash'd by
   stream

From ductile blocks, in bull's-hide bellows
   some
Admit the breezes, and discharge them
   back ;
Some dip the screeching bronzes in the pool:
With stithies planted on him Ætna groans.
They 'tween them with colossal force their
   arms   240
Upheave to measure, and with griping
   tongs
The iron turn and turn. Not otherwise,
(If we may tiny things compare with vast,)
An inbred passion of possessing spurs
Cecropian bees—in his own office each.
The towns are to the old a charge, and
   combs
To wall, and fashion their Dædalian roofs.
But, jaded, late at night betake them home
The younger, loaded on their legs with
   thyme ;
And on the arbute-berries all around   250
They feed, and blue-grey willows, casia too,
And blushing crocus, and the gummy lime,
And rust-hued martagons. With all is one
The rest from work, with all is one the toil.
At morning from the gates they sally
   forth ;—
Not anywhere delay :—again, when Eve
These same, from feed [recalled], at length
   hath warned
Forth from the champaign to withdraw,
   their homes
Then seek they, then their bodies they
   refresh ;
A hum arises, and they buzz around   260
Their borders and their thresholds. Then,
   when now
Within their couching-chambers they them-
   selves
Have ordered, all is stillness for the night,
And their own slumber holds their wearied
   limbs.
Nor sooth,—rain overhanging,—from the
   hives
Retire they over far, or trust the sky
When eastern gales are drawing on, but
   round
They safely water 'neath the city walls,
And rambles short essay, and pebbles oft,
As skiffs unsteady in the tossing wave,
Their ballast raise : therewith themselves
   they poise   271
Thro' unsubstantial clouds. Thou'lt marvel
   chief

From underground ;) the liquid ore he drain'd
Into fit moulds prepared ; from which he form'd
First his own tools ; then, what might else be
   wrought
Fusil or graven in metal."   *P. L.*, xi.

That this observance should have pleased
  the bees—
That neither do they riot in embrace,
Nor slothfully on Venus waste their frames,
Or bear their young with throes ; but by
  themselves
They cull their children in their mouth
  from leaves,
And honied herbage ; by themselves their
  king
And tiny Quirites they supply, and mould
Anew their palaces and waxy realms. 280
Oft, too, in roving thro' the flinty rocks
Their pinions they have chafed—yea, e'en
  their life
Beneath their load resigned ;—so great the
  love
Of flow'rs, and pride of gend'ring honey.
  Hence
Though these a span of narrow life befall,
(For no more than a seventh summer-tide
Is lengthened,) yet imperishable lasts
The lineage, and stands firm through many
  a year
The fortune of the house, and ancestors
Of ancestors are counted. Further, too,
Not thus their king do Egypt, and great
  Lydia, 291
And tribes of Parthians, and the Median
  [flood],
Hydaspes, venerate. The king un-
  harmed—
There dwells one spirit in them all ; when
  lost—
They've broken fealty, and the honeys
  heaped
Themselves have plundered, and to atoms
  rent
The fretwork of the combs. The guard of
  toils
Is he ; at him in wonder do they gaze,
And all, with humming full, around him
  stand,
And throng him close, and ofttimes lift
  him up 300
Upon their shoulders, and their frames to
  war
Expose, and seek through wounds a
  splendid death.
Some, from these marks, and following
  out
These instances, have said that in the bees
There dwells a portion of the heav'nly mind,
And draughts ethereal. For that deity
Pervades alike all lands, and tracts of sea,
·And sky sublime ; that hence the flocks,
  the herds,

Mankind, of savage creatures every tribe—
Each [being] for itself at birth derives 310
A subtile life. Moreover, to this source
All [living things] thereafter are reduced,
And at their dissolution are restored ;
That neither is there room for death, but
  quick
They wing their journey to the rank of star,
And mount them to the firmament on high.
  If ever thou their narrow home, and,
  stored
In treasure-cells, their honeys would'st un-
  seal,
First, sprinkled with a draught of waters,
  rinse
Thy mouth, and in thy hand before thee
  stretch 320
The piercing smoke. Their heavy produce
  twice
They gather ; twain the harvest-times ; as
  soon
As hath Taÿgete, the Pleiad maid,
Her comely visage to the lands revealed,
And with her foot hath spurned the Ocean-
  tides,
Disdained ; or when the self-same, as she
  flies
The constellation of the wat'ry Fish,
More melancholy from the sky sinks down
Within the winter-waves. In them dwells
  wrath
Past bound, and when annoyed their bane
  they breathe 330
Into their stingings, and their viewless bolts
They leave behind them, to the arteries
Firm fixed, and in the wound their lives
  lay down.
But if, in dread of rig'rous winter-tide,
Thou'lt both be sparing for the time to come,
And look with mercy on their shattered
  souls,
And broken fortunes ;—yet to fumigate
With thyme, and cut away the empty wax,
Who would demur? For often, unre-
  marked,
The lizard hath begnawed the combs, and
  cells, 340

---

282. Or : " and freely life."

316. The German critic quoted by Jahn observes, that the latter clause of verse 227 of the text comes in languidly after the former ; to which Voss replies, that it is only an amplification of the preceding idea. But surely this is a weak answer ; for it is at least as easy for an amplification to be languid as not. According to the view of some translators, the passage would be rendered thus :
" And take their station in the height of heaven ;"
which would give a stronger sense ; but it is by no means certain that *succedere* will bear the interpretation thus put upon it.

340. That is : beetles by cellfuls.

Uppiled with beetles, runaways from light,
And, at another's viands sitting down,
The [task-] exempted drone; or hornet fierce
Hath mixed among them with unbalanced arms;
Or moths—cursed crew; or, of Minerva loathed,
The spider in the door-way hath hung up
Her flowing toils. The more have they been drained,
So the more keenly all will strain to mend
A fallen people's wreck, and full will brim
The combs, and weave their magazines from flowers. 350
But if, (since our mischances, too, on bees
Hath life entailed,) their bodies shall be faint
With dismal sickness, which at once shalt thou
Be able by no doubtful marks to learn :—
Straight in the ailing is a diff'rent hue;
A grisly meagreness the visage mars;
Then from the dwellings carry they abroad
The carcases of those that lack the light,
And lead their doleful obsequies; or they
With legs entangled at the threshold hang,
Or lag indoors within their cloistered homes, 361
All both with hunger spiritless, and dull
With rivelled chillness : then a deeper tone
Is heard, and drawlingly they hum : as cold
At times on forests Auster growls; as booms
Chafed ocean with recoiling waves; as storms
In prisoned furnaces the rav'ning fire :—
Here will I counsel thee at once to burn
Galbanean scents, and honeys introduce
In water-pipes of reed, yea, cheering on,

And wooing them [in their] exhausted [state] 371
To their familiar food. And 'twill bestead
To blend bruised taste of gall, and roses dried,
Or sodden must enriched thro' plenteous fire,
Or [sun-] dried clusters from the Psithian vine,
And thyme of Attica, and centaur-plants,
Rank smelling. In the meads, too, is a flower,
For which the name *Amellus* swains have coined ;—
To those who seek an easy plant [to find] :
For lifts it from a single matted sod 380
A giant bush ; [of] golden [hue] itself,
But in the petals, which, full many a one,
Are shed around, faint twinkles purple tint
Of dusky violet. Oft with platted wreaths
Thereof the altars of the gods are trimmed ;
Harsh in the mouth its flavor ; this in dells
That have been pastured, do the shepherds cull,
And fast by Mella's serpentizing streams.
Stew roots of this in spicy wine, and serve
In baskets full the viands at their gates.
But if upon a sudden all his stock 391
Shall any [swain] have failed, nor, whence a race
Of new [-ly fostered] breed may be recalled,
Shall he possess [the means], it e'en is time
Th' Arcadian master's memorable plans
To ope, and how ere this from slaughtered steers
The tainted gore hath often yielded bees.
High tracing it from its primeval source,
The legend all will I unfold. For where
The Pella-named Canopus' blessèd race
Inhabits near the Nile, that stagnant lies
Through overflowing flood, and round their fields 402
Are carried in their painted skiffs ; and where
The quivered Persis' frontier presses close ;
And into seven separated mouths
Asunder runs, while flushing on, the stream,
E'en from the colored Indians borne adown,
And blooming Egypt, with its sable slime

---

345. See Spenser's beautiful description of Aragnoll's spinning his web to catch Clarion, in *Muiopotmos*, 357:

" And weaving straight a net with manie a fold
About the cave, in which he lurking dwelt,
With fine small cords about it stretched wide,
So finely sponne, that scarce they could be spide ;" &c.

The process of capture is gracefully described by Dryden :

" So the false spider, when her nets are spread,
Deep ambush'd in her silent den does lie ;
And feels far off the trembling of her thread,
Whose filmy cord should bind the struggling fly.
Then if at last she find him fast beset,
She issues forth, and runs along her loom :
She joys to touch the captive in her net,
And drag the little wretch in triumph home."
Ann. Mir., 180, 1.

400. " What wonder, in the sultry climes, that spread
Where Nile redundant o'er his summer bed
From his broad bosom life and verdure flings,
And broods o'er Egypt with his wat'ry wings,
If with advent'rous oar and ready sail
The dusky people drive before the gale ;
Or on frail floats to neighb'ring cities ride,
That rise and glitter o'er the ambient tide."
Gray, *Alliance of Education and Government*.
402. It is by no means certain that *stagnantem* is not active.

It fertilises :—all that country grounds
Infallible deliv'rance on this craft. 410
In the first place, a scanty spot is chosen,
And for these very services confined.
This, both with tiling of a narrow roof,
And with contracted walls, do they inclose,
And add four loopholes, with the light aslant
From the four winds. A calf then, arching now
His horns upon a brow of two years' age, is sought.
In him the nostrils twain, and breath of mouth,
While many a struggle he opposes, tight
Are blocked, and, slain by blows, his battered flesh 420
Through the unbroken hide is crushed to pulp.
Thus laid, they leave him in his cloistered hold,
And 'neath his ribs lay scraps of branches, thyme,
And fresh [-culled] casias. This is carried on
When Zephyrs first are chasing on the waves,
Before with earliest hues the meadows flush,
Before the prating swallow hangs her nest
Beneath the beams. Meanwhile acquiring heat,
Within the softened bones the juice ferments,
And, in surprising fashions to be seen, 430
Live creatures, destitute of feet at first,
And soon with pinions whizzing, swarm around,
And traverse more and more the subtile air :
Till, like a rainy-torrent, gushing forth
From clouds of summer, they have burst away ;
Or like the arrows from the driving chord,
If e'er light Parths commence the op'ning fights.
What deity, O Muses, what—struck out
This craft for our behoof? Whence took its rise
This new experience [on the part] of men ?

The shepherd Aristæus, taking flight
From Peneus' Tempe, when his bees were lost 442
(As [goes] the legend,) by disease alike
And hunger, melancholy took his stand
Hard by the holy [well-] head of the stream,
At its far bound, outpouring many a plaint ;
And in this strain his parent he addressed :
" Mother, Cyrene mother, who dost haunt
The lowest [regions] of this bubbling fount,
Why me from the all-glorious line of gods,
(If only, whom thou sayest, is my sire—
Thymbra's Apollo,) loathed of fates, hast borne ? 452
Or whither banished is thy love of us ?
Why would'st thou bid me hope for heav'n ?
Lo ! e'en
This very credit of my mortal life,
Which scarce the skilful ward of fruits and flocks
Had wrought me out, essaying every [art],
With thee for mother, do I quit. Nay come,
And with thy hand thyself my fruiting groves
Uproot ; bring hostile fire upon my stalls,
And kill my harvests ; burn my seeded crops, 461
And wield the lusty axe against my vines,
If such sore weariness of my renown
Hath seized thee." Now his mother heard the cry
Beneath the chamber of the deepsome flood.
Around her their Milesian wools her Nymphs
Were carding, with full hue of glassy-green
Ingrained :—e'en Drymo, Xantho, too, alike
Ligœa, and Phyllodoce—their locks
Out-streamed in lustre o'er their snowy necks ; 470
Nesæe, Spio too, Thalia too,

459. What Aristæus, with something of petulance, hypothetically called upon his mother to do, Sir Guyon absolutely effected for the " Bower of Bliss ;" *Faerie Queene*, ii. 12, 83:

" But all those pleasant bowres, and pallace brave,
Guyon broke downe with rigour pitilesse ;
Ne ought their goodly workmanship might save
Them from the tempest of his wrathfulnesse,
But that their blisse he turn'd to balefulnesse ;
Their groves he feld ; their gardins did deface ;
Their arbers spoyle ; their cabinets suppresse ;
Their banket-houses burne ; their buildings race ;
And, of the fayrest late, now made the fowlest place."

" O boundlesse woe,
If there be any black yet unknown griefe,
If there be any horror yet unfelt,
Unthought-of mischief in thy fiend-like power,
Dash it upon my miserable head :
Make me more wretch, more cursed if thou canst."
Marston, *Antonio and Mellida*, P. 2, i. 5.

---

427. *Hirundo* is a general name for several kinds of swallows. Perhaps Virgil alludes to the martin, as Shakespeare does in the following passage from *Macbeth*, i. 6:

" This guest of summer,
The temple-haunting martlet, does approve,
By his lov'd mansionry, that the heaven's breath
Smells wooingly here : no jutty, frieze, buttress,
Nor coigne of vantage, but this bird hath made
His pendent bed, and procreant cradle."

Cymodoce as well, Cydippe too,
And auburn [-tressed] Lycorias—one a
maid,
The other having then Lucine's first pangs
Experienced ; Clio too, and Beroe
Her sister, daughters of the Ocean both,
With gold both girdled, both with dappled
skins ;
And Ephyre, and Opis, and the Asian
[maid]
Deïope, and nimble Arethuse,
Her arrows laid aside at last. 'Mong
whom   480
Was Clymene relating th' idle pains
Of Vulcan, and th' intrigues and blissful
thefts
Of Mars, and down from Chaos reck'ning
o'er
The crowded loves of gods. By which her
song
Enchanted, while around their spindles
they
Their downy tasks spin off, his mother's
ears
Once more the wail of Aristæus struck,
And on their crystal thrones were all
amazed.
But ere the other sisters Arethuse,
Forth-gazing, lifted up her auburn head
Above the billow-crest ; and from afar :
" O scared not idly by so deep a groan,
Cyrene sister, he himself for thee,   493
Thy chief affection, Aristæus sad
By father Peneus' billow stands in tears,
And calls thee heartless by thy name." To
her
His mother, shocked in soul with strange
alarm,
Cries, " Lead, haste, lead him to us ; 'tis
allowed
For him to touch the thresholds of the gods."
At once does she enjoin the deepsome
floods   500
Far-wide to part asunder, where the youth
Might introduce his steps. But him around,
In mountain-fashion arched, the billow
stood,
And welcomed him within its bosom vast,
And sent him on beneath the stream. And
now,
In wonder gazing on his mother's court,
And wat'ry realms, and lakes in caves en-
jailed,

And rumbling groves, he went his way,
and stunned
At the vast coil of waters, all the floods,
Careering 'neath the mighty earth, he
viewed,   510
Dispread in various regions,—Phasis e'en,
And Lycus, and the [fountain-] head,
wherefrom
The deep Enipeus disembogues him first ;
Whence father Tiber, and whence Anio's
tides,
And, rife in rock, the booming Hypanis ;
Caicus, too, of Mysia, and, engilt
Upon his double horns on bull-like face,
Eridanus ; than which no other stream
Along the teeming tilths, with fiercer force
On flushes to the purple main. As soon
As he arrived within the chamber's roof,
With pumice hanging, and Cyrene learnt
Her offspring's causeless weepings, for his
hands   523
The sisters duly crystal springs present,
And bring him towels with a shaven nap.
Some load the boards with cates, and serve
and serve
The brimming goblets ; with Panchæan fires
Blaze up the altars : and his mother cries :
" Do thou take beakers of Mæonian wine ;
To Ocean pour we." She herself at once
Entreats both Ocean, sire of [all] things,
and the Nymphs,   531
The sister-train—-the hundred who the
woods,
The hundred who the rivers, haunt. Three
times
With crystal nectar Vesta in a glow
She sprent ; three times the blaze, shot up
aloft
To the dome-crest, flashed back : with
which presage
Her spirit bracing, thus herself begins :
" In the Carpathian gulf· of Neptune
dwells
A seer, the azure Proteus, he who spans

I burn to view th' enthusiastic wilds
By mortal else untrod. I hear the din
Of waters thundering o'er the ruin'd cliffs,
With holy reverence I approach the rocks,
Whence glide the streams renown'd in ancient
song.
Here from the desert down the rumbling steep
First springs the Nile ; here bursts the sounding
Po
In angry waves ; Euphrates hence devolves
A mighty flood to water half the east ;
And there, in gothic solitude reclin'd,
The cheerless Tanais pours his hoary urn."
    Armstrong, *Health,* b. ii.

539. " Proteus is shepheard of the seas of yore,
And hath the charge of Neptune's mighty heard :
An aged sire with head all frowy hore,
And sprinckled frost upon his deawy beard :

---

482. Goldsmith speaks of a more moral descrip-
tion of *furta* in the *Deserted Village :*
" The breezy covert of the warbling grove,
That only sheltered thefts of harmless love."

507. " Come now, ye Naiads, to the fountains lead ;
Now let me wander through your gelid reign.

The vasty ocean with his fish, and car
With double-footed coursers yoked. He now   541
Emathia's havens and his native land,
Pallene, is revisiting. To him
Both we the Nymphs look up with awe, and e'en
The agèd Nereus: for the prophet knows
All things which are, which were, which yet to come
Are trailing on; since so to Neptune good it seemed,
Whose monster-cattle and unsightly seals,
He pastures underneath the wat'ry-whirl.
By thee must he, my son, in fetters first
Be caught, that all the source of the disease
He may discover, and the issues bless.   552
For without force no counsels will he grant,
Nor him by praying may'st thou bend; brute force
And manacles, when captured, on him strain:
Round these at last will unavailing wiles
Be shattered. I myself will thee, what time
Shall Sol have kindled up meridian heats,
What time the herbage is athirst, and now
More welcome to the cattle is the shade,
Lead to the agèd [seer's] sequestered haunts,   561
Where, wearied, he betakes him from the waves;
That readily, in slumber as he lies,
Thou may'st assail him. But when with thy hands
And fetters thou shalt hold him tightly grasped,
Then divers shapes, and forms of savage beasts,

Will baffle thee. For in a trice will he
Become a bristly boar, and tigress swart,
And scale-clad dragon, and a lioness
With tawny neck; or piercing roar of flame
Will he discharge, and thus from out his bonds   571
Will drop, or, melted into waters thin,
Escape away. But how the more shall he
Transmute him into every guise, so much,
My son, the more do thou the griping chains
Strain tight, till such shall he become, with frame
Transformed, as thou beheldest him, when he
With sleep commenced was muffling up his eyes."
These speaks she, and ambrosia's flowing scent
Distils around, wherewith she overspread
Her son's whole body, and o'er him there breathed   581
From tresses trimly laid a musky air,
And o'er his limbs a lively vigor came.
There is a vasty cavern in the side
Of a heart-eaten mountain, whereinto
Full many a billow by the blast is forced,
And into curves receding splits itself;
At times for [storm-] caught seamen anchorage
Right safe: within doth Proteus screen himself
By the obstruction of a monster rock.   590
In ambush here the Nymph the stripling posts
Turned from the light away; takes she herself
Her station at a distance, gloomed in mists.
Now rav'ning Sirius, scorching thirsty Inds,
Was blazing, and in heav'n had fiery Sol
Accomplished his meridian round; the herbs

Who, when those pittiful outcries he heard
Through all the seas so ruefully resownd,
His charett swift in hast he thether steard,
Which with a teeme of scaly Phocas bownd
Was drawne upon the waves, that fomed him arownd."   Spenser, *F. Q.*, iii. 8, 30.

566. So Spenser says of Archimago; *F. Q.*, i. 2, 10:
" He then devisde himself how to disguise;
For by his mighty science he could take
As many formes and shapes in seeming wise,
As ever Proteus to himselfe could make:
Sometime a fowle, sometime a fish in lake,
Now like a foxe, now like a dragon fell:
That of himselfe he ofte for feare would quake,
And oft would flie away."

The attentive reader will no doubt remark the graphic turn with which this imitation concludes. The passage also calls to mind the lines in Milton's *Comus*:
" Boldly assault the necromancer's hall;
Where if he be, with dauntless hardihood,
And brandish'd blade rush on him; break his glass,

And shed the luscious liquor on the ground,
But seize his wand: though he and his cursed crew
Fierce sign of battle make, and menace high,
Or like the sons of Vulcan vomit smoke,
Yet will they soon retire, if he but shrink."

584. " His bowre is in the bottom of the maine,
Under a mightie rocke, gainst which doe rave
The roring billowes in their proud disdaine,
That with the angry working of the wave
Therein is eaten out a hollow cave,
That seemes rough masons hand with engines keene
Had long while laboured it to engrave:
There was his wonne."   *Faerie Queene*, iii. 8, 37.

587. Or: " Splits itself upon sequestered coves;"
but this rendering is hardly consistent with *tutissima*. See Heyne on *Æn.* l. 161.

Were with'ring, and in droughty channels warmed,
His beams were seething hollow streams to slime ;
When Proteus, seeking his accustomed caves,
Was coming from the billows. Him around   600
The wat'ry nation of the mighty deep
Disporting, scattered wide the bitter spray.
For slumber stretch themselves the seals, apart
Upon the strand ; himself (as doth at times
The guardian of a fold upon the mounts,
When evening from their grazing to the sheds
Brings home the calves, and by their bleatings heard
The lambkins whet the wolves), sits central down
Upon a cliff, and reckons o'er their tale.
O'er whom since now the vantage offered is
To Aristæus, having scarce allowed   611
The senior to lay down his jaded limbs,
With lusty shout he rushes on, and him
Surprises with the handcuffs as he lies.
He, not unmindful, on the other hand,
Of his own craft, transfigureth himself
Into all marvels of [created] things—
Both fire, and fearful beast, and flowing flood.
But when no guile discovers an escape,
Into himself, defeated, he returns,   620
And with the mouth of man at last he spake :
" Pray who, thou most presumptuous of youths,
Bade thee our habitations to approach ?
Or what," he cries, " hence seekest thou ?"
But he :
" Thou knowest, Proteus, knowest of thy-self,
Nor is one able thee to dupe in aught ;

---

601.   " But is not yonder Proteus' cave,
        Below that steep,
        Which rising billows brave?
It is : and in it lies the god asleep ;
        And, snorting by,
        We may descry
    The Monsters of the deep."
        Dryden, *Albion and Albanius*, iii.

617. " To dreadfull shapes he did himselfe trans-forme :
Now like a gyaunt ; now like to a feend ;
Then like a centaure ; then like to a storme,
Raging within the waves."   *F. Q.*, iii. 8, 42.

" Sudden the god a lion stands ;
He shakes his mane, he spurns the sands ;
Now a fierce lynx with fiery glare,
A wolf, an ass, a fox, a bear."   Gay, *F.*, i. 33.

But cease thy wishing [to make dupes of us].
The gods' injunctions following have we come,
In fallen circumstances hence to seek
Oracular replies." So much he spake.
To these the seer at length with effort vast
His eyeballs, flashing with a blue-green glare,   632
Rolled on him, and deep gnashing [with his teeth],
He thus with destinies his lips unlocked :
" 'Tis not the wrath of less than is divine
That vexeth thee : thou expiatest grievous crimes.
For thee doth Orpheus, in a piteous case
In nowise owing to his own desert,
These punishments, save fates withstand, awake,
And fiercely rages for his ravished bride.
She sooth, while headlong she was flying thee   641
Along the streams—a maiden doomed to die—
A monstrous water-snake before her feet,
Haunting the margents in the lofty grass,
Perceived not. But the Dryads' sister-choir
The highest regions of the mountains filled
With shrieking ; wept the Rhodopean towers,
Pangæan heights alike, and Rhesus' land
Mavortian, and the Getæ, Hebrus too,
And Attic Orithyia. He himself   650
Soothing on hollow shell his heart-sick love,
Thee, darling spouse, thee on the lonely shore
All by himself, thee at the dawning day,
Thee as it sank adown, was wont to chant.
Yea, jaws of Tæn'rus, gates of Dis profound,

---

635. See note on *Geo.* i. 115.

655. Pope's splendid allusion to this legend is well known ; but it must be quoted :
" But when, through all the infernal bounds
    Which flaming Phlegethon surrounds,
        Love, strong as death, the poet led
        To the pale nations of the dead,
What sounds were heard,
What scenes appear'd,
    O'er all the dreary coasts !
        Dreadful gleams,
        Horrid screams,
        Fires that glow,
        Shrieks of woe,
        Sullen moans,
        Hollow groans,
    And cries of tortured ghosts !
But hark ! he strikes the golden lyre ;
And see ! the tortured ghosts respire,
    See, shady forms advance !
Thy stone, O Sisyphus, stands still,
Ixion rests upon his wheel,
    And the pale spectres dance ;

And, glooming with a murky dread, the grove
He entered, and the Manes he approached,
And their terrific monarch, and the hearts
Unknowing how to melt at mortal prayers.
But by his strain aroused from lowest seats
Of Erebus, advanced the subtile shades,
And phantom-forms of those that lack the light; 662
As numerous [as] thousands of the birds
[That] bury them among the leaves, what time
Doth eve, or wintry shower drive them down
From mountains: mothers, husbands too, and frames
Of high-souled heroes that have done with life;
Boys, and unwedded maids, and striplings laid
On fun'ral-piles before their parents' eyes:
Whom round the sable ooze, and hideous reed 670
Of Cocyt, and with lazy wave the fen
Unlovely binds, and Styx, nine times out-poured
Between, confines them. Yea, astonied stood
The very homes and deepest hell of Death,
And, twisted through their locks with azure snakes,
The Furies; and restrained his triple mouth

The Furies sink upon their iron beds,
And snakes uncurl'd hang listening round their heads.
" But soon, too soon, the lover turns his eyes:
Again she falls, again she dies, she dies!
How wilt thou now the fatal sisters move?
No crime was thine, if 'tis no crime to love.
  Now under hanging mountains,
  Beside the falls of fountains,
  Or where Hebrus wanders,
  Rolling in mæanders,
    All alone,
    Unheard, unknown,
  He makes his moan;
  And calls her ghost,
  For ever, ever, ever lost!
  Now with furies surrounded,
  Despairing, confounded,
  He trembles, he glows,
  Amidst Rhodope's snows:
See, wild as the winds, o'er the desert he flies;
Hark! Hæmus resounds with the Bacchanals' cries—
    Ah see, he dies!
Yet even in death Eurydice he sung,
Eurydice still trembled in his tongue,
    Eurydice the woods,
    Eurydice the floods,
Eurydice the rocks, and hollow mountains rung."
    Ode on St. Cecilia's Day, st. 4, 6.

672. "Where rocks and rueful deserts are descried,
And sullen Styx rolls down his lazy tide."
    Garth, *Dispensary,* c. vi.

The gaping Cerberus, and in the breeze
The circuit of Ixion's wheel stood still.
And now, his steps retracing, all mishaps
He had avoided, and Eurydice, 680
Restored, was coming to the upper air,
Behind him following, (for Proserpine
This law had giv'n,) when sudden madness seized
The heedless lover,—pardonable sure,
If Manes knew to pardon;—short he stopped,
And back upon Eurydice, his own,
Now even 'neath the very verge of light,
Mindless, alas! and whelmed in soul, he looked.
There all his toil was squandered, and the league
Of the remorseless tyrant burst, and thrice
A crash was heard within Avernian pools.
'What,' cries she, 'both unhappy me and thee 692
Hath ruined, Orpheus,—frenzy what so wild?
Lo! call me back once more the ruthless Weirds,
And sleep is sealing up my swimming eyes.
And now farewell! I'm borne away, en-wrapt
In deep of night around, and stretching forth
To thee,—alas! not thine,—my weakly hands.'
She said, and on a sudden from his eyes,
As smoke commingled into subtile air,
She fled another way, nor him, in vain
Grasping at shades, and longing many a word 700
To utter, did she any further see;
Nor did Hell's ferryman allow him more

678. Sotheby has:
"And fixed in air Ixion's wheel reposed."
691. See Milton quoted *Æn.* i. v. 167.
693. "My eyes are going to bed, and leaden sleep
Doth draw the curtains o'er them."
    Shirley, *Love Tricks,* iv. 2.
" Peace rest on you! One sad tear every day,
For poor Alinda's sake, 'tis fit you pay.
A thousand, noble youth! And when I sleep
Even in my silver slumbers still I'll weep."
    J. Fletcher, *The Loyal Subject,* v. 2.
695. "So fare you well at once; for Brutus' tongue
Hath almost ended his life's history:
Night hangs upon mine eyes."
    Shakespeare, *Julius Cæsar,* v. 5.
700. "Was ever known
A man so miserably blest as I!
I have no sooner found the greatest good,
Man in this pilgrimage of life can meet,
But I must make the womb, where 'twas conceived,
The tomb to bury it, and the first hour it lives
The last it must breathe."
    Webster, *A Cure,* i. 2.

To cross the barrier fen. What should he do?
Whither should he betake himself, his spouse
Twice ravished from him? With what weeping move
The Manes, with what voice the gods?
She sooth
Now cold was floating in the Stygian bark.
They tell that he for sev'n whole months in course,
Beneath a heav'n-high rock, beside the wave
Of lonely Strymon, wept, and vented these [his woes] 710
'Neath icy grottoes, soothing tigresses,
And drawing with his minstrelsy the oaks:
As, mourning underneath a poplar shade,
The nightingale bemoans her missing brood,
Which [some] unfeeling ploughman, on the watch,
Hath ravished callow from the nest; but she
Weeps thro' the night, and, sitting on a bough,
Her piteous strain renews, and far and near
Fills every spot with melancholy plaints.
No Love, no joys of Hymen bent his soul;
Alone the Polar ice, and snowy Don, 721
And fields ne'er widowed of Rhipæan frosts,
He ranged, bewailing lost Eurydice,
And bootless grants of Dis: thro' which his task
The matrons of the Cicons scorned, amid
The holy rites of gods, and revel-feasts
Of slighted Bacchus, into atoms rent,
The stripling scattered o'er the spacious fields.
Then too the head, wrung off a marble neck,

When, bearing it upon his central tide, 730
Œagrian Hebrus rolled,—'Eurydice' the very voice
And death-cold tongue, 'Ah! poor Eurydice!'
As flies the spirit, called; 'Eurydice'
The banks re-echoed all throughout the stream."
These Proteus: and he plunged him with a bound
Within the deepsome sea, and where he plunged
The yesting wave he wreathed below his neck.
But not Cyrene; for unasked she spoke
The trembler: " Son, 'tis lawful from thy mind
To lay aside thy melancholy cares. 740
This is the whole occasion of the plague;
'Tis hence the Nymphs, with whom she used to hold
The dances in the lofty groves, have sent
The piteous desolation on thy bees.
Do thou thy gifts in lowly fashion spread,
Entreating reconcilement, and adore
Th' easy Napæans; for they will vouchsafe
Their pardon to thy vows, and bate their wrath.
But what should be the manner of thy suit

---

714. Milton briefly alludes to the nightingale; *P. L.*, b. vii. iv.:
" Nor then the solemn nightingale
Ceased warbling, but all night tuned her soft lays."
" All but the wakeful nightingale ;
She all night long her amorous descant sung."
" Where the love-lorn nightingale
Nightly to thee her sad song mourneth well."
Comus.
Thomson, more at length; *Spring*, 717, &c.:
" Oft when, returning with her loaded bill,
Th' astonish'd mother finds a vacant nest,
By the hard hand of unrelenting clowns
Robb'd, to the ground the vain provision falls;
Her pinions ruffle, and low-drooping scarce
Can bear the mourner to the poplar shade;
Where, all abandon'd to despair, she sings
Her sorrows through the night; and, on the bough
Sole-sitting, still at every dying fall
Takes up again her lamentable strain
Of winding woe; till, wide around, the woods
Sigh to her song, and with her wail resound."
The next stanza is quoted in note on *Æn.* ii. v. 727.

730–6. So Milton alludes to Orpheus in *Lycidas*:
" When, by the rout that made the hideous roar,
His goary visage down the stream was sent,
Down the swift Hebrus to the Lesbian shore."
" So when the Thracian furies Orpheus tore,
And left his bleeding trunk deform'd with gore,
His sever'd head floats down the silver tide,
His yet warm tongue for his lost consort cried;
Eurydice with quivering voice he mourn'd,
And Heber's banks Eurydice returned."
Gay, *Trivia*, ii. 293.
" ' Olympia! my Olympia's lost !' I cry.
' Olympia's lost !' the hollow vaults reply.
Louder I make my lamentable moan;
The swelling echoes learn like me to groan;
The ghosts to scream, as through lone a sles they sweep!
The shrines to shudder, and the saints to weep!"
Savage, *Wanderer*, c. ii.
" Cold is Cadwallo's tongue,
That hush'd the stormy main:
Brave Urien sleeps upon his craggy bed:
Mountains, ye mourn in vain
Modred, whose magic song
Made huge Plinlimmon bow his cloud-topt head.
On dreary Arvon's shore they lie,
Smear'd with gore, and ghastly pale:
Far, far aloof th' affrighted ravens sail;
The famish'd eagle screams, and passes by."
Gray, *Bard*, i. 3.
735. Thus Thomson, seizing the idea in v. 529, makes the genius of the Thames disappear in his own waters:
" He said; and plunged to his crystal dome,
While o'er his head the circling waters foam."
Poems on several Occasions.

I first will duly tell thee. Four choice
    bulls 750
Of passing form, who now for thee feed
    down
The green Lycæus' peaks, do thou choose
    out,
And with a neck untouched as many kine.
Four altars at the goddesses' high shrines
For these construct, and from their throats
    discharge
The holy blood, and in a leafy grove
The oxen's carcases themselves forsake.
Then, when the ninth Aurore shall have
    displayed
Her dawn, to Orpheus his funereal dues,
Lethean poppies, shalt thou pay, and thou
A sable ewe shalt butcher, and the grove
Visit again; Eurydice, appeased 762
By slaughtered heifer-calf, shalt thou
    adore."
No dallying: at once he puts in force
His mother's mandates. To the shrines he
    comes;
The indicated altars he uprears;
Four chosen bulls of passing form he leads,
And, with a neck untouched, as many kine.
Then, when the ninth Aurore had ushered
    in
Her dawn, to Orpheus his funereal dues
He pays, the grove, too, visits he again.
But here an unexpected prodigy, 772
And wondrous to be named, do they be-
    hold:—
Throughout the molten inwards of the
    beeves,

---

767. Milton in the same way repeats the execution of orders in the words of the orders themselves; *P. L.*, b. x. end.

Bees buzzing, from within the womb entire,
And bubbling forth from out their riven
    sides;
And, warping on, huge clouds; and stream-
    ing now
Together on the tree-crest, and adown
A cluster dropping from the buxom boughs.
    These verses on the management of
    fields 780
And cattle I was chanting, and on trees;
While mighty Cæsar at Euphrates deep
Thunders in war, and conqueror gives laws
Thro' acquiescing tribes, and aims to tread
A path to reach Olympus. At that hour
Me, Virgil, sweet Parthenope did nurse,
While rioting in tasks of fameless ease;
I, who have madrigals of shepherds played,
And, bold in youth, thee, Tityrus, have
    sung
Beneath a canopy of spreading beech. 790

---

777. We are indebted to the genius of Milton for this exquisite metaphor, which he applies to the motion of locusts, in illustrating that of the wicked angels, when flocking to the summons of Satan:

"As when the potent rod
Of Amram's son, in Egypt's evil day
Waved round the coast, up call'd a pitchy cloud
Of locusts, warping on the eastern wind,
That o'er the realm of impious Pharaoh hung,
Like night, and darken'd all the land of Nile."
                                    Paradise Lost, b. i.

If it be thought too great a liberty to render *trahi* by a neuter verb, this beautiful word must be abandoned, and the passage altered thus:

"And boundless clouds trailed on," &c.

In this case, too, line 84 must share a like fate, and be thus lowered:

"See trailed upon the wind," &c.

788. *Carmina lusi:* so in *Ecl.* i. v. 10; *Ludere quæ vellem.*

THE ÆNEID.

BOOK I.

*That [bard] am I, who erst attuned his lay
Upon the slender reed, and from the woods
Withdrawing, have compelled the neighb'ring fields
The tiller to obey, though greedy [he]:—
A welcome task to swains: but now Mars' dread*

ARMS and the man I sing, who erst from coasts
Of Troy to Italy and Lavinian shores,
By destiny a rover, came. Much he
Was tossed alike on lands and sea, through might

Those writers seem to have been hasty in their criticisms upon these first four lines, who pronounce them unworthy of the author of the *Æneid*. Able scholars are found to think them thoroughly Virgilian; and Forbiger thinks he sees plain evidence of genuineness in the word *at*. Had the writers in question, instead of saying that the passage was not Virgil's, said that it was a weak introduction to an epic poem, they would have been quite right; and doubtless no one would have been happier to agree with them than Virgil himself. It seems highly probable that he sent the lines in dispute, along with the work itself, to some friend, who showed them to others, and in this way they obtained currency as the unquestioned production of his pen. Thus from their genuineness, coupled with their great ingenuity, they crept into the text, from which they were most likely ejected by Tucca and Varius, though some manuscripts retained them still. One thing is pretty certain,—that Virgil, whose discretion and taste must be admitted, even by those who think meanly of his creative powers, would never, with his great original before him, have begun the *Æneid* with an *Ille ego*. At all events, Persius did not believe in the puerility, if he ever heard of it.

This opening reminds one of the introduction to the *Faerie Queene*:

"Lo! I, the man whose Muse whylome did maske,
As time her taught, in lowly shepheards weeds,
Am now enforst, a farre unfitter taske,
For trumpets sterne to chaunge mine oaten reeds,
And sing of Knights and Ladies gentle deeds:" &c.
See also *Shepheards Calender*, October, 55.

4. Cowley compares the sufferings of Charles the Second to those of Æneas, philosophising, *more suo*:

Of heav'nly Powers, for the rankling wrath
Of ruthless Juno; yea, and much he bore
Thro' war, till he a city built, and brought
His gods to Latium, whence the Latin race,
And Alban sires, and walls of lofty Rome.
O Muse, to me the reasons do thou tell,
What Pow'r aggrieved, or wherefore in a chafe,   11
The queen of gods should have enforced a man,
Marked for his piety, to undergo
Mishaps so many, meet so many toils.
Can wrath so grievous [dwell] in heav'nly minds?
There was an ancient city,—colonists
Of Tyre possessed it,—Carthage, right afront
Of Italy and Tiber's mouths afar,
Rich in resources, and in war's pursuits
Most truculent; the which is Juno said   20
Above all regions singly to have nursed,—
Samos postponed. Her arms [stood] here, here stood

" But, in the cold of want, and storms of adverse chance,
They harden his young virtue by degrees:
The beauteous drop first into ice does freeze,
And into solid crystal next advance.
His murder'd friends and kindred he does see,
And from his flaming country flee:
Much is he tost at sea, and much at land;
Does long the force of angry gods withstand:
He does long troubles and long wars sustain,
Ere he his fatal birthright gain.
With no less time and labour can
Destiny build up such a man,
Who's with sufficient virtue filled
His ruin'd country to rebuild."
Ode on Restoration.

" I am pursued; all the ports are stopt too;
Not any hope to escape; behind, before me,
On either side I am beset;—cursed fortune;
My enemy on the sea, and on the land too,
Redeemed from one affliction to another."
Beaumont and Fletcher, *The Custom of the Country*, ii. 4.

15. So Milton, *Par. Lost*, b. vi:
" In heavenly Spirits could such perverseness dwell?"

Her car. That this might to the nations prove
The seat of rule,—should Fates in any wise
Allow,—the goddess even then both aims,
And cherishes [her aim]. But she, in sooth,
Had heard that from the Trojan blood a strain
Would be descended, which her Tyrian towers
One day would overthrow; that hence a race,
Wide bearing empire, and in battle haught,
Would come for Libya's death-blow; that the Weirds 31
Ordained it thus. Saturnia, dreading this,
And mindful of the lasting war, which she
Had whilom waged at Troja, in behalf
Of her belovèd Argos : nor e'en yet
The reasons for her wrath, and cruel pangs
Had vanished from her mind ; bides treasured up
Within her deep of spirit the award
Of Paris, and her slighted beauty's wrong,
The hated lineage, too, and dignities 40
Of ravished Ganymede : o'er these inflamed,
Throughout the whole of ocean's surface tossed,
The Trojans, remnants from the Danai
And merciless Achilles, did she drive
Afar from Latium ; and thro' many a year
They wandered, hunted by the Destinies,
All seas around : of such colossal weight
[The labor] was to build the Roman race.
Scarce out of sight of the Sicilian land,
Their canvas for the deep were they, in glee,
Vouchsafing [to the breezes], and the foam
Of briny ocean dashing with their bronze ;
When Juno, harboring beneath her breast
Her deathless wound, these [vented] with herself : 54
" That I, discomfited, from my emprise

Should cease, nor have the pow'r from Italy
The monarch of the Teucri to debar !
Forsooth I am prohibited by fates !
Was Pallas able to burn up the fleet
Of Argives, and themselves below the deep
To whelm, for one man's fault, the madness e'en 61
Of the Oilean Ajax ? She herself,
Jove's speeding leven launching from the clouds,
Alike their vessels scattered, and upturned
The seas with storms ; him, blazes blasting forth
From his pierced bosom, in a whirl of wind
She clutched, and on a pointed rock impaled.
But I, who pace the empress of the gods,
Yea both the sister and the spouse of Jove,
Thro' years so many with a single clan 70
Am waging warfare. And may [mortal] wight
The pow'r of Juno worship furthermore,
Or humbly on her altars lay a gift ?"
Such [thoughts] the goddess in a heart incensed
Inly revolving, to the native land
Of rain-storms, spots with madding Austers big,—
Æolia,—comes. 'Tis here King Æolus,
Within a monster vault, the struggling winds
And blust'ring storms with sovereign sway controls,
And reins them in with fetters and a jail.
They in their anger with prodigious growl,
[Growl] of the mountain, thunder round their bars. 82
Sits Æolus in his citadel on high,
His sceptre wielding, and their passions soothes,
And cools their wrath ; [which] did he not, the seas,
And lands, and sky sublime, they would in sooth,
Careering swiftly, with them bear away,

---

25. " Daring men command and make their fates."
  Massinger, *The Bondman*, ii. 3.
" Consider of your sex's general aim,
  That domination is a woman's heaven."
  Middleton, *A Fair Quarrel*, ii. 2.

35. *Argis* may perhaps be an adjective here, though in an unusual form.

39. " *Juno*. But he shall rue and ban the dismal day,
Wherein his Venus bare the ball away ;
And heaven and earth just witnesses shall be,
I will revenge it on his progeny.
Pallas. Well, Juno, whether we be lief or loth,
Venus hath got the apple from us both."
  Peele, *The Arraignment of Paris*, ii. end.

" But if in heav'n a hell we find,
  'Tis all from thee,
  O jealousy,
Thou tyrant of the mind."
  Dryden, *Love Triumphant*, iii. 1.

58. " That which the Fates appoint must happen so,
Though heavenly Jove and all the gods say, No !"
  R. Greene, *Alphonsus*, i.i. end.

67. " Caught in a fiery tempest, shall be hurl'd
Each on his rock transfix'd, the sport and prey
Of wracking whirlwinds." Milton, *P. L.*, b. ii.

80. " Like as a boystrous winde,
Which in th' earthes hollow caves hath long been hid,
And shut up fast within her prisons blind,
Makes the huge element, against her kinde,
To move and tremble as it were aghast,
Untill that it an issew forth may finde ;
Then forth it breakes, and with his furious blast
Confounds both land and seas, and skyes doth overcast." Spenser, *Faerie Queene*. iii. 9, 15.

And sweep along the air. But, dreading this,
The sire almighty has in pitchy caves
Concealed them, and a pile and lofty mounts   90
Above them laid, and giv'n a monarch, who
By pact decreed should know, at his command,
Alike to check and give the slackened reins :
To whom then Juno prayerful used these words :
"O Æolus, (for 'tis to thee the sire
Of gods, and king of men, alike hath giv'n
To soothe the waves, and heave them by the wind,)
A nation, foe to me, the Tyrrhene main
Is sailing, Ilium into Italy
Conveying, and their conquered household-gods :   100
Strike fury in thy winds, and whelm their ships,
Deep sunken, or, dissundered, hunt them down,
And strew abroad their corses on the deep.
With me are twice sev'n Nymphs of passing form ;
Of whom [the maid], who fairest is in shape,
Dëiope, in steadfast marriage-bond
Will I unite, and consecrate thine own ;
That all her years, in company with thee,
For such deservings she may while away,
And make thee father with a lovely race."
These Æolus [returned her] in reply :
"Be thine, O queen, the task to search whate'er   112
May be thy wish ; to me, to undertake
Thy mandates is a law. 'Tis thou for me,
(Whatever this of realm [partakes],) 'tis thou
Dost sceptre win and Jove ; 'tis thou dost give
That I recline at banquets of the gods,
And makest me the lord of rains and storms."
When these were said, with spear-head, towards it veered,

The vaulted mountain on its flank he smote,
And straight the winds, as in battalion formed,   121
Where outlet is vouchsafed them, dash amain,
And in tornado blow throughout the lands.
They swooped upon the sea, and all at once
Both East, and South, and South-west, rife in storms,
Uproot it wholly from its deepest seats,
And volley mountain surges to the shores.
Ensues both cry of men and creak of ropes.
The clouds upon a sudden tear away
Both heav'n and day-light from the Trojans' eyes ;   130
Upon the deep broods collied night ; the poles
Thundered, and æther gleams with serried fires ;
And all threat instant death upon the crews.
Forthwith Æneas' limbs are with a chill
Unnerved ; he groans, and stretching both his hands
Forth to the stars, such accents with his voice
He utters : "O both thrice and four times blest,
To whom, before the presence of your sires,
'Neath Troja's stately walls, it fell by lot
To meet your doom ! O bravest of the race
Of Danai, O Tydeus' son, that I   141
On Ilian plains should not have fall'n, and poured
This spirit forth 'neath thy right hand, where fierce
Beneath the weapon of Æacides

---

105. See note on *Æn.* iv. v. 126.
112. "Ask noble things of me, and you shall find I'll be a noble giver."
   Webster, *The Duchess of Malfi*, v. 1.
119. "As when Dan Æolus, in great displeasure
   For losse of his deare Love by Neptune hent,
   Sends forth the winds out of his hidden threasure
   Upon the sea to wreake his full intent ;
   They, breaking forth with rude unruliment
   From all foure partes of heaven, doe rage full sore,
   And tosse the deepes, and teare the firmament,
   And all the world confound with wide uprore ;
   As if instead thereof they Chaos would restore."
   Spenser, *F. Q.*, iv. 9, 23.

121. "Straight" is plainly implied in *ac*, v. 82. See Wagner.
125. See note on *Geo.* i. v. 318 :
   "Nor slept the winds," &c.
130. "How like the day, that flattered us
   With cheerful light, are my desires fled hence,
   And left me here a prodigy of darkness,
   A walking herse, hung round about with night,
   Whose wings must one day cover all !"
   Shirley, *The Doubtful Heir*, iv. 2.
137. Shakespeare makes Pericles, under similar circumstances, address a prayer to the Deity ; *Pericles*, iii. 1 :
   "Thou God of this great vast, rebuke these surges, Which wash both heaven and hell ; and Thou that hast
   Upon the winds command, bind them in brass, Having call'd them from the deep ! O still thy deaf'ning,
   Thy dreadful thunders ; gently quench thy nimble, Sulphureous flashes."
142. "Could not the fretting sea
   Have rowled me up in wrinkles of his browe ?
   Is death growen coy ? or grim confusion nice ?
   That it will not accompany a wretch ?"
   Marston, *Antonio and Mellida*, P. 1, i. 1.

Is Hector lying, where Sarpedon huge,
Where, clutched together underneath his
  waves,
The Simois so many heroes' shields,
And helms, and gallant corses rolls along !"
  While he such [plaints] is venting, from
  the North
A roaring tempest strikes his sail ahead,
And lifts the billows to the stars. Their
  oars   151
Are shivered ; then swings off the prow,
  and shows
The broadside to the waves ; thereon pur-
  sues
A rugged mount of water in a pile.
These on the billow-summit hang ; to those
The yawning surge amid the waves unveils
The ground ; the tide is raving with the
  sands.
Three, swept away, upon the lurking rocks
Doth Notus whirl ; the rocks Italians call
"The Altars," which amid the billows lie,
A monster reef on surface of the main.
Three Eurus shoulders from the deep on
  shelves   162
And quicksands—pitiable to be seen—
And grides upon the shoals, and with a
  mound
Of sand encircles them. The one, which
  bare
The men of Lycia and Orontes staunch,
Before his very eyes a mountain sea
Strikes, [swooping] from above, upon the
  stern :
The pilot is dislodged, and, forward fallen,

149. "But let the ruffian Boreas once enrage
The gentle Thetis, and, anon, behold
The strong-ribb'd bark through liquid mountains
  cut,
Bounding between the two moist elements,
Like Perseus' horse : where's then the saucy boat,
Whose weak untimber'd sides but even now
Co-rivall'd greatness?—Either to harbour fled,
Or made a toast for Neptune."
    Shakespeare, *Troilus and Cressida*, i. 3.

Thomson has a fine passage, describing a scene
not very dissimilar ; *Winter*, 153 :
"Then issues forth the storm with sudden burst,
And hurls the whole precipitated air
Down in a torrent. On the passive main
Descends th' ethereal force, and with strong gust
Turns from its bottom the discolour'd deep.
Through the black night that sits immense around,
Lash'd into foam, the fierce conflicting brine
Seems o'er a thousand raging waves to burn.
Meantime the mountain-billows, to the clouds
In dreadful tumult swell'd, surge above surge,
Burst into Chaos with tremendous roar."

155.   "The proud waves took pleasure
To toss my little boat up like a bubble :
Then like a meteor in the air he hung ;
Then catched, and hugged him in the depth of
  darkness."
    J. Fletcher, *The Double Marriage*, iii. 3.

Is rolled along upon his head. But her
Three times the billow, in the selfsame
  spot,   171
Whirls, chasing her around, and in the
  flood
The rav'ning eddy gorges her. Appear
Men scattered, swimming in the mighty
  gulf,
The weaponry of heroes, planks alike,
And Troja's royal treasure thro' the waves.
Now the stout galley of Ilioneus,
Now that of brave Achates, [that] alike,
Wherein was Abas wafted, and wherein
The aged Aletes, mastered has the storm.
In the loose joinings of their ribs they all
Admit the hostile flood, and yawn with
  leaks.   182
Meanwhile felt Neptune that with mighty
  coil
Turmoiled was ocean, and a storm launched
  forth,
And from their lowest beds were tided back
The restful waters. Violently roused,
And, looking from the deep abroad, he
  raised
His peaceful head above the topmost wave.
Dispersed throughout the ocean he beholds
Æneas' fleet, the Trojans overwhelmed 190
By billows, and the downfall of the sky :
Nor did the wiles of Juno and her spleen
Escape her brother. To his presence he
Calls Eurus and the Zephyr ; such thereon
He speaks : " Hath such proud confidence
  of birth
Possessed you ? What now ! Heav'n and
  earth, ye Winds,
Without my sanction, dare ye to embroil,
And such colossal piles to raise ? Whom
  I—
But meeter 'tis to quell the troubled waves.
Henceforth to me with no like punishment

174. "We might descry a horred spectacle ;
The issue of black fury strowed the sea
With tattered carcases of splitting ships,
Halfe sinking, burning, floating, topsie turvie."
    Marston, *Antonio and Mellida*, P. 1, i. 1.

186. *Stagna* seems to refer to the still waters at
the bottom of the deep sea, which are not affected
by the wind on the surface. The storm was so
furious, that even these were involved in commotion and carried aloft.

188. So Milton, *P. L.*, b. xii. :
"And looking down to see the hubbub strange,
And hear the din."

"Down, ye angry waters all !
Ye loud-whistling whirlwinds, fall !
Down, ye proud waves ! ye storms, cease !
I command ye, be at peace !
Fright not with your churlish notes,
Nor bruise the keel of bark that floats."
    J. Fletcher, *The Pilgrim*, iii. 7.

Shall ye for your malpractices atone. 201
Speed flight, and to that king of yours say
   these :
'That not to him the lordship of the main,
And grisly trident are by lot assigned, .
But e'en to me. He holds the monster
   rocks,
Thy homes, O Eurus : in that court [of his]
Let vaunt him Æolus, and hold his sway
Within the bolted prison of the winds.'"
So spake he ; and more speedily than
   said
The swollen seas he stills, and puts to flight
The mustered clouds, and brings again the
   sun.   211
Cymothoe and Triton [both] at once,
Against them straining, from the pointed
   rock
Push off the galleys ; with his trident he
Heaves them himself, and opes the vasty
   Syrts,
And calms the ocean ; and on nimble
   wheels
He skims along the surface of the waves.
And as what time among a mighty mob
An insurrection oft hath started up,
And fumes the vulgar rabble in their souls ;
And now are flying brands and stones ;—
   their rage   221
Supplies them weapons ;—then if by a
   chance
Some sage, of weight through sanctity and
   worth,

They have descried, they hush [to peace],
   and stand
Beside him with their ears erect : he sways
Their spirits by his words, and soothes their
   breasts.
Thus wholly did the crash of ocean fall,
When once the sire, forth gazing on the
   seas,
And wafted on beneath a cloudless sky,
Controls his coursers, and upon the wing
Resigns the reins to his pursuing car. 231
The comrades of Æneas, wearied out,
What shores are nearest to them in their
   course
Strive earnestly to fetch, and to the coasts
Of Lybia turn themselves. There lies a
   spot
Within a far retreat : an isle a haven forms
By the projection of its sides, whereon
Is shattered every billow from the deep,
And into curves receding splits its form.
On this side and on that colossal rocks,
And twin [-like] cliffs rise tow'ring to the
   heaven ;   241
Beneath whose brow the waters far and near

---

202. "Begone, and tell your king, for his pre-
   sumption,
We'll lash him from our land with iron rods,
And drag him at our stirrup through the streets."
   Webster, *The Thracian Wonder*, iii. 1.

210. The calm is thus described by Thomson ;
Winter, 197-201 :
"All Nature reels, till Nature's KING, who oft
Amid tempestuous darkness dwells alone,
And on the wings of the careering wind
Walks dreadfully serene, commands a calm :—
Then straight air, earth, and sea are hush'd at
   once."

Milton elegantly makes the Morn equally potent ;
P. R., b. iv. :
"Thus pass'd the night so foul, till Morning fair
Came forth, with pilgrim steps, in amice grey ;
Who with her radiant finger still'd the roar
Of thunder, chased the clouds, and laid the
   winds."

214. So Dryden, of the escape of the British
fleet :
"It seem'd as there the British Neptune stood,
With all his hosts of waters at command,
Beneath them to submit th' officious flood,
And with his trident shoved them off the sand."
   Annus Mirabilis, 184.

223. As *vir*, v. 151, on some occasions means
hero, *i.e.*, a great man, what reason is there

that on others it may not mean a sage, *i.e.*, a wise
man ?
   "When the fire was raised
Of fierce sedition, and the cheek was swollen
To sound the fatal trumpet, then the sight
Of this your worthy captain did disperse
All those unfruitful humours, and even then
Convert you from fierce tigers to staid men."
   Webster, *Appius and Virginia*, ii. 2.

Such a reverend character may call to mind the
Village Preacher in Goldsmith's *Deserted Village* :
"Unskilful he to fawn, or seek for power
By doctrines fashion'd to the varying hour ;
Far other aims his heart had learn'd to prize,
More bent to raise the wretched than to rise."
"Truth from his lips prevail'd with double sway,
And fools, who came to scoff, remained to pray."
"As some tall cliff, that lifts its awful form,
Swells from the vale, and midway leaves the
   storm.
Though round its breast the rolling clouds are
   spread,
Eternal sunshine settles on its head."
The idea in this last fine image he may have
borrowed from Dryden, who says of Lord Chan-
cellor Hyde :
"Your brow, which does no fear of thunder know,
Sees rolling tempests vainly beat below."
Milton says of Beelzebub :
   "With grave
Aspect he rose, and in his rising seemed
A pillar of state ; deep on his front engraven
Deliberation sat, and public care ;
And princely counsel in his face yet shone
Majestic, though in pain."   *P. L.*, b. ii.

231. Or : "careering car."

235. *Vertuntur* is here supposed to carry a
middle sense.

239. See note on *Geo.* iv. v. 420.

Lie hush in safety. Then a scene with woods
That quiver from above, and, dark with shade
Terrific, doth a grove o'erhang. Beneath
The brow, that faced [the view] with beetling cliffs,
A grot : sweet waters are within, and seats
Of living stone, a homestead of the Nymphs.
Here [weather-] weary barks no fetters hold ;
No anchor moors them with its hookèd bite.
Hither Æneas with his seven ships, 251
From all the number mustered, enters in,
And, with an earnest yearning for the land
Debarked, the men of Troy the wished-for beach
Enjoy, and, dripping with the brine, their limbs
Upon the shore repose. And first from flint
Achates struck a sparkle, and the fire
Caught up in leaves, and round it he purveyed
Dry provender, and in the fuel seized
The flame. Then Ceres, tainted by the waves, 260
And implements of Ceres, fetch they forth,
All-wearied in condition, and their grain,
Recovered, they prepare alike to parch
With blazes, and to crush it in the quern.
  Meanwhile Æneas scrambles up a cliff,
And far and near a universal view
Throughout the deep he aims to take, if he
May any Antheus, tossed by storm, descry,
And Phrygian ships with oars in double tier,
Or Capys, or upon his lofty stern 270
Caïcus' arms. No bark within his ken,

Three harts espies he roving on the strand ;
These all their droves are following in the rear,
And thro' the dales there feeds a lengthened host.
He halted here, and in his hand his bow
And nimble shafts he seized, the weaponry,
Which staunch Achates used to bear. And first
The very leaders, porting high their heads
With branching horns, he prostrates ; then the rank and file ;
And, driving with his missives all the throng, 280
Disperses them among the leafy woods ;
Nor ceases, ere that he, their conqueror,
Sev'n giant corses levels to the earth,
And brings the number with the ships to match.
He next the haven seeks, and shares them out
To all his comrades. Thereupon the wines,
Which good Acestes in the casks had stowed
On Sic'ly's strand, and as they went their way
The hero had vouchsafed them, deals he out,
And soothes their mourning bosoms with the words : 290
"O comrades, (for we are not unaware
Of your misfortunes in the past ;) O ye,
Who weightier have endured, to these the god
Will also grant an end. Ye e'en the rage
Of Scylla, and her cliffs that deep within
Are booming, have approached ; ye e'en have proved
The rocks of Cyclops : rally ye your souls,
And rueful fear dismiss ; perchance e'en these

---

243. *Scena* properly means "background ;" but background is a very unrhythmical, unpoetical word.
"Its uplands sloping deck the mountain's side,
Woods over woods in gay theatric pride."
Goldsmith, *Traveller.*

252. "Betwixt the hollow hanging of a hill,
And crooked bending of a craggy rock,
The sails wrapt up, the mast and tacklings down,
She lies so close that none can find her out."
Marlowe, *Tamburlaine the Great*, P. 2, i. 2.

258. "And serewood from the rotten hedges took,
And seeds of latent fire from flints provoke."
Dryden, *Flower and Leaf*, 413, 4.

264. *Frangere saxo*, v. 179. See note on *Geo.* i. v. 267.

265. This may call to mind a passage in Milton's *P. R.*, b. ii. :
"Up to a hill anon his steps he rear'd,
From whose high top to ken the prospect round,
If cottage were in view, sheepcote, or herd ;
But cottage, herd, or sheepcote, none he saw ;
Only in a bottom saw a pleasant grove : " &c.

---

294.   "Let not thy eyes,
Although thy grief become them, be in love
With tears. I prophesy a joy shall weigh
Down all our sufferings. I see comfort break
Like day, whose forehead cheers the world."
Shirley, *The Brothers*, iii. 5.

"Leave this vain sorrow !
Things being at the worst begin to mend. The bee,
When he hath shot his sting into your hand,
May then play with your eyelid."
Webster, *The Duchess of Malfi*, iv. 1.

"He does bear his loss
With such a noble strength of patience, that,
Had Fortune eyes to see him, she would weep
For having hurt him, and, pretending that
She did it but for trial of his worth,
Hereafter ever love him."
Beaumont and Fletcher, *The Honest Man's Fortune*, i. 2.

298. "Wake, wake, and let not patience keep thee poor !
Rouse up thy spirit from this falling slumber !

Hereafter to remember it will joy.
Through changeful hazards, through so
   many risks   .   .   .   300
Of our condition, we to Latium steer,
Where homes of peace the Destinies reveal.
'Tis there permitted that the realms of
   Troy
May rise again. Endure, and keep your-
   selves
For prosp'rous issues." Such like with his
   voice
He speaks, and, sick at soul with huge
   concerns,
He hope upon his visage counterfeits,
A deep dejection smothers in his heart.
They gird them to the spoil and coming
   feast:
The hides they tear asunder from the ribs,
And bare the flesh. Some cut it into joints,
And while they quiver spear them on the
   spits;   312
Upon the strand bronze vessels others place,
And flames supply. They then with food
   recruit
Their pow'rs, and, stretched upon the turf,
   are filled
With ancient Bacchus, and with fatted
   game.
Soon as was hunger by the feast removed,
And boards were cleared away, in long
   discourse
After their lost companions they inquire,

   Make thy distress seem but a weeping dream,
   And this the opening morning of thy comforts."
      Middleton, *No Wit Like a Woman's*, i. 2.

304. " Stoop thou to th' world, 'twill on thy bosom
      tread;
   It stoops to thee, if thou advance thy head."
      Middleton, *Your Five Gallants*, iii. 2.

305. " There's nothing of so infinite vexation
   As man's own thoughts."
      Webster, *Vittoria Corombona*, v. 2.

308. " Though in your heart there rage a thousand
      tempests,
   All calmness in your looks."
      J. Fletcher, *The Queen of Corinth*, i. 1.

      " O thou for whom I drinke
   So deep of griefe, that he must only thinke,
   Not dare to speake, that would express my woe;
   Small rivers murmur; deep gulfes silent flow."
      Marston, *Sophonisba*, end.

      " While I am compassed round
   With mirth, my soul lies hid in shades of grief,
   Whence, like the bird of night with half-shut eyes,
   She peeps, and sickens at the sight of day."
      Dryden, *The Rival Ladies*, iii. 1.

   " But 'tis the wretch's comfort still to have
   Some small reserve of near and inward woe,
   Some unsuspected hoard of darling grief,
   Which they unseen may wail, and weep, and
      mourn,
   And, glutton-like, devour."
      Congreve, *Mourning Bride*, i. 1.

In doubt alike between their hope and fear,
Whether to hold that they are [still] alive,
Or undergo the final [pangs of death], 322
Or now, when called on, from a distance
   hear.
In chief the good Æneas now the fall
Of keen Orontes, now of Amycus,
And ruthless fates of Lycus, inly mourns;
And [mourns] brave Gyas, and Cloanthus
   brave.
And now there was an end, when Jupiter,
From cope of th' Empyrean gazing down
Upon the sail-winged ocean, and the lands
That lie [below], and shores, and spreading
   tribes,   331
So stood he still upon the crest of heaven,
And firmly fixed his eyes on Libya's
   realms.
And him, within his bosom such concerns
While casting, more [than usually] sad,
And o'er her glistening eyes bedewed with
   tears,
Venus accosts: "O thou, who dost th'
   affairs
Alike of men and deities control
With endless sovereignty, and with thy bolt
Dost overawe them, what such heinous
   [crime]   340
'Gainst thee could my Æneas perpetrate?
The Trojans what? To whom, while they
   have borne
So many deaths, the whole wide round of
   earth
Upon the score of Italy is barred?
Sure, that the Romans hence in time to
   come

321. " Chewing the food of sweet and bitter fancy."
      Shakespeare, *As You Like It*, iv. 3.

326.   " I've oft took him
   Weeping alone, poor boy, at the remembrance
   Of his lost friends, which, as he says, the sea
   Swallowed, with all their substance."
      Middleton, *More Dissemblers besides Women*, i. 2.

   " I have wept for ye, boys,
   And constantly, before the Sun awaked,
   When the cold dew-drops fell upon the ground,
   As if the Moon were discontented too,
   My naked feet o'er many a rugged stone
   Have walked, to drop my tears into the seas
   For your sad memories."
      Shirley, *St. Patrick for Ireland*, v. 2.

Æneas might have comforted himself by the
thought that
         " We must all die,
   All leave ourselves; it matters not where, when,
   Nor how, so we die well; and can that man that
      does so
   Need lamentation for him?"
      J. Fletcher, *Valentinian*, iv. 4.

330. " Fix here, and rest awhile your sail-stretched
      wings,
   That have outstript the winds."
      J. Fletcher, *The Prophetess*, ii. 3.

When years wheel by—that hence should chieftains rise,
From Teucer's blood recovered, who the sea,
Who lands, should hold with universal sway,—
Thou hast engaged. What counsel, O my sire,
Hath changed thee? Sooth herewith the set of Troy,   350
And her disastrous wreck I used to suage,
While balancing conflicting fates with fates.
The selfsame fortune at this hour pursues
My heroes, hunted by so many risks.
What end assign'st thou of their toils, great king?
Antenor, from the midst of Greeks escaped,
Could pierce in safety the Illyrian gulfs,
And inmost realms of Liburnis, and o'erpass
Timavus' spring, where through its outlets nine,
With thund'ring mountain-din, it flushes forth   360
A bursten sea, and with a roaring flood
O'erwhelms the fields. Here ne'ertheless did he
The city of Petavium found, and homes
Of Teucri, and a title to the race
Assigned, and fastened up the Trojan arms:
Now sepulchred in tranquil rest he sleeps.
We, thine own offspring, in whose favor thou
Dost nod [bestowal of] the height of heaven,
Our vessels—O unutterable!—lost,
Are, owing to the spleen of one, betrayed,
And severed far from Italy's coasts. Is this   371
The compliment to piety? Is't thus
That thou restorest us to sceptral sway?"
  Smiling on her, the sire of men and gods,
With mien, wherewith the welkin and the storms
He clears, the liplets of his daughter sipped;
Thereon such like he speaks: "Refrain from fear,
O Cytherea; stirless rest for thee
Thy people's destinies. Thou shalt behold
Lavinium's city and its promised walls,
And waft aloft to stars of heav'n high-souled   381
Æneas; neither me hath counsel changed.
He shall for thee—for I will it announce,
Since this concern is preying on thy mind,
And, farther [in the future] wheeling round

The secrets of the Destinies, will I]
Awake them—carry on a mighty war
In Italy, and furious clans shall crush,
And laws and cities for the people found;
Until third summer shall have him beheld
In Latium reigning, and three winter [-tides],   391
Have passed away for Rutuli subdued.
Moreo'er, the boy Ascanius, [he,] to whom
The surname of Iulus now is joined,
(Ilus it was, so long as Ilion's state
In empire stood), shall in his sway complete
Thrice ten great cycles with revolving months,
And from Lavinium's seat the kingly power
Translate, and rampart with a world of strength
Long Alba. Here now monarchy shall last
For full three hundred years 'neath Hector's line,   401
Till Ilia, priestess of a royal strain,
With child by Mars, shall at a birth present
A double progeny. Then Romulus,
In tawny cov'ring of a female wolf,
His nurse, rejoiced, [the sceptre of] the race
Shall undertake, and build Mavortian walls,
And Romans call them after his own name.
To these I set nor bounds nor times of power:
Dominion without end have I vouchsafed.
Nay, Juno fierce, who now the sea, and lands,   411
And sky, is vexing with alarm, shall change
Her counsels for the better, and with me
The Romans foster, of the universe
The masters, and a toga-mantled race.
'Tis thus decreed. As lustra glide away
An age shall come, what time Assarac's house
Shall Pthia and renowned Mycenæ grind
In bondage, and o'er conquered Argos rule.
Of glorious pedigree there shall be born
A Trojan, Cæsar, who his sovereign sway
Shall bound by ocean, by the stars his fame;   422
Julius, a title from Iulus great
Derived. Him thou hereafter in the sky,
When laden with the booties of the East,
Shalt welcome, free from care: he, too, with vows
Shall be invoked. Uncultured ages then
Shall grow to softness, battles laid aside.

---

348. Is not *omni ditione* like *omnem prospectum?* v. 180.

384. Or, of course more literally: "upon thee."

405. "Some powerful spirit instruct the kites and ravens
To be thy nurses! Wolves and bears, they say,
Casting their savageness aside, have done
Like offices of pity."
           Shakespeare, *Winter's Tale*, iii. 2.

412. Or: "in alarm."

Hoar Faith and Vesta, with his brother
  Remus
Quirinus, laws shall issue; dread with steel
And straitened links, War's portals shall
  be shut;   431
Within, the godless Furor, sitting down
Upon his felon armor, and enchained
With hundred knots of bronze behind his
  back,
Shall thunder grisly with a mouth of blood."
  These [words] he speaks; and him of
    Maia born
Despatches downward from the lofty [hea-
  ven],
In order that the lands, and that the towers
Of Carthage, new [ly raised], might open lie
For hostry to the Trojans; lest, of fate
Unknowing, Dido drive them from her
  bounds.   441
He wings his way along the vast of air
Upon the oarage of his wings, and quick
On Libya's coasts alighted. And he now
Discharges his injunctions; and their hearts
Of fierceness do the Tyrians lay aside,
At pleasure of the god. Among the first
The queen doth towards the Trojans enter-
  tain
A peaceful spirit and a kindly mind.
  But good Æneas, turning o'er thro' night
Full many [a thought], as soon as boun-
  teous dawn   451
Was deigned, resolved to sally forth, and
  search

The novel spots; what regions by the wind
He may have reached; to seek who tenant
  them;
(For wastes does he perceive)—or be they
  men,
Or savage creatures,—and to carry back
The facts discovered to his mates. The fleet
Within an amphitheatre of groves,
Beneath a vaulted cliff, encloistered round
With trees and fearful shades, he hides:
  himself,   460
Attended by Achates only, paces on,
A pair of javelins waving in his hand,
With breadth of steel. 'Fore whom amid
  the wood
His mother threw herself across his path,
Wearing the guise and garment of a maid,
And maiden's arms—one Sparta-born, or
  like
Harpalyce of Thrace, [who] tires her steeds,
And wingy Hebrus in her flight outstrips.
For on her shoulders, in the wonted mode,
A handy bow, as huntress, had she hung,
And giv'n the gales her locks to scatter
  round,   471
Bare at the knee, and with her flowing folds
Gathered in knot. And first is she to cry:
" Ho! youths, inform me if you've haply
  seen
One of my sisters straying here, begirt
With quiver, and the skin of dappled lynx,
Or with a shout the foaming boar's career
Hotly pursuing?" Venus thus; and thus
The son of Venus in reply began:
" Of sisters thine not one has been by me,
[Or] heard, or seen. Oh! whom shall I
  thee name,   481
Thou maid? For neither mortal is thy
  mien,
Nor doth thy voice a human being speak.

---

435. Spenser's description of Sir Guyon's binding
Furor is very fine. The hint is evidently taken
from this passage:

"Then him to ground he cast, and rudely hayld,
  And both his hands fast bound behind his backe,
And both his feet in fetters to an yron racke.

With hundred yron chaines he did him bind,
  And hundred knots, that did him sore constraine:
Yet his great yron teeth he still did grind
  And grimly gnash, threatning revenge in vaine:
His burning eyen, whom bloody strakes did staine,
  Stared full wide, and threw forth sparkes of fyre:
And, more for ranck despight than for great paine,
Shakt his long locks colourd like copper wyre,
And bitt his tawny beard to show his raging yre."
                            F. Q., ii. 4, 14, 15.

In the address to Peace in *Windsor Forest*, Pope
alludes to similar consequences of her reign:

" Exiled by thee from earth to deepest hell,
In brazen bonds shall barbarous discord dwell;
Gigantic pride, pale terror, gloomy care,
And mad ambition, shall attend her there;
There purple vengeance, bathed in gore, retires,
Her weapons blunted, and extinct her fires;
There hated envy her own snakes shall feel,
And persecution mourn her broken wheel;
There faction roar, rebellion bite her chain,
And gasping furies thirst for blood in vain."

452. *Constituit*, v. 309, must be anticipated
here, in order to make the meaning intelligible
in English.

---

474. Or: "reveal her."

482. Spenser must have had this passage in view
in the beautiful description of Belphœbe, which he
gives at great length: *Faerie Queene*, ii. 3, 21–31.
Trompart replies to her like Æneas, stanza 33:

" O goddesse, (for such I thee take to bee,)
For nether doth thy face terrestriall shew,
Nor voyce sound mortall; I avow to thee
Such wounded beast, as that, I did not see,
Sith earst into this forrest wild I came.
But mote thy goodlyhed forgive it mee,
To weete which of the gods I shall thee name,
That unto thee dew worship I may rightly frame."

  " By that heavenly form of thine,
    Brightest fair, thou art divine,
    Sprung from great immortal race
    Of the gods, for in thy face
    Shines more awful majesty
    Than dull weak mortality
    Dare with misty eyes behold,
    And live."

J. Fletcher, *The Faithful Shepherdess*, i. 1.

Oh! sure a goddess! Art thou Phœbus'
  sister?
Of the Nymphs' race art one? Propitious
  be,
And, whosoe'er [thou art], our travail ease;
And underneath what clime at last, within
What regions of the globe, we may be
  thrown,
Do thou instruct us. Ignorant alike
Of men and places, do we wander, driven
By tempest hither, and by mountain waves.
For thee shall many a sacrificial beast 492
Before thy altars fall by our right hand."
  Then Venus: "Verily, I do not deem
Myself deserving of such deep respect.
With Tyrian maids the custom is to bear
A quiver, and with purple buskin high
To swathe the legs. Thou Punic realms
  dost see,
The sons of Tyrus, and Agenor's town;
But Libyan are the lands, a race in war
Ungovernable. Dido bears the sway 501
Imperial, from the Tyrian city passed,
Her brother flying. Tedious is her wrong,
Its mazes tedious; but I will pursue
The points most prominent of her affairs.
  Her consort was Sychæus, in his land
The richest of Phœnicians, and beloved
With deep affection of his hapless [spouse];
To whom her father had [the damsel] given
Unsullied, and with virgin omens yoked.
But Tyrus' sovereignty her brother held—
Pygmalion—in his guilt before all else 512
A greater monster; between whom arose
Mad anger in the midst. That godless
  [wretch]—
[E'en] at the altar's front, and blind with
  love
Of gold,—Sychæus, off his guard,

> "A certain touch, or air,
> That sparkles a divinity beyond
> An earthly beauty."
> Ben Jonson, *The Alchemist*, iv. 1.

494. "Thereat she blushing said: 'Ah! gentle
  Squire,
Nor goddesse I, nor angell; but the mayd
And daughter of a woody nymphe.'"
  Faerie Queene, iii, 5, 36.

499. Notwithstanding Wagner's view of *genus*,
v. 339, the popular opinion seems to be right. The
effort to relieve the word of an awkwardness in
apposition gives a strained and disjointed appearance to the construction, an evil which would appear
to be worse from the other.

507. There does not seem to have been in his
case any
> "Strife
> Of pity and fury; but the gold
> Made pity faint, and fury bold."
> Middleton, *The Mayor of Queenborough*, ii. 1.

510. "The miserable have
No other medicine, but only hope."
Shakespeare, *Measure for Measure*, iii. 1.

In secret overpowers with the sword,
Regardless of his sister's loves. And long
He masked the deed, and he, the miscreant,
Pretending many [a counterfeit], beguiled
The heart-sick lover with a hollow hope.
But in her slumbers rose the very ghost
Of her unburied husband. Lifting up 523
His features, in a wondrous fashion wan,
He bared the bloody altars, and a breast
Pierced thro' and thro' with steel, and of
  her home
Unravelled all the hidden guilt. Then flight
To speed, and from her country to with-
  draw,
He counsels; and, as aidance for the route,
Old treasures he unbosoms from the earth,
An unknown weight of silver and of gold.
By these [disclosures] roused, her flight and
  mates 532
Dido prepared. Assemble they, in whom
Or ruthless hatred of the despot dwelt,
Or terror keen. [Some] ships, which were
  by chance
Equipped, they seize and freight with
  gold: the wealth
Of miserly Pygmalion o'er the main
Is borne:—a woman leader of the feat.
They reached the spots, where thou dost
  now perceive
The giant walls, and rising citadel 540
Of infant Carthage; and they purchased
  ground,—
([Called] *Byrsa* from the title of the act,)
What they could girdle round with [one]
  bull's-hide.
But, pray you, who are ye, or from what
  coasts
Have ye arrived, or whither hold your
  route?"
  To her, in such inquiring, sighing he,
And from his deep of bosom heaving voice:
"O goddess, if from their primeval source
Retracing them, I should proceed, and thou
Wert free to hear the records of our toils,
Eve first in cloistered heav'n would lull the
  day. 551
Us from time-honored Troy (if thro' your
  ears

519.   "Their best conscience
Is, not to leave 't undone, but keep 't unknown."
  Shakespeare, *Othello*, iii. 3.

522.   "Darkness itself
Will change night's sable brow into a sunbeam
For a discovery."
  Middleton, *The Spanish Gipsy*, ii. 2.

"Other sins only speak: murder shrieks out."
  Webster, *The Duchess of Malfi*, iv. 2.

539. *Nunc cernes* is rather a startling lection to
the reader of Virgil. There is good authority for
cernis, which is far preferable.

The name of Troy hath peradventure passed),
Borne over severed seas, by chance its own,
A storm hath drifted on the Libyan coasts.
I am the good Æneas, who my gods,
Reft from the foeman, carry in my fleet
With me, by fame beyond the sky renowned.
I Italy seek, my country, and a race
From highest Jove [derived]. With twice ten ships   560
Upon the sea of Phrygia I embarked,
My goddess-mother pointing out my path,
Pursuing oracles vouchsafed : scarce seven,
Rent by the waves and eastern blast, survive.
Myself unknown, in want, thro' Libya's wilds
Roam on, from Europe and from Asia driven."
   Nor brooking his outpouring further plaints,
Thus Venus interposed amid his grief :
" Whoe'er thou art, not hated, [as] I deem,
Of heav'nly pow'rs, thou draw'st the breath of life—   570
[Thou], who at Tyrus' city hast arrived.
Do thou but go thy way, and from this spot
Betake thee to the portals of the queen.
For I to thee announce thy mates returned,
And fleet restored, e'en wafted to [a port]
Of safety by the shifted northern gales ;—
Unless to bootless end the augur's art
Have my mistaken parents taught. Behold
[Those] twice six swans, exulting in a troop;
Whom, swooping from the empyrean clime,
Jove's bird was troubling in the open sky :

Now in a lengthful rank they either seem
To take their grounds, or gaze adown on those   583
Already taken. As, on their return,
They are disporting with their whirring wings,
And in a bevy have begirt the heavens,
And uttered forth their songs : not otherwise
Thy ships alike, and flower of thy [friends],
Or hold the haven, or with canvas full
Its mouth are ent'ring. Only go thy way,
And where the path conducts thee steer thy step."   591
She spake ; and, turning off, she flashed [a sheen]
Back from her carmine neck, and from her head
Ambrosial tresses heav'nly perfume breathed ;
Her garment to her foot-soles wimpled down,
And in her gait the goddess stood confessed.
When he his mother knew, with such address
Did he pursue her, as she takes her flight :
" For what dost thou, thou heartless too, so oft
With phantom spectres make thy son a sport ?   600
Why not vouchsafed to link right hand to right,
And real words to hear and speak in turn ?"
In such he chides, and towards the walls his step
Directs. But Venus, as they pace along,
Bescreened them in an atmosphere of gloom,
And with a thick investiture of mist

---

579. In this troublesome comparison, which has given rise to various conjectures, it would seem pretty certain that *capere terras* refers to *portum tenet*, and *despectare captas* to *subit ostia*. The views generally taken seem either to be strained, or to fail in parallelism. May not *despectare* refer to the vessels in the rear, who were contemplating those ahead of them already in port? Some of the swans had alighted, while the others were looking down on them in their stations on the ground. This is the view attempted to be expressed in the version.

Marston employs a similar image for another, and more natural purpose :

" Then looke as when a faulcon towres aloft
Whole shoales of foule, and flockes of lesser birds
Crouch fearefully, and dive, some among sedge,
Some creepe in brakes; so Massinissa's sword,
Brandisht aloft, tost 'bout his shining caske,
Made stoop whole squadrons."
                    Sophonisba, ii. 2.

581. So Milton, *P. L.*, b. xi. :

" The bird of Jove, stoop'd from his aery tour,
Two birds of gayest plume before him drove."

592. Parnell finely describes the companion of the Hermit turning into an angel :

" But scarce his speech began,
When the strange partner seem'd no longer man ;
His youthful face grew more serenely sweet ;
His robe turn'd white, and flow'd upon his feet ;
Fair rounds of radiant points invest his hair ;
Celestial odours breathe through purpled air ;
And wings, whose colours glitter'd on the day,
Wide at his back their gradual plumes display.
The form ethereal bursts upon his sight,
And moves in all the majesty of light."
                    The Hermit.

The passage may call to mind Milton's description of Eve :

" Grace was in all her steps, Heav'n in her eye,
In every gesture dignity and love." *P. L.*, b. 8.

Was Chaucer in Milton's mind ?—

" Lo, truely they written, that her seien,
That Paradis stood formèd in her eien
And with her richè beauty evermore
Strove love in her, aie which of hem was more."
                    Troilus and Cresseide, st. 117.

The goddess compassed them, lest any might
Avail to see them, or to touch, or plan
Delay, or reasons of their coming ask.
Herself to Paphos borne aloft departs, 610
And blithesome visits her own seats again ;
Where to her [honor stands] a fane, and glow
A hundred altars with Sabæan cense,
And [fragrance] breathe from girlonds fresh [ly culled].
Meanwhile they seized the way where points the path.
And now they scaled the hill, which beetles huge
The city o'er, and at the facing towers
Peers from above. Æneas marvels at the pile,
Erst Punic cabins ; marvels at the gates,
And at the din, and pavements of the streets. 620
The Tyrians hotly ply. Some stretch the walls,
And rear the citadel, and with their hands
Uproll the stones ; some fix upon a site
For homestead, and with furrow shut it in.
They statutes [pass], and magistrates elect,
And senate held in rev'rence ; others here
The harbors excavate ; here others lay
The deep foundations of a theatre,
And giant pillars from the rocks hew out,
The lofty garniture for coming scenes. 630
Such toil, as 'neath the sun employs the bees,
In early summer in the bloomy fields,
When they the full-grown offspring of the race
Lead forth, or when they fluid honeys pack,
And with the luscious nectar puff the cells ;
Or burdens of [the workers] coming in
Receive, or, in battalion formed, the drones,
A lazy cattle, banish from the cribs :
Work glows, and scented honeys smell of thyme.
" O happy ye, whose walls already rise !"
Exclaims Æneas, and he gazes up 641
Upon the city-heights. He moves him on,
Fenced in with cloud (a marvel to be told),
Among the midst, and mingles with the men,
Nor is perceptible to any [eye].
A grove in centre of the city stood,
In shadow full luxuriant, in which spot
At first, by surges and tornado tossed,
The Carthaginians dug an omen forth,
Which had the queenly Juno pointed out—

A sprightly courser's head ;—for in this way 651
[Was it foretokened] that the race would prove
Matchless in war and fruitful in resource,
Throughout [all] ages. Here a vasty fane
To Juno the Sidonian Dido reared,
In gifts and godhead of the goddess rich ;
Upon the steps whereof bronze thresholds rose,
And, linked with bronze, the timbers ;
creaked the hinge
With folding-doors of bronze. .'Twas in this grove
A novel feature soothed their first alarm ;
Here first Æneas safety dared to hope, 661
And better trust in his distressed estate.
For while he pores o'er every single [sight]
'Neath the vast temple, waiting for the queen ;
While, what [kind] fortune on the city rests,
And at the works of artists each with each
And toil of tasks, he marvels—he beholds
The fights of Ilium in their course [portrayed],
And wars, already all throughout the globe
Bruited abroad by rumor ; Atreus' sons,
And Priam, and Achilles, fell to both. 671
He paused, and weeping : " Now what spot," he cries,
" Achates, what the country on the earth,
That is not of our suff'ring full? Lo, Priam !
E'en here for merit are its own rewards ;
Tears are there for misfortunes, and the soul
[The woes] of mortals touch. Dismiss thy fears ;
To thee will this renown bring some relief."
In such wise speaks he, and his fancy feeds
With th' empty portrait, heaving many a groan, 680
And with a plenteous flow bedews his face.
For he beheld how Pergamus around

653. Few expressions in all Virgil's works have given more trouble to the commentators than *facilem victu.* Trapp very innocently wishes that he never had written it, and seems to be a little ashamed of his idolised author for having done so. His own interpretation supplies an excellent and consistent sense ; but few scholars will be found to endure his giving an active signification to a passive supine. It is better to regard the word as a substantive, being thus used in connection with *facilem* by Virgil himself in *Geo.* ii. v. 460. See *Æn.*, iii. 540.

658. The " timbers ;" *i. e.,* the "door-posts."

668. " Your brave gilt house, my lord, your honour's hangings,
Where all your ancestors, and all their battles,
Their silk and golden battles, are deciphered."
J. Fletcher, *The Loyal Subject,* ii. 1.

---

631. See notes on *Geo.* iv. 79, and 213, &c.

The battling Greeks were flying *here;*
   Troy's youth
Were hot pursuing; *there* the Phrygians
   [fled],
On pressed the plumed Achilles in his car.
Nor hence afar, with canvas white as snow,
The tents of Rhœtus does he recognise,
A-weeping, which in maiden sleep betrayed,
The bloody son of Tydeus made a waste
With butchery immense, and drove aloof
His fiery coursers to the camp, ere they
Had tasted of the provender of Troy, 692
And drank the Xanthus. In another part
The flying Troilus, with loss of arms—
Ill-fated youth! and not a match when joined
In duel with Achilles!—by his steeds
Is borne, and to the empty chariot cleaves
Upon his back, the reins engrasping still;
And neck and locks are trailed along the
   earth,
And with inverted spear the dust is scored.
Meanwhile were pacing onward to the fane
Of Pallas—not their friend—the Trojan
   dames 702
With streaming tresses, and her Robe they
   bare
In prayerful fashion sad, and with their breasts
Struck by their hands: the goddess, turned
   aloof,
Her eyes kept riveted upon the ground.
Thrice had Achilles round the Ilian walls
Dragged Hector, and his breathless corse
   for gold
Was selling. Then he sooth a heavy groan
Draws from his bosom's depth, when spoils,
   when cars, 710
And when the very body of his friend,
And Priam, stretching forth unweaponed
   hands,
He viewed. Himself he also recognized,
Mingled among the chieftains of the Greeks;

And th' Eastern lines, and swarthy Memnon's arms.
Leads files of Amazons with moony shields
Penthesilea frantic, and amidst
Her thousand [squadrons] is she all ablaze,
Her golden sashes clasping on beneath
A pap projecting,—[she,] the warrioress!
And dares, a maiden, to engage with men.
  While these by Dardan-sprung Æneas,—
   [scenes], 722
To claim his wonder,—are beheld; while
   he
Is senseless-struck, and, rooted [to the spot],
In one fixed gaze is clinging, to the fane
Queen Dido, in her beauty passing fair,
Advanced, a mighty retinue of youths
Close-thronging. Such as on Eurotas'
   banks,
Or through the brows of Cynthus, Dian plies
The dances, whom, a thousand mountain-
   nymphs 730
Attending, this and that side circle round.
Her quiver she upon her shoulder bears,
And, pacing, all the goddesses outtops;
Delights thrill thro' Latona's silent breast.
Such Dido was; such, blithe, she moved
   her on
Among the midst, intent upon her task,
And future realm. Then at the goddess'
   gates,
Amid the temple's vault, she, fenced with
   arms,
And on a throne high cushioned, took her
   seat. 739
She was dispensing to her subjects rights
And laws, and dealing evenly their toil
Of tasks in portions fair, or these by lot
Was drawing, when Æneas suddenly
Sees Antheus, and Sergestus, and the brave
Cloanthus, drawing nigh with throng immense,
And others of the Teucri, whom o'er sea
The inky hurricane had wide dispersed,
And carried far away to other coasts.
At once he was amazed himself, at once
Achates both with joy and fear was thrilled.
In eagerness they burned to link right
   hands; 751
But their uncertain state disturbs their
   minds.
They keep disguised, and by the hollow cloud

---

683. " There is a thousand Hectors in the field:
Now here he fights on Galathe his horse,
And there lacks work; anon, he's there afoot,
And there they fly, or die, like scaled sculls
Before the belching whale; then is he yonder,
And there the strawy Greeks, ripe for his edge,
Fall down before him, like the mower's swath;
Here, there, and every where, he leaves, and
   takes;
Dexterity so obeying appetite,
That what he will, he does; and does so much,
That proof is call'd impossibility."
   Shakespeare, *Troilus and Cressida*, v. 5.

687. Shakespeare alludes to this event in
Henry VI., iv. 2:
" Our scouts have found the adventure very easy:
That as Ulysses, and stout Diomede,
With slight and manhood stole to Rhœsus' tents,
And brought from thence the Thracian fatal steeds;
So we, well cover'd with the night's black mantle,
At unawares may beat down Edward's guard."

717.   " I'll take to me
The spirit of a man, borrow his boldness,
And force my woman's fears into a madness."
   J. Fletcher, *The Island Princess*, iii. 3.

726.   " A miracle!
I mean of goodness; for, in beauty, madam,
You make all wonders cease."
   Dryden, *All for Love*, iii. 1.

Enveloped, watch what chance [befalls]
    the men ;
Upon what shore the fleet they leave ; why
    come :
For deputies from all the galleys went,
Entreating favor, and amid a shout
The temple sought. As soon as entered in,
And in the presence of [the queen] was
    deigned
The liberty of speech, with gentle breast
Ilioneus their chieftain thus began :   761
" O queen, to whom hath Jove vouch-
    safed to build
A city new, and haughty hordes to curb
In equity, we wretched sons of Troy,
By tempests carried over every sea,
Beseech thee,—from our vessels bid avaunt
Their cursèd blazes, spare a holy race,
And take a nearer view of our estate.
We come not, either with the sword to
    waste   769
The household-gods of Libya, or to turn
The booties rifled from you to the shores :
[Dwells] no such violence within our soul,
Nor such high insolence in conquered men.
There is a spot,—'Hesperia' do the
    Greeks
By name entitle it,—an ancient land,
Puissant in arms and richness of its soil :
Œnotrian swains inhabited it [erst] ;
Now rumor [tells] that moderns 'Italy'
Have called the nation from their leader's
    name.   779
Our course was hitherward, when in a trice
Uprising from the billow, rife in storm,
Orion flung us upon viewless shoals,
And far with wanton Austers e'en thro'
    waves,—
Salt ocean mast'ring,—and through wayless
    rocks,
Dispersed us. Hither to your coasts we few
Have floated on. What race of men is this ?
Or what so wild a country tolerates
This usage ? From a hostelry of sand
Are we debarred ; wars wake they, and
    forbid   789

Our setting foot upon the foremost shore.
If ye the race of man, and mortal arms
Disdain, yet look for gods that mind [the
    deeds]
Of right and wrong. Æneas was our king,
Than whom none else more upright [lived],
Nor greater was in piety, or war
And arms; which hero if the Weirds preserve,
If he is feeding on the breath of heaven,
Nor yet reposes with the grisly ghosts,
No fear there is, lest it should thee repent
That thou had'st been the foremost to
    compete   800
In courtesy. [We] likewise cities have
Within the bourns of Sic'ly, aye and fields,
And famed Acestes from the blood of Troy.
Be it allowed our tempest-shattered fleet
To draw ashore, and timbers in the woods
To fit, and oars to dress ; if it is deigned
For Italy, with mates and king restored,
To steer ; that Italy and Latium we
In joy may seek. But if our safety all
Is reft away, and thee, most worthy sire
Of Teucri, doth the sea of Libya hold, 811
Nor hope of our Iulus now remains,—
Still to the straits of Sicily at least,
And to our settlements prepared, where-
    from
We have been carried hither, and to king
Acestes, [grant] we may repair." In such
Ilioneus : together all at once
The Dardans muttered with their voice
    [assent].
Then briefly Dido, downcast in her look,
Speaks forth : " Alarm dismiss ye from
    your heart,   820

---

782. " When with fierce winds Orion arm'd
Hath vex'd the Red Sea coast."
                        Milton, *P. L.*, b. i.

" The roughening deep expects the storm, as sure
As red Orion mounts the shrouded heaven."
                        Armstrong, *Health*, b. iii.

789. " The air's as free for a fly as an eagle."
                        Ben Jonson, *The New Inn*, ii. 2.

" A handful of poor naked men we are,
Thrown on your coast, whose arms are only
    prayer,
That you would not be more unmerciful
Than the rough seas, since they have let us l:ve
To find your charity."
                Shirley, *St. Patrick for Ireland*, i. 1.

792. " The eagle frowned, and shook his royal
    wings,
            And charged the fly
            From hence to hie :
Afraid, in haste the little creature flings,
            Yet seeks again,
Fearful, to perk him by the eagle's side :
            With moody vein,
The speedy post of Ganymede replied :
' Vassal, avaunt ! or with my wings you die :
Is't fit an eagle seat him with a fly ?' "
    R. Greene, *Menaphon's Roundelay*. See note
on line 820.

Ben Jonson thus winds up his tragedy of *Sejanus* :

" Let this example move the insolent man,
Not to grow proud and careless of the gods.
It is an odious wisdom to blaspheme,
Much more to slighten, or deny their powers :
For whom the morning saw so great and high,
Thus low and little 'fore the even doth lie."

816. *Liceat*, v. 551, is still understood.

820. " The fly craved pity ; still the eagle frowned :
            The silly fly,
            Ready to die,
Disgraced, displaced, fell grovelling to the ground :

O Teucer's sons, solicitudes shut out.
My painful state, and infancy of realm,
Such measures force me to devise, and wide
My frontiers with a sentry to defend.
Who knows not th' Æneads' race? Troy's
    city who?
Their gallantry alike and gallant men,
Or conflagrations of so great a war?
Not breasts so blunted do we Tyrians bear,
Nor yokes the Sun his coursers, turned
    aloof
So far from Tyrus' city. Whether ye 830
The great Hesperia and Saturnian fields,
Or Eryx' bourns and king Acestes, choose,
Safe through my succor I will you dismiss,
And aid you with my means. And do ye
    list
On equal terms with me to settle down
In these my realms?—The city which I
    build is yours ;
Draw up your ships ; the child of Troy
    and Tyre
With no distinction shall by me be used.
And would to heav'n your king himself
    were here,—
Æneas, driven by the selfsame blast ! 840
Assuredly throughout the shores true men
Will I despatch, and Libya's utmost bounds
Bid them examine, if a castaway
In any of its woods or towns he roams."
  By these her words excited in their
    soul,

Alike the brave Achates, and the sire
Æneas, now were burning long ere this
To burst away the cloud. Achates first
Æneas [thus] accosts : " O goddess-born,
What thought is now arising in thy mind ?
All safe thou see'st, thy fleet and mates
    restored.   851
One absent is, whom we ourselves saw
    whelmed
Amid the billow : to thy mother's words
All else replies." He scarce had spoken
    these,
When suddenly the mantling cloud itself
Asunder splits, and melts to open air.
Still stood Æneas, and in crystal sheen
Gleamed forth, in face and shoulders like
    a god.
For on her son his mother had herself
Becoming locks, and blooming light of
    'youth,   860
And in his eyes her sprightly graces,
    breathed :
Such beauty as to iv'ry hands impart ;
Or when is silver, or the Parian stone,
In yellow gold encased around. Then thus
The queen does he accost, and, unforeseen
By all, upon a sudden he exclaims :
" I, whom ye seek, am in your presence
    here,
Trojan Æneas, snatched from Libyan
    waves.
O [lady], who alone hast pity felt
For Troy's unutterable woes ; who us,
A remnant from the Greeks, now wearied
    out   870
By all the hazards both of land and sea,
In want of all things, in thy city, home,
Thy partners makest ! throughly thee to
    pay

  The eagle saw,
And with a royal mind said to the fly :
    ' Be not in awe ;
I scorn by me the meanest creature die ;
Then seat thee here.' The joyful fly up flings,
And sat safe-shadowed with the eagle's wings."
  R. Greene, *Menaphon's Roundelay.* See note
on line 792.

834. If the hypothetical idea contained in *seu* and
sive is to be continued in *vultis et*, of which construction there are many examples, the translation
must be altered thus :
    " And if you list
  On equal terms with me to settle down
  In these my realms, the city which I build
  Is yours."
" Come in, then, take possession of your own :
  My lands, my house, my goods, and all is your's."
  Webster, *The Weakest goeth to the Wall*, iv. 2.
The Trojans might safely have said :
    " Do your pleasure, Sir :
  Beggars must not be choosers."
  Beaumont and Fletcher, *The Honest Man's Fortune*, v. 3.

840. *Notus* here must mean a strong wind in
general, as the south wind would drive them *from*
and not *to* Africa.

842.   " A century send forth ;
  Search every acre in the high-grown field,
  And bring him to our eye."
                Shakespeare, *King Lear*, iv. 4.

857. " Not great Æneas stood in plainer day,
  When, the dark mantling mist dissolved away,
  He to the Tyrians show'd his sudden face,
  Shining with all his goddess mother's grace :
  For she herself had made his countenance bright,
  Breathed honour on his eyes, and her own purple
    light."
        Dryden, *Britannia Rediviva*, 128-133.

858. " Not Lollia Paullina, nor those blazing stars,
  Which make the world the apes of Italy,
  Shall match thyself in sun-bright splendency."
            Machin, *The Dumb Knight*, i. 1.

869.   " Dearest lady,
  Great in your fortune, greater in your goodness,
  Make a superlative in excellence,
  In being greatest in your saving mercy."
        Massinger, *The Duke of Milan*, iii. 3.
" Her goodness does disdain comparison,
  And, but herself, admits no parallel." *Ib.*, iv. 3.

873.   " 'Tis I am poor,
  For I have not a stock in all the world
  Of so much dust, as would contrive one narrow
  Cabin to shroud a worm."
            Shirley, *The Brothers*, iv. 5.

Meet thanks is not, O Dido, in our power,
Nor that of Dardan race,—where'er 'tis found
In any spot,—which scattered is thro'out
The mighty globe. O may the gods on thee
(If any pow'rs of heav'n regard the good,
If righteous dealing anywhere be aught,
A soul, too, that is conscious to itself   881
Of right,) the guerdons, thy desert, confer !
What so propitious ages gave thee birth ?
What such high parents gendered such [a child] ?
While rivers to the seas shall run, while shades
Shall sweep the mountains' jutting sides, while heaven
Shall feed the stars, [thy] glory and thy name,   887
And praises aye shall last, whatever lands
Call me." Thus having said, he clasps
His friend Ilioneus with his right hand,
And with his left Serestus ; then the rest ;
Brave Gyas also, and Cloanthus brave.
  Sidonian Dido was in wonder lost,
First at the presence of the hero, next
At his so striking fortune, and she thus
Spake from her lip : " What fortune, goddess-born,
Pursues thee onward through such grievous risks ?
What power drives thee to our savage coasts ?
Art thou that [world-renowned] Æneas, whom
To Dardan-sprung Anchises Venus boon

---

875. "Would thou hadst less deserved,
That the proportion both of thanks and payment
Might have been more ! Only I have left to say
More is thy due than more than all can pay."
       Shakespeare, *Macbeth*, i. 4.

878. "But to those powers above, that can requite,
That from their wasteless treasures heap rewards,
More out of grace than merits, on us mortals,
To those I'll ever pray, that they would give you
More blessings than I have skill to ask."
       May, *The Heir*, iv.

"Angels reward the goodness of this woman !"
       Massinger, *The Duke of Milan*, i. 3.

881. "As high and hearty as youth's time of innocence,
That never knew a sin to shape a sorrow by :
I feel no tempest, nor a leaf wind-stirring
To shake a fault ; my conscience is becalmed."
       Middleton, *A Game at Chess*, iv. 1.

"Every good deed sends back its own reward
Into the bosom of the enterpriser." *Ib.*, iii. 1.

884. "Happy the parents of so fair a child !"
       Shakespeare, *Taming of the Shrew*, iv. 5.

894.   "There is a minute,
When a man's presence speaks in his own cause,
More than the tongues of twenty advocates."
       Massinger, *The Fatal Dowry*, i. 1.

Bare at the wave of Phrygian Simois ?   901
Yea sooth I call to mind that Teucer came
To Sidon, banished from his country's bourns,
New kingdoms seeking by the aid of Bel :
Then Bel, my sire, was wasting Cyprus rich,
And conq'ror holding it beneath his sway.
From that time forward has to me been known
The Trojan city's fortune, and thy name,
And kings Pelasgic. He, thy foe, himself
Was used with praise distinguished to extol
The Teucri, and would have it he was sprung   911
From th' ancient stock of Teucrians. Then come,
O youths, advance ye underneath our roofs.
Like fortune me, too, tossed through many a toil,
Hath willed at last to settle on this land.
Not unacquainted with misfortune, I
The wretched learn to aid." Thus speaks she forth :
At once Æneas to the royal roofs
She leads ; at once within the fanes of gods
A sacrifice enjoins. Nor less meanwhile
She sends his mates on shore a score of bulls,   921
A hundred bristly backs of burly swine,
A hundred fatted lambkins with their dams,
The gifts and merry-making of the god.
But gorgeously with royal pomp the dome
Within is furnished, and amid the halls
The banquets they provide : — cloths wrought with skill,
And haughty scarlet ; massy silver plate
Upon the tables, and, embossed in gold,
The brave achievements of her sires, a chain
Of great occurrences, exceeding long,   931
Extended thro' so many [gallant] men,
From the commencement of her ancient race.
Æneas (for a father's love his mind
To be at rest allowed not), to the ships

---

916. "One, too, acquainted with calamities,
And from that apt to pity. Charity ever
Finds in the act reward, and needs no trumpet
In the receiver."
       J. Fletcher, *The Sea Voyage*, ii. 2.

"I hate to leave my friend in his extremities."
       J. Fletcher, *The Woman Hater*, ii. 1.

Gray, happily, of Virtue when schooled by Adversity :
"Stern, rugged nurse ! thy rigid lore
With patience many a year she bore :
What sorrow was, thou bad'st her know,
And from her own she learn'd to melt at others' woe."
       Hymn to Adversity.

Despatches fleet Achates in advance,
These [tidings] to Ascanius to report,
And to the town to lead [the youth] himself:
Stands [centred] in Ascanius every thought
Of his fond parent. Presents, furthermore,
Rescued from Ilium's wreck, he bids him
  bring ;—   941
A kirtle stiff with figures and with gold,
And, woven round with saffron-hued
  acanth,
A veil, the Argive Helen's brave attire,
Which from Mycenæ she, when Pergamus
She sought, and nuptials disallowed, had
  brought
Away, her mother Leda's wondrous gift.
Moreo'er, a sceptre, which Ilione,
Of Priam's daughters eldest, erst had
  borne ;
And for the neck a necklace strung with
  beads,   950
And, double with its jewels and with gold,
A diadem. Despatching these [behests],
His journey to the ships Achates bent.
  But Cytherea machinations new,
New schemes, is turning over in her breast;
That Cupid, changed in figure and in looks,
Should in the place of sweet Ascanius come,
And with the presents set the raging queen
Afire, and in her bones inweave his flame ;
Since sooth a house equivocal she fears,
And Tyrians double-tongued : fell Juno
  stings,   961
And towards the night unrest returns again.
She therefore in these words winged Love
  accosts :
"O son, my strength, my mighty pow'r
  alone,
O son, who bolts Typhæan of the highest
  sire
Disdainest, I to thee for refuge fly,
And humbly thy divinity entreat.
How brother thine, Æneas, round all shores
Is tossed upon the ocean, through the hate
Of Juno the unjust, is known to thee,   970
And in my grief thou oftentimes hast
  grieved.
Him the Phœnician Dido entertains,
And stays with luring accents ; and I dread
What turn Junonian hospitage may take :
In such a grave conjuncture of affairs
She will not be at rest. On which account
To trap the queen beforehand with my
  wiles,
And with the flame to vest her, I design,

Lest she through any influence of heaven
May change her [feelings], but in potent
  love   980
For my Æneas may with me be chained.
Now understand my notion [of the means],
Whereby thou may'st be able to effect
This [end]. The royal boy, my chief concern,
At summons of his darling sire prepares
To go to Sidon's city, bearing gifts,
The remnants from the deep and flames of
  Troy.
Him I, when drowsed in sleep, upon the
  high
Cythera, or upon Idalia's [mount],
Within my hallowed seat will hide away ;
Lest he in any wise avail to learn   991
My plots, or thwart them in the midst.
  Do thou
His mien, for not beyond a single night,
With cunning counterfeit, and, boy [thyself],
The well-known features of the boy assume ;
That when shall Dido, in the height of
  bliss,
Thee welcome to her bosom, in the midst
Of royal banquets and Lyæan juice ;
When she shall grant embraces, and imprint
Her luscious kisses, thou thy hidden fire
May'st inly breathe, and dupe her with thy
  bane."   1001
The words of his dear mother Love obeys,
And doffs his wings, and in Iulus' gait
Rejoicing trips along. But Venus o'er
Ascanius' limbs a stilly rest bedews,
And, nestled in her breast, the goddess lifts
[The sleeper] to Idalia's lofty groves,
Where downy marjoram, exhaling [scent],
Imbosoms him in flow'rs and balmy shade.
  And now, her word obeying, Cupid
  paced,   1010
And to the Tyrians bore the royal gifts,
Blithe, with Achates for a guide. When he
Arrives, beneath a prideful canopy,
The queen has just reposed her on a couch
Of gold, and throned her in the midst.
  Now sire
Æneas, now too Troja's youth collect,
And on the outspread purple all recline.

1006.   "Sleep, sleep, young angel!
          My care shall wake about thee."
                  Middleton, *The Spanish Gipsy*, iii. 3.
" When Venus would her dear Ascanius keep
  A prisoner in the downy bands of sleep,
  She odorous herbs and flowers beneath him
    spread,
      As the most soft and sweetest bed ;
  Not her own lap would more have charmed his
    head."   Cowley, *The Garden*.

961.   " They shall find,
   That to a woman of her hopes beguiled,
   A viper trod on, or an aspic's mild."
        J. Fletcher, *The Spanish Curate*, iv. 1.

The serving-men give waters for their hands,
And Ceres from the baskets fetch they forth,
And towels bring with shaven nap. Within
Handmaidens fifty, with whom rests the charge 1021
In long array the viands to dispose,
And magnify the household-gods with fires;
A hundred others, and as many youths
Of service, matches in their age, with cates
The boards to burden, and to set the cups.
Yea, too, the Tyrians thro' the merry halls
Together flocked in numbers, [e'en] enjoined
Upon the broidered sofas to recline.
They gaze in wonder at Æneas' gifts ;
In wonder at Iulus do they gaze, 1031
And at the glowing features of the god,
And his feigned accents ; at the kirtle too,
And veil, embroidered with the saffron-hued
Acanthus. Chief of all, the hapless one,
Abandoned to the coming plague, her soul
Cannot have sated, and by gazing grows
The hotter,—[she,] Phœnicia's dame,—and is alike
Excited by the boy and by his gifts.
When he upon Æneas's embrace 1040
And neck has hung, and cloyed the mighty love
Of his pretended sire, he seeks the queen.
She with her eyes, with all her soul she hangs
On him, and fonds him to her breast at times ;—
[She,] Dido,—wareless what a potent god
Was rooting down within her wretched self.
But mindful of his Acidalian mother he
By slow degrees Sychæus to efface
Begins, and by a living passion aims
To prepossess affections, now long since
At quiet, and a heart unused [to love].
As soon as in the banquet was a pause,
And boards were cleared, huge wassail-bowls they set, 1053
And crown the wine. A din throughout the courts
Arises, and along the spacious halls
Their voice they roll. Down burning cressets hang
From gilded ceilings, and the night with flames

Wax-torches overpower. Here the queen
A bowl, with jewels weighty and with gold,
Required, and brimmed it up with taintless wine,— 1060
Which Bel, and all from Bel were wont [to brim].
Then silence was observed throughout the courts.
" O Jove (for that thou grantest rights to guests
They tell), that this a happy day alike
To Tyrians, and the voyagers from Troy,
May prove, be it thy pleasure, and that this
May our descendants in remembrance hold.
Be present Bacchus, giver of delight,
And Juno kind ; and Tyrians, O do ye
The union solemnize in friendly mood."
She said, and of the liquors spilled a gift
Upon the board, and first, when spilled, [the rest] 1072
She reached as far as to her tip of lip ;
Then, rallying him, she it to Bitias gave.
He, nothing slack, drained off the foaming bowl,
And swilled him from the brimming gold.
Next [drank]
The other nobles. On his gilded lute
The tressed Iopas warbles o'er [the lay],
Which highest Atlas taught him. Chants this [bard]
The rambling Moon and travails of the Sun ;
Whence race of men, and flocks ; whence rain, and fires ; 1081
Arcturus, and the rainy Hyades,
And twain Triones ; wherefore speed so fast
To dip them in the ocean wintry Suns,
Or what delay withstands the laggard nights.

" As heaven with stars, the roof with jewels glows,
And ever living lamps depend in rows."
Pope, *Temple of Fame*.
" Her room
Outbraved the stars with several kinds of lights."
Webster, *Vittoria Corombona*, iii. 2.
1075. " Did I not find thee gaping, like an oyster
For a new tide? Thy very thoughts lie bare,
Like a low ebb ; thy soul, that rid in sack,
Lies moored for want of liquor."
Beaumont and Fletcher, *Bonduca*, i. 2.
1078. Bards in ancient times wore their hair very long. The reader may, perhaps, readily call to mind this element in the grand description of one of their number, in Gray's noble *Ode* :
" Robed in the sable garb of woe,
With haggard eyes the poet stood ;
(Loose his beard, and hoary hair
Stream'd, like a meteor, to the troubled air,)
And with a master's hand, and prophet's fire,
Struck the deep sorrows of his lyre."

1039. Or, perhaps : " deluded."
1056. " From the arched roof,
Pendent by subtle magic, many a row
Of starry lamps and blazing cressets, fed
With Naphtha and Asphaltus, yielded light
As from a sky." Milton, *P. L.*, b. I.

Redouble with acclaim the men of Tyre,
And Trojans second them. Yea too, the
   night
With diverse talk unhappy Dido eked,

1086. *The enthusiasm of his auditors, in so warmly clapping Iopas, shows that they would not have come under the lash of Lorenzo; Shakespeare, Merchant of Venice, v. 1:*
   "Therefore the poet
Did feign that Orpheus drew trees, stones, and
   floods;
Since nought so stockish, hard, and full of rage,
But music for the time doth change his nature:
The man that hath no music in himself,
Nor is not mov'd with concord of sweet sounds,
Is fit for treasons, stratagems, and spoils;
The motions of his spirit are dull as night,
And his affections dark as Erebus:
Let no such man be trusted."

And deep[ly] drank [of] passion, as she asks
Much about Priam, about Hector much;
Now, in what arms Aurora's son had come;
Now what were Diomedes' coursers; now,
How puissant was Achilles. "Nay then
   come,   1093
And from the first commencement tell us,
   guest,
The stratagems of Danai,"—she cries,—
" And hazards of thy [friends], and wan-
   d'rings thine ;
For now the seventh summer wafts thee on,
A roamer over every land and wave."

1089. *"My ears, my greedy eyes, my thirsty soul, Drank gorging in the dear delicious poison, Till I was lost, quite lost."*
   Smith, *Phædra and Hippolytus*, i. 1.

BOOK II.

ALL dropped to silence, and their faces kept
   [Firm fixed], on him attent. Then thus
   began
The sire Æneas from his lofty throne :
" Unspeakable, O queen, the grief thou
   bid'st
Renew; how Troja's wealth and piteous
   realm
The Greeks uprooted, and those saddest
   [scenes],
Which I myself have witnessed, and
   wherein
A leading part I bore. Such [miseries]
In telling, who of Myrmidons, or Dolopes,
Or [who,] the soldier of Ulysses stern,   10
Could keep from tears? And now the
   moistful night
Posts downward from the sky, and setting
   stars
Are urging slumbers. But if [thee enthrals]

Line 2. "And Expectation, like the Roman eagle, Took stand, and called all eyes."
   J. Fletcher, *The Prophetess*, iii. 1.

11. *"Then, sighing soft awhile, at last she thus :
O lamentable fall of famous towne,
Which raignd so many yeares victorious,
And of all Asia bore the soveraigne crowne,
In one sad night consumd and throwen downe !
What stony hart, that heares thy haplesse fate,
Is not emplerst with deepe compassiowne,
And makes ensample of mans wretched state,
That floures so fresh at morne, and fades at evening
   late !"* Spenser, *F. Q.*, iii. 9, 39.

*" My tears, like ruffling winds, locked up in caves,
   Do bustle for a vent."*
   Ford, *The Lover's Melancholy*, v. 1.

13. *" For now the streaky light began to peep,
   And setting stars admonish'd both to sleep."*
   Dryden, close of *Hind and Panther.*

So strong a passion our mishaps to learn,
And briefly hear of Troja's latest pang,
Although my soul at recollection quails,
And hath in woe recoiled, I will begin.
" Worn out by war, and baffled by the
   fates,
The chiefs of Danai,—so many years
Now gliding past,—a horse of mountain-
   size   20
By heav'nly handicraft of Pallas build,
And overlay its ribs with plank of fir :
An off'ring they pretend for their return.
That rumor spreads. Herein the chosen
   frames
Of heroes, culling them by lot, in stealth
Do they imprison in its darksome side,
And throughly its colossal vaultages,
And womb, with weaponed soldiery they
   fill.
" Within the view lies Tenedos, an isle
Full widely known by rumor, rich in
   wealth,   30
While Priam's realm endured, now but a
   bay,
And post of lame dependance for the ships.
Transported hither, on the lonely beach
They masked themselves. We deemed
   that they had gone,
And with the breeze had for Mycenæ made.
All Teucria therefore from her lengthened
   woe
Herself releases ; opened are the gates ;
It joys to go and view the Doric camp,

16. *" Remembrance wakes with all her busy train, Swells at my breast, and turns the past to pain."*
   Goldsmith, *Deserted Village.*

And spots forsaken, and a quitted shore.
Here the Dolopians' hosts, here pitched
  [his tent]   40
The fell Achilles; for their galleys here
The station; here in battailous array
To combat were they wont. Some stand
  amazed
At unespoused Minerva's deathful gift,
And marvel at the hugeness of the horse.
And first Thymœtes moves that it be
  brought
Inside the walls, and in the castle lodged;
Whether in guile, or now the fates of Troy
Decreed it so. But Capys and [the rest],
Within whose mind a sounder judgment
  [dwelt],   50
Or in the sea the ambush of the Greeks,
And their mistrusted off'rings, bid to fling,
And burn them up with blazes underlaid;
Or of the womb the vaulted lurking-holes
To bore and probe. The commons, un-
  resolved,
Into conflicting sentiments is split.
" There first ahead of all, with throng
  immense
Attending him, Laocoon, afire,
Down from the summit of the castle runs;
And from afar: 'O wretched citizens,   60
What such wild frenzy [this]? Do ye
  believe
Our foes withdrawn? Or think ye any gifts
Of Grecians are devoid of craft? Is thus
Ulysses known? Or, prisoned in this wood,
Achæans are concealed, or this is framed
An engine 'gainst our walls, to overpeer
Our homes, and on the city from on high
To pounce; or lurking lies some trick.
  The horse

---

44. It is very stiff to make *Minervæ*, v. 31, the dative case; nor is it at all according to the usage of Virgil, who continually uses the genitive under such circumstances; *e. g., Templum conjugis antiqui, Æn.* iv. 457. See also *Æn.* xi. 4, *Vota Deum.*

53. It is not meant that the same individuals recommended destruction both by water and fire; but that, of those who advocated the total destruction of the horse, some proposed the one and some the other; or, if this should not be consented to, at least *terebrare et tentare*, &c. This explains the use of *que*, for which if *ve* be read, an awkward uncertainty results from the use of the following *aut*.

66. " The prince's espials have informed me,
How the English, in the suburbs close intrench'd,
Wont, through a secret grate of iron bars
In yonder tower, to overpeer the city;
And thence discover, how, with most advantage,
They may vex us with shot, or with assault."
  Shakespeare, 1 *Henry VI.,* i. 4.
68. " There is a devilish cunning
  Expressed in this black forgery."
  Webster, *Appius and Virginia,* iii. 2.

Trust not, O Trojans! whatsoe'er that be,
I dread the Grecians, even bringing gifts.'
Thus having spoken, his prodigious spear
With lusty pow'rs upon the monster's side,
And on its paunch, with joinings arched,
  he hurled.   73
It quiv'ring stood, and from the womb
  convulsed
The vaults rang hollow, and gave forth a
  groan.
And if the gods' decrees, if reason not
  obtuse,
Had been [our blessèd lot], he had enforced
The marring of th' Argolic shrouds with
  steel;
And, Troy, thou would'st be standing now,
  and thou,
O Priam's stately castle, would'st remain.
" Behold, meanwhile, a stripling, with
  his hands   81
Pinioned behind his back, with lusty shout
Were Dardan shepherds haling to the king;
Who had, a stranger, of his free accord
Himself presented to them as they came,
That he this very [plot] might carry out,
And open Troja to Achaia's sons;—
Self-confident in spirit, and prepared
For either issue,—or to work his wiles,
Or fall before indubitable death.   90
From every quarter, in the zeal to see,
Poured round, the youth of Troja tides
  amain,
And vie in making of the prisoner sport.
Now hear the stratagems of Danai,
And from a single outrage learn them all.
For when amid our gaze, confused, un-
  armed,
He stood, and with his eyes the Phrygian
  hosts
Beheld around: 'Ah! now what land,'
  he cries,
' What seas can welcome me? Or what
  doth now
For hapless me at last remain, for whom
With Greeks no further is there any place;
Yea, too, the very Dardans in their rage
Vengeance with blood demand?' By which
  his moan   103
Our minds were wholly changed, and all
  assault

---

100. " Your melancholy mole is happy now;
He fears no officers, but walks invisible.
Would I were chamber-fellow to a worm!
The rooks have princely lives that dwell upon
The tops of trees; the owls and bats are gentlemen,
They fly, and fear no warrants: every hare
Outruns the constable: only poor man,
By nature slow and full of phlegm, must stay,
And stand the cursèd law."
  Shirley, *The Imposture,* v. 4.

Was stifled. We encourage him to speak:
From what blood sprung, or what he brings,
    to say,
Where his reliance as a pris'ner rests.
He these,—alarm at last discarded,—
    speaks:
"'Yea all to thee, O king, whate'er
    result,
Will I,' saith he, 'acknowledge in their
    truth;   110
Nor that I am of Argive race disown.
This first: nor if hath Fortune Sinon
    shaped
A wretch, shall she, unscrupulous, beside
Shape him a hollow and a lying [knave].
If haply in discourse hath reached thine ears
Such name as that of Palamede, from Bel
Descended, and his rumor-noised renown,
Whom the Pelasgi, 'neath a baseless charge,
Unguilty under evidence accursed,
Since he discountenanced their wars, sent
    down   120
To death :—they mourn him now when reft
    of light :—
Me as his comrade, e'en by link of blood
Allied, a needy father, hither sent
To warfare from its earliest date. While
    he
Stood firmly in his puissance unimpaired,
And flourished in the cabinets of kings,
We, too, both some repute and dignity
Have borne. As soon as through the jea-
    lous hate   130
Of cozening Ulysses,—[matters] not un-
    known
I speak,—from upper regions he withdrew,
Heart-broken, I my life in gloom and grief
Dragged out, and inly with resentment
    viewed
The downfall of my unoffending friend;

107. Or: "We encourage him to tell
From what blood sprung, or [message] what he
    brings,
To say what meant his confidence when caught."
113. "I am unfortunate, but not ashamed
    Of being so: No I let the guilty blush."
                Southern, *Oroonoko*, i. 2.
    "What! because we are poor
Shall we be vicious?"
        Webster, *Vittoria Corombona*, i. 2.
"To seem to be, and not be what I seem,
Are things my honest nature understands not."
                Dryden, *Cleomenes*, iii. 1.
130. Or: "jealousy."
131. "I could so roll my pills in sugared syllables,
And strew such kindly mirth o'er all my mischief,
They took their bane in way of recreation."
            Middleton, *A Game at Chess*, i. 1.
"Of all wild beasts preserve me from a tyrant,
And of all tame a flatterer."
            Ben Jonson, *Sejanus*, i. 2.

Nor held my peace,—a madman!—yea I
    vowed
That I, if any chance allowed, if e'er
To my paternal Argos I returned
A conqueror, would his avenger prove;
And by my words a bitter hate aroused.
Hence [fell] on me misfortune's earliest
    blight;
Hence ever used Ulysses to alarm   140
With fresh impeachments; hence he used
    to strew
Equivocal expressions through the mob,
And seek in complot means of [harm];
    nor, sooth,
He rested till, with Calchas for a tool,—
But yet why these distasteful truths do I
In vain unfold? Or wherefore you detain?
If all Achæans in one rank ye hold,
And this it is enough to hear, at once
Take vengeance : this the Ithacan would
    wish,
And Atreus' sons at heavy cost would buy.'
"But then we burn to question, and to
    seek   151
The reasons, unaware of villainies
So deep, and craft Pelasgic. Quaking he
Proceeds, and from a traitor-bosom speaks :
"'Oft longed the Danai their flight to
    plan,
Troy left behind, and with the lengthened
    war
Outwearied, to retire ;—and would to
    heaven
That they had done so! Often shut them in
A felon storm of ocean; Auster, too,
Alarmed them on their setting out. In
    chief,   160
When now this horse stood framed with
    maple beams,
All thro' the welkin thundered squalls of rain.
We, poised in doubt, Eurypylus despatch,
Who Phœbus' oracles consults, and he

136.   "Wrath covered carries fate:
    Revenge is lost if I profess my hate."
                Ben Jonson, *Sejanus*, i. end.
142.   "Your faith freighted
With lies, malicious lies : your merchant Mischief;
He that ne'er knew more trade than tales, and
    tumbling
Suspicions into honest hearts."
        J. Fletcher, *Thierry and Theodoret*, i. 1.
So Satan in Milton's *Paradise Lost*, b. v.:
            "And casts between
Ambiguous words and jealousies, to sound
Or taint integrity."
149.   "Truth laughs at death,
And terrifies the killer more than killed;
Integrity thus armless seeks her foes."
        J. Fletcher, *The Queen of Corinth*, iv. 3.
159. Milton so applies "felon" to the winds in
Paradise Lost, b. i., and *Lycidas*.

These drear announcements from the shrines brings back:
"By blood and by a butchered maid ye stilled
The winds, when first, O Greeks, to Ilium's shores
Ye came ; by blood must your return be sought,
And by an Argive life atonement made."
Which sentence, when it reached the commons' ears, 170
Their souls were mazed, and through their inmost bones
An icy shudder ran,—for whom the Fates Decree it, whom Apollo may demand.
Hereon the Ithacan, with vast ado,
Drags forth the prophet Calchas to the midst :—
What mean those intimations of the gods He importunes. And many now to me
The knave's unfeeling villainy presaged,
And silently the coming [issues] saw.
He twice five days is dumb, and, cloistered up, 180
Refuses to surrender any man
By word of his, and subject him to death.
He scarce at last, enforced by lusty calls
From th' Ithacan, by concert gives to voice
A vent, and for the altar me appoints.
All acquiesced ; and [woes], which for himself
Each held in dread, when shifted from [themselves]
For ruin of a single wretch, they bore.
And now the cursed day drew nigh ; for me Were holy rites prepared, and salted grains,
And fillets [to entwine] around my brows.
Myself I rescued, I avow, from death, 192
And burst my bonds ; and in an oozy pool
Through night-time hidden in the sedge I lurked,
Till they should grant their canvas [to the gale],
If haply they would grant it. Nor with me [Rests] any hope of seeing furthermore
My ancient country, nor my darling boys,

And parent sore-desired ; whom they perchance
E'en forfeits will exact for my escape, 200
And this my fault by death of hapless ones Atone. Then thee by gods above and Powers,
Who know my truth, by— (if there any be, Which anywhere to mortals may abide),—
Unsullied faith, I pray compassionate
Such grievous woes, compassionate a soul That undergoes [distresses] not deserved.'
" To these his tears do we vouchsafe him life,
And freely pity him. E'en first himself
From off the man his handcuffs, and the bonds 210
Tight-straitened, Priam orders to be loosed,
And thus in words of kindliness he speaks:
' Whoe'er thou art, the Grecians, lost, henceforth
Do thou forget ; thou shalt be ours ; and these
At my inquiry in their truth explain :
With what intent this pile of monster-horse Have they erected ? Who the architect ?
Or what seek they? What is the holy end ? Or what the enginery of war ?' He said.
The other, versed in wiles and Grecian craft, 220
Uplifted to the stars his bond-stript hands :
'Ye, deathless fires, and your divinity,
That may not be profaned, do I,' he cries,

205. "Do pity me !
Pity's akin to love." Southern, *Oroonoko*, ii. 2.
Laocoon might have said :
"Pray heaven it be no fault !
For there's as much disease, though not to th' eye,
In too much pity as in tyranny."
Middleton, *The Phœnix*, i. 1.

206. "The quality of mercy is not strained :
It droppeth as the gentle rain from heaven Upon the place beneath ; it is twice blessed :
It blesseth him that gives and him that takes ;
'Tis mightiest in the mightiest ; it becomes The thronèd monarch better than his crown."
Shakespeare, *Merchant of Venice*, iv. 1.

207. "If powers divine
Behold our human actions,—as they do,— I doubt not, then, but innocence shall make False accusation blush, and tyranny
Tremble at patience."
Shakespeare, *Winter's Tale*, iii. 2.

208. "A free confession of a fault wins pardon ;
But, being seconded by desert, commands it."
Massinger, *The Bondman*, iii. 4.

222. So Iago attests the stars; Shakespeare, *Othello*, iii. 3 :
"Witness, you ever-burning lights above !
You elements that clip us round about !"
"Then hear me, heaven, to whom I call for right,
And you, fair twinkling stars, that crown the night."
J. Fletcher, *The Faithful Shepherdess*, iv. 4.

172. "I have a faint cold fear thrills through my veins,
That almost freezes up the heat of life."
Shakespeare, *Romeo and Juliet*, iv. 3.

174. "Art thou a statesman,
And canst not be a hypocrite ? Impossible !"
Dryden, *Don Sebastian*, ii. 1.

186. "What man, when condemned,
Did ever find a friend ? Or who dares lend An eye of pity to that star-crossed subject,
On whom his sovereign frowns ?"
Massinger, *The Emperor of the East*, v. 1.

192. "To cheat the cheater, was no cheat, but justice."
Ben Jonson, *The Staple of News*, v. 1.

'Attest ; ye, altars and accursèd swords,
Which I escaped, and fillets of the gods,
Which I a victim bare ; 'tis free to me
The hallowed obligations of the Greeks
To cancel ; it is free to me to loathe the men,
And all [their plans] to bring beneath the light,
If any they disguise ; nor am I tied   230
By any laws of country. Do but thou
By thy engagements stand, and when thou'rt saved
Save thou thy credit, Troy, if I true [facts]
Adduce, if large [returns] I thee repay.
"'The Grecians' every hope and confidence
Upon the war commenced, for ever stood
By Pallas' aid. But truly from the [hour,]
That Tydeus' godless son, Ulysses, too,
Crime-planner, the Palladium, big with fate,
Essaying from her hallowed fane to wrest,—
The sentries of the highest tower slain,—
Engrasped the holy image, and with hands
Of blood the goddess' maiden wreaths presumed   243
To taint, thenceforth began to ebb away,
And, slowly sinking, to be carried back,
The hope of Grecians ; shattered were their powers ;
Estranged the goddess' mind. Nor tokens these
With doubtful omens did Tritonia deign.
The image scarce was planted in the camp :—
Flared bick'ring fires from its erected eyes,
And briny sweat coursed o'er its limbs ; and thrice   251
She,—wondrous to be told,—from earth sprang up,
Both buckler wielding and a quiv'ring lance.
Straight Calchas chanteth that the seas in flight
Should be attempted ; nor that Pergamus
Could be uprooted by Argolic arms,
Unless the omens they should seek anew
At Argos, and the deity restore,
Which o'er the main, and in their bending barks,

They with them have conveyed away.
And now,   260
Seeing that with the breeze they have sought out
Their home Mycenæ, arms and comrade-gods
Are they preparing, and upon the main,
Repassed, will unexpectedly be here :
So Calchas methodises the portents.
This figure for Palladium's sake, for sake
Of the offended godship, they, when warned,
Erected, to atone their rueful guilt.
Howbeit Calchas ordered to upraise
[Of] monster [bulk] this pile, with carpentry   270
Of sturdy woods, and stretch it out to heaven,
That through the gates it might not be received,
Or brought within the city ; nor the race
Beneath the ancient veneration guard.
For, if your hand profaned Minerva's gifts,
Then vast destruction (which presage may gods
The rather turn against himself !) to sway
Of Priam, and to Phrygians, would ensue.
But if by your own hands it mounted up
Upon the city, Asia uncompelled   280
With mighty war to Pelops' walls would come,
And these decrees our children's children wait.'
"By such a stratagem, and artifice
Of perjured Sinon is the tale believed ;
And they are caught by craft and forcèd tears,
Whom neither did the son of Tydeus,
Nor did Achilles, of Larissa ['s land],
No, not ten years reduced, no, not a thousand keels.
"Here to us wretches is another [scene]
Presented, graver, and more terrible by far,   290
And it dismays our unforeseeing breasts.
Laocoon, for Neptune fixed by lot
The priest, was butchering a giant bull

265. Though *digerit*, v. 182, seems scarcely to bear it, yet the context almost requires the line to be rendered thus :
" 'Tis thus that Calchas construes the portents."
276. "That, O ye Heavens, defend ! and turne away
From her unto the miscreant himselfe !"
Spenser, *Faerie Queene*, v. 8, 19.
280. Or, according to Wagner and Forbiger : "from afar."
283.   "Be murderous still ;
But, when thou strik'st, with unseen weapons kill."
Webster, *Appius and Virginia*, ii. 3.
"Treason has done his worst."
Shakespeare, *Macbeth*, iii. 2.

232.   "For great men,
Till they have gained their ends, are giants in
Their promises, but, those obtained, weak pigmies
In their performance."
Massinger, *The Great Duke of Florence*, ii. end.

233. "Oh heaven ! oh earth ! bear witness to this sound,
And crown what I profess with kind event,
If I speak true ; if hollowly, invert
What best is boded me to mischief !"
Shakespeare, *Tempest*, iii. 1.

Hard by the reverend altars. But, behold!
From Tenedos, along the calmy deeps,
(I shudder as I tell [the tale],) two snakes
With coils enormous lean upon the main,
And towards the shores at even pace advance ;
Whose breasts, among the billows reared aloft,
And crests blood-tinted, overtop the waves ;
Their other part sweeps ocean in the rear,
And arches in a fold their boundless chines :
A roar arises, with the briny flood   303
In foam. And now the lands they reached, and, stained
O'er eyes of flame with blood and fire, they licked
Their hissing mouths with bick'ring tongues. We fly
In all directions, bloodless at the sight.
They seek Laocoon in steady march ;
And first the tiny frames of his two sons
Each serpent, clipping them, infolds, and preys   310
Upon their wretched members with his fang.
Next, him [the father], coming up with aid,
And weapons bringing, do they clutch, and swathe
With giant rings. And now his midriff twice
Embracing, twice entwining round his neck
Their scaly backs, o'ertop him with their head
And necks on high. He straightway with his hands
To tear the knots asunder strains, bedrenched
Upon the wreaths with gore and sable bane ;
At once dread cries he raises to the stars :
Such roarings as, what time a bull hath fled
The altar, struck with wounds, and from his neck   322
Hath shaken out the undecisive axe.
But to the temple's summit with a glide
The dragons twain escape away, and seek
The tow'r of fell Tritonis, and beneath
The goddess' feet, and 'neath her disc of shield,
Are screened. Then sooth throughout their frighted breasts
Creeps strange alarm on all ; and for his crime
Laocoon they say had duly paid,   330
Who with his spear-head marred the holy wood,
And hurled against its back an impious lance,
That to its seat the image should be brought,

And power of the goddess be implored,
They shout at once. We rive the walls, and ope
The bulwarks of the city. Gird them all
To toil, and lay beneath its feet the roll
Of wheels, and hempen fetters on its neck
They strain. The fateful engine mounts the walls,
Teeming with weapons. Round it do the lads,   340
And lasses unespoused, chant holy [hymns],
And with their hand delight to touch the rope.
It steals along, and tow'ring up it glides
Upon the city's heart. O native land !
O Ilium, home of deities, and walls
Of Dardan sons renowned in war ! Four times
Within the very threshold of the gate
It halted, and from out the womb a clank
Four times the weapons gave. Yet press we on,
Unthinking, and with frenzy blind, and bring   350
The evil-omened monster to a stand
Within the hallowed citadel. Then, too,
With fates to come Cassandra opes her lips,
By mandate of the god not e'er believed
By Trojans. We the temples of the gods,
Ill-starred, to whom was that our latest day,
With festal leafage through the city deck.
"Meanwhile the heav'n is wheeled around, and Night
Swoops on from ocean, wrapping deep in gloom
Both earth, and sky, and Myrmidons' deceits.   360
Thro'out the city spread, to silence dropped
The Trojans : sleep infolds their jaded limbs.
And now the Argive host in marshalled ships
Was moving on from Tenedos, amid

---

353. Cassandra might have said :
"How you stand, gaping all
On your grave oracle, your wooden god there !"
But they would have replied :
"Then, sir, I'll tell you a secret :
Suspicion's but at best a coward's virtue."
             Otway, *Venice Preserved*, iii. end.

358.   " Ere the bat hath flown
His cloistered flight ; ere to black Hecate's summons
The shard-borne beetle, with his drowsy hums,
Hath rung night's yawning peal, there shall be done
A deed of dreadful note."
             Shakespeare, *Macbeth*, iii. 2.

The kindly stillness of the silent Moon,
In quest of the familiar shores, what time
Its fires the royal ship had hoisted up;
And, shielded by unfair decrees of gods,
The Danai, imprisoned in its womb,
The fir-wood bars too, Sinon frees by
   stealth. 370
These doth the opened horse to air restore,
And blithe withdraw them from the hollow
   wood
Thessander, Sthenelus too, foremost [they],
And dread Ulysses, sliding down a rope
Let fall, and Achamas, and Thoas,
And Peleus' grandson, Neoptolemus,
And first Machaon, Menelaus too,
And e'en Epeos, framer of the fraud.
They storm the city, buried in its sleep
And wine; the sentinels are put to death;
And thro' the open portals all their friends
Do they admit, and join their complice
   bands. 382
"The hour it was, wherein their maiden
   rest
Begins with heart-sick mortals, and steals
   on,
By gift of gods thrice-welcome. In my
   sleep,
Behold! before mine eyes in deepest woe

---

365.   "Up! I beseech thee,
Thou lady regent of the air, the Moon,
And lead me by thy light to some brave vengeance!"
    Middleton, *The Spanish Gipsy*, i. 3.

"Queen, and huntress, chaste and fair,
  Now the sun is laid to sleep,
Seated in thy silver chair,
  State in wonted manner keep:
Hesperus entreats thy light,
Goddess, excellently bright.

"Earth, let not thy envious shade
  Dare itself to interpose;
Cynthia's shining orb was made
  Heav'n to clear, when day did close:
Bless us then with wishèd sight,
Goddess excellently bright."
    Ben Jonson, *Cynthia's Revels*, v. 3.

386, &c. So Shakespeare makes Cassandra cry, when she sees Hector going to battle for the last time; *Troilus and Cressida*, v. 3:

"O farewell, dear Hector.
Look, how thou diest! Look, how thy eye turns
   pale!
Look, how thy wounds do bleed at many vents!
Hark, how Troy roars! How Hecuba cries out!
How poor Andromache shrills her dolours forth!
Behold, destruction, frenzy, and amazement,
Like witless antics, one another meet,
And all cry—Hector, Hector's dead, O Hector!"

"O Hamlet, what a falling off was there."
    Hamlet, i. 5.

"What a mockery hath death made thee! Thou
   look'st sad.
In what place art thou? in yon starry gallery?
Or in the cursèd dungeon?"
    Webster, *Vittoria Corombona*, v. 1.

Seemed Hector to be near me, and outpour
A flood of tears, dragged onward by the
   car,
As erst, and coaly-black with gory dust,
And through his swollen feet transpierced
   with thongs. 390
Ah, woe is me! in what a plight he was!
How altered from that Hector, who re-
   turns
Garbed in Achilles' spoils, or having hurled
Upon the ships of Greeks the Phrygian
   fires!—
A frowsy beard, and blood-beclotted locks,
Those wounds, too, wearing, which, full
   many a one,
Around his native walls did he receive.
Weeping myself, I, unaddressed, appeared
The hero to accost, and forth to draw
The mournful accents: 'O Dardania's light,
O stanchest hope of Trojans, what delays
So great have held thee back? From re-
   gions what, 402
O Hector sore-desired, dost come? How
   thee,
After the many deaths of thy own [friends],
After the changeful toils, alike of men,
And city, do we, worn to death, behold!
What shameful cause hath marred thy gentle
   looks?
Or why these wounds do I descry?' He
   naught;
Nor heeds me as I bootless [questions] ask:
But deeply from the bottom of his breast
Groans heaving: 'Ah! escape, O goddess-
   born, 411
And snatch thee from these blazes,' he ex-
   claims;
'The foe is in possession of the walls;
Down topples Troja from her stately height.
Enough for Priam and for country done.
Could Pergamus by right hand have been
   screened,
It even had been screened by this. To thee
Her holy rites and her Penates Troy
Intrusts: these take the comrades of thy
   fates;

---

403. It seems very stiff to connect *ut*, v. 283, with *defessi*, 285. Nor does the view seem consistent with the context, which in various ways expresses the desire to see Hector, with surprise and delight at the sight.

410. "Could words express the story I've to tell you,
Fathers, these tears were useless, these sad tears,
That fall from my old eyes. But there is a cause
We all should weep, tear off these purple robes,
And wrap ourselves in sackcloth, sitting down
On the sad earth, and cry aloud to heaven:
Heaven knows, if yet there be an hour to come,
Ere Venice be no more."
    Otway, *Venice Preserved*, iv. 2.

With these a city seek, [that city] grand,
Which, ocean traversed, thou shalt rear at last.' 421
So speaks he; and the fillets with his hands,
And Vesta puissant, and her deathless fire,
From th' inmost sanctuaries forth he brings.
"Meanwhile the city is by wide-spread woe
Turmoiled; and more and more,—although withdrawn,
And bowered in trees, the dwelling of my sire
Anchises stood retired,—wax bright the sounds,
And fear [ful din] of arms assails. From sleep
Am I aroused, and by ascent surmount 430
The roof-top's battlements, and stand thereby
With ears erected: as what time a blaze
On growing corn, with Austers fuming, falls;
Or torrent, rav'ning with a mountain flood,
The fields is whelming, whelming merry crops,
And toils of beeves, and woods sweeps headlong off,
The wareless shepherd all aghast is struck,
While hearing from a lofty crest of rock
The din. Then sooth the certainty was clear,
And open lie the stratagems of Greeks. 440
Now the vast palace of Deiphobus,
Through mastery of Vulcan, gave a crash;
Now next him is Ucalegon ablaze;
Sigeum's friths gleam far and wide with fire.
Out bursts both shriek of men, and clang of trumps:
Arms mad I seize; nor sense enough in arms;
But to collect a band for fight, and rush
In concert with my comrades to the tower,
My very soul is burning. Rage and wrath
My mind drive headlong, and [the thought] occurs, 450
That glorious [is the end], to die in arms.
"But lo! Pantheus, from darts of Greeks escaped,
Pantheus, the son of Othrys, of the tower
And Phœbus priest, himself, with his own hand,
The holy [vessels], and the conquered gods,
His little grandson, too, is dragging on,
And wildly presses to my doors with speed.
'In what position [stands] our highest weal,
Pantheus? What citadel are we to seize?'
I scarce had spoken these, when with a groan 460
He such returns: 'To Dardanie has come
Her final day, and her avoidless hour.
We have been Trojans, Ilium has been,
And the colossal fame of Teucer's sons.
Fierce Jove to Argos has translated all;
Greeks lord it in the burning town. Aloft,
Amid the city standing, men in arms
The horse outpours, and Sinon, conqueror,
Is blending conflagrations, while he scoffs.
Others are present at the double-op'ning gates, 470
As many thousands as have ever come
From great Mycenæ. Others have with arms
Blocked up the narrow passes of the streets,
Arrayed against us; stands the falcion's edge
With flashing point, drawn, ready for the death.
Scarce the first warders of the gates essay
Encounters, and, with blindfold Mars, oppose.'
By such announcements of Othryades,
And the [impulsive] power of the gods,
Upon the flames and weapons am I borne,
Whither the fell Erinys, whither din 481
Is summoning, and shriek upraised to heaven.

---

451. "Death gives eternity a glorious breath;
O to die honoured who would fear to die?"
Marston, *The Malcontent*, v. 3.

"When our souls shall leave this dwelling,
The glory of one fair and virtuous action
Is above all the scutcheons of our tomb,
Or silken banners o'er us."
Shirley, *The Traitor*, v. 1.

463. "Ay, thus we are; and all our painted glory
A bubble that a boy blows into the air,
And there it breaks."
Beaumont and Fletcher, *The Knight of Malta*, iv. 2.

"O horror, horror!
Egypt has been! our latest hour is come!
The queen of nations from her ancient seat
Is sunk for ever in the dark abyss;
Time has unrolled her glories to the last,
And now closed up the volume."
Dryden, *All for Love*, v. 1.

---

434. This description of the rush of a mountain-torrent is imitated by Spenser; *Faërie Queene*, ii. 11, 18:

"Like a great water-flood, that tombling low
From the high mountaines, threates to overflow
With suddein fury all the fertile playne,
And the sad husbandmans long hope doth throw
Adowne the streame, and all his vowes makes vayne;
Nor bounds nor banks his headlong ruine may sustayne."

444. So Dryden, of the Fire of London; *Annus Mirabilis*, 231:

"A key of fire ran all along the shore,
And lighten'd all the river with a blaze."

Attach themselves [to me as warrior-] mates
Rhipeus, and Epytus, all-great in arms,
Presented by the moon, and Hypanis,
And Dymas, and they cluster to my side,
The young Corœbus also, Mygdon's son.
He in those days to Troy by chance had
   come,
With frantic passion for Cassandra fired,
And as a son-in-law his succor brought
To Priam and the Phrygians;—hapless
   [youth] !   491
Who heeded not the warnings of his bride,
In frenzy. Whom when, serried close, I
   saw
To be for battle bold, I furthermore
Begin with these : ' O youths, ye breasts,
   thrice-brave
In vain, if [dwells] in you a fixed desire
To follow him who dares the last attempts,
What stands the fortune of the state ye see;
All have withdrawn, their shrines and altars
   left,—
The deities, by whom this realm had stood;
Ye help a burning city : let us die,   501
And charge upon the centre of the frays.
The only safety is for vanquished men
No safety to expect. 'Twas thus that madness
Was in the young men's souls infused.
   Thereon,—
As wolves, freebooters in a murky mist,
Whom hath the felon rage of appetite
Unkennelled, blindfold, and their quitted
   cubs
Look out for them with thirsty jaws,—
   through darts,
Thro' foes, on no uncertain death do we 510

Advance, and keep the central city's route :
Round hovers ebon Night with vaulted
   shade.
Who that night's havoc, who its deaths in
   speech
Develop may, or with his tears can match
Its suff'rings ? Down the agèd city falls,
That held dominion through so many years;
Full many corses motionless are strewn
At every step alike throughout the streets,
And thro' the houses, and the holy fanes
Of gods. Nor is it Teucer's sons alone 520
That pay amercements with their blood:
   at times,
E'en to the hearts of vanquished men re-
   turns
Their prowess, and their Grecian victors
   fall.
Grim woe on every side, on every side
Alarm, and many, many a shape of death.
" Androgeus first, with mighty throng of
   Greeks
Escorting him, presents himself to us,
In ignorance supposing we were troops
Allied, and, unaddressed, with friendly
   words
Accosts us : ' Hasten on, ye heroes ! Pray
What sloth so late delays you ? Others
   sack   531
And plunder burning Pergamus, [while] ye
Are now first coming from the lofty ships!'.
He said, and in a trice (for no replies
Were granted, worthy of sufficient trust,)
Perceived that he was fallen on the midst
Of enemies. He stood aghast, and back
His foot along with voice he checked, like
   one,

---

495.   " Fortune's browe hath frowned,
   Even to the utmost wrinkle it can bend :"
" Fortune my fortunes, not my minde shall shake."
   Marston, *Antonio and Mellida*, P. 1, iii.
" Fall what can fall, I dare the worst of fate.
Though the foundation of the earth should shrink,
The glorious eye of heaven lose his splendour,
Supported thus, I'll stand upon the ruins,
And seek for new life here."
         Massinger, *The Duke of Milan*, i. 3.
499. " When our great monarch into exile went,
Wit and religion suffer'd banishment:—
Thus once, when Troy was wrapp'd in fire and
   smoke,
The helpless gods their burning shrines forsook ;
They with the vanquish'd prince and party go,
And leave their temples empty to the foe."
   Dryden, *To the Lord Chancellor Hyde*, 17-23.
504.   " In our courage
And daring lies our safety."
      Massinger, *The Bondman*, iii. 3.
So Denham of the hunted stag in *Cooper's Hill* :
" Wearied, forsaken, and pursued, at last
All safety in despair of safety placed,
Courage he thence resumes, resolved to bear
All their assaults, since 'tis in vain to fear."

517.   " Behold those slaughters
The dry and withered bones of Death would bleed
   at !"
   Beaumont and Fletcher, *Valentinian*, iv. 4.
525. " I know death hath ten thousand several
   doors
For men to take their exits."
      Webster, *The Duchess of Malfi*, iv. 2.
      " The rugged Charon fainted,
And asked a navy, rather than a boat,
To ferry over the sad world that came."
        Ben Jonson, *Catiline*, i. 1.
533. It is a question whether the interrogative
form here would not be more effective :
          " Are ye
Now first arriving from the lofty ships?"
" Where was your soldiership? Why went not
   you out,
With all your right honourable valour with you?"
      J. Fletcher, *The Loyal Subject*, iv. 5.
536. "You put too much wind to your sail :
   discretion
And hardy valour are the twins of honour,
And, nursed together, make a conqueror."
      Beaumont and Fletcher, *Bonduca*, i. 1.

Who, as he presses on the ground, hath crushed
A snake, unlooked for in the thorny brakes,
And in his consternation suddenly 541
Hath started from him back, as he his wrath
Upraises, and his azure neck distends:
Not otherwise Androgeus, at the sight
Fear-smitten, was retreating. On we charge,
And on their serried arms are poured around,
And wareless of the place, and panic-seized,
In every quarter do we lay them low:
Upon the maiden effort Fortune breathes.
And here, in transport with success and soul, 550
Exclaims Corœbus: 'O my mates, where first
The path of safety Fortune shows, and where
Herself propitious she displays, let us
Pursue; change shields, and fit upon ourselves
The badges of the Grecians: [whether] guile,
Or gallantry, who questions in a foe?
Themselves shall give us arms.' Thus having said,
Thereon Androgeus' hairy-tufted helm,
And comely scutcheon of his shield he dons,
And suits an Argive's falchion to his side.
This Rhipeus, this [doth] Dymas e'en himself, 561
And [this] doth all the youth in merry mood;
With fresh [-won] spoils each arms himself.
We march,
Mixed up with Greeks,—the deity not ours;—
And many a battle through the darksome night,
Together hurtling, fight we hand to hand;
Numbers of Greeks we hurry down to hell.
Some fly in all directions to the ships,
And seek with speed the trusty shores.
Some mount
Once more in craven fear the giant horse,
And are ensconced in its familiar womb.
"Alas! 'tis nothing right that one presume 572
On deities unwilling. Lo! was dragged
With streaming locks the Priamean maid,
Cassandra, from Minerva's fane and shrines,
Stretching to heav'n her burning eyes in vain:—
Her eyes,—for bonds confined her dainty hands.

---

558. *Induitur*, v. 393, seems to be used in a middle sense.

Brooked not this sight in his bemaddened soul
Corœbus, and he flung himself, death-doomed,
Upon the centre of the squadron. One and all 580
We follow on, and charge with serried arms.
Here first from out the temple's stately cope
By darts of our own [friends] we're overwhelmed,
And a most pitiable massacre
Arises from the figure of our arms,
And misconception of our Grecian crests.
Then do the Danai with groanful sound,
And in their wrath at rescue of the maid,
Mustered from every quarter, make assault,—
Thrice-eager Ajax, and th' Atridæ twain,
And all the army of the Dolopes: 591
As, on the bursting of a hurricane,
The hostile winds at times in tourney meet,
Both Zephyrus, and Notus, Eurus too,
Blithe with his eastern steeds; the forests howl,
And with his trident foamy Nereus storms,
And wakes the waters from their lowest bed.
They too,—if any in the darkling night
By stratagem we routed thro' the gloom,
And chased all through the city,—[these] appear. 600
The first are they to recognize our shields,
And lying weapons, and to mark our tones,
As in their accent diff'ring from their own.
Straight by their number are we whelmed: and first
Corœbus, under Peneleus' right hand,
At th' altar of the goddess strong in war,
Sinks down; and Rhipeus falls, who stood among
The Teucrians the one most righteous man,
And carefullest of honor:—to the gods
It otherwise seemed good. Die Hypanis
Alike, and Dymas, by their mates transpierced. 611
Nor did thy deep religion, nor the wreath
Of Phœbus screen thee, Pantheus, in thy fall.
O Ilian ashes, and thou latest fire

---

579. "'Tis godlike in you to protect the weak."
Southern, *Oroonoko*, ii. 2.

608. "A goodness set in greatness:—how it sparkles
Afar off, like pure diamonds set in gold."
Middleton, *Women beware Women*, v. 1.

613. Or:
"Neither did thee, O Pantheus, in thy fall,
Thy deep religion, or Apollo's fillet, screen."

Of my own [friends]! I you to witness take,
That at your setting neither did I shun
The darts, nor any hazards from the Greeks;
And if the fates had [doomed] that I should fall,
I earned it by my hand. We thence are forced
Asunder: Iphitus and Pelias with myself;
Of whom was Iphitus now weighed with age, 621
And Pelias, lagging from Ulysses' wound:—
Straight called to Priam's palace by a shriek.
"But here vast fighting (as if no where else
Were other frays, none dying all thro'out
The city); Mars so unappeased, and Greeks,
On dashing to the palace, we descry;
The gates, too, leaguered by a tortoise-roof,
Advanced. The ladders grapple to the walls,
And at the very door-posts up the steps
They struggle, and their bucklers to the darts, 631
By their left hands o'ercanopied, oppose:
They grasp the battlements within their right.
The Dardans, on the other hand, the towers
And covered rooftops of the dome uproot.
With these for weapons, when the last they see,
Already at the very verge of death,
To guard them they prepare, and gilded beams,
The lofty beauties of their ancient sires,
Roll down. The rest with falchions drawn beset 640
The doors below; these [same] do they defend
In serried host. Our spirits are refreshed,
To give assistance to the king's abode,
With succor, too, the heroes to relieve,
And vigor to the vanquished to impart.
"There was an entrance, and mysterious doors,
And passage free thro' Priam's halls, from one

---

615. So Milton similarly makes Satan say; *Paradise Lost*, b. i.:
"For me be witness all the host of Heaven,
If counsels different, or dangers shunn'd
By me, have lost our hopes."

640. It should be particularly observed that verses 449, 450, allude to guards *inside* the doors; otherwise they would have been involved in the slaughter described in v. 465. This view makes v. 485 intelligible.

To other, and a portal in the rear,
Neglected; where Andromache ill-starred,
So long as the imperial sway endured, 650
Time after time, unretinued, was wont
To hasten to the parents of her spouse,
And to his father's sire to draw the lad Astyanax. I mount the battlements
Of th' highest roof, whence Teucer's wretched sons
Were hurling from the hand effectless darts.
A tower,—standing up in steepy [height],
And from the roof-tops stretched beneath the stars,
Whence used all Troy and galleys of the Greeks
To be descried, and the Achaian camp,—
Assailing it around with iron [there], 661
Where upmost stories offered weak'ning joints,
We root from its high bed, and force along.
This, toppling on a sudden, with a crash
Trails demolition, and upon the troops
Of Greeks far-wide falls down: but other [Greeks]
Succeed them; neither stones, nor any form
Of weapons in the meanwhile cease [to fly].
"Before the very entrance-court itself,
And at the outmost portal Pyrrhus bounds,
In weapons gleaming, and the sheen of bronze: 671
Such as when into light of day a snake,
On baleful grasses fed, whom, swollen out,
Cold winter was concealing 'neath the earth,
Now fresh from casted slough, and sleek with youth,
Rolls on his slippery chine with lifted chest,
Erected to the sun, and in his mouth
Is quiv'ring with a triply-cloven tongue.
Along with him the giant Periphas,
And, of Achilles' coursers charioteer, 680
His squire Automedon; along with him
All Scyros' youth advance beneath the dome,
And blazes volley to the roofs. Himself
Among the foremost, with his battle-axe
Engrasped, is bursting through the stubborn gates,
And tearing down the doors from off their hinge,
[Though] bound with bronze; and now,—when hewed away
The [cross-] beam,—hath he hollowed out the planks,
[Though] stable oak, and with a spacious gap

---

666. "When Greeks joined Greeks, then was the tug of war." Lee, *Rival Queens*, iv. 1.

A mighty op'ning made. Appears the
   dome 690
Within, and lengthful courts lie ope;
   appear
The private halls of Priam and the kings
Of olden days; and [warriors] clad in arms
Behold they standing in the foremost gate.
"But th' inner palace is with moanful
   sound,
And hubbub sad turmoiled, and in its
   depths
With women's wails the vaulted chambers
   shriek:
Their howling strikes the golden stars.
   Then dames
In panic thro' the vast apartments stray,
And, hugging, grasp the posts, and kisses
   print. 700
On presses Pyrrhus with his father's might;
Nor him can bolts nor guards themselves
   sustain.
Gives way the gate before the frequent ram,
And, wrenched from off the hinge, down
   sink the doors.
By pow'r a path is made: the Greeks, in-
   poured,
An entrance force, and massacre the first,
And wide with soldiery each spot they fill.
Not so [resistless], when from bursten dams
The foamy river hath escaped away,

And mastered in its gulf the barrier-
   mounds, 710
'Tis carried onward frantic in a pile
Upon the fields, and all throughout the
   plains
The cattle with their cotes it sweepeth off.
I Neoptolemus beheld myself
Insane with butchery, and in the gate
Atreus' twain sons; I Hecuba beheld,
And her one hundred daughters; Priam,
   too,
Among the altars staining with his blood
The fires, which he himself had sanctified.
Those fifty nuptial chambers, hope so great
Of children's children; doors, with foreign
   gold 721
And trophies haught, down tumbled to the
   ground:
Possess the Danai, where fails the flame.
"Perchance, too, what was Priam's
   doom thou may'st
Demand. What time the captured city's
   fall,
And palace-gates demolished, he beheld,
The foeman, too, amid his private halls,
His armor, long disused, the aged [sire]
Around his shoulders, shivering with eld,
Throws idly, and in bootless sword is girt,
And on the serried foemen is he borne, 731
Death-doomed. Amid the courts, and
   underneath
The naked vault of heav'n, an altar vast
There stood, and nigh, a very ancient bay,
O'er th' altar bending, and the household
   gods
Imbosoming in shade. Here Hecuba,
Her daughters, too, in vain the altars
   round,
As headlong pigeons in a murky storm,
Close nestled, and the figures of the
   gods
Embracing, sat. But Priam, e'en himself,
In youthful arms assumed when she be-
   held:— 740
'What such dread aim, O most unhappy
   spouse,
Hath driv'n thee to be harnessed in these
   arms?
Or whither rushest?' cries she: 'No such
   aid,

---

694. *Vident*, v. 485; *i.e.*, the besiegers see. See note on line 640.

697. "The tragic voice of women strikes mine ear."
    Shirley, *The Brothers*, v. 1.

698. "As he that strives to stop a suddein flood,
And in strong bancks his violence enclose,
Forceth it swell above his wonted mood,
And largely overflow the fruitfull plaine,
That all the countrey seemes to be a maine,¹
And the rich furrowes flote, all quite fordonne;
The wofull husbandman doth lowd complaine
To see his whole yeares labor lost so soone."
    Spenser, *F. Q.*, iii. 7, 34.

"So from the hills, whose hollow caves contain
The congregated snow and swelling rain,
Till the full stores their ancient bounds disdain;
Precipitate the furious torrent flows:
In vain would speed avoid, or strength oppose:
Towns, forests, herds, and men, promiscuous drown'd,
With one great death deform the dreary ground;
The echo'd woes from distant rocks resound."
    Prior, *Solomon*, b. ii.

"Well did he know
How a tame stream does wild and dangerous grow
By unjust force: he now with wanton play
Kisses the smiling banks, and glides away;
But, his known channel stopped, begins to roar,
And swell with rage, and buffet the dull shore;
His mutinous waters hurry to the war,
And troops of waves come rolling from afar;
Then scorns he such weak stops to his free source,
And overruns the neighbouring fields with violent course."
    Cowley, *Davideis*, b. i.

717. *Nurus*, v. 501, of course properly means "daughters-in-law;" of which, however, as Hecuba had only fifty, the word must be taken in a sense to include her fifty daughters as well. It evidently means the same as *natæ*, v. 515. In the same loose way *patres* is used, v. 579.

721. "Or where the gorgeous East with richest hand
Showers on her kings barbaric pearl and gold."
    Milton, *P. L.*, b. ii.

Nor guardians such as these, the crisis needs;
No, not if e'en my Hector now were here.
Hither, I pray, repair; this altar all
Will shield, or thou shalt die along with us.'
Thus having from her lips out-spoken, she
Recovered to her [side] the agèd [king],
And set him down upon the holy seat. 750
"But lo! from Pyrrhus' butchery escaped,
Polites, one of Priam's sons, through darts,
Through foes, flies o'er the lengthful colonnades,
And, wounded, traverses the empty halls.
Him fiery Pyrrhus with a hostile wound
Pursues, and now, this moment, in his hand
He clutches him, and spears him with his lance.
When he at last before his parents' eyes
And presence came, he dropped, and life outpoured
With floods of blood. Here Priam, though he now 760
Is grappled in the [very] midst of death,
Natheless forbore not, nor his voice and wrath
He spared: 'Yet may to thee for [this thy] guilt,'
He cries, 'for such audacious deeds, the gods
(If dwells there any righteousness in heaven,
Which may concern itself about the like),
Repay meet thanks, and guerdons due return;
Who in my presence forced me to behold
The murder of my son, and with his death
Hast fouled a father's sight. But ne'er was he, 770
From whom thou falsely sayest thou art sprung,—
Achilles,—such to Priam, [though] a foe,
But he a suitor's rights and trust revered,
And Hector's lifeless body for the grave
Restored, and passed me to my kingdom back.'
So spake the agèd [monarch], and a dart,

744. "This fighting fool wants policy."
Beaumont and Fletcher, *The Maid's Tragedy*, iii. end.
"*Duke.* Dost thou not shake?
Bianca. For what? to see a weak,
Faint, trembling arm advance a leaden blade?
Alas! good man, put up, put up; thine eyes
Are likelier much to weep, than arms to strike."
Ford, *Love's Sacrifice*, v. 1.

747. "Who would not die with all the world about him?" Ben Jonson, *Catiline*, iii. 1.

A feeble [dart], without a stroke, he hurled,
Which by the grating bronze was straight rebuffed,
And on the buckler's boss-tip idly hung.
T' whom Pyrrhus: 'Therefore these thou shalt report, 780
And go a messenger to Peleus' son,
My sire; to him my barbarous exploits,
And Neoptolemus degenerate,
Mind thou to tell. Now die!' He, saying this,
Up to the very altars dragged him on,
[All] in a quake, and slipping on his son's
Abundant blood, and in his left hand he
His tresses interlaced, and in his right
A flashing sword upraised, and plunged it deep
Up to the very handle in his side. 790
This the conclusion was of Priam's fates;
This end through fortune swept him off, while he
Beholds his Troy ablaze, and Pergamus
In ruins, o'er so many tribes and lands
Of Asia erst proud ruler. On the shore
His giant trunk is lying, and the head
Torn from the shoulders, e'en a nameless corse.

777. "Breathes there a spirit
In such a heap of age?"
Middleton, *The Spanish Gipsy*, v. 2.

784. A less cruel man than he might have said:
"The rigour and extremity of law
Is sometimes too, too bitter, but we carry
A chancery of pity in our bosom."
Ford, *Perkin Warbeck*, ii. 2.

797. The 'ideas in verses 557, 8, are partly embodied by Thomson in Massinissa's address to Sophonisba, act iv. 5:
"Nor a world combined
Shall tear thee from me, till outstretch'd I lie,
A nameless corse."
The same expression occurs in Spenser, *F. Q.*, iv. 8, 49:
"Therefore Corflambo was he cald aright,
Though namelesse there his bodie now doth lie."
There was none to cry over the hapless Priam:
"Call for the robin-redbreast and the wren,
Since o'er shady groves they hover,
And with leaves and flowers do cover
The friendless bodies of unburied men,
Call unto his funeral dole
The ant, the field-mouse, and the mole,
To rear him hillocks that shall keep him warm,
And, when gay tombs are robbed, sustain no harm."
Webster, *Vittoria Corombona*, v. 1.
His fate must call to mind Shirley's noble song:
"The glories of our blood and state
Are shadows, not substantial things;
There is no armour against fate;
Death lays his icy hand on kings:

v. 559—578. BOOK II. v. 578—593. 113

" But then it was that terrible dismay
First compassed me around. I stood
　　aghast. 799
Occurred the picture of my darling sire,
When I the king, in age his fellow, saw
His life outbreathing from a grisly wound ;
Occurred the lorn Creusa, and a home
Dismantled, and the young Iulus' fate.
I look abroad, and what about me be the
　　force
Examine. All have left me, wearied out,
And with a spring their bodies to the earth
Have launched, or giv'n them feebled to
　　the fires.
"And thus I now the single one survived,
When by the gates of Vesta harb'ring close,
And noiseless skulking in a lone retreat,
I Tyndaris espy. The brilliant fires 812
Gave me their light while wand'ring, and
　　around
Thro' every [object] carrying on mine eyes.
She at the Teucri, 'gainst herself incensed,
Upon account of Pergamus o'erthrown,
And at the vengeance of the Greeks, and
　　wrath
Of her abandoned spouse, in previous
　　dread,—
Of Troja [she], and of her native land
The common Fury,—had concealed herself,
And by the altars, loathed, was sitting down.
Fires kindled up within my soul ; succeeds
A rage my sinking country to avenge, 823
And penalties inflict, by guilt deserved.
' Forsooth shall she her Sparta, free from
　　harm,
Mycenæ of her fathers, too, behold,

And with a triumph won proceed a queen ?
Alike a nuptial union, and a home,
Her parents and her children shall she see,
Escorted by a bevy of the dames 830
Of Ilium, and by Phrygian serving-men ?
Shall Priam 'neath the falcion have suc-
　　cumbed ?
Shall Troy have burnt with fire ? The
　　Dardan strand
So many times have reeked with blood ?
　　Not so !
For though there's no renown, for mention
　　meet,
In chastisement of woman, nor enjoys
The conquest [any] honor, ne'ertheless,
For having quenched a guilty soul, and ta'en
The vengeance it deserves, shall I be
　　praised ;
And it will be a pleasure to have cloyed
A passion for retributory fire, 841
And satisfied the ashes of my friends.'
I such was casting, and in rage of soul
Was hurried onward, when my mother boon,
Never before so brilliant in mine eyes,
Herself presented visibly to me,
And 'mid the gloom in crystal sheen she
　　beamed ;
Displaying all the goddess, and in guise
And stature such as she is wont t' appear
To denizens of heav'n ; and me, engrasped
By my right hand, did she restrain, and
　　these 851
Moreover added from her rubied lip :

835.　　　　" 'Twas a manly blow :
　　The next thou giv'st, murder some sucking infant,
　　And then thou wilt be famous."
　　　　　Webster, *Vittoria Corombona*, v. 2.

Scepter and crown
　　Must tumble down,
And in the dust be equal made
With the poor crooked scythe and spade.
" Some men with swords may reap the field,
And plant fresh laurels where they kill ;
But their strong nerves at last must yield :
They tame but one another still :
　　Early or late,
　　They stoop to fate,
And must give up their murmuring breath,
When they, pale captives, creep to death.
" The garlands wither on your brow,
Then boast no more your mighty deeds !
Upon Death's purple altar now,
See, where the victor-victim bleeds :
　　Your heads must come
　　To the cold tomb ;
Only the actions of the just
Smell sweet, and blossom in their dust."
　　　The Contention of Ajax and Ulysses.
820. " Sith women's wits work men's unceasing
woes."
　　Peele, *The Arraignment of Paris*, iv. 1.
821. Surely there has been enough said of secrecy
already. *Secreta, latentem,* and *abdiderunt* may
fairly relieve *invisa* from a weakness.

　　　　　　　" 'Tis a woman :
A subject not for swords, but pity."
　　Beaumont and Fletcher, *Valentinian*, v. 8.
839.　" Fie ! Your sword upon a woman ?"
　　　　Shakespeare, *Othello*, v. 2.
" And none so much as blame the murderer,
But rather praise him for that brave attempt,
And in the chronicle enrol his name,
For purging of the realm of such a plague."
　　　　　Marlowe, *Edward the Second.*
Yet most people would have applied to him what
we are told by Q. Curtius (8, i. 52) that Clytus said
to Alexander :
　" Philip fought men, but Alexander women."
　　　　　Lee, *Rival Queens*, iv. 2.
840. *Expleo* in Virgil, and it would seem in all
other authors, always takes an accusative. In the
very next line, v. 587, *satiasse* commands the same
case. To resort, then, to a Græcism is worse than
needless. However, it must be confessed that
animum flammæ is a very awkward expression.
848. Literally, of course : " Owning herself a
goddess."
852. *Roseo ore,* v. 593, would so be rendered by
Milton. See *Comus* :
　　" Thrice upon thy finger's tip,
　　　Thrice upon thy rubied lip."

I

'My son, what such deep anguish rouseth up
Thy uncontrolled resentments? Why dost
    rage?
Or whither hath thy love of us withdrawn?
Wilt thou not first consider where thy
    sire
Anchises, worn with age, thou may'st have
    left?
Whether thy spouse Creusa be alive,
Ascanius, too, thy boy? round all of
    whom
The Grecian troops from every quarter
    rove;   860
And, did not my solicitude withstand,
Already would the flames have swept them
    off,
And hostile sword have drained them. Not
    for thee
Doth Spartan Tyndaris' detested face,
Or Paris, the rebuked ;—the ruthlessness
Of gods, of gods,—this realm doth over-
    throw,
And razes Troja from its crest. Behold!—
For all the mist, which now o'er thee
    dispread,
While gazing, dims thy mortal ken, and
    dank
Around bedarks thee, will I clear away; 870
Do thou no mandates of thy parent fear,
Nor her injunctions to obey refuse :—
Here, where disscattered heaps, and stones
    from stones
Asunder wrenched, thou viewest, and the
    smoke,
Upsurging with commingled dust, the walls
And their foundations, torn away,
With his colossal trident Neptune shakes,
And the whole city from its bed uproots.
Here Juno, trebly-furious, in the van
Maintains [possession of] the Scæan gates,
And, frantic, from the ships her fed'rate
    force,   881
With falcion girt, is calling. Now, observe,
Tritonian Pallas on the castle heights
Has ta'en her post, in storm-cloud gleam-
    ing forth
And Gorgon grim. . The Sire himself to
    Greeks
Courage and prosp'ring arms supplies;
    himself
The gods awakes against the Dardan arms.

Snatch flight, my son, and put an end to toil :
On no occasion shall I stand aloof,
And safe will set thee in thy father's gate.'
She said, and in the clustered shades of
    night   891
Herself she buried. Spectres dread appear,
And, foes to Troy, the mighty pow'rs of
    gods.
"Then, sooth, all Ilium seemed to me
    to sink
Upon the fires, and from its base Nep-
    tunian Troy
To be o'erturned : as e'en on mountain
    heights
An agèd ash, when hewed around by steel
And many an axe, in rivalry the swains
Press on to overthrow ; it ever threats,
And, forced to quiver, on its shaken crest
Its locks it nods, until, by slow degrees 901
Thro' wounds subdued, it deep hath groaned
    its last,
And, wrested from the brows, hath trailed
    a wreck.
I downward pass, and—deity my guide—
Amid the fire and foes am I brought clear :
Give place the weapons, and the flames
    retreat.
"And when I now am at the door ar-
    rived
Of my paternal seat, and ancient home,
My father, whom in chief I yearned to bear
Off to the lofty mounts, and chief I sought,
His life,—Troy razed,—refuses to prolong,
And banishment to brook. 'O ye, with
    whom   912
Your blood in age is unimpaired,' he cries,
'And firmly stand your pow'rs in native
    might,
Plan ye escape. If heav'n's inhabitants
Had willed that I should lengthen out my
    life,
This residence for me they would have saved.
Enough, and more !—one wreck have we
    beheld ;
A captured city, too, survived. Oh! thus,
My corpse, thus laid, addressing, ye depart.
I by [some] hand myself a death will find :

---

864. "Was this the face that launched a thousand
    ships,
And burnt the topless towers of Ilium ?"
    Marlowe, *Doctor Faustus*.
        "Why did Nature
Empty her treasure in thy face, and leave thee
A black, prodigious soul ?"
    Shirley, *The Wedding*, ii. 3.
865. Or : "Paris the condemned."

893. "Then let me stay ; and, father, do you fly :
Your loss is great, so your regard should be ;
My worth unknown, no loss is known in me.
Upon my death the French can little boast ;
In your's they will, in you all hopes are lost.
Flight cannot stain the honour you have won,
But mine it will, that no exploit have done.
You fled for vantage every one will swear,
But if I bow, they'll say it was for fear.
There is no hope that ever I will stay,
If the first hour I shrink and run away.
Here on my knee, I beg mortality,
Rather than life preserved with infamy."
    Shakespeare, *K. Henry V.*, iv. 5.

The foe will pity me, and seek the spoils.
Easy the loss of grave. This long time past
I, loathed by gods and worthless, stay the
　years,　　　　　　　　　　　　　924
Since me the sire of gods and king of men
Hath blasted with his levin-storms, and
　scathed
With fire.' In saying such he stiffly stood,
And fixed continued. On the other hand,
Dissolved in tears are we,—alike my spouse
Creusa, and Ascanius, even all　　　930
The household, lest my sire should be
　content
Our all to ruin with himself, and press
Upon the doom that hastens. He declines,
And to his aim, and in the selfsame seat,
He clings. Once more I'm hurried on to
　arms,
And deeply wretched do I long for death.
For what device, or what the chance was
　now
Vouchsafed? 'That I could stir a foot, O
　sire,
When thou wert left behind, could'st thou
　expect?
And hath so dark a guilt a father's lips 940
Escaped? If pleaseth it the gods above,
That out of so immense a city naught
Be left, and this [resolve] within thy mind
Is seated, and to Troja, doomed to die,
It joys to link alike thyself, and thine,—
The gate lies open to a death [like] that,
And Pyrrhus will anon be present here
From Priam's plenteous blood, [the mis-
　creant,]
Who slays a son before a father's eyes,
The father at his altars. Was't for this, 950
O mother boon, that me through darts,
　through fires,
Thou sav'st, that [I] amid our private halls
[Should look upon] a foeman; yea, that I
Ascanius, and my father, and Creusa near,
One butchered in the other's blood, should
　see?
Arms, heroes, bring my arms: their latest
　light
The conquered calls. Restore me to the
　Greeks;
Let me again go see the fights renewed:
We ne'er shall all this day die unavenged.'
"Thereon with steel am I begirt once
　more;　　　　　　　　　　　　　960
And I was introducing my left hand
Within my shield, adjusting it [thereto],
And bearing me outside the halls: but lo!
My feet embracing, in the threshold clung
My spouse, and young Iulus to his sire

Held out. 'If thou dost go to meet thy
　doom,
Snatch us too with thyself to every [risk]:
But if, from trial, any hope in arms
Assumed thou restest, first this home de-
　fend.
To whom is young Iulus, t' whom thy sire,
[To whom] am I too left, once called thy
　wife?　　　　　　　　　　　　　971
"Such venting loud, with moaning all
　the house
She filled, when rises up a prodigy,
A sudden one, and marv'llous to be told.
For 'mid his mourning parents' hands and
　lips,
Lo! from the summit of Iulus' head
A filmy tuft is seen to shed a light,
And, harmless at the touch, a flame to lick
His silky locks, and round his brows to
　feed.
We, flurried, quake with terror, and shake
　out　　　　　　　　　　　　　980
The blazing hair, and quench the holy fires
From water-springs. But sire Anchises
His eyes uplifted to the stars, in glee, and
　forth
He stretched his hands to heaven with his
　voice:
'Almighty Jove, if thou by any prayers
Art swayed, regard us,—[I entreat] but
　this;—
And if by goodness we deserve it, deign
Thy aid, then, sire, and stablish these
　portents.'
"Scarce these the agèd [man] had said:
　forthwith
With sudden crash it thundered on the left,
And, from the welkin shooting through the
　gloom,　　　　　　　　　　　　991
A meteor, trailing on a link [of light],
With plenteous sheen careered. This,
　gliding on
Above the highest roof-tops of the dome,
In Ida's forest do we see enshroud
Its brilliant form, and marking out the
　paths.
Then in long track its furrow sheds a gleam,
And wide the spots around with sulphur
　smoke.
Here sooth my sire, o'erpowered, to the
　air
Uplifts himself, and he accosts the gods, 1000
And venerates the holy star: 'Now, now

---

936. "'Tis time to die when 'tis a shame to live."
　　Middleton, *The Changeling*, v. 3.

985. "Can men's prayers,
Shot up to Heaven with such a zeal as mine are,
Fall back like lazy mists, and never prosper?"
　　J. Fletcher, *Beggar's Bush*, iii. 4.

989. "Forthwith" is the true force of *que*, v. 692.
996. More literally: "Its brilliant self."

l 2

Is no demur ; I follow you, and where
Ye lead am present. O my father's gods,
Save ye my family, my grandson save !
Yours this presage, and in your heav'nly will
Troy rests. I sooth submit, nor, son, do I
In company with thee decline to go.'
" He said. And through the city now the fire
Is heard in greater plainness ; closer, too,
The conflagrations roll along the heat. 1010
' Then come, dear father, place thee on my neck :
Myself will on my shoulders thee support ;
Nor shall that travail weigh me down.
Howe'er events
Shall fall, a single and a common risk,
A single safety, shall there be for both.
Let young Iulus my companion be,
And from afar my consort watch our steps.
Do ye, ye servants, in your minds give heed
To what I say. When from the city passed
There stands for you a knoll, and agèd fane
Of Ceres lorn, and, nigh, a cypress-tree,
Time-honored, by the reverence of our sires
Preserved through many a year. To this one spot   1023
From different [directions] will we come.
Do thou, my father, take within thy hand
The holy [emblems] and our country's gods :
For me, departed from so sore a war,
And slaughter fresh, to touch them were a crime,
Till I have washed me in a living stream.'
These having spoken, on my shoulders broad,   1030
And neck submissive, with a robe and hide
Of tawny lion am I overlaid,
And undertake my load. In my right hand
The young Iulus twined himself, and he
His father follows with no even steps :
Behind creeps on my consort. We are borne
Through spots of shade ; and me, whom heretofore
No weapons, showered on me, would affect,
Nor clustered Grecians from a hostile band,
Now every breath alarms ; starts every sound   1040

One poised [in doubt], and equally in dread
Alike for his companion and his load.
And now was I approaching to the gates,
And all the way appeared t' have overpassed,
When suddenly a frequent din of feet
Seemed to be present at my [very] ears ;
My father, too, forth peering through the gloom,
Cries out, ' Son, fly, my son ! they're drawing nigh !
Their blazing shields and gleaming bronze I see !'
'Twas here that, flurried [as I was], from me   1050
Some Power, ill my friend, (I know not what,)
Robbed my bewildered mind. For in my course
While I the by-ways track, and pass aside
Without the public quarter of the streets,
Ah ! whether reft away from me, ill-starred,
By destiny, my spouse Creusa paused ;
Or wandered from the path ; or, faint, sat down ;—
Is unresolved : thenceforward ne'er was she
To eyes of ours restored ; nor e'er did I
Upon the lost one cast a look behind, 1060

---

hearing the noise of battle, before his junction with the Duke of Albemarle :
" With such kind passion hastes the prince to fight,
And spreads his flying canvas to the sound ;
Him whom no danger, were he there, could fright,
Now, absent, every little noise can wound."
              Annus Mirabilis, 109.
So Denham of the hunted stag in *Cooper's Hill* :
" Now every leaf, and every moving breath,
Presents a foe, and every foe a death."

1044. Weise, with other editors, reads *vicem* instead of *viam* ; an emendation which yields a better sense, though it has been attacked as bad Latin. In answer to this objection it may be observed, in the first place, that Heyne, Brunck, Markland, and Weise ought to know good Latin from bad ; and, in the second, that even if they did not, it does not at all follow that, because Virgil has used *evitasse* in connection with *vices* elsewhere, he should be confined to such a conjunction for ever. He himself seems to apply *evado* to an exactly similar expression in book x., v. 316 :
           " Casus evadere ferri
Quod licuit parvo."
However, the reading *viam* is adhered to, not because *vicem* would be bad Latin, or because there is any indifference to its yielding a far better sense, but because it seems to have no authority whatever from manuscripts.

1049. " I see the blaze of torches from afar,
And hear the trampling of thick-beating feet :
This way they move."
           Dryden, *Don Sebastian*, iv. 1.

1060. It is quite true that he would not have seen her if he had ; but he speaks of her according to his subsequent experience ; as if he had said :

1002.   " Oh ! a cherubim
Thou wast, that did preserve me. Thou didst smile,
Infused with a fortitude from heaven."
           Shakespeare, *Tempest*, i. 2.

1026. *Sacra*, v. 717, evidently refers to the image of Vesta, the fillets and the fire, mentioned in verses 296, 7.

1040. Dryden borrows the idea in these lines, when speaking of the anxiety of Prince Rupert at

Or turn a thought, until we are arrived
At ancient Ceres' hill and hallowed seat.
All being mustered here at last, 'twas she
Alone was missing, and her mates, and son,
And consort, failed. Whom both of men and gods
In frenzy did I not upbraid ? Or what
More bitter in the city razed did I
Behold? Ascanius, and my sire Anchises,
And Teucrian Penates to my mates
Do I entrust, and in a winding glen 1070
Secrete them : I myself the city seek
Once more, and am begirt in gleaming arms.
Resolved am I all hazards to renew,
And all through Troja to return, and fling
Once more my head in face of risks. At first
The walls and darkling thresholds of the gate,
Whence I had issued forth, I seek again,
And backward trace my steps, marked through the gloom,
And scan them with my eye. The dread [of night] all round,
At once the very stillness fright my soul.
Thence home, if haply she her foot, if she
Had haply [thither] moved, do I myself 1082
Betake. The Danai had rushed within,
And all the dwelling occupied. Forthwith
The glutton fire is vollied by the wind
To the roof-crests ; up mount the flames ; the tide
Is raving to the breezes. I advance,
And Priam's dome revisit and the tower.
And now within the empty colonnades,
In Juno's sanctuary, sentries choice, 1090
Phœnix and cursed Ulysses, were the spoil
Close-guarding. Hither, [drawn] from every side,
Troy's treasure, rifled from the burning shrines,
E'en boards of gods, and massy bowls of gold,
And plundered gear, are heaped together. Boys,
And quaking dames, in long array stand round.

Yea, daring e'en to fling my words thro'out
The darkness, with a cry I filled the streets,
And in my grief redoubling all in vain,
Creusa o'er and o'er again I called. 1100
While searching, and in endless rage among
The city buildings, fraught with woe [to me],
The spectre and the phantom of herself,
Creusa, loomed upon me 'fore my eyes,
And larger than the [life-] known [form] her ghost.
Aghast was I, and stood my hair on end,
And clave articulation to my jaws.
She then on this wise me accosts,
And takes away my troubles by these words :
' Why joys it thee to give such ready way
To madding sorrow, O delightsome spouse?
These happen not without the will of gods ;
Nor is it granted thee to carry off 1113
Creusa as thy comrade, nor doth he,
The lord of high Olympus [this] allow.
For thee protracted wand'rings [are in store],
And ocean's spacious surface must be ploughed ;
And thou shalt at Hesperia's land arrive,
Where Lydian Tiber thro' the wealthy fields
Of heroes with a gentle current runs. 1120
There glad estate, and realm, and queenly bride,
Are purchased for thee : drive away thy tears
For thy beloved Creusa. Ne'er shall I
The Myrmidons', or Dolopes' proud seats
Behold, or shall I go to be a thrall
To Grecian matrons,—[I,] a Dardan dame,
And spouse to th' son of Venus the divine ;
But me the sovereign mother of the gods
Holds back within these coasts. And now farewell,
And guard affection for our common son.'
These words when she delivered, me in tears,

" I did not turn my eyes back to see if Creusa were behind, who was really missing, though I did not know it at the time." The translators, generally, fall into what appears to be a weakness, by their taking *respicio* in its tropical meaning. Freund, however, adopts what seems to be the right view. The poet means Æneas to say : " I never turned a look, nor a thought, behind upon my missing wife."

1080. " No ! all is hushed, and still as death : 'tis dreadful !"
Congreve, *Mourning Bride*, ii. 1.

1106. " All which when he unto the end had heard,
Like to a weake faint-hearted man he fared
Through great astonishment of that strange sight;
And, with long locks upstanding stiffly, stared
Like one adawed with some dreadfull spright."
Spenser, *F. Q.*, v. 7, 20.

1125. Cleopatra felt as Creusa :
" Know, sir, that I
Will not wait pinion'd at your master's court ;
Nor once be chastised with the sober eye
Of dull Octavia. Shall they hoist me up,
And show me to the shouting varletry
Of censuring Rome ? Rather a ditch in Egypt
Be gentle grave to me ! Rather on Nilus' mud
Lay me stark naked, and let the water-flies
Blow me into abhorring ! Rather make
My country's high pyramides my gibbet,
And hang me up in chains !"
Shakespeare, *Ant. and Cleop.* v. 2.

And longing many a [thought] to speak,
    she left,   1132
And back retreated into filmy air.
Three times I there essayed to throw my
    arms
Around her neck; three times in vain en-
    grasped,
The phantom-form escaped my hands, a
    match
For wanton winds, and likest wingy sleep.
"Thus I at length my mates,— the night
    far spent,—

1135. So Savage, in the *Wanderer,* canto ii.
The Hermit, on the sight of the shadow of his
wife Olympia, says:
"Still thus I urge (for still the shadowy bliss
Shuns the warm grasp, nor yields the tender kiss)
Oh, fly not! fade not! Listen to Love's call;
She lives!—no more I'm man!—I'm spirit all!
Then let me snatch thee!—press thee!—take me
    whole!
Oh, close!—yet closer! closer to my soul!
Twice round her waist my eager arms entwined,
And, twice deceived, my frenzy clasp'd the wind!"

Revisit. And I here in wonder find
A mighty number of companions strange
Had tided in, both dames and men,— a
    throng   1141
Mustered for banishment, a piteous horde.
From every side they flocked, in mind and
    means
Prepared [to voyage] to whatever lands
I pleased to lead them off across the
    main.
And now upon the brows of Ida's cope
The star of morn was rising, and the day
Was ush'ring in; the Greeks, too, held the
    gates'
Beleaguered thresholds; nor was any hope
Of succor granted [to us] : I gave way,
And with my sire upraised the mountains
    sought."   1151

1151. "This is the chance of fickle Fortune's
wheel:
A prince at morn, a pilgrim ere 't be night."
                       Robert Greene, *Alphonsus,* iv.

BOOK III.

"AFTER it seemed to heav'nly Powers meet
To raze the realm of Asia, and the race
Of Priam that deserved it not, and fell
Proud Ilium, and is smoking from the
    ground
All Neptune's Troja,— climes of banish-
    ment
Wide-severed, and unpeopled lands, are we
Enforced to seek by omens of the gods;
And underneath Antandros' self, and
    mounts
Of Phrygian Ida, we a navy build,
In doubt where fates may bear us, where
    'tis deigned   10
To settle down : and muster we our men.
The dawning summer scarcely had begun,—
Straight sire Anchises to resign the sails
To fates commanded ; when the shores and
    ports
Of my paternal land in tears I leave,
The plains, too, where [once] Troja stood.
    I'm borne
A banished man upon the deep with mates,
And son, Penates, and the mighty gods.

Line 4. " Troy, that art now nought but an idle
    name,
And in thine ashes buried low dost lie,
Though whilome far much greater then thy fame,
Before that angry gods and cruell skie
Upon thee heapt a direful destinie."
                        Spenser, *F. Q.,* iii. 9, 33.

"A martial land afar with spacious
    plains
Is peopled; (Thracians till it ;) whilom
    ruled   20
By fierce Lycurgus, hostelry of yore
To Troy, and their Penates leagued [with
    ours],
While Fortune stood. I'm hither borne,
    and found
Upon the winding shore my earliest walls,
With fates unfriendly ent'ring, and the
    name,
'Æneadæ,' from my own name I coin.
"I was performing their religious rites
In honor of my Dionæan mother,
And gods, the patrons of my tasks com-
    menced ;
And to the lofty monarch of the powers 30
That haunt the heav'ns, was slaying on the
    shore
A glossy bull. By chance a mound was
    nigh,

32. This whole legend of Polydorus is finely
imitated by Spenser, *F. Q.,* i. 2, 30, 31 :
" And thinking of those braunches greene to frame
    A girlond for her dainty forehead fit,
He pluckt a bough ; out of whose rifte there came
Smal drops of gory bloud, that trickled down the
    same.

" Therewith a piteous yelling voice was heard
Crying, ' O spare with guilty hands to teare

On top whereof were cornel shrubs, and bush
Of myrtle, bristling with the serried shafts
Of lances. I approached; and from the ground
As I an effort make to wrench away
A verdant thicket, that I might imbower
The altars with its branches rife in leaves,
A fearful prodigy do I behold,
And marvellous for story. For the tree,
Which first from out the ground with bursten roots 41
Is torn,—from this flow drops of jetty blood,
And with the gore the earth distain. My limbs
Chill terror shakes, and, icy-cold, my blood
Curdles with fear. Again do I press on
E'en of another [bush] a limber twig
To wrench away, and throughly to explore
The lurking reasons:—of [this] other, too,
The jetty blood comes coursing from the bark.
I, waking many [a thought] within my mind, 50
The rural Nymphs adored, and father Mars,
Who o'er the Getic fields presides, that they
Might duly to the visions grant success,
And lighten the portent. But when the third
Lance-shafts with greater effort I assail,
And strain with knees against opposing sand ;—
Shall I speak out, or shall I hold my peace?—
From the mound's base a tearful groan is heard,
And voice, sent forth, is wafted to my ears:
'Why, O Æneas, manglest thou a wretch?
Forbear thee from [a corse] now tombed; forbear 61

Polluting thy religious hands. To thee
No stranger, me hath Troja brought to light ;
[N]or is this blood-stream dripping from a tree.
Ah! fly fell regions, fly a miser shore.
For I am Polydorus. Here transpierced
An iron crop of weapons me hath screened,
And grown upon me with their pointed darts.'
Then sooth, with doubting fear in spirit crushed,
Aghast was I, and stood my hair on end,
And clave articulation to my jaws. 71
" This Polydore, with mighty weight of gold,
Unhappy Priam whilom had by stealth
Consigned to Thracia's monarch to be reared,
When now mistrusted he Dardania's arms,
And saw the city circled by a siege.
He, when the Trojans' pow'r was broken up,
And Fortune ebbed away, the interests
Of Agamemnon, and his conqu'ring arms,
Pursuing, thro' all obligation bursts, 80
Slays Polydore, and gains the gold by force.
To what dost thou not drive the hearts of men,
Cursed greed of gold ! When shudd'ring left my bones,

My tender sides in this rough rynd embard ;
But fly, ah ! fly far hence away, for feare
Least to you hap, that happened to me heare,
And to this wretched Lady, my dear love :
O too deare love, love bought with death too deare!'
Astond he stood, and up his heare did hove ;
And with that suddein horror could no member move."

40. Or: "wondrous to be mentioned."

61. "Forbear! What art thou that dost rudely press
Into the confines of forsaken graves?
Hath death no privilege?"
Ford, *Love's Sacrifice*, v. 4.

" What call unknown, what charms presume
To break the quiet of the tomb?
Who thus afflicts my troubled sprite,
And drags me from the realms of night?

Long on these mould'ring bones have beat
The winter's snow, the summer's heat,
The drenching dews, and driving rain!
Let me, let me sleep again.
Who is he, with voice unblest,
That calls me from the bed of rest?"
Gray, *Descent of Odin*.

64. "Forbear, if thou hast pity. Ah! forbear!
These groans proceed not from a senseless plant,
No spouts of blood run welling from a tree."
Dryden, *King Arthur*, iv. 1.

77. "Our hopes all come to this! our mighty hopes,
Huge as a mountain, shrunk into a wart."
Shirley, *Honoria and Mammon*, iii. 4.

83. " That cart arrest, and raise a common cry,
For sacred hunger of my gold I die."
Dryden, *Cock and Fox*, 253, 4.

Both here and in his translation of the *Æneid*,
Dryden renders *sacer* by "sacred:" surely this is to mislead. Chaucer merely says :
" My gold caused my mordre, soth to saine."
The Nonnes Preestes Tale.

" But when the bowels of the earth were sought,
Whose golden entrails mortals did espy,
Into the world all mischief then was brought,
This framed the mint, that coined our misery."
Drayton, *Pastorals*, iv. 22.

Timon of Athens was of a different stamp from Polymestor :
" What is here?
Gold? Yellow, glittering, precious gold! No, gods,

To chosen leaders of the populace,
And to my sire the first, the gods' portents do I
Report, and what may be their judgment ask.
With all the same decision :—to withdraw
From land by guilt profaned ; that hospitage
Defiled should be abandoned ; and that we
Should grant the southern breezes to the ships. 90
So Polydorus' fun'ral we perform,
And on the mound a heap of earth is piled.
The altars to the Manes mourning stand
With dun festoons, and cypress swart ; and, round,
The Trojan women with dishevelled hair, According to the custom. We present
Boats frothing with warm milk, and bowls of holy blood ;
The spirit, too, we bury in the grave,
And with loud voice the last [of calls] arouse.
" Then, when dependance first upon the main 100
Is [placed], and winds vouchsafe us seas appeased,
And woos soft chiding Auster to the deep,
My comrades launch the ships, and fill the shores :
Away from port we're swept, and lands and towns

I am no idle votarist. Roots, you clear Heavens !
Thus much of this will make black white ; foul, fair ;
Wrong, right ; base, noble ; old, young ; coward, valiant.
Ha ! you gods ! why this ? What this, you gods ? Why this
Will lug your priests and servants from your sides,
Pluck stout men's pillows from below their heads :
This yellow slave
Will knit and break religions ; bless th' accurs'd ;
Make the hoar leprosy ador'd ; place thieves,
And give them title, knee, and approbation,
With senators on the bench."
    Shakespeare, *Timon of Athens*, iv. 3.
    " Though I must grant,
Riches, well got, to be a useful servant,
But a bad master."
Massinger, *A New Way to Pay Old Debts*, iv. 1.
    " Conscience, my friends,
And wealth, are not always neighbours."
    The City Madam, v. 2.

94. Or : " sombre wreaths."

97. So Dryden, of the funeral rites of Arcite :

" Full bowls of wine, of honey, milk, and blood,
Were pour'd upon the pile of burning wood,
And hissing flames receive, and hungry lick the food.
Then thrice the mounted squadrons ride around
The fire, and Arcite's name they thrice resound,
' Hail and farewell ! they shouted thrice amain,
Thrice facing to the left, and thrice they turn'd again." *Palamon and Arcite*, 2265-71.

Retreat. A holy region 'mid the sea
Is peopled, full delightsome to the mother
Of Nereids, and Ægean Neptune, which,
While straying erst around the coasts and shores,
The Bowman with the lofty Gyaros
And Myconus enchained, and, unremoved,
Gave to be peopled, and to scorn the winds.
I'm wafted hither : this thrice-peaceful [land] 112
The wearied safely welcomes in its port.
Debarked, Apollo's city we adore.
King Anius, he, the same, the king of men,
And Phœbus' priest, with wreaths and holy bay
Brow-bound, comes up ; Anchises, his old friend,
He recognizes. We unite right hands
In hospitage, and pass beneath his roof.
" The temple of the god, of agèd stone
Upreared, I prayed : ' A home, our own, vouchsafe, 121
Thymbræan ! walls vouchsafe to weary [souls],
A lineage, too, and city that will last.
Guard thou the second Pergamus of Troy,
A remnant from the Greeks and fell Achilles.
Whom follow we ? Or whither biddest thou
To wend our way ? Where settlements to plant ?
Vouchsafe, O sire, thine oracle, and steal Within our souls.' I scarce had spoken these :
Upon a sudden all appeared to quake, 130
Alike the fane and bay-tree of the god,
And the whole mount to be convulsed around,
The tripod, too, to rumble in the shrines, Unveiled. We reverently fall to earth,
And voice is wafted onward to our ears :

---

108. Spenser seems to have drawn the idea of his *Wandering Islands* from this legend about Delos :

" For those same Islands, seeming now and than,
Are not firme land, nor any certein wonne,
But stragling plots, which to and fro doe ronne
In the wide waters ; therefore are they hight
The Wandering Islands." *F. Q.*, ii. 12, 11.

Milton alludes to it in illustration of a grand idea :
    " The aggregated soil
Death, with his mace petrific, cold and dry,
As with a trident smote, and fix'd as firm
As Delos, floating once."   *P. L.*, b. x.

124. Or :
" Guard thou her second Pergamus for Troy."

134.   " But of all, the burst
And the ear-deafening voice o' th' oracle,
Kin to Jove's thunder, so surpriz'd my sense,
That I was nothing."
    Shakespeare, *Winter's Tale*, iii. 1.

'Ye hardy sons of Dardanus, what land
First bare you from your parents' stock,
    the same
Within its fruitful lap shall welcome you,
Returned. Seek out your ancient mother.
    Here
Æneas' house shall rule o'er every coast,
And his sons' sons, and they who shall
    from them   141
Be born.' These Phœbus: and with
    mingled stir
Vast rose the joy, and all the body ask
What be that city, whither Phœbus calls
The rovers, and enjoins them to return?
My sire then, turning o'er the record-tales
Of men of old, cries : ' Listen, O ye chiefs,
And learn your hopes. Crete, isle of
    mighty Jove,
Amid the ocean lies, where [stands] the
    mount
Of Ida, and the cradle of our race.   150
A hundred mighty cities do they haunt,
Thrice-fruitful kingdoms, whence our eldest
    sire,—
If I aright remember [legends] heard,—
Teucer, to coasts Rhœtean first was borne,
And for his kingdom chose the site. Nor yet
Had Ilium and the tow'rs of Pergamus
Stood forth : they harbored in the lowest
    glens.
Hence [sprang] the mother, [she,] the
    denizen
Of Cybela, the bronzes, too, of Corybants,
And grove of Ida ; hence in holy [rites]
A trusty secresy ; and lions, yoked,   161
The chariot of their mistress underwent.
Then come, and where the mandates of
    the gods
Are leading follow we : let us appease
The Winds, and for the realms of Gnosus
    make.
Nor are they distant by a lengthful route :
Only let Jove be with us,—[day's] third dawn
Shall land our navy on the Cretan coasts.'
Thus having spoken, for the altars he
The dueful sacrifices slew,—a bull   170

To Neptune, unto thee a bull, Apollo
    fair,
A sable victim to [the god of] Storm,
To favorable Western gales a white.
" A rumor flies, that, from his father's
    realms
Expelled, Idomeneus the chief was gone,
And that abandoned were the shores of
    Crete,
Its homes from foeman free, and that its
    seats
Were standing for us all forlorn. We quit
Ortygia's havens, and across the deep
We fly, and, revelled over on its brows,
Naxos, and green Donusa, Olearos,   181
And snow-white Paros, and the Cyclad-
    isles,
Sprent o'er the main, and friths, with clus-
    tered lands
Thick-sown, we coast. Up springs the
    sailor-shout
In changeful rivalry ; the crews they
    cheer ;—.
' To Crete and our progenitors let us
Repair !' A breeze, uprising from astern
Attends us as we go, and we at last
Glide gently to the Curets' ancient coasts.
So, .eagerly, the wished-for city's walls
I plan, and ' Pergamean ' title it ;   191
The nation, too, rejoicing in the name,
I urge to love their hearths, and rear
    aloft
The castle with its roofs. And now the
    sterns
Were just up-hauled upon the thirsty beach ;
In marriage-rites, and new [ly granted]
    fields
The youth were tasked ; their rights and
    homes was I
Dispensing ;—when upon a sudden swooped
From [some] attainted region of the sky
On limbs a wasting, and alike on trees,
And seeded crops a pitiable plague,   201
And season rife with death. Their precious
    lives
They left, or healthless bodies trailed along.
Then Sirius 'gan to scorch the barren fields ;
Grass withered, and its food the sickly corn
Denied. Once more t' Ortygia's oracle
And Phœbus,—ocean meted back,—my
    sire
Advises to resort, and grace to crave ;
What close to our distressed estate he
    brings ;
Whence he enjoins our trying [to obtain]
Relief from suff'rings ; whither veer our
    course.

---

136. " But what have been thy answers, what but
    dark,
Ambiguous, and with double sense deluding,
Which they who ask'd have seldom understood,
And not well understood as good not known ?"
                                    Milton, *P. R.*, b. i.
146. Or : " chronicles."
157. Or : " valley-depths."
170. So Dryden, on the Restoration of King
    Charles the Second :
" A bull to thee, Portunus, shall be slain,
 A lamb to you, ye tempests of the main :
 For those loud storms, that did against him roar,
 Have cast his shipwreck'd vessel on the shore."
                            Astrea Redux, 121-4.

191. Or : " call it after Pergamus."

"'Twas night, and things of life thro'out
   the lands   212
Sleep held. The holy figures of the gods,
And Phrygian tutelars, which I with me
From Troy, and from amid the city-fires,
Had brought away, appeared before mine
   eyes
To stand hard by, in slumbers as I lay,
Plain in a flood of light, where full the moon
Through the inserted casements poured her
   [rays];
On this wise then t' accost me, and to take
Solicitudes away by these their words:
'Whate'er to thee, what time t' Ortygia
   borne   222
Apollo is prepared to utter, here
He chants, and sends us to thy dwelling-
   place,
Lo! unentreated. We,—Dardania burnt,—
Thee and thine arms who've followed;
   under thee
Who have the heaving ocean in thy ships
O'er-traversed; [we], the same, thy sons
   of sons,
That are to issue, to the stars will raise,
And to thy city sovereignty vouchsafe. 230
Do thou for giant [heroes] giant walls
Prepare, and quit not flight's protracted toil.
Thy homesteads must be changed: 'tis not
   these shores
Delian Apollo hath advised for thee,
Or hath he bid thee settle down in Crete.
There is a spot, ('Hesperia' do the Greeks
Entitle it by name;) an ancient land,
Puissant in arms and richness of its soil:
Ænotrian swains inhabited it [erst];
Now rumor [tells], that moderns 'Italy'
Have called the nation from the leader's
   name.   241
These are the rightful settlements for us;
Hence Dardanus was sprung, (sire Jasius,
   too;)
From the which chieftain [came] our race.
Come! rise!
And blithely to thy agèd sire these words,
Not to be called in doubt, report: 'Let him
Deep-search for Coryth and Ausonian
   lands:
The fields of Dicte Jove denies to thee.'
Thunderstruck by such sights and voice of
   gods,—   249

Nor lethargy was that; but in my sight
To recognize their looks, and banded hair,
And features present to me, did I seem:
Then trickled icy sweat from all my
   frame;—
I snatch my body from the couch, and
   spread
To heav'n my hands uplifted with my
   voice,
And off'rings pour untainted on the
   hearths.
The homage to completion brought, in joy
I certify Anchises, and the tale
Develop in its order. He avowed
The pedigree of doubt, and double sires,
Himself, too, by a modern misconceit 261
Of ancient spots misled; then saith: 'O
   son,
Experienced in the destinies of Troy,
Alone to me such fates Cassandra sang.
Now do I recollect that she foretold
That these were to our nation due, and oft
Hesperia, oft Italian realms, she named.
But who could fancy that the Teucer-race
Were to Hesperia's shores to come? Or
   whom
Could then the prophetess Cassandra move?
To Phœbus let us yield, and, warned [by
   him],   271
His better [counsels] follow.' Thus he
   speaks,
And we, exulting, in a throng obey
His word. This home, too, we forsake,
   and,—few
Behind us left,—give sail, and scud across
The waste of water in our hollow bark.
"Soon as the galleys occupied the deep,
Nor further now do any lands appear;
Sky all around, and all around the main;—
Then o'er my head a dingy rain-cloud came
To a nearstand, night bringing on and storm,
And 'gan the wave to crisp beneath the
   gloom.   282
Forthwith the winds roll on the sea, and rise
The mountain waters. Scattered here and
   there,
Thro'out the mighty ocean are we tossed.
Storm-clouds' enwrapped the day, and dark-
   ness dank

---

212. "Night, clad in black, mourns for the loss of
   day,
And hides the silver spangles of the air,
That not a spark is left to light the world;
Whilst quiet sleep, the nourisher of life,
Takes full possession of mortality:
All creatures take their rest in soft repose."
            Machin, *The Dumb Knight*, ii. 1.

228. Or: "O'er-measured."

250. See note on *Ecl.* v. 58.

253.   "How he shook the king,
Made his soul melt within him, and his blood
Run into whey! It stood upon his brow
Like a cold winter-dew."
            Beaumont and Fletcher, *Philaster*, i. 1.

263.   "O be of comfort!
Make patience a noble fortitude,
And think not how unkindly we are used:
Man, like to cassia, is proved best being bruised."
            Webster, *The Duchess of Malfi*, iii. 5.

Reft heav'n away, and from the rifted clouds
The fires redouble. From our course are we
Thrown out, and wander in the blindfold
    waves.
E'en Palinure himself denies that he   290
Can day from night discriminate in heaven,
Nor recollect his path amid the surge.
Three suns, thus doubtful from the dark-
    some murk,
We wander on the deep, as many nights
Without a star. Upon the day, the fourth,
Land first was seen to lift it [s form] at last,
To ope afar the mounts, and wreathe the
    smoke.
Sails lower; to the oars we rise; no stay;
The crews in straining whirl the foam, and
    sweep
The azure [waters]. Rescued from the
    waves,   300
The shores of Strophads welcome me the
    first.
The Strophads stand (by Grecian title
    called,)
Isles in the great Ionian, which the dread
Celæno, and the other Harpies haunt,
Since Phineus' palace was against them
    barred,
And former boards in terror they forsook.
No more distressful monster-form than
    these,
Nor any feller plague and scourge of gods
Hath reared it [s form] above the Stygian
    waves.
Maiden the faces of the wingèd [fiends],
All-foul their belly's flux, and pounced their
    hands,   311
Their features, too, with craving ever wan.
When, hither wafted, enter we the port,
Behold! in every spot blithe droves of
    beeves
We see along the champaigns, and a flock
Of goats, with keeper none, throughout the
    grass.
We charge them with the falcion, and the
    gods,
And Jove himself, invite to share and prey.
Then on the bending beach we both upraise
Our seats, and banquet on the rich repast.
But on a sudden with a fearful swoop   321
Down from the mountains stand the Har-
    pies by,
And with prodigious whizzings do they flap
Their wings, and rifle the repast, and all
Befoul with touch uncleanly: then [is heard]

An awful screaming 'mid a noisome smell.
Once more, within a far retreat, beneath
A vaulted rock, incloistered round with trees
And dreadful shadows, lay we out the
    boards,
And on the altars place anew the fire: 330
Once more from forth a diff'rent side of
    heaven,
And darksome shrouds, the whirring crew
    flits round
The prey with hooky claws; with lips defile
The banquet. Then the order to my mates
I issue forth, that they should take their
    arms,
And with the cursèd nation war be waged.
Nor otherwise than as enjoined do they,
And range their falcions, screened among
    the grass,
And hide away their bucklers out of sight.
So when, in swooping down, a din they
    raised   340
Along the winding shores, Misenus gives
A signal from his lofty post of watch
Upon his hollow bronze. My comrades
    charge,
And strange encounters they essay, to mar
The filthy birds of ocean with the sword.
But neither on their feathers any dint,
Nor wounds upon their backs do they re-
    ceive;
And, gliding 'neath the stars in sweepy
    flight,
The prey half-eaten, and their foot-tracks
    foul,
They leave. Alone upon a cliff all-high   350
Celæno perched, ill-boding prophetess,
And from her bosom vents she forth this
    strain:
'War, too, for slaughter of our beeves, and
    steers
Laid low, descendants of Laomedon,
Is 't war to bring upon us ye prepare,
And th' unoffending Harpies to expel
From their ancestral realm? Receive ye,
    then,

---
346. Shakespeare makes Ariel and his company equally invulnerable; *Tempest*, iii. 3:
    " You fools, I and my fellows
    Are ministers of fate: the elements,
    Of whom your swords are temper'd, may as well
    Wound the loud winds, or with bemock'd-at stabs
    Kill the still-closing waters, as diminish
    One dowle that's in my plume: my fellow-
        ministers
    Are like invulnerable."

351. Spenser torments Guyon with the same fiend:
    " Whiles sad Celeno, sitting on a clifte,
    A song of bale and bitter sorrow sings,
    That hart of flint asonder could have rifte."
                            F. Q., ii. 7, 23.

---
308. More literally: "wrath of gods."
310. Spenser, in the *Faerie Queene*, ii. 12, 36, calls them:
    " The hellish harpyes, prophets of sad destiny."
314. Or: "fat droves."

Within your souls, and these my words imprint :
What [fates] to Phœbus the almighty sire, Phœbus Apollo hath to me foretold ; 360
To you do I, of Furies eldest, [these] Disclose. Italia in your course ye seek, And,—winds invoked,—Italia shall ye reach,
And it will be allowed to enter port ;
But ne'er shall ye the granted city gird With walls, till fearful hunger, and the wrong
Of our blood-shedding force you with your jaws
Your tables to demolish, gnawed around.'
She said. And to the forest, on her wings Upborne, flew back. But in my mates, ice-cold 370
With sudden horror, did the blood congeal : Their spirits fell ; nor further now with arms,
But vows and orisons, they beg me sue
For peace ; or whether goddesses they be, Or fate-announcing and ill-boding birds.
My sire Anchises, too, with hands outstretched
From shore, the great divinities invokes, And sacrifices due appoints : ' Ye gods, Their threat'nings bid avaunt ! gods, turn aside
The like disaster, and, propitious, save 380 The holy.' Then the cable from the shore To wrench away, and sheets uncoiled to slack,
He orders. Southern gales the canvas swell : We scud along upon the yesting waves, Where wind alike and pilot wooed a course. Now looms amid the billow, rife in woods, Zacynthus, and Dulichium, Same too,
And Neritos, sublime with crags. We shun The rocks of Ithaca, Laertes' realms,
And ban the fell Ulysses' foster-land. 390 Soon, too, the Mount Leucata's stormy crests,
And, feared by mariners, is opened out Apollo. Him we weary seek, and reach The humble town. The anchor from the bow Is cast ; the sterns are resting on the shore.

---

371. " The pith of oracles Is to be then digested, when th' events Expound their truth, not brought as soon to light As uttered : Truth is child of Time."
Ford, *The Broken Heart*, iv. 3.

373. " For the dearth,
The gods, not the patricians, make it ; and Your knees to them, not arms, must help."
Shakespeare, *Coriolanus*, i. 1.

390. " Ban'd be those cosening arts that wrought our woe,
Making us wandering pilgrims to and fro."
Anonymous, *The Returne from Pernassus*, ii. 1.

" Thus having gained at last a land unhoped,
We both perform the cleansing rites to Jove,
And light the altars up for vows, and fame The shores of Actium with the sports of Troy.
My stript companions with the streaming oil 400
Practise their native wrestlings. Joy it is To have escaped so many Argive towns,
And through the midst of foes maintained a flight.
Meanwhile around the mighty year the sun Is wheeled, and icy winter frets the waves With northern blasts. A shield of hollow bronze,
Great Abas' load, upon the fronting posts I fix, and mark the action with the verse :
' THESE ARMS ÆNEAS FROM THE VICTOR GREEKS.' 409
I bid them then to quit the port, and take Their seats upon the thwarts. In rivalry The crews lash ocean, and the waters sweep. Straight put we out of sight the skyey peaks Of the Phæaces, and Epirus' shores
We coast, and enter the Chaonian port, And the tall city of Buthrotus reach.
" Here, past belief, a rumor of events
Lays hold upon our ears :—that Helenus, The son of Priam, rules thro' Grecian towns, He having gained the spouse and sceptral sway 420
Of Pyrrhus, sprung from Æacus's strain ;
And that Andromache had now once more Passed to a husband of her native land.
I was astounded, and my bosom burned With strange desire the hero to accost,
And ascertain events of such concern.
From port I sally, quitting ships and shores : When yearly feasts, by chance, and gifts of woe,
Before the city in a grove, fast by
The billow of pretended Simois, 430
Andromache was pouring to his ash [es] Libations, and was calling on the Shades At Hector's tomb, which of the em'rald turf,—
An empty [tomb],—a pair of altars, too,
A fountain-head for tears, she'd sanctified. When she descried me coming, and around The Trojan weapons in distraction saw,
Scared by the mighty wonders, stiff she grew
Amid the sight ; the heat her bones forsook ;
She falls ; and after a protracted time 440 Scarce speaks at last ; ' Dost thou, a real shape,

A real messenger, present thyself
To me, O goddess-born? Art thou alive?
Or if from thee boon light hath fled away,
Where is my Hector?' [Thus] she spake,
  and tears
Outpoured, and every spot with shrieking
  filled.
Scarce few [replies] to her, [in] frantic
  [mood],
Do I throw in, and troubled, with stray
  words
Ope wide [my lips]: 'Alive I am indeed,
And life thro' all extremities prolong. 450
Doubt not: for thou realities dost see.
Alas! what chance succeeds to thee, de-
  throned
From such a noble spouse? Or fortune what
Again doth visit, meet enough for thee?
Dost thou, Andromache of Hector, guard
The wedded bonds of Pyrrhus?' Down
  she cast
Her visage, and with lowered voice she
  spake:
'O singularly blest before all else,
The Priamean maid, at foeman's tomb,
'Neath Troja's stately walls decreed to die,
Who bore not any castings of the lot, 461
Nor, pris'ner, touched a conqu'ring mas-
  ter's bed!
We,—country burnt,—o'er severed waters
  borne,
The arrogance of th' Achillean brood,
And [that] disdainful youth, in slavery
A mother proving, have endured: who then,
Pursuing Leda-sprung Hermione,
And Spartan nuptials, me, his handmaid,
  e'en
To Helenus his lacquey handed o'er
To be possessed. But him, by mighty love
Of his betrothed, reft from him, set afire,
And hounded by the Furies of his crimes,
Orestes intercepts when off his guard, 473
And butchers at the altars of his sire.
At Neoptolemus' decease, a share
Of his dominions, ceded to him, fell
To Helenus; who, by their name, the plains
"Chaonian," and "Chaonia" all [the land]
From Trojan Chaon called; and Pergamus,
And this his Ilian castle on the heights 480
Erected. But to thee what winds, what
  fates,

Thy course have deigned? Or pray what
  god hath driven
Thee, wareless, to these coasts of ours?
How [fares]
The boy Ascanius? Does he [still] survive,
And feed upon the air? Whom hath to thee,
Now Troy — — — —. Yet in the boy
Dwells any feeling for a mother lost?
Say whether to the gallantry of old,
And manly courage, do alike his sire
Æneas, and his uncle Hector rouse him up?'
Such poured she forth in tears, and weep-
  ings long   491
In vain awaked: when, [issued] from the
  walls,
The hero-son of Priam, Helenus,
With numbers in his train, presents himself,
And recognises his own [friends], and blithe
Conducts us towards the palace, and his
  tears
Between his every word profusely sheds.
I move me forward, and a petty Troy,
And, made to ape the great, a Pergamus,
And thirsty brook with Xanthus' name,
  perceive,   500
And clasp the portals of a Scæan gate.
And none the less do Teucer's sons with me
Enjoy the friendly city. These the king
Within the wide piazzas entertained:
Amid the hall they tasted Bacchus' cups,—
With viands dished on gold,—and platters
  held.
" And now a day, and second day, passed
  by,
And breezes court the sails, the canvas, too,
Is puffed by swelling Auster:—in these
  words
Do I accost the prophet, and prefer   510
The like requests: ' O thou, of Troja born,
Interpreter of gods, who dost the will
Of Phœbus, who the tripods, Clarius' bays,
Who constellations dost perceive, and
  tongues
Of birds, and omens of the flighty wing,
Come tell; (for all my voyage hath to me
Religion fav'ring told, and, one and all,
The gods have urged me by their will to seek
Italia, and essay sequestered lands:
A strange portent, and fearful to be told,

---

445.   "Hector is gone!
Who shall tell Priam so, or Hecuba?
Let him, that will a screech-owl aye be call'd,
Go into Troy, and say there—Hector's dead:
There is a word will Priam turn to stone;
Make wells and Niobes of the maids and wives,
Cold statues of the youth; and in a word,
Scare Troy out of itself."
   Shakespeare, *Troilus and Cressida*, v. 11.

509.   "We owe this happiness
To you, fair princess, for whose safer passage
The breath of heaven did gently swell our sails,
The waves were proud to bear so rich a lading,
And danced to the music of the winds."
   Shirley, *The Young Admiral*, ii. 2.

520. "Thus like the sad presaging raven, that tolls
The sick man's passport in her hollow beak,
And in the shadow of the silent night
Doth shake contagion from her sable wings."
   Marlowe, *The Jew of Malta*, i.

Harpy Celæno chants alone, and threats
Disastrous anger and a famine foul ;) 522
What the chief dangers I am to avoid ;
Or, what pursuing, can I overcome
Distresses so intense ?' Here Helenus,—
Steers slaughtered first in wonted form,—
    entreats
With earnestness the favor of the gods,
And slacks the fillets of his hallowed head,
And me, O Phœbus, to thy thresholds he
Himself conducted by the hand, o'erawed
At thy abundant presence, and these
    [strains] 531
Then chants the priest from out his heav'nly
    lips :
" 'O goddess-born (for that thou dost
    proceed
With higher auspices throughout the deep,
Clear my conviction : thus the king of gods
The destinies allots, and rolls along
Thy fortunes; such the cycle that is wheeled:)
A few to thee from many a response,
That thou may'st safer traverse kindly seas,
And be enabled in Ausonia's port 540
To settle down, will I unfold ; for Fates
Bar Helenus the knowledge of the rest,
Saturnian Juno, too, forbids to speak.
First, Italy, which now thou deemest nigh,
Its ports, too, as at hand, O unaware,
To enter dost prepare, a distant route,
Unpathed, divides afar by distant lands.
First, e'en upon Sicilia's wave thy oar
Must needs be bent, and traversed in thy
    ships
The surface of Ausonia's briny main, 550
And hellish lakes, and Æan Circe's isle,
Ere thou canst rest thy city in a land
Secure. To thee the tokens will I name ;
Do thou preserve them treasured in thy
    mind.
What time by thee, [all] anxious, at the
    wave
Of a sequestered river, found beneath
The holms upon its bank, a monstrous sow,
That has produced a brood of thirty young,
Shall lie, white, on the ground reclining,
    white 559
Around her dugs the litter ;—that shall be
Thy city's site; *that*, rest assured from toils.
Nor do thou fear the future meal of boards :
The Weirds will find a way, and, when
    invoked,
Apollo will be with you. But these lands,
And border this of [yon] Italian shore,
Which, next thee, by our ocean's tide is
    drenched,
Avoid thou : one and all, by felon Greeks
The towns are peopled. Likewise here
    their walls

The Locri of Narycium have upreared,
And plains of Sallentines with soldiery 570
Lyctian Idomeneus beset. Here [stands]
That small Petelia, leaning on the wall
Of Philoctetes, Melibœan chief.
Yea, too, when wafted on across the seas,
Thy barks shall have reposed, and now thy
    vows,
With altars reared, on shore shalt thou
    discharge,
Be kerchiefed o'er thy tresses, muffled up
In crimson hood ; lest any adverse sight,
'Mid holy fires in homage to the gods,
Meet thee, and trouble the portents. This
    form 580
Of sacrifices let thy comrades, this
Thyself maintain ; in this religious rite
Let thy devout posterity abide.
But when set forward [on thy course] the
    wind
Shall thee have wafted to Sicilia's coast,
And strait Pelorus' narrows shall begin
To ope apart, the land upon thy left,
And left-side seas by doubling long be
    sought ;
The shore upon the right hand, and its
    waves,
Avoid. These spots, erst shattered by a
    shock, 590
And wreck enormous,—such a mighty change
Can long antiquity of age effect,—
Asunder sprang do they report, what time
Both lands uninterruptedly were one :
Into the midst with fury flushed the deep,
And rifted with its waves Hesperia's side
From Sic'ly's, and between the fields and
    towns,
Dissevered by a shore, with narrow tide
It flushes. Scylla doth the side upon the
    right,
The left Charybdis unappeased blockades,
And with its pit's profoundest whirl thrice
    sucks 601

575. More literally : "stood still."

599. Spenser gives a grand description of his
parallels to Scylla and Charybdis, the "Gulfe of
Greedinesse," and "Rock of Reproch ;" *Faerie
Queene*, ii. 12, 3-9:
" On th' other syde an hideous Rock is pight
    Of mightie magnes stone, whose craggie clift
    Depending from on high, dreadfull to sight,
    Over the waves his rugged armes doth lift,
    And threateneth downe to throw his ragged rift :
    On whoso cometh nigh ; yet nigh it drawes
    All passengers, that none from it can shift :
    For, whiles they fly that Gulfe's devouring iawes
They on the rock are rent, and sunck in helpless
    wawes. . . .

" They, passing by, that grisely mouth did see
    Sucking the seas into his entralles deepe,
    That seemd more horrible than hell to bee,
    Or that darke dreadfull hole of Tartare steepe."

The mountain billows into the abyss;
Again, too, in succession shoots them up
Beneath the air, and lashes with the surge
The constellations. But in darksome shrouds
A cave incloses Scylla, stretching out
Her jaws, and trailing ships upon the rocks.
Above,—her figure, that of human kind,
A damsel e'en, with beauteous bosom far
As to the groin; below,—of monster frame
A *Pistrix*, with the tails of dolphins linked
To womb of wolves. It meeter is for thee
Thro'out Trinacrian Pachynus' bounds 613
To coast, a loiterer, and tedious routes
To wheel around, than once to have descried
The hideous Scylla in her monstrous cave,
And cliffs that thunder with the dingy dogs.
Moreo'er, if any skill in Helenus
There dwell, if any credit in the seer,
If with the true Apollo stores his mind,
This single [warning], goddess-born, to thee 621
E'en before all, this single [warning] I
Will pre-declare, and re-announcing [this],
Again, and o'er again, will thee advise:
Great Juno's deity in chief with prayer
Adore; to Juno freely chant thy vows,
And overcome with gifts of humble suit
The puissant mistress: thus shalt thou at last,
In triumph, with Trinacria left astern,
Upon the bourns of Italy be launched.
When, hither wafted, thou shalt have attained 630
The Cuman city, and the sacred lakes,
And [depths] Avernian, booming with their woods,
The madding prophetess shalt thou behold;
Who in her deepest [seat of] rock the fates
Chants forth, and trusts to leaves her marks and words.
Whatever verses on the leaves the maid
Hath scored, she ranges into rhythmic form,

And quits them, cloistered up within the grot.
Abide they in their places undisturbed,
Nor from their rank depart. But [these] the same, 640
What time, upon the turning of the hinge,
A gentle breeze hath driven, and the gate
Deranged the tender leaflets, ne'er thenceforth
To catch them flutt'ring through the vaulted rock,
Nor to recall their postures, or unite
The verses, does she care: without advice
[Men] pass away, and loathe the Sibyl's seat.
Here be not any waste of time to thee
Of such concern,—though mates upbraid, and loud
The voyage summon to the deep the sails,
And their propitious bosoms thou canst fill,— 651
That thou should'st not the prophetess approach,
And with thy prayers entreat that she herself
May chant the heav'nly answers, and unlock
Her voice and lips with favor. She to thee
Italia's tribes, and battles doomed to come,
And by what means thou mayest every toil
Or shun, or suffer, will unfold, and grant,
When worshipped, a successful course.
These [truths]
Be they, whereof it is by voice of ours 660
Permitted thee to be advised. Up! quick!
And, great by thine exploits, raise Troy to heaven.'
"Which when the prophet thus with friendly lip
Spake forth, gifts thereupon, of weight with gold
And the veneer of iv'ry, to the ships
He bids be borne; and packs within their holds
A mass of plate, and basins of Dodone,
A coat of armor interlinked with rings,
And wrought with gold in triplet, and the cone
And waving plumes of helm distinguished, 670
Of Neoptolemus. There likewise be
His presents for my father. Steeds he adds,
And adds he guides; a rower-train supplies;
My mates the same time furnishes with arms.

---

616. Grander than Virgil is Milton's imitation of him in the description of Sin; *P. L.*, b. ii.:

"Before the gates there sat
On either side a formidable shape;
The one seem'd woman to the waist, and fair:
But ended foul in many a scaly fold,
Voluminous and vast; a serpent armed
With mortal sting: about her middle round
A cry of Hellhounds never ceasing bark'd
With wide Cerberian mouths full loud, and rung
A hideous peal; yet, when they list, would creep,
If aught disturb'd their noise, into her womb,
And kennel there; yet there still bark'd and howl'd
Within, unseen."

633. "Poetic fury, and historic storms."
Ben Jonson, *The Fox*, iv. 1.

"Meanwhile the navy to equip with sails
Anchises gave command, that no delay
Might be presented to a leading wind.
Whom Phœbus' seer with deep respect
   accosts:
'Anchises, honored with the haught em-
   brace
Of Venus! O solicitude of gods!   680
Twice rescued from the wrecks of Per-
   gamus,
Behold! Ausonia's land before thee [lies]:
This seize thou by thy sails. And yet past
   this
There's need for thee to glide along the
   deep.
That region of Ausonia is afar,
Which opes to thee Apollo. Go,' saith he,
'O blest in the devotion of thy son.
Why further am I carried on, and stay
By talk the rising southern gales?' Nor
   less
Andromache, at latest parting sad,   690
Brings robes embroidered with a thread of
   gold,
And Phrygian mantle for Ascanius;
Nor of the compliment comes short; and
   loads
[The youth] with woven gifts, and such
   she speaks:
'Accept these also, which to thee may
   stand
Memorials of my hands, my boy, and prove
The long affection of Andromache,
The spouse of Hector. Take thy [friends']
   last gifts,
O thou, to me the only picture left
Of my Astyanax! Thus eyes, thus hands,
Thus he his lips was wont to move; and
   now   701
In equal age along with thee would he
Be rip'ning into man.' On parting I, with
   tears
Upstarting, these addressed: 'Live happy
   ye,

Whose fortune is accomplished, now their
   own:
From one fate to another we are called.
For you is rest secured: no ocean-plain
Must needs be ploughed, nor have Ausonia's
   fields
Retreating ever backward, to be sought.
The likeness of the Xanthus, and a Troy
Ye see, which your own hands have shaped,
   beneath   711
More happy auspices, I pray to heaven!
And which may prove less open to the
   Greeks.
If ever Tiber, and the neighb'ring fields
Of Tiber, I shall enter, and the walls,
That are vouchsafed my nation, I shall view,
Our kindred cities in the days to come,
And neighbor peoples,—in Epirus [you],
[We] in Hesperia,—who have Dardanus
The selfsame founder, and the selfsame
   fates,   720
Both Troys will render in affection one:
Let this concern our children's children
   wait.'
"We're wafted forth along the deep,
   hard by
The neighb'ring heights Ceraunian, whence
   there [lies]
The path to Italy, and the shortest route
Across the waves. The sun swoops down
   meanwhile,
And darkling mounts are shaded o'er.
   We're stretched
Upon the bosom of a wished-for land,
Fast by the billow, having lotted oars,
And all around, along the droughty beach,
Our frames we tend: sleep dews our jaded
   limbs.   731
Nor yet upon her central circle Night,
Chased onward by the Hours, advanced:—
   not slow
Uprises Palinurus from his couch,
And searches all the winds, and in his ears
The breeze he catches; all the stars he
   marks,
As on they glide across the silent heaven,—
Arcturus, and the rainy Hyades,
And twin Triones; and he scans around
Orion armed with gold. What time he sees
That all lies settled in the calmy sky, 741
He gives a brilliant signal from the stern:
We strike th' encampment, and essay our
   route,

---

675. "Lay her before the wind! Up with her
      canvas,
    And let her work! The wind begins to whistle:
    Clap all her streamers on, and let her dance,
    As if she were the minion of the ocean!
    Let her bestride the billows till they roar,
    And curl their wanton heads!"
         J. Fletcher, *The Double Marriage*, ii. 1.

677. It is plain, from verse 481, that the wind was
   a "leading" one.

693. Or: "Nor of his dignity."

703. Classical heroes seem greatly addicted to
   tears, forgetting that a watery grief is scarce as
   deep as a dry:
   "Think not the worse, my friends, I shed not tears:
     Great griefs lament within."
         J. Fletcher, *Valentinian*, iv. 4.

731. "Gallants, the night growes old, and downy
      sleep
    Courts us to entertain his company;
    Our tyred limbes, brused in the morning fight,
    Intreat soft rest, and gentle husht repose."
         Marston, *Antonio and Mellida*, P. i. 2.

And spread the pinions of the sails. And now
Aurore was blushing, with the stars chased off,
When far away we see the glooming hills,
And lowly Italy. 'ITALIA!' first
Achates shouts aloud ; ITALIA hail
My comrades with a blithe hurrah ! Then sire
Anchises with a coronal bedecks 750
A mighty wassail-bowl, and brimmed it up
With taintless wine, and called upon the gods,
While standing on the lofty stern : 'Ye gods,
Of sea, and land, and storms the rulers, lend
A ready voyage by the wind, and breathe
Propitious.' 'Gin to swell the wished-for gales,
And opens out the haven, closer now,
And looms Minerva's fane upon the height.
The crews furl sails, and veer the prows to shore.
The haven by the billow from the East
Is bent into an arch ; the jutting cliffs 761
Are foaming with the briny spray. Itself
Lies hid ; launch out their arms with double pier
Rocks tower-shaped, and from the strand withdraws the fane.
Four horses here upon the grass, the first
Portent, perceived I browsing on the plain
At large, of snowy whiteness. And my sire
Anchises : ' War it is, O foreign land,
Thou dost forebode ! for war are horses armed ; 769
War threat these beasts. But still at times
The selfsame quadrupeds are wont to pass
Beneath the chariot, and harmonious reins
To suffer in the yoke : hope e'en of peace,'
He cries. We then entreat the holy powers
Of Pallas, thund'ring in her armor, who

First welcomed us rejoiced, and o'er our heads,
Before the altars, we with Phrygian hood
Are muffled ; and by rules of Helenus,
Which he had granted as of chief concern,
We duly to the Argive Juno burn 780
The ordered sacrifices. No delay :
Straight,—vows completed in due form,— the arms
Of the sail-mantled yards we [sea-] ward veer,
And quit the homesteads of the sons of Greeks,
And their mistrusted fields. Therefrom the bay
Of the Herculean—(if report be true),—
Tarentum is descried. Uplifts her [form]
Lacinium's goddess in the front, and heights
Of Caulon, and shipwrecking Scyllace. 789
Then far, [uprising] from the surge is kenned
Trinacrian Ætna, and the thund'ring growl
Of ocean, and the stricken rocks we hear
Far off, and broken noises at the shores ;
And deeps leap up, and with the tide the sands
Are mingled. And my sire Anchises :
' Sooth
This that Charybdis ; Helenus these cliffs,
These rocks of terror chanted. Rescue us, O crews !
And rise in even measure to your oars.'
No less than as enjoined do they : and first
His creaking prow did Palinurus veer 800
To the left waves ; the left with oars and winds
The squadron in a body sought. To heaven
Are we uplifted on the arched gulf,
And we the same,—the billow drawn away,—
Pass downward to the lowest Shades.
Three times
The cliffs gave thunder 'mid the hollow rocks,

803-9. " If after every tempest come such calms,
May the winds blow till they have wakened death ;
And let the labouring bark climb hills of seas,
Olympus-high, and duck again as low
As hell's from heaven !"
Shakespeare, *Othello*, ii. 1.
804. " What sands, what shelves, what rocks do threaten her ;
The forces and the nations of all winds,
Gusts, storms, and tempests : when her keel ploughs hell,
And deck knocks heaven !—then to manage her,
Becomes the name and office of a pilot."
Ben Jonson, *Catiline*, iii. 1.
806. " For do but stand upon the foaming shore,
The chiding billow seems to pelt the clouds ;
The wind-shak'd surge, with high and monstrous main,

745. " Light, the fair grandchild to the glorious sun,
Opening the casements of the rosy morn,
Makes the abashèd heavens soon to shun
The ugly darkness it embraced before,
And at his first appearance puts to flight
The utmost relics of the hell-born night."
Brewer, *Lingua*, iii. 6.
756. " The waves were proud to entertain our navy ;
The fish in amorous courtship danced about
Our ship, and no rude gale from any coast
Was sent to hang upon our linen wings,
To interrupt our wishes ; not a star
Muffled his brightness in a sullen cloud
Till we arrived."
Shirley, *The Young Admiral*, ii. 2.
758. Or : " shews."

K

Three times the spray, dashed up, and dewy stars
We saw. Meanwhile the wind hath with the sun
The weary left; and wareless of the path,
We towards the shores of Cyclops drift along. 810
"The port [lies] stirless from approach of winds,
And spacious in itself; but Ætna near
With awful wrack is thund'ring, and at times
Flings forth a cloud of blackness to the sky,
In smoke with pitchy whirl and glowing ash,
And shoots up balls of flames, and licks the stars.
At times the rocks and rifted bowels of the mount
It, belching, spouts aloft, and molten stones
Beneath the heav'ns with rumbling rolls around,
And from the bottom of its bed seethes up.
There is a legend, that, by leven-flash 821
Half-burnt, the body of Enceladus
Is whelmed beneath this pile, and, o'er him laid,
Huge Ætna blasts out flame from forges burst;
And, often as he shifts his weary side,
That all Trinacria with a growling quakes,
And overcasts the welkin with the smoke.
That night, in forests bowered, fell portents
We suffer, nor what cause creates the din
Perceive. For neither were there lights of stars, 830
Nor sheeny in the stellar firmament
The heav'ns, but fogs thro'out the sullen sky,
And dismal night confined the moon in cloud.
"And now the following day with infant Dawn
Was rising, and Aurore from heaven had chased
Dank shade; when suddenly from out the woods,
Wasted away by meagreness extreme;

The novel figure of an unknown man,
And pitiable in its garb, comes forth,
And humbly to the shores outspreads its hands. 840
We gaze upon him. Dread his filthiness,
His beard, too, wild, his wrapper tacked with thorns:
But in the rest a Greek, and ere the while
To Troy in native armor sent. And he,
What time the Dardan dress, and arms
Of Troy, he spied afar, awhile stopped short,
Affrighted by the sight, and stayed his step.
Anon he flung him headlong to the shores,
With weeping and entreaties: 'By the stars
Do I conjure you, by the gods above, 850
And this life-giving light of heav'n, away,
O Teucri, take me; to whatever lands
Transport me; this will be enough. I know
That I am one from out the Grecian ships,
And own that I the Ilian gods of home
In war assaulted: for the which, if be
So heinous the demerit of our crime,
Fling me in atoms on the waves, and 'neath
The mighty ocean plunge me; if I die,
'Twill be a pleasure to have died by hands
Of men.' He said, and folding round our knees, 861
And, writhing, to our knees he clinging held.
Who he may be we counsel him to tell,
From what descent he may have sprang; thereon,
What fortune hunts him onward to avow.
My sire himself, Anchises, his right hand,
No great delays presenting, gives the youth,
And with the ready pledge his mind assures.
These speaks he,—terror laid aside at last:
'I am from Ithaca, my native land, 870
The comrade of Ulysses evil-starred.
My name is Achemenides, to Troy,
My father Adamastus being poor,

Seems to cast water on the burning bear,
And quench the guards of the ever-fixed pole:
I never did like molestation view
On th' unchafed flood."
                Shakespeare, *Othello*, ii. 1.

812. Spenser briefly but finely alludes to Ætna, *F. Q.*, i. 11, 44:

"As burning Ætna from his boyling stew
Doth belch out flames, and rockes in peeces broke,
And ragged ribs of mountaines molten new,
Enwrapt in coleblacke clowds and filthy smoke,
That al the land with stench, and heven with horror, choke."

838. The account of Achemenides somewhat resembles Spenser's description of "Despair;" *F. Q.*, i. 9, 35:

"His griesie lockes, long growen and unbound,
Disordred hong about his shoulders round,
And hid his face; through which his hollow eyne
Lookt deadly dull, and stared as astound;
His raw-bone cheekes, through penurie and pine,
Were shronke into his iawes, as he did never dine.
His garment, nought but many ragged clouts,
With thornes together pind and patched was:" &c.

846. "As children wading from some river's bank,
First try the water with their tender feet;
Then, shudd'ring up with cold, step back again,
And straight a little further venture on,
Till at the last they plunge into the deep,
And pass at once what they were doubting long."
        Dryden, *The Maiden Queen*, v. 1.

(And would my fortune had remained!) set
 forth.
Here me, while they in consternation quit
The barb'rous dwelling, my unthoughtful
 mates:
Abandoned in the Cyclop's monster den.
The home it is of gore and bloody feasts;
Inside obscure, stupendous. He himself
Of giant height, and smites the lofty stars;
(Gods, such a plague, O bid avaunt from
 earth!) 881
Nor in his aspect bearable, nor meet
To be addressed by any one in speech.
Upon the entrails and the sable blood
Of hapless [wights] he feeds. I saw myself,
When from our number bodies twain, en-
 grasped
Within his monstrous hand, amid the den
He, bending backward, smashed against a
 rock,
And, spattered with the blood, the chamber
 swam.
I saw, when, dripping with the jetty gore,
Their limbs he craunched, and, warm be-
 neath his fangs, 891
Their joints they quivered. Neither un-
 chastised,
In sooth; nor did the like Ulysses brook,
[N] or was the Ithacan forgetful of himself
In such grave crisis. For the moment he,
Gorged with the cates, and buried in his
 wine,
His bended neck laid down, and stretched
 along
The cave, enormous, spewing up the gore,
And gobbets intermixed with bloody wine,
Throughout his slumber;—we, when we
 had prayed 900
The mighty Pow'rs, and lotted [each] their
 parts,
At once, on all sides, round are poured,
 and drill
With sharpened tool the eye, the monster
 [eye],
Which skulked alone beneath a scowling
 brow,
As Argive shield, or Phœbus' cresset huge;
And blithesome at the last our comrades'
 shades
Do we avenge. But fly, O wretched, fly,
And from the shore your cable burst away.

881. Or, perhaps more strongly:
"Gods, banish such a nuisance from the earth!"

899. If Virgil is somewhat coarse here, Spenser,
in his description of Errour, has no difficulty in
being still coarser; *Faerie Queene*, i. 1, 20:

'Therwith she spewd out of her filthie maw
A floud of poyson horrible and blacke,
Full of great lumps of flesh, and gobbets raw."

For what in guise, and howsoever vast,
Doth Polypheme within his vaulted cave
Pen in his fleecy flocks, and squeeze their
 teats, 911
A hundred other cursèd Cyclops dwell
In every quarter by these winding shores,
And through the lofty mountains rove.
 Third horns
Of Luna fill them now with light,
Since life in woods, among the lonely lairs
And haunts of savage creatures, do I drag,
And on the giant Cyclops from a cliff
I look abroad, and shudder at the din
Of feet and voice. An unnutritious food,—
Berries and stony cornels,—boughs purvey,
And grasses feed me with their roots up-
 torn. 922
Surveying all around, this fleet I first
Spied coming to the shores. To this did I
Resign myself, whatever it might prove.
Enough to have escaped the cursèd crew;
Do ye the rather take away this life
By any death whate'er.' He scarcely these
Had said, when from the mountain-crest
 himself
Perceive we, moving him among his flocks
With giant bulk,—the shepherd Poly-
 pheme,— 931
And seeking the familiar shores:—a mon-
 ster dread,
Misshapen, huge, whose eye is reft away.
A branchless pine within his hand controls,
And renders sure, his steps. His woolly
 ewes

920. If the secondary meaning of *infelicem*,
verse 649, be preferred, "miserable" can be substituted for "unnutritious," or "wretched sustenance" for *victum infelicem*.

"Behold, the earth hath roots;
Within this mile break forth a hundred springs:
The oaks bear mast, the briers scarlet hips;
The bounteous housewife, Nature, on each bush
Lays her full mess before you."
 Shakespeare, *Timon of Athens*, iv. 3.

931. "Behold the monster, Polypheme;
See what ample strides he takes,
The mountain nods, the forest shakes;
The waves run frighten'd to the shores;
Hark! how the thundering giant roars."
 Gay, *Acis and Galatea*.

934. Grander is Milton, *P. L.*, b. i.:
"His spear, to equal which the tallest pine
Hewn on Norwegian hills, to be the mast
Of some great ammiral, were but a wand,
He walk'd with."

Milton, however, may have borrowed the idea
from Cowley, as Dr. Johnson remarks on the
passage in the third book of his *Davideis*:

"His spear the trunk was of a lofty tree,
Which Nature meant some ship's tall mast
 should be."

Attend upon him;—that the only joy
And comfort of his woe. Soon as he touched
The deepsome billows, and the waters reached,
The dripping gore of his uprooted eye
Therefrom he washes, gnashing with his teeth   940
With groan [s]; and now he stalks through middle sea,
Nor yet the surge his tow'ring sides bedewed.
We far therefrom our flight in horror haste,—
Our suitor welcomed thus thro' his desert,—
And silently the cable cut away;
And, bending forward, sweep with rival oars
The waters. He perceived, and towards the sound
Of voice his steps he veered. But when no power
Is giv'n of reaching us with his right hand,
Nor is he able in pursuit to match   950
Ionian waves, a thund'ring yell he lifts,
Wherewith the deep and all its billows quaked,
And inly startled was Italia's land,
And bellowed Ætna through his winding vaults.
But from the forests and the lofty mounts
The Cyclops' brood, forth summoned, to the ports
Come swooping downward, and the strands they fill.
Descry we, vainly standing side by side,
With scowling eye-ball, Ætna's brother-train,
Porting to heav'n their tow'ring heads,—a dire   960
Assembly: as when on some lofty crest
Sky-mounting oaks, or cone-rife cypresses,
Have stood in group, the stately wood of Jove,
Or grove of Dian. Headlong drives us on
A keen alarm, for any point whate'er
T' uncoil the sheets, and spread the sails to winds
Of favor. Warn them, on the other hand,
The orders [giv'n] of Helenus that they
'Twixt Scylla and Charybdis,—either route
With trifling odds of death,—hold not their course.   970

Decreed it is that backward we direct
The canvas. But, behold! the northern gale,
From out Pelorus' narrow mansion sent,
Is present with us. I am wafted past
Pantagia's outlets in the living rock,
And Megarian bays, and Thapsus lying [low].
Such shores roamed over, coasting back again,
[To us] did Achemenides reveal,
The comrade of Ulysses evil-starred.
"Outstretched before Sicania's bay, there lies   980
An isle against Plemmyrium, rife in waves:
Its name the ancients have Ortygia called.
There is a legend, that Alpheus, stream
Of Elis, hither worked mysterious paths
Beneath the sea, who now, O Arethuse,
Is mingled with thy spring in Sic'ly's waves.
Enjoined, the sovereign powers of the spot
We worship; and I thence sail by,—too rich,—
The soil of stagnating Helorus. Hence
Pachynus' tow'ring cliffs, and jutting rocks
We graze; and, granted never by the fates
To be disturbed, looms Camarine afar,   992
And the Geloan champaigns, Gela, too,
Called by the title of its felon flood.
Thence stately Acragas far off displays
Colossal walls, of high-souled horses erst
The breeder. Thee, too, with accorded gales
I leave, palm-rife Seline, and skirt the shoals
Of Lilybeum, stern with viewless rocks.
Hence me the haven, and the joyless coast
Of Drepanum receive. Here, hunted on
By storms so many of the deep, alas!   1002
My father,—[he,] of every care and chance
The anodyne,—Anchises do I lose.
Here me, best father, wearied, dost thou leave;
Ah! vainly rescued from such grievous risks.
Nor did the prophet Helenus, what time
He many a fearful warning gave, foretell

---

936. "The day abhors me, and from me doth fly,
  Night still me follows, yet too long doth stay;"
"But what availeth either night or day?
  All's one to me, still day, or ever night;
  My light is darkness, and my darkness light."
                  Drayton, *First Legend*.

946. Or: "vying."

979. It is difficult to believe that Virgil ever wrote verses 690, 691. However, as they are received into the text, *infelicis* must be translated as in v. 613; that is, in the sense in which Achemenides used, and not as Æneas would use it. The latter would have employed *pellacis*, or some other uncomplimentary term, to raise anger rather than pity.

983. So Milton, *Arcades*:

"Of famous Arcady ye are, and sprung
  Of that renownèd flood, so often sung,
  Divine Alpheus, who by secret sluice
  Stole under seas, to meet his Arethuse."

These woes to me; no, not Celæno dread.
This was my last distress, this was the goal
Of longsome voyages. Departed hence,
A god hath borne me onward to your coasts." 1012

Thus sire Æneas,—all on him attent,—
Alone recounted the decrees of gods,
And told his voyages. He hushed at last,
And here,—conclusion made,—he came to rest.

BOOK IV.

But, smitten long erewhile by passion sore,
The queen her wound is nursing in her veins,
And she is wasted by a viewless fire.
The hero's lofty worth, and lofty pride
Of his descent, are ofttimes to her mind
Returning; in her breast deep printed cling
His features and his words; nor doth unrest
Vouchsafe a peaceful slumber to her limbs.
The next Aurore with Phœbus' torch the lands
Was scanning, and the moistful shade from heaven 10
Had chased away, when, scarcely in her mind,
She thus her sister, one with her in soul,
Accosts: "O Anna, sister [mine], what dreams
Appal me, poised [in doubt]! How strange
The guest, [who] has at our abodes arrived!
Of what a noble bearing in his mien!
Of what a gallant heart and arms! I deem
In sooth, (nor idle the belief,) that he
The offspring is of gods. Degen'rate souls

Fear proves. Ah! by what fates has he been tossed! 20
What battles, carried to their close, he sang!
If rested not within my mind [resolve],
Firm and unshaken, not to wish to yoke
Myself to any in the marriage-bond,
Since my first love betrayed me, duped by death;
Had there been no disgust at bed and torch,
To this one weakness I could haply stoop.
O Anna, (for I will avow [the truth,])
Since the decease of my unhappy spouse,
Sychæus, and that household gods with blood, 30
[Spilt] by a brother, were besprent, this man
Alone hath warped my feelings, and hath forced
A falt'ring soul: I recognise the tracks
Of former passion. But I would to heaven,
That either deepest earth for me would first
Gape open, or that the almighty sire
Would hurl me with his leven to the shades,
The ghastly shades of Erebus, and night

Line 4. If "multa," v. 3, must be rendered more literally, a dull substitute for "lofty" is easily found.

9. "The morrow next, so soon as Phœbus' lamp
Bewrayed had the world with early light,
And fresh Aurora had the shady damp
Out of the goodly heven amoved quight."
    Spenser, *Faerie Queene*, iii. 10, 1.

See note on line 846.

12. "There's never man nor woman that e'er loved,
But chose some bosom friend, whose close converse
Sweetened their joys, and eased their burdened minds
Of such a working secret."   May, *The Heir*, ii.

19. "And live a coward in thine own esteem,
Letting 'I dare not' wait upon 'I would,'
Like the poor cat i' the adage."

The adage is:
"The cat loves fish, but dares not wet her feet."
See Payne Collier on Shakespeare, *Macbeth*, i. 7.

"A donative he hath of every god:
Apollo gave him lockes; Jove his high front;
The god of eloquence his flowing speech;
The feminine deities strowed all their bounties

And beautie on his face; that eye was Juno's;
Those lips were his that wonne the golden ball;
That virgin-blush, Diana's: here they meete,
As in a sacred synod."
    Marston, *Insatiate Countesse*, i.

"Feare is my vassall; when I frowne he flyes:
A hundred times in life a coward dies." *Ib.*, iv.

20. "She loved me for the dangers I had passed,
And I loved her that she did pity them."
    Shakespeare, *Othello*, i. 3.

23. "Were she the abstract of her sex for form,
The only warehouse of perfection;
Were there no rose nor lily but her cheek,
No music but her tongue, virtue but her's,
She must not rest near me. My vow is graven
Here in my heart, irrevocably breathed;
And when I break it—"
    Beaumont and Fletcher, *The Knight of Malta*, v. 2.

37. "You greater powers, guard me from violence,
And from a wilful fall I'll keep myself:
High Jupiter, the venger of foul sin,
With angry thunder strike me to the deepest,
And darkest shades of hell, when I consent
To soil my unstained faith."
    Beaumont and Fletcher, *The Faithful Friends*, ii. 2.

Profound, before that thee, O Modesty,
I outrage, or thy laws I break. He, who
First linked me to himself, hath borne away
My loves: let him possess them in his heart,
And guard them in the grave." Thus
speaking forth,
She filled her bosom with her starting tears.
Anna replies: "O thou than light of day
More precious to thy sister, wilt thou all
alone
Be wasted mourning in a lasting youth?
Nor darling sons, nor Venus' guerdons
know?
That ash or buried Manes reck of this,
Dost thou imagine? Be it, hitherto, 50
While sick at heart, no lovers thee have
swayed,
No, not in Libya, not erenow at Tyre ;—
Iarbas scorned, and other chieftains, whom
The Afric land, in triumphs rich, supports:
Wilt thou e'en fight against a welcome love?
Nor to thy mind occurs it, on whose fields
Thou'st settled? This side, the Gætulian
towns,
A horde that cannot be o'ercome in war,
Unreined Numidians, too, encircle thee,
And the inhospitable Syrt ; on that, 60
A country waste with drought, and far and
wide
Barcæans raging. Wherefore name the wars

That spring from Tyrus, and a brother's
threats?
In sooth I deem that, with the deities
Their guardians, Juno in their favor, too,
This course have Ilium's galleys by the
breeze
Held [hither]. What a city, sister, thou
Shalt this behold ! what kingdoms to arise
From such a union! With the Trojans'
arms
[On ours] attending, with what grand ex-
ploits 70
Shall Carthaginian glory rear her [head] !
Do thou but crave indulgence from the gods,
And,—off'rings of propitiation made,—
Free scope to hospitality accord,
And pleas for his detention net around,
While sorely on the ocean winter storms,
And water-rife Orion, and his ships
Are shattered; while not practicable heaven."
By these her words she kindled up a soul
With passion fired, and to a wav'ring mind
Imparted hope, and disengaged reserve. 81
They in the first place to the shrines re-
pair,
And grace throughout the altars crave ; they
slay,
According to the custom chosen, ewes
Of two years old to law-enacting Ceres,
And Phœbus, and to the Lyæan sire ;
'Bove all to Juno, whose concern are ties
Of marriage. Fairest Dido, e'en herself,
A saucer holding in her right hand, pours
Full in the centre of a heifer's horns, 90
Gloss-white ; or, 'fore the features of the
gods,
She paces by the altars rich, and day
Renews with gifts, and, poring with her
lips apart,
Within the opened bosoms of the beasts,
Their throbbing entrails she consults. Alas!

---

39. "'Tis one thing to be tempted, Escalus,
Another thing to fall."
Shakespeare, *Measure for Measure*, ii. 1.

"She that has no temptation set before her,
Her virtue has no conquest: then would her
constancy
Shine in the brightest goodness of her glory,
If she would give admittance, see and be seen,
And yet resist and conquer : there were argument
For angels."
Middleton, *More Dissemblers besides Women*,
i. 2.

" Whiteness of name, thou must be mine."
J. Fletcher, *The Elder Brother*, iv. 3.

45. So Gray's Bard passionately expresses his
affection for his murdered comrades :
" Dear lost companions of my tuneful art,
Dear as the light that visits these sad eyes,
Dear as the ruddy drops that warm my heart,
Ye died amidst your dying country's cries."
Shakespeare varies the image. Brutus says to
Portia ;
" You are my true and honourable wife ;
As dear to me as are the ruddy drops
That visit my sad heart."
Julius Cæsar, ii. 1.

47. "I am but the shadow of myself without thee."
Shirley, *The Politician*, ii. 1.

"Life without love is load ; and time stands still :
What we refuse to him, to death we give ;
And then, then only, when we love, we live."
Congreve, *The Mourning Bride*, ii. end.

---

63. The strict meaning of *germani*, v. 44, can
scarcely be intended here.

81. "I am lost,
Utterly lost ! My faith is gone for ever !
My fame, my praise, my liberty, my peace,
Changed for a restless passion ! O hard spite,
To lose my seven years' victory at one sight !"
Middleton, *More Dissemblers besides Women*,
i. 3.
"O that I
Have reason to discern the better way,
And yet pursue the worse !"
Massinger, *The Unnatural Combat*, iv. 1.

It had been better advice for Anna to have said :
"Therefore I charge you,
As you have pity, stop those tender ears
From his enchanting voice ; close up those eyes,
That you may never catch a dart from him,
Nor he from you."
Beaumont and Fletcher, *A King and no King*, ii. 1.

The soothsayers' unknowing minds! What boot
Her vows the raver? What the shrines? Meanwhile
Upon her marrow preys the gentle flame,
And silent lives the wound beneath her breast.
Unhappy Dido is consumed, and roams 100
Through the whole city, frantic: like a hind,
By arrow pierced, which, heedless, hath afar
Among the woods of Crete a shepherd shot,
While hunting her with weapons, and hath left
The wingy steel, unconscious; she in flight
The forests and the lawns of Dicte scours:
The deadly shaft is clinging to her flank.
Æneas now she brings with her throughout
The central buildings, and Sidonian wealth
Exhibits, and a city to his hand; 110
Begins to utter, and amid the word
Stops short. Now looks she for the self-same feasts,
As day is sinking, and to Ilium's toils
Once more to listen in her wildness craves,
And hangs once more upon the speaker's lips.
Then, when they have withdrawn, and in her turn
The darkling moon extinguishes her light,
And, as they sink, the stars are urging sleep,
She lonely in her empty palace mourns,
And on the couch, [which he had] left, lies down: 120
Him absent absent she both hears and sees.
Or in her lap Ascanius she, bewitched
By the resemblance of his father, stays,
If she could cheat unutterable love.
Uprise not tow'rs commenced; their arms the youth
Ply not, or havens, or defensive works,
In war secure, provide; hang broken off
Their labors, and the walls' embattled heights
Immense, and enginery made match for heaven.
Whom soon as the belovèd spouse of Jove 130

---

101. Dido was the reverse of Viola's sister, who
" Never told her love,
But let concealment, like a worm i' th' bud,
Feed on her damask cheek; she pined in thought,
And, with a green and yellow melancholy,
She sat like patience on a monument,
Smiling at grief."
Shakespeare, *Twelfth Night*, ii. 4.

" She, sir,
That walks here up and down an empty shadow;
One that for some few hours
But wanders here, carrying her own sad coffin,
Seeking some desert place to lodge her griefs in."
J. Fletcher, *The Sea Voyage*, iv. 2.

102. " Looke as a well-growne stately headed bucke,
But lately by the woodman's arrow strucke,
Runs gadding o'er the lawnes, or nimbly strayes
Among the combrous brakes a thousand wayes;
Now through the high wood scowrs, then by the brooks,
On every hill side, and each vale he lookes,
If 'mongst their store of simples may be found
An hearbe to draw and heale his smarting wound."
Browne, *Brit. Past.*, ii. 4.

This simile may call to the reader's mind the pathetic description of the wounded stag in *As You Like It*, ii. 1:
" To-day, my lord of Amiens, and myself,
Did steal behind him, as he lay along
Under an oak, whose antique root peeps out
Upon the brook that brawls along this wood:
To the which place a poor sequestered stag,
That from the hunters' aim had ta'en a hurt,
Did come to languish; and, indeed, my lord,
The wretched animal heav'd forth such groans,
That their discharge did stretch his leathern coat
Almost to bursting; and the big round tears
Cours'd one another down his innocent nose
In piteous chase: and thus the hairy fool,
Much marked of the melancholy Jaques,
Stood on the extremest verge of the swift brook,
Augmenting it with tears."

111. " How her heart beats!
Much like a partridge in a sparhawk's foot,
That with a panting silence does lament
The fate she cannot fly from."
Massinger, *The Unnatural Combat*, v. 1.

114, 15. " But all the while that he these speeches spent,
Upon his lips hong faire Dame Hellenore
With vigilant regard and dew attent,
Fashioning worldes of fancies evermore
In her fraile witt, that now her quite forlore:
The whiles unwares away her wondring eye
And greedy eares her weake hart from her bore."
Spenser, *Faerie Queene*, iii. 9, 51.

" Wherein I spoke of most disastrous chances,
Of moving accidents, by flood and field;
Of hair-breadth scapes i' th' imminent deadly breach;
Of being taken by the insolent foe,
And sold to slavery; of my redemption thence,
And portance in my travels' history;—
Wherein of antres vast, and desarts idle,
Rough quarries, rocks, and hills whose head touch'd heaven.
. . . . . . These things to hear
Would Desdemona seriously incline. . . . .
She'd come again, and with a greedy ear
Devour up my discourse."
Shakespeare, *Othello*, i. 3.

119. " Her chamber's but a coffin of a larger Volume, wherein she walks so like a ghost,
'Twould make you pale to see her."
Shirley, *The Cardinal*, iv. 2.

" Strong is my love to thee; for every moment
I'm from thy sight, the heart within my bosom
Mourns, like a tender infant in its cradle,
Whose nurse had left it."
Otway, *Venice Preserved*, iii. 1.

126. " Alack! when once our grace we have forgot,
Nothing goes right; we would, and we would not."
Shakespeare, *Measure for Measure*, iv. 4.

Perceived to be enchained by such a plague,
Nor character to stand in passion's way,
Saturnia Venus in such words accosts :
" Distinguished praise, in sooth, and splen-
  did spoils
Ye carry off, both thou and [that] thy boy !
Mighty and notable the pow'r divine,
If by the cunning of a pair of gods
One woman is subdued ! Nor doth it so
Escape my notice, that [these] walls of ours
Thou, dreading, hast suspected held the
  domes   140
Of stately Carthage. But what limit shall
  there be ?
Or to what end now struggles so severe ?
Why do we not the rather endless peace
And covenanted nuptial rites promote ?
Thou hast what thou hast sought with all
  thy soul :
The loving Dido burns, and hath imbibed
The frenzy through her bones. Then, let
  us rule
This nation jointly, and with equal sway ;
Be it allowed her, to a Phrygian spouse
To be a slave, and, as a dowry given, 150
The Tyrians to resign to thy right hand."
To her (for she perceived that she had
  spoken
With feigned intent, in order that the realm
Of Italy she might to Libyan coasts
Divert,) thus Venus in reply began :
" Who madly would such [terms as these]
  decline ?
Or liefer would with thee engage in war ?
If only fortune may attend the scheme,
Which thou announcest. But by fates am I
Borne onward, doubtful whether Jove may
  will   160
That one should be the city for the men
Of Tyre, and for the refugees from Troy ;
Or would approve the nations being blent,
Or leagues cemented. Thou his consort
  art :
Thine is the privilege to sound his mind
By prayer. Go forward ; I will follow."
  Then
The royal Juno thus caught up [the word] :
"With me shall rest that task. Now by
  what plan
What presseth on us can be brought to pass,

132. " No ! I must downward, downward ! Though
repentance
Could borrow all the glorious wings of grace,
My mountainous weight of sins would crack their
pinions,
And sink them to hell with me."
          Massinger, *The Renegade*, iii. 2.
142. Or : " Or whither with a struggle so severe ?"
148. Or : " This a joint nation."
     Or : " auspices."

In few, — attend ! — I thee will teach.
Æneas,   170
And with him, Dido thrice-unblest, prepare
To go a hunting to the wood, what time
To-morrow's Titan shall have brought to
  light
His infant dawn, and with his beams un-
  veiled
The globe. On these will I a black'ning
  shower
With blended hail, while flutter plumes, and
  glades
They girdle with th' inclosure, from above
Outpour, and with my thunder will I wake
All heav'n. On every side the retinue
Shall fly amain, and in the gloom of night
Shall they be mantled. At the self-same
  grot   181
Shall Dido and the Trojan prince arrive.
There I shall be, and, if I have thy sure
  assent,
In lasting marriage will I her unite,
And consecrate her his for ever. Here
Shall Hymenœus be." Opposing not
Her suitress, Cytherea acquiesced,
And at the crafts that were devised she
  smiled.
  Meanwhile Aurora rising Ocean left.
Forth issues from the gates at beam of day,
Uprisen, chosen youth ; nets wide of mesh,
Toils, hunting lances with a breadth of steel,
And Massylæan horsemen sally forth, 193
And keenly-scented force of hounds. The
  queen,
Delaying in her chamber, at the gates
The princes of the Tyrians wait, and, badged
With purple and with gold, her palfrey
  stands,

188. " The gods assist just hearts ; and states, that
trust
Plots before Providence, are lost like dust."
               Marston, *Sophonisba*, ii. 1.
" A woman's tongue, I see, some time or other,
Will prove her traitor."
               Ford, *The Fancies*, iv. 1.
194. Prior seems to have had this passage in his
view while describing Abra in *Solomon*, b. ii. :
" Thy King, Jerusalem ! descends to wait
Till Abra comes. She comes ; a milk-white steed,
Mixture of Persia's and Arabia's breed,
Sustains the nymph : her garments flying loose,
(As the Sydonian maids or Thracian use)
And half her knee and half her breast appear,
By art, like negligence, disclosed, and bare :
Her left hand guides the hunting courser's flight,
A silver bow she carries in her right,
And from the golden quiver at her side
Rustles the ebon arrow's feather'd pride ;
Sapphires and diamonds on her front display
An artificial moon's increasing ray.
Diana, huntress, mistress of the groves,
The favourite Abra speaks, and looks, and
moves."

And fiercely champs the foaming bits. At last
Forth comes she,—thronging her a mighty train,—
Invested in a Sidon hunting-cloak   200
With purfled edge. Her quiver is of gold;
Her locks in knot are gathered into gold;
A golden brooch her robe of crimson binds
Beneath. Moreo'er her Phrygian retinue
And gay Iulus pace along. Himself,
Æneas, passing fair beyond the rest,
Moves on their comrade, and the trains unites:
Like as, when Lycia in her wintry plight,
And Xanthus' rivulets, Apollo quits,
And Delos of his mother goes to view, 210
The dances, too, renews; and, mingled round
The altars, Cretes alike, and Dryopes,
And painted Agathyrsi, shout amain;
[The god] himself on brows of Cynthus walks,
And with the velvet leaf his streaming hair
He presses, as he shapes it, and with gold
He braids; his weapons on his shoulders clang.
No tardier than he Æneas paced:
Such striking beauty from his peerless mien
Beams forth. As soon as at the lofty mounts   220
And pathless lairs they are arrived, behold!
Wild she-goats, from a height of rock dislodged,
Down scampered from the brows; on th' other side
The stags the open champaigns scour [full] speed,
And dusted squadrons huddle in their flight,
And leave the mountains. But the boy Ascanius
Amid the vallies in his mettled horse
Rejoices; and now these in race, now those,
Outstrips, and prays be granted to his vows
A foaming boar among the listless flocks,
Or tawny lion to descend the mount.   231
    Meanwhile with uproar vast the heav'n begins

To be turmoiled. Ensues with mingled hail
A rain-storm; and the retinue of Tyre
In every quarter, and the youth of Troy,
And Venus' Dardan grandson, through the fields
Sought diff'rent shelters in their fear. Down swoop
The torrents from the mounts. The self-same grot
Do Dido and the Trojan leader reach.
And Tellus first, and Juno, patroness   240
Of wedlock, give the signal: levens flashed,
And witness to the union was the sky,
And on the highest summit shrieked the Nymphs.
That day first proved the source of death,
And first, of her misfortunes. Nor is she
By outward form [s] or reputation swayed,

Crosse Knight and Una in Spenser's *Faerie Queene*, b. i. c. i. 6, 7:
  " Thus as they past,
The day with cloudes was suddeine overcast,
And angry Iove an hideous storme of raine
Did poure into his lemans lap so fast,
That everie wight to shrowd it did constrain;
And this faire couple eke to shroud themselves were fain.

" Enforst to seeke some covert nigh at hand,
A shadie grove not farr away they spide,
That promist ayde the tempest to withstand;
Whose loftie trees, yclad with sommers pride,
Did spred so broad, that heavens light did hide,
Not perceable with power of any starr:
And all within were pathes and alleies wide,
With footing worne, and leading inward farr:
Faire harbour that them seems; so in they entred ar."

240. So Milton, *Paradise Lost*, b. ix.:
" Earth trembled from her entrails, as again
In pangs; and Nature gave a second groan;
Sky lour'd; and, muttering thunder, some sad drops
Wept at completing of the mortal sin."
How different the image of nuptial love before the fall!—
  " To the nuptial bower
I led her blushing like the morn: all Heaven,
And happy constellations, on that hour
Shed their selectest influence; the Earth
Gave sign of gratulation, and each hill;
Joyous the birds; fresh gales and gentle airs
Whispered it to the woods, and from their wings
Flung rose, flung odours from the spicy shrub."
      Milton, *P. L.*, b. 8.

242. " Well, heaven forgive him, and forgive us all!
Some rise by sin, and some by virtue fall."
      Shakespeare, *Measure for Measure*, ii. 1.

245. " Thick darkness dwells upon this hour; integrity,
Like one of heaven's bright luminaries, now
By error's dullest element interposed,
Suffers a black eclipse."
      Middleton, *A Game at Chess*, iv. 4.
          " To err but once
Is to be undone for ever."
        Anything for a Quiet Life, i. 1.

---

217. Or: "upon his shoulders thunder arms."

224. "Alate we ran the deer, and through the lawnds
Stripped with our nags the lofty frolic bucks,
That scudded 'fore the teasers like the wind."
      Robert Green, *Friar Bacon*, opening lines.

227.   " Out of brave horsemanship
Arise the first sparks of glowing resolution,
That raise the mind to noble action."
        Webster, *The Duchess of Malfi*, i. 2.

232. This passage may call to mind the Red

138   v. 171—178.   THE ÆNEID.   v. 178—197.

Nor Dido now clandestine love designs:
A marriage does she call it; with this name
Before her frailty she a curtain weaves.
  Straight Rumor runs thro' Libya's mighty
    towns;—   250
Rumor, than whom there is none other ill
More fleet. By volubility she thrives,
And vigor musters to her in her march.
A pigmy through alarm at first, anon
She rears her [form] to air, and o'er the
    ground
She stalks, and hides her head among the
    clouds.
Her, Earth her dam, embittered at the
    wrath

---

249. Or, in the soft parlance of modern laxity:
"Before her indiscretion weaves a veil."
"Who wooed in haste, and means to wed at leisure."
  Shakespeare, *Taming of the Shrew*, iii. 2.
So Dryden, *Hind and Panther*, 353, 4:
"Then by a left-hand marriage weds the dame,
Covering adultery with a specious name."
        "With what cunning
This woman argues for her own damnation!"
  Beaumont and Fletcher, *The Knight of Malta*,
    iii. 4.
       "How, in a moment,
All that was gracious, great, and glorious in her,
And won upon all hearts, like seeming shadows
Wanting true substance, vanished!"
  Massinger, *The Picture*, iv. 3.

250. Contention is thus described by Thomson;
  Liberty, iv. 33:
"Contention led the van: first small of size,
But soon dilating to the skies she towers!
Then, wide as air, the livid Fury spread,
And, high her head above the stormy clouds,
She blazed in omens, swell'd the groaning winds
With wild surmises, battlings, sounds of war:
From land to land the maddening trumpet blew,
And poured her venom through the heart of man."

253. So Parnell says of the ills in Pandora's box:
"From point to point, from pole to pole they flew,
Spread as they went, and in the progress grew."
                                            Hesiod.

And Dryden, of the origin of the Fire of London:
"Then in some close-pent room it crept along,
And mouldering as it went, in silence fed;
Till th' infant monster, with devouring strong,
Walk'd boldly upright with exalted head."
                          Annus Mirabilis, 218.

"The flying rumours gather'd as they rolled,
Scarce any tale was sooner heard than told;
And all who told it added something new,
And all who heard it made enlargements too!
In every ear it spread, on every tongue it grew."
And again:
"But straight the direful trump of slander sounds;
Through the big dome the doubling thunder
    bounds;
Loud as the burst of cannon rends the skies,
The dire report thro' every region flies.
In every ear incessant rumours rung,
And gathering scandals grew on every tongue."
                     Pope, *Temple of Fame.*

Of gods, the youngest sister, as they tell,
To Cœus and Enceladus, brought forth,
Swift on her feet and on her nimble wings:—
A monster dread, a giantess, in whom   261
As many be the feathers on her frame,
So many wakeful eyes [there lie] beneath,—
A marvel to be told,—so many tongues,
Mouths just so many babble, up she pricks
So many ears. By night she flies 'twixt
    heaven
And earth a-midway, whizzing through the
    gloom,
Nor down to balmy slumber drops her eyne.
By day she sits a spy, or on the ridge
Of [some] roof-top, or on the lofty towers,
And mighty cities with alarm she fills; 271
As firm a grasper of the false and wrong,
As herald of the true. She then with maze
Of prate the people filled brimful, in glee,
And facts and fictions in an equal sort
She chanted: "That Æneas had arrived,
From blood of Troja sprung, to whom, as
    spouse,
The lovely Dido deigns herself to link;
That now the winter-tide, however long,
In mutual dalliance they enjoy, of realms
Unmindful, and by shameless passion
    thralled."   281
These [tales] eachwhere the loathsome
    goddess spreads
Upon the people's tongues. She straight
    to king
Iarbas wheels aside her course, and fires
His mind with tattle, and heaps up his
    wrath.

---

260. "For Fame hath many wings to bring ill
  tidings."
       Massinger, *The Duke of Milan*, i. 3.
"Such was her form, as ancient bards have told:
Wings raise her arms, and wings her feet infold:
A thousand busy tongues the goddess bears,
And thousand open eyes, and thousand listening
    ears."   Pope, *Temple of Fame.*

272. This line was rendered in the first edition:
"As much a stickler for the false and wrong."

279.   "Sleep shall not seize me,
Nor any food befriend me but thy kisses,
Ere I forsake this desert. I live honest!
He may as well bid dead men walk. I humbled,
Or bent below my power! let night-dogs tear me,
And goblins ride me in my sleep to jelly,
Ere I forsake my sphere!"
      J. Fletcher, *Thierry and Theodoret*, i. 1.

283.   "But, great man,
Every sin thou committ'st shews like a flame
Upon a mountain; 'tis seen far about,
And, with a big wind made of popular breath,
The sparkles fly through cities! here one takes,
Another catches there, and in short time
Waste all to cinders: but remember still,
What burnt the valleys first came from the hill."
  Middleton, *Women beware of Women*, iv. 1.

He, sprung from Hammon, by a ravished Nymph
Of Garama, a hundred vasty fanes
To Jupiter throughout his spacious realms,
A hundred altars, reared ; and wakeful fire
Had sanctified, the gods' undying watch ;
And with the blood of flocks their floor is rich,   291
And blooming [stand] the gates with damasked wreaths.
And he, soul-crazed, and with the bitter tale
Afire, is said, at th' altars' front, amid
The gods' immediate pow'rs, in many a prayer
Jove humbly to have sued with hands upturned :
"Almighty Jove, to whom the Moorish race,
Now banqueting on broidered couches, pours
Lenæan sacrifice, dost these behold ?
Or thee, my father, when thou launchest forth   300
Thy levens, do we idly hold in awe ?
And is it random flashes in the clouds
Appal our minds, and empty thunders blend ?
The woman, who, a rover in our bourns,
A paltry city for a fee hath built,
To whom a sea-board to be ploughed, to whom, too, we
The jurisdiction of the spot have deigned,
Hath our espousals spurned, and as her lord
Æneas hath she welcomed to her realm.
And now *that* Paris, with his half-man train,   310
With Lydian turban underneath his chin,
And dripping tresses tied, the spoil enjoys :
We off'rings to thy fanes forsooth present,
And cherish an unprofitable tale."
[The suitor,] while in accents such he prays,
And holds the altars, the almighty heard,
And towards the royal city turned his eyes,
And to the lovers, of their better name
Forgetful ; then thus Mercury accosts,
And such injunctions gives : " Post quick, my son !   320
The Zephyrs call, and sail upon thy wings,
And the Dardanian prince, who loiters now
In Tyrian Carthage, and the cities, deigned
By Fates, regardeth not, do thou address,
And through the nimble gales bear down my words :
' His fairest mother vouched him not to us
The like, and from the arms of Greeks for this
Twice claims him ; but that he might prove the man,
To govern Italy, with princedoms big,
And storming in the battle ; his descent   330
From Teucer's lofty lineage to evince,
And the whole world to force beneath his rule.
If him no glory of such noble deeds
Enkindles, nor for sake of his own fame
Himself in toil engages, does the sire
T' Ascanius grudge the towered-heights of Rome ?
What [end] does he design ? Or with what hope
Is he delaying 'mong a hostile clan,
Nor casts a thought upon his Auson race,
And fields Lavinian ? ' Let him sail !' This is
The point ; let this the message be from us."
He said. Prepared the other to obey
His sovereign father's mandate ; and he first
Upon his feet ties ancle-gear of gold,   344
Which high upon its pinions, whether o'er
The waters, or the lands, at even pace

---

286.   " Old Cham,
Whom Gentiles Ammon call, and Libyan Jove."
Milton, *Paradise Lost*, b. iv.

301. " Terrify babes, my lord, with painted devils :
I am past such needless palsy."
Webster, *Vittoria Corombona*, iii. 2.

" Look to 't, for our anger
Is making thunder-bolts.
Thunder ! in faith,
They are but crackers."   *Ibid.*, ii. 1.

309. " Laying her duty, beauty, wit, and fortunes,
On an extravagant and wheedling stranger,
Of here and everywhere."
Shakespeare, *Othello*, l. 1.

310.   " A raw young fellow,
One never trained in arms, but rather fashioned
To tilt with ladies' lips than crack a lance ;
Ravish a feather from a mistress' fan,
And wear it as a favour."
Massinger, *The Bondman*, i. 1.

313.   " But that it were profane
To argue heaven of ignorance or injustice,
I now should tax it."
The Emperor of the East, v. 1.

328. Or: " frees," " saves."

333.   " Othello's occupation's gone."
Shakespeare, *Othello*, iii. 3.

346.   " Now I go, now I fly,
Malkin my sweet spirit and I.
O what a dainty pleasure 'tis
To ride in the air
When the moon shines fair,
And sing and dance, and toy and kiss !
Over woods, high rocks, and mountains,
Over seas, our mistress' fountains,
Over steeples, towers, and turrets
We fly by night, 'mongst troops of spirits."
Middleton, *The Witch*, iii. end.

" But here's a little flaming cherubim,
The Mercury of heaven, with silver wings,

With the fleet blast convey him. Then his wand
He takes. Herewith he summons forth from Hell
The ghastly spirits, others sends adown
Beneath the rueful realms of Tartarus; 350
Grant slumbers and withdraws them, and the eyes
At death unseals. Relying upon this,
He hunts the storms, and swims through troublous clouds.
And now, on wing, the peak and steepy sides
Of painful Atlas he descries, he, who
The firmament upon his summit props ;—
Atlas, whose piny head is ever ringed
With sullen clouds, and beat by wind and rain.
Snow, showered down, his shoulders kerchiefs; then
Floods headlong hurtle from the old man's chin, 360
And stiffened stands in ice his bristly beard.
Here first, while leaning on his balanced wings,
Cyllenius halted; hence with his whole frame
He flung himself head-foremost to the waves,
Like to a bird, which round the shores, around
The fishy rocks flies low the surface nigh.
Not elsewise flew between the earth and heaven,
And Libya's sandy shore and breezes passed,

Impt for the flight to overtake his ghost,
And bring him back again."
                Southern, *Isabella*, end.

358. Like Milton's description of the region beyond Lethe:
"Beyond this flood a frozen continent
Lies dark and wild, beat with perpetual storms
Of whirlwind and dire hail, which on firm land
Thaws not, but gathers heap, and ruin seems
Of ancient pile." *P. L.*, b. ii.

360. Spenser gives Winter a beard not unlike to that of Atlas:
"Lastly came Winter cloathed all in frize,
Chattering his teeth for cold that did him chill;
Whilst on his hoary beard his breath did freese;
And the dull drops that from his purpled bill
As from a limbeck did adown distill."
                F. Q., vii. 7, 31.

"For scarce her chariot cut the easie earth,
And journeyed on, when Winter with cold breath
Crosseth her way, her borrowed haire did shine
With glittering isickles all christaline;
Her browes were perewigged with softer snow,
Her russet mantle fringed with ice below."
           Marston, *Entertainement*, l. 25.

363. "A station like the herald Mercury
New-lighted on a heaven-kissing hill."
            Shakespeare, *Hamlet*, iii. 4.

From his maternal grandsire coming down,
The Cyllene child. When first with pinioned soles 370
He touched the kraals, Æneas founding towers,
And dwellings newly raising, he espies.
Ay e'en had he, with yellow jasper starred,
A sword, and with the Tyrian purple blazed
A mantle, from his shoulders wimpled down;
Which presents had the wealthy Dido made,
And parted out the warp with filmy gold.
He instantly assails him: "Dost thou now
Foundations of the stately Carthage lay?
And, wife-besotted, art thou rearing up 380
Her beauteous city? Ah! of sovereignty
And thine estate forgetful! He himself,
The ruler of the gods, sends me to thee
From bright Olympus down, who by his nod
Wheels round the heav'n and earth; himself commands
To bring these orders thro' the nimble gales:
'What [end] dost thou design? Or with what hope
Dost while away thine hours in Libyan lands?
If thee no glory of such noble deeds
Affecteth, nor for sake of thine own fame
Thou dost thyself engage in toil, regard 391
Ascanius rising, and the prospects of thine heir
Iulus, [he,] to whom Italia's realm
And Roman land are due.'" In such a strain
Cyllenius having spoken, mortal ken
Amid his speech he quitted, and afar
He faded into subtile air from view.
But sooth Æneas, wildered at the sight,
Was dumb-struck, and his hair was raised on end
With terror, and his voice within his jaws

369. Milton's description of Raphael's descent from heaven somewhat resembles this of Mercury; *Paradise Lost*, b. v.:
"Down thither prone in flight
He speeds, and through the vast eternal sky
Sails between worlds and worlds, with steady wing
Now on the polar winds, then with quick fan
Winnows the buxom air. . . .
. . . At once on the eastern cliff of Paradise
He lights."

380. "Where is your understanding,
The noble vessel that your full soul sailed in,
Ribbed round with honours? Where is that? 'Tis ruined!
The tempest of a woman's sighs has sunk it."
      J. Fletcher, *The Bloody Brother*, ii. 1.

386. "A thousand leagues I have cut through empty air,
Far swifter than the sailing rack that gallops
Upon the wings of angry winds, to seek thee."
      J. Fletcher, *Women Pleased*, iv. 3.

Stood fixed. He burns to make escape by flight, 401
And leave the blissful regions, thunderstruck
At such grave warning and behests of gods.
Alas! what can he do? With what address
Now venture to approach the raging queen?
What introductions first should he adopt?
And now to this side, now to that, he shifts
His active spirit, and to sundry points
He hurries it, and whirls it round thro' all.
While wav'ring, this to him the worthier view 410
Appeared: he Mnestheus and Sergestus calls,
And brave Cloanthus:—"That the fleet by stealth
They should equip, and muster at the shore
The crews, their arms get ready, and what ground
For this his sweeping change of plan there be,
They should disguise; that he himself meanwhile,
(Since Dido, best [of beings,] nothing knew,
And she would not expect that loves so warm
Could be dissolved,) approaches would essay,
And what the softest seasons of address, 420
What course was fitting to the case." With speed
His mandate do they all in glee obey,
And put in force his orders. But the queen
His stratagems—a lover who can dupe?—
Divined, and was the foremost to perceive
His coming movements, fearing all [though] safe.
The same ungodly Rumor, as she fumes
Announced to her that furnished was the fleet,
And that a voyage was prepared. She storms,
Of reason void, and, fired, in revel-rage 430
Through all the city runs: as [fury-] roused
At holy [emblems] moved, a raver-maid,
What time triennial orgies goad her on,
When heard is Bacchus, and Cithæron calls
By night with shouting. She at last accosts
Æneas in these accents, unaddressed:

---

405. More literally: "Now dare to come about."
429. "Pigmie cares
Can shelter under patience' shield, but gyant griefes
Will burst all covert."
Marston, *Antonio and Mellida*, P. 2, ii. 3.

"Hast hoped, O traitor, thou could'st e'en disguise
Such heinous wickedness, and steal away
In silence from my land? Nor doth my love
Hold thee, nor thee a right hand plighted erst, 440
Nor Dido, doomed by felon death to die?
Nay, e'en 'neath winter's star dost thou equip
Thy fleet, and haste amid the northern blasts
To voyage through the deep, O heartless? What?
Were it thou did'st not seek strange lands, and homes
Unknown, and ancient Troy remained, would Troy
Thro' billowy ocean in thy ships be sought?
Me fliest thou? I [pray] thee by these tears,
And thy right hand, (since to my wretched self
Naught else I now have left,) by our embrace, 450
By bridal [joys] begun, if well at all
Of thee I have deserved, or aught of mine
Hath proved of charm to thee, compassionate
A falling house, and [thee] I pray, if still
Be any room for prayers, divest thyself
Of such a thought as that. On thy account
Loathe me the Libyan clans and Nomads' kings;
The Tyrians are incensed; on thy account,
The selfsame, is my honor blotted out,
And former character, whereby alone 460

---

437. "Thy shallow artifice by its suspicion,
And, like a cobweb veil, but thinly shades
The face of thy design."
"Thou, like the adder, venomous and deaf,
Hast stung the traveller, and after hear'st
Not his pursuing voice; even when thou think'st
To hide, the rustling leaves and bended grass
Confess, and point the path which thou hast crept." Congreve, *The Mourning Bride*, v. 1.

455. "Spite of my rage and pride,
I am a woman and a lover still." *Ibid.*, iv. 1.

460. "I see my leprosy unveiled; that sin,
Which, with my loss of honour, first engaged
My misery, is with a sunbeam writ
Upon my guilty forehead."
Shirley, *The Imposture*, v. 3.

"She was once an innocent,
As free from spot as the blue face of heaven,
Without a cloud in 't: she is now as sullied
As is that canopy, when mists and vapours
Divide it from our sight, and threaten pestilence."
Ford, *The Fancies*, v. 1.

"What delight has man
Now at this present for his plea ant sin
Of yesterday's committing? 'las, 'tis vanished,
And nothing but the sting remains within him!"
Middleton, *The Widow*, iii. 2.

Was I approaching towards the stars. To whom
Dost thou abandon me in death's embrace,
O guest?—since this the only name remains
From [that of] husband. Why do I delay?
Is't till Pygmalion, [my own] brother, raze
[These] walls of mine, or me his pris'ner hale
The Gætulan Iarbas? If at least
I any offspring, sired of thee, had owned
Before thy flight, if sported in my hall
For me some infantine Æneas, who 470
Might thee, tho' but in face, repeat, I sooth
Should not appear quite captived and forlorn."
She said. He at Jove's warnings kept his eyes
Unmoved, and with a struggle 'neath his heart
Unrest kept down; at last in [words] a few
He answers: "Ne'er will I, O queen, disown
That [in those favors], which, full many a one,
In language thou hast power to recount,
Thou [nobly] hast deserved [of me]; nor shall it irk
Elissa in my memory to bear, 480
So long as I am mindful of myself,
So long as animation sways these limbs.
Upon the question will I speak few [words].
I neither hoped to cover this retreat
By act of stealth, (form no [such fancy] thou,)
Nor e'er affected torches of a spouse,
Or entered into contracts [such as] these.
If Destinies would let me pass my life
'Neath my own rule, and of my free accord

To lull my woes to rest, Troy's city chief,
And the dear relics of my [countrymen],
Should I be cherishing; the lofty domes
Of Priam would remain, and with my hand 493
I re-arising Pergamus had built
For vanquished men. But now great Italy
Grynian Apollo, Italy the lots
Of Lycia, have commanded me to grasp.
This is my passion, this my native land.
If thee, a lady of Phœnicia, towers
Of Carthage, and a Libyan city's sight 500
Engages, what, I pray thee, means the grudge
At Teucri settling down in Auson land?
Our right it is, too, foreign realms to seek.
Me does my sire Anchises' troubled ghost,
As oft as with dank shades the night enwraps
The lands, as oft as fiery stars arise,
In slumbers warn and startle; me my boy,
Ascanius, and his precious person's wrong,
Whom of Hesperia's realm and destined fields
I cheat. Now e'en the courier of the gods,
From Jove himself despatched,—the head of both 511
I take to witness,—thro' the nimble gales
Hath carried down his orders. I myself
The deity in open light beheld
Ent'ring the walls, and in these ears his voice
Absorbed. Cease thou t' inflame alike myself
And thee with thy complainings: Italy,
With no free choice of mine, do I pursue."
Him, speaking such, long since askance she views,
Hither and thither rolling round her eyes,
And scans him wholly with her silent looks,
And, set ablaze, on this wise speaks she forth: 522
"Neither a goddess mother was to thee,
Nor Dardanus the founder of thy race,

---

461. "Fight well, and thou shalt see, after these wars,
Thy head wear sunbeams, and thy feet touch stars."
Massinger, *The Virgin Martyr*, ii. 3.

"No! you have let me stain my rising virtue,
Which else had ended brighter than the sun."
Lee, *The Rival Queens*, iv. 2.

462. Or: "about to die."

485. "Lay not that flattering unction to your soul,
That not your trespass, but my madness speaks."
Shakespeare, *Hamlet*, iii. 4.

486. "Let weak statesmen think of conscience;
I am armed against a thousand stings, and laugh at
The tales of hell and other worlds: we must
Possess our joys in, and know no other
But what our fancy every minute shall
Create to please us."
Shirley, *The Politician*, i. 1.

"But it does not
Add to the graces of your royal person,
To tread upon a lady thus dejected
By her own grief."

"Strike out a lion's teeth, and pare his claws,
And then a dwarf may pluck him by the beard:
'Tis a gay victory!" Shirley, *Chabot*, iii. 1.

510. "With devotion's visage,
And pious action, we do sugar o'er
The devil himself.", Shakespeare, *Hamlet*, iii. 1.

"Doth she make religion her riding-hood
To keep her from the sun and tempest?"
Webster, *The Duchess of Malfi*, ii. 3.

"A plea which will but faintly take thee off"
"From this leviathan scandal that lies rolling
Upon the crystal waters of devotion."
Middleton, *A Game at Chess*, ii. 1.

516. "Rid me of this my torture, quickly, there!
My madam with the everlasting voice,—
The bells in time of pestilence ne'er made
Like noise, or were in that perpetual motion!"

"A lawyer could not have been heard! nor scarce
Another woman, such a hail of words
She has let fall." Ben Jonson, *The Fox*, iii. 2.

Traitor! but bred thee, jagged with flinty cliffs,
The Caucasus, and Hyrcanian tigresses
Their dugs approached. For why do I pretend?
Or to what deeper [wrongs] reserve myself?
At our weeping did he heave a groan?
Bent he his eyes? O'erpowered, shed he tears? 530
Or hath he pity for a lover felt?
Before what [insults] what shall I prefer?
Now, now, nor highest Juno, nor the sire
Saturnian with impartial eyes views these.
Trust nowhere safe! An outcast on the beach,
A beggar, have I harbored, and, a fool,
Enthroned him in the partnership of realm;
His missing fleet, his mates, from death redeemed.
Ah! fired by furies am I hurried! Now
The seer Apollo, now the Lycian lots, 540
Now, too, the courier of the gods, despatched

525. "I have been gulled in a shining carbuncle,
A very glowworm, that I thought had fire in't,
And 'tis as cold as ice."
Beaumont and Fletcher, *Wit at Several Weapons*, ii. 2.

"Honour you've little, honesty you've less;
But conscience you have none."
Dryden, *The Duke of Guise*, iv. 1.

"Thou seed of rocks, will nothing move thee, then?"
J. Fletcher, *The Bloody Brother*, iii. 1.

"Are you marble?
If Christians have mothers, sure they share in
The tigress' fiercenees; for, if you were owner
Of human pity, you could not endure
A princess to kneel to you, or look on
These falling tears which hardest rocks would soften,
And yet remain unmoved."
Massinger, *The Renegade*, iii. 5.

"Be sure
You credit anything, the light gives light to,
Before a man. Rather believe the sea
Weeps for the ruined merchant, when he roars;
Rather the wind courts but the pregnant sails,
When the strong cordage cracks; rather, the sun
Comes but to kiss the fruit in wealthy autumn,
When all falls blasted."
Beaumont and Fletcher, *The Maid's Tragedy*, ii. 2.

526. "Thou almost mak'st me waver in my faith,
To hold opinion with Pythagoras,
That souls of animals infuse themselves
Into the trunks of men: thy currish spirit
Govern'd a wolf, who, hang'd for human slaughter,
Even from the gallows did his fell soul fleet,
And, whilst thou lay'st in thy unhallow'd dam,
Infus'd itself in thee; for thy desires
Are wolfish, bloody, starv'd, and ravenous."
Shakespeare, *Merchant of Venice*, iv. 1.

"When did the tiger's young ones teach the dam?
Oh! do not learn her wrath; she taught it thee:
The milk, thou suck'dst from her, did turn to marble:
Even at thy teat thou hadst thy tyranny."
Titus Andronicus, ii. 3.

From Jove himself, brings dread commands through air.
That is, forsooth, a task for Pow'rs above!
That care arouses them at their repose!
I neither stay thee, nor thy words refute.
Begone! Pursue Italia with the winds!
Seek kingdoms o'er the billows! Sooth I hope
That thou 'mid rocks, if aught the holy Powers
Avail, [the cup of] punishment wilt drain,
And by her name wilt 'Dido!' often call.
Absent I'll dog thee with my sooty flames;
And when cold death shall from the soul my limbs 552
Have sundered, I, a ghost, in every spot
Will haunt thee. Retribution shalt thou pay,
Thou caitiff! I shall hear, and this report
Shall come to me below the deepest shades."
She with these words the parley in the midst
Breaks off, and, sick at heart, escapes the air,
And turns away, and flings her from his eyes,
Leaving him falt'ring grievously thro' fear,
And making ready many [a word] to speak.
Her maids upraise her, and her fainting limbs 562
Into her couching-chamber, marble-fraught,
Bear off and lay them down upon a couch.
But good Æneas, though the suff'ring [queen]
To soothe by comforting does he desire,
And by his words to turn away her woes,
Upheaving many a sigh, and in his soul
Impaired by mighty passion, still fulfils
The gods' behests, and seeks again the fleet.

546. "Hence from my sight, thou venom to my eyes!
Would I could look thee dead, or with a frown
Dissect thee into atoms, and then hurl them
About the world, to cast infection,
And blister all they light on!"
Marmion, *The Antiquary*, iv. 1.

548. "Do you know who dwells above, sir,
And what they have prepared for men turned devils?
Did you never hear their thunder? Start and tremble
When their fires visit us? Death sitting on your blood,
Will nothing wring you then, do you think?"
J. Fletcher, *The Humourous Lieutenant*, iv. 5.

562. "My life, like to a bubble i' th' aire,
Dissolved by some uncharitable winde,
Denyes my body warmth: your breath
Has made me nothing."
Rawlins, *The Rebellion*, i. 1.

570. "He walks away,
And if he find her dead at his return,
His pity is soon done; he breaks a sigh
In many parts, and gives her but a piece on 't."
Middleton, *Women beware of Women*, iii. 1.

Then sooth the Teucri bend [to toil], and
   launch   571
The lofty galleys all throughout the strand.
Smeared, floats the keel, and leafy oars
   they bring,
And heart of oak, unfashioned, from the
   woods,
In zeal for flight. These flitting might you
   see,
And from out all the city pouring forth :
E'en as, what time a monster heap of spelt
The emmets waste, of winter-tide in mind,
And in their dwelling lay it up in store ;
A sable army marches o'er the plains, 580
And bear in loads the booty thro' the grass
By straitened track ; some push the moun-
   tain-grains,
Against them straining with their shoulders;
   some
The squadrons rally, and chastise delays ;
With travail every path is in a glow.
What, Dido, was thy feeling then, the like
Perceiving ! Or what groanings did'st thou
   heave,
What time the shores in ferment far and
   wide
Thou ! spied'st from thy castle-crest, and
   saw
The ocean all turmoiled before thine eyes
With such loud shoutings ! O unfeeling
   love,   591
To what dost thou not drive the hearts of
   men !
To have recourse again to tears, again
To try him by entreaty, is she forced,
And humbly bow her spirit to her love,
Lest she should any [course] leave unes-
   sayed,
To bootless purpose [then] about to die.
" Anna, thou seest that [all] is hurried on
Throughout the shore ; they round from
   every side
Have mustered ; now the canvas courts the
   gales,   600
And on the sterns the sailors in delight
Have set their chaplets. Seeing I this pang,
So grievous, have been able to await,
I shall be able to support it too,
O sister. Still, do thou this one request
Perform, O Anna, for my hapless self.
For [yon] arch traitor honored thee alone ;
His hidden feelings even he to thee
Intrusted ; thou alone wert wont to know

---

578. " Black ants in teams come darkening all the
   road,
Some call to march, and some to lift the load ;
They strain, they labour with incessant pains,
Press'd by the cumbrous weight of single grains."
                      Parnell, *The Flies.*

The soft approaches to the man, and times
   [Of speech]. Go, sister, and in humble
   form   611
My haughty foe accost : ' I did not swear
At Aulis with the Greeks to overthrow
The Trojan nation, or did I a fleet
To Pergamus, despatch ; nor of his sire
Anchises th' ashes and the shades have I
Uprooted :—why declines he to allow
My words to sink within his churlish ears ?
[Say] whither is he rushing ? This last
   boon
To me, his wretched lover, let him grant :
That he should wait alike an easy flight,
And leading winds. I am not craving
   now   622
The former union, which he hath betrayed ;
Nor that his beauteous Latium he should
   lack,
And realm forego : an idle hour I seek,
Reprieve and room for frenzy, till my fate
May teach me, overborne, to bear the
   smart.'
As a last favor this do I entreat ;—
Have pity on a sister !—which [request]
When thou shalt have accorded to me,
   thee,   630
Full recompensed, at death will I requite."
In [accents] such she prayed, and weep-
   ings such
Her sister, in most miserable plight,
Both carries and recarries back. But he
By weepings none is moved, or any words

---

610. " I'll try each secret passage to his mind,
And love's soft bands about his heart-strings wind."
           Dryden, *Conquest of Granada,* iii. 1.
              " Oh, my sister,—
Fate fain would have it so,—persuade, entreat !
A lady's tears are silent orators."
              J. Fletcher, *Love's Cure,* v. 3.
611. " A heavy heart bears but a humble tongue."
           Shakespeare, *Love's Labour's Lost,* v. 2.
627. Or : " how to grieve."
631. That is,—that nothing but the gratitude of
a whole life could suffice to repay the obligation.
This is by no means satisfactory ; but the fact is,
that it seems impossible to know here what Virgil
either meant or wrote. The reading given by
Weise is founded, not upon manuscript, but on a
conjecture of Heyne's. But, though it were safe to
settle an author's text on the base of fancy, is not
cumulatâ sorte more like prose than poetry ? To
pay a favour back with " augmented capital " is
even very questionable prose.

635. " But neither bended knees, pure hands held
   up,
Sad sighs, deep groans, nor silver-shedding tears,
Could penetrate her uncompassionate sire."
          Shakespeare, *Two Gentlemen of Verona,* iii. 1.
              " My kind sister,
Thy tears are of no force to mollify
This flinty man."
          Heywood, *A Woman Killed with Kindness.*

In pliancy he heeds : the Weirds withstand,
And blocks the god the hero's gentle ears.
And as when, sturdy in its agèd trunk,
An oak do Alpine tempests from the north,
With blowings now on this side, now on
    that,   640
In mutual tourney struggle to uproot ;
A din arises, and the lofty leaves
Bestrew the earth, on shaking of its bole ;
It grapples to the rocks itself, and high
As with its summit to the gales of heaven,
So low it stretches with its root to hell :
Not otherwise, with never ceasing words
On this and that side is the hero pealed,
And in his noble breast deep feels his
    pangs :
His soul unshaken bides ; vain tears are
    shed.   650
Then sooth ill-fortuned, startled at her
    fates,
Prays Dido for her death : it irketh her
To gaze upon the canopy of heaven.
That she more readily may her design
Accomplish, and the light forsake, she saw,
When on the incense-burning altars she
Her off'rings placed,—appalling to be
    told,—
The holy fluids blacken, and the wines,
Outpoured, to turn them into loathsome
    gore.
This sight to none, no, not her sister e'en,
Did she divulge. Moreover, stood within
    the dome   661
A shrine of marble to her former spouse,
Which she with wonderful respect revered,
With snowy wools and festal leafage hung.
Hence voices, and the accents of her lord,
As calling, seemed distinctly to be heard,
What time the darkling night enchained
    the lands,
And, lone upon the gable-heights, the owl
With dirge funereal often would complain,
And spin her lengthful hootings to a wail.
And many a prophecy, besides, of holy
    seers   671
With awful warning fills her with alarm.

"A south wind
Shall sooner soften marble, and the rain,
That slides down gently from his flaggy wings,
O'erflow the Alps, than knees, or tears, or groans,
Shall wrest compunction from me."
            Massinger, *The City Madam*, v. 3.
648. So Milton, in *Paradise Lost*, b. ii. :
    "Nor was his ear less peal'd
With noises loud and ruinous."
653. So Cato says, in Addison's *Cato*, iv. 4 :
"O Lucius! I am sick of this bad world ;
The daylight and the sun grow painful to me."
671. Or, if *priorum*, v. 464, be read : "of seers
of yore."

Himself the fell Æneas in her sleep
The raver baits; and ever to be left
[All] lonely to herself she ever seems,
Unretinued, a longsome way to wend,
And seek the Tyrians in a land forlorn.
As troops of Furies madding Pentheus
    sees,
The sun, too, double, and a Thebes twofold
Appearing ; or, of Agamemnon [sired],
Orestes, chased on stages, as he flies   681
His mother, armed with brands and sooty
    snakes,
And vengeful Diræ in the threshold sit.
So, when she took the Furies to her
    breast,
O'erwhelmed with anguish, and resolved to
    die,
The time and manner with herself she
    weighs,
And in [these] words her sister, woe-begone,
Accosting, in her visage masks her plan,
And plants the calm of hope upon her
    brow :
"A way, O sister,—give thy sister joy !—
Have I discovered, which may him restore
To me, or me, his lover, free from him. 692
Near ocean's limit and the setting sun,
The utmost region of the Æthiops lies,
Where monster Atlas on his shoulder
    wheels
The Empyrean, gemmed with blazing stars.
Therefrom to me there hath been pointed
    out
A priestess of the Massylæan clan,
The guardian of the Hesp'rids' fane, and
    who   699
His banquets to the dragon used to serve,
And watch the holy branches on the tree,
Besprinkling fluid honies [o'er his food],

679. Armstrong uses the same illustration to
magnify the horrors of another species of madness,
—that which results from intemperance :
"But such a dim delirium, such a dream
Involves you ; such a dastardly despair
Unmans your soul as maddening Pentheus felt,
When, baited round Cithæron's cruel sides,
He saw two suns, and double Thebes ascend."
                          Health, b. iv.
682.   "*Orestes.* Now, now
I blaze again ! See there ! Look where they
    come,—
A shoal of Furies ! How they swarm about me !'
My terror ! Hide me ! Oh, their snakey locks !
Hark how they hiss ! See, see their flaming brands !
Now they drive full at me ! How they grin,
And shake their iron whips ! My ears ! What
    yelling !"   Philips, *The Distrest Mother*, end.
696. Shakespeare beautifully expresses the idea
conveyed by *stellis ardentibus aptum*, v. 482:
Merchant of Venice, v. 1 :
"Sit, Jessica : look how the floor of heaven
Is thick inlaid with patines of bright gold."
                                                L

And drowsy poppy. Pledges she herself
That she by spells can free what minds she
   lists,
But loose can launch on others grievous
   pains ;
Arrest the water in the floods, and turn
The stars aback ; and she the ghosts by
   night
Evokes : earth roaring underneath thy feet
Wilt thou behold, and ashes coming down
From mountains. I attest the gods and thee,
Dear sister, and thy darling head, that I
To sorc'rous arts unwillingly resort. 712
Do thou in private a funereal pile
In th' inner court beneath the air upraise,
And the man's armor, which the godless
   [wretch]
Fixed in the couching chamber left, and all
His dress, the bridal bed, too, wherein I
Was ruined, lay thereon. To blot away
All, all memorials of the cursèd man
Delights me, and the priestess [this] en-
   joins,"   720
   These words she having uttered, held
   her peace ;
At once her features wanness overspreads.
Still Anna deems not that her sister cloaks
Her death beneath the strange religious
   rites,
Nor such wild frenzies harbors in her mind,
Or does she weightier [evils] apprehend
Than at Sychæus' death. She therefore
   makes
The ordered preparations. But the queen,—
A pyre in th' inner court beneath the air
Upraised immense, of pines and plank of
   oak,—   730
Lays out alike the spot with coronals,
And decks it with the deathly leaf. Above,
His garments, and the falcion left behind,
His image, too, she places on the bed,
Not wareless of the future. Stand the
   altars round ;
And with dishevelled locks the priestess
   thrice
Forth thunders from her mouth a hundred
   gods,
Both Erebus, and Chaos, Hecat too,
Threefold, the maid Diana's triple forms.
And sprinkled she the mimic waters of the
   spring   740

711. The swearing by the head was a common oath in many countries. Though no longer a custom in these, Spenser puts it into the mouth of one of his characters:

" Then I avow, by this most sacred head
  Of my dear foster-childe."
                     Faerie Queene, iii. 2, 33.

712. More literally :
" For sorc'rous arts unwillingly am girt."

Avernian ; and, by moonlight mown with
   hooks
Of bronze, are sought the herbs of downy
   growth,
With sap of sable poison ; and is sought,
Wrenched from the forehead of a new-
   foaled colt,
And ravished from the dam, the [mole of]
   love.
[The queen] herself with salted meal, and
   hands
Religious, near the altars, with one foot
Stript of its [sandal-] bands, in robe ungirt,
About to die, to witness calls the gods,
The stars, too, of her destiny aware :   750
Thereon,—if any Pow'r, impartial e'en
And mindful, holds the lovers worth a care,
[Who're tied] by no fair contract,—him she
   prays.
'Twas night, and jaded bodies peaceful
   sleep
Were snatching to them through the earth,
   and woods
And raging seas had gone to rest, when stars
In mid career are rolled, when every field
Is hushed. The cattle, and enamelled
   birds,
E'en those which far and wide the crystal
   meres,
And those which lands, with briars brist-
   ling, haunt,   760
In slumber laid beneath the stilly night,
Their sorrows were assuaging, and the
   hearts,
Forgetful of their travails. But not so,

754. The stillness of the world at night is finely described by Dr. Young, *Night Thoughts*, i. 18-25:

" Night, sable goddess ! from her ebon throne,
  In rayless majesty, now stretches forth
  Her leaden sceptre o'er a slumbering world.
  Silence, how dead ! and darkness, how profound !
  Nor eye, nor listening ear, an object finds ;
  Creation sleeps. 'Tis as the general pulse
  Of life stood still, and nature made a pause ;
  An awful pause ! prophetic of her end."

" Sweet sleep charm his sad senses, and gentle
    thoughts
  Let fall your flowing numbers here, and round
    about
  Hover, celestial angels, with your wings,
  That none offend his quiet !"
               Shirley, *The Maid's Revenge*, v. 3.

758. " All birds that in the stream their pinions dip,
  Or from the brink the liquid crystal sip,
  Or show their beauties to the sunny skies,
  Here waved their plumes that shone with varying
    dyes ;
  But chiefly he, that o'er the verdant plain
  Spreads the gay eyes, which grace his spangled
    train ;
  And he who, proudly sailing, loves to show
  His mantling wings and neck of downy snow."
        Sir William Jones, *The Seven Fountains*.

Unblest of spirit, the Phœnician dame;
Nor is she ever melted into sleep,
[N] or in her eyne or bosom welcomes night.
Redouble her distresses, and once more,
Again uprising does her passion storm,
And surge with her resentments' mighty tide.
Thus then she broods upon [her lot], and thus 770
Within her bosom with herself revolves:
"Lo! what is it I do? Shall I once more
My former suitors, ridiculed, essay,
And nuptials with the Nomads humbly crave,
Whom I so often have already scorned
As husbands? Shall I therefore Ilian barks,
And worst behests of Teucer's sons attend?
Is it because it joys them that erewhile
By my assistance they have been relieved,
And duly with the grateful there abides
The obligation from a former act? 781
But grant I willed it,—who'll allow it me?
Or, loathed, admit me to their haughty ships?
Alas! O lady lost, dost thou not know,
Or not as yet perceive the perjuries
Of the Laomedontian race? What then?
Shall I, alone in flight, accompany
Their chuckling seamen? Or, by Tyrians thronged 788
And all my people's host, be wafted on,
And, whom from Sidon's city scarce did I
Unroot, shall I again lead o'er the deep,
And bid them give the canvas to the gales?
Nay, rather perish as thou hast deserved,
And with the falcion turn away the pang!
Thou, overpowered by my tears, thou first
Dost lade a raver, sister, with these ills,
And fling her to the foe. 'Twas not allowed,
A life of marriage void, without a fault,
To lead, in fashion of a savage beast,
Nor such anxieties to touch! The faith,
Pledged to Sychæan ash [es], is not kept!"
Such grievous plaints she vented from her breast. 802
Æneas on the lofty stern, now fixed
Upon departure, sleep was snatching, now
With preparations orderly arranged.
To him the figure of the god in dreams
Itself presented, in the selfsame guise
Returning, and again thus seemed to warn;

764. "Wrongs done to love
Strike the heart deeply: none can truly judge on't
But the poor sensible sufferer whom it racks
With unbelievèd pains."
Middleton, *The Witch*, i. 1.
788. Or: "A crew triumphant!"
801. "Angels themselves must break that promise
Beyond the strength and patience of angels."
Massinger, *The Fatal Dowry*, v. 2.

In all like Mercury, alike in voice,
And hue, and amber locks, and limbs adorned 810
With youth: "O goddess-born, canst sleep prolong
Beneath this crisis? Nor what dangers thence
May thee environ, madman! dost perceive?
Nor hearest thou propitious Zephyrs breathe?
That [woman] wiles and awful wickedness
Is in her breast revolving, bent on death,
And surges with resentments' fitful tide.
Art thou not posting hence in headlong haste,
Whilst thou to post in headlong haste hast power?
Forthwith shalt thou behold the sea turmoiled 820
With ships, and grisly torches glare; forthwith
The shores with blazes in a glow, if thee,
Delaying in these regions, shall the Dawn
Have touched. Uprouse thee then! break off delays!
A vacillating and capricious thing
Is woman ever." He, thus having said,
Himself commingled with the sable night.
Then sooth Æneas, by the sudden gloom
Affrighted, tears away his frame from sleep,
And importunes his comrades: "Quick awake! 830
My men, and take your stations on the thwarts;
Unclew the sails with speed! A god, despatched
From th' empyrean high, to hasten flight,
And cut away the twisted hawsers, lo!
Once more is urging on. We follow thee,
O holy one of gods, whoe'er thou art,

825. "Mutability,
All faults that may be nam'd, nay that hell knows,
Why hers, in part, or all: but rather all;
Nor e'en to vice
They are not constant, but are changing still
One vice, but of a minute old, for one
Not half so old as that."
Shakespeare, *Cymbeline*, ii. 5.
"And yet, believe me, good as well as ill,
Woman's at best a contradiction still."
Pope, *Moral Essays*, Ep. ii. 269.
"A creature fond and changing, fair and vain,
The creature, 'Woman,' rises now to reign."
Parnell, *Hesiod*.
"Oh! women have fantastic constitutions,
Inconstant in their wishes, always wavering,
And never fixed." Otway, *Venice P.*, iii. 1.
835. "I feel now
That there are Powers above us, and that 'tis not
Within the searching policies of man
To alter their decrees."
Beaumont and Fletcher, *The False One*, v. 1.

L 2

And thy behests once more obey with joy.
O be thou present, and benignly aid,
And stars in heav'n propitious bring." He
  spake,
And tears his blade of lightning from the
  sheath,   840
And with drawn steel the hawsers smites.
  At once
The selfsame fervor holds them all. They
  hale alike,
And hurry; they the shores have left; the
  main
Lies hid beneath the galleys; forcing, they
Whirl up the foam, and sweep the azure
  [seas].
And now first sprent the lands with virgin
  light

Aurora, leaving Tithon's saffron bed.
Soon as the queen from posts of watch
  beheld
The light wax white, and with its balanced
  sails
The navy under way, and shores and ports
Unpeopled, without rower, she perceived,
Both thrice and four times on her dainty
  breast   852
Deep struck with hand, and rent in amber
  locks;
"Alas the day! O Jove, shall this man
  go?"
She cries, "and shall an alien ridicule
Our realm? Will they not fetch their
  armor forth,
And, [poured] from all the city, give him
  chase,
And others drag down galleys from the
  docks?
Go quick! bring blazes, set the sails, ply
  oars!—
What do I say? Or where am I? My
  brain   860
What madness turns? Unhappy Dido!
  Now
Do thy ungodly doings sting thee? Then
'Twas meet [they should] when thou the
  sceptral sway
Vouchsafedst.—Lo! right hand and troth
  [of one],
Who with him, they assert, his country's
  gods
Is bringing! Who upon his shoulders bare
A father spent with age!—His body seized
Could I not have dislimbed, and o'er the
  waves
Have scattered it? [Could I] not his com-
  peers,
Not,—have annihilated with the steel 870
Ascanius' very self, and served him up
To be a banquet on his father's boards?

---

844. As the enemies of the Castle of Temperance concealed the Earth:
"So huge and infinite their numbers were,
That all the land they under them did hyde."
    Spenser, *Faerie Queene*, ii. 11, 5.

845. So Spenser, *F. Q.*, i. 2, 7. See also i. 11, 51:
"Now when the rosy-fingred Morning faire,
Weary of aged Tithones saffron bed,
Had spread her purple robe through deawy aire."

Shakespeare has numberless descriptions of day-break of great beauty; *e. g., Romeo and Juliet,* ii. 3:
"The grey-ey'd morn smiles on the frowning night,
Checkering the eastern clouds with streaks of light;
And flecked darkness like a drunkard reels
From forth day's pathway, made by Titan's wheels:
Now ere the sun advance his burning eye,
The day to cheer, and night's dark dew to dry;"
&c.

And again, in the same Play, iii. 5:
    "Look, what envious streaks
Do lace the severing clouds in yonder east:
Night's candles are burnt out, and jocund day
Stands tiptoe on the misty mountain-tops."

"See, the day begins to break,
And the light shoots like a streak
Of subtle fire; the wind blows cold,
Whilst the morning doth unfold,
Now the birds begin to rouse,
And the squirrel from the boughs
Leaps to get him nuts and fruit;
The early lark, that erst was mute
Carols to the rising day
Many a note and many a lay."
    J. Fletcher, *The Faithful Shepherdess,* iv. 4.

"Mild rides the Morn in orient beauty dress'd,
An azure mantle, and a purple vest,
Which, blown by gales, her gemmy feet display,
Her amber tresses negligently gay:
Collected now her rosy hand they fill,
And, gently wrung, the pearly dew distil.
The songful Zephyrs, and the laughing Hours,
Breathe sweet, and strew her opening way with flowers."
    Savage, *Wanderer,* c. iv.

And shortly after, of Sunrise:
"Now, in his tabernacle roused, the Sun
Is warn'd the blue ethereal steep to run;

While on his couch of floating jasper laid,
From his bright eye Sleep calls the dewy shade.
The crystal dome transparent pillars raise,
Whence, beam'd from sapphires, living azure plays;
The liquid floor, inwrought with pearls divine,
Where all his labours in mosaic shine:
His coronet a cloud of silver-white;
His robe with unconsuming crimson bright,
Varied with gems, all heaven's collected store!
While his loose locks descend, a golden shower."

855.   "Have I no spleen,
Nor anger of a woman? Shall he build
Upon my ruins, and I, unrevenged,
Deplore his falsehood?"
    Massinger, *The Picture*, iii. 6.

868. "No! let me know the man that wrongs me so,
That I may cut his body into motes,
And scatter it before the Northern blast."
Beaumont and Fletcher, *The Maid's Tragedy*, ii. 1.

But doubtful th' issue of the fray had proved.—
It might have proved so : whom had I to fear,
About to perish ? Torches on their camp
I might have flung, and filled their decks with flames,
And son and father with the race have quenched !
Aye even have myself bestowed them !— Sun !
Who scannest with thy fires all tasks of earth, 879
And thou, agent and witness of these woes,
O Juno ! Hecat, too, in crossing paths
By night invoked thro' cities with a howl ;
And O ye vengeful Furies, and ye gods
Of perishing Elissa, hear ye these,
And turn your pow'r divine, that is their due,
To [these] my wrongs, and listen to our prayers !
If needs must be his cursèd person touch
The ports, and float to land, and thus the fates
Of Jove exact, this issue is decreed :—
Yet worried by the warfare and the arms
Of [some] bold clan, an exile from his bourns, 891
Wrenched from Iulus's embrace, may he
Crave aid, and see the ignominious deaths
Of his own [people] ! nor when he himself
Shall have surrendered, [laid] beneath the terms
Of [some] unrighteous peace, may he enjoy
His realm or light desired, but let him fall
Before his day, and [lie] amid the sand
Unsepulchred ! These [boons] I beg ; this word,
My latest, with my blood outpour. 900
Then ye, O Tyrians, harass with your hate
The brood and all its progeny to come,
And to my ash [es] offer up these gifts.
Between the nations let there be no love,
Nor leagues ! Rise ! some avenger from our bones,
The Dardan settlers to pursue with fire
And falcion, now, hereafter, at what time
Soe'er shall pow'rs impart them [unto thee].
The curse of shores antagonist to shores,
To billows waves, to armor arms, I pray :
May both themselves and their descendants war !" 911
These speaks she, and her mind to every side
She shifted, seeking, soon as in her power,
To break away the [thread of] loathly light.
She Barce then, Sychæus' nurse, in brief
Accosted ; for her own the sable ash
In her time-honored land possessed : "Dear nurse,
My sister Anna hither lead to me ;
Tell her to haste her person to bedew
With water of the brook, and with her bring 920
The victims and atonements pointed out :
Thus let her come ; and thy own brows do thou
Thyself envelop with religious band.
The sacrifices to the Stygian Jove,
Which, in due form commenced, have I prepared,
It is my purpose to complete, and put
An end to my distresses, and the pyre
Of Dardan bust abandon to the flame."
On this wise does she speak. The other sped
Her step with agèd woman's zeal. But scared, 930
And at her monstrous undertakings wild,
Dido, her blood-shot eyeball rolling round,
And dashed with blotches o'er her quiv'ring cheeks,
And wan at coming dissolution, bursts
Within the inner portals of the dome,
And in her frenzy mounts the lofty pyre ;
The Dardan falcion, too, does she unsheathe,—
Not for these services a boon acquired.
Here, soon as on the Ilian gear, and bed
Well-known, she gazed, awhile in tears and thought 940
Delaying, she both laid her on the couch,
And spake her latest words : "O relics dear,
While doom and deity allowed, receive

---

899. "Let him be lost, no eye to weep his end,
Nor find no earth that's base enough to bury him !"
J. Fletcher, *Rule a Wife and Have a Wife*, iii. 5.

905. "Arise, black vengeance, from thy hollow cell !
Yield up, O love, thy crown, and hearted throne,
To tyrannous hate ! Swell, bosom, with thy fraught,
For 'tis of aspics' tongues."
        Shakespeare, *Othello*, iii. 3.

914. So Amavia prays, in Spenser's *Faerie Queene*, ii. 1, 36:
"Come, then ; come soon ; come, sweetest Death,
And take away this long lent loathed light."

921. Or : "The beasts and the."

928.   "*Hecate.* Is the heart of wax
Stuck full of magic needles ?
  Stadlin. 'Tis done, Hecate.
  Hec. And is the farmer's picture and his wife's
Laid down to th' fire yet ?
  Stad. They're a-roasting both too."
        Middleton, *The Witch*, i. 2.

This soul, and free me from these troubles! I
Have lived, and that career, which had my
   fate
Assigned, have run; and now this shade of
   mine
Majestic 'neath the earth shall wend its
   way.
A passing glorious city have I reared;
My walls have seen; a husband having
   venged,
I've from a hostile brother penalties   950
Exacted: blest, alas! too blest,
Had but the Dardan keels ne'er touched
   our shores!"
She said; and,—pressed upon the couch
   her lips,—
"Die shall we unavenged; but let us die!"
   she cries,
" Thus, thus it joys to pass to shades below.
This conflagration with his eyes let drink
The barbarous Dardanian from the deep,
And with him bear the omens of our death."
   She said; and in the midst of such [her
   words]
Her train behold her sunk beneath the
   steel,   960
The sword, too, frothing with the gore,
   and sprent
Her hands. A shrieking mounts the lofty
   halls;
Wild revels Rumor thro' the city shocked;
With moans, and groan, and women's howl,
   the roofs
Are ringing; thunders heav'n with mighty
   wails:
No otherwise, than if from foes let loose
All Carthage were to fall or agèd Tyre,
And raging blazes were to be enwreathed
Throughout the gables both of men and
   gods.
Her sister breathless heard, and, terrified,

944. "I fall to rise: mount to thy Maker, spirit!
Leave here thy body: Death hath her demerit."
   Marston, *Insatiate Countesse*, v. 5.

947. "Through darkness diamonds spread their
richest light."
   Webster, *Vittoria Corombona*, iii. 2.

959. Or: "below the shades."

966. "So from a spark, that kindled first by chance,
With gathering force the quickening flames
   advance;
Till to the clouds their curling heads aspire,
And towers and temples sink in floods of fire."
   Pope, *Temple of Fame*.

The translation of the second *per* in this idiomatic
passage would involve the supply of a weak ellipsis.

970. "Which when that warriour heard, dismount-
ing straict
From his tall steed, he rusht into the thick,
And soone arrived where that sad Pourtraict
Of death and dolour lay, halfe dead, halfe quick:

In flurried haste, while marring with her
   nails   971
Her features, and her breasts with clenchèd
   hands,
Darts through the midmost, and the dying
   [queen]
Loud calls by name: " O sister, was it
   this?
In cunning didst thou seek me? Was it
   this
That pile funereal, was it this the fires
And altars had in store for me? Whereof
In chief shall I forlorn complain? Hast
   thou
Thy sister for a comrade scorned at death?
Would thou had'st called me to the selfsame
   doom!   980
One anguish and one hour had with the
   sword
Swept both of us away. With these [my]
   hands
Did I e'en rear it, and our country's gods
Call with my voice, that I should thee,
   thus laid,
O heartless one, have failed? Thyself and
   me
Thou hast, O sister, quenched, thy people
   too,
And the Sidonian sires, and city thine.
Give me with waters clean to wash her
   wounds;
And should there any parting breath above
Still wander, I will catch it with my lips."

In whose white alabaster brest did stick
A cruell knife that made a griesly wownd,
From which forth gusht a stream of gore-blood
   thick,
That all her goodly garments staind arownd,
And into a deepe sanguine dide the grassy grownd."
   Spenser, *F. Q.*, ii. 1, 39.

974. "What shall she do? She to her brother runs,
His cold and lifeless body does embrace;
She calls to him that cannot hear her moans,
And with her kisses warms his clammy face."
   Cowley, *Constantia and Philetus*.

981. " First will I sing thy dirge,
Then kiss thy pale lips, and then die myself,
And fill one coffin and one grave together."
   Beaumont and Fletcher, *The Knight of the
   Burning Pestle*, iv. 5.

989. "She stirs; here's life!
Return, fair soul, from darkness, and lead mine
Out of this sensible hell! She's warm, she breathes!
Upon thy pale lips I will melt my heart,
To store them with fresh colour."
   Webster, *The Duchess of Malfi*, iv. 2.

990. " His palled face, impictured with death,
She bathed oft with teares and dried oft:
And with sweet kisses suckt the wasting breath
Out of his lips like lillies pale and soft.
And oft she cald to him, who answerd nought,
And onely by his lookes did tell his thought."
   Spenser, *Astrophel*.

Thus speaking, she had climbed the lofty
  steps, 991
And, her half-living sister clasping round,
She hugged her in her bosom with a groan,
And stanched the jetty blood-streams with
  her robe.
The other, efforts having made to lift
Her heavy eyeballs, swoons away again:
Deep plunged beneath her breast, the
  wound
Is gurgling. Thrice she, lifting up her
  [form],
And leaning on her elbow, raised [her-
  self];
Thrice backward was she rolled upon the
  bed, 1000
And with her wand'ring eyes through lofty
  heaven
She sought the light, and groaned when it
  was found.

Then Juno, the almighty, in her ruth
At her long anguish and laborious death,
Sent Iris from the Empyrean down,
To disengage the struggling soul, and limbs
Enfettered [with it]: for that, seeing she
Nor by her destiny, nor death deserved,
Was dying, but ill-starred before her day,
And by a sudden frenzy-passion fired, 1010
Not yet had Proserpine the golden lock
From off the summit of her head with-
  drawn,
And to the Stygian Orcus doomed the
  head.
So dewy Iris on her saffron wings,
Along the sky a thousand motley hues
Abstracting from the sun afront, flies down,
And near, above the head, she stood:
" This lock,
Devote to Dis, enjoined I carry off,
And thee from that thy body I release."
Thus speaks she, and the lock with her
  right hand 1020
She cuts; and all the heat at once dissolved,
And to the breezes sped the life away.

992. " Eyes, look your last!
Arms, take your last embrace! and lips, Oh! you
The doors of breath, seal with a righteous kiss
A dateless bargain to engrossing death!"
  Shakespeare, *Romeo and Juliet*, v. 3.

1002. "*Antoninus.* Then with her dies
The abstract of all sweetness that's in woman!
Let me down, friend, that, ere the iron hand
Of death close up mine eyes, that may at once
Take my last leave both of this light and her:
For, she being gone, the glorious sun himself
To me's Cimmerian darkness.
  Macrinus. Strange affection!
Cupid once more hath changed his shafts with
  Death,
And kills, instead of giving life."
  Massinger, *The Virgin Martyr*, iv. 3.

1022. " O she is gone! the talking soul is mute!
She's hushed, no voice of music now is heard!
The bower of beauty is more still than death;
The roses fade, and the melodious bird,
That waked their sweets, has left them now for
  ever." Lee, *The Rival Queens*, v. 1.

  " So, fare thee well!
Now boast thee, Death! In thy possession lies
A lass unparalleled. Downy windows, close;
And golden Phœbus never be beheld
Of eyes again so royal!"
  Shakespeare, *Antony and Cleopatra*, v. 2.

BOOK V.

MEANWHILE Æneas with the navy now
His mid [-sea] voyage straight was holding
  on,
And the dun billows with the northern gale

Was cleaving, looking back upon the walls,
  which now
Are glaring with unblest Elissa's flames.
What reason may have lighted up a fire,
So great, lies hidden; but the grievous
  pangs

Line 2. Virgil often uses *medius* to indicate a distance from the extremity, be it greater or less. For instance, in *Æn.* iii. v. 665, Polyphemus *graditur per æquor jam medium*; yet, *necdum fluctus latera ardua tinxit*. So here, the word is employed loosely, to express Æneas being well out at sea. However, it would seem better not to attempt too strict a version of the word, especially as "mid-sea" may well carry with it a similar looseness of meaning.

3. There are numberless instances of Virgil's using the names of winds in a lax way, according as the necessities of the metre required. See note on *Æn.* i. l. 841. Yet, perhaps, *Aquilo* may here be employed deliberately in its accurate signification. In *Æn.* iv. v. 310, to take *Aquilonibus* in the sense of wind generally would plainly be to

weaken the force of Dido's sarcasm; and so, in the present case, the same word is probably repeated with design. The Trojans were in such a hurry to be gone, that they went even with a foul wind. However, *Aquilo* would not be so much a-head as *Boreas.*

4. " They, looking back, all th' eastern side beheld
Of Paradise, so late their happy seat,
Waved over by that dreadful brand! the gate
With dreadful faces throng'd, and fiery arms.
Some natural tears they dropp'd, but wip'd them
  soon:
The world was all before them, where to choose
Their place of rest, and Providence their guide."
  Milton, *P. L.*, end.

From outrage offered to a mighty love,
And knowledge what can frantic woman do,
Through sad foreboding lead the Trojans'
  minds. 10
  Soon as their galleys occupied the deep,
Nor any land now further meets [the
  view] ;—
Seas all around, and all around the sky ;—
Above his head a dingy rain-cloud came
To a near stand; Night bringing on and
  storm;
And 'gan the wave to crisp beneath the
  gloom.
E'en Palinure, the pilot, from the stern
On high: "Ah! why have storm-clouds
  so immense
Wrapt heav'n? Or what, sire Neptune,
  dost prepare?" 19
Thus having said, thereon he gives command

To reef the sails, and ply with lusty oars,
And veers diagonally to the wind
The folds [of canvas], and suchlike he
  speaks :
"High-souled Æneas, not, tho' Jove to me
Should pledge himself as surety, could I
  hope
That 'neath this sky Italia we could fetch.
Athwart us shifted, bluster, and uprise
In concert from the inky West, the winds,
And into cloud the ether is condensed : 29
We neither have the pow'r to struggle on
Against them, nor the effort e'en to make.
Since Fortune lords it, follow we [her lead],
And whither she is calling bend our course.
Nor deem I far, trustworthy, brotherly,
The coasts of Eryx, and Sicilia's ports,
If only in a duly mindful mood,
The stars observed I calculate again."
Then good Æneas: "Sooth I long have
  seen
That thus the winds exact, and that in vain
Against them thou dost strive : Shape
  course by sails ! 40
Can any land to me more welcome prove,
Or where the rather I would fain put in
My shattered ships, than that which guards
  for me
The Dardan-sprung Acestes, and the bones
Of sire Anchises bosoms in its lap ?"
When these were spoken, they the havens
  seek,

---

8. "*Lopez.* Methinks a woman dares not—
   Roderigo.   Thou speak'st poorly ;
   What dares not woman when she is provok'd ?
   Or what seems dangerous to love or fury ?"
                    Fletcher, *The Pilgrim,* iii. 1.

' "The effects of violent love are desperate."
                    Massinger, *A Very Woman,* v. 4.

10. "I cannot change, as others do,
    Though you unjustly scorn ;
   Since that poor swain that sighs for you,
    For you alone was born.

   "No, Phillis, no, your heart to move
    A surer way I'll try ;
   And, to revenge my slighted love,
    Will still love on, will still love on, and die.

   "When, killed with grief, Amyntas lies,
    And you to mind shall call
   The sighs that now unpity'd rise,
    The tears that vainly fall,

   "That welcome hour, that ends this smart,
    Will then begin your pain ;
   For such a faithful tender heart
    Can never break, can never break in vain."
                    Earl of Rochester, *Constancy.*

18. One of the oldest descriptions of a storm in
the English language (before Chaucer's *Canterbury
Tales*) is to be found in Gower's *Confessio Amantis,*
b. viii. :
   "Whan thei were in the sea amid,
    Out of the north thei see a cloude,
    The storme arose, the wyndes loude
    Thei blewen many a dredefull blaste,
    The welken was all ouercaste :
    The derke night the sonne hath vnder,
    There was a great tempest of thunder.
    The moone, and eke the sterres bothe
    In blacke cloudes thei hem clothe,
    Whereof their bright loke thei hide."

"If by your art, my dearest father, you have
Put the wild waters in this roar, allay them ;
The sky, it seems, would pour down stinking pitch,
But that the sea, mounting to the welkin's cheek,
Dashes the fire out."   Shakespeare, *Tempest,* i. 2.

"Hie therefore, Robin, overcast the night ;
The starry welkin cover thou anon
With drooping fog, as black as Acheron."
                Midsummer Night's Dream, iii. 2.

21. "As when the seaman sees the Hyades
    Gather an army of Cimmerian clouds,
    (Auster and Aquilon with wingèd steeds,
    All sweating, tilt about the watery heavens,
    With shivering spears enforcing thunder-claps,
    And from their shields strike flames of lightning,)
    All-fearful folds his sails, and sounds the main,
    Lifting his prayers to the Heavens for aid
    Against the terror of the winds and waves."
        Marlowe, *Tamburlaine the Great,* iii. 2.

27. "From every several quarter of the sky
    The thunder roars, and the fierce lightnings fly
    One at another, and together dash
    Volley on volley, flash comes after flash,
    Heaven's light looks sad, as they would melt away,
    The night is come i' th' morning of the day :
    The card'nal winds He makes at once to blow,
    Whose blasts to buffets with such fury go :" &c.
                        Drayton, *Noah's Flood.*

"The flattering wind, that late with promis'd aid
From Candia's bay th' unwilling ship betray'd,
No longer fawns beneath the fair disguise,
But like a ruffian on his quarry flies :
Tost on the tide she feels the tempest blow,
And dreads the vengeance of so fell a foe."
                        Falconer, *Shipwreck,* ii. 3.

29. "At first a dusky wreath they seem to rise
    Scarce staining ether ; but by swift degrees,
    In heaps on heaps, the doubling vapour sails
    Along the loaded sky, and mingled deep
    Sits on th' horizon round a settled gloom."
                        Thomson, *Spring.*

And fav'ring Zephyrs swell the sails. The fleet
Is quickly wafted through the gulf, and they at last
Are borne delighted to the well-known strand.
But from a lofty mountain-crest afar 50
Amazed at their approach, and barks allied,
Acestes meets them, bristling in his darts,
And in an Afric she-bear's skin ; whom bore
A Trojan mother, gendered by the flood Crimisus. Of his ancient fathers he,
Not mindless, gives them joy on their return,
And entertains them, glad, with rural wealth,
And cheers the weary with his kindly means.
What time next gairish day with infant dawn
The stars had chased aloof, from all the shore 60
His mates Æneas to assembly calls,
And from a hillock-pile [these words] he speaks :
"Great Dardans, issue from the lofty blood
Of gods, the yearly cycle is fulfilled,
With months completed, from the time that we
My god-like sire's remains and bones in-hearsed
In earth, and mournful altars sanctified.
And now the day, unless I am deceived,
Is nigh, which ever bitter, ever blest,—
Thus ye, O gods, have willed it !—I shall hold. 70

This were I in Gætulian Syrts to pass,
A banished man, or on the Argive sea,
And in Mycenæ's city overta'en,
Still yearly vows, and anniversary
Processions, in due course would I dis-charge,
And pile the altars with their rightful gifts.
Now further ; at the ashes and the bones
E'en of my sire himself,—not sooth, I deem,
Without the mind, without the will, of gods,—
Are we arrived, and wafted down [the deep], 80
The ports of friendship enter. Therefore come !
And let us all this jovial feast observe ;
Entreat the Winds ; and that it be his will
That I should every year these holy rites

71. It seems very unnatural to make *hunc*, v. 51, to depend upon an elliptical verb, which it is merely gratuitous to understand. Neither is it easy to see what the reference to *Æn.* vii. v. 611 has to do with the matter.
The devotion of Æneas to the memory of his father is like that of Lord Surrey to his mistress :
" Let me whereas the sunne doth parche the grene,
  Or where his beames do not dissolue the yse :
In temperate heate where he is felt and sene :
In presence prest of people madde or wise :
Let me in hye, or yet in low degree ;.
In longest night, or in the shortest daye :
In clearest skie, or where cloudes thickest be ;
In lusty youth, or when my heeres are graye :
Let me in heaven, in earth, or els in hell,
In hyll or dale, or in the foming flood,
Thrall, or at large, aliue whereso I dwell,
Sicke or in health, in euill fame or good :
Hers will I be."   *Song* xii.
The same idea is similarly handled by Turberville in *A Vow to Serve Faithfully.*

74. "'Tis true, fair daughter ; and this blessed day
Ever in France shall be kept festival :
To solemnise this day, the glorious sun
Stays in his course, and plays the alchymist :
Turning with splendour of his precious eye
The meagre cloddy earth to glittering gold :
The yearly course, that brings this day about,
Shall never see it but a holyday."
                        Shakespeare, *King John*, iii. 1.

82. " *Duke.* What brow looks sad, when we com-mand delight ?
We shall account that man a traitor to us
That wears one sullen cloud upon his face !
I'll read his soul in't, and, by our bright mistress,
Than which the world contains no richer beauty,
Punish his daring sin.
  Leontio.   He will deserve it,
Great sir, that shall offend with the least sadness !
Or, were it so possess'd, yet your command,
That stretches to the soul, would make it smile,
And force a bravery. Severe old age
Shall lay aside his sullen gravity,
And revel like a youth ; the forward matrons,
For this day, shall repent their years and coldness
Of blood, and wish again their tempting beauties,
To dance like wanton lovers."
                        Shirley, *The Duke's Mistress,* i. 1.

69. "'Tis not a cypresse-bough, a count'nance sad,
A mourning garment, wailing elegie,
A standing herse in sable vesture clad,
A toombe built to his name's eternitie,
   Although the shepheards all should strive
     By yearly obsequies,
   And vow to keepe thy fame alive
     In spite of destinies,
That can suppresse my griefe :
   All these and more may be,
Yet all in vaine to recompence
   My greatest losse of thee.

" Cypresse may fade, the countenance be changed,
A garment rot, an elegie forgotten,
A herse 'mongst irreligious rites be ranged,
A toombe pluckt down, or else through age be rotten :
   All things th' impartial hand of fate
     Can rase out with a thought :
   These have a sev'ral fixèd date,
     Which, ended, turne to nought.
Yet shall my truest cause
   Of sorrow firmely stay,
When these effects the wings of time
   Shall fanne and sweepe away."
                        Browne, *Shepheard's Pipe,* Ecl. iv.

Present, what time my city is upreared,
In temples consecrated to himself.
Twain head of beeves to you the Troja-
 born
Acestes grants, by reckoning for each ship:
Invite ye household gods, and country-
 gods,
To banquet, and [the gods] which doth our
 host   90
Acestes worship. Further, if to men
Shall ninth Aurora have a kindly day
Brought forth, and with her beams unveiled
 the globe,
The op'ning contests of the speeding ship
I to the sons of Teucer will propose;
And he who in the foot-race is of might,
And he who, venturesome in pow'rs, or
 stalks
Superior in the dart and nimble shafts,
Or trusts him the encounter to commence
With gauntlet raw ;—let one and all be
 here,   100
And wait the guerdons of a well-earned
 palm.
All guard your lips, and ring your brows
 with sprigs."
Thus having said, his temples he bedecks
With myrtle of his mother. Helymus
Doth this, doth this Acestes ripe of age,
Doth this the boy Ascanius; follows whom
The other youth. He from th' assembly
 passed
With many a thousand to the tomb, [him-
 self]
The centre, in a vast attending throng.
Here duly in libation pouring out   110
Twain drinking-vessels with unmingled
 wine,
He spills them on the ground, with new
 milk twain,
Twain with religious blood; and strews
 bright flowers,
And speaks the like: " Hail, sainted sire,
 once more !
Hail, O ye ashes, to no end regained,
And spirit of my father, and his shade !
'Twas not allowed to me Italia's bourns,
And destined fields, nor Auson Tiber ['s
 stream],
Whate'er it be, with thee to seek." He
 these
Had spoken, when from out the deepest
 shrine   120
A slipp'ry serpent, huge, sev'n rings, sev'n
 folds

·121. See notes on *Geo*. iii. 570.
" Lo ! the green serpent, from his dark abode,
 Which ev'n imagination fears to tread,
 At noon forth issuing, gathers up his train

Trailed onward, gently bosoming the tomb,
And through the altars gliding on; whose
 chine
Did spots of azure, and, bedropped with
 gold,
[Each] scale a levin-flash set all afire :
As, with the sun afront, the rainbow flings
Upon the clouds a thousand motley hues.
Æneas was astounded at the sight.
It, as with lengthful train at last it glides
Among the saucers and the burnished cups,
Both tasted of the banquet, and again,
Unharmful, 'neath the basement of the
 tomb   .   132
Retreated, and the altars, feasted on,
Forsook. So much the more does he renew
The sacrifices to his sire commenced,
Uncertain whether he should deem it were
The Genius of the place, or of his sire
Th' attendant. Slaughters he twain two-
 year ewes,
In customed fashion, and as many swine,
And just so many bullocks, swart of back ;
The wines, too, from the saucers he out-
 poured,   141
And called upon the great Anchises' soul,
And Manes, from the Acheron released.
Yea too, his comrades, as to each belonged
Th' ability, in joy their off'rings bring,
The altars burden, and the bullocks slay.
In order bronzen [vessels] others set,
And, scattered all along the turf, they place
Live coals beneath the spits, and roast the
 flesh.

The looked-for day arrived, and Phaeton's
 steeds   150

In orbs immense, then, darting out anew,
Seeks the refreshing fount; by which diffus'd,
He throws his folds."   Thomson, *Summer*.
150, 151. Drummond, charmingly of the day when
he was to meet his mistress :
" Phœbus, arise,
 And paint the sable skies
 With azure, white, and red ;
 Rouse Memnon's mother from her Tython's bed,
 That she may thy career with roses spread.
 The nightingales thy coming eachwhere sing,
 Make an eternal spring.
" This is that happy morn,
 That day, long-wishèd day,
 Of all my life so dark,
 (If cruel stars have not my ruin sworn,
 And fates my hopes betray,)
 Which (purely white) deserves
 An everlasting diamond should it mark.
" The winds all silent are ;
 And Phœbus in his chair
 Ensaffroning sea and air,
 Makes banish every star,
 Night like a drunkard reels
 Beyond the hills, to shun his flaming wheels.
 The fields with flow'rs are deck'd in every hue,
 The clouds with orient gold spangle their blue."
                          Sonnets, &c., i. 36.

Now bare the ninth Aurore in cloudless
  light ;
And rumor, and renowned Acestes' name,
The neighborhood had roused. In merry
  throng
They full had filled the shores, the Ænead
  sons
To view, part even to compete prepared.
The prizes first are placed before their eyes,
And in the centre of the cirque are set,—
Religious tripods, chaplets too of green,
And palms, as guerdon for the conquerors,
And arms, and robes with purple throughly
  dyed, 160
A talent ['s weight] of silver and of gold ;
And from the centre of the knoll the trump
Sounds forth the games begun. [Well]
  matched, commence

" How often have I bless'd the coming day,
  When toil remitting lent its turn to play,
  And all the village train, from labour free,
  Led up their sports beneath the spreading tree :
  While many a pastime circled in the shade,
  The young contending as the old survey'd ;
  And many a gambol frolick'd o'er the ground,
  And slights of art and feats of strength went
    round,
  And still, as each repeated pleasure tir'd,
  Succeeding sports the mirthful band inspir'd."
          Goldsmith, *Deserted Village*, 15-24.

" Were you to encounter
Those ravishing pleasures, which the slow-paced
  hours
(To me they are such) bar me from, you would,
With your continued wishes, strive to imp
New feathers to the broken wings of Time,
And chide the amorous sun for too long dalliance
In Thetis' watery bosom."
          Massinger, *The Renegado*, v. 8.

Gifford here quotes a fine passage from Tomkis'
Albumazar :
" How slow the day slides on ! When we desire
  Time's haste, he seems to lose a match with
    lobsters ;
  And when we wish him stay, he imps his wings
  With feathers plumed with thought."

" Oh, why so long should I my joys delay ?
  Time, imp thy wings, let not thy minutes stay,
  But to a moment change the tedious day.
  The day! 'twill be an age before to-morrow ;
  An age, a death, a vast eternity."
          Lee, *Theodosius*, iii. 2.

" With what a leaden and retarding weight
Does expectation load the wings of Time !"
          Mason, *Elfrida*.

151. Ben Jonson gives a grand description of a
day, the exact reverse of this. Lentulus says to
Cethegus :
" It is, methinks, a morning full of fate !
  It riseth slowly, as her sullen car
  Had all the weights of sleep and death hung at it !
  She is not rosy-finger'd, but swoll'n black ;
  Her face is like a water turn'd to blood,
  And her sick head is bound about with clouds,
  As if she threaten'd night ere noon of day !"
          Catiline, i. 1.

The op'ning contests with their weighty oars
Four galleys, chosen out of all the fleet.
The wingy Pristis Mnestheus drives with
  crew
Of mettle,—Mnestheus, an Italian soon,
From which his name the line of Memmius
  [springs] ;
And Gyas huge Chimæra, of huge bulk,
A structure like a city, which with tier 170
Threefold the Dardan youth force on ; the
  oars
In triple rank arise ; Sergestus, too,
From whom the Sergian house preserves its
  name,
Is in the mighty Centaur borne along ;
In sea-green Scylla, too, Cloanthus, whence
Thy pedigree, Cluentius son of Rome.
There lies afar within the main a rock,
Afront the foamy shores, which, under-sunk
At times, is by the swelling billows lashed,
When wintry north-west winds eclipse the
  stars, 180
When calm 'tis hushed, and from th' un-
  ruffled wave
A level is uplifted, e'en a rest,
Thrice-welcome to the divers loving sun.
Here sire Æneas reared a goal of green,
[Formed] out of leafy ilex, to the crews
A mark, whence they might know to turn
  them back,
And when to veer around their longsome
  course.
Their stations then by lot do they select ;
The captains, too, themselves upon the
  sterns
With gold and purple graced, gleam forth
  afar. 190
The other youth in poplar leaf are dressed,
And, o'er their naked shoulders smeared
  with oil,
Begin to shine. Down sit they on the
  thwarts,
And arms are strained to oars. Upon the
  stretch
They wait the sign, and drains their bound-
  ing hearts
A throbbing tremor, and ambitious lust
Of praises. Then, what time the shrilly
  trump
Gave forth its clang, from their own sta-
  tions all,—
There's no delay,—sprang forward : strikes
  the sky
The sailor-shout ; by indrawn arms con-
  vulsed, 200

170. Or : " The labor of a city ;" for no one
seems to know which meaning was in the poet's
mind when he penned the ambiguous phrase, *Urbis
opus*.

The waters foam; in measure plough they in
The furrows, and throughout asunder yawns,
Uptorn by oars and trident beaks, the sea.
In no such hurry in the two-horse race
Have chariots seized the field, and dash amain
When started from the goal; nor charioteers
O'er yokes, thus darting, shook the waving reins,
And, bending forwards, o'er the lashes hang.
Then with the clapping and hurrah of men,
And zeal of cheerers, every grove rings out
In concert, and the voice th' imprisoned shores 211
Volley along; the stricken hills with shout
Rebound. Shoots forth ahead before the rest,
And glides away upon the foremost waves,
Amid the hurly and the din, Gyas; whom next
Cloanth pursues, superior in his oars;
But ties him by its weight his plodding pine.
Astern of these, at even interval,
Pristis and Centaur struggle to secure
The leading place. And [this] now Pristis holds; 220
Now, worsted, giant Centaur by her slips;
Now both abreast and with linked stems are borne,
And plough with lengthful keel the briny seas.
And they were now approaching to the rock,
And gaining goal, when Gyas in the van,
And in mid sea the winner, with his voice
Accosts Mencetes, helmsman of his ship:
" Pray whither on the right dost swerve so far?
Steer hitherward a passage! Hug the shore,
And let thy blade the crags upon the left
Graze close; the deep let others keep !"
He said : 231
But, dreading hidden rocks, Mencetes veers
His bow aside to billows of the main.
" Whither art thou departing wide away?
Make for the rocks, Mencetes !" with a shout
Gyas once more recalled him: and, behold!
He views Cloanthus bearing down astern,
And holding closer. Th' other, e'en between
The ship of Gyas and the booming rocks,

Shaves, further in, a course upon the left,
And in a trice the leader passes by, 241
And gains safe seas,—the goal behind him left.
Then sooth up kindled in the stripling's bones
Tow'ring vexation, neither did his cheeks
Lack tears; and he the slow Mencetes,
Forgetful of his dignity alike,
And of his comrades' safety, on the sea
Down tumbles headlong from the lofty stern.
Himself the steersman to the helm succeeds,
Himself the captain; and he cheers the crew, 250
And turns the rudder-handle to the shores.
But when, encumbered, from the lowest bed
[Of ocean] he is scarce at last restored,
Now old, and dripping in his reeking gear,
Mencetes seeks the summit of the rock,
And on an arid crag sat down. At him,
Both [as he falls and swims, the Teucri laughed,
And laugh as he disgorges from his chest
The briny waters. Here a joyous hope
Was lighted up within the hindmost pair,
Sergestus [e'en] and Mnestheus, to pass by 261
The lagging Gyas. Seizes first the space
Sergestus, and the rock approaches : still
Nor by a whole preceding keel was he
The foremost,—foremost by a part ;—a part
His rival Pristis presses with her beak.
But, midship pacing down among his men
Themselves, does Mnestheus cheer them on:
" Now! now!
Uprise ye to your oars, Hectorean mates,
Whom I in Troy's last destiny chose out
My comrades; now those energies put forth,
Now spirits [those], which in Gætulia's Syrts 272
Ye exercised, and in Ionia's sea,
And Malea's coursing waves. I, Mnestheus, now
The leading [prizes] do not seek, nor aim
To win! yet oh !—but those let gain the day,

---

244. " But 'tis a grief of fury, not despair!
And if a manly drop or two fall down,
It scalds along my cheeks, like the green wood,
That sputt'ring in the flame works outward into tears." Dryden, *Cleomenes*, i. 1.
256. " I feel a hand of mercy lift me up
Out of a world of waters, and now sets me
Upon a mountain, where the sun plays most,
To cheer my heart, even as it dries my limbs."
Middleton, *No Wit like a Woman's*, ii. 3.
Where he probably might have thought with Colax, in Randolph's *Muses' Looking-Glass*, iii. 3 :
" He's a good friend will pardon his friend's errors,
But he's a better takes no notice of them."

---

228. *Mihi*, v. 162, is of course the *dativus ethicus*, but so thoroughly idiomatical, that a literal translation of it would involve an intolerable, and scarce intelligible, weakness. Under the circumstances in which it appears, some such term as "pray" would probably be used in English, and it is therefore introduced; but it is not offered as a correct translation.

To whom, O Neptune, thou hast this vouch-
    safed :
Shame be it to have come in last ! This
    win,
My countrymen, and bid the crime avaunt !"
They in the height of struggle forward bend:
With giant strokes the bronze-bound galley
    thrills,   281
And, underneath, the surface is withdrawn.
Then quick-repeated panting shakes their
    joints,
And droughty lips ; sweat flows in runnels
    down
On every side.   Mere chance the heroes
    brought
The wished-for fame.   For, frenzied in his
    soul,
While towards the rocks Sergestus further in
Close drives his stem, and threads th' un-
    righteous space,
Ill-starred, he stuck upon the jutting rocks.
Shocked were the cliffs, and on a pointed
    crag   290
The struggling oars asunder snapped aloud,
And, dashed against it, hung the bow. Up
    spring
The crew together, and with thund'ring
    shout
They force aback ; and stakes with iron
    shod,
And poles with sharpened end, do they
    produce,
And gather in the gulf the broken oars.
But Mnestheus blithe, and through success
    itself
More alert, with fleet advance of oars,
And winds invoked, the easy waters seeks,
And runs along upon the open sea.   300
As, in a cavern on a sudden roused,
A dove, whose home and charming nestlings
    [lie]
Within a shroud-abounding pumice rock,
Is wafted to the fields upon the wing,
And, startled, with her pinions in the vault
A mighty flapping does she raise ; anon,
Gliding athwart the calmy air, she skims
A limpid course, nor stirs her nimble wings:
Thus Mnestheus, thus the Pristis' self, in
    flight
Cuts through the utmost seas ; thus, as she
    scuds,   310
Her very moment carries her along.
And first Sergestus does he leave behind,
As he is struggling on the lofty rock

And scanty shoals, and vainly calling aid,
And learning to career with broken oars.
Thence Gyas, and Chimæra's self, of bulk
Colossal, overtakes he : she gives way,
Since of her pilot she has been bereft.
And now alone, upon the very goal,
Cloanthus is ahead : whom he pursues 320
And presses, struggling with his might and
    main.
Then sooth redoubles shout, and one and
    all
Spur on the chaser with their zealous cheers,
And rings again the welkin with their peals.
These deem it a disgrace, should they not
    keep
Their rightful honor and the glory gained,
And life are willing to exchange for praise.
Those their success supports : they have the
    power,
Since pow'r they seem to have. And haply
    they
With even beaks the prizes would have
    ta'en,   330
Had not, both hands outstretching to the
    deep,
Cloanth alike his prayers outpoured, and
    called
The deities to [share] his vows : " Ye gods
To whom belongs the lordship of the main,
Across whose seas I run, for you with joy
I on this strand a snowy bull will set
Before your altars, debtor to my vow,
And entrails on the briny waves cast forth,
And spill the fluid wines."   He said ; and
    him
Beneath the deepest waves heard all the
    choir   340
Of Nereids, and of Phorcus, and the maid
Panope ; and the sire Portunus' self
With giant hand impelled him as he speeds.
She, quicker than south blast and wingy
    shaft,

328. *Possunt quia posse videntur*, v. 231. This
does not appear to be a very felicitous remark in
this place ; for the *hos* were beaten. Taken strictly,
it is false ; taken loosely, it does not apply. It
might, to be sure, be true to say, that, in their own
estimation,
" They can, because they seem as if they could :"
but this turns what is generally considered to be a
wise and terse saying into a very dull observation.
Compare Beaumont and Fletcher, *Philaster*, ii. 1:
    " Think so, and 'tis so."
Also Dryden, *Cleomenes*, i. 1:
" Peace, peace, good grandmother, he lives already,
And conquers, too, in saying he will try."
And Rowe, *Ambitious Stepmother*, i. :
" The wise and active conquer difficulties
By daring to attempt 'em : sloth and folly
Shiver and shrink at sight of toil and hazard,
And make th' impossibility they fear."

288. That is : " scanty."
298. Or : *agmine celeri*, " rapid line."
313. *Alto*, v. 220, seems scarcely a well-chosen
term, as the rock appears to have been of no height ;
in fact, no more than barely emergent.

Flies to the land, and in the haven deep
Herself she harbored. Then Anchises'
    son,—
The throng all summoned in accustomed
    form,—
The winner, by a herald's lusty voice,
Cloanth pronounces, and with verdant bay
Betrims his brows; and presents for the
    ships,   350
Three bullocks each, and wines he grants
    to choose,
And carry off a silver-talent vast.
Special distinctions on the captains' selves
Confers he : on the winner, wrought in
    gold,
A cloak, round which in double waving line
Full much of Melibœan purple ran ;
And, interwove therein, the royal boy
On leafy Ida tires the nimble stags
With dart and chase, alert, like one that
    pants,
Whom Jove's fleet armor-bearer, wafted
    high   360
From Ida, kidnapped in his hooky claws ;
Aged guards their hands stretch idly to the
    stars,
And storms the bay of hounds upon the
    gales.
But who next held in prowess second rank,—
To him a coat of mail, with burnished rings
Enlinked, and triply laced with gold, which
    he
Himself had from Demoleos reft away,
In conquest by the ravening Simois,
'Neath stately Ilium, on the hero he
Bestows to wear, an honor and safeguard
In arms. This scarcely bore, of many a fold,
Phegeus and Sagaris, the serving men, 372
Sore straining with their shoulders ; but
    [therein]
Bedight, Demoleos erst would rout in chase
The straggling Trojans. Gifts the third he
    makes
Twain basins [wrought] of bronze, and
    drinking-boats,

In silver finished, and with figures crisp.
And thus now guerdoned all, and in their
    wealth
Elate, brow-wreathed with purple bands,
    they paced :
When from the felon rock with ample skill
Scarce wrenched,—oars missing, and dis-
    abled in one tier,—   381
His flouted ship, without repute, Sergest
Was working on. As oft a snake, sur-
    prised
Upon the elevation of a road,
O'er whom athwart the bronze-shod wheel
    hath passed,
Or, heavy with his blow, [some] passenger
Hath left half-dead, and mangled with a
    stone,—
All vainly flying, with his body forms
Extended wreaths; in [one] part truculent,
And blazing with his eyes, and rearing high
His hissing neck ; part, crippled by the
    wound,   391
Firm holds him back, while resting on his
    knots,
And coiling up his form on his own limbs.
With such like oarage was the plodding
    bark
Advancing : still her sails she sets,
And enters in full sail the [harbor's] mouth.
Æneas with the promised gift presents
Sergestus, blithe at rescue of his ship,
And mates returned. To him a female
    slave
Is giv'n, not wareless of Minerva's works,
Pholoe, a Crete by race, twin sons, too,
    at her breast.   401
This contest closed, the good Æneas
    moves
On to a grassy level, which the woods
Upon the winding hills on every side
Imbowered, and in centre of the dale
The cirque [as] of a theatre there lay ;

387. "We have scotched the snake, not killed it."
            Shakespeare, *Macbeth*, iii. 2.

391. "Behind the general mends his weary pace,
    And sullenly to his revenge he sails :
So glides some trodden serpent on the grass,
    And long behind his wounded volume trails."
            Dryden, *Annus Mirabilis*, cxxiii.

Falconer uses the image to illustrate a very dif-
ferent fact ; *Shipwreck*, iii. 2:
" Awhile the mast, in ruins dragg'd behind,
    Balanc'd th' impression of the helm and wind :
The wounded serpent, agoniz'd with pain,
    Thus trails his mangled volume on the plain."

406. .   "In a pleasant glade
With mountaines rownd about environed
And mightie woodes, which did the valley shade,
And like a stately theatre it made,
Spreading itself into a spatious plaine."
            Spenser, *F. Q.*, iii. 5, 39.

---

359. "One like Actæon, peeping through the grove,
Shall by the angry goddess be transform'd,
And, running in the likeness of an hart,
By yelping hounds pull'd down, shall seem to die."
            Marlowe, *Edward II.*

362. "Twice was he seene in soaring eagles shape,
And with wide winges to beat the buxome ayre ;
Once, when he with Asterie did scape ;
Againe, when as the Trojane boy so fayre
He snatcht from Ida hill, and with him bare :
Wo ndrous delight it was there to behould
How the rude shepheards after him did stare,
Trembling through feare least down he fallen
    should,
And often calling to him to take surer hoald."
            Spenser, *Faerie Queene*, iii. 11, 34.

Whither, along with many a thousand men,
Repaired the hero, in th' assemblage [he]
The midmost, and upon a seat upraised
He sat him down. With prizes here he
      woos   410
The spirits, who may haply list to strive
In nimble foot-race, and the guerdons sets.
From all sides flock the Teucrians and
      mixed
Sicilians : Nisus and Euryalus
The foremost [candidates] ; Euryalus,
Marked for his beauty and a blooming
      youth ;
Nisus, for chaste affection for the boy.
Whom next there followed, royal [ly de-
      rived]
From Priam's peerless stock, Diores : him
Salius, and with him Patron, of whom one
An Acarnanian was, the other [born]   421
From Arcad blood of Tegeæan strain.
Then two Sicilian striplings, Helymus
And Panopes, inured to woods, the aged
Acestes' comrades : many a one beside,
Whom fame hath in her mystery concealed.
Amidst of whom then thus Æneas spake :
"These welcome in your minds, and turn
      thereto
Your glad attention. Of this throng shall
      none
Withdraw, by me unguerdoned. I will
      give   430
Twain Gnosian missiles, bright with burn-
      ished steel,
And, silver-chased, a battle-axe to bear :
This one distinction shall there be for all.
The foremost triad prizes shall receive,

And with the yellow olive round their head
Be bound. The leading winner let possess
A courser, badged with trappings ; let the
      next
An Amazonian quiver, aye and full
Of Thracian arrows, which with breadth of
      gold
A belt embraces, and a buckle clasps   440
Beneath with rounded jewel ; let the third
With this Argolic helm retire content."
When these were said their station take
      they up,
And in a moment, on a signal heard,
Seize on the stages, and the barrier quit,
Forth flushing like a show'r : the furthest
      [bounds]
At once they mark. Ahead starts off, and
      far
'Fore all the rest shoots Nisus forth, more
      fleet
Than e'en the winds and levin-wings. Next
      him,
But with a lengthened interval the next, 450
On presses Salius ; with a distance left,
Then after him Euryalus the third ;
And Helymus Euryalus pursues ;
Close on whose very person next, lo ! flies,
And heel now chafes with heel, Diores,
      pressing
Upon his shoulder ; and, if there remained
More stages he might pass him, stealing off
The leader, and [the issue] leave in doubt.
And now well-nigh the limit of the stage,
And, wearied, hard upon the very bound
Were they arriving ; when on slippery
      blood   461
Slides ill-starred Nisus, where from
      butchered steers
It, spilled by chance, the ground and
      em'rald grass
Had wetted from above. 'Twas here the
      youth,
Now conqueror triumphant, failed to keep
His steps, that staggered on the trampled
      ground ;
But headlong, both upon the filthy soil,
And hallowed gore itself, he toppled down.
He still, not mindless of Euryalus,

"And overhead
Insuperable highth of loftiest shade,
Cedar, and pine, and fir, and branching palm,
A silvan scene ; and, as the ranks ascend
Shade above shade, a woody theatre
Of stateliest view."   Milton, *P. L.*, iii.

"'Twas an horrid pile
Of hills, with many a shaggy forest mix'd,
With many a sable cliff and glittering stream.
Aloft, recumbent o'er the hanging ridge,
The brown woods wav'd ; while ever-trickling
   springs
Wash'd from the naked roots of oak and pine
The crumbling soil ; and still at every fall
Down the steep windings of the channel'd rock
Remurmuring rush'd the congregated floods
With hoarser inundation ; till at last
They reach'd a grassy plain, which from the skirts
Of that high desert spread her verdant lap,
And drank the gushing moisture, where, confin'd
In one smooth current, o'er the lilied vale
Clearer than glass it flow'd. Autumnal spoils,
Luxuriant spreading to the rays of morn,
Blush'd o'er the cliffs, whose half-encircling mound
As in a sylvan theatre enclos'd
That flowery level."
   Akenside, *Pleasures of the Imagination*, ii. 274-
292.

448. "Every body" is not quite so dignified in
English as *omnia corpora* in Latin.

457. The poet himself is as ambiguous here as he
hypothetically intended the issue to be.

469. "The trees grow up, and mix together freely,
The oak not envious of the sailing cedar,
The lusty vine not jealous of the ivy
Because she clips the elm ; the flowers shoot up,
And wantonly kiss one another hourly,
This blossom glorying in the other's beauty,
And yet they smell as sweet, and look as lovely."
      Fletcher, *Lover's Progress*, i. 1.

Nor of their loves: for planted he himself
In face of Salius, rising through the slime:
But lay the other, whirled on clotted sand.
On shoots Euryalus, and, conqueror 473
By service of his friend, first place he holds,
And flies with clap and favoring acclaim.
Next Helymus comes up, and now third palm,
Diores. Here the whole assembled throng
Of the vast hollow, and the sires' front view,
With lusty cries does Salius fill, and claims
That his distinction, filched away by craft,
Should be restored him.   Guards Euryalus
His popularity and graceful tears; 482
More winning, too, the merit, when it comes
In a fair form. His help affords, and loud
Shouts forth with thund'ring voice Diores, who
Has to a palm succeeded, and in vain
Has reached the final prizes, if the first
Distinctions upon Salius are bestowed.
Then sire Æneas saith: "Your gifts to you
Secure abide, O youths, and from its rank
None stirs a palm : to me be it allowed
To pity my unfaulty friend's mishap." 492
Thus having said, an Afric lion's hide,
Immense, to Salius gives he, burdensome
With shag and gilded claws.   Here Nisus cries:
"If for the worsted be such fine rewards,
And thou dost feel compassion for the fallen,
What worthy gifts wilt thou to Nisus grant,
Who have by merit earned the leading crown,
Had not the [same] unfriendly fortune me,
The which hath Salius, swept [therefrom] away?" 501
And at the same time with these words he showed
His face and limbs, befouled with soaking soil.

---

482. "Graceful;" or "decent."
Macbeth says of himself:
"I have bought
Golden opinions from all sorts of people." Act i. 7.
" Hear, ye fair daughters of this happy land,
Whose radiant eyes the vanquish'd world command,
Virtue is beauty: but when charms of mind
With elegance of outward form are join'd,
When youth makes such bright objects still more bright,
And fortune sets them in the strongest light;
'Tis all of Heaven that we below may view,
And all, but adoration, is your due."
Young, *Force of Religion*, i. 9-16.

492. "'Tis something to be pitied of a king."
Marlowe, *Edward the Second.*

The sire thrice-worthy smiled at him, and bade
A buckler forth be brought, the art on art
Of Didymaon, from the holy gate
Of Neptune by the Greeks plucked down: with this
Choice boon the peerless youth does he present.
Thereon, when were the races closed, and he
Went through [the distribution of] the gifts:
"Now if there valor be in any wight, 511
And ready resolution in his breast,
Let him appear and raise aloft his arms,
With [cestus-] banded hands." He thus-wise speaks,
And of the fight the double prize lays down;—
A bullock for the conqu'ror decked in gold
And wreaths ; a falcion and distinguished helm,
As comforts for the conquered. No delay!
Straight Dares rears his front with giant powers,
And lifts him with the vast applause of men: 520
He who alone was customed to maintain
The conflict against Paris ; and the same
Fast by the tomb, where greatest Hector lies,
The conqu'ror Butes of colossal frame,
Who in descent from the Bebrycian race
Of Amycus did vaunt him, felled to earth,
And stretched him dying on the tawny sand.
Such Dares for the op'ning combat lifts
His stately head, and shows his shoulders broad,
And, arms outstretching, tosses them by turns, 530
And with his buffets cuffs the gales. For him
There is another sought: nor is there one
Out of a host so great makes bold to meet
The man, and draw the gauntlets on his hands.
Therefore alert, and deeming one and all
Held from the palm aloof, he stood before
Æneas' feet ; nor making more demur,
Then with the left hand seizes by his horn
The bull, and speaks on this wise:
"Goddess-born,
If no one dares to trust him to the fray, 540
What period to my standing [here]? How long
Is it becoming I should be delayed?
Bid me lead off my guerdon." One and all
At once with voice the Dardans cheered, and begged
That to the hero should be given up

[The prizes] that were pledged. Severely here
Acestes chides Entellus with his speech,
As next upon the emerald couch of turf
Along with him he sat: "Entellus, erst
Of champions gallantest without avail, 550
Such noble gifts, in so submissive mood,
With naught of struggle, to be carried off
Wilt thou allow? Where now that god of our's,
Thy master, Eryx, chronicled in vain?
Where thy renown throughout all Sicily,
And those thy trophies hanging from thy roofs?"
He quick to these: "Not love of praise, nor fame,
Hath yielded, banished by alarm; but sooth,
Ice-cold through sluggish eld, my blood is dull,
And pow'rs worn-out are freezing in my frame. 560
If I,—what I had whilom, and wherein
That caitiff yonder trusting brags,—if now
I had that youth, not sooth by prize
Allured, and by a lovely bull, would I
Have come: nor do I of the guerdons reck."
Thus having said, thereon he in the midst
A pair of gauntlets of stupendous weight
Flung down, wherein fierce Eryx for the frays
Was used to wield his hand, and strain his arms
Within the stubborn hide. Their souls were in amaze: 570
Of such huge oxen sev'n prodigious hides
Were stiff with lead and iron stitched within.
'Fore all is Dares wonder-struck himself,

---

559. "Vilarezo
Was once, as you are, sprightly, and though I say it,
Maintain'd my father's reputation,
And honour of our house, with actions
Worthy our name and family; but now,
Time hath let fall cold snow upon my hairs,
Plough'd on my brows the furrows of his anger,
Disfurnish'd me of active blood, and wrapt me
Half in my sear-cloth."
Shirley, *Maid's Revenge*, i. 2.

561. "Age has not yet
So shrunk my sinews, or so chill'd my veins,
But conscious virtue in my breast remains.
But had I now
That strength, with which my boiling youth was fraught;
When in the vale of Balasor I fought,
And from Bengale their captive monarch brought;
When elephant 'gainst elephant did rear
His trunk, and castles justl'd in the air;
My sword the way to victory had shown,
And ow'd the conquest to itself alone."
Dryden, *Aurungzebe*, act. ii.

And far aloof declines; and, great of soul,
The offspring of Anchises both the weight,
And very folds enormous of the hides,
To this side, and to that, turns o'er and o'er.
Thereon the agèd [hero] such like words
Fetched from his bosom: "What if one had seen
The gloves and arms of Hercules himself,
And the sad combat on this very strand?
These arms thy brother Eryx whilom wore;
(With blood thou seest and spattered brains yet dyed;) 583
In these against the great Alcides stood;
To these was I inured, while better blood
Imparted strength, nor yet did jealous eld,
On both my temples sprent, wax grey.
But if
The Trojan Dares these our arms declines,
And this with good Æneas is resolved,
My counsellor Acestes sanctions [this], 590
The combats let us even make. The hides
Of Eryx I for thee forego,—dismiss
Thy fears,—and thou thy Trojan gauntlets doff."
These having said, he flung a double robe
From off his shoulders; and his limbs huge joints,
His monstrous bones and shoulders, laid he bare,
And stood a giant on the central sand.
Then did the father, from Anchises sprung,
Bring forward even gauntlets, and entwined
The hands of both with weapons of a size.
Straight each erect on tiptoe stood, and reared 601
His arms undaunted to the gales above.
Far backward from the blow their lofty heads
Withdrew they, and commingle hands with hands,
And goad the fray: in nimbleness of feet
Superior one, and trusting in his youth;
The other, powerful in limbs and bulk,
But 'neath the trembler totter sluggish knees;
Asthmatic panting shakes his giant joints.
The champions 'tween them bandy many a stroke 610
All vainly, many on their hollow side
Redouble they, and from their chest give forth

---

587. He might truly have said with Amyclas in Ford's *Broken Heart*, i. 2:

"See lords, Amyclas your king is ent'ring
Into his youth again. I shall shake off
This silver badge of age, and change this snow
For hairs as gay as are Apollo's locks;
Our heart leaps in new vigour."

M

Prodigious crashes, and around their ears
And temples wanders the repeated hand;
Their cheeks are crackling 'neath the iron
    blow.
Stands in his weight Entellus, and, un-
    stirred
In the same posture, merely with his frame,
And eyes upon the watch, the strokes
    escapes.
The other, as who storms a stately town
With enginery, or round the mountain
    towers   620
Sits under arms, now these, now inlets
    those,
And all the ground, with skilfulness ex-
    plores,
And with diverse assaults in vain persists.
Entellus, rising up, his right hand showed,
And lifted it aloft: the other quick
Foresaw the buffet swooping from above,
And, with his nimble body slipped aside,
    withdrew.
His strength Entellus squandered on the
    wind,
And, self-moved, heavy he, and heavily,
Himself to earth with vasty weight falls
    down;   630
As sometimes in its hollowness down falls
Either on Erymanth or Ida vast,
From roots upwrenched, a fir. Together
    rise
In zeal the Trojans and Sicilia's youth:
Ascends their outcry to the heav'n; and
    first
Acestes hurries up, and from the ground
Uplifts in pity his coeval friend.

But not foreslowed, nor daunted by his fall,
The hero fiercer to the fight returns,
And wrath wakes strength. Then kindles
    might his shame,   640
And conscious prowess, and he hotly hunts
The headlong Dares all throughout the
    plain,
Now with the right hand blows redoubling,
    now
E'en with the left. Nor stay, nor rest: as
    storms
With plenteous hail on housetops rattle,—so
With crowding blows the hero with each
    hand
Oft smites and chases Dares. Then the sire
Æneas, wrath to go to further lengths,
Entellus, too, to fume with soul of gall,
Permitted not, but put an end to fight, 650
And fainting Dares rescued, soothing him
With words, and speaks the like: "Un-
    happy man!
What such wild frenzy seized thy soul?
    Dost thou
Not feel his strength is foreign, and the
    powers
Of heav'n are changed? Submit thee to a
    god!" He said:
And straight broke off their combats with
    the speech.
But him his trusty peers, as weakly knees
He drags, and flings to either side his head,
And from his mouth discharges clotted gore,
And teeth in blood commingled, to the
    ships   660
Conduct; and, summoned, helm and sword
    receive;

---

626. Spenser makes even the wind created by a giant's blow of terrific energy:
" The geaunt strooke so maynly mercilesse,
That could have overthrowne a stony towre;
And, were not hevenly grace that did him blesse,
He had been pouldred all, as thin as flowre;
But he was wary of that deadly stowre,
And lightly lept from underneath the blow;
Yet so exceeding was the villein's powre,
That with the winde it did him overthrow,
And all his sences stoond, that still he lay full low."   *F. Q.,* i. 7, 12.

628. Marlowe has a different image:
" And make your strokes to wound the senseless light." *Tamburlaine the Great,* iii. 3.

631. Spenser illustrates such a fall in no common-place way:
" As when a vulture greedie of his pray,
Through hunger long that hart to him doth lend,
Strikes at an heron with all his bodies sway,
That from his force seemes nought may it defend;
The warie fowl, that spies him toward bend
His dreadfull souse, avoydes it, shunning light,
And maketh him his wing in vaine to spend;
That with the weight of his own weeldlesse might
He falleth nigh to ground, and scarse recovereth flight."   *F. Q.,* iv. 3.

643. *Ille,* v. 457, does not admit of a close translation.
    " So they
Doubly redoubled strokes upon the foe."
    Shakespeare, *Macbeth,* i. 2.

645. " Yet nought thereof was Triamond adredde,
Ne desperate of glorious victorie;
But sharpely him assayld, and sore bestedde
With heapes of strokes, which he at him let flie
As thicke as hayle forth poured from the skie:
He stroke, he soust, he foynd, he hewd, he lasht,
And did his yron brond so fast applie,
That from the same the fierie sparkles flasht,
As fast as water-sprinkles gainst a rocke are dasht."
    Spenser, *F. Q.,* iv. 3, 25.

654. This argument was used by Duessa to Sansloy, but without effect:
" 'Yea but,' quoth she, ' he beares a charmed shield,
And eke enchaunted armes, that none can perce;
Ne none can wound the man, that does them wield.'
'Charmd or enchaunted,' answered he then ferce,
'I no whitt reck; ne you the like need to reherce.'"   *F. Q.,* i. 4, 50.

656. Such seems to be the force of *que, et.*

The palm and bull resign t' Entellus. Here
The conqueror, triumphant in his soul,
And with the bull elate, cries: "Goddess-
  born,
And ye, O Teucer's sons, learn these,—alike
What were my powers in a youthful frame,
And from what death recalled ye Dares
  save."
He said, and took his stand against the face
Of the confronted bull, which stood hard by
The guerdon of the fight, and, with right
  hand   670
Drawn backward, full in centre of his horns
He poised the felon gauntlets, lifted high,
And dashed them on the bones,—the
  brain burst ope.
Is felled, and lifeless, quiv'ring, sinks to
  earth the ox.
He o'er him from his breast such words
  outpours:
"This nobler life, O Eryx, I to thee
In lieu of Dares' death, repay; a conqu'ror
  here,
My gauntlets and my craft I lay aside."
Forthwith Æneas in the nimble shaft
Woos those to strive, who peradventure list,
And lays down prizes; and with giant hand
A mast from out Serestus' ship uprears, 682
And on a cord, passed through, a wingèd
  dove,
Whereto their weapons they may aim, he
  hangs
From the tall mast. Together flocked the
  men,
And th' in-cast lot a helm of bronze received.
And first, with fav'ring cheer, before them all
Leaps forth the station of Hippocoon,
The son of Hyrtacus: whom Mnestheus,
  late
The winner in the naval strife, pur-
  sues,—   690
Mnestheus, with verdant olive bound.
Eurytion third,
Thy brother, O thrice-glorious Pandar,
  who,
Commanded erst to violate the league,
First hurled thy weapon in the midst of
  Greeks.

---

666. "Old as I am, and quenched with scars and
  sorrows,
Yet would I make this withered arm do wonders,
And open in an enemy such wounds
Mercy would weep to look on."
  J. Fletcher, *Valentinian*, iv. 4.

674. In the short space of nine lines, from v. 473-
481, Virgil uses *taurus*, *juvencus*, and *bos* of the
same beast: yet they all differ.

688. In this strong sense *exit* is used, *Geo.* i. v.
116. *Consequitur*, v. 494, therefore, must not be
rendered tamely.

The last, and at the bottom of the helm,
Acestes settled down, e'en venturing he
With hand of his to try the toil of youths.
Then arch with lusty strength their buxom
  bows
The heroes, each according to his might,
And from their quivers draw their weapons
  forth.   700
And, foremost through the heav'n, with
  twanging cord,
The shaft of young Hyrtacides disparts
The wingy gales, swoops straightway, and
  is fixed
Within the timber of the fronting mast.
The mast it quivered, and the startled
  bird
Betrayed her apprehension by her wings,
And every [spot] with mighty clapping
  rang.
Next, active Mnestheus with his in-drawn
  bow
Took up his stand, aloft directing aim,
And eyes and arrow levelled both at once.
But, pitiable, he the bird herself   711
Had not the power with the steel to strike:
The knots and flaxen ligatures he burst,
Wherewith she, foot-enfettered, from the
  mast
On high was hanging. She to southern
  gales,
And clouds of blackness, fled on wing
  away.
Then quickly, long erewhile upon his bow,
In readiness, his weapons keeping stretched,
Eurytion called his brother to his vows,
As now he watched her blithe in empty
  heaven;   720
And, clapping with her wings, he pierced
  the dove
Beneath a sable cloud. She breathless falls,
And leaves her life among th' empyreal
  stars,
And as she falls brings home the fastened
  shaft.
Palm missed, alone remained Acestes, who
Still shot his weapon to the airy gales,
The sire exhibiting alike his skill,
And ringing bow. Here offered is to view
A sudden prodigy, and doomed to prove
Of grave presage. The mighty issue [this!
Explained thereafter, and their late por-
  tents   731
Alarming prophets sang. For, as it flies
Among the wat'ry clouds, the shaft took
  fire,
And scored a pathway with the flames, and
  spent,
To subtile winds withdrew: as oft, from
  heaven

Unsphered, athwart it shoot the flying stars,
And tresses trail. With thunder-stricken souls
Stood fixed, and supplicated heav'nly powers,
The heroes of Trinacria and Troy.
Nor does thrice-great Æneas the portent
Decline; but clasping glad Acestes, he
Loads him with handsome gifts, and speaks the like: 742
"Sire, take them: for Olympus' mighty king
Hath willed that thou, by such presagements placed
Above the lot, the honors bear away.
This present of the aged Anchises' self
Shalt thou possess,—a bowl with figures graved,
Which Thracian Cisseus whilom to my sire
Anchises for a noble gift had giv'n to bear,
Of his affection standing-proof and pledge."
Thus having spoken, he enrings his brows
With verdant bay, and at the head of all
The foremost conqueror Acestes names.
Nor does the good Eurytion grudge the prize, 754
Borne off before him, though 'twas he alone
That from the lofty heav'n struck down the bird.
Next stalks in guerdons he who burst the bands;
The last, who pierced with wingy bolt the mast.
But sire Æneas,—not yet closed the strife,—
To him the guardian and companion [squire] 760
Of young Iulus calls,—the son of Epytus;
And thus bespeaks his confidential ear:
"Go haste thee, and Ascanius (if he now
His boyish squadrons with him hath prepared,
And the manœuvres of their steeds arranged,)
In honor of his grandsire, tell," saith he,
"To bring his troops, and show himself in arms."
Himself bids all the scattered throng withdraw
From th' ample cirque, and open stand the plains.
On march the boys, and 'fore their parents' view 770
Shine uniformly on their bridled steeds:
Whom all the youth of Sicily and Troy,
As they advance, in admiration cheer.
The hair of all in customed form was pressed
With shaven chaplet. Carry they a pair
Of cornel spear-shafts, tipped with steel; a part
Upon the shoulder burnished quivers; runs
From summit of the chest, about the neck,
A pliant collar of entwisted gold.
Of riders companies in number three, 780
And commandants by threes pace to and fro;
The youths, each following in twelves, with band
Divided gleam, with masters, too, alike.
One was a line of youths, which, triumphing,
The little Priam led, his grandsire's name
Recalling, thy illustrious descent,
Polites, doomed Italians to advance;
Whom bears a Thracian horse of piebald hue,
With blots of white, his forefoot fetlocks white,
A brow, too, white displaying, tow'ring high. 790
The second, Atys, whence the Atii
Of Rome their pedigree have carried down;—
The little Atys, e'en a boy beloved
By boy Iulus. Last, and past them all
In figure lovely, is Iulus borne
Upon a Sidon palfrey, which to him
The beauteous Dido had vouchsafed, to be
Of her affection standing-proof and pledge.
The other youths are on Sicilian steeds
Of aged Acestes carried. Welcome with applause 800
The fearful lads, and as they gaze rejoice
The sons of Dardanus, and recognise
The features of their ancient sires. As soon
As all th' assemblage, and their [parents'] eyes,
Delighted they survey upon their steeds,
A signal to them by a shout, as they
Stood ready, gave the son of Epytus
From far, and sounded with his whip. Apart
They shot [in] even [ranks], and troops by threes
Broke up in sundered squadrons, and again,
When summoned, they their marches wheeled about, 811
And hostile weapons tilted. Thereupon
Fresh charges they commence, and fresh retreats,
Confronted on the grounds, and rings in rings
Alternate they entangle, and awake
The mimicry of battle under arms.
And now their backs do they expose in flight,
Now in hostility reverse their darts;

Peace made, in company now ride. As erst,
'Tis said, the Labyrinth in lofty Crete 820
A passage had, inweaved with blinding walls,
And, puzzling by a thousand ways, a cheat,
Where might annul the tokens of advance
Unmarked and irretrievable mistake.
In course none else the Teucri's sons their steps
Involve, and weave their flights and frays in sport ;
Like dolphins, which, in swimming through dank seas,
Cut the Carpathian and the Libyan [main],
And gambol through the waves. This style of tilt,
And tourneys these, Ascanius first, what time 830
He Alba Longa girt with walls, renewed,
And taught the ancient Latins to observe
In form wherein the boy himself, wherein
Troy's youth with him [observed it]. Th' Albans taught
Their [sons] ; hence highest Rome in after days
Received it, and the homage to their sires
Maintained ; and now it is entitled "Troy,"
The boys "The Trojan Band." Thus far the games
Were kept in honor of the sainted sire.
  Here Fortune, shifted, altered first her faith. 840
The while with diff'rent pastimes by the tomb
Are they observing annivers'ry [rites],
Saturnian Juno Iris sent from heaven
To Ilium's fleet, and as she hies she breathes
The winds upon her, stirring many [a thought],
Not yet englutted with her old revenge.
The other, hasting on her passage o'er
The bow with thousand hues, by none beheld,—

820. Fletcher compares the world to a labyrinth :
" The world's a labyrinth, where unguided men
Walk up and down to find their weariness :
No sooner have we measur'd with much toil
The crooked path, with hope to gain our freedom,
But it betrays us to a new affliction."
        The Night-Walker, iv. 6.
See Akenside, *Pleasures of the Imagination*, iii. 1-5.

840. " Daughter, thou seest how Fortune turns her wheel.
We that but late were mounted up aloft,
Lull'd in the skirt of that inconstant Dame,
Are now thrown headlong by her ruthless hand,
To kiss that earth whereon our feet should stand."
        Heywood, *Foure Prentises of London*, I. I.

848. Spenser makes Clarion still gayer than Iris :

With nimble flight down posts the maid.
She views
The mighty throng, and scans the shores, and sees 850
The ports abandoned, and the navy left.
But, far secluded on the lonely beach,
The Trojan women wept Anchises lost,
And on the deep, deep sea all gazed in tears.

" Lastly his shinie wings as silver bright,
Painted with thousand colours passing farre
All painters skill, he did about him dight :
Not half so manie sundrie colours arre
In Iris bowe ; ne Heaven doth shine so bright,
Distinguished with manie a twinckling starre ;
Nor Junoes bird, in her ey-spotted traine,
So manie goodly colours doth containe."
        Muiopotmos, 12.

Milton grandly describes the descent of Raphael :
" Down thither prone in flight
He speeds, and through the vast eternal sky
Sails between worlds and worlds, with steady wing
Now on the polar winds, then with quick fan
Winnows the buxom air ; till, within soar
Of towering eagles, to all the fowls he seems
A phœnix, gazed by all as that sole bird,
When, to enshrine his reliques in the sun's
Bright temple, to Egyptian Thebes he flies.
At once on th' eastern cliff of Paradise
He lights, and to his proper shape returns
A seraph wing'd : six wings he wore to shade
His lineaments divine ; the pair that clad
Each shoulder broad came mantling o'er his breast
With regal ornament ; the middle pair
Girt like a starry zone his waist, and round
Skirted his loins and thighs with downy gold
And colours dipp'd in Heaven ; the third his feet
Shadow'd from either heel with feather'd mail,
Sky-tinctured grain." *P. L.*, b. v.

" Meantime refracted from yon eastern cloud,
Bestriding earth, the grand ethereal bow
Shoots up immense ; and every hue unfolds,
In fair proportion running from the red,
To where the violet fades into the sky."
        Thomson, *Spring*.

Akenside thus beautifully paints Fiction :
" Let Fiction come, upon her vagrant wings
Wafting ten thousand colours through the air,
Which, by the glances of her magic eye,
She blends and shifts at will, through countless forms,
Her wild creation."
        Pleasures of the Imagination, i. 14-18.

854. Even Colin at first sight of the sea was not more alarmed than these timid ladies :
" ' So to the sea we came ; the sea, that is
A world of waters heaped up on hie,
Rolling like mountaines in wide wildernesse,
Horrible, hideous, roaring with hoarse crie.'
' And is the sea,' quoth Coridon, ' so fearfull ?'
' Fearful, much more,' quoth he, ' then hart can fear :
Thousand wyld beasts with deep mouthes gaping direfull
Therein stil wait poore passengers to teare.
Who life doth loath, and longs death to behold,
Before he die, alreadie dead with feare,
And yet would live with heart half stonie cold,
Let him to sea, and he shall see it there.

"Alas! that should to weary [hearts] remain
So many shoals, and such expanse of sea!"—
One cry with all. A city they entreat;
It irks the toil of ocean to endure.
She therefore flung herself among the midst,
In harming not unversed, and mien alike
And garment of the goddess lays aside.
She Beroë becomes, the agèd wife 862
Of Tmaros-born Doryclus, [one] to whom
Had birth, and erst a name, and sons belonged ;
And thus amid the Dardans' mothers she
Intrudes herself: "O wretched, whom no hand,"
She cries, "of Grecia in the war had haled
To doom beneath your native city's walls !
O hapless nation, for destruction what
Does Fortune hold thee back ? Since Troja's wreck 870
The seventh summer now is wheeled, while seas,
While every land, so many rocks, devoid
Of hospitage, and stars, we having spanned
Are wafted on ; while we through ocean vast
Italia flying chase, and by the waves
Are rolled along. Here Eryx' brotherbourns,
Our host Acestes, too : what hinders us
From founding walls, and giving citizens
Their city ? O my country! and, in vain
Delivered from the foe, ye household gods!
Shall none e'ermore be called the walls of Troy ? 881
Nowhere shall I behold Hectorean streams,
The Xanthus and the Simois ? Nay come,
And burn ye up with me the cursèd ships.
For through my sleep to me Cassandra's ghost,
The prophetess, seemed blazing brands to give.
Here seek ye Troy ; here lies the home," she cries,

And yet as ghastly dreadfull, as it seemes,
Bold men, presuming life for gain to sell,
Dare tempt that gulf, and in those wandring stremes
Seek waies unknowne, waies leading down to hell.'"
    Spenser, *Colin Clouts Come Home Again.*

See note on *Æn.* 8, v. 109, where the quotation is continued.

875. "But me, not destined such delights to share,
My prime of life in wand'ring spent and care;
Impell'd with steps unceasing to pursue
Some fleeting good, that mocks me with the view ;
That like the circle bounding earth and skies,
Allures from far, yet, as I follow, flies ;
My fortune leads to traverse realms alone,
And find no spot of all the world my own."
    Goldsmith, *Traveller.*

"For you ; now is the moment for the deed
To be accomplished : be there no demur
With such grave presages. Lo! altars four 890
To Neptune : e'en the god himself the brands
And heart supplies." These saying, she, the first,
Engrasps with vehemence the felon fire,
And with right hand uplifted from afar
She it with effort brandishes and flings.
Roused were the minds, and paralyzed the hearts
Of th' Ilian women. Here from many, one,
Who was by birth the eldest, Pyrgo, [she]
Of Priam's sons so many royal nurse :
"No Beroë [is this] for you ; this, dames,
Is no Rhœtean wife of Doryclus. 901
Mark ye the tokens of a heav'nly grace,
And glowing eyes ; what air is hers, what looks,
And tone of voice, nay gait as she proceeds !
I e'en myself erewhile left Beroë,
At parting, sick, impatient that alone
From such a service she should lacking be,
Nor rightful off'rings to Anchises bring."
These [words] she uttered : but the dames, at first
In vacillation and with evil eyes, 910
Began to view the ships ; in doubt between
A wretched passion for the present land,
And realms that summon by the fates :
what time
Along the sky the goddess raised her [form]
On pinions of a poise, and in her flight
A bow colossal scored beneath the clouds.
Then, sooth, astounded by the prodigies,
And frenzy-driv'n, in chorus do they yell,
And pillage from the inmost hearths their fire.
Some rob the altars ; leaf, and sprigs, and brands, 920
They fling together. Vulcan fumes with reins

---

921. Glover thus graphically describes the burning of the Persian camp:
"The word is giv'n. They seize
The burning fuel. Sparkling in the wind,
Destructive fire is brandish'd.
Now devastation, unconfined, involves
The Malian fields. Among barbarian tents
From diff'rent stations fly consuming flames.
The Greeks afford no respite ; and the storm
Exasperates the blaze. To ev'ry part
The conflagration like a sea expands,
One waving surface of unbounded fire,
In ruddy volumes mount the curling flames

Let loose through banks, and oars, and painted sterns
Of fir. A courier to Anchises' tomb,
And [to] the benches of the theatre,
Eumelus, brings the tidings that the ships
Were in a blaze; and they themselves behind
See sooty ashes flutt'ring in a cloud.
And first Ascanius, as he gaily led
His cavalry manœuvres, in such guise,
Keen on his charger, sought the troubled camp; 930
Nor can the breathless masters hold him back.
"What this strange frenzy? At what [object] now,
At what is it you aim?" cries he. "Alas!
My wretched countrywomen! It is not
The foeman, and the hostile camp of Greeks,—
'Tis your own hopes ye burn. Lo! 'here am I,
Your own Ascanius!" He before their feet
His empty helmet flung, wherewith bedight
In sport the mimicry of war he waked.
At once Æneas hastes, at once the hosts
Of Teucer's sons. But they in fear thro'out
The severed shores, in all directions fly 942

Apart, and woods, and, be they anywhere,
The vaulted rocks clandestinely they seek.
They're sick of their emprise and of the light,
And their own [friends] repentant recognize,
And Juno from their bosom is dislodged.
Howbeit did not upon this account
The flames and burnings their ungoverned might
Lay by: beneath the smoking timber lives
The oakum, spewing lazy smoke, and slow
Upon the galleys preys the smould'ring heat, 952
And all throughout their hull descends the plague:
Nor heroes' strength nor in-poured floods avail.
Then good Æneas from his shoulders tears
His garment off, and calls the gods to aid,
And stretches out his hands: "Almighty Jove,
If not as yet the Trojans to a man
Thou dost abhor, if thy good will of old
At all regards the travails of mankind;
Grant now my fleet, O sire, to 'scape the flame, 961
And save the Trojans' slender state from doom;
Or do thou,—what remains,—by hostile flash
To death, if I deserve it, send me down,

To heav'n's dark vault, and paint the midnight clouds.
So, when the north emits his purpled lights,
The undulated radiance, streaming wide,
As with a burning canopy invests
Th' ethereal concave. Œta now disclos'd
His forehead, glittering in eternal frost:
While down his rocks the foamy torrents shone.
Far o'er the main the pointed rays were thrown;
Night snatch'd her mantle from the Ocean's breast;
The billows glimmer'd from the distant shores."
Leonidas, b. xii.

Ariel tells Prospero of the scene of magic fire which he conjured up:
"I boarded the king's ship; now on the beak,
Now in the waist, the deck, in every cabin,
I flam'd amazement: sometimes, I'd divide,
And burn in many places; on the topmast,
The yards and bowsprit, would I flame distinctly,
Then meet, and join. Jove's lightnings, the precursors
O' the dreadful thunder-claps, more momentary
And sight-out-running were not: the fire and cracks
Of sulphurous roaring the most mighty Neptune
Seem to besiege, and make his bold waves tremble,
Yea, his dread trident shake."
Shakespeare, *Tempest*, i. 2.

941. "Fear soon is settled in a woman's breast."
Drayton, *Edward to Alice*.

942. "For if the least imagin'd overture
But of conceiv'd revolt men once espy,
Straight shrink the weak; the great will not endure;
Th' impatient run; the discontented fly;
The friend his friend's example doth procure,
And all together haste them presently,

Some to their home, some hide; others that stay
To reconcile themselves, the rest betray."
Lord Salisbury's Speech to King Richard.
Daniell, *Civil War*, ii. 34.

945. Polydore is smart on Monimia:
"Intolerable vanity! your sex
Was never in the right; ye are always false
Or silly; even your dresses are not more
Fantastic than your appetites; you think
Of nothing twice; opinion you have none;
To-day ye are nice, to-morrow none so free;
Now smile, then frown; now sorrowful, then glad;
Now pleased, now not; and all you know not why!
Virtue you affect; inconstancy's your practice."
Otway, *Orphan*, i. 2.

952. Dryden of the Fire of London:
"In this deep quiet, from what source unknown,
Those seeds of fire their fatal birth disclose
And first few scattering sparks about were blown,
Big with the flames that to our ruin rose.
"Then in some close-pent room it crept along,
And, smouldering as it went, in silence fed;
Till th' infant monster, with devouring strong,
Walk'd boldly upright with exalted head."
Annus Mirabilis, 217, 18.

964. See Charles's address to Heaven; *Ann. Mir.* 262:
"Or if my heedless youth has step'd astray,
Too soon forgetful of Thy gracious hand,
On me alone Thy just displeasure lay,
But take Thy judgments from this mourning land."

And with thy right hand whelm me here."
He scarce
These [words] had uttered, when with sluicy rains
A pitchy storm beyond example raves,
And thrill with thunder steeps and plains of earth.
From the whole welkin dashes down a shower,
Confused with water, and in deepest black
With huddled southern gales; and from above   971
The ships are brimmed; the half-charred timbers reek;
Till every fire is quenched, and all the keels,
With loss of four, are rescued from the plague.
But sire Æneas, by the sore mischance
Deep-shocked, was now to this side, now to that,
Within his bosom shifting weighty cares,
Debating whether he should settle down
On Sic'ly's fields, forgetful of the fates,
Or aim at reaching the Italian coasts. 980

Then agèd Nautes, whom in special wise
Tritonian Pallas taught, and famous made
With plenteous science, offered these replies,—
Or what the gods' high anger might presage,
Or what the scheme of destinies demand;—
And he, Æneas cheering with these words,
Begins: "O goddess-born, where'er the Fates
May draw us and withdraw us follow we;
Whatever shall befortune, every hap
Is by endurance to be overcome.   990
Thou hast a Dardan of a heav'nly line,
Acestes: him take thou, and knit with thee
Frank partner in thy plans. To him consign
Who, from the galleys lost, are in excess,

"Meanwhile the South wind rose, and, with black wings
Wide-hovering, all the clouds together drove
From under Heaven; the hills to their supply
Vapour, and exhalation dusk-and moist,
Sent up amain; and now the thicken'd sky
Like a dark ceiling stood; down rush'd the rain
Impetuous."   Milton, *P. L.*, xi.

"He, when deep-rolling clouds blot out the day,
And thunderous storms and solemn gloom display,
Pours down a watery deluge from on high,
And opens all the sluices of the sky:
High o'er the shores the rushing surge prevails,
Bursts o'er the plain, and roars along the vales:
Dashing abruptly, dreadful down it comes,
Tumbling through rocks, and tosses, whirls, and foams:
Meantime, from every region of the sky,
Red burning bolts in forky vengeance fly;
Dreadfully bright o'er seas and earth they glare,
And bursts of thunder rend th' encumbered air."
      Broome, *Paraphrase on Ecclus.*, 43.

974. Dryden calls the ships, destroyed by fire in the Dutch war, "martyrs":

"Restless he pass'd the remnant of the night,
Till the fresh air proclaim'd the morning nigh:
And burning ships, the martyrs of the fight,
With paler fires beheld the eastern sky."
      Annus Mirab., st. 102.

976. "Then comes my fit again: I had else been perfect:
Whole as the marble, founded as the rock;
As broad and general as the casing air:
But now I am cabin'd, cribb'd, confin'd, bound in
To saucy doubts and fears."
      Shakespeare, *Macbeth*, iii. 4.

Shakespeare makes Reignier bear calamity with a brave heart:

"I am a soldier, and unapt to weep,
Or to exclaim on fortune's fickleness."
      1 Henry VI., v. 3.

986.   "Cure her of that:
Canst thou not minister to a mind diseas'd;
Pluck from the memory a rooted sorrow;
Raze out the written troubles of the brain;
And with some sweet oblivious antidote
Cleanse the stuff'd bosom of that perilous grief
Which weighs upon the heart?"
      Shakespeare, *Macbeth*, v. 3.

988. Churchill inculcates similar obedience to Honour:
"If Honour calls, where'er she points the way,
The sons of Honour follow and obey."
      The Farewell.

990.   "In struggling with misfortunes
Lies the true proof of virtue. On smooth seas
How many bauble boats dare set their sails,
And make an equal way with firmer vessels!
But let the tempest once enrage that sea,
And then behold the strong-ribb'd argosie,
Bounding between the ocean and the air,
Like Perseus mounted on his Pegasus.
Then where are those weak rivals of the main?
Or to avoid the tempest fled to port,
Or made a prey to Neptune: even thus
Do empty show and true-priz'd worth divide
In storms of fortune."
      Dryden, *Troilus and Cressida*, i. 1.

Rowe makes Jane Shore give utterance to the following pathetic soliloquy:
"Yet, yet endure, nor murmur, oh! my soul:
For are not thy transgressions great and numberless?
Do they not cover thee like rising floods,
And press thee like a weight of waters down?
Does not the hand of righteousness afflict thee?
And who shall plead against it? Who shall say
To Power Almighty, Thou hast done enough?
Or bid his dreadful rod of vengeance stay?
Wait then with patience, till the circling hours
Shall bring the time of thy appointed rest,
And lay thee down in death. The hireling thus
With labour drudges out the painful day,
And often looks with long-expecting eyes
To see the shadows rise, and be dismissed."
      Jane Shore, act v.

"Remember patience is the Christian's courage.
Stoics have bled, and demigods have died:
A Christian's task is harder:—'tis to suffer."
      Walpole, *Mysterious Mother*, iv. 4.

And who are weary of our grand emprise
And thine estate, alike the aged, advanced
In years, and sea-worn matrons ; and what-
  e'er
Is weakly with thee, and afraid of risk,
Cull out, and let them have,—the weary
  [souls],—
Their ramparts in these lands ; their city
  they   1000
Shall call 'Acesta' by a licensed name."
By such expressions of his agèd friend
Afire, then sooth is he o'er all his cares
Distracted in his soul. And ebon Night
Upon her two-horse chariot borne, the
  heavens
Enchained ; thereon appeared from out the
  sky
Down gliding, th' apparition of his sire
Anchises, on a sudden pouring forth
Such words : " O son, to me than life
  erewhile,
While life remained, more dear ; O son,
Experienced in the destinies of Troy, 1011
At Jove's commandment am I hither come,
He who the fire hath banished from thy
  ships,
And pitied thee at last from heav'n on
  high.
Th' advice obey, which now [in] fairest
  [shape]
The agèd Nautes gives ; do thou choice
  youths,
The bravest hearts, to Italy transport.
A race of steel, and savage in their guise,
By thee in Latium is to be subdued.
Yet first the nether homes of Dis approach,
And through the depths Avernian seek,
  my son,   1021
Converse with me. For have no hold of me
The godless Tartarus, or rueful shades ;

1004. "'Twas when bright Cynthia with her silver
car,
  Soft stealing from Endymion's bed,
  Had call'd forth ev'ry glitt'ring star,
  And up th' ascent of heav'n her brilliant host
    had led.
  Night with all her negro train
  Took possession of the plain ;
  On an herse she rode reclin'd
  Drawn by screech-owls slow and blind.
  Close to her with printless feet,
  Crept Stillness in a winding sheet.
  Next to her deaf Silence was seen,
  Treading on tip-toes over the green ;
  Softly, lightly, gently she trips,
  Still holding her fingers seal'd to her lips."
            Smart, *Ode* xiv. 1.

1016. " For know, an honest statesman to a prince
Is like a cedar planted by a spring ;
  The spring bathes the tree's root, the gratefull
    tree
  Rewards it with its shadow."
       Webster, *Dutchesse of Malfy*, iii. 2.

But sweet assemblies of religious [souls],
Elysium, too, do I frequent. Thee hither-
  ward
The taintless Sybil with abundant blood
Of sable flocks shall lead. Then all thy race,
And what the walls be giv'n thee, thou
  shalt learn.
And now farewell : dank Night is wheeling
  round
Her central orbit, and the ruthless Dawn
Hath breathed upon me with his panting
  steeds."   1031
He spake, and sped like smoke to subtile
  air.
Æneas cries : " Hence whither dost thou
  rush ?
Whither dost fling away ? Whom fliest
  thou ?
Or who from our embraces thee debars ?"
Pronouncing these, the embers he awakes
And slumb'ring fires ; and Pergamean Lar,
And hoary Vesta's shrine, with sacred meal
And brimful censer humbly he adores.
Forthwith his comrades, and Acestes first,
He summons, and of Jupiter's command,
And his dear sire's injunctions, throughly he
Apprises them, and what decision now 1043

1027-9. Perhaps the reader may here be reminded
of Miranda, who says to Prospero :
           " You have often
  Begun to tell me what I am ; but stopp'd,
  And left me to a bootless inquisition ;
  Concluding, *Stay, not yet*."
           Shakespeare, *Tempest*, i. 2.

1029. Spenser finely describes Night in her airy
progress :
" Where griesly Night, with visage deadly sad,
  That Phœbus chearefull face durst never vew,
  And in a foule blacke pitchy mantle clad
  She findes forth comming from her darksome mew ;
  Where she all day did hide her hated hew.
  Before the door her yron charet stood,
  Already harnessed for iourney new,
  And cole-black steedes yborne of hellish brood,
  And on their rusty bits did champ, as they were
    wood."   *F. Q*., i. 6, 20.
" For Night's swift dragons cut the clouds full fast,
  And yonder shines Aurora's harbinger,
  At whose approach ghosts, wand'ring here and
    there,
  Troop home to church-yards : damned spirits all,
  That in cross-ways and floods have burial,
  Already to their wormy beds are gone ;
  For fear lest day should look their shames upon,
  They wilfully themselves exile from light,
  And must for aye consort with black-brow'd
    Night."
  Shakespeare, *Midsummer Night's Dream*, iii. 2.

1030. " But, soft ! methinks I scent the morning
air.
     . . . . Fare thee well at once !
  The glow-worm shows the matin to be near,
  And 'gins to pale his ineffectual fire :
  Adieu, adieu, adieu ! Remember me."
           Shakespeare, *Hamlet*, i. 5.

Stands settled in his mind. To his designs
No stay ; nor does Acestes disallow
His orders. For the city they enrol
The dames, and willing commons set aside,
Souls craving naught of high renown.
   Themselves
The thwarts renew, and in the ships replace
The timbers, gnawed by flames around ;
   they fit
Both oars and cordage ; in their number
   scant,   1051
But all alive their gallantry for war.
Meanwhile Æneas with a plough scores out
The city, and by lot assigns their homes ;
This bids be "Ilium," and these spots be
   "Troy."
Trojan Acestes in the kingship joys,
And institutes a Forum, and grants rights
To summoned sires. Then, neighb'ring on
   the stars,
On Eryx' crest there founded is a seat
T' Idalian Venus ; and t' Anchises' tomb
A priest and grove, wide-holy, is attached.
And now nine days the nation all observed
The feast, and on the altars sacrifice   1063
Was offered ; gentle breezes laid the seas,
And freshening Auster, breathing on them,
   woos
Once more upon the deep. There rises up
A mighty weeping through the winding
   shores ;
In mutual embrace both day and night
Do they retard. Now e'en the very dames,
The very men, to whom erst grim appeared
The aspect of the sea, and insupportable
The will of heav'n, desirous are to go, 1072
And all the travail of a flight endure :
Whom good Æneas cheers with kindly
   words,
And to Acestes, linked by blood, in tears

1051. " Joy, joy, I see confest from every eye :
   Your limbs tread vigorous, and your breasts beat
      high.
   Thin tho' our ranks, tho' scanty be our bands,
   Bold are our hearts, and nervous are our hands.
   With us, truth, justice, fame, and freedom close,
   Each singly equal to a host of foes."
            Brooke, *Gustavus Vasa*, iii. end.

1067. Of these tiresome dames it might have been
said :
" Had women navigable rivers in their eyes,
   They would dispend them all. I'll tell thee,
   These are but moonish shades of griefs or fears :
   There's nothing sooner dry than women's tears."
         Webster, *Vittoria Corombona*, v.

1072. " Philosophers their pains may spare, ,
      Perpetual motion where to find ;
   If such a thing be anywhere,
      'Tis, woman, in thy fickle mind."
           Charles Cotton, *The False One*.

See note on *Æn.* iv. v. 569.

Entrusts. Three calves to Eryx, and to
   Storms
A ewe-lamb, he to slaughter then enjoins,
And hawser [s] in succession to be loosed.
Himself, enwreathed upon his head with
   leaves
Of olive trimmed, far standing on the
   bow,   1080
A paten holds, and flings the entrails forth
Upon the briny waves, and fluid wines
Outpours. The wind, uprising from astern,
Attends the voyagers. In rivalry
The crews lash ocean, and the waters
   sweep.
But Venus meanwhile, worried by her
   cares,
Neptune accosts, and from her breast out-
   pours
Such plainings : " Juno's weighty wrath,
   her gall,
Not to be glutted, me, O Neptune, force
To stoop to every prayer :—[she] whom
   nor length   1090
Of time, nor any piety doth melt ;
Nor is she, by the sovereignty of Jove
And by the Fates [though] beaten down,
   at rest.
'Tis not enough that she in cursèd hate
Hath from the bosom of the Phrygians'
   race
Their city eaten out, nor dragged them on
Through every punishment :—of ruined
   Troy
The remnant, ashes, and the bones she
   hunts.
The grounds of such outrageous frenzy she
May know. Thou wert my witness late
In Libyan surges what a pile she raised
Upon a sudden ; seas all blent with
   heaven,   1102
In vain relying on Æolian storms :
In thy own realm adventuring this. Lo !
   e'en
By Trojan matrons, forced all through the
   crime,

Juno was as hard as Shylock, with whom, in
favour of Antonio, was no
" Glancing an eye of pity on his losses,
   That have of late been huddled on his back ;
   Enough to press a royal merchant down,
   And pluck commiseration of his state
   From brassy bosoms, and rough hearts of flint,
   From stubborn Turks and Tartars, never train'd
   To offices of tender courtesy."
      Shakespeare, *Merchant of Venice*, iv. 1.

1090. Venus could not have said with the Duchess
of York :
" A beggar begs that never begged before."
        Shakespeare, *K. Richard II.*, v. 3.

1091. See note on *Ecl.* i. *l.* 85.

She hath in shameful wise burnt up their ships,
And, through the loss of fleet, constrained [their lord]
To leave his comrades to an unknown land.
For what remains, I crave it be allowed
For thee to grant safe canvas through the waves; 1110
Laurentine Tiber it may be allowed
To reach; if I admissible [requests]
Am urging, if the Weirds those walls vouchsafe."
Then the deep sea's Saturnian tamer these
Delivered: "It is altogether right
That thou, O Cytherea, shouldest trust
Upon my realms, whence drawest thou thy birth.
I've earned it, too: I oft the frenzies quelled
And such wild madness both of sky and sea.
Nor is it less upon the lands (the Xanthus
And Simois to witness do I call,) 1121
Hath thine Æneas been a care to me.
What time, in chase of Troja's breathless hosts,
Achilles hurtled them against the walls,
Gave many a thousand to their doom, and groaned
Choked rivers, nor could Xanthus find a path,
And disembogue him in the main:—then I
Æneas, while with Peleus' gallant son

Engaged,—no matches or his gods, or powers,—
Seized in a hollow cloud; although I yearned 1130
To overthow from its foundation, reared
By hands of mine, the walls of Troy foresworn.
Now, too, my mind abides with me the same:
Dispel thy fear; in safety shall he reach
Avernus' havens, which thou dost desire.
One only shall there be, whom, missing, he
Shall in the eddy seek; a single life
For many shall be giv'n." By these his words
When he to gladness calmed the goddess' breast,
His coursers does the father yoke in gold,
And foaming curbs upon the beasts he sets,
And from his hands threw all the reins away. 1142
In sea-green chariot airily he flies
Along the surface-seas: down sink the waves,
And 'neath his thund'ring axle ocean's plain
Is in its swell upon the waters laid;

1126. Drayton, of the overthrow in the Red Sea:
" Death is discern'd triumphantly in arms
On the rough seas his slaughtery to keep,
And his cold self in breath of mortals warms,
Upon the dimpled bosom of the deep.
There might you see a chequer'd ensign swim
About the body of the envy'd dead,
Serve for a hearse or coverture to him,
Erewhile did waft it proudly 'bout his head:
The warlike chariot turn'd upon the back,
With the dead horses in their traces ty'd,
Drags their fat carcass through the foamy brack,
That drew it late undauntedly in pride.
There floats the barb'd steed with his rider drown'd,
Whose foot in his caparison is cast,
Who late with sharp spurs did his courser wound,
Himself now ridden with his strangled beast."
Moses his Birth and Miracles, iii. 41–56.

Glover, finely of the destruction of the Persians:
" Down the Thalian steep
Prone are they hurry'd to th' expanded arms
Of Horrour, rising from the oozy deep,
And grasping all their members, as they fall.
The dire confusion like a storm invades
The chafing surge. Whole troops Bellona rolls
In one vast ruin from the craggy ride.
O'er all their arms, their ensigns, deep-engulf'd;
With hideous roar the waves for ever close."
Leonidas, viii. end.

1140. " He said no more, but bade two Tritons sound
Their crooked shells, to spread the summons round.
Through the wide caves the blast is heard afar;
With speed two more provide his azure car,
A concave shell; two the thinn'd coursers join:
All wait officious round, and own th' accustom'd sign.
The god ascends; his better hand sustains
The three-forked spear, his left directs the reins.
Through breaking waves the chariot mounts him high;
Before its thundering course the frothy waters fly.
He gains the surface; on his either side
The bright attendants, rang'd with comely pride,
Advance in just array, and grace the pompous tide." Hughes, *Court of Neptune*, end.

1146. " So when th' assuming god, whom storms obey,
To all the warring winds at once give way,
The frantic brethren ravage all around,
And rocks, and woods, and shores, their rage resound;
Incumbent o'er the main, at length they sweep
The liquid plains, and raise the peaceful deep.
But when superior Neptune leaves his bed,
His trident shakes, and shows his awful head;
The madding winds are hush'd, the tempest cease,
And every rolling surge resides in peace."
Congreve, *Birth of the Muse*.

W. Thompson ascribes the same power to May in his beautiful Hymn, st. 2:
" At thy approach the wild waves' loud uproar,
And foamy surges of the madd'ning main
Forget to heave their mountains to the shore,
Diffused into the level of the plain.

Flee off the storm-clouds from the waste of sky.
Then [loom] the motley figures of his train,
Immense sea-monsters, and the elder choir
Of Glaucus and Palæmon Ino-born, 1150
And nimble Tritons, and all Phorcus' host.
Keeps Thetis on the left, and Melite,
And Panope the maid, Nesæe, Spio, too,
Thalia also, and Cymodoce.
  Here through the sire Æneas' anxious mind

For thee the halcyon builds her summer's nest;
For thee the ocean smooths her troubled breast,
Gay from thy placid smiles, in thy own purple drest."

1155. This whole account of the Trojans leaving Sicily will be involved in great confusion, unless the reference of *hic*, v. 827, be rightly understood. As it stands, it would seem to be connected with the preceding history of Neptune and Venus: but this view seems quite inadmissible. The state of the case appears to be this: While Æneas was making arrangements for the colony, which he was to leave behind him, composed of the infirm of both sexes, silly women and cowards, Venus solicits the friendly aid of Neptune, which is freely accorded. The sea had been rough, the winds unruly, and the sky threatening; but these were all reduced to moderation (v. 820, 1,) by the interference of the god. This change of weather took place just after the completion of the funeral feast in honor of Anchises (v. 763, 4); so that Æneas sets sail with as fair a wind as could be,—*Auster;* Cumæ being nearly due north of Eryx. The breeze, which had been freshening, was still too light to admit of much progress by sailing, so that they had hitherto trusted to their oars; but now, at a certain point of their voyage (probably soon after they had set out)—*hic*, —they set the sails.
  But how came they to *tack?*—for sailors never tack with a fair wind; and yet *Auster* was fair; and, moreover, we are told, *ferunt sua flamina classem.* There seems to be but one way out of this serious difficulty, a difficulty which does not seem to have been noticed by the commentators. Though the wind was fair for going from the west of Sicily to Campania, yet it might have been foul for getting out of Eryx, and clear of the land to the open sea. So far they tacked, and then—but not till then— the *flamina* could be said to be *sua*. If this explanation of the matter be considered too refined, it is not easy to see how Virgil is to be screened from the charge of ignorance or carelessness. One need be neither sailor nor yachtsman to comprehend the dilemma in which a poet of unquestionable learning, and of no little caution, must otherwise be involved.
  There seems to be no difficulty about the general meaning of the passage from *Attolli* to *detorquentque;* but it is not sure that *fecere pedem* is translated aright. It is very objectionable to employ technical terms in a poem further than is absolutely necessary; yet this last expression, strictly perhaps, should have been rendered, "they belayed the sheet," or, "they made a tack." This, at least, is certain, that they did something or other with the sheet, with a view to tacking: and what, if not belaying it? In nautical language the whole proceeding, it is probable, would be thus expressed: They stepped the masts, bent the sails on the yards, tacked about while in stays, let fly, now the port,

Thrill soothing joys in turn. He bids with speed
That all the masts be hoisted up, yards stretched
To sails. They fastened all at once the sheet,
And equally their canvas-folds upon the left,
Now on the right, unloose; they all at once
The lofty yard-arms veer and veer aback:
Waft their own gales the fleet. The first 'fore all, 1162
The serried squadron Palinurus led:
Towards him the rest were bid to aim their course.
And now well-nigh the zenith-goal of heaven
Dank Night had gained; in calm repose their limbs
The sailors had unbent, stretched 'neath the oars
Along the painful seats; when Somnus, light,
Down gliding from the empyrean stars,
Sundered the sullen air, and forced apart
The shades, thee seeking, Palinure, to thee,
Unfaulty, bearing rueful dreams; 1172

now the starboard, sheets, and braced the yards sharp up on either hand.
  The tutor should impress upon the uninitiated student, that the "sheet" of a sail is *not* its spread of canvas, but the rope which is attached to one or both of its lower corners, in order to extend it and maintain its position.

1157. "High on the slipp'ry masts the yards ascend,
  And far abroad the canvas wings extend."
    Falconer, *Shipwreck*, i.

1165. Rowe thus alludes to this ominous hour:
  " The setting sun descends
Swift to the western waves; and guilty Night,
Hasty to spread her horrors o'er the world,
Rides on the dusky air.—And now it comes,
The fatal moment comes, e'en that dread time,
When witches meet to gather herbs on graves,
When discontented ghosts forsake their tombs,
And ghastly roam about, and doleful groan."
    Ulysses, iii.

1168. Rawlins introduces Evadne praying for Giovanno a more merciful exercise of the god's power than he exhibited towards the unhappy pilot:
" Thou silent god, that with the leaden mace
Arresteth all (save those prodigious birdes)
That are Fate's heraulds to proclaime all ill;
Deafe Giovanno, let no fancied noyse
Of ominous screech-owles, or night ravens voice,
Affright his quiet sences: let his sleepe
Be free from horrour, or unruly dreames,
That may beget a tempest in the streames
Of his calm reason: let 'em run as smooth,
And with as great a silence, as those doe
That never tooke an injurie: where no wind
Had yet acquaintance: but like a smooth cristall,
Dissolv'd into a water that never frown'd,
Or knew a voyce but musicke."
    The Rebellion, act iv. 1.

And on the lofty stern the god sat down,
To Phorbas like, and from his lips out-
  pours
These accents: "Palinure, Iasus' son,
The waters of themselves waft on the
  fleet;
Staid breathe the gales; the hour is giv'n
  to rest:
Lay down thy head, and steal thy flagging
  eyes
From toil. E'en I myself a little while
Will in thy stead thy duties undertake."
To whom, with effort heaving up his
  eyes,
Saith Palinurus; "Is it me the face 1182
And restful surges of the calmy sea
Thou bidd'st not know? Is't me this
  marvel trust?
Why sooth am I Æneas to confide
To guileful southern gales, aye, duped so
  oft
By the delusion of a cloudless sky?"
Such words he uttered, and attached
  [thereto],
And clinging, no where let the tiller go,
And kept his eyes [turned] towards the
  stars. Behold! 1190
The god a branch, in dew of Lethe soaked,
And drowsed with efficacy from the Styx,
Above both temples waves, and, as he
  stays,
Unstrings his swimming eyeballs. Scarcely
  first
Had unanticipated rest unbent
His joints, when, leaning o'er him from
  above,

1191. T. Warton has a different image:
"On this my pensive pillow, gentle Sleep,
Descend, in all thy downy plumage drest:
Wipe with thy wing those eyes that wake to
  weep,
And place thy crown of poppies on my breast."
    Ode, i. 1.
Fletcher a different magic. In his beautiful
pastoral poem, *The Faithful Shepherdess*, he in-
troduces the "Sullen Shepherd," with Amaryllis
in his arms, and saying:
"From thy forehead thus I take
These herbs, and charge thee not awake,
Till in yonder holy well
Thrice, with powerful magic spell
Fill'd with many a baleful word,
Thou hast been dipp'd. Thus, with my cord
Of blasted hemp, by moonlight twin'd,
I do thy sleepy body bind.
I turn thy head unto the east,
And thy feet unto the west,
Thy left arm to the south put forth,
And thy right unto the north.
I take thy body from the ground,
In this deep and deadly swound,
And into this holy spring
I let thee slide down by my string"
    Act iii. 1, 1–16.

With a wrenched piece of stern, and with
  the helm,
He flung him forward on the crystal waves,
Head-foremost, and upon his mates in
  vain
Oft calling. He himself, winged, on the
  wing, 1200
Upraised his [form] to subtile air. Not
  less
Careers its voyage safe upon the main
The fleet, and through sire Neptune's
  words of pledge
Is wafted unalarmed. And now it e'en,
Borne on, was drawing nigh the Sirens'
  rocks,
Erst stern, and with the bones of many
  bleached;—
Then hoarse afar with th' ever-chafing
  sea
The rocks were booming;—when the
  father felt
That, through her pilot lost, his reeling
  ship
Warped off,—himself e'en steered her in
  the nighted waves, 1210
Upheaving many a groan, and in his soul

1205. The Nymph of the Derwent seems to
have been hardly less dangerous in Damon's view:
"Within our Darwin, in her rockie cell,
A nymph there lives, which thousand boyes
  hath harm'd;
All as she gliding rides in boats of shell,
Darting her eyes, (where spite and beauty dwell:
Ay me, that spite with beautie should be
  arm'd!)
Her witching eye the boy and boat hath
  charm'd.
No sooner drinks he down that pois'nous eye,
But mourns and pines: (ah piteous crueltie!)
With her he longs to live; for her he longs to
  die." P. Fletcher, *Piscatory Eclogues*, v. 5.

1210. The gallant soldier seems to have become
an able seaman, so as not to have needed the warn-
ing of Chromis:
"Ah, foolish lads, that think with waves to play,
And rule rough seas, which never knew com-
  mand!
First in some river thy new skill essay,
Till time and practice teach thy weakly hand.
A thin, thin plank keeps in thy vital breath:
Death ready waits. Fond boyes, to play with
  death!"
    P. Fletcher, *Piscatory Eclogues*, iv. 16.

"Inur'd to peril, with unconquer'd soul,
The chief beheld tempestuous oceans roll
O'er the wild surge, when dismal shades preside,
His equal skill the lonely bark could guide;
His genius, ever for th' event prepared,
Rose with the storm, and all its dangers shared."
    Falconer, *Shipwreck*, i. 2.

1211. "He must not float upon his watery bier
Unwept, and welter to the parching wind,
Without the mead of some melodious tear."

The idea in this beautiful passage of Milton's

Shocked at the misadventure of his friend:
"O thou, who to a sky and ocean bright

(*Lycidas*) is borrowed from Ben Jonson's *Cynthia's Revels*, i. 1:

"Vouchsafe me, I may do him these last rites,
But kiss his flower, *and sing some mourning strain*
Over his wat'ry hearse*."*

See Gifford's note. No excuse is needed for transcribing the charming dirge a little farther on:

"Slow, slow, fresh fount, keep time with my salt tears;
   Yet slower yet; O faintly, gentle springs:
List to the heavy part the music bears,
Woe weeps out her division, when she sings.
     Droop herbs and flowers,
     Fall grief in showers,
     Our beauties are not ours;
     O, I could still,
Like melting snow upon some craggy hill,
     Drop, drop, drop, drop,
Since nature's pride is now a wither'd daffodil."

This lament of Æneas over Palinurus may remind

O'ermuch hast trusted, naked shalt thou lie,
O Palinurus, on an unknown strand !"

Shakespeare's readers of the exquisite address of Pericles to his dead queen, when committing her to a watery grave:

"No light, no fire: th' unfriendly elements
Forgot thee utterly; nor have I time
To give thee hallow'd to thy grave, but straight
Must cast thee, scarcely coffin'd, in the ooze;
Where for a monument upon thy bones
And aye-remaining lamps, the belching whale
And humming water must o'erwhelm thy corpse,
Lying with simple shells."

Why Æneas should make no remark about the loss of the rudder and piece of stern seems hard to explain; his steering his ship without a rudder is still more unintelligible. Even in modern days, with all the advantages of nautical and mechanical skill, the loss of a rudder occasions no small concern to a ship's company.

The language of the story seems to be much better than the construction of it. Surely there was no "*dignus vindice nodus*" in the case.

BOOK VI.

So speaks he weeping, and upon the fleet
Let loose the reins, and softly gains at last
Cumæ's Eubœan coasts. They veer around
The prows towards ocean; then with gripping fang
The anchor firmed the ships, and fringe the shores
Their arching sterns. A band of youths springs forth
In fervor on Hesperia's strand. Some seek
The seeds of fire concealed in veins of flint;
Some scour wild creatures' matted shrouds,
The forests; and discovered floods reveal.   10
But good Æneas to the tow'rs, whereon

Line 8. Milton alludes to other artificial modes of striking a light:

"While the winds
Blow moist and keen, shattering the grateful locks
Of these fair spreading trees; which bids us seek
Some better shroud, some better warmth to cherish
Our limbs benumb'd, ere this diurnal star
Leave cold the night, how we his gather'd beams
Reflected may with matter sere foment;
Or by collision of two bodies, grind
The air attrite to fire."   *P. L.*, x. end.

Apollo guardian sits aloft, and far
To th' awful Sibyl's cloisters,—cavern huge,—
Repairs; in whom a giant intellect
And spirit does the Delian seer inbreathe,
And opes [events] to come. They enter now
The groves of Trivia, and his gilded domes.
   Dædalus, as goes the legend, as he flies
The realms of Minos on his sweepy wings,
Adventuring to trust him to the sky,   20
Along a wontless region floated off
To th' icy Bears, and on the Chalcian height
Alighted airily at last. Restored
To these lands first, O Phœbus, unto thee
He sanctified the oarage of his wings,
And reared a monster fane. Upon the doors
Androgeus' death; then, penalties to pay
Ceropians doomed,—O piteous plight !—by sevens
Each year the bodies of their progeny;
Stands,—drawn the lots,—the urn. On th' other side,   30

12. "Its uplands sloping deck the mountain's side,
Woods over woods in gay theatric pride;
While oft some temple's mould'ring tops between
With memorable grandeur mark the scene."
                        Goldsmith, *Traveller.*

Upraised from Ocean, answers Gnosus' land.
Here the inhuman passion for a bull,
And, prostituted through an artifice,
Pasiphaë; and her confounded birth,
And twain-shaped imp, the Minotaur, stands there,
Memorials of her execrable lust;
Here is that toilful work of his abode,
And its inextricable maze. But sooth,
The mighty passion of the royal maid
Commiserating, Dædalus himself   40
The cheats and windings of the dome unclewed,
Directing random footsteps by a thread.
Thou, too, a leading share in such a noble work,
Might grief allow, O Icarus, would'st hold.
He twice essayed upon the gold to grave
Thy fall; twice dropped thy father's hands.
Yea, all
They in succession with their eyes would scan,
Had not Achates, in advance despatched,
Been present now, and, in his company,
Priestess of Phœbus and the Trivian [maid],
Deiophobe of Glaucus [daughter], who   51
Such like pronounces to the king: "This hour
Exacteth not these gazings for itself;
Now to be slaying from the herd untouched
Sev'n steers were meeter, just as many ewes
Of two years' old, in customed fashion culled."
Having addressed Æneas in such words
(Nor do the men the holy rites enjoined
Delay), the Teucri to the lofty fane
The priestess calls. Th' Eubœan cliff's huge side   60
Is scooped into a cavern, whither lead

Wide avenues a hundred, hundred gates,
Whence just as many voices sally forth,
The Sibyl's answers. To the threshold they
Were come, when cries the maid: "To claim the fates
'Tis time: the god! behold the god!" With whom,
While [words] the like she speaks before the doors,
Upon a sudden neither mien, nor hue
Are uniform, nor trim remained her locks;
But heaving stands her breast, and, frenzy-wild,   70
Her heart is swelling up: and she appears
Enlarged [in figure], neither utt'ring [tone]
Of mortals, seeing she is breathed upon
By now a closer power of the god.
"Dost thou betake thee idly to thy vows
And prayers, Troy-born Æneas?" she exclaims;
"Dost thou betake thee idly? for erethen
Shall not yawn open the enormous jaws
Of the astounded mansion." And the like
She having spoken held her peace. Ice-cold   80
Throughout the hardy bones of Teucer's sons
A shudder ran, and prayers the monarch pours
From out his bosom's depth: "O Phœbus, who
Hast ever pitied Troja's weighty woes,
Who Paris' Dardan shafts and hands didst aim
Against the body of Æacides;
So many seas, vast lands encircling, I
Have entered,—thou my guide,—and, far withdrawn,
The clans of the Massylians, and the fields,
Dispread in front by Syrtes; now at last   90
The flying coasts of Italy we grasp.
May Troja's fate have followed us thus far!
O ye, too, it is lawful now to spare
The Pergamean race,—e'en all ye gods
And goddesses, to whom hath stood opposed

---

38. "A stately palace he forthwith did build;
Whose intricate innumerable ways,
With such confused errours, so beguil'd
Th' unguided entrers with uncertain strays,
And doubtful turnings kept them in delays;
With bootless labour leading them about,
Able to find no way, nor in, nor out."
        Daniel, *Complaint of Rosamond.*

"Well knew'st thou what a monster I would be,
When thou didst build this labyrinth for me,
Whose strange meanders, turning ev'ry way,
Be like the course wherein my youth did stray:
Only a clue doth guide me out and in,
But yet still walk I circular in sin."
        Drayton, *Rosamond to King Henry.*

45. "'Tis strange my master should be yet so young
A puppy, that he cannot see his fall,
And got so near the sun."
        J. Fletcher, *The Noble Gentleman,* i. 1.

61. Yalden, in his fine *Hymn to Darkness,* xiii.:

"In caves of night, the oracles of old
Did all their mysteries unfold:
Darkness did first Religion grace,
Gave terrours to the god, and reverence to the place."

72.   "The Pythian goddess
Is dumb and sullen, till with fury fill'd
She spreads, she rises, growing to the sight,
She stares, she foams, she raves; the awful secrets
Burst from her trembling lips, and ease the tortur'd maid."   Smith, *Phædra and Hippolytus,* i. 1.

Our Ilium and Dardania's high renown.
Do thou too, O most holy prophetess,
Foresightful of futurity, vouchsafe,—
Realms not undue to my own fates I claim,—
That Teucri may in Latium settle down,
And wand'ring gods and hunted Pow'rs of
  Troy.   101
I then to Phœbus, and the Trivian [maid],
A fane of solid marble will appoint,
And days of festival from Phœbus' name.
Thee also there awaits within my realm
A stately sanctuary; for I here
Thy oracles and mystical replies,
Pronounced to my own nation, will lay up,
And chosen men, boon [maiden], sanctify.
Only to leaves thy verses do not trust, 110
Lest, troubled, they may flit abroad, the
  sport
Of sweepy winds: pray chant them thou
  thyself."
An end he made of speaking with his lips.
But not as yet of Phœbus tolerant,
Wild raves the prophetess within the cave,
If she the mighty god from out her breast
Can shake: so much the more he tires her
  mouth
Of fury, taming down her hagard heart,
And by his pressure moulds her [to his will].
And now the dome's one hundred vasty
  gates   120
Flew open of their own accord, and waft
The prophetess' replies through air: "O
  thou,
Who art at last discharged from mighty risks
Of sea, yet heavier though the land remain.
Into Lavinium's realms the Dardan sons
Shall come;—chase this disquiet from thy
  breast;—
But that they'd come they shall not also wish.
Wars, dreadful wars, and with a flood of
  blood

The Tiber in a foam do I perceive.
To thee shall not a Simois, nor Xanthus,
Nor camp of Dorians [there] be lacking
  found;   131
A new Achilles there is now secured
In Latium, aye himself a goddess' son.
Neither shall Juno, to the Teucri linked,
In any quarter be aloof; whilst thou
In humble fashion, in thy state of want,—
What nations of the Itali, or what
The cities [thou] shalt not have craved!
  The cause   138
Of such a grievous woe once more a bride,
The hostess of the Teucri, and once more
Foreign espousals. Yield thou not to woes;
But, in their face, the bolder go, as thee
Thy fortune shall allow. The foremost path
Of safety, which thou dost imagine least,
Shall from a Grecian city be disclosed."
  In such like accents from her shrine
  chants forth
The Cuman Sibyl dreadful mysteries,
And through the cave rebellows, with the
  dark
The true enwrapping. O'er the frenzied
  [maid]
These curbs Apollo shakes, and plies his
  goads   150
Beneath her breast. As soon as paused her
  rage,
And madding lips reposed, hero Æneas
Begins: "No phase of toils, O maid, to
  me
Arises strange or unexpected: all
Have I forestalled, and in my mind ere now
Gone o'er them with myself. One thing I
  crave:
Since here the portal of the hellish king
Is said [to lie], and, fraught with murk, the
  fen,
From Acheron o'erflowed, that it may prove
My lot to wend my journey to the gaze

---

98. "Thou fathom'st the deep gulf of ages past,
    And canst pluck up with ease
  The years when thou dost please:
Like shipwreck'd treasures, by rude tempests cast
    Long since into the sea,
  Brought up again to light and public use by thee.
    Nor dost thou only dive so low, but fly
  With an unwearied wing the other way on high,
    Where fates among the stars do grow;
      And there, with piercing eye,
  Through the firm shell and the thick white dost spy
      Years to come a-forming lie,
  Close in their sacred secundine asleep,
      Till hatch'd by the sun's vital heat,
    Which o'er them yet does brooding set,
      They life and motion get,
    And, ripe at last, with vigorous might
  Break through the shell, and take their everlasting
    flight." Cowley, *Pindaric Odes*, The Muse.

127. "But e'en shall wish that they had never
  come."

139. Hermia says to Helena:
  "You, mistress, all this coil is long of you."
Shakespeare, *Midsummer Night's Dream*, iii. 2.

142. The Bastard to King John:
  "Be great in act, as you have been in thought;
  Let not the world see fear, and sad distrust,
  Govern the motion of a kingly eye:
  Be stirring as the time: be fire with fire:
  Threaten the threat'ner; and outface the brow
  Of bragging horror; so shall inferior eyes,
  That borrow their behaviours from the great,
  Grow great by your example, and put on
  The dauntless spirit of resolution."
            Shakespeare, *King John*, v. 1.

"Whate'er it be, be thou still like thyself,
And sit thee by our side: yield not thy neck
To fortune's yoke, but let thy dauntless mind
Still ride in triumph over all mischance."
            3 *K. Henry VI.*, iii. 3.

And presence of my darling sire; that thou
Would'st teach the route, and ope the holy
gates. 162
Him I through flames and thousand chasing
darts
Saved on these shoulders, and from 'mid
the foe
Recovered; he attended on my path;
All seas along with me, and all the threats
Alike of ocean and of sky, he bore;—
Infirm, beyond the strength and lot of eld.
Yea that in lowly guise I thee should seek,
And thresholds thine approach, imploring
me, 170
The selfsame charges gave. Both son and
sire,
Kind [maid], compassionate, I entreat;
(For thou canst all things, nor hath Hecat
thee
In vain appointed o'er Avernian groves;)
If Orpheus could his consort's ghost evoke,
Resting on Thracian lute and tuneful
strings;
If Pollux ransomed by alternate death
A brother; goes, too, and returns the way
so oft;—
Why mighty Theseus, why Alcides, name?
My birth, too, is from Jupiter supreme."
In accents such he sued, and th' altars
held, 181
When thus the prophetess began to speak:
"O sprung from blood of gods, thou child
of Troy,
Son of Anchises, easy the descent
T' Avernus; night and day lies ope the gate
Of ghastly Dis: but to recall the step,
And to effect escape to upper air,—
This is the difficulty, this the toil.

The few, whom Jove hath in his kindness
loved,
Or glowing merit lifted to the sky, 190
The children of the gods, have had the
power.
All intervening [regions] forests hold,
And Cocyt, gliding with his black embrace,
Environs them. But if such deep desire,
If yearning so intense possess thy mind,
Twice o'er the Stygian pools to float, twice
view
The murky Tartarus, and thee it joys
To yield thy spirit to the wild emprise,
Receive what needs must be accomplished
first.
There lurks within a shady tree a bough
Of gold, alike in leaves and lither spray,
To Juno of the nether world pronounced
Devote: this all the grove imbow'rs, and
shades 203
With darkling glens inclose. But 'tis not
deigned
Beneath the hidden [spots] of earth to pass,
Before one shall have cropped away the
sprigs
With golden tresses from the tree. This gift,
Her own, to be presented to herself
Hath beauteous Proserpine ordained. The
first

Our prison strong; this huge convex of fire
Outrageous to devour, immures us round
Ninefold; and gates of burning adamant,
Barr'd over us, prohibit all egress.
These pass'd, if any pass, the void profound
Of unessential night receives him next,
Wide gaping, and with utter loss of being
Threatens him, plunged in that abortive gulf.
If thence he scape into whatever world,
Or unknown region, what remains him less
Than unknown dangers, and as hard escape?"
Par. Lost, ii.

---

176. Julio attributes a similar power to his fair
one's voice:
"And when she speaks, oh, angels, then music
(Such as old Orpheus made, that gave a soul
To agèd mountains, and made rugged beasts
Lay by their rages; and tall trees, that knew
No sound but tempests, to bow down their
branches,
And hear and wonder; and the sea, whose surges
Shook their white heads in heaven, to be as
midnight
Still and attentive) steals into our souls
So suddenly and strangely, that we are
From that time no more ours, but what she
pleases!" Fletcher, *The Captain*, ii. 1.

184. "But easy is the way and passage plaine
To Pleasure's pallace; it may soone be spide,
And day and night her dores to all stand open wide."
Spenser, *F. Q.*, ii. 3, 41.

"But many shapes
Of Death, and many are the ways that lead
To his grim cave, all dismal." Milton, *P. L.*, xi.
188. "Long is the way
And hard, that out of Hell leads up to light;

190. "How just our pride, when we behold those
heights!
Not those ambition paints in air, but those
Reason points out, and ardent virtue gains,
And angels emulate; our pride how just!
When mount we? when these shackles cast? when
quit
This cell of the creation? this small nest,
Stuck in a corner of the universe,
Wrapt up in fleecy cloud and fine-spun air?
Fine-spun to sense; but gross and feculent
To souls celestial; souls ordain'd to breathe
Ambrosial gales, and drink a purer sky:
Greatly triumphant on Time's further shore,
Where virtue reigns, enrich'd with full arrears;
While pomp imperial begs an alms of peace."
Young, *The Complaint*, N. 6.

"To chase each partial purpose from his breast;
And through the mists of passion and of sense,
And through the tossing tide of chance and pain,
To hold his course unfaltering, while the voice
Of Truth and Virtue, up the steep ascent
Of nature, calls him to his high reward,
The applauding smile of Heaven."
Akenside, *Pleasures of Imagination*, i. 160-6.

Plucked off, fails not a second [bough] of
 gold,   210
And with like metal does the shoot begin
To leaf. Aloft then search it with thine
 eyes,
And duly cull it with thy hand when found.
For freely it will follow of itself,
And readily, if thee the Weirds invite:
Thou else wilt not have pow'r by any
 strength
To master it, nor wrench it off with stub-
 born steel.
Moreo'er, lies dead the body of thy friend,—
Alas! thou know'st it not,—and thy whole
 fleet
It taints with death, while my advices thou
Art seeking, and delaying in my door.
In his own resting-place consign him first,
And hearse him in the grave. Bring sable
 flocks: 223
Be these the first atonements. Thus at last
The groves of Styx, and realms impassable
To living [beings], thou shalt view." She
 said,
And with a tightened lip she dumb became.
Æneas, downcast in his eyes, with
 mournful look,
Fares on, the cavern leaving, and in mind
Revolves the hidden issues with himself;
To whom the stanch Achates comrade
 goes,   231
And firms his footsteps, [filled] with like
 concerns.
Much they between them in diverse dis-
 course
Conferred,—what lifeless mate the pro-
 phetess
Could mean, what body was to be ingraved,
And they Misenus on the droughty beach,
When came they, see by death unworthy
 killed;—
Misenus, son of Æolus, than whom
None else more eminent with bronze to
 rouse
The crews, and Mars to kindle with the
 strain.   240
Of mighty Hector he had been the mate;
Round Hector, e'en with clarion and with
 spear
Distinguished, was he wont to meet the
 frays.

As soon as him the conquering Achilles
Berobbed of life, t' Æneas Dardan-born
Had the thrice-gallant hero joined himself
As comrade, following no meaner [fates].
But then, while haply he on hollow shell
With music fills the seas, and in his strain
To contests madly challenges the gods, 250
The jealous Triton,—if 'tis worth belief,—
Had plunged the hero, 'mongst the rocks
 surprised,
Upon the foamy billow. Therefore all
With lusty outcry shouted round; in chief
The good Æneas. Then the Sibyl's
 orders,—
There's no delay,—in tears do they des-
 patch,
And th' altar of the sepulchre to pile
With trees, and stretch it forth to heav'n,
 they strive.
The route is taken to an ancient wood,
Wild creatures' lofty lairs. Down fall
 pitch-pines;   260
With axes stricken does the ilex ring;
And ashen timbers, and the splitting oak
Is cleft with wedges; towards it roll they
 on
Huge mountain-ashes from the mounts.
 Yea too,
Æneas, 'mid such toils the foremost, cheers
His mates, and with like weapons is
 equipped,
And these himself within his own sad heart
Revolves, while gazing on the boundless
 wood,
And thus with voice he prays: "Would
 heav'n that now
To us that golden branch upon the tree 270
Would show itself within a grove so vast!
Since all with truth,—alas! with too much
 [truth],—
Of thee the prophetess, Misenus, spake."
These [words] he scarce had uttered, when
 by chance
Two doves, before the hero's very face,
Swooped from the firmament upon the wing,

---

248. Misenus was not so modest, and perhaps not so skilful, as P. Fletcher represents Thelgon in one of his charming Eclogues:

" I have a pipe, which once thou loved'st well,
 (Was never pipe that gave a better sound,)
Which oft to heare, fair Thetis from her cell,
 Thetis, the queen of seas, attended round
With hundred nymphs, and many powers that
 dwell
In th' ocean's rocky walls, came up to heare,
And gave me gifts, which still for thee lye hoarded
 here."   *Piscatory Eclogues*, i. 19.

269. Notwithstanding all that Wagner says, *forte* (v. 186) seems to make nonsense of the passage. Nor does the objection to *voce*,—for which there is very good authority,—seem to be worth very much.

---

221. Or: "and dost on my threshold hang." But it is not easy to preserve the metaphor in *pendes*, without conveying the notion of a different kind of dependence from that which the poet had in view.

236. *Atque* (v. 162) has almost the force of "straightway." See Wagner, *Quæst. Virg.* xxxv. 22.

And lighted down upon the sward of green.
Then does the highest hero recognize
His mother's birds, and blithe he prays:
" Be ye,
O [be] my guides, if any path there lies,
And steer through air your passage to the
    groves,   281
Where shades the precious bough the
    fruitful soil.
And thou, O goddess-mother, fail me not
In my uncertain state." Thus having said,
He checked his footsteps, watching what
    the signs
They furnish, whither they proceed to pass.
In feeding they so far advance on wing,
As could the eyes of those pursuing keep
Within their view. Thereon, what time
    they came
Up to Avernus' noisome-smelling jaws, 290
They mount them fleet, and through the
    crystal air
Gliding away, upon the perch desired,
Atop the double tree, they settle, whence
A chequered sheen of gold throughout the
    boughs
Gleamed back. As mistletoe is wont in
    woods
In cold of winter to be green with leaf
New [-horn], (which soweth not its native
    tree,)
And with its saffron offspring to enring
The rounded branches: suchlike was the
    guise
Of the gold leafing on the shady holm; 300

The foil thus tinkled in the balmy breeze.
Æneas in a moment seizes it,
And, eager, breaks away the coying [bough],
And bears it to the Sibyl-seer's abode.
    Nor less meanwhile Misenus on the shore
The Teucri wept, and paid the latest [dues]
To thankless ashes. First, with pitch-pines
    rich
And oak cut up, a mighty pyre they reared;
Whose sides they interlace with sombre
    leaves,
And deathly cypresses in front erect,   310
And grace it o'er with gleaming arms. A
    part
Warm waters, and bronze vessels, surging up
Through flames, prepare, and wash and
    oint the corpse
Of him death-cold. Up springs a groan.
    They then
The limbs, bewept, upon a couch lay down,
And o'er them fling his purple wardrobe,
    wraps
Well known. Some underwent the mighty
    bier,—
Sad service,—and in fashion of their sires
A torch, laid underneath, averted held.
Together huddled are consumed their gifts
Of incense, viands, jars with oil outpoured.
Soon as the ashes had fall'n in, and slept
The flame, with wine they moistened the
    remains   323
And spongy embers; and the gathered
    bones
In bronzen casket Corinæus urned.
    The same thrice circled with the crystal wave
His comrades, sprinkling them with filmy
    dew,
And branch of blessèd olive, and the men
He purified, and spake the latest words.

---

287. Spenser makes use of the same agency to bring the heart-broken Squire to Belphœbe:
" The same he tooke, and with a riband new,
    In which his ladies colours were, did bind
About the turtle's necke, that with the vew
Did greatly solace his engrieved mind.
All unawares the bird, when she did find
Herselfe so deckt, her nimble wings displaid,
And flew away as lightly as the wind:
Which sodaine accident him much dismaid;
And, looking after long, did mark which way she straid,
But whenas long he looked had in vaine,
Yet saw her forward still to make her flight,
His weary eie return'd to him againe,
Full of discomfort and disquiet plight,
That both his iuell he had lost so light,
And eke his deare companion of his care.
But that sweet bird departing flew forthright,
Through the wide region of the wastfull aire,
Untill she came where wonned his Belphebe fair."
                                        F. Q., iv. 8, 7, 8.

293. *Geminâ*, rather than *geminæ*, has the authority of the best manuscripts. *Geminæ* looks very awkward and intrusive, while it is doubtful that Virgil ever uses the word at all with an ellipsis of the noun.
    There seems to be as little doubt about the meaning as about the lection. It would be an abrupt weakness, quite below the poet, to introduce the

element of a fork in the tree in this way; indeed to mention it at all would be trifling. He is all along dwelling upon the double character of the tree, in consequence of the presence of an extraneous branch.

317.   " Most worthy soldiers,
Let me entreat your knowledge to inform me
What noble body that is, which you bear
With such a sad and ceremonious grief,
As if ye meant to woo the world and nature
To be in love with death."
            Beaumont and Fletcher, *Bonduca*, v. 1.

329. P. Fletcher beautifully makes Love, or Charity, perform such offices; *Purple Island*, ix. 46:
" And when the dead, by cruel tyrants' spite,
    Lie out to rav'nous birds and beasts expos'd,
His yearnful heart pitying that wretched sight,
    In seemly graves their weary flesh enclos'd,
    And strew'd with dainty flow'rs the lowly hearse;
    Then all alone the last words did rehearse,
Bidding them softly sleep in his sad sighing verse."

But good Æneas rears of massy bulk 330
The barrow, and the hero's arms, his own,
Both oar and trump, beneath a skyey mount;
That which "Misenus" now from him is called,
And holds through ages his undying name.
These [rites] discharged, in haste he carries out
The Sibyl's orders. Stood a cavern deep,
And huge with chasm enormous, rife in crags,
Fenced by a pitchy mere and gloom of woods;
O'er which no flying creatures could, unscathed,
A voyage steer upon their wings: such steam, 340
Forth flushing from its murky jaws, would waft
Its form to th' arch of heav'n; wherefrom the spot

336. "An hydeous hole al vaste, withouten shape
Of endless depth, orewhelmde with rugged stone,
Wyth ougly mouth, and grisly jawes doth gape,
And to our sight confounds it selfe in one.
Here entred we, and geding forth, anone
An horrible lothly lake we might discerne
As black as pitche that cleped is Averne.
A deadly gulfe where nought but rubbish grows,
With fowle black swelth in thickned lumpes lies,
Which up in the ayer such stinking vapors throwes,
That over there may fly no fowle but dyes,
Choakt with the pestilent savours that aryse."

This extract is made from a very early imitation of Virgil by Sackville, called "Induction to A Mirrour for Magistrates."
Spenser makes Night, at Duessa's request, carry Sansfoy to hell to be healed by Æsculapius, in which account he finely imitates Virgil, but with some grand original touches:

"Thence turning backe in silence softe they stole,
And brought the heavie corse with easie face
To yawning gulfe of deepe Avernus hole:
By that same hole an entrance dark and bace,
With smoake and sulphur hiding all the place,
Descends to Hell: there creature never past,
That backe retourned without heavenly grace:
But dreadful furies, which their chaines have brast,
And damned sprights sent forth to make ill men aghast.

"By that same way the direfull dames do drive
Their mournefull charett, fild with rusty blood,
And downe to Plutoe's house are come b:live:
Which passing through, on every side them stood
The trembling ghosts with sad amazed mood,
Chattring their iron teeth, and staring wide
With stonie eies: and all the hellish brood
Of fiends infernall flockt on every side,
To gaze on erthly wight, that with the Night durst ride."
F. Q., i. 5, 31, 2.

339. "All that were made for man's use fly this desert:
No airy fowl dares make his flight over it,
It is so ominous.
Serpents and ugly things, the shames of nature,
Roots of malignant tastes, foul standing waters."
J. Fletcher, *The Sea Voyage*, i. 3.

The Grecians have entitled by the name
"Aornos." Here four bullocks, swart of back,
First sets the priestess, and upon their brow
The wines pours over, and the topmost hairs
Cropping amid the centre of their horns,
She places them upon the holy fires,—
The first libations,—calling with her voice
On Hecat, puissant both in heaven and hell.
Knives others plant beneath [their throats], and catch 351
The milk-warm blood in bowls. Æneas, e'en
Himself, a female lamb of sable fleece,
Unto the mother of the Fury-train,
And her high sister, with the falcion stabs;
A barren cow, too, Proserpine, to thee.
Then to the Monarch of the Styx he founds
His nightly altars, and the flesh entire
Of bulls he lays upon the flames, rich oil
O'er burning entrails pouring down. But lo!
Just at the rays and dawn of th' infant sun,
The ground is rumbling underneath their feet, 362
And 'gan the heights of forests to be stirred,
And dogs were seen to yell throughout the gloom,—
The goddess drawing nigh. "Far, oh! far hence
Avaunt, profane!" loud cries the prophetess,
"And from the grove entire withdraw; and thou
Start forward on thy way, and from its sheath
Tear forth the falcion. Now for courage need,
Æneas, now for steady heart." Thus much
She having uttered, frantic plunged herself 371
Within the open cave. His guide, as she
Proceeds, he matches with undaunted steps.
Ye gods, whose sway is o'er the ghosts, and ye,
Still Shadows; Chaos, too, and Phlegethon;
Spots silent far and wide in night;—to me
Be it allowed what has been heard to speak;

362. "But loe, while thus amid the desert darke,
We passed on with steppes and pace unmette:
A rumbling roar confusde with howle and bark
Of dogs, shoke all the ground under our feete,
And stroke the din within our ears so deepe
As halfe distraught unto the ground I fell,
Besought retourne, and not to visite hell."
Sackville, *Induction*, 28.

364. Or, if gender must be observed:
"And through the gloom were bitches seen to howl."
See note on *Geo.* i. l. 648.

Be it allowed with your assent to ope
The things, in deep of earth and darkness sunk.
    They fared in gloom beneath the lonely night, 380
Through shade, and through the tenantless abodes
And empty realms of Dis. As by the fitful moon,
Beneath her sullen light, a route is [ta'en]
In woods, when Jove hath buried heav'n in shade,
And inky Night from Nature stripped her hue.
Before the court itself, and hell's first jaws,

380.   "The bottom of a well
At midnight, with but two stars on the top,
Were broad day to this darkness."
        Shirley, *The Lady of Pleasure,* iv. 1.

383.   "O thievish Night,
Why shouldst thou, but for some felonious end,
In thy dark lantern thus close up the stars,
That Nature hung in heaven, and fill'd their lamps
With everlasting oil, to give due light
To the misled and lonely traveller?"

"I did not err; there does a silver cloud
Turn forth her silver lining on the night,
And casts a gleam over this tufted grove."
        Milton, *Comus.*

"Now black, and deep, the night begins to fall,
A shade immense. Sunk in the quenching gloom,
Magnificent and vast, are Heaven and Earth.
Order confounded lies; all beauty void:
Distinction lost; and gay variety
One universal blot: such the fair power
Of light, to kindle and create the whole.
Drear is the state of that benighted wretch,
Who then, bewilder'd, wanders through the dark,
Full of pale fancies, and chimeras huge;
Nor visited by one directive ray,
From cottage streaming, or from airy hall."
        Thomson, *Autumn.*

385. Or, more literally: "from objects reft their hue."

Savage has the same idea and its reverse. Speaking of the sun:
"What gay, creative power his presence brings!
Hills, lawns, lakes, villages!—the face of things,
All night beneath successive shadows miss'd,
Instant begin in colours to exist."
        The Wanderer, c. iv.

386-395. Spenser has different occupants of the gates of hell:

"At length they came into a larger space,
That stretcht itself into an ample playne;
Through which a beaten broad highway did trace,
That streight did lead to Plutoes griesly rayne:
By that wayes side there sate infernall Payne,
And fast beside him sat tumultuous Strife;
The one in hand an yron whip did strayne,
The other brandished a bloody knife;
And both did gnash their teeth, and both did threaten life.

"On th' other side in one consort there sate
Cruell Revenge, and rancorous Despight,
Disloyall Treason, and hart-burning Hate;
But gnawing Gealousy, out of their sight

Have Woe and vengeful Cares their pallets laid; 387

Sitting alone, his bitter lips did bight;
And trembling Fear still to and fro did fly,
And found no place where safe he shroud him might:
Lamenting Sorrow did in darkness lye;
And Shame his ugly face did hide from living eye.

"And over them sad Horror with grim hew
Did alwaies sore, beating his yron wings;
And after him owles and night-ravens flew,
The hateful messengers of heavy things."
        F. Q., ii. 7, 20-2.

387. "Vengeful Cares."

"And first within the portche and jawes of hell
Sate diepe Remorse of Conscience, al besprent
With teares; and to her selfe oft would she tell
Her wretchednes, and cursing never stent
To sob and sigh: but ever thus lament
With thoughtful care, as she that all in vayne
Would weare and waste continually in payne.

"Her iyes unsteadfast rolling here and there,
Whurld on eche place, as place that vengeauns brought,
So was her minde continually in feare,
Tossed and tormented with the tedious thought
Of those detested crymes which she had wrought:
With dreadful cheare and lookes thrown to the skye,
Wyshyng for death, and yet she could not dye."
        Sackville, *Induction,* 32, 3.

"O conscience! into what abyss of fears
And horrors hast thou driven me; out of which
I find no way, from deep to deeper plunged."
        Adam's Soliloquy, Milton, *P. L.,* ix.

"Thoughts, my tormentors, arm'd with deadly stings,
Mangle my apprehensive tenderest parts,
Exasperate, exulcerate, and raise
Dire inflammation, which no cooling herb
Of med'cinal liquor can assuage,
Nor breath of vernal air from snowy Alp.
Sleep hath forsook and given me o'er
To death's benumbing opium as my only cure:
These faintings, swoonings of despair,
And sense of Heaven's desertion."
        Samson Agonistes.

"No—'tis the tale which angry conscience tells,
When she with more than tragic horrour swells
Each circumstance of guilt; when stern, but true,
She brings bad actions forth into review;
And, like the dread hand-writing on the wall,
Bids late Remorse awake at Reason's call;
Arm'd at all points bids scorpion Vengeance pass,
And to the mind holds up Reflection's glass;
The mind which, starting, heaves the heartfelt groan,
And hates that form she knows to be her own."
        Churchill, *The Conference.*

"O! it is monstrous! monstrous!
Methought the billows spoke, and told me of it;
The winds did sing it to me; and the thunder,
That deep and dreadful organ-pipe, pronounc'd
The name of Prosper; it did bass my trespass."
        Shakespeare, *Tempest,* iii. 3.

"O coward conscience, how dost thou afflict me!
The lights burn blue. It is now dead midnight.
Cold fearful drops stand on my trembling flesh.
What do I fear? myself? there's none else by.

And wan Diseases haunt, and rueful Eld,
And Fear, and Hunger, counselling to crime,
And grisly Want,—shapes awful to be seen,— 390
And Death, and Toil; then Death's own kinsman, Sleep,
And guilty Joys of soul, and doomful War

Richard loves Richard; that is, I am I.
Is there a murderer here? No:—yes; I am:
Then fly!—What? from myself? Great reason: why?
Lest I revenge. What? myself on myself?
Alack! I love myself. Wherefore? for any good,
That I myself have done unto myself?
Oh, no! alas! I rather hate myself
For hateful deeds committed by myself.
I am a villain: yet I lie, I am not.
Fool, of thyself speak well:—Fool, do not flatter.
My conscience hath a thousand several tongues,
And every tongue brings in a several tale,
And every tale condemns me for a villain.
Perjury, foul perjury, in the high'st degree,
Murder, stern murder, in the dir'st degree,
All several sins, all used in each degree,
Throng to the bar, crying all,—Guilty! guilty!"
K. Richard III., v. 3.

388. "Wan Diseases."
" Immediately a place
Before his eyes appear'd, sad, noisome, dark;
A lazar-house it seemed; wherein were laid
Numbers of all diseased; all maladies
Of ghastly spasm, or racking torture, qualms
Of heartsick agony, all feverous kinds,
Convulsions, epilepsies, fierce catarrhs,
Intestine stone and ulcer, colic-pangs,
Demoniac frenzy, moping melancholy,
And moonstruck madness, pining atrophy,
Marasmus, and wide-wasting pestilence,
Dropsies, and asthmas, and joint-racking rheums.
Dire was the tossing, deep the groans.   Despair
Tended the sick busiest from couch to couch;
And over them triumphant Death his dart
Shook, but delay'd to strike, though oft invok'd
With vows, as their chief good and final hope."
Milton, *P. L.*, b. xi.

391. "At last this odious offspring whom thou seest,
Thine own begotten, breaking violent way,
Tore through my entrails, that, with fear and pain
Distorted, all my nether shape thus grew
Transform'd. But he my inbred enemy
Forth issued, brandishing his fatal dart,
Made to destroy. I fled, and cried out *Death!*
Hell trembled at the hideous name, and sigh'd
From all her caves, and back resounded *Death!*"
Ibid., b. ii.

392. "Hateful confounders both of blood and laws,
Vile orators of shame, that plead delight;
Ungracious agents in a wicked cause,
Factors for darkness, messengers of night,
Serpents of guile, devils that do unite
The wanton taste of that forbidden tree,
Whose fruit once pluck'd, will show how foul we be."
Daniel, *Complaint of Rosamond.*

" Have mercy, Heaven! how have I been wandering,
Wandering the way of lust, and left my Maker!

Upon the fronting sill, and iron cells
Of Furies, and Disunion wild, enwreathed
Upon her snaky hair with gory bands.
Amidst it spreads its boughs and agèd arms
An elm umbrageous, huge; which haunt, they tell
Fantastic Dreams in clusters occupy,
And grapple to it under every leaf.
And many a portentous form beside 400
Of divers brutes are stalling in the doors,—
Centaurs, and Scyllæ of a double guise,
And hundred-handed Briareus, and beast
Of Lerna, hissing dread, and, armed with flames,
Chimæra; Gorgons, Harpies, too, and shape
Of the three-bodied Ghost. Here grasps his sword
Æneas, scared with sudden fear, and its drawn edge
Against them he presents as they advance;
And had not his companion in her lore
Reminded him that they were subtile sprites, 410
Without a body, hovering around
Beneath the hollow phantom of a form,
He would have hurtled on them, and in vain
Have cut asunder spectres with a sword.

How have I slept like cork upon a water,
And had no feeling of the storm that toss'd me!
Trod the blind paths of death! forsook assurance,
Eternity of blessedness, for a woman!"
Fletcher, *The Island Princess*, iv. 5.

398. Dryden gives a lively description of dreams in a passage which he introduces into his translation of Chaucer's *Nones Preestes Tale:*
" Dreams are but interludes, which Fancy makes;
When monarch Reason sleeps, this mimic wakes:
Compounds a medley of disjointed things,
A mob of robbers, and a court of kings.
Light fumes are merry, grosser fumes are sad:
Both are the reasonable soul run mad.
And many wondrous forms in sleep we see,
That neither were, nor are, nor e'er can be.
Sometimes forgotten things long cast behind
Rush forward to the brain, and come to mind.
The nurse's legends are for truth receiv'd,
And the man dreams but what the boy believ'd."
The Cock and the Fox, 325.

" I talk of dreams;
Which are the children of an idle brain,
Begot of nothing but vain fantasy;
Which is as thin of substance as the air,
And more inconstant than the wind, who wooes
Even now the frozen bosom of the north,
And, being anger'd, puffs away from thence,
Turning his face to the dew-dropping South."
Shakespeare, *Romeo and Juliet*, i. 4.

410. " Alas! good venturous youth,
I love thy courage yet, and bold emprise;
But here thy sword can do thee little stead."
Milton, *Comus.*

414. Ariel, seeing Alonzo and his company draw their swords, cries:

Hence lies the path that leadeth to the waves
Of the Tartarean Acheron. Troubled here
With mire and gorge prodigious, seethes a gulf,
And into Cocyt belches all its sand.
These waters and the floods a ferryman,
Terrific, guards, of fearful filthiness,— 420
Charon; upon whose chin full much of hoary hair
Neglected lies; stand [stiff] his eyes in flame;
Down from his shoulders hangs his frowsy garb
In knot. Himself his shallop with a pole
Shoves on, and tends the sails, and carries o'er
The bodies in his boat of rusty hue,
Now old; but flush and green the god's old age.
Hither the throng, all tiding to the banks,
Kept rushing,—dames, and husbands, and the forms
Of high-souled heroes, that have done with life; 430
Boys, and unwedded maids, and striplings, laid
On piles before the presence of their sires:

> "You fools! I and my fellows
> Are ministers of fate; the elements
> Of whom your swords are temper'd, may as well
> Wound the loud winds, or with bemock'd-at stabs
> Kill the still closing waters, as diminish
> One dowle that's in my plume."
> Shakespeare, *Tempest*, iii. 3.

416. "Four infernal rivers, that disgorge
Into the burning lake their baleful streams:
Abhorred Styx, the flood of deadly hate;
Sad Acheron, of sorrow black and deep;
Cocytus, named of lamentation loud,
Heard on the rueful stream; fierce Phlegethon,
Whose waves of torrent fire inflame with rage:
Far off from these, a slow and silent stream,
Lethe, the river of oblivion, rolls
Her watery labyrinth; whereof who drinks
Forthwith his former state and being forgets,
Forgets both joy and grief, pleasure and pain."
Milton, *P. L.*, b. ii.

427. "Age had not shed
That dust of silver o'er his sable locks,
Which spoke his strength mature beyond its prime,
Yet vigorous still; for from his healthy cheek
Time had not cropt a rose, or on his brow
One wrinkling furrow plough'd; his eagle eye
Had all its youthful lightning."
Mason, *English Garden*, b. ii.

428. "Gape, earth, and let the fiends infernal view
A hell as hopeless, and as full of fear,
As are the blasted banks of Erebus,
Where shaking ghosts, with ever howling groans,
Hover about the ugly ferryman,
To get a passage to Elysium."
Marlowe, *Tamburlaine the Great*, v. 2.

432. "First, Moloch, horrid king, besmear'd with blood
Of human sacrifice, and parents' tears;

As numerous as in the earliest cold
Of Autumn, in the forests gliding, fall
The leaves; or numerous as birds to land
Together flock them from the gulf profound,
When the chill year is chasing them across
The deep, and driving them to sunny climes.
They stood, beseeching they might be the first
To make the passage over, and outstretched 440
Their hands with yearning for the farther bank.
Yet, takes the surly boatman in now these,
Now those; but others, banished far aloof,
Debars he from the strand. Æneas, sooth,
In wonderment, and by the bustle moved,
Saith: "Tell me, O thou maiden, what imports
The flocking to the river? Or what seek
The ghosts? Or by what diff'rence these the banks
Forsake, those sweep with oars the leady shoals?"
To him thus shortly th' agèd priestess spake: 450
"Sired of Anchises, most undoubted child
Of gods, Cocytus' pools profound thou seest,
And fen of Styx, by whose divinity
Are gods afraid to swear, and swear untruth.
All this which thou descriest is a throng,
Unholpen and ungraved; yon ferryman
Is Charon; these, whom wafts the wave, the tombed.

Though, for the noise of drums and timbrels loud,
Their children's cries unheard, that passed through fire
To his grim idol." Milton, *P. L.*, b. i.

438. "Part loosely wing the region, part more wise
In common, ranged in figure, wedge their way,
Intelligent of seasons, and set forth
Their airy caravan, high over seas
Flying, and over lands, with mutual wing
Easing their flight; so steers the prudent crane
Her annual voyage, borne on winds; the air
Floats as they pass, fann'd with unnumber'd plumes." *Ibid.*, b. vii.

"When Autumn scatters his departing gleams,
Warn'd of approaching Winter, gather'd, play
The swallow people; and toss'd wide around,
O'er the calm sky, in convolution swift,
The feather'd eddy floats: rejoicing once,
Ere to their wintry slumbers they retire;
In clusters hung, beneath the mouldering band,
And where, unpierced by frost, the cavern sweats;
Or rather into warmer climes convey'd,
With other kindred birds of season."
Thomson, *Autumn*.

Nor is it giv'n to carry them across
The banks of terror, and the brawling floods,
Before their bones have in their homes reposed. 460
A hundred years they stray and hover round
These shores: thereon admitted, they at last
The pools sore wished-for come to view again."
Anchises' offspring paused, and checked his steps,
Revolving many a thought, and from his soul
Compassionated their unrighteous lot.
There spies he sad, and lacking rite of death,
Leucaspis, and the Lycian navy's chief,
Orontes; whom, together borne from Troy
O'er gusty waters, Auster overwhelmed,
Ingulfing in the tide both ship and men.
Lo! pilot Palinurus moved him on: 472
Who in the Libyan voyage late, while he
Remarks the stars, had fallen off the stern,
Flung forth amid the waves. Him, sorrow-struck,
When he with difficulty recognized
In depth of gloom, he thus accosts him first:
" Who, Palinure, of gods reft thee from us,
And whelmed thee 'neath the middle of the sea?
Come say. For, not ere then found false, my soul 480
By this one answer hath Apollo duped;
Who chanted that thou shouldest on the deep
Be safe, and at Ausonia's bourns arrive.
Behold! is this his plighted faith?" But he:
" Nor thee hath Phœbus' oracle misled,
O prince, Anchises' son, nor did a god
In ocean plunge me: for the helm, by chance
Through my excessive energy wrenched off,
Whereto I grappled, its appointed guard,
And steered our courses, in my headlong fall 490

474. " Orion's shoulders and the Pointers serve
   To be our loadstars in the lingering night;
   The beauties of Arcturus we behold:
   And though the sailor is no bookman held,
   He knows more art than ever bookmen read."
   Robert Greene, *A Looking-Glass for London.*
490. " I saw your brother,
   Most provident in peril, bind himself
   (Courage and hope both teaching him the practice)
   To a strong mast, that lived upon the sea;
   Where, like Arion on the dolphin's back,
   I saw him hold acquaintance with the waves."
   Shakespeare, *Twelfth Night*, i. 2.

I with me dragged away. By felon seas
I swear, that I no such intense alarm
On my behalf conceived, as lest thy ship,
Of tackle robbed, of pilot dispossessed,
Should fail thee in such heaving mountain-waves.
Three wintry nights throughout the boundless seas
Did Notus bear me forceful o'er the tide:
On dawn the fourth scarce Italy I kenned,
High from the billow-top. By slow degrees
I swam to land; was now securing spots
Of safety, if a ruthless crew, as I 501
With reeking gear was cumbered, and with hands
Inbent was clutching jaggy crests of rock,
Had not with steel assailed me, and in ignorance

495. " Fail thee," or " founder."
Wolsey similarly protests his fidelity to his king:
   " I do profess,
That for your highness' good I ever labour'd
More than mine own: that aim I have, and will.
Though all the world should crack their duty to you,
And throw it from their soul; though perils did
Abound, as thick as thought could make them, and
Appear in forms more horrid; yet my duty,
As doth a rock against the chiding flood,
Should the approach of this wild river break,
And stand unshaken yours."
   Shakespeare, *K. Henry VIII.*, iii. 2.

500. " *Francisco.*   Sir, he may live:
I saw him beat the surges under him,
And ride upon their backs; he trod the water,
Whose enmity he flung aside, and breasted
The surge most swoln that met him; his bold head
'Bove the contentious waves he kept, and oar'd
Himself with his good arms in lusty stroke
To the shore, that o'er his wave-worn basis bow'd,
As stooping to relieve him: I not doubt
He came alive to land.
   Alonzo.   No, no, he's gone."
   Shakespeare, *Tempest*, ii. 1.

501. " I know among you some have oft beheld
A blood-hound train, by Rapine's lust impell'd,
On England's cruel coast inpatient stand,
To rob the wanderers wreck'd upon their strand,
These, while their savage office they pursue,
Oft wound to death the helpless plunder'd crew,
Who, 'scap'd from ev'ry horror of the main,
Implor'd their mercy, but implor'd in vain."
   Falconer, *Shipwreck*, c. ii.

" Then we're deliver'd twice: first from the sea,
And then from men, who, more remorseless, prey
On shipwreck'd wretches, and who spoil and murder
Those whom fell tempests and devouring waves
In all their fury spared."
   Lillo, *Fatal Curiosity*, i. 3.

503. *Mons* (from *emineo*,) is strictly any prominence. Here (v. 360) it cannot mean "mountain," as Palinurus could not have reached the top of a mountain, while struggling for life in the water.

A prize imagined. Holds me now the surge,
And bandy me the winds about the shore.
Thee therefore by the joysome light and gales
Of heaven ; by thy father, I entreat ;
By hopes of rising Iulus, from these woes
Deliver me, unconquered [prince] ; or earth   510
Do thou cast o'er me,—for thou hast the power,—
And seek out Velia's havens ; or do thou,
If any means exist, if any [means]
Thy goddess-mother hath to thee disclosed,
(For not, I deem, without the will of gods,
O'er floods so mighty, and the Stygian fen,
Dost thou prepare to float,) thy right hand lend
A wretch, and carry me away with thee
Along the waves, that I, at least in seats
Of peacefulness in death, may be at rest."
The like he'd spoken, when the like began
The prophetess : " Whence this so dread desire,   522
O Palinure, to thee? Shalt thou, ungraved,
The Stygian waters, and the rigid tide
Of the Eumenides behold, or bank,
Unauthorised, approach ? Cease thou to hope
That deities' decrees are warped by prayer.
But take in heedful mood [these] words [of mine],
Of thy sore plight the comforts : for thy bones
Shall neighbor [nations] far and wide throughout   530

Their cities, by portents from heav'n enforced,
Appease, and rear a tomb, and at the tomb
Present their yearly off'rings, and the place
The deathless name of Palinure shall hold."
By these her words his cares were chased away,
And banished from his dreary heart awhile
Its anguish : joys he in a name-sake land.
    So they complete their route commenced, and near
The river ; whom when from that quarter now
The boatman from the Stygian wave espied
Advancing through the silent grove, and foot
Directing to the bank, on this wise he   542
Is foremost to accost them with his speech,
And chides them, unassailed : " Whoe'er thou art,
Who armor-clad art marching on our streams,
Come, say, why com'st thou ?—now,—from yonder spot,—
And check thy step. The place of Shades is this,
Of Sleep and drowsy Night : 'twere felony
To waft live bodies in the Stygian bark.
Nor sooth have I rejoiced that I took in
Alcides passenger upon the pool ;   551
Nor Theseus and Pirithous, though they
Were sired of gods, and unsubdued in might,
He with his hand the hellish warder sought
For fetters,—from our very monarch's throne,—
And dragged him quaking : these, to force away
Our mistress from the couching-hall of Dis,
Addressed themselves." In answer whereunto
Spake briefly the Amphrysian prophetess :
" Here no such ambush ; cease to be disturbed ;   560

506. " Bandy," or " racket."
" Ha ! total night and horrour here preside ;
  My stunn'd ear tingles to the whizzing tide :
It is their funeral knell ! And, gliding near,
Methinks the phantoms of the dead appear,
But lo ! emerging from the wat'ry grave,
Again they float incumbent on the wave ;
Again the dismal prospect opens round,
The wreck, the shore, the dying, and the drown'd.
And see, enfeebled by repeated shocks,
Those two, who scramble on th' adjacent rocks,
Their faithless hold no longer can retain :
They sink o'erwhelm'd, and never rise again."
              Falconer, *Shipwreck*, c. iii.

511. There is no small pathos and power in Young's account of his committing Narcissa (Mrs. Temple) to the grave in France ; where her corpse fared as ill as did that of Palinurus :
" Denied the charity of dust to spread
  O'er dust ! A charity their dogs enjoy !
What could I do ? What succour ? What resource ?
With pious sacrilege a grave I stole ;
With impious piety that grave I wronged ;
Short in my duty ; coward in my grief !
More like her murderer, than friend, I crept,
With soft-suspended step, and muffled deep
In midnight darkness, whisper'd my last sigh."
              Complaint, N. iii.

535.   " When humbly thus
The great descend to visit the afflicted,
When thus unmindful of their rest they come,
To soothe the sorrows of the midnight mourner,
Comfort comes with them, like the golden sun,
Dispels the sullen shades with her sweet influence,
And cheers the melancholy house of care."
              Rowe, *Jane Shore*, act ii.

" You saw but sorrow in its waning form,
  A working sea, remaining from a storm ;
When the now weary waves roll o'er the deep,
And faintly murmur ere they fall asleep."
              Dryden, *Aurungzebe*, iv. 1.

" In thy serener shades our ghosts delight,
    And court the umbrage of the night ;
  In vaults and gloomy caves they stray,
But fly the morning's beams, and sicken at the day."
              Yalden, *Hymn to Darkness*, st. 6.

Nor do our weapons violence import.
Let the colossal porter in his den,
For ever barking, scare the bloodless shades;
Chaste Proserpine her uncle's palace keep.
Trojan Æneas, marked for piety
And arms, is passing to his father down
To lowest shades of Erebus. If thee
No thought of such high piety affects,
Yet thou this branch, (uncovers she the branch
That lurked beneath her robe;) should'st recognise." 570
Then from its spleen down sinks his swelling heart:
Nor more to these. He looking in amaze
At th' awful present of the fateful spray,
After long interval beheld, towards these
His dingy vessel turns, and nears the bank.
Thereon the other spirits, which along
The lengthful thwarts were sitting, flings he down,
And clears the gangways: at the same time takes
Within the hold the huge Æneas. Groaned
The cobbled shallop underneath the weight,
And, rife in leaks, took in the fen in floods. 581
At last, across the river, free from harm,
Both prophetess and hero he debarks
In ooze unsightly, and on sea-green sedge.
    Huge Cerberus with triple-throated bay
Peals through these kingdoms, in his fronting den
Couching immense. To whom the prophetess,
His necks now seeing bristle with their snakes,
With honey drowsed and drug-besprinkled grains,
A bolus throws. With madding hunger he

Three gullets op'ning, snaps up what was thrown, 591
And his huge chine unbraces, stretched on earth,
And, monstrous, all throughout his den is spread.
Æneas grasps the entrance,—[deep in sleep]
The sentry buried,—and he quick escapes
Beyond the rivage of the stream, that knows
Of no return. Forthwith are voices heard,
And mighty crying, and the ghosts of babes,
That weep within th' immediate threshold, whom,
Without their sharing in a life of charm,
And ravished from the breast, black day hath reft, 601
And plunged in dissolution premature.
Next these are they, who on a truthless charge
Were doomed to death. Nor, sooth, are these their homes
Assigned without a lot, without a judge:
Investigator Minos shakes the urn;
He both a council of the voiceless calls,
And gains a knowledge of their lives and sins.
Then the next regions hold the wailful ones,
Who to themselves have death, while free from guilt, 610

---

580. "The princely York himself, alone a freight,
The Swiftsure groans beneath great Gloster's weight." Dryden, *Astræa Redux*, 234.

587. Of course one is reminded here of Satan's address to Death, in Milton:

"Whence and what art thou, execrable shape!
That dar'st, though grim and terrible, advance
Thy miscreated front athwart my way
To yonder gates? Through them I mean to pass,
That be assur'd, without leave ask'd of thee!
Retire, or taste thy folly; and learn by proof,
Hell-born! not to contend with spirits of Heaven."
P. L., b. ii.

590. Spenser makes Night, under similar circumstances, independent of the druggist's aid:

"Before the threshold dreadfull Cerberus
His three deformed heads did lay along,
Curled with thousand adders venomous;
And lilled forth his bloody flaming tong.

At them he gan to reare his bristles strong,
And felly gnarre, untill Dayes enemy
Did him appease: then downe his taile he hong,
And suffered them to passen quietly:
For she in Hell and Heaven had power equally."
F. Q., i. 5, 34.

Odin is equally potent:

"Uprose the King of men with speed,
And saddled straight his coal-back steed;
Down the yawning steep he rode,
That leads to Hela's drear abode.
Him the Dog of Darkness spied,
His shaggy mouth he open'd wide,
While from his jaws, with carnage fill'd,
Foam and human gore distill'd;
Hoarse he bays with hideous din,
Eyes that glow and fangs that grin;
And long pursues, with fruitless yell,
The father of the powerful spell."
Gray, *Descent of Odin*, 1-12.

608. "Let guilty men remember, their black deeds
Do lean on crutches made of slender reeds."
Webster, *Vittoria Corombona*, end.

"A thousand stings are in me! O, what vile prisons
Make we our bodies to our immortal souls!
Brave tenants to bad houses: 'tis a dear rent
They pay for naughty lodging!"
Middleton, *The Spanish Gipsy*, iii. 1.

610. "Beneath the beech, whose branches bare,
Smit with the lightning's livid glare,
O'erhang the craggy road,
And whistle hollow as they wave;
Within a solitary grave,
A slayer of himself holds his accurs'd abode.

Procured by their own hand, and, loathing light,
Have cast away their lives. How would they wish

"Lower'd the grim morn, in murky dies,
Damp mists involv'd the scowling skies,
And dimm'd the struggling day;
As by the brook that ling'ring laves
Yon rush-grown moor with sable waves,
Full of the dark resolve he took his sullen way.
" I mark'd his desultory pace,
His gestures strange, and varying face,
With many a mutter'd sound:
And ah! too late aghast I view'd
The reeking blade, the hand embru'd;
He fell, and groaning grasp'd in agony the ground."
             T. Warton, *Ode*, vi. 1-3.
" Forbear, forbear;
Think what a sea of deep perdition whelms
The wretch's trembling soul, who launches forth
Unlicens'd to eternity. Think, think:
And let the thought restrain thy impious hand.
The race of man is one vast marshall'd army,
Summon'd to pass the spacious realms of Time;
Their leader the Almighty. In that march,
Ah! who may quit his post?"   Mason, *Elfrida*.
" Who flies from life confesses
He flies from something that appears so dreadful
He dares not face it. Is it guilt or virtue
That thus shrinks back and trembles at to-morrow?
Yes, this is meanness, and alone regards
Its selfish ease; virtue is never leagued
With its base dictates."
             Mickle, *Siege of Marseilles*, iv. 2.

612. " Ay, but to die, and go we know not where
To lie in cold obstruction, and to rot;
This sensible warm motion to become
A kneaded clod; and the delighted spirit
To bathe in fiery floods, or to reside
In thrilling regions of thick-ribbed ice;
To be imprison'd in the viewless winds,
And blown with restless violence round about
The pendent world; or to be worse than worst
Of those, that lawless and incertain thoughts
Imagine howling !—'tis too horrible !
The weariest and most loathed worldly life,
That age, ache, penury, and imprisonment,
Can lay on nature, is a paradise
To what we fear of death."
             Shakespeare, *Measure for Measure*, iii. 1.
" To be, or not to be,—that is the question:
Whether 'tis nobler in the mind, to suffer
The slings and arrows of outrageous fortune,
Or to take arms against a sea of troubles,
And, by opposing, end them? To die,—to sleep,—
No more ;—and, by a sleep, to say we end
The heart-ache, and the thousand natural shocks
That flesh is heir to,—'tis a consummation
Devoutly to be wish'd. To die ;—to sleep ;—
To sleep ! perchance to dream :—ay, there's the rub;
For in that sleep of death what dreams may come,
When we have shuffled off this mortal coil,
Must give us pause: there's the respect
That makes calamity of so long life.
For who would bear the whips and scorns of time,
The oppressor's wrong, the proud man's contumely,
The pangs of despis'd love, the law's delay,
The insolence of office, and the spurns
That patient merit of the unworthy takes,

In air aloft now even penury,
And sore distresses to endure ! The law
[Of hell] withstands them, and th' unlovely fen
With melancholy billow binds them fast,
And, nine times poured between, Styx hems them in.
Nor far from this, on every side dispread,
Are shown " The Mourning Fields :" so call they them by name.
Here those, whom callous love with ruthless waste   620
Hath eaten to the core, sequester'd paths
Bescreen, and myrtle-thicket bowers round :
Their woes forsake them not in death itself.
He Phædra in these regions, Procris too,
And moanful Eriphyle, pointing out
The wounds from her unfeeling son, descries ;
Evadne also, and Pasiphäe.
To these Laodamia comrade goes,
And Cænis, erst a youth, a woman now,
E'en changed again by fate to shape of yore.   630
Among whom Dido, the Phœnician dame,
Fresh from her wound, was wand'ring in a spacious grove.

When he himself might his quietus make
With a bare bodkin? Who would fardels bear,
To grunt and sweat under a weary life ;
But that the dread of something after death,—
The undiscover'd country, from whose bourn
No traveller returns,—puzzles the will,
And makes us rather bear those ills we have,
Than fly to others that we know not of?
Thus conscience does make cowards of us all."
             Hamlet, iii. 1.

620. " Then hastens onward to the pensive grove,
The silent mansion of disastrous love.
Here Jealousy with jaundic'd look appears,
And broken slumbers, and fantastic fears.
The widow'd turtle hangs her moulting wings,
And to the woods in mournful murmurs sings.
No winds but sighs there are, no floods but tears ;
Each conscious tree a tragic signal bears :
Their wounded bark records some broken vow,
And willow-garlands hang on every bough."
             Garth, *Dispensary*, vi. 242-50.

632. " Hence, all you vain delights,
As short as are the nights,
Wherein you spend your folly !
There's nought in this life sweet,
If man were wise to see't,
But only melancholy :
Oh, sweetest melancholy !
Welcome, folded arms, and fixed eyes,
A sigh that piercing, mortifies,
A look that's fasten'd on the ground,
A tongue chain'd up without a sound !
Fountain-heads, and pathless groves,
Places which pale passion loves !
Moonlight walks, when all the fowls
Are warmly hous'd, save bats and owls !

Near whom as soon as Troja's hero stood,
And recognized her dim among the shades ;—
As who in th' infant month or sees, or thinks
That he has seen, among the clouds the moon
Arising ;—tears he dropped, and with sweet love
Addressed her : "Hapless Dido, was then true
The news which me had reached, that thou wert dead,
And through the sword had sought the closing [scene] ? 640
Alas ! was I to thee the cause of death ?
By stars I swear, by deities above,
And if lies any faith in deep of earth,
I loth, O queen, departed from thy shore.
But me the gods' commands, which force me now

A midnight bell, a parting groan !
These are the sounds we feed upon ;
Then stretch our bones in a still gloomy valley ;
Nothing's so dainty sweet as lovely melancholy."
    J. Fletcher, *The Nice Valour*, iii. 3.
Any one can see Milton's obligations to this exquisite song for some of the ideas in *Il Penseroso*.
636.   " Or fairy elves,
Whose midnight revels, by a forest side,
Or fountain, some belated peasant sees,
Or dreams he sees, while overhead the moon
Sits arbitress, and nearer to the earth
Wheels her pale course."
    Milton, *P. L.*, b. i. end.
"For what I see, or only think I see,
Is like a glimpse of moonshine, streak'd with red :
A shuffled, sullen, and uncertain light,
That dances through the clouds, and shuts again."
    Dryden, *Cleomenes*, iv. 1.
638. " Such is the fate unhappy women find,
And such the curse entail'd upon our kind,
That man, the lawless libertine, may rove
Free and unquestion'd through the wilds of love ;
While woman, sense and nature's easy fool,
If poor weak woman swerve from virtue's rule,
If, strongly charm'd, she leave the thorny way
And in the softer paths of pleasure stray,
Ruin ensues, reproach and endless shame,
And one false step entirely damns her fame.
In vain with tears the loss she may deplore,
In vain look back on what she was before ;
She sets, like stars that fall, to rise no more."
    Rowe, *Jane Shore*, act. i. end.
645. " So spake the Fiend, and with necessity,
The tyrant's plea, excused his devilish deeds."
    Milton, *P. L.*, b. iv.
"A fellow that makes religion his stalking-horse,
He breeds a plague : thou shalt poison him."
    Marston, *The Malcontent*, iv. 3.
    " Come, you shall not labour
To extenuate your guilt, but quit it clean :
Bad men excuse their faults ; good men will leave them :
He acts the third crime that defends the first."
    Ben Jonson, *Catiline*, iii. 2.

To travel through these shades, through regions rife
In thorns through fallowness, and night's abyss,
Constrained by their behests ; nor could I deem
That this such grievous anguish I on thee
Could bring by my departure. Stay thy step, 650
And from our gaze withdraw not thou thyself.
Whom fliest thou ? This [time], that I
Address thee, is by destiny the last."
With suchlike words Æneas tried to soothe
The soul afire, and fixing stern regards ;
And tears he waked. The other, turned aloof,
Her eyes kept riveted upon the ground ;
Nor is in visage by his speech commenced
More influenced, than if she stood a flint
Unyielding, or Marpesian rock. At last
She tore herself away, and in her hate 661
Retreated to the shady forest, where
Her former consort echoes to her griefs,
And her affection does Sychæus match.
Nor less Æneas, by her fate unkind
Struck to the heart, pursues her weeping far,
And feels compassion for her as she goes.
Therefrom he toils along the route assigned.
And now they occupied the utmost fields,
Which, set apart, the famed in battle haunt. 670
Here meets him Tydeus, here, renowned in arms,
Parthenopæus, and the wan Adrastus' ghost.
Here, sorely wept 'mong denizens of air,
And fall'n in fight, the sons of Dardanus :
All whom as he perceives in long array,

"The devil can cite Scripture for his purpose."
    Shakespeare, *Merchant of Venice*, i. 3.
"And, oftentimes, excusing of a fault
Doth make the fault the worse by the excuse."
    King John, iv. 2.
"Gospel is in thy face and outward garb,
And treason on thy tongue."
    Dryden, *The Duke of Guise*, iv. 1.
656. " Small griefs find tongues ; full casks are ever found
To give, if any, yet but little sound ;
Deep waters noiseless are ; and this we know
That chiding streams betray small depth below."
    Herrick, *Amatory Odes*, xlviii.
Had she condescended a word, she might have said :
    " If impious acts
Have left thee blood enough to blush,
I'll paint it on thy cheeks."
    Fletcher, *Spanish Curate*, iii. 3.
659. *Silex* is always feminine in Virgil.

He o'er them groaned; e'en Glaucus,
  Medon, too,
Also Thersilochus, Antenor's children three,
And, consecrate to Ceres, Polyphæte;
Idæus, too, still grasping car, still arms.
Round stand the spirits right and left in
  crowds. 680
Nor is't sufficient to have seen him once;
It joys to linger to the last, and move
Their step with his, and of his coming learn
The reasons. But the chieftains of the
  Greeks,
And Agamemnon's phalanxes, when they
Beheld the hero and his gleaming arms
Among the shadows, quake with deep
  alarm.
Some turn their backs, as erst they sought
  the ships;
Others a puny exclamation raise:
The cry begun deludes them as they gape.
  And here the son of Priam he beholds,
Deiphobus, torn all throughout his form,
And mercilessly mangled on his face,— 693
His face, and both his hands, and temples
  robbed
Of ravished ears, and, maimed with seem-
  less wound,
His nostrils. Him thus scarce he recognized,
As quakes he, and the dread infliction hides;
And with familiar tones he speaks him first:
" Deiphobus, of might in arms, thou seed
From lofty blood of Teucer, who hath
  chosen 700
Such bloody vengeance to inflict? To
  whom
Was such great pow'r o'er thee allowed?
  To me
Brought rumor [word] on [that] last night
  that thou,
Worn out with mighty slaughter of the
  Greeks,
Down sankest on a jumbled charnel-heap.

Then I myself upon Rhœteum's shore
A tomb, an empty [tomb], upreared, and
  thrice
With thund'ring voice upon thy Manes
  called.
Thy name and weapons guard the spot;
  thee, friend,
I was unable to descry, and lay [in earth],
At my departure from our native land."
Whereto the son of Priam : " Naught, my
  friend, 712
On thy part hath been left [undone]; all
  [debts]
Hast thou to thy Deiphobus discharged,
And to his corse's shades. But me my
  fates,
And [that] Laconian [woman's] deathful
  guilt,
Have plunged in these misfortunes. It is
  she
Hath these memorials left. For, our last
  night
How 'mid unreal joys we passed, thou
  know'st,
And thou must needs remember it too
  well. 720
What time with bound the doomful horse
  o'erleaped
High Pergamus, and, pregnant in its
  womb,
Brought infantry in armor on us; she,
A dance pretending, led the Phrygian
  dames,
Enacting Bacchanalian revels round:
Herself, the midmost, held a monster
  torch,
And from the castle summit hailed the
  Greeks.
Then me, forespent with sorrows, and with
  sleep
Weighed down, my luckless couching-
  chamber held,

---

681. The smiths in the house of Riches were equally astonished at the sight of Sir Guyon:
" But when an earthly wight they present saw
Glistring in armes and battaïlous array,
From their whot work they did themselves with-
  draw
To wonder at the sight; for, till that day,
They never creature saw that cam that way:
Their staring eyes sparckling with fervent fyre,
And ugly shapes did nigh the man dismay,
That, were it not for shame, he would retyre."
  Spenser, *F. Q.*, ii. 7, 37.

705. As Rowe makes Slaughter do:
" The dreadful business of the war is o'er;
And Slaughter, that from yester morn till ev'n,
With giant steps, passed striding o'er the field,
Besmear'd and horrid with the blood of nations,
Now weary sits among the mangled heaps,
And slumbers o'er her prey."
  Tamerlane, ii. 1-6.

718. " Here lay Duncan,
His silver skin lac'd with his golden blood;
And his gash'd stabs look'd like a breach in nature
For Ruin's wasteful entrance."
  Shakespeare, *Macbeth*, ii. 3.

728, 9. He had no one to raise the warning
voice:
" While you here do snoring lie,
  Open-ey'd Conspiracy
  His time doth take:
  If of life you keep a care,
  Shake off slumber and beware:
  Awake! awake!" *Tempest*, ii. 1.

" ' Sleep no more!
Macbeth does murder sleep,'—the innocent sleep:
Sleep, that knits up the ravell'd sleave of care,
The death of each day's life, sore labour's bath,
Balm of hurt minds, great nature's second course,
Chief nourisher in life's feast." *Macbeth*, ii. 2.

And overwhelmed me, as I lay, a rest, 730
Balmy and deep, and likest to the still
Of death. Meanwhile my exemplary wife
All weapons from the house clears quite away,
And from my head had filched my trusty sword.
Inside the house she Menelaus calls,
And opes the doors: sooth hoping this would prove
A signal service to her loving [lord],
And that the scandal of her old misdeeds
Could thus be blotted out. Why thee delay?
They burst within the hall of sleep; is joined 740
In company with them Æolides,
Encourager of crimes. O gods! the like
Requite ye to the Grecians if, with lip
Religious, vengeance I demand in turn.
But thee, with life endowed, what accidents,—
Come, tell me in thy turn,—have hither brought?
Art come, enforced by wand'rings of the deep,
Or by a warning from the gods? Or thee
What fortune harasses, that drear abodes,

731. "Shake off this downy sleep, death's counterfeit." *Macbeth*, ii. 3.
732. Helen well deserves Marston's satire:
'Sooner hard steel will melt with southern winds,
A seaman's whistle calm the ocean,
A town on fire be extinct with tears,
Than women, vowed to blushless impudence,
With sweet behaviour and soft minioning,
Will turn from that where appetite is fixed."
Malcontent, iv. 3.
735. This miserable murderess scarce deserves to be connected with any allusion to Lady Macbeth:
"Come, come, you spirits
That tend on mortal thoughts, unsex me here,
And fill me, from the crown to the toe, top-full
Of direst cruelty! Make thick my blood;
Stop up th' access and passage to remorse,
That no compunctious visitings of nature
Shake my fell purpose, nor keep peace between
Th' effect and it! Come to my woman's breasts,
And take my milk for gall, you murd'ring ministers,
Wherever in your sightless substances
You wait on nature's mischief! Come, thick night,
And pall thee in the dunnest smoke of hell,
That my keen knife see not the wound it makes,
Nor heaven peep through the blanket of the dark,
To cry, *Hold! hold!*" · Act i. 5.
749. "See'st thou the dreary plain, forlorn and wild,
The seat of Desolation, void of light,
Save what the glimmering of these livid flames
Casts pale and dreadful?" Milton, *P. L.*, b. i.
"This is the place, by his commands, to meet in:
It has a sad and fatal invitation:
A hermit, that forsakes the world for prayer
And solitude, would be timorous to live here.

Without a sun, spots troublous, thou should'st reach?" 750
At this, a turning point of their discourse,
Aurora in her rosy four-horse car
Had now mid heav'n in her empyreal race
O'erpassed; and haply all the granted time
Would they have whiled away in such employs;
But him the Sibyl, his companion, warned,
And briefly [thus] addressed: "The night swoops on,
Æneas; we in weeping spend the hours.
This is the spot, where into branches twain
The pathway splits itself. The right [is that], 760

There's not a spray for birds to perch upon;
For every tree that overlooks the vale
Carries the mark of lightning, and is blasted.
The day, which smiled, as I came forth, and spread
Fair beams about, has taken a deep melancholy,
That sits more ominous in her face than night:
All darkness is less horrid than half light.
Never was such a scene for death presented:
And there's a ragged mountain peeping over,
With many heads, seeming to crowd themselves
Spectators of some tragedy."
  Shirley, *The Court Secret*, iv. 2.

750. Or: "Sun-lacking, spots of trouble."
752. "*Naiis*. Behold the rosy dawn
    Rises in tinsell'd lawn,
    And smiling seems to fawn
      Upon the mountains.
  Cloe. Awakèd from her dreams,
    Shooting forth golden beams,
    Dancing upon the streams,
      Courting the fountains."
Drayton, *The Muses' Elysium*, Nymphal iii.
"Is it so much, and yet the morn not up?
See yonder, where the shame-fac'd maiden comes!
Into our sight how gently doth she slide,
Hiding her chaste cheeks, like a modest bride,
With a red veil of blushes!"
  Fletcher, *The Woman-Hater*, i. 1.
757, 8. "The clock upbraids me with the waste of time." Shakespeare, *Twelfth Night*, iii. 1.
760. "Eternity, the various sentence past,
Assigns the sever'd throng distinct abodes,
Sulphureous or ambrosial: what ensues?
The deed predominant! The deed of deeds!—
Which makes a Hell of Hell, a Heaven of Heaven.
The goddess, with determin'd aspect, turns
Her adamantine key's enormous size
Through destiny's inextricable wards,
Deep driving every bolt, on both their fates.
Then, from the crystal battlement of Heaven,
Down, down she hurls it through the dark profound,
Ten thousand thousand fathom; there to rust,
And ne'er unlock her resolution more.
The deep resounds; and Hell, through all her glooms,
Returns, in groans, the melancholy roar."
  Young, *Complaint*, N. ix.

v. 541—558. BOOK VI. v. 558—574. 191

Which stretches 'neath the walls of mighty Dis;
By this the route t' Elysium lies for us;
But punishments of wicked [souls] the left
Works out, and sends them to accursèd Hell."
Deiphobus in answer : " Storm thou not,
Great priestess ; I shall pass away, fill up
The tale, and be restored to gloom. Go thou,
Our pride ! go, better fates enjoy !" Thus much
He said, and at the word his footsteps wheeled.
Æneas on a sudden looks behind, 770
And 'neath a cliff upon the left he sees
A spacious hold, engirt with triple wall,
Which, ravening with its scorching flames, the flood,
Tartarean Phlegethon, beclips, and whirls
The booming rocks. A gate there is in front,
Colossal, and of solid adamant
Its pillars ; that no might of men, not e'en
The heav'nly ones themselves, may have the power
To root them from their base with steel.
There stands
[Up-mounting] to the gales an iron keep;
And, sitting down, Tisiphone, with robe
Blood-spattered, tucked beneath, the vestibule 782
Unsleeping sentinels both night and day.
Hence groans are heard, and felon lashes ring ;

The clank of iron and the trail of chains.
Æneas paused, and, startled by the din,
Stood still. " What forms of guilt [are these], O maid ?—
Speak forth !—or by what vengeance are they plagued ?
What such distressful wailing to the air ?"
Then thus the prophetess began to speak :
"O famous prince of Teucri, it to none 791
Is lawful in his purity to plant
A foot upon the cursèd sill ; but me
When o'er the groves Avernian Hecat placed,
Herself explained the vengeance of the gods,
And she escorted me through every [spot].
These does the Gnosian Rhadamanthus hold,
Thrice-rigid realms, and punishes and hears
Their crafty sins, and forces them to own
What crimes, committed in the uppei world, 800
Each [soul], in unavailing secrecy
Exulting, hath deferred to death ['s] late [hour].
Forthwith the guilty ones Avengeress
Tisiphone, accoutred with a scourge,
Torments in mockery, and stretching out
In her left hand her grisly snakes, she calls
The ruthless squadrons of the sister-crew.
At last then, grating on dread-jarring hinge,
The cursèd gates are oped. Dost see what guise

---

772. " At last appear
Hell bounds, high reaching to the horrid roof,
And thrice threefold the gates ; threefold were brass,
Three iron, three of adamantine rock,
Impenetrable, impaled with circling fire,
Yet unconsumed." Milton, *P. L.*, b. ii.

773. " Horrors beneath, darkness in darkness, Hell
Of Hell, where torments behind torments dwell ;
A furnace formidable, deep, and wide,
O'er-boiling with a mad sulphureous tide,
Expands its jaws, most dreadful to survey,
And roars outrageous for the destin'd prey.
The sons of light scarce unappall'd look down,
And nearer press Heaven's everlasting throne."
Young, *Last Day*, b. iii.

774. See note on l. 416.

780. " Methinks Suspicion and Distrust dwell here,
Staring with meagre forms through grated windows ;
Death lurks within, and unrelenting punishment ;
Without, grim danger, fear, and fiercest pow'r,
Sit on the rude old tow'rs and Gothic battlements :
While horror overlooks the dreadful wall,
And frowns on all around."
Rowe, *Lady Jane Grey*, act iii.

784. A touching picture of a prisoner's woe from Chaucer; *Knighte's Tale*. Speaking of Palamon, 1281, 2 :

" The pure fetters on his shinnes grete
Were of his bitter salte teres wete."

802. " Cut off even in the blossoms of my sin,
Unhousel'd, disappointed, unanel'd ;
No reckoning made, but sent to my account
With all my imperfections on my head :
O, horrible ! O horrible ! most horrible !"
Shakespeare, *Hamlet*, i. 5.

" Yet down his cheeks the gems of pity fell,
To see the helpless wretches that remain'd,
There left through delves and deserts dire to yell ;
Amaz'd, their looks with pale dismay were stain'd,
And, spreading wide their hands, they meek repentance feign'd.

" But ah ! their scorned day of grace was past,
For (horrible to tell !) a desert wild
Before them stretch'd, bare, comfortless, and vast,
With gibbets, bones, and carcasses defil'd.
There nor trim field, nor lively culture smil'd ;
Nor waving shade was seen, nor fountain fair ;
But sands abrupt on sands lay loosely pil'd,
Through which they floundering toil'd with painful care,
Whilst Phœbus smote them sore, and fir'd the cloudless air."
Thomson, *Castle of Indolence*, end.

809. " Before the gates there sat
On either side a formidable shape :
The one seem'd woman to the waist, and fair,

Of sentry in the entrance sits? What shape
The threshold guards? With fifty pitchy
    chasms   811
Terrific, Hydra fiercer holds within
His seat. Then Tartarus itself opes twice
So deep adown the steep, and stretches forth
Beneath the darkness, as the upward gaze
To th' empyrean firmament of Heaven.
Here Terra's ancient progeny, the brood
Titanian, dashed by lightning down, are
    rolled
At bottom of the pit. Here, too, I saw
Aloeus' twins, huge bodies, who with hands
Attempted to demolish mighty heaven, 821
And Jove thrust out from his ancestral
    realms.
I saw, too, paying penalties severe,
Salmoneus, while he apes the fires of Jove,
And peals of Heav'n. He, drawn by
    coursers four,
And cresset brandishing, through states of
    Greeks,
And through the city of mid Elis, rode
In triumph, and the worship of the gods
Claimed to himself,—the madman!—who
    the storms,
And flash inimitable, with his bronze 830

And tramp of horn-hoofed steeds would
    counterfeit.
But the almighty sire, 'mid massy clouds
His levin-bolt elanced,—not torches he,
Nor smoky lights from pitchy pines;—and
    him
Headforemost in a wild tornado hurled.
Moreover, Tityus, too, the foster-child
Of Earth all-teeming, was there to behold;
Whose frame through nine whole acres is
    dispread;
A monstrous vulture, too, with hooky bill
The deathless liver pecking, and the flesh
That teems for punishments, both roots
    them up   841
For cates, and nestles 'neath his tow'ring
    chest:
Nor to the inwards, bourgeoning anew,
Is any respite granted. Wherefore name
The Lapithæ, Ixion, and Pirithous?
O'er whom there beetles black a [rock of]
    flint,
Now, now about to topple o'er, and like
One falling. Shine 'neath lofty couches boon
Their golden props, and banquets are
    served up
With kingly lavishness before their view.
The eldest of the Furies near reclines 851
And bars their touching with their hands
    the boards,
And rises up, her brand uplifting high,
And thunders with her mouth. Here they
    by whom
The brotherhood were loathed, while life
    endured;
Or parent buffeted, or craft inwove

But ended foul in many a scaly fold,
Voluminous and vast; a serpent arm'd
With mortal sting. About her middle round
A cry of hellhounds never ceasing bark'd
With wide Cerberian mouths full loud, and rung
A hideous peal; yet, when they list, would creep,
If aught disturb'd their noise, into her womb,
And kennel there; yet there still bark'd and howl'd,
Within, unseen."   Milton, *P. L.*, b. ii.

818. "For such a numerous host
Fled not in silence through the frighted deep,
With ruin upon ruin, rout on rout,
Confusion worse confounded; and Heaven-gates
Pour'd out by millions her victorious bands
Pursuing."   *Ibid.*, b. ii.

821. "He it was, whose guile
Stirr'd up with envy and revenge, deceived
The mother of mankind, what time his pride
Had cast him out of Heaven, with all his host
Of rebel angels: by whose aid, aspiring
To set himself in glory above his peers,
He trusted to have equall'd the Most High,
If he opposed; and, with ambitious aim
Against the throne and monarchy of God,
Raised impious war in Heaven, and battle proud,
With vain attempt. Him the Almighty Power
Hurl'd headlong flaming from the ethereal sky,
With hideous ruin and combustion, down
To bottomless perdition, there to dwell
In adamantine chains and penal fire,
Who durst defy the Omnipotent to arms."
                                    Ibid., b. i.

824. "What devil art thou, that counterfeits
heaven's thunder?"
        Webster, *The Duchess of Malfi*, iii. 5.

830. Drayton, speaking of David's skill on the lyre, says that the birds strained themselves
        "To imitate the inimitable touch."
                                David and Goliath.

840. No such very imaginary scene in warm regions:
"A surface hideous, delug'd o'er with blood,
Beyond my view illimitably stretch'd,
One vast expanse of horror. There supine,
Of huge dimension, cov'ring half the plain,
A giant corse lay mangled, red with wounds
Delv'd in th' enormous flesh, which, bubbling, fed
Ten thousand thousand grisly beaks and jaws,
Insatiably devouring."   Glover, *Leonidas*, b. xi.

852. "But on they roll'd in heaps, and, up the trees
Climbing, sat thicker than the snaky locks
That curl'd Megæra. Greedily they plucked
The fruitage fair to sight, like that which grew
Near that bituminous lake where Sodom flamed;
This more delusive, not the touch but taste,
Deceived. They, fondly thinking to allay
Their appetite with gust, instead of fruit,
Chew'd bitter ashes, which the offended taste
With spattering noise rejected: oft they essay'd,
Hunger and thirst constraining: drugg'd as oft,
With hatefulest disrelish writhed their jaws,
With soot and cinders fill'd."   Milton, *P. L.*, b. x.

856, 7. "How often in contempt of laws,
        To sound the bottom of a cause,
        To search out ev'ry rotten part,
        And worm into its very heart,

Against a client ; or they who, alone,
Have brooded o'er the riches they have gained,
Nor set aside a portion for their kin ;—
Which is the vastest multitude ;—and who
For their adultery were put to death ; 861
And who have godless arms pursued, nor feared
The right hands of their masters to beguile :—
In durance they their punishment await.
Seek not to be informed what punishment ;
Or what the shape [of pain], or fate, hath whelmed

> Hath he ta'en briefs on false pretence,
> And undertaken the defence
> Of trusting fools, whom in the end
> He meant to ruin, not defend."
>   Churchill, *The Duellist*, b. iii.

" I have seen some of his profession
Out of a case as plain, as clear as day,
Pick out such hard, inextricable doubts,
That they have spun a suit of seven years long,
And led their hood-wink clients in a wood,
A most irremeable labyrinth,
Till they have quite consum'd them."
   May, *The Heir*, act iv.

858. " A thousand black tormentors shall pursue thee,
Until thou leap into eternal flames,
Where gold, which thou adorest here on earth,
Melted, the fiends shall pour into thy throat."
   Fletcher and Shirley, *The Night Walker*, ii. 4.

From a noble passage of Ben Jonson's :
" Good morning to the day ; and next, my gold !
Open the shrine, that I may see my saint,
Hail the world's soul, and mine! More glad than is
The teeming earth to see the long'd-for sun
Peep through the horns of the celestial Ram,
Am I to view thy splendor darkening his :
That lying here, amongst my other hoards,
Shew'st like a flame by night, or like the day
Struck out of Chaos, when all darkness fled
Unto the centre. O thou son of Sol,
But brighter than thy father, let me kiss
With adoration thee, and every relick
Of sacred treasure in this blessed room."
   The Fox, i. 1, 1-13.
Also see Ford's *City Madam*, iii. 3.

861. " Groans are too late : sooner the ravisher
Whose soul is hurled into eternal frost,
Stung with the force of twenty thousand winters,
To punish the distempers of his blood,
Shall hope to get from thence, than those avoid
The certainty of hell where he is."
   Fletcher and Shirley, *The Night Walker*, iv. 5.

862. " Be virtuous ends pursu'd by virtuous means,
Nor think th' intention sanctifies the deed :
That maxim, publish'd in an impious age,
Would loose the wild enthusiast to destroy,
And fix the fierce usurper's bloody title ;
Then bigotry might send her slaves to war,
And bid success become the test of truth ;
Unpitying massacre might waste the world,
And persecution boast the call of Heaven."
   Johnson, *Irene*, iii. 8.

Their subjects. Others roll a monster rock,
And hang distended on the spokes of wheels.
The ill-starred Theseus sits, and sit he will
For ever ; Phlegyas, too, in depth of woe,
Puts all in mind, and with a thund'ring voice 871
Bears witness through the shades : 'Learn righteousness,
When warned, and not to slight the gods !'
This [wretch]
Hath sold away a native land for gold,
And over it a tyrant master placed ;
Made statutes, and unmade them, for his fee.
Another hath assailed a daughter's bed,
And barred espousals. All of them have dared
Gigantic guilt, and what they dared have gained.
[No,] not although I had a hundred tongues, 880

869. " Prayers there are idle, death is woo'd in vain :
In midst of death poor wretches long to die :
Night without day or rest, still doubling pain :
Woes spending still, yet still their end less nigh :
The soul there restless, helpless, hopeless lies :
There's life that never lives, there's death that never dies."
   P. Fletcher, *Purple Island*, vi. 37.

" A dungeon, horrible on all sides round,
As one great furnace flamed ; yet from those flames
No light ; but rather darkness visible
Served only to discover sights of woe,
Regions of sorrow, doleful shades, where peace
And rest can never dwell ; hope never comes,
That comes to all ; but torture without end
Still urges, and a fiery deluge, fed
With ever-burning sulphur unconsumed."
   Milton, *P. L.*, b. i.

" Or for ever sunk
Under yon boiling ocean, wrapp'd in chains ;
There to converse with everlasting groans,
Unrespited, unpitied, unreprieved,
Ages of hopeless end."   *Ibid.*, b. ii.

874. Shirley, of similar guilt :
" Does he call treason justice? Such a treason
As heathens blush at, nature and religion
Tremble to hear : to fight against my country !
'Tis a less sin to kill my father, there,
Or stab my own heart : these are private mischiefs
And may in time be wept for ; but the least
Wound I can fasten on my country makes
A nation bleed." *The Young Admiral*, iii. 1.

" But view them closer, craft and fraud appear ;
E'en liberty itself is barter'd here.
At gold's superior charms all freedom flies ;
The needy sell it, and the rich man buys."
   Goldsmith, *Traveller*.

" O Portius, is there not some chosen curse,
Some hidden thunder in the stores of heaven,
Red with uncommon wrath, to blast the man
Who owes his greatness to his country's ruin ?"
   Addison, *Cato*, i. 1, 21-24.

And hundred mouths, and iron voice, could I
All shapes of their enormities embrace,
All titles of their punishments recount."
These words when Phœbus' agèd priestess spake :—
" But come now, seize the pathway, and complete
The undertaken service : let us haste !"
She cries. " The walls do I discern, upreared
In forges of the Cyclops, and the gates
With their confronting archway, where these gifts
Do our injunctions bid us to lay down." 890
She said, and, footing on with even step
Along the darkness of the paths, they grasp
The intervening space, and near the doors.
Upon the entrance does Æneas seize,
And dews his person o'er with water fresh,
And on the fronting threshold pins the branch.
At length, these [duties] having been discharged,
The service of the goddess done, they reached
The gladsome regions and the charming greens,

882. In Ford's First Play the following sublime passage occurs ; '*Tis Pity*, iii. 6:
" There is a place,
(List, daughter) in a black and hollow vault,
Where day is never seen ; there shines no sun,
But flaming horror of consuming fires ;
A lightless sulphur, chok'd with smoky fogs
Of an infected darkness : in this place
Dwell many thousand thousand sundry sorts
Of never-dying deaths ; there damnèd souls
Roar without pity ; there are gluttons fed
With toads and adders ; there is burning oil
Pour'd down the drunkard's throat ; the usurer
Is forc'd to sup whole draughts of molten gold ;
There is the murderer for ever stabb'd,
Yet can he never die ; there lies the wanton
On racks of burning steel, whilst in his soul
He feels the torment of his raging lust."

899. " With greater light Heaven's temples opened shine ;
Morns smiling rise, evens blushing do decline ;
Clouds dappled glister, boisterous winds are calm,
Soft zephyrs do the fields with sighs embalm ;
In silent calms the sea hath hush'd his roars,
And with enamour'd curls doth kiss the shores ;
All-bearing Earth, like a new-married queen,
Her beauties heightens, in a gown of green
Perfumes the air, her meads are wrought with flow'rs,
In colours various, figures, smelling, pow'rs ;
Trees wanton in the groves with leavy locks,
Here hills enamell'd stand, the vales, the rocks,
Ring peals of joy; here floods and prattling brooks,
(Stars' liquid mirrors,) with serpenting crooks,
And whispering murmurs, sound unto the main,
The golden age returned is again."
Drummond, *Flowers of Sion*.

And blessèd mansions of the happy groves.
Here does a more expansive atmosphere,
Yea with a glitt'ring sheen, the plains enrobe, 902
And their own sun, the stars their own, they know.
Some play their limbs upon the turfy lists,
In frolic strive, and on the golden sand
Engage in wrestle ; others with their feet
Strike up the dances, and their sonnets sing.
Moreo'er, the Thracian priest with lengthful garb
Answers the sev'n varieties of tones
In rhythmic strains ; and now the same he strikes 910
With fingers, now with quill of iv'ry. Here

" Their glittering tents he pass'd, and now is come
Into the blissful field, through groves of myrrh,
And flowering odours, cassia, nard, and balm ;
A wilderness of sweets ; for Nature here
Wanton'd as in her prime, and play'd at will,
Her virgin fancies pouring forth more sweet,
Wild above rule or art, enormous bliss."
Milton, *P. L.*, b. v.

900. " O sacred innocence that sweetly sleeps
On turtles' feathers, whilst a guilty conscience
Is a black register, wherein is writ
All our good deeds and bad, a perspective
That shews us hell !"
Webster, *The Duchess of Malfi*, iv. 2.

904. Milton makes both Angels and Devils engage in earthly games : even Virgil, in his necessary ignorance, did not venture so far as this.
A scene similar to this is described by Sir William Jones in his " Seven Fountains :"
" Then in a car, by snow-white coursers drawn,
They led him o'er the dew-besprinkled lawn,
Through groves of joy and arbours of delight,
With all that could allure his ravish'd sight ;
Green hillocks, meads, and rosy grots he view'd,
And verdurous plains with winding streams bedew'd.
On every bank, and under every shade,
A thousand youths, a thousand damsels play'd ;
Some wantonly were tripping in a ring
On the soft border of a gushing spring ;
While some, reclining in the shady vales,
Told to their smiling loves their amorous tales."

" Sometimes with secure delight
The upland hamlets will invite,
When the merry bells go round,
And the jocund rebecks sound
To many a youth and many a maid,
Dancing in the chequer'd shade ;
And young and old come forth to play
On a sunshine holy-day."
Milton, *L'Allegro*.

907. " O the pleasure of the plains !
Happy nymphs and happy swains
(Harmless, merry, free, and gay,)
Dance and sport the hours away."
Gay, *Acis and Galatea*, 1-4.

911. How charming is Spenser !
" Eftsoones they heard a most melodious sound,
Of all that mote delight a daintie eare,
Such as attonce might not on living ground,
Save in this paradise, be heard elsewhere :

v. 648—659.   BOOK VI.   v. 659—674.   195

The ancient strain of Teucer, fairest race,
The high-souled heroes, born in better years,
E'en Ilus, and Assaracus, and Dardanus,
Troy's founder. He from far in wonder views
The warriors' armor and their phantom cars.
Their spears stand firmly planted in the earth,
And all around unyoked throughout the plain
Their horses feed. What zest for cars and arms
Resided in them living, what concern   920
In feeding glossy coursers, that the same
Pursues them when in earth inhearsed.
Behold!
Descries he others on the right and left
Throughout the herbage feasting, and in choir
Glad Pæan hymning 'mid a spicy grove
Of bay; whence from above [in] fullest [tide]
The river of Eridanus is rolled

Right hard it was for wight which did it heare,
To read what manner musicke that mote bee;
For all that pleasing is to living eare
Was there consorted in one harmonee;
Birdes, voices, instruments, windes, waters, all agree.
" The ioyous birdes, shrouded in chearefull shade,
Their notes unto the voice attempred sweet;
Th' angelicall soft trembling voyces made
To th' instruments divine respondence meet;
The silver-sounding instruments did meet
With the base murmure of the waters fall;
The waters fall with difference discreet
Now soft, now loud, unto the wind did call;
The gentle warbling wind low answered to all."
F. Q., ii. 12, 70, 1.

922. This idea is beautifully embodied by P. Fletcher:
" Thomalin, mourn not for him; he's sweetly sleeping
In Neptune's court, whom here he sought to please;
While humming rivers, by his cabin creeping,
Rock soft his slumbering thoughts in quiet ease."   *Piscatory Eclogues*, ii. 17.

926. Chatterton well describes the descent of a river, and its subsequent emergence:
" On Tiber's banks, Tiber, whose waters glide
In slow meanders down to Gaigra's side;
And, circling all the horrid mountain round,
Rushes impetuous to the deep profound;
Rolls o'er the ragged rocks with hideous yell;
Collects its waves beneath the earth's vast shell.
There for a while in loud confusion hurl'd,
It crumbles mountains down, and shakes the world;
Till borne upon the pinions of the air,
Through the rent earth the bursting waves appear;
Fiercely propell'd the whiten'd billows rise,
Break from the cavern, and ascend the skies."
The Death of Nicou, 1-12.

Along the forest. Here the band [of those,
Who] in their fighting for their native land
Have suffered wounds; and who were taintless priests,   930
While life endured; and who were holy bards,
And strains, of Phœbus worthy, spoke; or they,
Who by discovered arts have life refined,
And who have others mindful of them made
By their deserving it:—with all of these
Their brows are circled by a snowy wreath.
Whom, flocking round, the Sibyl thus addressed;
'Fore all Musæus: for a num'rous throng
Have him their centre, and to him look up,
Above them standing by his shoulders high:—   940
" Say, happy souls, and thou thrice-worthy bard,
What tract, what place, contains Anchises?
We
On his account have come, and mighty streams
Of Erebus sailed over." Straight to her
Reply in few the hero thus returned:
" To none there is a fixed abode: we dwell
In shady bow'rs; and couches of the banks,

---

929. " Welcome, my son! here lay him down, my friends,
Full in my sight, that I may view at leisure
The bloody corse, and count those glorious wounds.
How beautiful is death, when earned by virtue!
Who would not be that youth? What pity is it
That we can die but once to serve our country?"
Addison, *Cato*, iv.

931. " From yonder realms of empyrean day
Bursts on my ear th' indignant lay:
There sit the sainted sage, the bard divine,
The few, whom Genius gave to shine
Through every unborn age and undiscover'd clime."
Gray, *Ode for Music*, ii.

" The poet's eye, in a fine frenzy rolling,
Doth glance from heaven to earth, from earth to heaven;
And, as imagination bodies forth
The forms of things unknown, the poet's pen
Turns them to shapes, and gives to airy nothing
A local habitation and a name."
Shakespeare, *Midsummer Night's Dream*, v. 1.

947. The British poets abound in descriptions of such scenes as are here only briefly touched upon: the difficulty is in the selection. To quote but a few:
" A gardein saw I, full of blosomed bowis,
Upon a river, in a grene mede,
There as sweetnesse evermore inough is,
With flowres white, blewe, yelowe, and rede,
And cold welle streames, nothing dede,
That swommen full of smale fishes light,
With finnes rede, and scales silver bright:" &c.
Chaucer, *Assembly of Foules*, st. 27.

O 2

And meadows, fresh with runnels, do we haunt.
But ye, if thus the fancy in your heart
Inclines you, overpass this brow, and I 950
Forthwith will set you in an easy path."
He said, and in the front advanced his step,
And from above the glist'ring plains points out:
They thereupon the topmost summits leave.
But sire Anchises, deep in verdant glen,
The souls confined, and fated to advance
To upper light, was passing in review,
With earnestness reflecting; and by chance
Was counting all the number of his kin,
And dear descendants, and the destinies
And fortunes of the men, their manners too,
And their achievements. And when he beheld, 962
Advancing in his front along the grass,
Æneas, he in eagerness both hands
Outstretched, and tears were jetted o'er his cheeks,

And from his lips dropped forth the voice:
"Hast thou
Arrived at last, and hath thy piety,
Awaited by a parent, overcome
The painful journey? Is it deigned, my son,
To look upon thy features, and to hear 970
Familiar accents, and return them? Thus
In sooth I judged within my mind, and deemed
That it would happen, reckoning up the times;
Nor me hath my anxiety misled.
Borne [o'er] what lands, and o'er how spacious seas,
Do I receive thee! By how grievous risks
Betossed, my son! What terror have I felt,
Lest Libya's realms might do thee aught of harm!"
But he: "Me, sire, thy [ghost], thy rueful ghost,
Oft, oft appearing, these abodes hath forced
To near: my ships are riding in the Tyrrhene sea. 981
Vouchsafe to link right hand, vouchsafe, O sire;
And steal thee not away from our embrace."
In such wise speaking, at the same time he
Bewet his features with a flood of tears.
Three times he there essayed to throw his arms
Around his neck; three times, in vain engrasped,
The phantom-form escaped his hands, a match
For wanton winds, and likest wingy sleep.
Meanwhile Æneas sees within a vale, 990
That stretched in curve away, a grove retired,
And shrubs in thickets rustling, and the stream
Of Lethe, which along the homes of peace
Flows on. Round this uncounted states and tribes

" Fresh shadowes, fit to shroud from sunny ray:
Fair lawnds, to take the sunne in season dew:
Sweet springs, in which a thousand nymphs did play;
Soft-rombling brookes, that gentle slomber drew;
High-reared mounts, the lands about to view;
Low-looking dales, disloigned from common gaze,
Delightful bowres, to solace lovers trew;
False labyrinthes, fond runners eyes to daze;
All which, by Nature made, did Nature selfe amaze.

" And all without were walkes and alleyes dight
With divers trees enrang'd in even rankes;
And here and there were pleasant arbors pight,
And shadie seates, and sundrie flowring bankes."
        Spenser, *F. Q.*, iv. 10, 24, 5.

" I know a bank whereon the wild thyme blows,
Where oxlips and the nodding violet grows;
Quite over canopied with lush woodbine,
With sweet musk-roses, and with eglantine:
There sleeps Titania, some time of the night,
Lull'd in these flowers with dances and delight;
And there the snake throws her enamell'd skin,
Weed wide enough to wrap a fairy in."
        Shakespeare, *Midsummer Night's Dream*, ii. 2.

" Consent to be my mistress, Celestina,
And we will have it spring-time all the year:
Upon whose invitations, when we walk,
The winds shall play soft descant to our feet,
And breathe rich odours to re-pure the air;
Green bowers on every side shall tempt our stay,
And violets stoop to have us tread upon 'em.
The red rose shall grow pale, being near thy cheek,
And the white, blush, o'ercome with such a forehead.
Here laid, and measuring with ourselves some bank,
A thousand birds shall from the woods repair,
And place themselves so cunningly behind
The leaves of every tree, that while they pay
Us tribute of their songs, thou shalt imagine
The very trees bear music, and sweet voices
Do grow in every arbour."
        Shirley, *The Lady of Pleasure*, v. 1.

977, 8. Or, more literally:
        " How have I dreaded, lest
In aught the realms of Libya thee might harm!"

985. The ancient Epic poets could scarce have comprehended the Dauphin, when he says to Lord Salisbury:

" Let me wipe off this honourable dew,
That silverly doth progress on thy cheeks:
My heart hath melted at a lady's tears,
Being an ordinary inundation;
But this effusion of such manly drops,
This shower, blown up by tempest of the soul,
Startles mine eyes, and makes me more amaz'd
Than had I seen the vaulty top of heaven
Figur'd quite o'er with burning meteors."
        Shakespeare, *King John*, v. 2.

Were flitting; and,—as when among the
   meads
The bees in cloudless summer [-hour] alight
On chequered blossoms, and are streamed
   around
White lilies,—hums with music all the plain.
Æneas shudders at the sudden sight,
And in his ignorance does he demand 1000
The reasons :—what may be those floods
   beyond,
Or who the persons, in a host so vast
Have filled the banks. Then sire Anchises
   [thus] :
" The souls, to whom are other bodies due
By destiny, at Lethe's river-wave
Care-chasing draughts and long oblivion
   drink.
Hereof in sooth to give thee an account,
And spread them out before thy view, the
   line
Of my [descendants] to recount, long since
[Have] I desire[d]; that thou the more
   with me   1010
In Italy discovered may'st rejoice."
" O father, is it then to be conceived
That any spirits to the world above
Pass hence uplifted, and again return
To sluggish bodies? In these wretched
   [souls]
What so portentous passion for the light ?"
" I sooth will tell, nor keep thee poised [in
   doubt],
My son :" Anchises catches up [the speech],
And duly each particular unfolds.
   " Firstly; the sky, and lands, and wat'ry
   plains,   1020
And sheeny ball of Luna, and the stars
Titanian, soul within supports, and mind,
Shed through the members, stirs the mass
   entire,
And with the mighty framework blends
   itself.
Thence birth of men and cattle, and the
   lives

Of flying creatures, and the monster forms,
Which 'neath its marble surface breeds the
   deep.
A fiery energy and heav'nly source
Resides within these principles, so far
As harmful bodies clog them not, nor blunt
   them   1030
Earth-gendered joints and perishable limbs.
Hence fear they and desire, they grieve and
   joy ;
Nor do they peer abroad upon the heavens,
Confined in darkness and a gloomy jail.
Yea too, when with its latest ray hath life
Left them, yet do not from the woeful ones
Their every ill, nor all their body-plagues
Depart entirely. And it needs must be
That many a fault, long grown up with their
   growth,
In wondrous ways should deep within them
   root.   1040
Hence are they disciplined by punishments,

1030. The English idiom absolutely demands a negative in the positive clause in v. 732; otherwise a meaning the reverse of the poet's will be conveyed.

" O ignorant poor man ! What dost thou fear,
   Lock'd up within the casket of thy breast ?
What jewels and what riches hast thou there ?
   What heav'nly treasure in so weak a chest ?
" Look in thy soul, and thou shalt beauties find,
   Like those which drown'd Narcissus in the flood :
Honour and pleasure both are in thy mind,
   And all that in the world is counted good.
" Think of her worth, and think that God did mean
   This worthy mind should worthy things embrace :
Blot not her beauties with thy thoughts unclean,
   Nor her dishonour with thy passion base.
" Kill not her quick'ning pow'r with surfeitings ;
   Mar not her sense with sensuality ;
Cast not her wit on idle things ;
   Make not her free-will slave to vanity.
" And when thou think'st of her eternity,
   Think not that death against her nature is :
Think it a birth : and when thou go'st to die,
   Sing like a swan, as if thou went'st to bliss."
                Sir John Davies, *Immortality of the Soul*.
" Yet man, fool man ! *here* buries all his thoughts ;
   Inters celestial hopes without one sigh.
Prisoner of Earth, and pent beneath the Moon,
   Here pinions all his wishes ; wing'd by Heaven
To fly at infinite, and reach it there,
   Where seraphs gather immortality
On life's fair tree, fast by the throne of God."
" A soul immortal, spending all her fires,
   Wasting her strength in strenuous idleness,
Thrown into tumult, raptur'd or alarm'd,
   At aught this scene can threaten or indulge,
Resembles ocean into tempest wrought,
   To waft a feather, or to drown a fly."
                   Young, *The Complaint*, N. i.

1041.   " I am thy father's spirit,
Doom'd for a certain term to walk the night,
And, for the day, confin'd to lasting fires,

996. Spenser, beautifully of Clarion :
" There he arriving, round about doth flie,
From bed to bed, from one to other border ;
And takes survey, with curious busie eye,
Of every flowre and herbe there set in order ;
Now this, now that, he tasteth tenderly,
Yet none of them he rudely doth disorder,
Ne with his feete their silken leaves deface ;
But pastures on the pleasures of each place."
                      Muiopotmos, st. 22.
1006. See note on line 416.

1008.   " The hour's now come ;
The very minute bids thee ope thine ear ;
Obey, and be attentive."
                Shakespeare, *Tempest*, i. 2.
See note, *Æn.* v. 1027-9.

And penalties of crimes of old pay out.
Some gibbeted are spread to empty winds;
From others underneath the monstrous gulf
Their wickedness ingrained is washed away,
Or is burnt out by fire. We each endure
His proper Manes ; then we are dismissed
Throughout the wide Elysium, and we few
The gladsome fields possess : till length of day[s],—

Till the foul crimes, done in my days of nature,
Are burnt and purg'd away."
     Shakespeare, *Hamlet*, i. 5.

1044. Spenser magnificently introduces Pilate in the infernal regions, washing his hands, but in vain :

" He lookt a little further, and espyde
Another wretch, whose carcas deepe was drent
Within the river, which the same did hyde:
But both his hands, most filthy feculent,
Above the water were on high extent,
And faynd to wash themselves incessantly,
Yet nothing cleaner were for such intent,
But rather fowler seemed to the eye :
So lost his labour, vaine and ydle industry.

" The knight, him calling, asked who he was?
Who, lifting up his head, him answerd thus :
' I Pilate am, the falsest judge, alas !
And most unjust ; that, by unrighteous
And wicked doome,'" &c. *F. Q.*, ii. 7, end.

Crashaw, on the original act itself :

" My hands are wash'd, but, O the water's spilt,
That labour'd to have wash'd thy guilt :
The flood, if any be that can suffice,
Must have its fountain in thine eyes."

" What hands are here? Ha ! they pluck out mine eyes !
Will all great Neptune's ocean wash this blood
Clean from my hand? No ; this my hand will rather
The multitudinous seas incarnadine,
Making the green—one red."
    Shakespeare, *Macbeth*, ii. 2.

1046. " Nor custom, nor example, nor vast numbers
Of such as do offend, make less the sin.
For each particular crime a strict account
Will be exacted, and that comfort which
The damned pretend, fellows in misery,
Takes nothing from their torments: every one
Must suffer in himself the measure of
His wickedness." Massinger, *The Picture*, iv. 1.

1049. " Deceit and artifice ! the turn's too sudden :
Habitual evils seldom change so soon,
But many days must pass, and many sorrows,
Conscious remorse and anguish must be felt,
To curb desire, to break the stubborn will,
And work a second nature in the soul."
     Rowe, *Ulysses*, act i.

In Ford's Play '*Tis Pity*, the Friar thus touchingly addresses the guilty Giovanni ; act i. 1 :

" Hie to thy father's house : there lock thee fast
Within thy chamber ; then fall down
On both thy knees, and grovel on the ground ;
Cry to thy heart ; wash every word thou utter'st
In tears (and if't be possible) in blood :
Beg Heaven to cleanse the leprosy of lust
That rots thy soul ; acknowledge what thou art—
A wretch, a worm, a nothing : weep, sigh, pray,
Three times a day, and three times every night."

The round of time complete,—hath blotted out   1050
Th' incorporated stain, and taintless left
The heaven-born intelligence, and fire
Of uncompounded spirit. All of these,
When they have through a thousand years rolled round
The wheel [of Time], to Lethe's flood the god
Forth summons in a mighty host ; to wit,
That, void of memory, the vault above
They may again revisit, and begin
To wish into their bodies to return." 1059
 Anchises said, and on he draws his son,
The Sibyl with him too, within the midst
Of the assemblies, and the humming crowd ;
And fixes on a hillock, whence them all
In long array he can in front review,
And learn their lineaments as they advance.
" Now come ! what fame upon our Dardan race

Mason follows up the Christian idea thus beautifully :
      " O flinty Edgar,
What ! will this penitence not move thee? Know
There is a rose-lipp'd seraph sits on high,
Who ever bends his holy ear to earth,
To mark the voice of penitence, to catch
Her solemn sighs, to tune them to his harp,
And echo them in harmonies divine
Up to the throne of Grace." · *Elfrida*.

1051. " *Merlin*. But follow thou the whispers of thy soul,
That draw thee nearer Heaven ;
And, as thy place is nearest to the sky,
The rays will reach thee first, and bleach thy soot.
 Philidel. In hope of that I spread my azure wings,
And wishing still,—for yet I dare not pray,—
I bask in daylight, and behold with joy
My scum work outward, and my rust wear off."
     Dryden, *King Arthur*, ii. 1.

1059. " Heavens ! can you then thus waste, in shameful wise,
Your few important days of trial here?
Heirs of eternity ! yborn to rise
Through endless states of being, still more near
To bliss approaching, and perfection clear,
Can you renounce a fortune so sublime,
Such glorious hopes, your backward steps to steer,
And roll, with vilest brutes, thro' mud and slime !
No ! no !—Your heaven-touch'd heart disdains the sordid crime !"

" Not less the life, the vivid joy serene,
That lighted up these new-created men,
Than that which wings th' exulting spirit clean,
When just deliver'd from his fleshly den,
It soaring seeks its native skies agen :
How light its essence ! how unclogg'd its powers,
Beyond the blazon of my mortal pen !
Ev'n so we glad forsook the sinful bowers,
Ev'n such enraptur'd life, such energy was ours."
   Thomson, *Castle of Indolence*, ii. end.

1062. *Sonantem*, v. 753, must not be rendered too strongly : see vv. 703-9.

Attends hereafter, what posterity
From the Italian nation us awaits,—
Distinguished spirits, and about to pass
Into our name,—I will explain in speech,
And in thy destinies will tutor thee. 1071
"Yon youth, thou seest, who on his
   headless spear
Is leaning, holds by lot the nearest post
To light. He foremost to the stars of
   heaven,
Commingled with Italian blood, shall rise,—
Silvius, an Alban title, thy last child ;
Whom late to thee, in thy old age, thy
   spouse
Lavinia shall bring forth within the woods,
A king, and sire of kings, from whom our
   line
Shall rule in Alba Longa. He the next
Is Procas, of the Trojan race the pride,
And Capys [too], and Numitor, and he,
Who thee shall in his name reflect, Silvius
Æneas, equally for piety   1084
Or arms distinguished, if at any time
He Alba shall receive to rule. What youths!
Behold what mighty pow'rs do they display!
E'en shaded with the civic oak, they bear
Their temples. These Nomentum shall for
   thee,
And Gabii, and Fidenæ's city ; these 1090
Shall plant upon the hills Collatia's towers,
For praise of chastity renowned ; and add
Pometii the haughty, and the Fort
Of Inuus, and Bola, Cora too.
These then shall be their names ; the lands
   are now
Without a name. Yea too, in company
With his grandsire, Mavortian Romulus
Shall join him ; whom shall of Assarac's
   blood

1069. The idea in *ituras*, v. 758, seems to be that which Sir John Davies combats here :
" Nor in a secret cloister doth he keep
  These virgin-spirits, till their marriage-day ;
Nor locks them up in chambers, where they sleep
  Till they awake within these beds of clay."
     Immortality of the Soul, section 5.
But Thomson avails himself of it in *Alfred*, ii. 3 :
" From those eternal regions bright,
  Where suns that never set in night
    Diffuse the golden day,
  Where Spring unfading pours around,
  O'er all the dew-impearled ground,
    Her thousand colours gay :
O ! whether on the fountain's flowery side,
  Whence living waters glide,
    Or in the fragrant grove
Whose shade embosoms Peace and Love,
New pleasures all your hours employ,
And ravish every sense with every joy :
Great heirs of empire yet unborn
Who shall this island late adorn !
A monarch's drooping thought to cheer,
  Appear ! appear ! appear !"

His mother Ilia bring to light. Dost thou
   not see
How double plumes are standing from his
   head,   1100
And e'en the father of the gods above
Now stamps him with a dignity, his own ?
Behold ! beneath his auspices, my son,
That glorious Rome her sovereignty shall
   bring
To match with earth, her gallantry with
   heaven,
And singly for herself her seven heights
With rampart girdle, happy in a race
Of heroes : as the Berecynthian dame
Is wafted in her chariot, crowned with
   towers,
Through Phrygia's cities, blithe with birth
   of gods,   1110
A hundred grandsons folding in her arms,
All denizens of heav'n, all tenanting
The heights empyreal. Hither both thine
   eyes
Now turn ; this nation view, e'en Romans
   thine.
This Cæsar is, and all Iulus' strain,
Decreed to pass beneath the mighty cope
Of heav'n. This is the man, this he, whom
   thou
Dost often, often hear to thee is pledged,—
Augustus Cæsar, offspring of a god ;
He who shall found the age of gold again
In Latium, o'er the territories ruled 1121
By Saturn erst ; and past the Garamants
And Indians shall his sovereignty extend.
Without the constellations lies their land,
Without the pathways of the year and sun,
Where heav'n-supporting Atlas whirls the
   pole
Upon his shoulder, chased with blazing
   stars.
At his approach e'en now both Caspian
   realms,
And the Mæotian land, are struck aghast

1125. " In climes beyond the solar road,
 Where shaggy forms o'er ice-built mountains
    roam,
The Muse has broke the twilight gloom,
To cheer the shivering native's dull abode."
     Gray, *The Progress of Poesy*.

1127. " Even from the fiery-spangled veil of heaven."
    Marlowe, *Tamburlaine the Great*, v. 2.

Dr. Young has somewhere "blossomed with stars," Milton's " powdered with stars," *P. L.*, b. vii., may have been taken from Sackville's *Induction*, st. 9 :
" Then looking upward to the heavens beames,
With nightes starres thicke powdred every where,
Which erst so glistened with the golden streames,
That chearefull Phebus spred downe from his
   sphere."

At answers of the gods, and troubled be
The flurried outlets of the sev'nfold Nile.
Nor did in sooth Alcides overpass 1132
So wide [a span] of earth, although he
    pierced
The bronzen-footed hind, or tranquillized
The groves of Erymanth, and Lerna forced
To shudder through his bow: nor he who
    sways
His team with reins, encircled with the vine,
In conquest,—Liber, driving tigers down
From Nysa's lofty crest. And do we still
Demur to spread our fame by our exploits?
Or is it fear, that bars our settling down
Upon Ausonia's land?"   "But who is he
Afar, distinguished by the olive-sprays,
Bearing the holy things?" "I know the
    locks   1144
And frosty chin of Roma's monarch, who
The city first shall stablish by his laws;
From petty Cures, and a poor estate,
Commissioned to majesty sway. To whom
Shall Tullus next succeed, he who shall
    break
The quiet of his native land, and rouse 1150
To arms his restful subjects, and the hosts,
To triumphs now unused. Whom follows
    close
Too vauntful Ancus, now, e'en now, o'er-
    much
Rejoicing in mob-breath. And dost thou
    list

The Tarquin monarchs, and the haughty
    soul
Of vengeful Brutus, and the fascial rods,
Recovered, to behold? The consul's sway
And ruthless axes he shall first receive;
And, [though] a father, shall his sons,
    strange wars
Arousing, to their punishment, for sake 1160
Of beauteous freedom, call. Unhappy man!
Howe'er posterity these deeds shall brook,
The love of country, and a boundless lust
Of praises, shall prevail. Moreover too,
The Decii, and the Drusi far away,
And, unrelenting with his axe, behold
Torquatus; and, the standards bringing
    back,
Camillus. But those sprites, whom thou
    perceiv'st
Gleaming in weapons uniform, in heart
Knit now, and while in night they're over-
    whelmed,—   1170
Alas! how sore the war between them, if
The light of life they shall have reached!
    How sore
The battles and the carnage they shall wake!
From Alpine piles, and from Monœcus'
    tower,
The sire-in-law down swooping; son-in-law,

1159. "*Raymond.* What 'treason is it to redeem
    my king,
And to reform the state?
    Torrismond.   That's a stale cheat:
The primitive rebel, Lucifer, first us'd it,
And was the first reformer of the skies."
            Dryden, *Spanish Fryar*, v.

1161. "Beauteous freedom." The Tarquins
would have said:
            " Now mince the sin,
And mollify damnation with a phrase."
            Dryden, *Spanish Fryar*, v.

1162. "Brook," or, perhaps, "tell." The meaning of the passage seems to be this. It is as if
Anchises had said: "I am aware that this act of
Brutus is questionable, and that hereafter it will be
freely canvassed, and by some as freely condemned.
But, notwithstanding this difference of opinion, I
believe that the upholders of Brutus will at last
carry the world with them. The love of country,
and the desire for the approval of good men, will
be pronounced paramount to all considerations of
private interest or affection."

1163, 4. "Though the desire of fame be the last
    weakness
Wise men put off."
            Massinger, *A Very Woman*, v. 4.

Gifford, in a note on this passage, says that
Massinger and Milton (who calls fame, "That
last infirmity of a noble mind,") were probably both
indebted to Tacitus: "*Quando etiam sapientibus
cupido gloria novissima exuitur.*" Hist. xi. 6.

1171. "If you can look into the seeds of time,
And say, which grain will grow, and which will
    not."   Shakespeare, *Macbeth*, i. 3.

1147, 8. "And, as in cloudy days, we see the sun
Glide over turrets, temples, richest fields,
All those left dark, and slighted in his way,
And on the wretched plight of some poor shed,
Pours all the glories of his golden head:
So heavenly virtue on this envied lord
Points all his graces." Shirley, *Chabot*, iv. 1.

1153, 4. "O popular applause! What heart of man
Is proof against thy sweet seducing charms?
The wisest and the best feel urgent need
Of all their caution in thy gentlest gales;
But swell'd into a gust,—who then, alas!
With all his canvas set, and inexpert,
And therefore heedless, can withstand thy
    pow'r?" Cowper, *Task*, b. ii.

" Foe to restraint, unpractis'd in deceit,
Too resolute, from nature's active heat,
To brook affronts, and tamely pass them by;
Too proud to flatter, too sincere to lie,
Too plain to please, too honest to be great,
Give me, kind Heav'n, an humbler, happier state;
Far from the place where men with pride deceive,
Where rascals promise, and where fools believe;
Far from the walk of folly, vice, and strife,
Calm, independent, let me steal through life,
Nor one vain wish my steady thoughts beguile
To fear his lordship's frown, or court his smile."
            Churchill, *Night*.

"Wilt thou assign the flatteries, whereon
The reeling pillars of a popular breath
Have rais'd thy giant-like conceit?"
Beaumont and Fletcher, *The Laws of Candy*, i. 2.

With troops to meet him, from the East supplied !
Do not, my sons, do not familiarize
Such grievous battles to your minds, nor turn
Your lusty strength against your country's bowels :
And thou the first, do thou forbear, who draw'st 1180
Thy lineage from Olympus ; fling away
The weapons from thy hand, O my own blood !
That [warrior] to the lofty Capitol,
A conqueror, on Corinth triumphed o'er,
Shall drive his chariot, marked by slaughtered Greeks.
This Argos shall uproot, Mycenæ, too,
[The seat] of Agamemnon, aye and e'en
A child of Æacus, Achilles' seed,
The powerful in armor, having venged
The ancestors of Troja, and Minerva's fane, 1190
That was disgraced. Who, mighty Cato, thee,
Or thee, O Cossus, could unmentioned leave?
Who could the race of Gracchus? Or [those] twain,
Two levin-bolts of war, the Scipios,
The scourge of Libya? And Fabricius,
A master [spirit] in a petty sphere ?
Or thee, Serranus, sowing in thy trench ?
Whither, O Fabii, hurry wearied me ?
Thou art that " Maximus," who dost alone

For us by dallying retrieve the state. 1200
Others more tenderly shall model out
Their breathing bronzes, truly I believe ;
Shall living features from the marble draw ;
Plead causes better ; and the heav'n's career
Map out with wand, and rise of stars describe :
Do thou, to rule the nations 'neath thy sway,
Remember, Roman ! these shall be thy arts :—
E'en to obtrude upon them terms of peace,
To spare the prostrate, and to crush the proud."
Thus sire Anchises ; and, in their amaze,
He these subjoins : " See how Marcellus, badged 1211
With trophies from the gen'ral, stalks along
And, conq'ror, all the heroes overtops !
He shall the state of Rome, while tumult vast
Is troubling it, support ; he, mounted on his steed,
Shall quell the Pœni and revolting Gaul,
And the third captured arms shall hang aloft
To sire Quirinus." And Æneas here :—
For pacing by his side he saw a youth,
Peerless in figure and in gleaming arms,
But little blithe his forehead, and his eyne
With downcast look :—" Who, sire, is he, who thus 1222
Accompanies the warrior as he goes ?
His son ? Or any of his mighty stock
Of grandsons ? What a buzz of retinue

1179. " See, see, the pining malady of France !
Behold the wounds, the most unnatural wounds,
Which thou thyself hast given her woful breast !
O, turn thy edged sword another way ;
Strike those that hurt, and hurt not those that help ;
One drop of blood, drawn from thy country's bosom,
Should grieve thee more than streams of foreign gore." Shakespeare, 1 K. Hen. VI., iii. 3.

" Every wound
We give our country is a crimson tear
From our own heart. They are a viperous brood
Gnaw through the bowels of their parent."
Shirley, The Politician, iv. 2.

1197. " Cromwell, I charge thee, fling away ambition :
By that sin fell the angels."
Shakespeare, King Henry VIII., iii. 2.

" You have worth,
Richly enamelled with modesty ;
And, though your lofty merit might sit crown'd
On Caucasus, or the Pyrenæan mountains,
You choose the humbler valley, and had rather
Grow a safe shrub below, than dare the winds,
And be a cedar."
Randolph, The Muses' Looking-Glass, iii. 2.

" Trust me, I prize poor virtue with a rag
Better than vice with both the Indies."
Beaumont and Fletcher, The Faithful Friends, iv. 4.

1202. " Breathing :" that is, of course, seemingly alive : as Spenser represents Minerva working a Butterfly :

" Emongst these leaves she made a butterflie,
With excellent device and wondrous slight,
Fluttring among the olives wantonly,
That seem'd to live, so like it was in sight :
The velvet nap which on his wings doth lie,
The silken downe with which his backe is dight,
His broad outstretched hornes, his hayrie thies,
His glorious colours, and his glistering eies."
Muiopotmos, 42.

" Such are thy pieces, imitating life
So near, they almost conquer in the strife."
Dryden, Ep. to Sir G. Kneller.

" Still to new scenes my wandering muse retires,
And the dumb show of breathing rocks admires ;
Where the smooth chisel all its force has shown,
And soften'd into flesh the rugged stone."
Addison, Letter to Lord Halifax.

" Beneath yon storied roof, where mimic life
Glows to the eye, and at the painter's touch
A new creation lives along the walls."
Murphy, The Orphan of China, act ii.

1225, 6. So Gray of Queen Elizabeth :
" Girt with many a baron bold
Sublime their starry fronts they rear ;
And gorgeous dames and statesmen old,
In bearded majesty, appear.

Around! His bearing in himself how grand!
But ebon Night is hov'ring round his head
With sullen shade." The sire Anchises then
    began,
With eyedrops starting forth : "O son,
    seek not
The weighty sorrows of thy kin. The
    Fates   1230
Shall but just hold him to the view of earth,
Nor farther let him live. O'ermuch to you
Rome's race had puissant seemed, ye gods
    above,
If these your boons had ever-during proved.
What grievous groans of warriors will that
    field,
By Mars' majestic city, send abroad !
Aye, too, what obsequies, O Tiberine,
Shalt thou behold, when thou shalt glide
    along
By his fresh grave ! Nor shall there any
    youth
Of Ilian race his Latin ancestors   1240
To such a lofty pitch with hope upraise :
Nor ever shall the land of Romulus
In any nursling vaunt herself so high.
Ah piety ! Ah faith of olden days !
And thou, O right hand, unsubdued in war !
Not with impunity would any [knight]
Have tilted on to meet him, cased in arms,
Or when afoot against the foeman he would
    march,
Or gore with spurs his foaming charger's
    flanks.
Alas ! O youth, for pity meet ! If thou
Thy felon destinies in any wise   1251
Canst burst away, Marcellus thou shalt be.
By handfuls give me lilies ; let me strew
Their gaudy blossoms, and uppile the shade

In the midst a form divine !
Her eye proclaims her of the Briton line:
Her lion-fort, her awe-commanding face,,
Attemper'd sweet to virgin grace."
        The Bard, iii. 2.

1231. " He has a victory in 's death : this world
Deserved him not. How soon he was translated
To glorious eternity ! 'Tis too late
To fright the air with words ; my tears embalm
him."   Shirley, *Chabot*, end.

1244. " Oh, thou art gone, and gone with thee all
    goodness,
The great example of all equity,
(Oh, thou alone a Roman, thou art perished !)
Faith, fortitude, and constant nobleness !
Weep, Rome ! weep, Italy ! Weep all that knew
    him."   J. Fletcher, *Valentinian*, iv. 4.

1254. " Ye valleys low, where the mild whispers
    rise
Of shades, and wanton winds, and gushing
    brooks,
On whose fresh lap the swart-star sparely looks ;
Throw hither all your quaint enamell'd eyes,
That on the green turf suck the honied showers,
And purple all the ground with vernal flowers.

Of my descendant with these gifts at least,
And an unprofitable duty pay."
Thus they at large throughout the region
    range
In spacious plains of air, and all survey.
Through each whereof when had Anchises
    led
His son, and fired his spirit with the love
Of coming fame, he next the hero tells 1261
The battles, which thereafter should be
    waged ;
Informs him also of Laurentine clans,
And city of Latinus ; and the means,
Whereby each toil he may or shun or bear.
Two gates there are of Sleep, whereof
    the one
Is said to be of horn, through which is
    given
A ready outlet to the real shades :
The other, lustrous, finished off with sheen
Of iv'ry ; but [by this] to th' upper world
Fantastic visions do the Manes send. 1271
When with these words Anchises then escorts
His offspring, and the Sibyl by his side,
And lets them out by th' iv'ry gate,—he
    treads
The pathway to the galleys, and his mates
Revisits ; then straight bears him through
    the shore
To Caiet's port. The anchor from the bow
Is cast ; the sterns are resting on the
    strand.

Bring the rathe primrose that forsaken dies,
The tufted crow-toe, and pale jessamine,
The white pink, and the pansy freak'd with jet,
The glowing violet,
The musk rose, and the well-attired woodbine,
With cowslips wan that hang the pensive head,
And every flower that sad embroidery wears :
Bid Amaranthus all his beauty shed,
And daffodillies fill their cups with tears,
To strew the laureat hearse where Lycid lies."
                Milton, *Lycidas*.

        " With fairest flowers,
While summer lasts, and I live here, Fidele,
I'll sweeten thy sad grave. Thou shalt not lack
The flower, that's like thy face, pale primrose ; nor
The azur'd harebell, like thy veins ; no, nor
The leafy eglantine, whom not to slander,
Outsweeten'd not thy breath. The ruddock would,
With charitable bill," " bring thee all this ;
Yea, and furr'd moss besides, when flowers are none,
To winter-guard thy corse."
        Shakespeare, *Cymbeline*, iv. 2.

1256. " Hung be the heavens with black, yield day
    to night !
Comets, importing change of times and states,
Brandish your crystal tresses in the sky,
And with them scourge the bad revolting stars,
That have consented unto Henry's death !
Henry the Fifth, too famous to live long !
England ne'er lost a king of so much worth."
        Shakespeare, 1 *King Henry VI.*, i. 1, 1-7.

BOOK VII.

Thou, also, to our shores, Æneau nurse,
Caieta, at thy death undying fame
Hast giv'n; and now thy glory guards thy
  home,
And in the great Hesperia does thy name
Thy bones mark out, if that is any boast.
But good Æneas,—her funereal rites
Duly discharged, the barrow of the tomb
Upraised,—when once the mountain seas
  reposed,
Pursues his voyage under sail, and quits
The haven. Breathe the breezes on the night,
Nor does the silver moon their course
  forbid;   11
The ocean gleams beneath her dancing
  ray.
The nearest shores to Circe's land are grazed,
Wherein the wealthy daughter of the Sun
The groves, that must not be approached,
  makes ring
With ceaseless song, and in her prideful
  domes
Burns musky cedar for her nightly lamps,
Trav'lling the filmy warp with whistling
  reed.
Hence groans are clearly heard, and lions'
  wrath,   19
Rejecting chains, and roaring late at night;

Line 8. "And weary waves, withdrawing from the
    fight,
  Lie lull'd and panting on the silent shore."
            Dryden, *Annus Mirabilis*, 98.

11, 12. "Now through the passing cloud she seems
    to stoop,
  Now up the pure cerulean rides sublime.
  Wide the pale deluge floats, and streaming mild
  O'er the sky'd mountain to the shadowy vale,
  While rocks and floods reflect the quivering gleam,
  The whole air whitens with a boundless tide
  Of silver radiance, trembling round the world."
            Thomson, *Autumn*.

  "But soft! the golden glow subsides;
    Her chariot mounts on high;
    And now in silver'd pomp she rides
      Pale regent of the sky."
            Cunningham, *The Contemplatist*, 7.

12. Or, by less displacement of the Latin words:
"Gleams underneath her bickering light the deep."

14. "Within the navel of this hideous wood,
  Immured in cypress shades a sorcerer dwells,
  Of Bacchus and of Circe born, great Comus,
  Deep skill'd in all his mother's witcheries;
  And here to every thirsty wanderer
  By sly enticement gives his baneful cup,
  With many murmurs mix'd, whose pleasing poison
  The visage quite transforms of him that drinks,
  And the inglorious likeness of a beast
  Fixes instead, unmoulding reason's mintage,
  Character'd in the face. This have I learnt,
  Tending my flocks hard by i' the hilly crofts,
  That brow this bottom glade: whence night by
    night
  He and his monstrous rout are heard to howl,
  Like stabled wolves, or tigers at their prey,
  Doing abhorred rites to Hecate
  In their obscured haunts of inward bowers.
  Yet have they many baits, and guileful spells,
  To inveigle and invite the unwary sense
  Of them that pass unweeting by the way."
            Milton, *Comus*.

See Ben Jonson's magnificent Witch scene in
The Masque of Queens, enacted before James I.,
1609.

16. "Can any mortal mixture of earth's mould
  Breathe such divine, enchanting ravishment?
  Sure something holy lodges in that breast,
  And with these raptures moves the vocal air
  To testify his hidden residence.
  How sweetly did they float upon the wings
  Of silence, through the empty-vaulted night,
  At every fall smoothing the raven down
  Of darkness, till it smil'd! I have oft heard
  My mother Circe with the Syrens three,
  Amidst the flowery-kirtled Naiades,
  Culling their potent herbs and baleful drugs;
  Who, as they sung, would take the prison'd soul,
  And lap it in Elysium."   Milton, *Comus*.

19. "Whiles we stood here securing your repose,
  Even now, we heard a hollow burst of bellowing,
  Like bulls, or rather lions; did it not wake you?
  It struck mine ear most terribly."
            Shakespeare, *Tempest*, ii. 1.

  "Silence and solitude are every where.
  Through all the gloomy ways, and iron doors,
  That hither lead, nor human face nor voice
  Is seen or heard. A dreadful din was wont
  To grate the sense, when entered here, from
    groans,
  And howls of slaves condemned; from clink of
    chains,
  And crash of rusty bars and creaking hinges:
  And ever and anon the sight was dashed
  With frightful faces, and the meagre looks
  Of grim and ghastly executioners."
            Congreve, *The Mourning Bride*, v.

  "He knows her shifts and haunts;
  And all her wiles and turns; the venom'd plants
  Wherewith she kills; where the sad mandrake
    grows,
  Whose groans are deathful; the dead-numbing
    nightshade,
  The stupefying hemlock, adder's tongue,
  And martagan; the shrieks of luckless owls
  We hear, and croaking night-crows in the air!
  Green-bellied snakes, blue fire-drakes in the sky,
  And giddy flitter-mice with leathern wings!
  The scaly beetles, with their habergeons,
  That make a humming murmur as they fly!
  There in the stocks of trees white faies do dwell,
  And span-long elves that dance about a pool,
  With each a little changeling in their arms!
  The airy spirits play with falling stars,
  And mount the sphere of fire to kiss the moon!
  While she sits reading by the glow-worm's light,
  Or rotten wood, o'er which the worm hath crept,
  The baneful schedule of her nocent charms,
  And binding characters, through which she wounds
  Her puppets, the sigilla of her witchcraft."
            Ben Jonson, *The Sad Shepherd*, ii. 2.

And bristly boars and bears within their stalls
Are raging ; howl, too, shapes of monster wolves ;
Which from the guise of men the goddess grim,
Circe, had by her pow'rful herbs transshaped
To visages and forms of savage beasts.
Which such portents that Troja's holy sons
Might not endure, when wafted into port,
Nor near the shores accursèd, Neptune filled
Their sails with fav'ring winds, and sped their flight,
And carried them beyond the seething shoals.   30
And now 'gan flush with beams [of light] the main,
And from the lofty welkin saffron Morn
In rosy chariot gleamed ; when fell the gales,
And every blast sank suddenly to rest,
And on the lazy surface strain the oars.
And here a grove immense Æneas spies
From forth the ocean. Through the midst thereof
[The god] of Tiber in his charming stream,
With racing eddies, and of golden hue
With plenteous sand, bursts onward to the sea ;   40
And motley birds around and overhead,
Used to the banks and channel of the tide,
The welkin were enchanting with their song,
And flutt'ring through the grove. To bend their course,
And veer the prows to land, he bids the crews,
And enters in delight the shady flood.
  Come now, O Erato, who were the kings,
What crises of affairs, the posture what
Of ancient Latium, when a foreign host
Their fleet first landed on Ausonian coasts,
Will I unfold, and from the first retrace 51
The sources of the fray : thou, thou, thy bard,
Teach, goddess ! I will sing of dreadful wars,
Will sing of battles, and of princes, forced
To death by passions, and the Tyrrhene band,
And whole Hesperia mustered under arms.
A higher train of subjects rises up
For me ; a higher task I undertake.
  The king Latinus fields and towns, at rest
In lengthful peace, in years now stricken, ruled.   60
That he of Faunus and a Laurent Nymph,
Marica, was begotten, we receive.
To Faunus Picus father was ; and he

26, 7. "You spotted snakes, with double tongue,
   Thorny hedge-hogs, be not seen ;
   Newts, and blind-worms do no wrong :
   Come not near our fairy queen.
      Philomel, with melody
      Sing in our sweet lullaby :
   Lulla, lulla, lullaby ; lulla, lulla, lullaby ;
   Never harm, nor spell, nor charm,
   Come our lovely lady nigh ;
   So, good night, with lullaby.

   Weaving spiders, come not here ;
   Hence, you long-legg'd spinners, hence ;
   Beetles black, approach not near ;
   Worm, nor snail, do no offence."
         Shakespeare, *Midsummer Night's Dream*, ii. 3.

   " I know thy trains,
Though dearly to my cost, thy gins, and toils ;
Thy fair enchanted cup, and warbling charms,
No more on me have power ; their force is null'd :
So much of adder's wisdom have I learn'd,
To fence my ear against thy sorceries."
                     Milton. *Samson*.

28. Similarly Guyon escapes the "Rock of Reproch :"

" So forth they rowed ; and that ferryman
With his stiffe oares did brush the sea so strong,
That the hoare waters from his frigot ran,
And the light bubbles daunced all along,
Whiles the salt brine out of the billowes sprong."
            Spenser, *Faerie Queene*, ii. 12, 10.

43. " The briddes singen, it is no nay,
      The sperhauk and the popingay,
        That joie it was to here ;
      The throstel cok made eke his lay,
      The wode dove upon the spray,
        He sang ful loude and clere."
            Chaucer, *Rime of Sir Thopas*, 10.

   " The warblers lively tunes essay,
The lark on wing, the linnet on the spray,
While music trembles in their songful throats ;
The bullfinch whistles soft his flute-like notes,
The bolder blackbird swells sonorous lays ;
The varying thrush commands a tuneful maze :
Each a wild length of melody pursues,
While the soft-murmuring, amorous wood-dove coos ;
And, when in spring these melting mixtures flow,
The cuckoo sends her unison of woe."
            Savage, *The Wanderer*, c. v.

53. " So much the rather thou, celestial Light,
Shine inward, and the mind through all her powers
Irradiate ; there plant eyes, all mist from thence
Purge and disperse, that I may see and tell
Of things invisible to mortal sight."
            Milton, *P. L.*, b. iii.

57. " Thee I revisit now with bolder wing,
Escap'd the Stygian pool, though long detain'd
In that obscure sojourn, while in my flight
Through utter and through middle darkness borne,
With other notes than to the Orphean lyre,
I sung of Chaos and eternal Night ;
Taught by the heavenly muse to venture down
The dark descent, and up to reascend,
Though hard and rare."   *Ibid.*

Relates that thou, O Saturn, wast his sire ;
Thou art remotest founder of the race.
By the decree of gods, a son to him
And issue male was none; e'en as it dawned,
'Twas ravished from him in the prime of
   youth.
His palace, and his tenements so vast,
An only daughter kept, now ripe for man,
Now fit for marriage in completed years.
Her, many from great Latium, and through-
   out   72
Entire Ausonia, courted ; Turnus courts,
Before all other [suitors] passing fair,
Of pow'r through ancestors on ancestors ;
Whom to have linked to her as son-in-law
The royal consort sped with wondrous zeal:
But signs of gods with manifold alarms
Withstand. There was a "Laurel" 'mid
   the dome,
Within its deep recesses, consecrate   80
In locks, and during many a year with awe
Enguarded ; which, when lighted on, the
   sire
Latinus, when he reared his maiden towers,
Himself was rumored to have sanctified
For Phœbus, and therefrom the name,
"Laurentines," on the settlers to have fixed.
The topmost crest hereof did clustering
   bees,—
A marvel to be told !—with mighty hum
Across the limpid welkin borne, invest,
And, with their feet in one another's linked,
A swarm hung sudden from a bough in leaf.
Straight cries a seer : "A foreign hero we
Behold approaching, and a host in quest 93
Of the same quarters from the selfsame parts,
And lording o'er us from the castle height."
Moreover, while the altars with religious
   links
The maid Lavinia kindles, as she stands
Beside her father, she appeared,—oh,
   dread !—
With her long tresses to catch up the fire,
And through her whole apparel to be burnt
In crackling flame, alike in royal locks
Ablaze, ablaze in diadem, adorned   102
With jewelry; then smoky to be wrapt
In ruddy light, and all throughout the dome
To scatter Vulcan. This in sooth was held
[A] dread [portent], and wondrous to be
   seen :
For chanted they that she would brilliant
   prove
In fame and fortunes ; but that it presaged
To her own people a momentous war.
But, anxious at the prodigies, the king 110
The oracles of Faunus, his prophetic sire,
Approaches, and consults the groves
By deep Albunea, which of woodland
   [streams]
The noblest, from its holy well-head brawls,
And, dark, breathes out fell pestilential
   reek.
Herefrom the clans of Italy, and all
Œnotria's land in their perplexities
Seek answers. Hither when his gifts the
   priest
Hath brought, and underneath the stilly
   night,
On skins of butchered ewes outspread, lain
   down,   120
And slumbers courted ; many a spectral
   shape,
In wondrous fashions flutt'ring, he beholds,
And sundry voices hears ; enjoys he too
The converse of the gods, and from Avernus'
   depths
Accosts the Ach'ron. Here then e'en himself
The sire Latinus, seeking for replies,
A hundred woolly ewes of two years old
Slew duly, and upon the skin thereof,
And fleeces spread, he cushioned lay. A
   voice
Is sudden from the lofty grove returned :
"Seek not in Latin marriage-ties to wed

---

79. *Laurus*, however, is the "bay-tree."

80. "For it had been an auncient tree
   Sacred with many a mysteree,
   And often crost with the priestes crewe,
   And often hallowed with holy-water dewe."
         Shepheards Calender, Februarie.

102.   "'Tis well ! so great a beauty
   Must have her ornaments. Nature adorns
   The peacock's tail with stars ; 'tis she attires
   The bird of paradise in all her plumes ;
   She decks the fields with various flowers ; 'tis she
   Spangled the heavens with all those glorious
      lights :
   She spotted the ermine's skin ; and arm'd the fish
In silver mail. But man she sent forth naked,
Not that he should remain so, but that he,
Indued with reason, should adorn himself
With every one of these. The silk-worm is
Only man's spinster ; else we might suspect
That she esteem'd the painted butterfly
Above her master-piece. You are the image
Of that bright goddess, therefore wear the jewels
Of all the east ; let the Red Sea be ransack'd
To make you glitter."
   Randolph, *The Muses' Looking-Glass*, iv. 1.

112. "As those Druids taught, which kept the
      British rites,
And dwelt in darksome groves, there counselling
   with sprites." Drayton, *Polyolbion*, s. i. 34, 5.

124. "Oh ! bear me to the vast embowering shades,
To twilight groves, and visionary vales ;
To weeping grottoes, and prophetic glooms ;
Where angel forms athwart the solemn dusk
Tremendous sweep, or seem to sweep along ;
And voices more than human, through the void
Deep-sounding, seize th' enthusiastic ear !"
                    Thomson, *Autumn*.

Thy daughter, O my offspring, neither trust
The nuptial union that has been arranged.
Come foreign sons-in-law, who by their
    blood   134
Our reputation to the stars may waft,
And from whose root our children's chil-
    dren, all
Beneath their feet, where Sol, careering
    back,
Each Ocean views, both rolled and ruled
    shall see."
These father Faunus' answers and his
    warnings,
Vouchsafed him in the still of night, him-
    self   140
Latinus shuts not up within his lip;
But, flitting round far-wide, had Rumor
    now
Through towns Ausonian wafted them away,
When the Laomedontian youth fast moored
Their navy to the margent's turfy rise.
    Æneas, and the leading chiefs, and fair
Iulus, lay their bodies down beneath
The branches of a stately tree, and set
In order their repast, and wheaten cakes
Along the grass they place beneath the
    feast;—   150
'Twas thus that did he, Jupiter, inspire;—
And with wild fruits the corny board enrich.
Here th' other [cates] by chance devoured,
    what time
To turn their teeth upon the scanty bread
The dearth of diet forced them, and profane
With hand and jaws presumptuous the disc
Of fateful cake, nor spare its quarters broad:
"Ho! e'en our boards are we devouring!"
    cries
Iulus, nor indulging further jests.
That speech, when heard, first brought an
    end of woes;   160
And from the speaker's lips straight caught
    it up
His sire, and, mazed at th' oracle, he
    paused.
Forthwith, "Hail! land by fates my due,
    and ye,"
He cries, "O trusty household gods of Troy,
All hail! Our home is here, our country
    this.
For sire Anchises suchlike mysteries
Of fates,—I now recall it,—hath to me
Bequeathed: 'What time shall hunger thee,
    my son,
To shores unknown conveyed, when be
    thy cates
Consumed, compel thy tables to devour,—
Then, wearied out, remember to expect 171

---

145. Latin: "from."   154. "Bitings on."

Thy homes, and there to plant with [thy
    own] hand
Thy maiden roofs, and found them with a
    trench.
This was that hunger; this the crowning
    [act]
Awaited us, to set a bound to woes.
Then come, and gladsome with the Sun's
    first light—
What spots, or who the men that hold
    them, where
The city of the nation,—let us trace,
And [regions,] branching from the harbor,
    seek.
Now saucers in libation pour ye forth 180
To Jove, and with your orisons invoke
My sire Anchises, and the wines replace
Upon the boards." Thus having spoken
    forth,
He then his temples with a leafing bough
Enwreathes, and both the Genius of the
    place,
And Tellus, foremost of the gods, and
    Nymphs,
And Floods, unknown as yet, he prays;
    then Night,
And Night's arising signs, and Ida's Jove;
And next the Phrygian Mother he invokes,
And both his parents both in heaven and
    hell.
Then the almighty father thrice from heaven
Aloft in brightness thundered; and, afire
With rays of sheen and gold, within his
    hand   193
He, shaking it himself, from heaven dis-
    played
A cloud. Here suddenly a rumor's spread
Through Troja's squadrons, that the day
    was come,
Wherein the walls, their due, they might
    uprear.
In rivalry the banquet they renew,
And, at the mighty prodigy rejoiced,

---

176. As if he had said:
"Hence, loathed Melancholy,
  Of Cerberus and blackest Midnight born,
In Stygian cave forlorn,
  'Mongst horrid shapes, and shrieks, and sights
    unholy,
Find out some uncouth cell
  Where brooding Darkness spreads his jealous
    wings,
And the night-raven sings:
There under ebon shades and low-brow'd rocks
As rugged as thy locks,
  In dark Cimmerian desert ever dwell."
        Milton, *L'Allegro.*
193. "Right against the eastern gate,
  Where the sun begins his state,
  Robed in flames, and amber light,
  The clouds in thousand liveries dight."
        Ibid.

They set the wassail-bowls, and crown the wines.   200
What time next Day, with earliest torch arisen,
Surveyed the lands, the nation's city, and its bourns,
And shores, in groups dissevered search they out ;—
That these are plashes of Numicius' spring,
That this the river Tiber, that here dwell
The gallant Latins. Then Anchises' son
A hundred envoys, culled from every rank,
To the majestic palace of the king
Commands to march, all decked with Pallas' sprays,
And bear the hero presents, and entreat 210
Peace for the Teucri. No demur : they haste,
[As] ordered, and with rapid steps are borne.
Himself scores out the walls with lowly trench,
And builds upon the spot ; and on the shore
Their homes, the first, in fashion of a camp,
Encompasses with battlements and mound.
And now their journey having spanned, the towers
Of the Latini, and their lofty roofs,
The youths began to see, and near the wall.
Before the city, boys, and, in the bloom 220
Of early age, the youth are trained on steeds,
And tame their chariot[-courser]s on the dust ;
Or strain the restive bows, or limber bolts
Launch by [the dint of] arms, and in the race
And fight give challenge : when upon his steed
Borne in advance, to th'agèd monarch's ears
A courier brings the news, that giant men
In strange apparel had arrived. He gives
Commandment, that within the palace they
Should be invited, and he in the midst 230
Upon his throne ancestral took his seat.
A dome, majestical, immense, upraised
Aloft upon a hundred pillars, stood

Upon the city's crest, the royal court
Of Laurent Picus, awful from its woods,
And rev'rence of the fathers. Here to take
Their sceptres, and first fasces to upraise,
Was the auspicious usance of the kings ;
This sainted building was their senate-hall,
These the apartments for their holy feasts ;
Here, on the slaughter of a ram, the sires
At stretching boards were wont to seat them down.   242
Yea, too, the statues of their ancestors of yore,
In line, of cedar old,—both Italus,
And sire Sabinus, planter of the vine,
Holding a hooky bill below his bust,
And Saturn aged, and twain-faced Janus' form,
Were standing in the court ; and other kings
From the beginning, who the wounds of war
In fighting for their country's sake endured.
And many arms, moreo'er, on holy posts,
Cars captived, hang, arched battle-axes too,
And plumes of casques, and massy bars of gates,   253

> Or forms the pillars' long-extended rows,
> On which the planted grove, the pensile garden, grows.
> The workmen here obey the master's call,
> To gild the turret, and to paint the wall ;
> To mark the pavement there with various stone,
> And on the jasper steps to rear the throne.
> The spreading cedar, that an age had stood,
> Supreme of trees, and mistress of the wood,
> Cut down and carv'd, my shining roof adorns,
> And Lebanon his ruin'd honour mourns."
>   *Prior, Solomon,* b. ii.

243. " Oft let me range the gloomy aisles alone,
Sad luxury! to vulgar minds unknown.
Along the walls where speaking marbles show
What worthies form the hallow'd mould below ;
Proud names, who once the reins of empire held ;
In arms who triumph'd, or in arts excell'd ;
Chiefs, grac'd with scars, and prodigal of blood ;
Stern patriots, who for sacred freedom stood ;
Just men, by whom impartial laws are given ;
And saints, who taught, and led, the way to Heaven."   Tickell, *On the Death of Addison.*

" Those are the models of the ancient world,
Left like the Roman statues to stir up
Our following hopes ; the place itself puts on
The brow of majesty, and flings her lustre
Like the air newly lighten'd."
                Fletcher, *The Noble Gentleman,* i. 1.

250. " Patriots have toil'd, and in their country's cause
Bled nobly : and their deeds, as they deserve,
Receive proud recompense. We give in charge
Their names to the sweet lyre. Th' historic Muse,
Proud of the treasure, marches with it down
To latest times ; and Sculpture, in her turn,
Gives bond in stone and ever-during brass
To guard them, and t' immortalise her trust."
                          Cowper, *Task,* v.

---

200. The following song is introduced by Beaumont and Fletcher in a similar scene in *Valentinian,* v. 8:

" God Lyæus, ever young,
Ever honour'd, ever sung,
Stain'd with blood of lusty grapes,
In a thousand lusty shapes,
Dance upon the mazer's brim,
In the crimson liquor swim ;
From thy plenteous hand divine,
Let a river run with wine :
God of youth, let this day here
Enter neither care nor fear !"

233. " From furthest Africa's tormented womb
The marble brought erects the spacious dome,

And darts, and shields, and beaks from vessels wrenched.
Himself with his Quirinal augur-staff,
And scanty "trabea" short-girded, sat,
And in his left hand the "ancile" bare—
Picus, steed-tamer: whom, with golden wand
When struck, and metamorphosed by her drugs,
His wooer Circe, witched by passion, made
A bird, and powdered o'er his wings with hues. 261
Within such holy building of the gods,
And sitting on th' hereditary throne,
Latinus to his presence in the dome
The Teucri summoned, and to them these [words],
When entered in, he first from peaceful lip
Delivered : "Say, ye sons of Dardanus !—
For neither are we unaware
Or of your city, or of your race ; and known
By rumor, on the main your course ye steer,— 270
What seek ye, what the reason, or whereof
In want, your galleys to the Auson shore
Thro'out so many azure seas hath brought?
Whether it be by misconceit of course,
Or driv'n by tempests, such as, many a one,
In deep of ocean mariners endure,
Within the margents of our river ye
Have come, and in the harbor lie at rest :
Fly not our hospitality, nor yet
Be strangers to the Latins, Saturn's race,
Not righteous by controlment nor by laws,
Themselves restraining of their free accord,
And by the usance of their ancient god. 283
And sooth I mind me,—the tradition goes
Dim somewhat through [the lapse of] years, —that thus
The elders of Auruncans noised it, how,
Sprung from these countries, Dardanus pierced through
As far as the Idæan towns of Phrygia,
And Thracian Samos, which now Samothrace
Is called. Him, hence set out from Tyrrhene seat 290
Of Coryth, now upon a throne receives
The golden palace of the starry sky, ..

And of the altars of the gods he swells
The number." He had spoken, and his speech
Ilioneus thus followed with his voice :
"O king, of Faunus the distinguished son,
Nor, tossed by billows, hath a murky storm
Forced us to enter on your lands, nor star,
Or shore, misled us from our line of route :
We all, of purpose and with willing minds,
Are wafted to this city, driv'n from realms,
The greatest whilom, which, in his career
From farmost heaven, used the Sun to view.
From Jove the fountain of our race ; in Jove, 304
Their ancestor, the Dardan youth rejoice.
Our king himself, from Jove's sublimest strain,
Troy-born Æneas, sent us to thy courts.
How fierce a storm, from fell Mycenæ burst,
O'er Ida's plains hath swept ; forced by what fates,
Each sphere of Europe and of Asia clashed ;— 310
E'en he hath heard, if exiles any man
The end of earth, in ocean tided back ;
And if the zone of the unrighteous Sun,
Amid four zones dispread, cuts any off.
Borne from that deluge o'er so many seas,
Immense, a scanty home for country-gods,
And shore secure from harm, we crave, and, free
To every being, water e'en and air.
We not discreditable to your realm
Shall prove ; nor yours be noised a light renown ; 320
Or thankfulness for such a noble deed
Die off ; nor shall it irk Ausonia's sons
That Troy within their lap they had received.
By [our] Æneas' destinies I swear,
And his right hand of power, whether any man
In troth, or war and arms, hath proved it, us
Hath many a nation, many (—scorn us not,
That, of our own accord, upon our hands
The fillets we advance, and words of prayer,—)

Soars o'er th' eternal funds of hail and snow,
And leaves Heaven's stormy magazine below.
Thence through the vast profound of Heaven she flies,
And measures all the concave of the skies."
Pitt, *On the Death of Earl Stanhope*.

---

282. " The rest, we live
Law to ourselves : our reason is our law."
Milton, *P. L.*, b. ix.

292. " But see, my Muse, if yet thy ravish'd sight
Can bear that blaze, that rushing stream of light,
Where the great hero's disencumber'd soul
Springs from the Earth to reach her native pole.
Boldly she quits th' abandoned cask of clay,
Freed from her chains, and towers th' ethereal way ;

329. Ilioneus seems to have been a good, wise, gentle, yet vigorous character (see *Æn.* i. v. 521; ix. 501, 569) ; possessed of a mind like that described by Ben Jonson in a graceful poem entitled " *The Picture of the Mind:*"

" Not swelling like the ocean proud,
But stooping gently, as a cloud,
As smooth as oil pour'd forth, and calm
As showers, and sweet as drops of balm.

A clan both sought, and with themselves
  desired 330
To link. But us the oracles of gods,
To search out thoroughly these lands of
  yours,
By their behests have forced. Hence
  Dardanus
Arose ; Apollo hither claims us back,
And hurries us with his sublime commands
To Tyrrhene Tiber, and the saintly streams
Of the Numician spring. He gives to
  thee,
Moreo'er, a former Fortune's trifling gifts,
Remnants recovered from a blazing Troy.
From this gold [cup] his sire Anchises used
To pour libations at the altars ; this 341
Was Priam's ornament, when he their rights
To summoned commons, in accustomed
  form
Would grant :—both sceptre, and the reverend cap,
And robes, the travail of the Ilian dames."
At such expressions of Ilioneus
Latinus keeps his features downward fixed
In gaze, and moveless to the ground he
  cleaves,
While rolling round his eyeballs on the
  stretch.
Neither the broidered purple moves the
  king, 350
Neither does Priam's sceptre move so much,
As o'er his daughter's spousal bonds and
  bed
He muses, and old Faunus' prophecy
Revolves within his bosom :—that this
  [prince],
Who from a foreign seat hath issued forth,
That son-in-law is by the fates foreshown,
And to the realm with equal auspices
Is summoned ; that to him a line will rise,
In prowess eminent, and one to grasp
The whole of earth by valor. He at last
Exclaims in gladness : " Prosper may the
  gods 361
Our undertakings, and their own presage !
That shall be granted, Trojan, that you
  list ;
Nor do I scorn the presents. Not to you,—
Latinus ruler,—breast of fruitful land,
Or wealth of Troy, lacking shall be found.
Let but Æneas, e'en his very self,—

" Smooth, soft, and sweet, in all a flood,
  Where it may run to any good ;
  And where it stays, it there becomes
  A nest of odorous spice and gums.
" In action, winged as the wind ;
  In rest, like spirits left behind
  Upon a bank, or field of flowers,
  Begotten by the wind and showers."
      Underwoods, iv. 15-17.

If such a deep affection for us there exists ;
If to be linked in hospitage he speeds,
And be entitled our ally,—arrive ; 370
Nor let him shudder at the looks of friends.
To me a portion will it be of peace
T' have touched the right hand of your
  prince. Do ye
In answer to your king my message now
Return. I have a daughter, whom to wed
With husband of our race, nor oracles
From my paternal shrine, nor prodigies,
Full many, from the sky allow : that here
Shall sons-in-law appear from foreign
  coasts,
That this remains for Latium, do they
  chant ;— 380
Who by their blood our reputation to the
  stars
May waft. That this is he [whom] fates
  demand,
I both imagine, and,—if aught of truth
My mind presages,—wish." These having
  said,
Coursers from all his stud the father culls :
Stood thrice a hundred, sleek in lofty stalls.
At once for all the sons of Teucer he
Commands in order to be led, caparisoned
In purple and embroidered trappings,
  [steeds]
Of wingy foot. Down dangling from their
  chests 390
Hang golden poitrells ; covered o'er with
  gold,
The yellow gold they champ beneath their
  teeth.
A chariot for Æneas absent, and in yoke
A pair [of horses] from celestial seed,
Fire puffing from their nostrils, of *their*
  strain,
Which cunning Circe, stealing from her
  sire,
Raised spurious from a substituted dam.
The comrades of Æneas, with such gifts
And sayings of Latinus, raised on high
Upon their steeds, return, and peace bring
  home. 400
But lo ! from the Inachian Argos back
Returning was the ruthless spouse of Jove,
And, wafted onward, occupied the air ;
When blithe Æneas and the Dardan fleet
From out the welkin in the distance she,
Even from Sicily's Pachynus, spied.
She sees that buildings they are rearing
  now,
Now trusting to the land ; that they their
  ships

371. Or :
" Nor friendly countenances let him dread."

Had quitted. Stung with poignant smart
 she stood :
Then, tossing to and fro her head, these
 words   410
Outpours she from her breast : "Ah !
 loathsome brood,
And fates of Phrygians to our fates op-
 posed !
Could they not on Sigean plains have fallen?
Could they not, captived, have been cap-
 tive led ?
Did not the blazing Troy its heroes burn?
Amidst the fights, and through the midst
 of fires,
A path they have discovered. But, I ween,
My deity at last exhausted lies,
Or I, with rancor glutted, have reposed.
Yea, even from their country shaken forth,
Throughout the billows I in spite have
 dared   421
To chase them, and to set my face against
The refugees all through the deep ; on
 Teucer's sons
Are squandered pow'rs alike of sky and sea.
What booted me the Syrts or Scylla? what
The vast Charybdis? They are lodged
 within
The Tiber's wished-for channel, uncon-
 cerned
At ocean and at me. The pow'r had Mars
To wreck the ruffian brood of Lapithæ ;
The sire of gods himself delivered up 430
The ancient Calydon to Dian's wrath ;—
What curse so direful either Lapithæ,
Or Calydon, deserving? But sooth I,
Jove's sovereign spouse, who naught un-
 tried could leave,
Ill-fortuned, who myself to every [plan]
Have turned, am by Æneas overmatched !
But if my godhead is not great enough,
I certes should not scruple to entreat
Whatever anywhere there be : if I

Can't bend the deities above, I'll rouse 440
The Ach'ron. Grant it will not be vouch-
 safed
To bar them from the Latin realms, and
 by the fates
Lavinia rests unchangeably his bride :
Yet 'tis allowed to stay it, and to heap
Impediments against such high events ;
Yet 'tis allowed the subjects of both kings
To ruin. At this cost of their own [friends],
Let sire-in-law and son-in-law unite.
With Trojan and Rutulian blood shalt thou
Be dowered, damsel, and Bellona thee 450
Awaits, thy bridesmaid ; nor, with torch
 impregned,
Hath nuptial fires Cisseis teemed alone :
Yea shall *her* birth the same to Venus
 prove,—
Another Paris e'en, and brands of death
Once more against the re-arising Troy."
 These words when she pronounced, she
 direful sought
The earth. Baleful Allecto from the seat

440, 1. See note on l. 418.

 " By the sulphureous damps,
That feed the hungry and incessant darkness,
Which curls around the grim Alastor's back,
Mutter again, and with one powerful word
I'll call an host up from the Stygian lakes,
Shall waft thee to the Acherontic fens ;
Where, chok'd with mists as black as thy im-
 postures,
Thou shalt live still a-dying."
 Fletcher, *The Fair Maid of the Inn*, iii. 1.

 " I can call spirits from the vasty deep."
 Shakespeare, 1 *King Henry IV.*, iii. 1.

450. " The greatest curse brave men can labour
 under
Is the strong witchcraft of a woman's eyes."
 Fletcher, *The Lover's Progress*, iv. 3.

452. So Henry VI. to Gloster (Richard III.) :
" And thus I prophesy,—that many a thousand,
Which now mistrust no parcel of my fear ;
And many an old man's sigh, and many a widow's,
And many an orphan's water-standing eye,—
Men for their sons', wives for their husbands' fate,
And orphans for their parents' timeless death,—
Shall rue the hour that ever thou wast born.
The owl shriek'd at thy birth, an evil sign ;
The night-crow cried, aboding luckless time ;
Dogs howl'd, and hideous tempest shook down
 trees ;
The raven rook'd her on the chimney's top,
And chattering pies in dismal discords sung.
Thy mother felt more than a mother's pain,
And yet brought forth less than a mother's hope."
 Shakespeare, 3 *King Henry VI.*, v. 6.

457. " Forth from this place of dread, Earth to appal
Three Furies rushed at the angels' call.
One with long tresses doth her visage mask,
Her temples clouding in a horrid cask :
Her right hand swings a brandon in the air,
While flames and terror hurleth every where ;
Pond'rous with darts, her left doth bear a shield,
Where Gorgon's head looks grim in sable field.

---

418. "*First Magician.* But we, that can
Command armies from hell for our design,
And blast him, now stand idle and benumb'd,
And shall grow here ridiculous statues ! I'll
Muster my fiends.

Second Magician. And if I have not lost
My power, the spirits shall obey, to drown
This straggler, and secure this threaten'd island.

Archimagus. Stay ! Which of you can boast
 more power than I ?
For every spirit you command, my spells
Can raise a legion. You know I can
Untenant hell, dispeople the wide air
Where, like innumerable atoms, the black genii
Hover, and jostle one another. All
That haunt the woods and waters, all i' the dark
And solitary chambers of the earth,
Break through their adamantine chains, and fly
Like lightning to my will."
 Shirley, *St. Patrick for Ireland*, i. 1.

Of the dread goddesses, and murk of hell,
She wakes; whose heart's [delight are]
    woeful wars,
And wrath, and stratagems, and harmful
    crimes.   460
E'en doth her very father Pluto hate,
Her hellish sisters hate, the fiend: she
    turns herself
Into so many visages, so fell her forms,
She burgeons grisly with so many snakes.
Whom Juno in these accents instigates,
And speaks the like: "To me vouchsafe
    this toil,
Thine own, O maiden sprung from Night,
    this task,—
That our respect or reputation, rent
In pieces, from their ground may not
    retreat;
Nor that the Æneadæ should have the
    power   470
To importune Latinus for the match,
Or gain a footing in Italian coasts.
Thou brethren, knit in soul, canst arm to
    frays,
And households rack with hatred: lashes
    thou
On dwellings, and the brands of death
    [canst] bring;

Thou hast a thousand names, a thousand
    arts
Of harming. Ransack thy prolific breast;
Dash into atoms their adjusted peace;
Sow crimes [the germs] of warfare; let
    the youth
Their weapons wish, and beg at once, and
    seize."   480
    Allecto then, with Gorgon poisons
    baned,
At first to Latium and the stately roofs
Of the Laurentine king repairs, and down
Upon Amata's silent threshold sat;
Whom, o'er th' arrival of the Teucer-host
And spousal [rights] of Turnus, as she
    flames,
Alike her woman-cares and spleen in fer-
    ment kept.
At her the goddess from her dingy locks
One serpent launches, and within her
    breast,
To her heart's core, she plunges it beneath;
That, madding with the monster, all the
    court   491
She may embroil. He, gliding 'tween her
    robes
And glossy breast, is rolled with contact
    none,
And 'scapes the raver, as he breathes
    within
An adder soul: becomes the lusty snake
Entwisted gold about her neck, becomes
A band of stretching fillet, and entwines
Her locks, and slimy strays throughout her
    limbs.
And while the first contagion, as it steals

Her eyes blaze fire and blood, each hair 'stills
    blood,
Blood thrills from either pap, and where she stood
Blood's liquid coral sprang her feet beneath;
Where she doth stretch her arm is blood and
    death."
    Drummond, *The Shadow of the Judgment*.
See note on l. 418.

458. Wagner's reading *dearum* (v. 324) seems to
have better authority than *sororum*, which Weise
adopts; but if the latter be preferred, the version
must be varied thus:
    "Of the dread Sisters, and the murk of hell."

461. "Soon as these hellish monsters came in sight,
    The Sun his eye in jetty vapours drown'd,
    Scar'd at such hell-hounds' view: Heaven's mazed
        light
    Sets in an early evening: Earth astound,
    Bids dogs with howls give warning: at which
        sound
    The fearful air starts, seas break their bound,
    And frighted fled away; no sands might them
        impound." P. Fletcher, *Purple Island*, xii. 39.

    "Think of thy sin;
    It is the heir-apparent unto hell,
    And has so many, and so ugly shapes,
    His father Pluto and the Furies hate
    To look on their own birth."

"Besides 'tis so abhorr'd of all that's good,
    That when this monster lifts his cursed head
    Above the earth, and wraps it in the clouds,
    The sun flies back, as loth to stain his rays
    With such a foul pollution; and night,
    In emulation of so black a deed,
    Puts on her darkest robe to cover it."
        Marmion, *The Antiquary*, iii. 1.

477. "Over their heads a black distemper'd sky,
    And through the air let grinning Furies fly;
    Charg'd with commissions of infernal date,
    To raise fell Discord and intestine Hate;
    From their foul heads let them by handfuls tear
    The ugliest snakes and best-lov'd favourites there;
    Then whirl them (spouting venom as they fall)
    'Mongst the assembled numbers of the hall;
    There into murmuring bosoms let them go,
    Till their infection to confusion grow;
    Till such bold tumults and disorders rise,
    As when the impious sons of Earth assail'd the
        threaten'd skies." Otway, *Windsor Castle*.

483. "Then with expanded wings he steers his
        flight
    Aloft, incumbent on the dusky air
    That felt unusual weight; till on dry land
    He lights, if it were land, that ever burn'd
    With solid, as the lake with liquid fire."
            Milton, *P. L.*, b. i.

489. Imitated by Cowley, where he makes Envy
take possession of Saul:
    "With that she takes
    One of her worst, her best-beloved snakes:
    'Softly, dear worm! soft and unseen,' said she,
    'Into his bosom steal, and in it be
    My viceroy.'"   *Davideis*, b. i.

P 2

With moistful poison, thrills her senses
  through,   500
And round her bones inweaves the flame;
  nor yet
Her mind throughout her bosom felt the
  fire;
In gentler strain, and in the customed
  mode
Of mothers, spake she, shedding many a
  tear
Over her daughter and the Phrygian match:
" To Trojan exiles is Lavinia given
[In marriage] to be led, O thou her sire?
Nor dost compassionate alike thy child,
And thy own self? Nor dost compas-
  sionate
A mother, whom the traitor will forsake
With the first northern breeze, a pirate-
  knave,   511
Seeking the depths,—the damsel carried off?
Sooth not on this wise doth the Phrygian
  swain
Pierce Lacedæmon, and hath borne away
Ledæan Helen to the Trojan towns!
Where is thy saintly faith? where old
  regard
For thy own [friends], and right hand
  deigned so oft
To kinsman Turnus? If a son-in-law 518
For the Latini from [some] foreign land
Is sought, and that is settled, and on thee
The mandates of thy father Faunus weigh;
Sooth every land, which independent lies
Distinct from sway of ours, a foreign [land]
I deem, and that the gods intend it thus.
E'en Turnus, if his family's first source
Be backward traced, hath Inachus,
Acrisius, too, his fathers, and [his town,]
Central Mycenæ." When by these her
  words
Latinus having vainly tried, she sees
That firm he stands opposed, and deep had
  sunk   530
Into her inwards the adder's rageful bane,
And wholly through her spreads; then
  sooth unblest,
By monster goblins roused, past wont she
  raves
Crazed through the boundless city: as at
  times,
A top that flies beneath the twisted thong,

Which striplings in a spacious ring, around
Unpeopled halls, in frolic earnest, ply:
It, driven by the whip, is borne along
In wheeling courses; o'er it stand amazed
The inexperienced and unbearded groups,
In admiration at the spinning box: 541
The lashes give it life. Than that career
No slower, she throughout the midst of
  towns,
And ruffian mobs is driven. Yea moreo'er,
Into the forests,—Bacchus' spirit feigned,—
Attempting deeper guilt, and deeper rage
Commencing, off she flies, and hides away
Her daughter in the mountains, rife in
  leaves,
That she may wrest the marriage from the
  sons
Of Teucer, and the [hymeneal] torches
  stay;   550
" Evoe Bacchus," screaming, yelling forth,
" That thou alone art worthy of the maid;
For that the tender ivy-shafts she takes
For thee, that thee she circles in the dance,
For thee she fosters her devoted hair."
The rumor flies; and, by the Furies fired
Within their bosom, drives the selfsame
  glow
The matrons all at once strange roofs to
  seek.
Their homes have they abandoned; to the
  winds
They give their necks and locks. But other
  [dames]   560
With thrilling shrieks the welkin fill, and
  wield
Vine-girdled lances, wrapped about in
  skins.
Herself among the midmost in her heat
A blazing pine upbears, and chants the
  match
Of Turnus and her daughter, rolling round
A blood-shot eye, and sudden fiercely
  cries:
" Ho! list ye Latin dames, where'er ye be:
If in your duteous spirits any love
For your unfortunate Amata dwells,
If some concernment for a mother's right

---

502. Or: " through her whole breast caught up the fire."

535. Surely this is no elegant comparison, though it cannot be more elegantly expressed. The idea of a queen racing about the town, like a whip-top, is ludicrous, if not mean. Shakespeare draws an illustration from school-boy sports, which is more dignified, and far more ingenious:

" In my school-days, when I had lost one shaft,
I shot his fellow of the selfsame flight
The selfsame way, with more advised watch,
To find the other forth; and by advent'ring both,
I oft found both: I urge this childhood proof,
Because what follows is pure innocence.
I owe you much; and, like a wilful youth,
That which I owe is lost: but if you please
To shoot another arrow that self way
Which you did shoot the first, I do not doubt,
As I will watch the aim, or to find both,
Or bring your latter hazard back again,
And thankfully rest debtor for the first."
      The Merchant of Venice, i. 1.

Deep preys upon you, loose your tressy
    bands,   571
Take up the orgy-rites along with me."
    Suchlike 'mid woods, 'mid wild beasts'
        lonely [lairs]
Allecto baits the queen on every side
With goads of Bacchus. When she seemed
    enough
First transports to have whetted, and the
    plan
And all Latinus' court o'erthrown; straight
    hence
The sullen goddess on her raven wings
Is wafted to the bold Rutulian's walls,—
Which city Danae is said t' have built 580
For her Acrisian settlers,—onward borne
Upon the sweepy southern gale. The spot
Was Ardea erst by our forefathers called ;
And Ardea still remains a noble name ;
But its prosperity is of the past.
Here Turnus in his stately palace now
In ebon night was snatching mid repose.
Allecto doffs grim face and rageful limbs ;
Transshapes her into haggish lineaments,
And scores her frowsy brow with wrinkles ;
    dons   590
Hoar tresses with a fillet ; then inweaves
A sprig of olive ; Calybe becomes
The priestess-crone of Juno and her fane,
And to the youth before his eyes herself
With accents these presents : "O Turnus,
    wilt thou bear
That toils so many should be spent in vain,
And that thy sceptre should be signed
    away
To Dardan emigrants? The king to thee
The match and dowry, purchased by thy
    blood,
Denies, and for his realm a foreign heir
Is sought. Go now! to thankless jeopardy
Expose thee, flouted [man]! the Tyrrhene
    ranks   602

---

584. If *tenet* be read with Wagner and Forbiger,
instead of *manet* (v. 412), the passage must be
altered thus:
    "Preserves a noble name."

585. Or: "hath passed away."

590. "These many ruts and furrows in thy cheek
    Proves thy old face to be but champion ground
    Tilled with the plough of age."
            Randolph, *Hey for Honesty*.
See Dyce's Middleton, ii. 73.
Like the crone which Gay describes in Fable 23,
Pt. i.:
    "A wrinkled hag, of wicked fame,
    Beside a little smoky flame
    Sat hovering, pinch'd with age and frost :
    Her shrivell'd hands, with veins emboss'd,
    Upon her knees her weight sustains,
    While palsy shook her crazy brains."

Lay prostrate ; shelter Latins by a peace.
These e'en to thee, while thou in still of
    night
Shouldst lie, th' all-powerful Saturnian
    [queen]
Herself hath bid me openly to speak.
Then rouse thee up! and that the youth be
    armed,
And from the gates marched out, thou,
    blithe at arms,
Make ready ; and the Phrygian chieftains,
    who
Have ta'en their station in the lovely flood,
And their bepainted barks to ashes burn.
The sovereign power of the heav'nly
    [gods]   612
Commands. Let king Latinus e'en him-
    self,—
Save that to grant the match, and with his
    word
Comply, he gives assurance,—Turnus feel,
And at the last make proof of him in arms."
    The youth, here jeering the divineress,
Thus op'ning words from lip in turn replies :
"The news, that ships to Tiber's wave are
    borne,
Hath not, as thou imaginest, escaped 620
Mine ears ; (forge not for me such great
    alarms ;)
Nor royal Juno mindless is of us.
But, crushed by dotage, and past bearing
    truth,
Thy eld, O mother, worries thee with cares
All idly, and amid the arms of kings
Mocks a divineress with phantom dread.
Thy province is, the statues of the gods,
And temples, to defend ; let wars and
    peace

---

623. "'Dotard,' said he, 'let be thy deepe advise ;
    Seemes that through many yeares thy wits thee
        faile,
    And that weake eld hath left thee nothing wise.'"
                Spenser, *F. Q.*, ii. 3, 16.

"But thou, since Nature bids, the world resign ;
'Tis now thy daughter's daughter's time to shine."
            Parnell, *Elegy to an Old Beauty*.

"I pardon thee th' effects of doting age ;
Vain doubts, and idle cares, and over-caution ;
The second non-age of a soul more wise ;
But now decay'd and sunk into the socket,
Peeping by fits, and giving feeble light."
            Dryden, *Don Sebastian*, v. 1.

624. "Thy brows and cheeks are smooth as waters
        be
When no breath troubles them : believe me, boy,
Care seeks out wrinkled brows and hollow eyes,
And builds himself caves to abide in them."
        Beaumont and Fletcher, *Philaster*, ii. 3.

Turnus seems scarce to have remembered that
"Who scorns at eld peels off his own young hairs."
            Ben Jonson, *Sad Shepherd*, ii. 2.

Men carry on, by whom should wars be waged."
At such his words Allecto into wrath 630
Blazed out. But in the stripling, as he speaks,
A sudden shiver seizes on his joints ;
Stiff stood his eyeballs: with so many snakes
The Fury hisses, and so dread a shape
Presents it['s form]. Then, rolling eyes of fire,
As falters he, and further [words] he seeks
To speak, she thrust him back, and lifted up
Twain serpents from her tresses, and her thongs
Made ring, and these subjoins with rageful mouth :
" Behold ! by dotage I am crushed, whom eld, 640
Past bearing truth, amid the arms of kings
Bemocks with phantom dread ! Look thou to these :
Here am I from the awful Sisters' seat ;
Battles and death I carry in my hand."
Thus having spoken, at the youth she launched
A brand, and, smoking with a sooty light,
Her torches fastened deep within his breast.
His sleep huge shudd'ring breaks, and bones and joints
Sweat, bursten forth from his whole body, bathes.
" Arms !" mad he yells ; for arms through couch and halls 650
He searches. Storms a passion for the sword,

635. " But she thereat was wroth, that for despight
The glauncing sparkles through her bever glared,
And from her eies did flash out fiery light,
Like coles that through a silver censer sparkle bright." Spenser, *F. Q.*, v. 6, 38.

645. " Some Fury,
From burning Acheron, snatch'd a sulphur brand,
That smok'd with hate, the parent of red murder,
And threw it in her bosom."
Massinger, *Parliament of Love*, v. 1.

650. " A horse ! a horse ! my kingdom for a horse !"
Shakespeare, *K. Richard III.*, v. 6.

651. " O save me from the tumult of the soul,
From the wild beasts within ! For circling sands,
When the swift whirlwind whelms them o'er the lands ;
The roaring deeps that to the clouds arise,
While through the storm the darting lightning flies ;
The monster brood to which this land gives birth ;
The blazing city and the gaping earth ;
All deaths, all tortures, in one pang combined,
Are gentle to the tempest of the mind."
Masinissa, in Thomson's *Sophonisba*, i. 5.

And cursèd rage for warfare ; wrath 'bove all :
As when with mighty din, a fire of twigs
Is laid beneath a surging caldron's sides,
And with the heat up leap the waters ; raves
The fluid's steamy tide within, and high
With foam o'erflows ; nor can the billow now
Contain itself ; flies sooty rack to air.
An expedition therefore to the king
Latinus, on the outrage done to peace, 660
Enjoins he on the chieftains of the youths,
And orders arms to be prepared to guard
Italia, from their bourns to oust the foe :
" That he is coming on, a match for both,
Both Teucer's sons and Latins." When these words
He uttered, and the gods to [share] his vows
He called, in rivalry the Rutuli
Cheer them to arms. This—rouses matchless pride
Of shape and youth ; that—his ancestral kings ;
Another—his right hand of brilliant deeds.
While Turnus fills the Rutuli with daring soul, 671
Allecto 'gainst the Trojans set herself
In nimble motion on her Stygian wings ;
With fresh manœuvre having spied the spot
Wherein upon the strand Iulus fair
With ambush, and in chase, the savage beasts
Was hunting. Here a sudden furiousness
Upon his hounds the maid of Cocyt darts,
And dews their nostrils with familiar scent,
That they in mettle might a hart pursue :
Which proved the leading cause of woes, and fired 681
The spirits of the peasantry for war.
The hart was of surpassing shape, and huge

672. So Drayton of " Mischief ;"
" She, with a sharp sight and a meagre look,
Was always prying where she might do ill,
In which the fiend continual pleasure took,
(Her starved body plenty could not fill)
Searching in every corner, every nook ;
With winged feet, too swift to work her will,
Furnish'd with deadly instruments she went,
Of ev'ry sort, to wound where so she meant.

" Having a vial fill'd with baneful wrath,
(Brought from Cocytus by that cursed sprite)
Which in her pale hand purposely she hath,
And drops the poison upon every wight."
The Barons' Wars, ii. 4-6.

682. " Now
Doth dogged war bristle his angry crest,
And snarleth in the gentle eyes of peace."
Shakespeare, *K. John*, iv. end.

With horns, which, ravished from the
   mother's pap,
The sons of Tyrrheus fostered, Tyrrheus,
   too,
Their sire, to whom the royal herds submit,
And far and wide the wardship of the
   plain
Is trusted. Him, accustomed to their sway,
Their sister Silvia, with a world of pains
His antlers interlacing with soft wreaths,
Was wont to trick them out, and comb the
   beast, 691
And wash him in the crystal spring. He,
   tolerant
Of hands, and to his master's table used,
Would wander in the forests, and again
To the familiar thresholds, of himself,
Betake him home, however late at night.
Him, straying far, Iulus' madding hounds,
As he is hunting, started up, what time
[The stag] by chance adown the fav'ring
   stream
Was floating, and upon the emerald bank
His heats assuaging. E'en himself, afire
With love of special praise, Ascanius,
   aimed 702
Shafts from his arching bow : nor was the
   god
Not present to his right hand as it swerves:
And, shot with mighty whizzing both along

The belly, and along the flank, careered
The arrow. But the wounded beast within
His well-known shelter homeward fled,
   and passed
Groaning beneath the cotes, and with his
   plaint, 709
Bloody and suitor-like, filled all the house.
First sister Silvia, smiting with her hands

706. Sackville introduces a wounded hart, to
illustrate the "griefe of conscynce:"
" Like to the dere that stryken with the dart
Withdrawes himselfe into some secrete place,
And feeling green the wound about his hart,
Startles with panges tyl he fall on the grasse,
And in great feare lyes gasping there a space,
Furth braying sighes as though eche pange had
   brought
The present death which he doeth dread so oft."
Complaynt of Henrye D. of Buckingham, st. 34.

Not very dissimilarly, Pope:
" What are the falling rills, the pendent shades,
The morning bowers, the evening colonnades,
But soft recesses for th' uneasy mind
To sigh unheard in to the passing wind !
So the struck deer, in some sequester'd part,
Lies down to die (the arrow in his heart) ;
There hid in shades, and wasting day by day,
Inly he bleeds, and pants his soul away."
                                A Fragment.

711. Silvia was as tender-hearted as the Prioresse
in the prologue to the Canterbury Tales:
" Of smale houndes hadde she, that she fedde
With rosted flesh, and milk, and wastel brede.
But wept she if on of hem were dede,
Or if men smote it with a yerde smert :
And all was conscience and tendre herte."
                                        Chaucer.

Thyrsis, in a Bucolic of Herrick's, is equally
miserable from a similar cause :
" I have lost my lovely steer,
That to me was far more dear
Than thee kine which I milk here ;
Broad of forehead, large of eye,
Party-colour'd like a pie,
Smooth in each limb as a die ;
Clear of hoof, and clear of horn,
Sharply pointed like a thorn ;
With a neck by yoke unworn,
From the which hung down by strings,
Balls of cowslips, daisy rings,
Interplac'd with ribbonings :
Pardon, Lacon, if I weep ;
Tears will spring where woes are deep."
Hesperides : Pastoral and Descriptive, x.

Andrew Marvell has a charming poem on the
like subject:
" The wanton troopers riding by,
Have shot my Fawn, and it will dye.
Ungentle men ! they cannot thrive,
Who kill'd thee. Thou ne'er didst alive
Them any harm : alas ! nor cou'd
Thy death yet do them any good."
" With sweetest milk and sugar first
I it at mine own fingers nurs'd ;
And as it grew, so every day
It wax'd more white and sweet than they."
" It is a wondrous thing, how fleet
'Twas on these little silver feet !

---

690. " At early dawn the youth his journey took,
And many a mountain pass'd and valley wide,
Then reach'd the wild ; where, in a flowery nook,
And seated on a mossy stone, he spied
An ancient man : his harp lay him beside.
A stag sprung from the pasture at his call,
And, kneeling, lick'd the wither'd hand that tied
A wreath of woodbine round his antlers tall,
And hung his lofty neck with many a flow'ret
   small." Beattie, Minstrel, b. ii. 25.

702. " But now the monarch murderer comes in,
Destructive man ! whom Nature would not arme,
As when in madness mischief is foreseen,
We leave it weaponless for fear of harme.

" For she defencelesse made him, that he might
Less readily offend ; but art armes all,
From single strife makes us in numbers fight ;
And by such art this royall stagg did fall.

" He weeps till grief does even his murd'rers pierce :
Grief which so nobly through his anger strove,
That it deserv'd the dignity of verse,
And had it words, as humanly would move.

" Thrice from the ground his vanquish'd head he
   rear'd,
And with last looks his forrest walks did view ;
Where sixty summers he had rul'd the heard,
And where sharp dittany now vainly grew :

" Whose hoary leaves no more his wounds shall
   heale ;
For with a sigh (a blast of all his breath)
That viewless thing, call'd life, did from him steale,
And with their bugle hornes they winde his
   death." Davenant, Gondibert, i. 2, 52-6.

Her arms, aid summons, and together calls
The sturdy peasants. They,—for skulked
   the plague
Grim in the stilly forests,—unforeseen
Are present; one with firebrand burnt at
   end
Equipped, one with the knots of weighty
   club:
Whate'er is found by each in narrow search,
Their anger makes a weapon. Tyrrheus
   calls   718

> With what a pretty skipping grace,
> It oft would challenge me the race;
> And when 't had left me far away,
> 'Twould stay, and run again, and stay.
> For it was nimbler much than hinds,
> And trod as if on the four winds.
> " I have a garden of my own,
> But so with roses overgrown,
> And lillys, that you would it guess
> To be a little wilderness;
> And all the spring-time of the year
> It only loved to be there.
> Among the beds of lillys I
> Have sought it oft, where it should lye;
> Yet could not, till itself would rise,
> Find it, although before mine eyes.
> For in the flaxen lillys' shade
> It like a bank of lillys laid.
> Upon the roses it would feed,
> Until its lips ev'n seem'd to bleed;
> And then to me 't would boldly trip,
> And print those roses on my lip.
> But all its chief delight was still
> On roses thus itself to fill;
> And its pure virgin limbs to fold
> In whitest sheets of lillys cold."
> " O help! O help! I see it faint
> And dye as calmly as a saint.
> See how it weeps! The tears do come,
> Sad, slowly, dropping like a gum.
> So weeps the wounded balsam; so
> The holy frankincense doth flow.
> The brotherless Heliades
> Melt in such amber tears as these."
>   *The Nymph complaining for the Death of
>   her Fawn.*

715. "Thus as he spoke, loe! with outrageous cry
A thousand villeins rownd about them swarmd
Out of the rockes and caves adioyning nye;
Vile caitive wretches, ragged, rude, deformd,
All threatning death, all in straunge manner armd;
Some with unweldy clubs, some with long
   speares,
Some rusty knives, some staves in fier warmd:
Sterne was their looke; like wild amazed steares,
Staring with hollow eies, and stiffe upstanding
   heares."   Spenser, *F. Q.*, ii. 9, 13.

718. So Spenser of the "salvage man," who
rescued Calepine:

" Yet armes or weapon had he none to fight,
Ne knew the use of warlike instruments,
Save such as sudden rage him lent to smite."
                                   F. Q., vi. 4, 4.

" Infernal discord, hideous to behold,
Hangs like its evil genius o'er the city,
And sends a snake to every vulgar breast,
From several quarters the mad rabble swarm,
Arm'd with the instruments of hasty rage,

His troops, as he by chance a four-cleft oak
Was splitting up with wedges driven home,
Breathing ferociously, with axe engrasped.
But the fell goddess, from her spying-place
The season for her mischief having gained,
Seeks the cote's lofty roofs, and from the
   crest
Of its ridge-height the shepherd-signal
   sings,
And on her winding horn her hellish voice
She strains: wherewith straight quivered
   every grove
And deep, deep forests rang. E'en heard
   it far
The lake of Trivia, heard it Nar, the stream
With sulph'rous water white, and Veline
   springs;   730
And anxious mothers folded to their breasts
Their children. Then, sooth, posting to
   the sound,
Wherewith the fearful horn its signal gave,
With weapons seized from every quarter,
   troop
The dauntless swains: yea too the Trojan
   youth
T' Ascanius aid outpour from open camp.
They marshalled have their lines. Not
   now in rustic fray
With sturdy clubs, or stakes with burning
   tipped,
'Tis fought; but they with doubtful steel
   engage,
And bristles far and near a darkling crop
Of swords unsheathed; and bronzes, sun-
   struck, gleam,   741

> And in confus'd disorderly array,
> Most formidable march: their differing clamors,
> Together join'd, compose one deaf'ning sound;
> ' Arm, arm,' they cry."
>   Rowe, *The Ambitious Stepmother*, act v. 9-17.

727. " My poor heart trembles like a timorous leaf,
Which the wind shakes upon his sickly stalk,
And frights into a palsy."
                Shirley, *The Brothers*, iv. 5.

Allecto's voice produced both effects.

731. Goldsmith uses the idea to illustrate the attachment of the Swiss for their mountain-homes:

" And as a child, when scaring sounds molest,
Clings close and closer to the mother's breast,
So the loud torrent, and the whirlwind's roar,
But bind him to his native mountains more."
                                      The Traveller.

741. " He spake: and, to confirm his words, out
   flew
Millions of flaming swords, drawn from the thighs
Of mighty Cherubim; the sudden blaze
Far round illumined Hell."
                          Milton, *P. L.*, b. i.

" The flights of whistling darts make brown the sky,
Whose clashing points strike fire, and gild the
   dusk." Dryden, *Troilus and Cressida*, v. 2.

And fling their radiance underneath the clouds:
As when a billow with the rising gale
Begins to whiten, by degrees the sea
Uprears itself, and higher lifts its waves;
Then tow'rs to heaven from its deepest bed.
A stripling here, before the battle's front,
With whizzing arrow, who of Tyrrheus' sons
Was eldest, Almo low is laid; for clave
Beneath his throat the bolt, and choked with blood   750
The passage of his moistful voice, and life
Of thread. [Falls] many a corse of warriors round,
And elderly Galæsus, while himself
He offers mediator for a peace;
Who was the one most righteous man [of all],
And erst the richest in Ausonia's fields.
Five flocks of bleating ones to him, five herds,
Came home, and earth with hundred ploughs he turned.
Now whilst these [deeds] are going on throughout
The plains,—impartial Mars,—the goddess, made   760
Mistress of her engagement, when with blood
The warfare she imbrued, and set abroach
The deaths of their first fight, Hesperia quits,
And, turned away along the gales of heaven,
In triumph Juno speaks with haughty tone:
" Lo! stablished for thee by a rueful war,
Disunion! Say, for friendship let them meet,
And leagues compact! Since I with Auson blood
Have dewed the Trojans, this I e'en thereto
Will add, if I may have thy sure assent:
The neighbor cities by reports will I   771
To battles drive, and fire their souls with love
Of madding Mars, that they all round for aid
May come; throughout the fields I'll scatter arms."
Then Juno in reply: " Of frights and guile
There is an overflow. [Firm] stand the grounds
For warfare; with their weapons hand to hand
Are they engaged. The arms, which chance first gave,
Their maiden blood hath dyed. Such marriages,
And such connubial rites, let solemnise   780
The peerless son of Venus, and the king
Latinus' self. That thou o'er airs of heaven
With further liberty shouldst range, wills not
That father, of most high Olympus lord:
Off from [these] regions! I, if any [change Of] fortune in my toils remains, will set it straight
Myself." Such words Saturnia spoke. But she
Uplifts her pinions, hissing with their snakes,
And seeks Cocytus' seat, forsaking heights
Aloft. There is a spot 'mid Italy,   790
Beneath the lofty mountains, of renown,
And blazoned by report in many a coast,—
Amsanctus' glens. This, dark with clustered leaves,
A forest's side confines on either hand,
And, brawling in the midst, a flood gives forth

" The setting sun,
With yellow radiance, lightened all the vale;
And, as the warriors moved, each polished helm,
Corslet, or spear, glanced back his gilded beams.
The hill they climbed, and, halting at its top,
Of more than mortal size, towering, they seemed
An host angelic, clad in burning arms."
      Home, *Douglas*, iv. 1.

755. " So spake the seraph Abdiel, faithful found
Among the faithless, faithful only he:
Among innumerable false unmoved,
Unshaken, unseduced, unterrified,
His loyalty he kept, his love, his zeal;
Nor number, nor example, with him wrought
To swerve from truth, or change his constant mind,
Though single."   Milton, *P. L.*, b. v. end.

759. " Now,"—*atque*, v. 540,—see Wagner, Quæs. Virg. 35, 22.

760. " This battle fares like to the morning's war,
When dying clouds contend with growing light:
What time the shepherd, blowing of his nails,
Can neither call it perfect day nor night.
Now sways it this way, like a mighty sea,
Forc'd by the tide to combat with the wind;
Now sways it that way, like the selfsame sea
Forc'd to retire by fury of the wind:
Sometime, the flood prevails; and then, the wind:
Now, one the better; then, another best;
Both tugging to be victors, breast to breast,
Yet neither conqueror, nor conquered:
So is the equal poise of this fell war."
  Shakespeare, 3 *King Henry VI.*, ii. 5.

---

788.   " At last his sail-broad vans
He spreads for flight, and in the surging smoke
Uplifted spurns the ground; thence many a league,
As in a cloudy chair, ascending rides,
Audacious; but, that seat soon failing, meets
A vast vacuity. All unawares,
Fluttering his pennons vain, plumb down he drops
Ten thousand fathom deep."
      Milton, *P. L.*, b. ii.

A din from rocks and writhing eddy. Here
The fearful cave and vents of grisly Dis
Are shown, and from the bursten Acheron
A vasty whirlpool opes its plagueful jaws;
Whereinto the Erinys being plunged,—
The loathly fiend,—discumbered earth and
    heaven.   801
  Nor less the meanwhile the Saturnian
    queen
Upon the warfare sets a crowning hand.
Rush from the battle to the city all
The host of shepherds, and the slain bring
    back,
Young Almo, and the marred Galæsus'
    form;
And sue the gods, Latinus too conjure.
Turnus is present, and amid the charge
Of murder, and their heat, the horror he
Redoubles:—"That the Teucri to the
    realm   810
Were summoned; that the Phrygian brood
    was blent
With them; that he was banished from the
    court."
Then they, whose mothers, ecstasied by
    Bacchus,

797. Glover has a fine description of the Cave of the Furies:

                "Around it slept
A stagnant water, overarch'd by yews,
Growth immemorial, which forbade the winds
E'en to disturb the melancholy pool.
To this, the fabled residence abhorr'd
Of Hell-sprung beings, Demonax, himself
Predominating demon of the place,
Conducts the sev'n assassins. There no priest
Officiates; single there, as Charon grim,
A boatman wafts them to the cavern's mouth.
They enter, fenc'd in armour; down the black
Descent, o'er moist and lubricated stone,
They tread unstable. Night's impurest birds
With noisome wings each loathing visage beat;
Of each the shudd'ring flesh through plated steel
By slimy efts, and clinging snakes, is chill'd;
Cold, creeping toads beset th' infected way."
                      Athenaid, b. xiv.
See note on *Æn.* vi. *l.* 336.

800. "So saying he dismiss'd them: they with speed
Their course through thickest constellations held,
Spreading their bane. The blasted stars look'd wan,
And planets, planet-struck, real eclipse
Then suffer'd. Th' other way Satan went down
The causey to Hell-gate. On either side
Disparted Chaos overbuilt exclaim'd,
And with rebounding surge the bars assail'd,
That scorn'd his indignation: through the gate,
Wide open and unguarded, Satan pass'd
And all about found desolate."
                      Milton, *P. L.*, b. x.

813.   "Down they rush
From Nysa's vine-empurpled cliff, the dames
Of Thrace, the Satyrs, and the unruly Fauns,
With old Silenus, reeling through the crowd
Which gambols round him, in convulsions wild

In dances caper in the wayless woods,—
For not unweighty was Amata's name,—
From every quarter mustered, coalesce,
And importune for Mars. Straight all
    cursed war,
In spite of omens, spite of oracles
Of gods, heav'n's pleasure set aside, de-
    mand.
In rivalry the palace of the king   820
Latinus they beset. He, as a rock
Of sea unstirred, withstands them: like
A rock of sea, when comes a thund'ring
    crash,
The which, with many a billow baying
    round,
Maintains itself by its own weight: the cliffs
And foamy rocks are roaring round in vain,
And, dashed against its side, the ocean-weed
Is showered back. But when no pow'r is
    given
Their resolution blind to overrule,
And at fell Juno's beck events proceed;
The father, earnestly attesting gods   831
And empty gales, cries: "Welaway! we're
    crushed
By destinies, and overborne by storm!
Ye shall yourselves with sacrilegious blood
Pay these amercements, O unhappy [men].
Thee, Turnus, impious wretch, thee shall
    abide
Sore punishment, and thou with vows too
    late

Tossing their limbs, and brandishing in air
The ivy-mantled thyrsus, or the torch
Through black smoke flaming, to the Phrygian
    pipe's
Shrill voice, and to the clashing cymbals, mix'd
With shrieks and frantic uproar."
      Akenside, *Hymn to the Naiads*, 283-99.

821. "So have I seen a rock's heroic breast,
Against proud Neptune, that his ruin threats,
When all his waves he hath to battle prest,
And with a thousand swelling billows beats
The stubborn stone, and foams, and chaffs, and
    frets,
To heave him from his root, unmoved stand;
And more in heaps the barking surges band,
The more in pieces beat, fly weeping to the
    strand."
    G. Fletcher, *Christ's Triumph over Death*, xxiii.

            "All your attempts
Shall fall on me like brittle shafts on armour,
That break themselves; or waves against a rock,
That leave no sign of their ridiculous fury
But foam and splinters."
        Massinger, *The Fatal Dowry*, v. 2.

826. "A place there is, where proudly rais'd there
    stands
A huge aspiring rock, neighb'ring the skies,
Whose surly brow imperiously commands
The sea his bounds, that at his proud feet lies;
And spurns the waves, that in rebellious bands
Assault his empire, and against him rise."
              Daniel, *Civil War*, ii. 48.

The gods shalt worship. For to me my rest 838
Is gained, and wholly in the threshold [lies]
The haven ; of a happy death I'm robbed."
Nor speaking further, he himself shut up
Within the dome, and left the reins of state.
There was a custom in Hesperian Latium,
The which, from that day ever forth, the towns
Of Alba holy have observed, now Rome
Observes it, noblest of [created] things,—
When Mars arouse they to the opening fights ;
Or be it on the Getæ they prepare
To wage with might a tear-deserving war,
Or on Hyrcanians, or the Arab [tribe]s ; 850
Or 'gainst the Inds to march, and track the Dawn,
And standards from the Parths to redemand.
Two gates there are of War,—so call they them
By name,—from rev'rence hallowed, and the awe
Of Mars ferocious: shut them hundred bolts
Of bronze, and iron's deathless strength ; nor stirs

The guardian Janus from the threshold. These,—
When with the fathers rests a fixed resolve
For fight, himself in Quirine " trabea,"
And Gabine cincture, badged,—the grating doors,— 860
Unbars the consul ; he himself proclaims
The battles ; follows then the other youth,
And bronzen trumpets with a hoarse accord
Together blast. Then in this fashion e'en
Against the Æneads was Latinus pressed
War to declare, and open back the gates
Of sorrow. From their touch the father shrank,
And, turned aloof, the loathsome service fled,
And buried him within the darkling gloom.
Then, gliding down from heav'n, the queen of gods 870
The lagging portals forced her very self
With her own hand, and on their wheeling hinge
War's iron-banded gates Saturnia brast.
Burns, unaroused and moveless hitherto,
Ausonia. Some afoot prepare to march
Along the plains ; some, high on stately steeds,
Dust-covered storm : all arms demand.
Some—furbished shields and sheeny javelins scour
With oily lard, and whet upon the hone
Their battle-axes, and it joys to bear 880
The standards, and to hear the bray of trumps.

---

838. " I am a weak old man, so poor and feeble,
That my untoward joints can scarcely creep
Unto the grave, where I must seek my rest."
Ford, *The Lover's Melancholy*, v. end.
" These eyes, like lamps whose wasting oil is spent,
Wax dim, as drawing to their exigent ;
Weak shoulders, overborne with burd'ning grief,
And pithless arms, like to a wither'd vine,
That droops his sapless branches to the ground !—
Yet are these feet, whose strengthless stay is numb,
Unable to support this lump of clay,
Swift-winged with desire to get a grave,
As witting I no other comfort have."
Shakespeare, 1 *King Henry VI.*, ii. 5.

840. Thus losing the end of Pomfret's desires:
" Then I'd not be with any trouble vex'd,
Nor have the evening of my days perplex'd ;
But by a silent and a peaceful death,
Without a sigh, resign my agèd breath."
The Choice, end.

And Goldsmith's touching hopes :
" In all my wand'rings round this world of care,
In all my griefs,—and God has giv'n my share,—
I still had hopes my latest hour to crown,
Amid these humble bow'rs to lay me down ;
To husband out life's taper at the close,
And keep the flame from wasting by repose."
Deserted Village.

He was much in the position of Macbeth :
" Had I but died an hour before this chance,
I had liv'd a blessed time ; for, from this instant,
There's nothing serious in mortality :
All is but toys ; renown, and grace is dead ;
The wine of life is drawn, and the mere lees
Is left this vault to brag of."
Shakespeare, *Macbeth*, ii. 3.

871. " Thus saying, from her side the fatal key,
Sad instrument of all our woe, she took ;
And, towards the gate rolling her bestial train,
Forthwith the huge portcullis high updrew ;
Which, but herself, not all the Stygian powers
Could once have moved : then in the keyhole turns
The intricate wards, and every bolt and bar
Of massy iron or solid rock with ease
Unfastens. On a sudden open fly
With impetuous recoil and jarring sound
The infernal doors, and on their hinges grate
Harsh thunder, that the lowest bottom shook
Of Erebus." Milton, *P. L.*, b. ii.

875-81. " Ther mayst thou see devising of harneis
So uncouth and so riche, and wrought so wele
Of goldsmithry, of brouding, and of stele ;
The sheldes brighte, testeres, and trappures :
Gold-hewen helmes, hauberkes, cote-armures ;
Knightes of retenue, and eke squieres,
Nailing the speres, and helmes bokeling,
Gniding of sheldes, with lainers lacing :
Ther as nede is, they weren nothing idel :
The fomy stedes on the golden bridel
Gnawing, and fast the armurers also
With file and hammer priking to and fro ;
Yemen on foot, and communes many on
With shorte staves, thicke as they may gon ;
Pipes, trompes, nakeres, clariounes,
That in the bataille blowen blody sounes."
Chaucer, *Knightes Tale.*

E'en five great cities on their anvils reared
New forge them arms,— the powerful Atine,
And Tiber haughty, Ardea, and the sons
Of Crustumeria, and, with turrets crowned,
Antemnæ. Cov'rings for their heads secure
They hollow, and of withes bend wicker-
　work
For bucklers ; others cuirasses of bronze,
Or burnished greaves of pliant silver, mould.
To this the pride of share and pruning-hook,
To this all passion for the plough, gave
　way :　　　　　　　　　　　　　　891
The falchions of their fathers they recast
In forges. And the trumpets now ring
　forth ;
The watchword, sign for battle, passes on.
His helm one [warrior] seizes from the roofs
In anxious haste ; another to their yokes
Drives on his neighing steeds, and in a
　shield,
And, triply laced with gold, a habergeon,
Is dight, and belted with a trusty sword.
　Now open Helicon, O goddesses,　　900
And quicken ye my lays :—·what kings by
　war
Were roused, what brigads, following each,
　filled up
The champaign ; with what warriors even
　then
Bloomed Italy's boon land, with weapons
　what
It blazed : for ye alike remember, maids
Divine, and can recount them : scarce to us
The subtle breath of legend steals along.
　The foremost enters on the battle, fierce
From Tyrrhene coasts, despiser of the gods,
Mezentius, and his troops he arms. His son
Next to him, Lausus, [one] than whom none
　else
Was fairer, save Laurentine Turnus' form :
Lausus, steed-tamer, and the vanquisher 913
Of savage beasts, from Agyll's city leads,
That vainly followed him, a thousand men ;
　worthy
T' have been more happy in a father's rule,
And not Mezentius to have had his sire.
　Next these, along the herbage, marked
　　by palm,
His chariot, and his conq'ring steeds dis-
　plays,

Sprung from fair Hercules, fair Aventine ;
And on his scutcheon wears his father's
　badge,　　　　　　　　　　　　　921
A hundred snakes, and Hydra, adder-girt :
Whom in a wood on Aventinus' hill
The priestess Rhea, hidden in his birth,
Brought into being 'neath the climes of
　light,—
A woman intermingled with a god,—
As soon as,—Geryon slain,—Laurentine
　fields
The conquering Tirynthius reached, and
　bathed
His Spanish heifers in the Tuscan flood.
They javelins in their hands and felon pikes
For battles bear, and fight with slender
　blade　　　　　　　　　　　　　931
And lance Sabellian. He himself, afoot,
A lion's monstrous cov'ring winding round,
In fearful shag unkempt, with snowy tusks
Accoutred on his head, thus passed inside
The royal palace, bristling, and engirt
Around his shoulders with Herculean garb.
　Then brothers twain the walls of Tiber
　　leave,
The nation from their brother Tiber's name
Entitled,—e'en Catillus and fierce Coras,—
　youth　　　　　　　　　　　　　940
Of Argos, and before the battle's van,
Amid the thick of arms, are borne along :
As when two cloud-engendered Centaurs
　swoop
Down from [some] mount's high summit,
　Homole
And snowy Othrys in their fleet career
Forsaking : yields to them as they ad-
　vance
The spacious forest, and the bushy shrubs
Retire before them with a thund'ring crash.
　Nor absent was the founder of the town
Præneste, whom hath every age believed
Of Vulcan sired, 'mong rural folks a prince,
And on the hearth discovered,—Cæculus.
Him does a peasant host from far and near
Accompany, e'en heroes, who the tall　954
Præneste, and who Gabine Juno's fields,
And icy Anio, and the Hernic rocks,
With runnels dewy, haunt ; whom thou
　dost feed,
O rich Anagnia, whom sire Amasene.
For all of these do neither arms, nor shields,
Or chariots, clang : the greatest part sling
　balls　　　　　　　　　　　　　960
Of bluish lead ; some wield a pair of darts
In hand, and tawny caps of wolf-skin wear,
Screen for the head : their left foot-soles
　unshod

909.　　　" The immortal powers
　Protect a prince, though sold to impious acts,
　And seem to slumber till his roaring crimes
　Awake their justice ; but then, looking down,
　And with impartial eyes, on his contempt
　Of all religion, and moral goodness,
　They, in their secret judgments, do determine
　To leave him to his wickedness, which sinks him,
　When he is most secure."
　　　　　Massinger, *The Roman Actor*, iii. 1.

924. That is, of course : "in clandestine birth."

Messapus next, steed-tamer, Neptune's son,
Whom it was not allowed to mortal man,
Either by fire or steel, to overthrow,
His clans long while inactive, and his hosts
Unused to war, calls suddenly to arms,
And takes in hand again the falchion.
These— 970
Fescinnia's bands and low Falisci; those
Hold Soract's summits and Flavinian fields,
And, with its mount, the lake of Ciminus,
And groves Capenian. In their number matched
They marched, and sang their monarch: as at times
The snowy swans among the calmy clouds,
What time from feeding they betake them home,
And through their lengthful necks melodious notes
Give forth; the river rings and Asia's mere,
Far stricken. Nor would any deem that bands, 980
Bronze-armed, of such a mighty host were blent,
But from the deepsome gulf a skyey cloud
Of screaming birds was hurried to the shores.
  Lo! Clausus, from the Sabines' ancient blood,
Leading a mighty host, and he himself
Great as a mighty host, from whom is now
Both Claudian tribe and family dispread
Through Latium, since for share hath Rome been given
To Sabines. [Marches forth] along with him
A num'rous Amiternan band, and old 990
Quirites, of Eretum all the band,
And of the olive-rife Mutusca; who
Nomentum['s] city, who the Rosean fields
Of the Velinus, who the rugged cliffs
Of Tetrica, and mount Severus, and
Casperia haunt, and Foruli, and flood
Of the Himella; they who Tiber drink
And Fabaris; they whom chilly Nursia sent,
And Horta's hosts, and Latin clans, and those

---

964. *Instituere* (v. 690) is plainly an aorist.
975. " At which command the Powers militant
   That stood for Heaven, in mighty quadrate join'd
  Of union irresistible, moved on
  In silence their bright legions, to the sound
  Or instrumental harmony, that breathed
  Heroic ardour to adventurous deeds
  Under their godlike leaders."
                         Milton, *P. L.*, b. vi.

Whom Allia sev'ring, — luckless title!—
flows between: 1000
As many as the surges that are rolled
Upon the surface of the Libyan sea,
When gruff Orion in the wintry waves
Is hid; or when at early sun are parched
The serried ears, or on the Hermus' plain,
Or Lycia's golden fields. Their targes ring,
And by the tramp of feet the earth is scared.
  Next, [of the line] of Agamemnon, foe
Of Troja's name, Halesus in his car
His coursers yokes, and on to Turnus hastes
A thousand gallant tribes: who Massic [fields], 1011
In Bacchus fruitful, with their harrows turn;
And whom th' Auruncan sires from lofty hills,
And near the Sidicinian plains, despatched;
And those who Cales quit, and borderer
By Volturn's shoaly river, and alike
The rough Saticulan, and Osci's bands.
Their weapons slender javelins be; but these
It is their fashion with elastic strap
To fit. Their left hands does a target screen; 1020
In close encounter they have hookèd swords.
  Nor in our lays shalt they unmentioned pass,
O Œbalus, whom Telon on the nymph
Sebethis to have sired is said, what time
He Capreæ, the Teleboans' realms,
Possessed, now elderly: but e'en the son,
Not satisfied with his paternal fields,
Held even then far-wide beneath his sway
The tribes of the Sarrastes, and the plains
Which Sarnus dews, and they who occupy
Rufræ, and Batulum, and Celenna's fields,
And whom the apple-rife Abella's walls
O'erpeer: in Teuton fashion are they used
Their shafts to hurl; the cov'rings for whose heads— 1034
The rind from off the cork-tree reft; and gleam
Their bronzen bucklers, gleams their sword of bronze.
  Thee, too, the mount-fraught Nersæ to the frays
Despatched, O Ufens, famous in renown
And happy arms; whose nation, passing wild,
And used to constant hunting of the woods,
Was the Æquiculan with stubborn clods.
In arms they work the earth, and it delights 1042
To bring together booty ever fresh,
And live by plunder. And moreo'er there came

From the Marruvian clan a priest, with leaf
And blessèd olive o'er his helmet trimmed,
By the commission of his prince Archippus,
Thrice-gallant Umbro; who on adder brood,
And hydras breathing noisomely, was wont
To sprinkle slumbers both with charm and hand,   1050
And lull their wrath, and ease their bites with skill.
But not to salve the Dardan spear-point's blow
Had he the virtue; neither booted him
Against his wounds enchantments, bringing sleep,
And simples, gathered in the Marsian mounts.
Anguitia's woodland thee, thee Fucinus
With glassy wave, thee crystal meres, bewept.

1051. Music produces the same effect on man as on beast: at least, so the poets say. Shakespeare and Dryden have been already quoted; Congreve thus:

" Music alone with sudden charms can bind
  The wandering sense, and calm the troubled mind.
Begin the powerful song, ye sacred Nine,
  Your instruments and voices join;
Harmony, peace, and sweet desire,
  In every breast inspire.
Revive the melancholy drooping heart,
And soft repose to restless thoughts impart.
  Appease the wrathful mind,
  To dire revenge and death inclin'd:
With balmy sounds his boiling blood assuage,
And melt to mild remorse his burning rage.
'Tis done; and now tumultuous passions cease;
  And all is hush'd, and all is peace.
The weary world with welcome ease is blest,
  By music lull'd to pleasing rest."
                            Hymn to Harmony.

1056, 7. " Lament, ye nymphs, and mourn, ye wretched swains;
Stray, all ye flocks, and desert be, ye plains;
Sigh, all ye winds, and weep, ye crystal floods;
Fade, all ye flowers, and wither all ye woods.
I mourn Pastora dead: let Albion mourn,
And sable clouds her chalky cliffs adorn."
              Congreve, *The Mourning Muse of Alexis.*

" A spring, now she is dead! of what? of thorns,
Briers and brambles? thistles, burs, and docks?
Cold hemlock, yew? the mandrake, or the box?
Did not the whole earth sicken when she died?
As if there since did fall one drop of dew,
But what was wept for her? or any stalk
Did bear a flower, or any branch a bloom,
After her wreath was made? In faith, in faith,
You do not fair to put these things upon me,
Which can in no sort be: Earine,
Who had her very being and her name,
With the first knots or buddings of the spring,
Born with the primrose and the violet,
Or earliest roses blown; when Cupid smiled,
And Venus led the Graces out to dance,
And all the sweets and flowers in Nature's lap
Leap'd out, and made their solemn conjuration,
To last but while she lived! Do not I know

Marched, too, the offspring of Hippolytus,
Thrice lovely, to the battle, Virbius, whom,
A noble [soul], his mother Aricia sent,
Reared in Egeria's groves, the reeking banks   1061
Around, where, unctuous and appeaseable,
The altar of Diana [stands]. For they
Report in legend that Hippolytus,
As soon as by a stepdame's craft he fell,
And glutted by his blood his sire's revenge,
To atoms torn by his bewildered steeds,
To empyrean stars again, and 'neath
The upper gales of heaven, came, recalled
By sovereign simples and Diana's love.
Thereon th' almighty father, in his wrath
That any mortal from the shades below
Should to the light of life arise, himself
The Phœbus-sired inventor of such salve
And craft, with levin-bolt to Stygian waves
Hurled down. But Trivia, boon, Hippolytus   1076
Incloisters in sequestered cells, and him
To nymph Egeria and her grove consigns,
Where solitary in Italian woods
Unnoted he might pass his life, and where
By change of name he Virbius might be.
Whence also from the fane and hallowed groves   1082
Of Trivia horn-hoofed horses are debarred;
For that upon the shore the car and youth
They, scared at ocean-monsters, overturned.
The son upon the surface of the plain
Plied not a whit the less his fiery steeds,
And in his chariot to the battles rushed.

How the vale wither'd the same day? How Dove,
Dean, Eye, and Erwash, Idel, Snite, and Soare,
Each broke his urn, and twenty waters more,
That swelled proud Trent, shrunk themselves dry? that since
No sun or moon, or other cheerful star
Look'd out of heaven, but all the cope was dark,
As it were hung so for her exequies!
And not a voice or sound to ring her knell;
But of that dismal pair, the screeching owl,
And buzzing hornet! Hark! hark! hark! the foul
Bird! how she flutters with her wicker wings!
Peace! You shall hear her screech."
              Ben Jonson, *The Sad Shepherd*, i. 2.

1085. So the Souldan's horses, at sight of the light issuing from Prince Arthure's shield:

" Such was the furie of these headstrong steeds
Soon as the infants sunlike shield they saw,
That all obedience both to words and deeds
They quite forgot, and scornd all former law:
Through woods, and rockes, and mountaines, they did draw
The yron charet, and the wheeles did teare,
And tost the Paynim without feare or awe;
From side to side they tost him here and there,
Crying to them in vaine that nould his crying heare."   Spenser, *F. Q.*, v. 8, 41.

Himself among the van, of passing shape,
Turnus is all in motion, grasping arms,
And by a head entire above them stands:
On whom, all hairy with a triple crest,
A lofty morion a Chimæra props,   1093
Ætnean blazes puffing from her jaws:
The louder she, and wilder with her baleful fires,
The fiercer wax the frays with gushing blood.
Moreo'er an Io, with uplifted horns,
His glossy buckler badged with gold, [she] now
With hair thick-covered, now a heifer,—brave
Device!—and Argus guardian of the maid,
And, pouring from a graven urn his stream,
Her father Inachus. There follows on
A cloud of footmen, and the scutcheoned hosts   1103
Are thronged throughout the plains, e'en Argive youth,
And the Auruncan bands, the Rutuli,
And old Sicanians, and Sacranian files,
And with their painted shields Labici; who
Thy glades, O Tiberine, and holy marge
Of the Numicius plough, and work with share
The hills of Rutuli, and Circe's crest:
Over which fields Anxurian Jove presides,   1111
And, joying in her holy grove of green,

Feronia, where lies Satura's black wash,
And icy through the valley-beds a path
The Ufens seeks, and in the sea is hid.
Besides these, from the Volscian clan arrived
Camilla, leading on a troop of horse,
And hosts in bloom of bronze, a warrioress.
Not to Minerva's distaff or her frails
Was she accustomed with her lady hands,
But battles sore, a maiden, to endure,   1121
And in career of feet t' outstrip the winds.
She, or on topmost stalks of standing corn,

1113. *Saturæ palus* may possibly mean the "Pontine Marshes."

"When o'er this world, by equinoctial rains
Flooded immense, looks out the joyless Sun,
And draws the copious steam; from swampy fens,
Where putrefaction into life ferments,
And breathes destructive myriads: or from woods,
Impenetrable shades, recesses foul,
In vapours rank and blue corruption wrapt,
Whose gloomy horrors yet no desperate foot
Has ever dared to pierce; then, wasteful, forth
Walks the dire power of pestilent Disease.
A thousand hideous fiends her course attend,
Sick nature blasting, and to heartless woe,
And feeble desolation, casting down
The towering hopes and all the pride of man."
Thomson, *Summer*.

1114. "The fruitful valleys laced with silver rills."
Browne, *Brit. Past.*, b. ii. s. 3.

1122. "Softly gliding as I go,
With this burthen full of woe,
Through still silence of the night
Guided by the glow-worm's light,
Hither am I come at last.
Many a thicket have I past;
Not a twig that durst deny me,
Not a bush that durst descry me
To the little bird that sleeps
On the tender spray; nor creeps
That hardy worm with pointed tail,
But if I be under sail,
Flying faster than the wind,
Leaving all the clouds behind,
But doth hide her tender head
In some hollow tree, or bed
Of seeded nettles; not a hare
Can be started from his fare
By my footing; nor a wish
Is more sudden; nor a fish
Can be foynd with greater ease
Cut the vast unbounded seas,
Leaving neither print nor sound,
Than I, when nimbly on the ground
I measure many a league an hour."
J. Fletcher, *The Faithful Shepherdess*, iv. 2.

"How like the nimble winds, which play upon
The tender grass, yet press it not, or fly
Over the crystal face of smoothest streams,
Leaving no curl behind them; or the tide
The yellow-feather'd Hymen when he treads
Upon the air's soft bosom, doth she pass,
Observ'd with admiration! Why, she makes
Motion the god of every excellence."
Beaumont and Fletcher, *The Faithful Friends*, iv. 3.

1092. Smart, describing William the Conqueror:
"Like a god,
Refulgent stood the conqueror: on his troops
He sent his looks enliv'ning as the sun's,
But on his foes frown'd agony and death.
On his left side in bright emblazonry
His falchion burn'd; forth from his sevenfold shield
A basilisk shot adamant; his brow
Wore clouds of fury: on that with plumage crown'd
Of various hues sat a tremendous cone:
Thus sits high-canopied above the clouds,
Terrific beauty of nocturnal skies,
Northern Aurora: she thro' th' azure air
Shoots, shoots her trem'lous rays in painted streaks
Continual, while waving to the wind
O'er Night's dark veil her lucid tresses flow."
The Hop-Garden, b. i.

1100. "In vaine he fears that which he cannot shonne:
For who wotes not that womans subtiltyes
Can guylen Argus, when she list misdonne?
It is not yron bandes, nor hundred eyes,
Nor brasen walls, nor many wakefull spyes,
That can withold her wilfull-wandring feet:
But fast goodwill, with gentle courtesyes,
And timely service to her pleasure meet,
May her perhaps containe that else would algates fleet."
Spenser, *F. Q.*, iii. 9, 7.

Untouched, would fly, nor in her race had harmed

1124. " Here she was wont to go! and here! and here!
Just where those daisies, pinks, and violets grow:
The world may find the spring by following her;
For other print her airy steps ne'er left.
Her treading would not bend a blade of grass,
Or shake the downy blow-ball from his stalk!
But like the soft West-wind she shot along,
And where she went the flowers took thickest root,
As she had sow'd them with her odorous foot."
　　　　　　　Ben Jonson, *Sad Shepherd*, i. 1.

" Love's wings so justly heave
The body up, that as our toes shall trip
Over the tender and obedient grasse,
Scarce any drop of dew is dasht to ground."
　　　　　　　Marston, *Sophonisba*, iv. 1.

" I've seen him run swifter than starting hinds,
Nor bent the tender grass beneath his feet:
Swifter than shadows fleeting o'er the fields;

Their tender ears; or through the central main,
Poised on the heaving wave, would wend her way,
Nor in its surface dip her nimble soles.
Her all the youth, from houses and from fields
Outpoured, and crowd of dames, in wonder view,
And towards her gaze, while marching, open-mouthed,　　　　　　1130
With thunder-stricken minds;—how royal pride
Of purple drapes her glossy shoulders; how
A pin of gold her hair together binds;
Her Lycian quiver how she bears herself,
And shepherd-myrtle, headed with a point.

Nay, even the winds, with all their stock of wings,
Have puffed behind, as wanting breath to reach him."　　　　Lee, *Rival Queens*, ii. 1.

BOOK VIII.

WHEN Turnus hoisted up the flag of war
From the Laurentine castle, and the trumps
With grating clangor brayed, and when he roused
His mettled steeds, and when he brandished arms;
Forthwith excited are their souls: at once
All Latium bands together by an oath
In wild unrest, and storms the frantic youth.
The leading generals, Messapus [e'en]

Line 1. " Then straight commands, that at the warlike sound
Of trumpets loud and clarions be uprear'd
His mighty standard. That proud honour claimed
Azazel as his right, a cherub tall;
Who forthwith from the glittering staff unfurl'd
The imperial ensign; which, full high advanced,
Shone like a meteor streaming to the wind,
With gems and golden lustre rich emblazed,
Seraphic arms and trophies; all the while
Sonorous metal blowing martial sounds:
At which the universal host up sent
A shout, that tore Hell's concave, and beyond
Frighted the reign of Chaos and old Night.
All in a moment through the gloom were seen
Ten thousand banners rise into the air
With orient colours waving: with them rose
A forest huge of spears; and thronging helms
Appear'd, and serried shields in thick array,
Of depth immeasurable." Milton, *P. L.*, b. i.

3. " The trumpet, with its Mars-inciting voice
The wind's broad breast impetuous sweeping o'er,
Fill'd the big note of war."
　　　　　　　Glover, *On Sir Isaac Newton*.

And Ufens, and, despiser of the gods,
Mezentius, muster aid from every side,　10
And of the tillers rob the spacious fields.
E'en to the city of great Diomede
Is Venulus commissioned, to entreat
His aid, and,—that in Latium Teucer's sons
Were settling down, Æneas in his fleet
Arrived, and his defeated household-gods
Was bringing in, and giving out that he
Was by the destinies the king required,—
To give him information,—and that many a state
To the Dardanian hero link themselves,
And far and wide through Latium that his name　　　　　　　21
Is waxing great. By these beginnings what
Designs he, what, if Fortune should attend,
The issue of the contest he desires,
More clearly to himself than to the king
Turnus, or king Latinus, [must] appear.
Through Latium such: which as he fully sees,
The hero [of] Laomedontian [line]
Is wav'ring in a mighty tide of cares,
And now to this side, now to that, he shifts
His active spirit, and to sundry points　31

31. " Faster than spring-time showers, comes thought on thought;
And not a thought but thinks on dignity."
　　　　　Shakespeare, 2 *K. Henry VI.*, iii. 1.

He hurries it, and whirls it round through all :
As when within the water's bronzen lips
The dancing light, rebounded from the sun,
Or from reflection of the beaming moon,
Through every region flutters far and near;
And now beneath the air is glanced aloft,
And strikes the ceiling of the highest roof.
'Twas night, and jaded forms of life thro'out

33. " I shook for fear, and yet I danced for joy;
I had such motions as the sun-beams make
Against a wall, or playing on a water,
Or trembling vapour of a boiling pot,—
That's not so good ; it should have been a crucible
With molten metal : she had understood it."
Ben Jonson, *The Staple of News*, ii. 1.

Parnell has a beautiful image, in illustration of an idea not very dissimilar:

" His hopes no more a certain prospect boast,
And all the tenor of his soul is lost:
So when a smooth expanse receives imprest
Calm Nature's image on its watery breast,
Down bend the banks, the trees depending grow,
And skies beneath with answering colours glow :
But if a stone the gentle sea divide,
Swift ruffling circles curl on every side,
And glimmering fragments of a broken sun,
Banks, trees, and skies, in thick disorder run."
The Hermit.

See P. Fletcher's *Purple Island*, c. v. 47.

" A spacious lake below expanded lies,
And lends a mirror to the quiv'ring skies.
Here pendent domes, there dancing forests seem
To float and tremble in the waving gleam."
Langhorne, *Studley Park.*

The water in the text is said to have " bronzen lips," as the edges of the vessel, which confines it, are of bronze. *Sole* (v. 23) is the image of the Sun.

39. " The curfew tolls the knell of parting day,
The lowing herd wind slowly o'er the lea,
The ploughman homeward plods his weary way,
And leaves the world to darkness and to me.

" Now fades the glimmering landscape on the sight,
And all the air a solemn stillness holds,
Save where the beetle wheels his droning flight,
And drowsy tinklings lull the distant folds:

" Save that, from yonder ivy-mantled tower,
The moping owl does to the moon complain
Of such as, wandering near her secret bower,
Molest her ancient solitary reign."
Gray, *Elegy*, 1-3.

" 'Tis night, dead night, and weary Nature lies
So fast, as if she never were to rise.
No breath of wind now whispers through the trees,
No noise at land, nor murmur in the seas ;
Lean wolves forget to howl at night's pale noon,
No wakeful dogs bark at the silent moon,
Nor bay the ghosts that glide with horror by,
To view the caverns where their bodies lie.
The ravens perch, and no presages give,
Nor to the windows of the dying cleave ;
The owls forget to scream ; no midnight sound
Calls drowsy Echo from the hollow ground.
In vaults the walking fires extinguish'd lie ;
The stars, heav'n's sentries, wink and seem to die:
Such universal silence spreads below,
Through the vast shades where I am doomed to go."
Lee, *Theodosius*, v. 2, 1-16.

All lands, the race of fowls and flocks, deep sleep
Enthralled : when sire Æneas on the bank,
And underneath the vault of icy heav'n,
In bosom troubled by the rueful war,
Lay down, and through his limbs gave late repose.
To him the Genius of the place himself,
[The god] of Tiber, from his charming stream,
In years advanced, among the poplar leaves

" Come, sleep, O sleep! the certain knot of peace,
The baiting-place of wit, the balm of woe,
The poor man's wealth, the prisoner's release,
Th' indifferent judge between the high and low."
Sir Philip Sidney, *Astrophel and Stella*, xxxix.

" The drowsy night grows on the world, and now
The busy craftsman and o'erlabour'd hind
Forget the travel of the day in sleep:
Care only wakes, and moping pensiveness;
With meagre discontented looks they sit,
And watch the wasting of the midnight taper.
Such vigils must I keep, so wakes my soul,
Restless and self-tormented."
Rowe, *Jane Shore*, ii. 3-10.

44. " But gentle Sleepe envyde him any rest ;
Instead thereof sad sorow and disdaine
Of his hard hap did vexe his noble brest,
And thousand fancies bett his ydle braine
With their light wings, the sights of semblants vaine."
Spenser, *F. Q.*, iii. 4, 54.

" Here silken slumbers and refreshing sleepe
Were seldom found ; with quiet mindes those keepe,
Not with disturbed thoughts ; the beds of kings
Are never prest by them : sweet rest inrings
The tyred body of the swarty clowne,
And oft'ner lies on flocks than softest downe."
Browne, *Britannia's Pastorals*, ii. song 1.

" When night bids Sleep,
Sweet nurse of nature, o'er the senses creep,
When Misery herself no more complains,
And slaves, if possible, forget their chains,
Though his sense weakens, though his eyes grow dim,
The rest, which comes to all, comes not to him.
E'en at that hour Care, tyrant Care, forbids
The dew of sleep to fall upon his lids,
From night to night she watches at his bed ;
Now, as one mop'd, sits brooding o'er his head ;
Anon she starts, and, borne on raven's wings,
Croaks forth aloud,—'Sleep was not made for kings.'"
Churchill, *Gotham*, b. iii.

The friends of Æneas might here have wished for him what Valentinian's attendants desired for their emperor:

" Care-charming Sleep, thou easer of all woes,
Brother to Death, sweetly thyself dispose
On this afflicted prince ; fall, like a cloud,
In gentle showers ; give nothing that is loud
Or painful to his slumbers ; easy, sweet,
And as a purling stream, thou son of Night,
Pass by his troubled senses ; sing his pain,
Like hollow murmuring wind or silver rain :
Into this prince gently, oh, gently slide,
And kiss him into slumbers like a bride."
J. Fletcher, *Valentinian*, v. 2.

Appeared to lift him up,—with sea-green
    garb
Fine lawn enveloped him, and shady reed
His tresses veiled;—then to accost him thus,
And take away his troubles by these words:
  "O gendered from the race of gods,
    thou who   52
Dost Troja's city from her foes restore
To us, and everlasting Pergamus
Dost guard; O looked-for on Laurentine
    ground
And Latin fields, here [lies] for thee assured
Thy home, assured Penates; shrink thou
    not,
Nor be affrighted by the threats of war:
All spleen and wrath of gods have passed
    away.
And now by thee,—lest thou shouldst deem
    that sleep   60
Shapes these its baseless [visions],—found
    beneath
The holms upon my bank, a monstrous sow,
That has produced a brood of thirty young,
Shall lie, white, on the ground reclining,
    white
Around her dugs the litter; this shall prove
Thy city's site; this, rest assured from toils:
From which [event] within thrice ten re-
    turning years
Ascanius shall the city Alba build,
Of glorious name. No doubtful [truths] I
    chant.
Now by what means what presses on may'st
    thou   70
In triumph execute, in [words] a few,—
Give heed,—I thee will teach. Arcadia's
    sons
In these our coasts,—a race from Pallas
    sprung,
Who [following] king Evander as his
    mates,
Who following on his banners, have a site
Selected, and upon the mountains built
A city, Pallanteum, from the name
Of Pallas their progenitor,—these war
Unceasingly protract with Latium's race:
These to thy camp adjoin as thine allies,
And leagues compact. I thee will lead
    myself   81

Along my banks and runnel straight, that
    thou
The tide opposing mayest with thy oars,
Upborne, surmount. Come, rouse thee,
    goddess-born!
And when first stars are setting duly bring
Thy prayers to Juno, and her wrath and
    threats
By humble vows o'ercome. A conqueror
To me shalt thou pay homage. I am he,
Whom thou descriest with a brimming
    flood
Grazing the banks, and sev'ring fruitful
    tilths,   90
The azure Tiber, to the heav'ns a stream
Thrice welcome. Here to me a stately fane,
The head of lofty cities, towers forth."

88. This patronage of Æneas by father Tiber
was plainly not quite a disinterested affair (see
lines 92, 3): his civilities had partly their origin in
vanity, as those of the river-god in Fletcher's
Faithful Shepherdess were due to another selfish
cause:
  " I am this fountain's god: below
    My waters to a river grow,
    And 'twixt two banks with osiers set,
    That only prosper in the wet,
    Through the meadows do they glide,
    Wheeling still on every side,
    Sometimes winding round about,
    To find the evenest channel out.
    And if thou wilt go with me,
    Leaving mortal company,
    In the cool streams shalt thou lie,
    Free from harm as well as I.
    I will give thee for thy food
    No fish that useth in the mud;
    But trout and pike, that love to swim,
    Where the gravel from the brim
    Through the pure streams may be seen;
    Orient pearl fit for a queen
    Will I give, thy love to win,
    And a shell to keep them in:
    Not a fish in all my brook
    That shall disobey thy look;
    But, when thou wilt, come sliding by,
    And from thy white hand take a fly:
    And, to make thee understand
    How I can my waves command,
    They shall bubble whilst I sing,
    Sweeter than the silver string."   Act iii. 1.

89. " O, could I flow like thee, and make thy
    stream
My great example, as it is my theme!
Though deep, yet clear; though gentle, yet not
    dull;
Strong without rage, without o'erflowing full."
This celebrated allusion to the Thames, in Sir
John Denham's *Cooper's Hill*, is imitated by Prior,
speaking of the same river:
  " Serene, yet strong; majestic, yet sedate;
    Swift without violence, without terror great."
                                Carmen Seculare.
Even Hamilton must copy it, when writing an
Inscription on a Dog:
  " Calm, though not mean; courageous without
    rage;
    Serious, not dull, and without thinking sage."

---

51.   " She bids you
  Upon the wanton rushes lay you down,
  And rest your gentle head upon her lap,
  And she will sing the song that pleaseth you,
  And on your eyelids crown the god of sleep,
  Charming your blood with pleasing heaviness;
  Making such difference 'twixt wake and sleep,
  As is the diff'rence betwixt day and night,
  The hour before the heav'nly-harness'd team
  Begins his golden progress in the east."
        Shakespeare, 1 *K. Henry IV.*, iii. 1.

The River spoke; then in a pool profound
He plunged him, diving to its bed. The
    night
And sleep Æneas left: he rises up,
And as he gazes on the dawning beams
Of th' empyrean sun, in hollow hands
The water duly from the flood upbears,
And such-like words outpours to heav'n:
"O Nymphs, 100
Laurentine Nymphs, whence streams have
    birth, and thou,
O father Tiber, with thy holy tide,
Receive Æneas, and do ye at last
From dangers screen him. In whatever
    spring
Thy lake holds thee, who dost compassion
    feel
For our misfortunes; from whatever ground
In fullest beauty thou art gushing forth;
Aye with my homage, ever with my
    gifts,
Shalt thou be honored, O horn-bearing
    flood,
Lord of Hesperian waters. O be thou 110
But present, and more nigh to me confirm
Thy heav'nly intimations!" Thus he
    speaks,
And galleys twain of double bank he culls
From out the navy, and with oarage fits:
The same time furnishes the crews with
    arms.
But lo! an unexpected, and to view
A wondrous omen:—fair along the wood,
Like-hued with her white offspring, down
    there lay,
And on the bank of green is spied, a sow:
Which good Æneas sooth to thee, to thee
Slays, sovereign Juno, off'ring holy rites,
And places at thy altar with her brood. 122
Tiber that night, however long it proves,
His swelling river calmed, and, tiding back
With noiseless billow, so he came to rest,
That he, in fashion of a gentle plash
And stilly fen, might lay his surface low
Upon the waters, so that from the oar
Might strain be absent. Therefore they
    their course,
Commenced, speed forward with a cheering
    shout. 130
Glides through the streams the ointed fir;
    and waves
Are wond'ring, wonders th' unaccustomed
    grove
At shields of warriors gleaming from afar,
And painted galleys swimming on the flood.
They with their rowing night alike and day
Tire out, and lengthful reaches overpass,
And are by sundry trees imbowered, and
    thread
The verdant forests on the surface calm.
The sun the central circle of the sky
Had scaled, ablaze, what time from far the
    walls, 140
And castle, and the houses' scattered roofs,
Do they behold, which now the Roman power
Hath matched with heaven: then the
    scant domains
Evander held. They speedily their prows
Veer towards them, and the city they ap-
    proach.

And not a bynding ozyer bow'd his head,
But on his roote him bravely carryed:
No dandling leafe plaid with the subtill ayre,
So smooth the sea was, and the skye so fayre."
    Browne, *Britannia's Pastorals*, ii. 1.

" Calm were the elements, night's silence deep,
    The waves scarce murmuring, and the winds
    asleep." Dryden, *Absalom and Achitophel*.

125. " Either side
Was fenc'd by trees high-shadowing. The front
Look'd on a crystal pool, by feather'd tribes
At ev'ry dawn frequented. From the springs
A small redundance fed a shallow brook,
O'er smoother pebbles rippling just to wake,
Not startle Silence, and the ear of Night
Entice to listen undisturb'd."
    Glover, *Leonidas*, b. ii.

140. " Mark, how th' all-kindling orb
Meridian glory gains!
Round Meru's breathing zone he winds oblique
O'er pure cerulean plains:
His jealous flames absorb
All meaner lights, and unresisted strike
The world with rapt'rous joy and dread.
Ocean, smit with melting pain,
Shrinks, and the fiercest monster of the main
Mantles in caves profound his tusky head,
With sea-weeds dank and coral spread.
Less can mild Earth and her green daughters bear
The Moon's wide wasting glare:
To rocks the panther creeps; to woody night
The vulture steals his flight;
E'en cold cameleons pant in thickets dun,
And o'er the burning grit th' unwinged locusts
    run." Sir William Jones, *Hymn to Surya*.

---

124. " Quoth he: 'Slide billows smoothly for her
    sake,
Whose sight can make your aged Nereus young,
For her fair passage even alleys make,
And as the soft winds waft her sails along,
Sleek ev'ry little dimple of the lake,
Sweet Sirens, and be ready with your song.'"
    Drayton, *Barons' Wars*, iii. 47.

" Here waxt the windes dumbe (shut up in their
    caves),
As still as midnight were the sullen waves,
And Neptune's silver ever-shaking brest
As smooth as when the halcyon builds her nest.
None other wrinckles on his face were seene
Than on a fertile meade, or sportive greene,
Where never plow-share ript his mother's wombe,
To give an aged seed a living tombe:
Nor blinded mole the fatning earth e'er stirr'd,
Nor boyes made pitfals for the hungry bird.
The whistling reeds upon the water's side
Shot up their sharp heads in a stately pride,

By chance that day a yearly sacrifice
The Arcad king t' Amphitryon's great son,
And to the gods, was off'ring up before
The city in a grove. Along with him
Pallas his son, along with him were all
The foremost of the youths, and humble
   senate,   151
Presenting frankincense; and milk-warm
   blood
Was steaming at the altars. When tall ships
They saw, and that amid the shady grove
They towards them stole, and leaned on
   noiseless oars;
They're startled by the sudden sight, and
   all,—
The boards abandoned,—in a body rise.
Whom gallant Pallas to break off the rites
Forbids, and, with a weapon seized, himself
To meet them flies, and from a knoll afar:
" O youths, what cause hath forced you to
   essay   161
Our unknown pathways? Whither are ye
   bound?"
He cries: " Who [are you by] your race?
   Wherefrom,
Your home? Is't peace ye hither bring, or
   arms?"
Then sire Æneas from the lofty stern

---

156. So Spenser beautifully describes Colin's astonishment at the first sight of a ship (see note *Æn.* v. *l.* 854):

" For, as we stood there waiting on the strond,
Behold, an huge great vessell to us came,
Daunicng upon the waters back to lond,
As if it scornd the daunger of the same:
Yet was it but a wooden frame and fraile,
Glewed together with some subtile matter.
Yet had it armes and wings, and head and taile,
And life to move itselfe upon the water.
Strange thing! how bold and swift that monster was,
That neither car'd for wynd, nor haile, nor raine,
Nor swelling waves, but thorough them did passe
So proudly, that she made them roare againe."
   Colin Clouts Come Home Again.

T. Warton's swain is as much astonished as Pallas and his companions:

" Sudden a burst of brightness smote my sight,
From arms and all th' imblazonry of war
Reflected far, while steeds, and men, and arms
Seem'd floating wide, and stretch'd in vast array
O'er the broad bosom of the big-swoln flood
That dashing roll'd its beamy waves between.
The banks promiscuous swarm'd with thronging
   troops;
These on the flood embarking, those appear'd
Crowding the adverse shore, already past.
All was confusion, all tumultuous din.
I trembled as I look'd, tho' far above,
And in one blaze their arms were blended bright
With the broad stream, while all the glist'ring scene
The morn illum'd, and in one splendour clad."
   Eclogue iv.

Thus speaks, and from his hand holds out
   a branch
Of peaceful olive: " Sons of Troy, and
   arms
Unfriendly to the Latins, dost thou see;
Whom they by overbearing war have driven
To exile. We Evander seek. Bear these,
And tell him that Dardania's chosen chiefs
Have come, entreating for a league of
   arms."   172
Amazed was Pallas, at so great a name
Deep-struck: " O disembark, whoe'er thou
   art,"
Saith he, " and face to face my sire address,
And pass beneath our dwellings as a guest;"
And by the palm he caught him, and right
   hand
Engrasping, clung thereto. As on they
   paced,
The grove they enter, and the river quit.
Æneas then the king with friendly words
Accosts: " O best of Grecia's sons, to
   whom   181
Hath Fortune willed that I should offer
   prayer,
And stretch before me boughs with fillet
   trimmed;
In sooth I have no apprehension felt,
For that thou [wert] a leader of the Greeks,
An Arcad also, and that from thy root
With Atreus' double offspring thou wert
   linked;
But me my merit, and the holy oracles
Of gods, and kindred fathers, thy renown
Noised through the lands, have knit to
   thee, and brought   190
By fates, a willing [suitor]. Dardanus,
Of Ilium's city the primeval sire
And founder, from Electra, (as the Greeks
   report,)
Of Atlas daughter sprung, to Teucer's sons
Is wafted; gave Electra to the light
The highest Atlas, who the balls of heaven
Upon his shoulder props. You have for sire

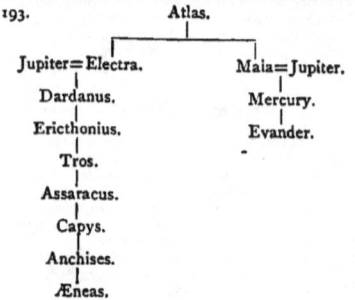

193.

Mercurius, whom, conceived, fair Maia bore
On Cyllene's icy crest ; but Maia, if at all
Repose we trust in [legends we have] heard,
Atlas, the self-same Atlas, sires, he who
The constellations of the sky upholds. 202
Thus branches off the pedigree of both
From the one blood. Relying upon these,
Not [through] ambassadors, nor through address,
Have I first proofs of thee devised : myself,
Myself, and my own life, have I myself
Exposed, and come a suitor to thy courts.
The selfsame Daunian clan, that pesters thee
With felon war, if us they may expel, 210
Believe that naught is lacking, but that they
May all Hesperia wholly bring beneath
Their yoke, and hold the sea, which doth above,
And that which doth below against it wash.
Receive, and grant us, troth. There be with us
Breasts bold in war ; there be [brave] souls,
And youth in actions tried." Æneas said.
The other on the speaker's face and eyes,
And his whole person with his eye long since
Kept poring. Then he thus few [words] returns : 220
" How thee, O gallantest of Teucer's sons,
I welcome, and delighted recognize !
How I thy mighty sire Anchises' words,
And voice, and visage, recollect ! For I
Remember that in visiting the realms
Of Hesione his sister, Priamus,
The offspring of Laomedon, in quest
Of Salamis, came farther on to see
Arcadia's icy bourns. Then dawn of youth
My cheeks was mantling over with its bloom ; 230
And I with wonder gazed upon the chiefs
Of Teucer's sons ; I gazed with wonder, too,
On th' offspring of Laomedon himself :
But statelier than all Anchises walked.
My spirit burned with youthful love t' accost
The hero, and to link right hand to right.
I went up to him, and in eagerness
'Neath Pheneus' walls I led him. He to me
A noted quiver and its Lycian shafts,

---

235. " Pardon, dread princess, that I made some scruple
To leave a valley of security,
To mount up to the hill of majesty,
On which, the nearer Jove, the nearer lightning.
What knew I, but your grace made trial of me ;
Durst I presume to embrace, where but to touch
With an unmanner'd hand, was death ? The fox,
When he saw first the forest's king, the lion,
Was almost dead with fear ; the second view
Only a little daunted him ; the third,
He durst salute him boldly."
    Massinger, *The Virgin-Martyr*, i. 1.

At his departure gave, a mantle too, 240
With gold inwove, and twain gold bits, which now
My Pallas hath. Then both,—that which ye seek,—
Right hand by me united is in league ;
And soon as ever shall to-morrow's dawn
Restore her to the lands, with succor I
Will send you blithe away, and with my means
Will help. Meanwhile these holy [rites],
—since ye
Have hither come as friends, — [these] yearly [rites],
Which to delay were crime, do ye observe
In kindness with us, and yourselves e'en now 250
Accustom to the boards of your allies."
When these were said, the viands and the cups,
Which were withdrawn, he bids to be replaced,
And he himself upon a turfy seat
The men disposes, and distinguished by a cushion
And hide of shaggy lion, he receives
Æneas, and invites him to a throne
Of maple. Then choice youths in rivalry,
And th' altar-priest, bear roasted flesh of bulls,
And heap in baskets labored Ceres' gifts,
And Bacchus they purvey. Æneas feasts,
And with him Troja's youth, upon the chine
And cleansing inwards of a solid ox. 263
  As soon as hunger was removed, and checked
Desire of eating, king Evander saith :
" Not these our yearly [rites] on us, these feasts
In customed form, this altar of a power
So mighty, hath a superstition vain,
And heedless of the ancient gods, enjoined :
From cruel dangers saved, O Trojan guest,
Perform we them, and honors earned renew. 271
Now firstly, poised on crags, this rock behold :
How are the masses scattered far abroad,
And stands forlorn the mansion of the mount,
And cliffs have trailed a vasty wreck !
Here stood
A cave, withdrawn within a huge recess,
Which the half-human Cacus' awful shape
Would occupy, by sunbeams unapproached :

---

277. Or, taking *semihominis* in its physical meaning—a doubtful view—
" Which the dread shape of Cacus, half a man."

And aye with murder fresh the ground was warm,
And, pinned upon the prideful gates, the heads
Of men hung ghastly with their rueful gore.
This monster's sire was Vulcan : of that [sire]
The sooty flames disgorging from his mouth,
With giant bulk he moved him on. Time brought
To us, too, at the last, as fain we wished,
The succor and arrival of a god.
For th' arch-avenger with the death and spoils
Of triple Geryon proud, Alcides, came,
And conqu'ror drove this way his monster bulls :
Beeves occupied alike the vale and stream.
But Cacus' spirit, through the furies wild,
Lest aught there had been or of crime, or craft,
Unhazarded or unessayed, four bulls
Of peerless figure from the grounds drives off,
As many heifers of surpassing shape ;
And these,—lest any footmarks lie with hoofs
Direct,—dragged towards the cavern by the tail,
And, hurried with their tracks upon the paths
Reversed, he hid within the gloomy rock.
No traces for the searcher cave-ward led.
Meanwhile when now his satiated droves
Amphitryo's son was shifting from their grounds,
And making ready a retreat, the beeves
At their departure low, and all the wood
Was filled with plaints, and with their cry the hills
Were quitted. Of the kine did one return
The sound, and bellowed 'neath the monster den,
And balked the hope of Cacus [though] injailed.
Here sooth Alcides' choler had blazed out
In frenzies from his inky gall. He grasps
His weapons in his hand and [club of] oak,
Weighted with knots, and at full speed he seeks
The skyish mountain heights. Then first our men
Saw Cacus quailing, and in eyes dismayed.

Straight posts he fleeter than the eastern gale,
And seeks the cave : Fear lent his feet her wings.
Soon as he shut him up, and, when the chains
Were brast, he lowered down the monstrous stone
Which hung thro' iron and his father's skill,
And strengthened with a bar, secured the doors :
Lo ! storming in his soul Tirynthius came,
And, every inlet scanning, to and fro
He flung his glances, gnashing with his teeth.
Thrice, hot with anger, scans he the whole mount
Of Aventinus ; thrice the rocky gates,
Essays in vain ; thrice, weary, in the vale
Sat down. There stood a pointed [cliff of] flint,—
The rocks cut sheer on every quarter,—o'er
The cavern's chine uprising, to be seen
Of passing height, for nests of boding birds
Meet homestead. This, as beetling with its crest,
'Twas leaning towards the river on the left,
He on the right, against it straining, shook,
And, loosened, wrenched from out its deepest roots ;
Then suddenly thereto an impulse gave ;
With which his impulse in its length and breadth
Peals Æther, leap apart the banks, and back
The river runs affrighted. But the den,
And royal court of Cacus, stript of roof,
Appeared enormous, and the shady vaults
Lay open deep within : not otherwise
Than if by any power deep within
Should yawning earth unlock her hellish homes,
And ghastly realms reveal, by gods abhorred,
And from above the hideous pit be kenned,
And Manes shudder at the light let in.

280

292

302

312

320

331

341

311. "But for that damn'd magician, let him be girt
With all the grisly legions that troop
Under the sooty flag of Acheron ;
Harpies and Hydras, or all the monstrous forms
'Twixt Africa and Ind,—I'll find him out,
And force him to return his purchase back,
Or drag him by the curls to a foul death,
Curs'd as his life." Milton, *Comus.*

316. Spenser has the same idea in more places than one :
"Thereto fear gave her wings, and need her courage taught." *F. Q.*, iii. 7, 26.
"It needlesse was to bid the flood pursue ;
Anger gave wings."
  Browne, *Britannia's Pastorals,* ii. 3.
"*Mistrust* now wing'd his feet, then raging ire,
'For speede comes ever lamely to desire.'"
  Ibid. ii. 4.

346. Dryden plainly borrows the idea, to illustrate the mischief done to ships by a cannonade ; *Annus Mirabilis,* 128 :
"Their open'd sides received a gloomy light,
Dreadful as day let into shades below."

v. 247—266. *BOOK VIII.* v. 266—285. 231

Therefore, surprised in unexpected day
Upon a sudden, and injailed inside
The hollow rock, and raising wontless roars,
Alcides whelms him from above with darts,
And every weapon summons to [his aid],
And him with stocks and monster stones
he plies. 352
But he,—for neither is there furthermore
Now any flight from danger,—from his jaws
Prodigious smoke,—a marvel to be told,
Spews forth, and wraps his home in blinding murk,
The eyes of view bereaving, and enspheres
Within the den a smoky night,—with fire
The darkness blent. Alcides brooked it not
In passion, and himself e'en through the fire
He flung with headlong spring, where thickest smoke 361
Its billow drives, and with a pitchy cloud
The vasty cavern waves. He Cacus here
In darkness, idle burnings spewing, grasps,
Twisting him to a knot, and grappling screws
His started eyeballs, and his blood-dry throat.
Forthwith is opened, with its doors wrenched off,
The grisly dwelling; and the stolen kine,
And plunder oath-denied, are to the heaven
Displayed, and by the feet the shapeless corse 370
Is dragged abroad. Their hearts cannot be cloyed
By poring o'er the fearful eyes, the face, and breast,

With bristles shaggy, of the demi-brute,
And at the blazes quenched within his jaws.
Thenceforward is the worship solemnised,
And glad posterity have kept the day;
Potitius, too, the leading founder was,
And, guardian of the rite to Hercules,
Pinarius' house. This altar in the grove
He reared, which ever ' Greatest ' shall be called 380
By us, and which shall greatest ever be.
Then come, O youths, do ye, in sacrifice
For such high merits, with the leaf enring
Your tresses, and the cups in your right hands
Stretch forth, and call upon our common god,
And wines present him freely." He had said,
When twain-hued poplar with Herculean shade
Both decked his locks, and, laced with leafage, hung;
A holy goblet, too, his right hand filled.
At once they all upon the board in joy
Pour out libations, and the gods entreat.
Meanwhile in th' empyrean sinking down
The eve is nigher brought: and now the priests 393
And, at their head, Potitius, marched along,
With skins, according to their fashion, clad,
And torches carried. They renew the feast,
And welcome off'rings of the second board
Present, and with their laden dishes pile
The altars. Then the Salian [priests] for chants

Ben Jonson, speaking of Rome:
" She builds in gold, and to the stars,
As if she threaten'd heav'n with wars;
And seeks for hell in quarries deep,
Giving the fiends, that there do keep,
A hope of day."
        Catiline, Chorus, end of act i.
Gifford traces this to Petronius Arbiter. (See T. Petronii Arb. Satyricon. Amstel. 1669, p. 431.)

351. *Ramis* (v. 250) as plainly means *trunks* of trees, as *molaribus* does not mean *mill*-stones.

355. P. Fletcher, of the Dragon:
" Out of his gorge a hellish smoke he drew
That all the field with foggy mist enwraps:
As when Tiphæus from his paunch doth spew
Black-smothering flames, roll'd in loud thunder-claps;
The pitchy vapours choke the shining ray,
And bring dull night upon the smiling day." *Purple Island*, xii. 23.

370. " Come forth, you seed of sulphur, sons of fire!
Your stench it is broke forth! Abomination
Is in the house." Ben Jonson, *Alchemist*, v. 1.

371, 2. " And after, all the raskall many ran,
Heaped together in rude rablement,
To see the face of that victorious man,
Whom all admired as from Heaven sent,

And gaz'd upon with gaping wonderment.
But when they came where that dead dragon lay,
Stretcht on the ground in monstrous large extent,
The sight with ydle feare did them dismay,
Ne durst approch him nigh, to touch, or once essay.

" Some feard, and fledd; some feard, and well it fayned:
One, that would wiser seeme then all the rest,
Warnd him not touch, for yet perhaps remaynd
Some lingring life within his hollow brest,
Or in his wombe might lurke some hidden nest
Of many dragonettes, his fruitfull seede;
Another saide, that in his eyes did rest
Yet sparckling fyre, and badd thereof take heed:
Another said, he saw him move his eyes indeed.

" One mother, wheras her foolehardy chyld
Did come too neare, and with his talants play,
Halfe dead through feare, her little babe revyled,
And to her gossips gan in counsell say:
' How can I tell, but that his talants may
Yet scratch my sonne, or rend his tender hand?
So diversly themselves in vaine they fray;
While some more bold to measure him nigh stand,
To prove how many acres he did spred of land."
        Spenser, *F. Q.*, i. 12, 9-11.

The blazing altars round, appear en-
wreathed 400
Upon their brows with poplar branches :
this—
A choir of striplings, that—of agèd [sires],
Who in their hymn the lauds of Hercules,
And his achievements, celebrate : how first
His step-dame's monster-forms and pair
of snakes,
Crushing them in his hand, he strangled;
how
In war choice cities he, the same, o'erthrew,
Both Troja and Œchalia ; how sore toils,
A thousand, under king Eurystheus, he
Endured through doom of Juno the unjust.
" Thou, O unconquerable [hero, slay'st]
The children of the cloud, of double limb,
Hylæus e'en, and Pholus, with thy hand :
Thou the monstrosities of Crete dost slay,
And lion huge beneath Nemea's rock. 415
At thee have quaked the Stygian pools ;
at thee
Hell's porter, cow'ring o'er half-eaten bones
Within his gory cavern ; neither thee
Have any shapes, not e'en Typhæus, scared,
A giant grasping weapons ; not devoid
Of pow'r of thought did thee beset around
The snake of Lerna with his host of heads.
All hail ! indisputable son of Jove, 423
Thou glory added to the pow'rs divine !
Alike to us, and thine own holy [rites],
Draw near propitious with a fav'ring step."
The like [exploits] they celebrate in songs :
Above them all do they subjoin the cave
Of Cacus, e'en himself too, puffing forth
With blazes. All the woodland with the din
Rings out in concert, and the hills rebound.
Thereon,—the holy services complete,—
They all betake them to the city back. 433
On fared the monarch, overwhelmed with
age,
And in his company Æneas, and his son
Close kept he to him as he foots along,
And eased the way with manifold discourse.
Æneas marvels, and his ready eyes
Round all he throws, and by the spots is
charmed,

And one by one in joy both searches out,
And hears, the legends of the men of yore.
Then king Evander, founder of the tower
Of Rome : " These groves the native
Fauns and Nymphs 443
Were used t' inhabit, and a race of men
Born from the boles [of trees] and sturdy
oak :
Who had nor rule, nor elegance [of life] ;
Nor bulls to yoke, or gather wealth, they
knew,
Or spare their gains : but branches and
the chase,
Rugged in sustenance, purveyed support.
First Saturn came from empyrean heaven,
Flying Jove's arms, and from his wrested
realm 451
An exile. He the race untaught, and spread
Through lofty mountains, settled, and
their laws
Vouchsafed, and 'Latium' chose them to
be called,
Since *latent* in these coasts he safe had
lain.
The golden age, whereof they tell, was
'neath that king :
He so in calm of peace the nations ruled ;
Till step by step a worse, and tarnished
age,
And rage for war, and lust of gain ensued.
Then came the Auson host, and Sic'ly's
clans ; 460
And Saturn's land too often laid aside
Her name. Then kings, and Tybris, rough
with frame
Immense ; from whom have we Italians next
The river by the title Tyber called ;
Old Albula hath lost its real name.
Myself, forth driven from my native land,
And following the ocean's utmost [bounds],
Almighty Fortune and resistless Fate
Have in these regions placed, and me have
forced
My mother nymph Carmentis' warnings
dread, 470
And her inspirer-god Apollo." Scarce
These [words] were spoken : then advanc-
ing on
He shows him both the altar, and the gate,
Which Romans by the name "Carmental"
call,

---

411. This transition from the third to the second person is copied by Milton ; as is remarked in Trollope's Anthon's Virgil :
" Both turn'd, and under open sky adored
The God that made both sky, air, earth, and
heaven,
Which they beheld ; the moon's resplendent globe,
And starry pole : Thou also mad'st the night,
Maker Omnipotent, and Thou the day."
 P. L., b. iv.

422. Spenser has a grand description of a Dragon, and the Red Cross Knight's victory over him ; *F. Q.*, i. 11, 8-14, &c.

468. 459. " But violence can never longer sleep
Than human passions please. In ev'ry heart
Are sown the sparks that kindle fiery war :
Occasion needs but fan them, and they blaze."
Cowper, *Task*, b. v.

468. " Since fate inevitable
Subdues us, and omnipotent decree,
The victor's will." Milton, *P. L.*, b. ii.

The Nymph Carmentis' compliment of old,
Presageful prophetess, who chanted first
That the Æneadæ would great become,
And Pallanteum famous. Farther on
The mighty grove, which mettled Romulus
Entitled the "Asylum," and beneath 480
An icy cliff "Lupercal" points he out,
According to Parrhasian fashion called
From the Lycæan Pan. E'en, too, does he
Point out the hallowed Argiletum's wood,
And calls the place to witness, and the death
Of his guest Argus he explains. Thence leads
To the Tarpeian hold and Capitol,
Now golden, bristling erst with savage brakes.
Already then dread rev'rence for the spot
The quaking peasants awed; already then
They shuddered at the forest and the rock.
"This grove, this hill," saith he, "with leafy crest,— 492
What god, it is unsure,—a god doth haunt:
Th' Arcadians hold that Jove himself they've seen,
When oft his darkling Ægis he would shake
In his right hand, and thunder-clouds arouse.
Moreover these two towns with scattered walls,
Remnants and records of the men of old,
Thou see'st. *This* castle father Janus,— *that*,
Did Saturn build: Janiculum of one, 500
Saturnia of the other, was the name."
With such like talk between them up they came
To poor Evander's palace, and at large
His herds saw lowing both throughout
The Roman Forum and the grand Carine.
When reached they his abodes; "These gates," saith he,
"Alcides conqu'ror entered: him this court
Received. O guest, dare riches to despise,
And mould thee also worthy of the god:
And come not churlish to our poor estate."
He said, and 'neath his narrow mansion's roof 511
The great Æneas led, and set him down,
Cushioned upon a carpeting of leaves,
And on the skin of a Libystine bear.
Night posts, and folds the earth with ebon wings.
But Venus, not in mind without a cause
A mother scared, and by Laurentines' threats,
And ruffian uproar roused, Vulcan accosts,
And from her husband's golden bed she these begins,
And o'er her accents breathes a heav'nly love: 520
"While in their warfare the Argolic kings
Were laying waste the fated Pergamus,
And, doomed to fall by hostile flames, its towers,
Not any succor for its wretched [sons],
Not weapons of thy skill and power I asked;
Nor thee, O dearest consort, or thy toils,
Have I been willing idly to employ;
Though both to Priam's sons full much I owed,
And oft Æneas' sore distress had wept.
He now at Jove's behests hath settled down
On the Rutulians' coasts: then I the same
A suitress come, and of thy deity, revered
By me, arms crave, a mother for a son.
Thee Nereus' daughter, thee Tithonus' spouse 534
Could bend by tears. Behold, what hordes combine,
What towns with bolted gates the falchion whet

---

481. As the Arcadians in Greece called Pan *Lycæus* from their mountain of that name, which was sacred to him, as being his supposed haunt; so Evander and his Arcadians in Italy, having consecrated the cave in the Palatine Mount to Pan, called it *Lupercal* from *lupus*; *Lycæus* being akin in form to λυκος, and hence suggesting the word *lupus*.

488. *Nunc* and *olim* (v. 348) might now be interchanged with too much truth:

"Fall'n, fall'n, a silent heap; her heroes all
Sunk in their urns; behold the pride of pomp,
The throne of nations fall'n; obscur'd in dust;
E'en yet majestical."

"Rent palaces, crush'd columns, rifled moles,
Fanes roll'd on fanes, and tombs on buried tombs."   Dyer, *Ruins of Rome.* 16.

508. "Yet once a-day drop down a gentle look
On the great molehill, and with pitying eye
Survey the busy emmets round the heap,
Crowding and bustling in a thousand forms
Of strife and toil, to purchase wealth and fame,
A bubble or a dust: then call thy thoughts
Up to thyself to feed on joys unknown,
Rich without gold, and great without renown."
                    Watts, *True Monarchy.*

509. "Pleasure has charms: but so has Virtue too.
One skims the surface, like the swallow's wing,
And scuds away unnotic'd. T'other nymph,
Like spotless swans in solemn majesty,
Breasts the pale surge, and leaves long light behind."   Walpole, *Mysterious Mother*, ii. 4.

515.   "For now began
Night with her sullen wings to double-shade
The desert."   Milton, *P. R.*, b. i. end.

Glover has a different image:

"In sable vesture, spangled o'er with stars,
The Night assum'd her throne."
                    Leonidas, ix. 1, 2.

'Gainst me, and [for] the overthrow of mine!"
She said, and in her snowy arms, this side
And that, the goddess, as he hesitates,
Infolds him warmly with a soft embrace.
He suddenly received the wonted flame,
And the known heat his marrow pierced, and coursed 542
Through melting bones. No less than when at times
With flashing thunder burst, the chink of fire,
In brightness gleaming, races through the clouds.
His spouse perceived it, blithesome in her wiles,
And of her beauty conscious. Then the sire,
Enchained in everlasting passion, speaks :
"Why seekest thou for reasons from the deep?
Whither, O goddess, hath thy trust in me
Departed? Had there been the like concern, 551
Then also lawful had it been for us
To arm the Trojans ; nor th' almighty sire,
Nor destinies forbade that Troy should stand,
And Priam through ten other years survive.
And now, if thou to battle dost prepare,
And this is thy resolve, engage can I
Whate'er there be of travail in my craft,

In iron what is able to be wrought,
Or in the flux electrum, how so far 560
As fires and blasts have force : by suing cease
To cast a doubt upon thy pow'rs." These words
He having said, the wished embraces gave,
And, thrown upon the bosom of his spouse,
He courted balmy slumber through his limbs.
Then soon as maiden rest, in mid career
Of night, now chased away, had banished sleep,
When first the dame, on whom to nurture life
By distaff and Minerva scant 'tis laid,
The embers and the drowsèd fires awakes,
Night adding to her work, and by the lights
Her maids with tedious task she plies, that she 572
Unsullied may be able to maintain
Her husband's bed, and tiny children rear :
Not otherwise, nor slower in that hour,
The lord of fire springs up from downy couch
To his artistic works. An isle, hard by
Sicania's side and the Æolian Lipare,
Is elevated, steep with smoking rocks ;
'Neath which a cave, and, eaten to the heart 580
By Cyclops' forges, its Ætnean dens
Thunder, and lusty dints, on stithies heard,
Return a groan, and hiss within the vaults
The Chalybs' bars, and in the furnaces
Fire pants ;—the home of Vulcan, and the land
" Vulcania " by its title. Hither then
The lord of fire came down from heav'n on high.
Iron were working in their monster den
The Cyclops,—Brontes e'en, and Steropes,
And, stript in limbs, Pyracmon. In their hands, 590
Unfashioned, with a part now burnished off,
A levin-bolt there lay ; full many which

---

544. Spenser employs the idea for a similar purpose :

"As the bonilasse passed bye,
  Hey, ho, the bonilasse !
She rovde at mee with glauncing eye,
  As cleare as the cristall glasse : ....
Or as the thonder cleaves the cloudes,
  Hey, ho, the thonder !
Wherein the lightsome levin shroudes ;
  So cleaves thy soul asonder."
              Shepheards Calender, August.

Differently in *Faerie Queene*, iii. 11-25 :

"'Tis listening fear and dumb amazement all :
When to the startled eye the sudden glance
Appears far south, eruptive through the cloud ;
And falling slower, in explosion vast,
The thunder raises his tremendous voice.
At first, heard solemn o'er the verge of Heaven,
The tempest growls ; but, as it nearer comes,
And rolls its awful burden on the wind,
The lightnings flash a larger curve, and more
The noise astounds : till overhead a sheet
Of livid flame discloses wide : then shuts,
And opens wider ; shuts and opens still
Expansive, wrapping ether in a blaze.
Follows the loosen'd, aggravated roar,
Enlarging, deepening, mingling ; peal on peal
Crush'd horrible, convulsing heaven and earth."
                          Thomson, *Summer*.

" Her cheeks bewraying
As many amorous blushings, which brake out
Like forced lightning from a troubled cloud."
       Shirley, *The Maid's Revenge*, i. 2.

569. " Minerva, skilful goddess, train'd the maid
To twirle the spindle by the twisting thread ;
To fix the loom, instruct the reeds to part,
Cross the long weft, and close the web with art."
                          Parnell, *Hesiod*.

592. " Above our atmosphere's intestine wars
Rain's fountain-head, the magazine of hail ;
Above the northern nests of feather'd snows,
The brew of thunders and the flaming forge
That forms the crooked lightning : above the caves,
Where infant tempests wait their growing wings,
And tune their tender voices to that roar,
Which soon, perhaps, shall shake a guilty world ;
Above misconstrued omens of the sky,
Far-travell'd comets' calculated blaze ;
Elance thy thought, and think of more than man."
              Young, *The Complaint*, N. ix.

From the whole welkin doth the father hurl
Adown upon the lands : part incomplete
Remained. Three rayons of the writhen shower,
Three, had they added, of the wat'ry cloud,
Of vermeil fire and wingèd Auster three.
Now flashes horror-fraught, and din and fear,
They in their work were blending, anger too,
With dogging flames. Elsewhere for Mars
They both a chariot and its flying wheels 601
Were speeding, wherewithal he rouses men,
Wherewith the cities ; and the Ægis, dread
Inspiring, the impassioned Pallas' arms,
In rivalry with scales of snakes and gold
Were furbishing, and serpents interlinked,
And e'en the Gorgon on the goddess' breast,
Her eyeballs rolling, with a severed neck.
" Away with all ! " he cries, " and put aside
The toils that are commenced, ye Cyclops, [brood]
Of Ætna, and attention hither turn :   611
Arms for a gallant hero must be made.
There's now employment for your powers, now
For lively hands, now for all master-skill :
Fling, fling away delays ! " Nor more he said ;
But they all promptly bent [them to the task],
And shared alike the travail. Run in rills
Bronze and a mine of gold, and wounding steel
In the huge furnace melts. A mighty shield
They bring to shape, a single one, to meet
The Latins' every dart ; and sevenfold disks
Dovetail in disks. In gusty bellows some
Admit the breezes, and discharge them back ;   623
Some dip the screeching bronzes in the pool,
With their implanted stithies groans the cave.
They 'tween them with gigantic force their arms
Upheave to rhythmic measure, and they turn,
And turn again, with griping tongs the block.
While these in coasts Æolian Lemnos' sire   629
Hastes on, Evander from his lowly home
Boon light awakes, and early songs of birds

622. "And eke the breathfule bellowes blew amaine."   Spenser, *F. Q.*, iv. 5, 36.
See note on *Geo.* iv. *l.* 235.

631. Wagner says : " *Audivi tamen homines rusticanos affirmantes, sæpe se hirundinum garrientium strepitu e somno excitari.*" There is no doubt that many others also have been awaked in the same way ; the author certainly has suffered the annoyance himself. Martens and swallows are exceedingly noisy at break of day, especially when engaged in building.
The British poets contain many passages of great beauty, descriptive of the early morning music of the feathered creation :

" Me mette thus in my bed all naked,
And looked forth, for I was waked
With smale foules a great hepe
That had afraied me out of my slepe,
Through noise and sweetness of hir song ;
And as me mette, they sat among
Upon my chamber roofe without
Upon the tyles over all about."
                Chaucer, *Booke of the Dutchesse*.

" Wake now, my love, awake ; for it is time ;
The rosy Morne long since left Tithons bed,
Allready to her silver coche to clyme ;
And Phœbus gins to shew his glorious hed.
Hark ! how the cheerefull birds do chaunt their laies,
And carroll of loves praise.
The merry larke hir mattins sings aloft ;
The thrush replyes ; the mavis descant playes ;
The ouzell shrills ; the ruddock warbles soft ;
So goodly all agree, with sweet consent,
To this dayes merriment."
                Spenser, *Epithalamion*.

" Then from her burnish'd gate the goodly glitt'ring east
Gilds every lofty top, which late the humorous night
Bespangled had with pearl, to please the morning's sight :
On which the mirthful quires, with their clear open throats,
Unto the joyful morn so strain their warbling notes,
That hills and valleys ring, and even the echoing air
Seems all compos'd of sounds, about them every where."   Drayton, *Polyolbion*, Song xiii.

595. " He saw them in their forms of battle ranged,
How quick they wheel'd, and flying behind them shot
Sharp sleet of arrowy showers against the face
Of their pursuers."   Milton, *P. R.*, b. iii.

" Now the storm begins to lour,
 (Haste, the loom of hell prepare,)
 Iron sleet of arrowy shower
   Hurtles in the darken'd air."
                Gray, *Fatal Sisters*, 1.

" Nay more, my lord, the masks are made so strong,
That I myself upon them scaled the heavens,
And boldly walked about the middle region ;
Where, in the province of the meteors,
I saw the cloudy shops of hail and rain,
Garners of snow, and crystals full of dew ;
Rivers of burning arrows, dens of dragons,
Huge beams of flames, and spears like firebrands."   Brewer, *Lingua*, ii. 6.

618. " High on the plain, in many cells prepared,
That underneath had veins of liquid fire
Sluiced from the lake, a second multitude
With wondrous art founded the massy ore,
Severing each kind, and scumm'd the bullion dross :
A third as soon had form'd within the ground
A various mould, and from the boiling cells
By strange conveyance fill'd each hollow nook."
                Milton, *P. L.*, b. i.

Beneath the roof. Up springs the agèd [king],
And with a tunic o'er his limbs is robed,

" Now Morn, her rosy steps with eastern clime
Advancing, sow'd the earth with orient pearl,
When Adam waked, so custom'd ; for his sleep
Was aery light, from pure digestion bred,
And temperate vapours bland, which the only sound
Of leaves and fuming rills, Aurora's fan,
Lightly dispersed, and the shrill matin song
Of birds on every bough."
　　　　　　　　　Milton, *P. L.*, b. v. 1-8.

" To hear the lark begin his flight,
And singing startle the dull night,
From his watch-tower in the skies,
Till the dappled dawn doth rise ;
Then to come, in spite of sorrow,
And at my window bid good morrow,
Through the sweet-briar, or the vine,
Or the twisted eglantine ;
While the cock, with lively din,
Scatters the rear of darkness thin,
And to the stack, or the barn-door,
Stoutly struts his dames before." *L'Allegro.*

" The breezy call of incense-breathing morn,
The swallow twittering from the straw-built shed,
The cock's shrill clarion, or the echoing horn,
No more shall rouse them from their lowly bed." Gray, *Elegy*, 5.

" Lull'd by the drowsy din in sleep I lay,
Till from the East pale gleam'd the dubious day ;
Till chanticleer his merry notes begun,
Thrice clapt his wings, and call'd the lingering Sun.
Rous'd by his orisons from sweet repose,
I shook off slumbers as the morning rose ;
The morning rose, but shed a languid light,
And down in ocean sunk the queen of night.
Then jackdaws chatter'd on the chimney high ;
And cranes pursued their voyage thro' the sky . .
Perch'd on a tree that nigh my chamber grew,
The kite began her lamentable pew,
Whereby the dawning of the day I knew."
Fawkes, *Translation of Gawin Douglas' Winter.*

To this and Douglas' other beautiful poem, on May, it is easy to see that Milton owed no small obligations.

" Hark ! hark ! the lark at heaven's gate sings,
　And Phœbus 'gins arise,
His steeds to water at those springs
　On chalic'd flowers that lies ;
And winking Mary-buds begin
　To ope their golden eyes ;
With every thing that pretty is :
　My lady sweet, arise ;
Arise, arise." Shakespeare, *Cymbeline*, ii. 3.

" How is't each bough a several music yields ?
The lusty throstle, early nightingale,
Accord in tune, though vary in their tale ;
The chirping swallow call'd forth by the sun,
And crested lark doth his division run ?
The yellow bees the air with murmur fill,
The finches carol, and the turtles bill ?"
　　　　　　　　Ben Jonson, *Vision of Delight.*

" See, the day regins to break,
And the lights shoot like a streak
Of subtle fire ; the wind blows cold,
Whilst the morning doth unfold ;

And Tyrrhene laces round his footsoles binds ;
He then below his side and shoulders belts
His Tegeæan falchion, winding back
A leopard's skin, down wimpled from the left.
Yea, too, twain watch-dogs from his lofty door
Precede, and company their master's step.
His guest Æneas' cell and private [haunts]
The hero sought, in mind of their discourse,
And of the service [he had] pledged. No less　　　　　　　　　　　　　　　　　642
Æneas early moved him forth : to that—
Pallas his son, to this—Achates went
As henchman. They on meeting knit right hands,
And in the centre of the court sit down,
And conversation free enjoy at last.
The king first these : " O Trojans' highest chief,
Who while unharmed, I sooth will never own
That whelmed are Troja's fortunes or her realm ;　　　　　　　　　　　　　　　　　　650
Scant in proportion to such high renown
Be our abilities for aid of war.
On this side by the Tuscan stream are we
Hemmed in, closes the Rutulan on that,
And round our rampart clatters with his arms.
But I to thee prodigious tribes, and camps,
Rich in dominion, purpose to attach ;
Which safety unexpected fortune shows :
Thou bring'st thee hither at the Weirds' demand.
Not far away from this is peopled, reared
Of agèd stone, Argylla's city's seat ;　　　661
Where erst a Lydian race, renowned in war,
Upon Etruscan mountains settled down.

　Now the birds begin to rouse,
And the squirrel from the boughs
Leaps, to get him nuts and fruit ;
The early lark, that erst was mute,
Carols to the rising day
Many a note and many a lay."
　J. Fletcher, *The Faithful Shepherdess*, iv. 5.

" What bird so sings, yet does so wail ?
O, 'tis the ravish'd nightingale.
Jug, jug, jug, jug, tereu she cryes,
And still her woes at midnight rise.
Brave prick-song ! Who is't now we hear ?
None but the lark so shrill and clear ;
Now at heaven's gates she claps her wings,
The morn not waking till she sings.
Hark, hark, with what a pretty throat
Poor robin redbreast times his note ;
Hark, how the jolly cuckoes sing
Cuckoe, to welcome in the Spring."
　　　　　　Lilly, *Alexander and Campaspe.*

See Weber's note on " Song by *Delight* ;" Ford's *Sun's Darling*, ii. 1.

This [city], blooming thro'out many a year,
The king Mezentius subsequently held
With prideful tyranny and felon arms.
Why name th' unutterable murders, why
The tyrant's furious doings? May the gods
Keep them in store for his own head and
   race !
Nay e'en dead bodies he to living linked,
Both yoking hands with hands, and face
   with face,—   671
A kind of rack,—and, with the gleet and
   gore
While streaming, in calamitous embrace,
He thus destroyed them by a ling'ring
   death.
But, wearied out at last, his citizens
In his unutterable frenzy, armed
Beleaguer both himself and palace round,
His partners slay, fire volley to his roofs.
He, 'mid the carnage 'scaping, fled for aid
To the Rutulians' lands, and by the arms
Of his host Turnus is he screened. For this
In righteous fury all Etruria rose :   682
Their prince for vengeance with immediate
   war
They redemand. To these their thousands I
Will thee, Æneas, as their captain join.
For storm throughout the shore their serried
   ships,
And crave t' advance the colors; holds
   them back

---

667. Barbarossa would have been a match for
him:
     " Come, mighty vengeance !
 Stir me, grim cruelty : the rack shall groan
 With new-born horrors ! I will issue forth,
 Like midnight pestilence : my breath shall strew
 The streets with dead ; and havock stalk in gore.
 Hence pity ! Feed the milky thought of babes ;
 Mine is of bloodier hue."
               Brown, *Barbarossa*, 4, end.

675. Churchill beautifully illustrates the duty of
kings:
 " The hive is up in arms—expert to teach,
 Nor, proudly, to be taught unwilling, each
 Seems from her fellow a new zeal to catch :
 Strength in her limbs, and on her wings despatch,
 The bee goes forth ; from herb to herb she flies,
 From flow'r to flow'r, and loads her lab'ring
    thighs
 With treasur'd sweets: robbing those flow'rs,
    which left,
 Find not themselves made poorer by the theft ;
 Their scents as lively, and their looks as fair,
 As if the pillager had not been there.
 Ne'er doth she flit on Pleasure's silken wing,
 Ne'er doth she, loit'ring, let the bloom of Spring
 Unrifled pass, and on the downy breast
 Of some fair flow'r indulge untimely rest.
 Ne'er doth she, drinking deep of those rich dews,
 Which chymist Night prepar'd, that faith abuse
 Due to the hive, and, selfish in her toils,
 To her own private use convert the spoils.
 Love of the stock first call'd her forth to roam,
 And to the stock she brings her booty home."
                       Gotham, b. iii.

An agèd soothsayer, the destinies
Declaring : ' O Mæonia's chosen youth,
Flower and prowess of the men of yore,
Whom righteous anger hurtles on the foe,
And with resentment due Mezentius fires ;
For no Italian is it right to tame   693
So great a nation : foreign leaders choose.'
Then camped th' Etruscan army on this
   plain,
Alarmed by warnings of the pow'rs divine.
Tarchon himself his envoys hath to me,
And kingdom's diadem with sceptre sent,
And the regalia he consigns, that I
His camp should enter, and the Tyrrhene
   rule   700
Assume. But me my age, through chill-
   ness slow,
And by long years outworn, and pow'rs
   too late
For gallant [deeds], the sovereignty be-
   grudges. I
My son would counsel to it, did not he,
Through a Sabellian mother blent [in race],
Hence draw a portion of his native land.
Do thou, to whose both years and birth the
   Weirds
Are kind, whom gods demand, commence
   [the task],
O Trojans and Italians' bravest chief.
To thee, moreover, I my Pallas here,   710
Our hope and consolation, will attach.
'Neath thee his master, warfare to endure,
And Mars' momentous work, thy feats to
   view,
Let him inure himself, and thee regard
In wonder from his earliest years. To
   him
Two hundred Arcad knights, the youths'
   choice strength,
Will I assign ; as many, too, to thee
In his own name will Pallas.' He these
   [words]
Had scarcely said, when down-fixed kept
   their eyes
Anchises' son Æneas, and the stanch   720
Achates ; and were thinking many a pain-
   ful [thought]
With their drear heart ;—had Cytherea not
A token given from the open heaven.
For on a sudden, quivered from the sky,
A levin-flash with pealing comes, and all
Appeared to go to ruin in a trice,
And a Tyrrhenian trumpet-blast to bray

---

701.   " Stay, pitying Time . . . .
   Comes manhood's feverish summer, chill'd full
    soon
 By cold autumnal care, till wintry age
 Sinks in the frore severity of death."
                  Mason, *English Garden*, b. ii.

Throughout the sky. They upward look.
Again, and [yet] again a crashing chides
Stupendous. Armory amid a cloud,   730
In a transparent quarter of the heaven,
Throughout the clear to glisten they perceive,
And, clashed, to thunder. In their souls the rest
Were mazed ; but Troja's hero knew the sound,
And pledges of his goddess-mother. Then
He speaks : "Nay do not, host, sooth do not seek
What issue may the prodigies import :
'Tis I am by Olympus claimed. This sign
My goddess-mother chanted she would send,
Should war assail me, and Vulcanian arms
Along the gales would for my succor bring.
Alas! how vast the slaughter for ill-starred
Laurentines is at hand! What penalties to me   743
Shalt thou, O Turnus, pay! How many shields
Of warriors shalt thou 'neath thy waves, and helms,
And gallant corses, father Tiber, roll!
Battles let them demand, and break the leagues !"
These words when he delivered, from his seat
On high he lifts himself, and first he wakes
The altars, drowsed with Herculean fires ;
And yestern Lar, and lowly household gods
He glad approaches ; butcher two-year ewes
According to the custom culled, alike   753
Evander, Trojan youth alike. Then he
Thence paces to the galleys, and his mates
Again he visits : from whose number those,
Who may his person follow to the wars,
In chivalry surpassing, he selects ;
The rest are wafted on the forward flood,
And lazily float down the fav'ring stream,
To come t' Ascanius with the news, alike
Of their estate, and of his father. Steeds
Are giv'n the Teucri, to the Tyrrhene fields
Repairing ; one they lead, without the lot
[Selected] for Æneas ; which all o'er   765
A lion's tawny hide caparisons,
All brightly gleaming with its claws of gold.
A rumor flies, throughout the petty town

Suddenly noised, that cavalry were quick
Advancing to the Tyrrhene monarch's shores.   770
Their vows the matrons in alarm repeat,
And nearer to the danger draws the fear,
And more enlarged now looms the form of Mars.
Then sire Evander, clasping the right hand
Of one upon departure, [to him] clings,
Weeping insatiably, and such he speaks :
"Oh! that to me past years would Jove restore !
Such as I was, what time the foremost rank
Beneath Præneste's self I prostrate laid,
And piles of shields in conquest set afire,
And Herilus its king with this right hand
'Neath Tart'rus sent ! To whom at birth three lives   782
His dam Feronia,—dreadful to be told !—
Had granted, triple armor to be swayed ;
He thrice was to be overthrown for death :
Whom yet this right hand then of all his lives
Bereft, and stript him of as many arms.
I nowhere now should from thy sweet embrace
Be torn away, my son ; nor e'er Mezentius,
On this his neighbor's person heaping scorn,   790
So many ruthless deaths by steel had caused,
Had widowed of so many citizens
My city. But do ye, O heav'nly powers,
And thou, of gods the highest ruler, Jove,
I pray, have pity on th' Arcadian king,
And hear a father's prayers: If your divinities,
If fates reserve my Pallas safe for me,
If doomed to see him, and to meet in one I live ;—
For life I sue : I will submit to bear
Whatever travail ye may list. But if   800
Any accurst disaster, Fortune, thou
Dost threaten, — now, oh! now, would heav'n that I

730, 1., Odd as this expression may appear, it is not more so than Spenser's "luckless luckie maid," which is to be found somewhere in the *Faerie Queene.*

768. Chaucer has an effective simile, to illustrate the spread of Rumor:
 "For if that thou
Threw in a water now a stone,
Well wost thou it will make anone

A little roundell as a cercle,
Paraventure as broad as a coverell,
And right anone thou shalt see wele,
That whole cercle will cause another whele,
And that the third, and so forth brother,
Every cercle causing other,
Broader than himselfe was,
And thus from roundell to compas,
Ech about other going,
Causeth of others stering,
And multiplying evermo,
Till it be so farre go,
That it at both brinkes bee,
Although thou may it not see."
 House of Fame, b. ii.

A pitiless existence might abridge,
Whilst my anxieties are doubtful, whilst
The expectation of the future [rests]
Unsure ; while thee, belovèd boy, my sole
And late delight, in my embrace I hold ;
Lest heavier tidings wound my ears."
    These words
The father at their latest parting poured :
The servants bear him swooning to his
    courts.   810
And so the cavalry had issued now
From opened gates : Æneas 'mid the van
And stanch Achates ; then Troy's other
    lords :
Pallas himself in centre of his troop,
Distinguished in his cloak and painted
    arms :
Like as, when in the wave of ocean bathed,
Hath Lucifer, whom Venus loves before
The other fires of stars, upraised in heaven
His holy visage, and the gloom dispersed.
The matrons quaking stand upon the walls,
And follow with their eyes the dusty cloud,
And their bronze-gleaming bands. They
    through the brakes,   822
Where [lies] the nearest bound'ry of their
    route,
March forward under arms. Up springs
    the shout,
And, — squadron marshalled, — with a
    prancing din
The hoof [of horses] shakes the crumbling
    plain.
Huge stands a grove by Cære's icy stream,
By rev'rence of the fathers far and near
[Deemed] holy : on its every side have [this]
The hollow hills incloistered, and the grove
With sombre fir surround. The legend goes
That for Silvanus, god of fields and flock,
The old Pelasgi sanctified alike   833
The thicket and a day,—they who the first
The Latin territories erst possessed.
Not far hence Tarcho and the Tyrrhenes safe
Were keeping their encampment in [these]
    grounds,
And all the legion from the lofty hill
Could how be seen, and through the
    spacious fields
It stretched. The sire Æneas, and the
    youth,   840

For battle chosen, hitherward advance,
And, jaded, both their steeds and bodies
    tend.
But Venus, goddess bright, 'mid skyey
    clouds,
Bringing her gifts, was drawing nigh ; and
    when
Her son within a vale retired afar,
Sequestered by the chilly stream, she saw,
She in such words addressed him, and
    herself
Presented to him unbesought : "Behold !
Completed by my consort's promised skill,
My boons ; that ne'er henceforward, O my
    son,   850
Either Laurentines haught, or Turnus fierce,
May'st thou demur to champion to the
    frays."
She spoke, and the embraces of her son
Did Cytherea seek ; the armor she
Laid beaming underneath a fronting oak.
He with the goddess' presents, and a grace
So noble, in delight, cannot be palled,
And o'er them one by one his eyes he
    rolls,
And marvels, and between his hands and
    arms
Turns o'er and o'er the helmet, dread with
    plumes,   860
And flames disgorging ; and the doomful
    sword,
The hauberk stiff with bronze, blood-tinted,
    huge,
As when a dingy cloud begins to flame
In sunbeams, and from far it flashes back ;
Then, of electrum and of gold refined,
The burnished greaves, and spear, and
    buckler's work,
That beggared all description. There the
    tale
Of Italy, and triumphs of the Romans, not
Unknowing of the seers, and unaware
Of time to come, the lord of fire had
    framed ;   870
There all the lineage of the future stock
Down from Ascanius, wars too fought in
    course.
And he had formed a cub-delivered wolf,
In Mars's verdant cave lain down ; twin
    boys,
Disporting as they hang around her dugs,
And licking unalarmed the dam ; her[self],

---

819. Or: " His holy face, and broken up the gloom."
821. " Methinks, they through the middle region
    come ;
    Their chariots hid in clouds of dust below,
    And o'er their heads their coursers' scatter'd some
    Does seem to cover them like falling snow."
            Davenant, *Gondibert*, iii. 3.
825. " The fleet hoof rattles o'er the flinty way."
            Mason, *Elfrida*.

867.   " Yet look, how far
The substance of my praise doth wrong this shadow
In underprizing it, so far this shadow
Doth limp behind the substance."
        Shakespeare, *Merchant of Venice*, iii. 2.

" Description cannot suit itself in words."
                K. Henry V., iv. 2.

With rounded neck bent back caressing them
By turns, and shaping with her tongue their forms.
Nor far hence Rome, and Sabine maidens, seized
Despite of law in session of the Cirque,
While grand Circensian [games] are held, had he   881
Subjoined, fresh war too, rising in a trice
On the Romulidæ, and Tatius aged,
And rigid Cures. Next, the selfsame kings,—
The strife between them laid aside,—afront
Jove's altar, and the saucers holding, stood,
And with a butchered sow cemented leagues.
Not far therefrom had nimble four-horse cars
Dissevered Metus [wrenched] diverging ways;—
But thou, O Alban, wouldest to thy words
Have stood !—and th' entrails of the traitor knave   891
Was Tullus haling through the wood, and, sprent,
The brambles were distilling with his blood.
Porsenna, too, was bidding them admit
The ousted Tarquin, and with mighty siege
Beleaguering the city ; th' Æneadæ
Were rushing to the sword in freedom's cause.
Him, like to one that cannot brook [the sight],
And like to one that threatens, you might view ;
Since Cocles ventured to uproot the bridge,
And Clœlia swam the flood,—her fetters burst.   901
At top, the sentry of Tarpeia's tower,
Stood Manlius before the fane, and held
The lofty Capitolian [heights], and fresh
The palace bristled with Romulian straw.
And flutt'ring here in gilded colonnades,
A goose of silver chanted that the Gauls
Were present in the threshold ; Gauls along the brakes
Were present, and were seizing on the tower,
Screened by the dark and boon of shady night :   910

Of gold their tresses, and of gold their gear ;
In cloaks of plaid they sparkle ; then with gold
Their milk-white necks are hooped ; they each a pair
Of Alpine jav'lins brandish in their hand,
With lengthened bucklers shielded o'er their forms.
Here dancing Salii, and Luperci stript,
And woolly caps, and targes dropped from heaven,
He'd beaten out ; chaste led the holy [rites]
Throughout the city dames in easy cars.
Hence at a distance he moreover adds 920
The homes of Tart'rus, lofty gates of Dis,
And crimes' amercements ; thee, too, Catiline,
Dangling upon an overhanging rock,
And at the Furies' features in a quake ;
Sequestered, too, the holy ones ; to these
Cato dispensing laws. Amid these [scenes]
A golden model of the swelling main
Extended wide ; but with a frosted wave
Foamed [seas of] azure ; and in silver round
The brilliant dolphins into circle swept
The waters with their tails, and cut the tide.   931
Within the centre, vessels beaked with bronze,
The frays of Actium, was there to behold ;
And all Leucate with embattled Mars
You might see glow, and waves beam forth in gold.
On this side, leading on the Itali
To fights, Augustus Cæsar with the sires,

922. Ben Jonson has a noble description of the circumstances under which Catiline met his end. Space forbids the insertion of more than a part of the whole passage :
" Which Catiline seeing, and that now his troops
Cover'd that earth they had fought on with their trunks,
Ambitious of great fame to crown his ill,
Collected all his fury, and ran in
Arm'd with a glory high as his despair,
Into our battle like a Libyan lion
Upon his hunters, scornful of our weapons,
Careless of wounds, plucking down lives about him,
Till he had circled in himself with death :
Then fell he too, t' embrace it where it lay.
And as in that rebellion 'gainst the gods,
Minerva holding forth Medusa's head,
One of the giant brethren felt himself
Grow marble at the killing sight, and now
Almost made stone, began to inquire, what flint,
What rock it was, that crept through all his limbs,
And ere he could think more, was that he feared :
So Catiline, at the sight of Rome in us,
Became his tomb : yet did his look retain
Some of his fierceness, and his hands still moved,
As if he labour'd yet to grasp the state
With those rebellious parts." *Catiline*, end.

897. " And thou, fair Freedom, taught alike to feel
The rabble's rage, and tyrant's angry steel ;
Thou transitory flow'r, alike undone
By proud contempt, and favour's fost'ring sun ;
Still may thy blooms the changeful clime endure !
I only would repress them to secure ;
For just experience tells, in ev'ry soil,
That those who think must govern those that toil ;
And all that freedom's highest aims can reach
Is but to lay proportion'd loads on each.
Hence, should one order disproportion'd grow,
Its double weight must ruin all below."
                            Goldsmith, *Traveller*.

And people, gods of home, and mighty gods,
Standing upon the elevated stern ;
Whose brows two flames auspiciously dis-
   charge,   940
And his paternal star is on his head
Displayed. Upon another part, with winds
And gods propitious, is Agrippa lifted high,
His squadron leading on : whose temples
   shine,—
Proud badge of war,—with naval chaplet
   beaked.
That side, with foreign pow'r and motley
   arms,
Antonius, conqu'ror from Aurora's hordes,
And shore of crimson, Egypt and the
   powers
Of Orient, and the farthest Bactra, brings
Along with him ; and follows,—O dis-
   grace !—   950
Th' Egyptian paramour. Together all
Are hurtling, and is wholly in a froth,
Uptorn with oars drawn back and trident
   beaks,
The surface [of the sea]. The deeps they
   seek :
Thou would'st believe were floating on the
   main
Uprooted Cyclades, or lofty mounts,
Justling with mounts : with such stupend-
   ous weight
The crews in towered ships are pressing on.
The hempen blaze by ' hand, and wingy
   steel
Is by their javelins scattered : Neptune's
   fields   960
With slaughter fresh are waxing red. The
   queen
Amidst them with her country's timbrel
   calls
Her hosts ; nor yet e'en from behind per-
   ceives
Twain snakes : and monster gods of every
   breed,
Barker Anubis, too, 'gainst Neptune [ranged],
And Venus, and against Minerva, grasp
Their weapons. Storms in centre of the fray
Mavors, embossed in steel, and from the
   sky
The rueful Furies ; and in mantle rent
In joy stalks Discord, whom with bloody
   scourge   970

---
950. " *Cleopatra.* Your lord, the man who serves
   me, is a Roman.
Octavius. He was a Roman till he lost that name,
To be a slave in Egypt."
                     Dryden, *All for Love*, iii. 1.
957. " Through Bosporus, betwixt the justling
   rocks."   Milton, *P. L.*, b. ii. end.
970. " Discord she wills ; the missile ruin flies :
   Sudden, unnatural debates arise,

Bellona dogs. The Actian [god] Apollo
   these
Perceiving, bending was his bow from high :
With that affright all Egypt and the Inds,
Each Arab, all the Sabans turned their
   backs.
The queen herself was seen,—the winds
   invoked,—
To set the sails, and now, e'en now, to
   slack
The loosened ropes. Her 'mid the havoc wan
At coming death, the lord of fire had made
To be by billows and Iapyx borne ;
But on the other side, with giant frame
Nile mourning, and his bosom spreading
   out,   981
And calling, in the fulness of his robe,
Into his sea-green lap and shroudy floods
The conquered [foes]. But Cæsar, borne
   along
In three-fold triumph to the walls of Rome,
Was consecrating to Italian gods,—
His deathless vow,—three hundred proudest
   shrines,
Through the whole city. Streets with joy,
   and sports,
And acclamation, ring. In all the fanes
A choir of matrons, altars in them all ;
Before the altars slaughtered bullocks
   strewed   991
The earth. He, sitting in the snowy gate
Of glist'ring Phœbus, th' off'rings of the
   tribes
Reviews, and fits them to the prideful doors :
March conquered nations in a lengthful
   train,   .

Doubt, mutual jealousy, and dumb disgust,
Dark-hinted mutterings, and avow'd distrust ;
To secret ferment is each heart resign'd ;
Suspicion hovers in each clouded mind ;
They jar, accus'd accuse, revil'd revile,
And warmth to warmth oppose, and guile to guile :
Wrangling they part, themselves themselves betray ;
Each dire device starts naked into day ;
They feel confusion in the van with fear ;
They feel the king of terrors in the rear."
               Savage, *Wanderer*, c. v.

" *Scar.*   Yond' ribald hag of Egypt,
Whom leprosy o'ertake ! i' the midst o' the fight,—
When vantage like a pair of twins appear'd.
Both as the same, or rather ours the elder,—
The brize upon her, like a cow in June,
Hoists sails and flies.
    Eno.   That I beheld : mine eyes
Did sicken at the sight on't, and could not
Endure a further view.
    Scar.   She once being loof'd,
The noble ruin of her magic, Antony,
Claps on his sea-wing, and like a doting mallard,
Leaving the fight in height, flies after her ;
I never saw an action of such shame :
Experience, manhood, honour, ne'er before
Did violate so itself."
       Shakespeare, *Antony and Cleopatra*, iii. 8.
                                                  R

As diff'rent in their tongues, as in the guise
Of garb and arms. Here Mulciber the
    race
Of Nomads, and loose-girdled Africans,
Here Leleges, and Carians, Gelons too,
With arrows armed, had fashioned. Passed
    along   1000
Euphrates, now the gentler in his waves;
And, farthest of mankind, the Morini,

And Rhine two-horned, and Dahœ unsub-
    dued,
Araxes, too, that held a bridge in scorn.
 The like o'er Vulcan's shield, his parent's
    gifts,
He views in wondermcnt, and of events
Unknowing, in the portraiture delights,
As he upon his shoulder raises up
Of sons of sons alike the fame and fates.

BOOK IX.

Now in a quarter severed far while these
Are being done, Saturnian Juno down
Sent Iris from the sky to Turnus bold.
By hazard then in sire Pilumnus' grove
Was Turnus sitting in a hallowed dale.
To whom Thaumantias from her coral mouth
Thus spake : "O Turnus, that, which to
    thy wish
Not one of gods could venture to engage,
Hath circling time, lo! brought thee of
    itself.
Æneas,—town, and mates, and navy left,—
The Palatine Evander's realm and court 11
Is seeking.   Nor [is this] sufficient : he
To Corythus' remotest towns hath pierced,
And arms a band of Lydians, levied boors.
Wherefore dost thou demur? 'Tis now
    the hour
Thy coursers, now thy chariots, to demand :
Break all delays, and storm his troubled
    camp."
She said, and into heav'n upraised herself
Upon her balanced wings, and in her flight
A spacious bow she scored beneath the
    clouds.   20
Knew her the youth, and lifted to the stars
Both hands, and with such accent[s] as she
    flies

Pursued her : "Iris, pride of heav'n, who
    thee,
Shot from the clouds, to me sent down to
    earth ?
Whence this so brilliant weather in a trice ?
Heav'n in the zenith do I see dispart,
And straying through the firmament the
    stars.
I follow omens of such high import,
Whoe'er thou art that callest me to arms."
And, thuswise having spoken, to the wave
He forward went, and from the eddy-face
Its waters he updrew, in many a prayer 32
Craving the gods, and loaded heav'n with
    vows.
 And now the army all thro' open plains

Line 6. Warner, beautifully of the color of Rosamond's lips :

"With that she dasht her on the lippes,
    So dyed double red ;
Hard was the heart that gaue the blow ;
    Soft were those lips that bled."
        Albion's England, b. viii. ch. 41.

20. "Have ye not seen, in gentle even-tide,
When Jupiter the earth hath richly shower'd,
Striding the clouds, a bow dispredden wide
As if with light invowe, and gaily flower'd
With bright variety of blending dies?
White, purple, yellow melt along the skies,
Alternate colours sink, alternate colours rise."
        W. Thompson, *Hymn to May,* 22.

23. "Hail, many-coloured messenger, that ne'er
Dost disobey the wife of Jupiter ;
Who, with thy saffron wings, upon my flowers
Diffusest honey-drops, refreshing showers :
And with each end of thy blue bow dost crown
My bosky acres, and my unshrubb'd down,
Rich scarf to my proud earth ; why hath thy queen
Summon'd me hither, to this short-grassed green?"
        Shakespeare, *Tempest,* iv. 1.

" O speak again, bright angel ! for thou art
    As glorious to this night, being o'er my head,
    As is a winged messenger of heaven
Unto the white-upturned wond'ring eyes
Of mortals, that fall back to gaze on him,
When he bestrides the lazy-pacing clouds,
And sails upon the bosom of the air."
        Romeo and Juliet, ii. 2.

28. P. Fletcher pleasantly introduces one of his fishermen, expressing the like pious obedience :

"As late upon the shore I chanc'd to play,
I heard a voice, like thunder, loudly say :
'Thirsil, why idle liv'st? Thirsil, away, away !'
Thou God of seas, thy voice I gladly heare ;
Thy voice (thy voice I know) I glad obey :
Only do thou my wand'ring wherry steer,
    And when it errs, (as it will eas'ly stray,)
    Upon the rock with hopeful anchor stay ;
Then will I swim where's either sea or shore,
Where never swain or boat was seen afore."
        Piscatory Eclogues, ii. 18, 19.

34.   "And now went forth the morn,
Such as in highest heaven array'd in gold

v. 26—36. BOOK IX. v. 36—59. 243

Marched rich in horses, rich in broidered gear
And gold. Messapus doth the leading lines,
The rear do Tyrrheus' youthful sons, restrain;
Prince Turnus in the centre of the host
Is in continued motion, grasping arms,
And by a head entire above them stands.
As, rising from his sev'n abated streams,
Deep through the still the Ganges; or when Nile 42
With batt'ning flood is ebbing from the plains,
And now hath buried him within his bed.
Here, sphered with sable dust, a sudden cloud
Do Teucer's sons descry, and gloom to rise
Upon the plains. First from the fronting mound
Cries out Caicus: "O ye citizens,

Empyreal; from before her vanish'd Night,
Shot through with orient beams; when all the plain,
Cover'd with thick embattled squadrons bright,
Chariots, and flaming arms, and fiery steeds,
Reflecting blaze on blaze, first met his view."
   Milton, *P. L.*, vi. 12-18.
" He look'd and saw what numbers numberless
The city-gates outpour'd, light-armed troops,
In coats of mail and military pride;
In mail their horses clad, yet fleet and strong,
Prancing their riders bore, the flower and choice
Of many provinces from bound to bound.
He saw them in their forms of battle ranged,
How quick they wheel'd, and flying behind them shot
Sharp sleet of arrowy showers against the face
Of their pursuers, and overcame by flight;
The field all iron cast a gleaming brown:
Nor wanted clouds of foot, nor on each horse
Cuirassiers all in steel for standing fight,
Chariots, or elephants indorsed with towers
Of archers; nor of labouring pioneers
A multitude with spades and axes arm'd
To lay hills plain, fell woods, or valleys fill,
Or where plain was, raise hill, or overlay
With bridges rivers proud, as with a yoke."
   P. R., b. iv.
Glover in graphic terms describes the Persian host:
   " Five thousand horse,
Caparison'd in streak'd or spotted skins
Of tigers, pards, and panthers, form'd the van;
In quilted vests of cotton azure-dyed,
With silver spangles deck'd, the tawny youth
Of Indus rode; white quivers loosely cross'd
Their shoulders; not ungraceful in their hands
Were bows of glist'ning cane; the ostrich lent
His snowy plumage to the tissued gold,
Which bound their temples. Next a thousand steeds
Of sable hue on argent trappings bore
A thousand Persians, all select; in gold,
Shap'd as pomegranates, rose their steely points
Above the truncheons; gilded were the shields,
Of silver'd scales the corslets; wrought with gems
Of price, high-plum'd tiaras danc'd in light.
In equal number, in resembling guise,
A squadron follow'd; save their mail was gold,
And thick with beryls edg'd their silver shields."
   Athenaid, iv. 11-29.

What mass is volumed with a pitchy murk?
Bring quick the sword, give jav'lins, mount the walls! 50
The foe is here, come on!" With lusty shout
The Teucri mask themselves by all the gates,
And man the walls. For thus, on taking leave,
Thrice great in arms, Æneas had enjoined:
" If any fortune should befall meanwhile,
They should not venture to array their line,
Nor trust the field; that they should merely guard
The camp and walls in safety through the trench.
Therefore, although t' engage the hand do shame
And wrath incite, natheless they bar the gates 60
Against them, and his orders prompt perform,
And, armed, in hollow towers wait the foe."
Turnus, when flying forward he'd outstripped
The plodding host, by twenty chosen knights
Escorted, and unlooked for, nears the town;—
Whom bears a Thracian steed with spots of white,
And screens a golden helm with crimson plume.
"Who shall he be, O youths, along with me,
That first against the foeman—? Lo!"
he cries;
And, upward whirling it, his jav'lin shoots
Into the gales, the prelude of the fight, 71
And stately bears him onward o'er the plain.
His mates receive [the movement] with a shout,
And follow with a dreadful grating yell.
They marvel at the Trojans' sluggish hearts,
That they their persons to the righteous field
Commit not, that the men confronting arms
Do not advance, but their encampment hug.
On this and that side chafed does he survey
Upon his horse their rampires, and approach
Throughout the wayless [wilds] he seeks.
   And like 81
A wolf in ambush by a full sheep-fold,

---

82. In a passage, which is marked by one of the blots on his *Paradise Lost*, Milton represents Satan as vaulting over the boundaries of Paradise. As he uses the like illustration of the marauding wolf, he carries the simile farther than Virgil:
   " High over-leap'd all bound
Of hill or highest wall, and sheer within
Lights on his feet. As when a prowling wolf

When growls he at the cotes, and winds
   and rains
Enduring, past the middle of the night :
Safe 'neath their dams the lambs their
   bleatings ply :
He, fierce and felon in his anger, storms
Against the absent ; tortures him the rage
Of rav'ning, gathered from a length of time,
And jaws, unmoist with blood :—not other-
   wise
In the Rutulian, gazing on the walls   90
And camp, wrath kindles ; in his hardy
   bones
Vexation blazes up :—by what device
He may essay an entrance, and what course
Dislodge the cloistered Teucri from their
   trench,
And pour them out upon the plain. The
   fleet
Which, joined to their encampments' side,
   lay hid,
Fenced round with ramparts and the river-
   waves,
He storms, and calls on his exulting mates
For burnings, and, in ardor, fills his hand
With flaring pine. Then truly [to the toil]
They lean them ; Turnus' presence spurs
   them on ;   101
And all the youth are armed with grisly
   links.
They've sacked the hearths ; the smoky
   torch throws pitchy light,
And Vulcan jumbled ashes to the stars.
   What deity, O Muses, warded off
So felon burnings from the Teucri ? who
Such mighty blazes from the ships repelled ?
Say ye. Of old the credence in the fact ;
But the tradition [runs] from year to year.
What time upon the Phrygian Ida first 110
Æneas built his navy, and prepared
To seek the depths of sea, 'tis said, herself,
The Berecynthian mother of the gods,
Great Jove accosted in these terms :
   " My son,
Grant to a suitress what thy parent dear,
Olympus tamed, from thee doth claim. I
   own
A piny forest, loved through many a year.
A grove there stood upon the mountain's
   crest
Whither my holy [rites] they used to bear,
With swart pitch-pine and maple timbers
   dark :   120
These I upon the Dardan youth, when he

Whom hunger drives to seek new haunt for prey,
Watching where shepherds pen their flocks at eve,
In hurdled cotes amid the fields secure,
Leaps o'er the fence with ease into the fold."
         P. L., b. iv.

A navy needed, cheerfully bestowed.
Now me, uneasy, troubles troubling fear :
Dispel my apprehensions, and herein
Allow by prayers a parent to avail :—
That neither broken down by any course,
Nor hurricane of wind, they be subdued.
May it bestead that they upon our mounts
Were sprung." To her on th' other hand
   her son,
Who wheels the constellations of the world :
" O mother, whither callest thou the fates ?
Or what dost seek for these ? Shall vessels
   framed   132
By mortal hands enjoy immortal right ?
And sure through unsure risks Æneas run ?
To what divinity is privilege
So great conceded ? Still, when done with
   [risks],
The goal and ports Ausonian they shall gain
Hereafter, whichsoever shall have 'scaped
The billows, and the Dardan chief have
   borne
To fields Laurentine I, their mortal shape
Will take away, and of the mighty main 141
Bid them be goddesses ; as Nereus-born
Doto and Galatea cleave apart
The foaming ocean with their breast." He
   spoke ;
And that this is established, by the floods,
His Stygian brother's, by the banks, that boil
With pitch and with a sooty gulf, he nods,
And by his nod made all Olympus quake.
Accordingly the day engaged was come,
And the due seasons had the Destinies 150
Fulfilled ; when th' outrage [done] by Tur-
   nus warned
The Mother, from her holy barques to drive
The brands aloof. Here first against their
   eyes
Strange light there glared, and from the
   Dawn appeared
To scud across the sky a mighty cloud,
And Ida's choirs ; thereon a fearful voice
Drops forth along the gales, and fills the
   hosts
Of Trojans and Rutulians : " Be not ye
In anxious haste, O Teucer's sons, to guard
My vessels, neither arm your hands : the seas
It sooner will to Turnus be vouchsafed
To burn to ashes than my holy pines.
Go ye, enfranchised, go, the goddesses
Of ocean ; 'tis the Mother bids." And
   straight the sterns   164
Each burst away their fetters from the banks,
And after dolphins' fashion, with their beaks
Plunged down, the bottom of the waters
   seek.
Hence, — marvellous portent !— as many
   prows,

O'erlaid with bronze, as whilom on the strand
Had rested, just so many maiden forms 170
Reissue, and are wafted on the deep.
  Mazed were the minds of Rutulans; Messapus
Was e'en himself appalled, with troubled steeds;
And halts the stream hoarse-booming, and his step
[The god] of Tiber from the deep recalls.
But not bold Turnus confidence forsook:
Yea he their spirits raises by his words,
Yea chides them too: "'Tis at the Trojans aim
These prodigies; from them hath Jove himself
His wonted help withdrawn; [their ships] nor darts, 180
Nor fires of Rutuli, await. The seas
Are therefore pathless to the Teucer-race,
Nor is there any hope of flight; one half
Their means is cut away: the land, more-o'er,
Is in our hands; so many thousand arms
Italian nations bring. Naught me affray,
(If Phrygians make of any public vaunt,)
The doomful oracles of gods. Enough
To fates and Venus granted, that the fields
Of rich Ausonia have the Trojans touched;
On th' other hand my fates as well have I,—
With falchion to uproot the cursèd race,
My bride reft from me; nor affects that pang
Th' Atridæ only, nor is it allowed 194
Mycenæ only on their arms to seize.
But 'tis enough that they have fallen once:—
For them t' have *sinned* before had been enough,
[Then] loathing deep well nigh all womankind:—
To whom this trust in intervening trench,
And hindrances of dykes, thin screens of death, 200
Give confidence. But have they not beheld
The walls of Troja, framed by Neptune's hand,
Sink down in flames? But ye, O chosen ones!
Who with the sword to break their rampart through
Makes ready, and along with me assails
Their quaking camp? With me there is no need
Of Vulcan's armor, nor a thousand keels,
Against the Teucri. Let Etruscans all
Forthwith unite themselves as their allies.
The darkness and Palladium's dastard theft,— 210

The sentries of the fortress-summit slain,—
They need not fear; nor shall we be enwombed
Within a horse's darksome paunch: in light,
Before the world, 'tis fixed with fire to wrap
Their walls around. I'll force them to conclude
That they with Danai have no concern,
And with Pelasgic youth, whom Hector stayed
To the tenth year. Now, therefore, since is past
The better part of day, for what remains,
Rejoicing in our bravely sped affairs, 220
Your bodies tend, O heroes, and expect
The fight to be prepared." Meanwhile, the gates
With watch of sentries to beset, the charge
Is given to Messapus, and the walls
To ring with fires. Twice seven Rutulans,
The mounds with soldiery to keep, are culled:
But follow each of these a hundred youths,
Crimson with plumes, and glistering in gold.
Patrol they, and the courses change, and spread
Along the turf, indulge in wine, and tilt
The wassail-bowls of bronze. Glare up the fires; 231
The sleepless night the sentries spend in play.
  These from the trench above the Trojans view,
And occupy the heights in arms: more'oer,
Restless with dread, they scrutinize the gates
The bridges, too, and outer works unite:
They weapons bring together. Spur them on
Mnestheus and keen Serestus, whom the sire
Æneas, should misfortunes ever call,
Decreed to be commanders of the youths,
And managers of state. All through the walls 241
The legion, having portioned out by lot
The risk, their vigil keeps, and executes
Their courses,—what should be maintained by each.

---

222. The overwhelming weight of manuscripts forces one to read *parari* and not *parati* (v. 156). It is well that such is the case; as the verse has a sad jingle of *ps* as it stands; but with the other reading would have a jingle of *ats* besides.

231. "Now night her course began, and, over Heaven
Inducing darkness, grateful truce imposed
And silence on the odious din of war.
Under her cloudy covert both retired,
Victor and vanquish'd. On the foughten field
Michael and his Angels prevalent
Encamping, placed in guard their watches round
Cherubic waving fires." Milton, P. L., b. vi.

Nisus there was, the sentry of a gate,
Thrice-keen in arms, of Hyrtacus the son ;
Whom huntress Ida had as comrade sent
T' Æneas,—quick with dart and nimble shafts ;
And by his side Euryalus his mate.
Than whom of Æneadæ none other stood
More fair, nor [fairer] donned the arms of Troy ; 251
The stripling, marking his unrazored lips
With bloom of youth. With these the love was one,
And side by side upon the frays they dashed :
Then, too, with common post the gate they kept.
Saith Nisus : "Do the gods this glow infuse
Within our spirits, O Euryalus ?
Or doth his dread desire to each become
A god ? 'Tis either fight, or something grand,
My soul now long since drives me to essay ;
Nor is it satisfied with calm repose. 261

Thou seest what [full] reliance on their state
The Rutuli possesses. Here and there
Lights twinkle ; they, in sleep and wine unstrung,
Have laid them down ; the regions far and wide
Are hushed. Learn further what I meditate,
And what design now rises in my mind.
Æneas hither to be called do all,
Both commons and the fathers, warmly pray, 269
And men to be despatched [to him] to bear
Undoubted tidings. If, what I for thee
Demand, they promise, seeing for myself
The glory of th' achievement is enough,—
Meseems that I can underneath yon hill
Find out a passage to the walls and domes
Of Pallanteum." In astonishment
Euryalus was lost, pierced thro' and thro'
With lofty passion for renown : at once
In these addresses he his glowing friend :
"Me, then, thy comrade in thy grand emprise, 280
O Nisus, dost disdain to link ? Shall I
Send thee alone upon such heavy risks ?

---

252. "Among the rest, that all the rest excelld,
A dainty boy there wonn'd, whose harmlesse yeares
Now in their freshest budding gently sweld ;
His nimph-like face nere felt the nimble sheeres ;
Youth's downy blossome through his cheeke appeares."
In Spenser's Works, *Brittain's Ida*, c. i. 2.

"Comus. Were they of manly prime, or youthful bloom ?
Lady. As smooth as Hebe's their unrazor'd lips."
Milton, *Comus*.

253. "And shine as you exalted are :
Two names of friendship, but one star :
Of hearts the union, and those not by chance
Made, or indenture, or leas'd out t' advance
 The profits for a time.
No pleasures vain did chime,
Of rhymes, or riots at your feasts,
Orgies of drink, or feign'd protests :
But simple love of greatness and of good,
That knits brave minds and manners more than blood." Ben Jonson, *Underwoods*, 88, iv.

259-261. "Imagination of some great exploit
Drives him beyond the bounds of patience."
Shakespeare, 1 *K. Henry IV.*, i. 3.

Perhaps Nisus thought that
 "Virtue, if not in action, is a vice."
 Massinger, *The Maid of Honour*, i. 1.

Marlowe makes the Duke of Guise say, in *The Massacre at Paris*:
"Now, Guise, begin those deep-engendered thoughts
To burst abroad those never-dying flames,
Which cannot be extinguish'd but by blood.
Oft have I levell'd, and at last have learn'd
That peril is the chiefest way to happiness,
And resolution honour's fairest aim.
What glory is there in a common good,
That hangs for every peasant to achieve ?
That like I best, that flies beyond my reach.
Let me to scale the high Pyramides,

And thereon set the diadem of France ;
I'll either rend it with my nails to nought,
Or mount the top with my aspiring wings,
Although my downfall be the deepest hell."
264. "Wide o'er all
The dusky plain, by the fires half extinct,
Are seen the soldiers, roll'd in heaps confus'd,
The slaves of brutal appetite."
 Smollett, *The Regicide*, v. 3.,

265, 6. Stillness at night is well described by Brown :
"All, all is hushed. Throughout the empty streets
Nor voice, nor sound ; as if the inhabitants,
Like the presaging herds, that seek the covert
Ere the loud thunder rolls, had inly felt
And shunned the impending uproar.
"There is a solemn horror in the night, too,
That pleases me : a general pause through nature :
The winds are hushed. And as I passed the beach
The lazy billows scarce could lash the shore :
No star peeps through the firmament of heaven."
 Barbarossa, iii. 1.

273. "And choose we still the phantom through the fire,
O'er bog, and brake, and precipice, till death ?
And toil we still for sublunary pay ?
Defy the dangers of the field and flood,
Or, spider-like, spin out our precious all,
Our more than vitals spin (if no regard
To great futurity) in curious webs
Of subtle thought, and exquisite design ;
(Fine net-work of the brain !) to catch a fly !
The momentary buz of vain renown !
A name ; a mortal immortality !"
 Young, *Complaint*, N. vi.

282. "However, I with thee have fix'd my lot ;
Certain to undergo like doom : if death
Consort with thee, death is to me as life ;
So forcible within my heart I feel
The bond of nature draw me to my own ;
My own in thee, for what thou art is mine ;

Not so my sire Opheltes, used to wars,
Hath trained me up, amid Argolic dread
And toils of Troja nurtured ; nor with thee
Have I in such a way demeaned myself,
High-souled Æneas and his latest fates
While following. Here there dwells, there
   dwells a soul,
A scorner of the light, and deems that fame,
Whereat thou aimest, cheaply bought with
   life." 290
Nisus to these : " Sooth nothing of the kind
From thee I feared ; nor is it decent, no !
So me in triumph may to thee restore
Great Jove, or whosoe'er with kindly eyes
Views these ! But should there any,—thou
   perceiv'st
How many [risks] in such a crisis [lie] ;—
Should any, either accident or god,
To misadventure hurry me away,
I would that thou shouldst overlive : thy age
Is worthier of life. One let there be   300
Who may entrust me to accustomed earth,
Reft from the fray, or ransomed by a price ;
Or, this should any Fortune disallow,
One, who may to [my] absent [corse] dis-
   charge
Its obsequies, and grace it with a grave.
Nor to thy wretched mother could I prove
The spring of woe so deep ; who thee, [dear]
   boy,—
Alone of many mothers daring it,—
Pursues, nor recks of great Acesta's domes."
But he : " To idle purpose dost thou weave
Thy flimsy pleas, nor my resolve, now
   changed, 311
Withdraws from its position. Let us haste !"
He cries. The sentries he at once awakes ;
They take their places, and the courses keep.
The station being left, he paces on
As Nisus' mate, and seek they out the prince.
The rest of living things through all the
   lands

   Our state cannot be sever'd ; we are one,
One flesh ; to lose thee were to lose myself."
      Adam to Eve: Milton, *P. L.*, b. ix.

290. " ' I'll go,' said I, ' once more I'll venture all ;
   'Tis brave to perish by a noble fall.' "
      Pomfret, *Love Triumphant over Reason.*

        " 'Tis the danger crowns
A brave achievement." May, *The Heir*, act ii.

299. " Thou art too covetous of another's safety ;
   Too prodigal and careless of thine own."
      Massinger, *The Bashful Lover*, ii. 6.

317. " Mydnight was cum, and every vitall thing
With swete sound slepe theyr weary lyms did rest,
The beastes were still, the lytle byrdes that syng
Now sweetely slept besides theyr mothers brest :
The olde and all were shrowded in theyr nest.
The waters calme, the cruel seas did ceas,
The wudes, the fyeldes, and all thynges held theyr
   peace.

With sleep their cares were light'ning, and
   their hearts
Forgetful of their toils. The Trojans' lead-
   ing chiefs,
Their chosen youth, a consultation held   320
Upon the highest int'rests of the realm,—
[To wit,] what they should do, or who
   should now
T' Æneas be a messenger. They stand
On lengthful lances resting, and their shields
Engrasping in the midst of camp and plain.
Then Nisus, and with him Euryalus,
Forthwith to be admitted warmly beg :
" That their affair was weighty, and would
   prove
Worth the delay." Iulus first received
The flurried [youths], and Nisus bade to
   speak.   330
Then thus the son of Hyrtacus : " O list
With minds unbiassed, ye Æncan sons,
Nor let these [propositions], which we bring,
Be judged of from our years. The Rutuli,
In slumber and in wine unstrung, are
   hushed :
The quarter for a stratagem have we
Ourselves espied, which lieth to the view
Upon the double roadway of the gate,
That [stands] the nearest to the sea. Their
   fires
Are stayed, and starward is the collied
   smoke   340

" The golden stars wer whyrlde amyd theyr race,
And on the earth did laugh with twinkling lyght,
When eche thing nestled in his restyng place,
Forgat dayes payne with pleasure of the nyght :
The hare had not the greedy houndes in sight,
The fearfull dear of death stood not in doubt,
The partrydge dremt not of the falcons foot.

" The ougly beare nowe myndeth not the stake,
Nor how the cruell mastyves do hym tear ;
The stag lay still unroused from the brake,
The fomy boar feard not the hunters speare.
All thing was still in desert, bush, and brear.
With quyet heart now from their travailes rest ;
Soundly they slept in midst of all their rest."
      Sackville, *Complaynt of Henrye D. of*
        Buckingham, 79-81.

" All things were husht, each bird slept on his
   bough,
And night gave rest to him, day tir'd at plough :
Each beast, each bird, and each day-toyling wight,
Receiv'd the comfort of the silent night."
      Browne, *Britannia's Pastorals*, i. 3.

" Lo ! midnight from her starry reign
   Looks awful down on earth and main,
   The tuneful birds lie hush'd in sleep,
With all that crop the verdant food,
With all that skim the crystal flood,
Or haunt the caverns of the rocky steep.
No rushing winds disturb the tufted bowers,
No wakeful sound the moonlight valley knows,
Save where the brook its liquid murmur pours,
And lulls the waving scene to more profound
   repose."   Akenside, *Ode to Sleep*, ii. 2, 2.

Upraised. If ye allow us to employ
The chance, to seek Æneas, and the walls
Of Pallanteum, here anon with spoils,—
Vast carnage wrought,—us present will you
 see.
Nor doth the road mislead us as we go:
Below the darkling valleys we have seen,
In ceaseless chase, the outskirts of the town,
And gained a knowledge of the stream
 throughout."
Here, weighed with years, and in his judgment ripe,
Aletes: "O ye gods of fatherland, 350
Beneath whose providence Troy ever rests,
Ye still intend not clean to wipe away
The Teucri, seeing ye [to them] have brought
Such souls, and breasts so stanch within
 their youths."
Thus saying, he the shoulders and right
 hands
Of both engrasped, and with his tears his
 face
And lips bedewed. "To you, O heroes,
 what,
What worthy guerdons for these deeds of
 praise
Could I deem possible to be repaid?
First the most honorable will the gods, 360
And your own merits, render; then the rest
Anon the good Æneas will return,
Aye and Ascanius, in the flow'r of age,
Not e'er unmindful of so high desert."
"Yea, you do I, whose only safety lies
In the recov'ry of my sire,"—[th' address]
Takes up Ascanius,—"by the mighty gods
Of home, and Assarac's domestic god,
And hoary Vesta's shrines, conjure; whatever chance
And trust I have, I place it in your breasts:
Recall my sire, restore his presence: naught
 is sad 371
With him regained. Two goblets will I give,
In silver finished, and with figures crisp,
Which from Arisba crushed my father took;
And tripods twain; of gold two talents huge;
An ancient bowl, which Sidon's Dido gave.
But if to seize Italia, and enjoy
Her sceptres, shall to me a victor fall,
And to prescribe th' allotment of the spoil:—
Thou sawest on what steed, in armor what,
Marched Turnus [all] in gold:—that very
 [steed], 381
The scutcheon and the crimson plumes,
 will I

371. "For since mine eie your ioyous sight did mis,
 My chearfull day is turnd to chearelesse night,
 And eke my night of death the shadow is:
 But welcome now, my light, and shining lampe of
 blis!" Spenser, F. Q., l. 3, 27.

Reserve from the allotment, even now,
O Nisus, thy rewards. Besides, my sire
Will twice six ladies' persons, passing choice,
And captives grant, and their own arms
 with all;
Above these [gifts], whatever of domain
E'en king Latinus doth himself possess.
But thee, whom my own age is following on
With closer stages, youth to be revered, 390
With my whole bosom do I welcome now,
And my companion clasp for every risk.
No honor shall be sought in my exploits
Without thee; whether peace or war I make,
On thee [shall rest] my deepest trust of deeds
And words." To whom in answer suchlike
 speaks
Euryalus: "No day shall have evinced
That I for such bold ventures am no match:
Let only fav'ring Fortune fall no foe.
But I from thee 'bove every boon one thing
Entreat: a mother of the ancient strain 401
Of Priamus have I, whom, woe-begone,
Not Ilium's land, not king Acestes' walls
Withheld from going forth along with me.
Her, in unconsciousness of this our risk,
Whate'er it is, and [left] without farewell,
I now am quitting: Night and thy right hand
My witness be, that I could not endure
A parent's tears. But, I entreat, do thou
Console her helpless, and assist her lorn.

392. "O, I have suffered
 With those that I saw suffer."
 Shakespeare, *Tempest*, i. 2, 5, 6.

399. There is high authority for reading *haut*,
instead of *aut*, in v. 283, which appears to make the
whole passage more like Virgil than the lection of
Heyne, Weise, and others. A colon after *tantum*
gives it a stiff air, and joining the word with *arguerit* does not seem to mend the matter much.
See Forbiger's satisfactory comment.

"The intent, and not the deed,
Is in our power: and therefore who dares greatly
Does greatly." Brown, *Barbarossa*, v. 2.

403. Or, observing the Latin order:
"Not Ilium's land withheld from going forth
Along with me, not king Acestes' walls."

410. The poor lady might perhaps have answered
her noble comforter as Leonato did Antonio:

"I pray thee, cease thy counsel,
Which falls into mine ears as profitless
As water in a sieve; give not me counsel;
Nor let no comforter delight mine ear,
But such a one whose wrongs do suit with mine.
Bring me a father that so lov'd his child,
Whose joy of her is overwhelm'd like mine,
And bid him speak to me of patience;
Measure his woe the length and breadth of mine,
And let it answer every strain for strain;
As thus for thus, and such a grief for such
In every lineament, branch, shape, and form;
If such a one will smile, and stroke his beard;
Call sorrow joy; cry hem, when he should groan;
Patch grief with proverbs: make misfortune drunk
With candle-wasters; bring him yet to me,

This hope of thee [O] let me bear away: 411
The bolder shall I march to every chance."
With smitten mind the Dardan sons shed tears;
'Fore all the fair Iulus; and his soul
The picture of a filial duty touched:
Then thus speaks forth: "Assure thyself that all
Shall worthy prove of thy immense emprise:
For *that* thy mother shall be [such] to me,
And fail alone Creusa's name, nor small
The gratitude is waiting such a birth. 420
Whatever chances follow thy exploit,
By this my head I swear, whereby my sire
Before me used, what I engage to thee
On thy return, and with success, these same
On both thy mother and thy race shall wait."
Thus speaks he, weeping o'er him; he at once
His gilded falchion from his shoulder doffs,
Which with surprising skill Lycaon, [son]
Of Crete, had made, and fitted, handy [-formed],
With iv'ry sheath. To Nisus Mnestheus gives 430
A shaggy lion's hide and spoils; [with him]
Aletes stanch exchanges helm. Forthwith
In armor clad they march: whom, pacing on,
The band of chieftains all, alike of young
And agèd, to the gates attend with prayers.
Aye fair Iulus, too, beyond his years
Bearing both gallantry and manly thought,
Injunctions many gave to be conveyed
T' his father: but the breezes scatter all,
And, purposeless, bestow them on the clouds. 440
They, sallying forth, the trenches overpass,
And through night's shade the camp, their foe, they seek,

And I of him will gather patience.
But there is no such man: for, brother, men
Can counsel, and speak comfort to that grief,
Which they themselves not feel; but, tasting it,
Their counsel turns to passion, which before
Would give perceptial medicine to rage,
Fetter strong madness in a silken thread,
Charm ache with air, and agony with words.
No, no; 'tis all men's office to speak patience
To those that wring under the load of sorrow,
But no man's virtue, nor sufficiency,
To be so moral, when he shall endure
The like himself: therefore give me no counsel:
My griefs cry louder than advertisement."
Shakespeare, *Much Ado about Nothing*, v. 1.

414. " He hath a tear for pity, and a hand
Open as day for melting charity."
2 *K. Henry IV.*, iv. 4.

442. Shakespeare has a fine description of a camp by night:

Yet first of many doomed to be the death.
At every step, in slumber and in wine
Throughout the grass dispread, they bodies view!
In upward posture chariots on the shore;
Among the traces and the wheels the men;
Together lying arms, together wines.
First from his lip thus spake Hyrtacides:
"Euryalus, with our right hand we must be bold: 450
Th' occasion now invites us of itself:
Here lies the route. Do thou,—lest any hand
May lift itself against us from the rear,—
Be on the watch, and keep a far look-out.
These [regions] I a wilderness will make,
And by a spacious pathway lead thee on."
So speaks he, and subdues his voice; at once
With sword attacks proud Rhamnes, who, by chance
On elevated cushions pillowed up,
From his whole chest was slumber puffing forth; 460
The same a king, and [he] to Turnus, king,
Most welcome augur: but by augur's art
He could not stave destruction off. Hard by
Three lacqueys, heedlessly among their arms
While lying, and the squire of Remus, he
Destroys; his charioteer, too, finding him
Just at his very steeds; and with the sword
Their lolling necks he severs; then of head
Despoils their lord himself, and leaves the trunk
With blood sob-breathing: warmed with sable gore, 470
The earth and couches reek. Moreo'er, he slays both Lamyrus

" Now entertain conjecture of a time,
When creeping murmur, and the poring dark,
Fill the wide vessel of the universe.
From camp to camp, through the foul womb of night,
The hum of either army stilly sounds,
That the fix'd sentinels almost receive
The secret whispers of each other's watch.
Fire answers fire; and through their paly flames
Each battle sees the other's umber'd face.
Steed threatens steed, in high and boastful neighs
Piercing the Night's dull ear; and from the tents
The armorers, accomplishing the knights,
With busy hammers closing rivets up,
Give dreadful note of preparation.
The country cocks do crow, the clocks do toll,
And the third hour of drowsy morning name."
K. Henry V., iv. chorus.

444. They probably had such thoughts as these:
" Now, Sleep, still child of sable-hooded night,
Befriend us! From the dark Lethean cell
Up-conjure all thy store of drowsy charms!
Lock fast their lids, o'erpower each torpid sense,
That they awake not ere the deed be done."
Hartson, *Countess of Salisbury*, v. 2.

471. " The slaughter then all measure did surpasse;
Whilst victors rag'd, bloud from each hand did raine;

And Lamus, and the young Serranus, who
Full much had revelled on that night, in
mien
Distinguished, and was lying, in his limbs
O'ermastered by a fulness of the god.
O happy man! if he without a pause
Had made that revel even with the night,
And eked it out till daylight :—as, unfed,
A lion, raising through the crowded folds
Alarms,—for spurs him hunger mad,—both
grinds 480
And rends the unresisting flock, and dumb
With terror; roars he with a mouth of
blood.
Nor less the carnage of Euryalus :
He too himself, afire, fumes on throughout,
And in the midst a num'rous, nameless
throng,
E'en Fadus and Herbesus he attacks,
And Rhesus, Abaris too, unaware :—
Rhœtus awake, and viewing all; but he
Behind a mighty wassail-bowl in fear
Ensconced himself : in whose confronting
breast 490
He, close upon him, as he rises up,
Hid his whole blade, and with abundant
death
Withdrew it. Th' other spews the crimson
life,
And wines, commingled with the blood,
returns,
In dying. He upon his stratagem
In ardor presses on; and now advanced
Up to the comrades of Messapus. There
He saw the failing of their latest fire,

And duly tethered horses cropping grass :
When briefly such like Nisus,—for he felt
That he by too great slaughter and desire
Was led away,—saith, "Let us cease; for
nears 502
Th' unfriendly light. Of vengeance there
is spent
Enough; a path is made among the foes."
Both many arms of heroes, finished off
With massive silver, do they leave behind,
And bowls together, and fair figured stuffs.
Euryalus th' accoutrements of Rhamnes
[grasps],
His belt, too, golden in its studs, which
gifts
To Remulus of Tibur whilom sent 510
The passing wealthy Cædicus, what time
He, absent, would unite him [to himself]
In hospitage ; the other at his death
Bequeaths them to his grandson to pos-
sess ;—
After his death the Rutuli in war,
And in engagement, won them :—these he
grasps,

501, 2. " Danger without discretion to attempt
Inglorious, beast-like, is."
Spenser, *F. Q.*, iii. 11, 23.

" Some fortitude is seen in great exploits,
That justice warrants, and that wisdom guides ;
All else is towering phrensy and distraction."
Addison, *Cato*, ii.

" Be advis'd :
Heat not a furnace for your foe so hot,
That it do singe yourself. We may outrun,
By violent swiftness, that which we run at,
And lose by over-running. Know you not,
The fire, that mounts the liquor till it run o'er,
In seeming to augment it, wastes it. Be advis'd :
I say again, there is no English soul
More stronger to direct you than yourself ;
If with the sap of reason you would quench,
Or but allay, the fire of passion."
Shakespeare, *K. Henry VIII.*, i. 1.

" But as it is not the mere punishment,
But cause, that makes a martyr, so it is not
Fighting, or dying, but the manner of it,
Renders a man himself. A valiant man
Ought not to undergo, or tempt a danger,
But worthily, and by selected ways :
He undertakes with reason, not by chance.
His valour is the salt to his other virtues :
They are all unseason'd without it."
Ben Jonson, *New Inn*, iv. 3.

" Temper your heat,
And lose not, by too sudden rashness, that
Which, be but patient, will be offer'd to you.
Security ushers ruin ; proud contempt
Of an enemy three parts vanquish'd, with desire
And greediness of spoil, have often wrested
A certain victory from the conqueror's gripe.
Discretion is the tutor of the war,
Valour the pupil."
Massinger, *Maid of Honour*, i. 3.

502, 3. " The silent hours steal on,
And flaky darkness breaks within the east."
Shakespeare, *K. Richard III.*, v. 3.

The liquid rubies dropping downe the grasse,
With scarlet streames the fatall fields did staine."
Stirling, *Jonathan*, 83.

489. Had Rhœtus been more fortunate, he would
have been paralleled by Braggadocchio.
" To whom she thus.—But ere her words ensewd,
Unto the bush her eye did suddein glaunce,
In which vaine Braggadocchio was mewd,
And saw it stirre : she lefte her percing launce,
And towards gan a deadly shafte advaunce,
In minde to marke the beast. At which sad
stowre,
Trompart forth stept, to stay the mortall chaunce,
Out crying: 'O ! whatever hevenly powre,
Or earthly wight thou be, withold this deadly howre !
" O ! stay thy hand ; for yonder is no game
For thy fiers arrowes, them to exercize ;
But loe ! my lord, my liege, whose warlike name
Is far renownd through many bold emprize ;
And now in shade he shrowded yonder lies.'
She staid : with that he crauld out of his nest,
Forth creeping on his caitive hands and thies ;
And standing stoutly up, his lofty crest
Did fiercely shake, and rowze as comming late from
rest." Spenser, *F. Q.*, ii. 3, 34, 5.

493. The tutor might do well to point to v. 349,
as evidence that *purpureus* does not necessarily
mean," purple."

And vainly to his gallant shoulders suits.
He then Messapus' trimly fitting helm,
And graced with plumes, puts on him.
  From the camp
They draw away, and safety seek to gain.
Meanwhile the horse, sent on from La-
  tium's city   521
While the remainder of the host in line
Is ling'ring on the plains, were on the march,
And to king Turnus bringing on replies,—
Three times a hundred, all equipped in
  shields,
With Volscens chief. And they were near-
  ing now
The camp, and ent'ring on the mounds,
  what time
These winding by the left-hand path from far
Descry they, and his helm Euryalus
Hath in the glimm'ring shade of night be-
  trayed   530
Unthoughtful, and, confronted to the beams,
Flashed back. 'Twas not for naught the
  glimpse was gained.
Aloud shouts Volscens from the squadron:
  "Halt!
Ye warriors! What the object of your
  march?
Or who are ye in arms? Or whither hold
Your course?" They make no effort at reply,
But hasten on their flight upon the woods,
And trust the night. The horse oppose
  themselves
At byways known on this side and on that,
And ev'ry outlet with a guard invest.   540
There was a thicket, bristling wide with
  brakes
And sable ilex, which had serried thorns
Choked up in ev'ry quarter; fitfully
The pathway shone among the darkened
  walks.
The gloom of branches, and his cumbrous
  spoil,
Euryalus obstruct, and his alarm
Conducts him from his line of route astray.
Off Nisus starts: and now, not knowing
  [this],
He had escaped the foemen, and the spots,
Which since from Alba's name were "Al-
  ban" called:—   550
Then king Latinus [there] had lofty stalls:—
When [still] he stood, and towards his
  absent friend
In vain looked back: "Ill-starred Euryalus,
Thee in what quarter have I left? Or where
Shall I pursue, again unrav'lling all
The tangled pathway of the cheating wood?"
At once e'en backward his examined steps
He tracks, and wanders through the stilly
  brakes.

He hears the horses, hears the din and signs
Of those pursuing. Nor was long the time
In th' interval, when reaches to his ears
A shouting, and he sees Euryalus,
Whom at this moment doth the squadron all,
Through the deception of the place and
  night,
With wild'ring hubbub on a sudden seize,
O'erwhelmed and struggling [much,] full
  much in vain.
What should he do? With power what,
  what arms,
The stripling to deliver should he dare,
Or, death-doomed, fling him on the midst
  of swords,
And speed by wounds a glorious death?
  In haste   570
A javelin hurling with his in-drawn arm,
Up-gazing on the lofty Moon, he thus
Prays with his voice: "Do thou, O god-
  dess, thou
Propitious aid our task, O pride of stars,
And thou Latonian guardian of the groves;
If any off'rings to thy altars e'er
On my behalf my father Hyrtacus
Hath brought, if any by my hunts myself
Have added, or upon thy dome hung up,
Or fastened to thy holy pediments;   580
This troop do thou allow me to confound,
And guide my missiles through the gales."
He said;
And, as he strains with his whole frame,
  he hurls
The steel. The winging spear asunder
  smites
The shades of night, and swoops upon the
  back
Of Sulmo, turned away, and there is
  snapped,
And through his midriff shoots with rifted
  wood.
He's rolled along, disgorging from his breast
The fevered tide, death-cold, and smites
  his flanks

---

574. "As Cynthia, from her wave-embattel'd
  shrouds
Op'ning the west, comes streaming thro' the clouds,
With shining troops of silver-tressed stars
Attending on her, as her torch-bearers;
And all the lesser lights about her throne
With admiration stand as lookers on;
Whilst she alone, in height of all her pride,
The queen of light along her sphere doth glide."
  Drayton, *Charles Brandon to Queen Mary of
    France.*

589. "Death-cold. Yes, Felisarda, he is gone,
  that in
The morning promis'd many years; but death
Hath in few hours made him as stiff, as all
The winds of winter had thrown cold upon him,
And whisper'd him to marble."
  Shirley, *The Brothers,* iv. 5.

With long [-drawn] sobs. [In] diff'rent
  [quarters] round   590
They gaze. Thereby the keener, he, the
  same,
Lo! poised another javelin from his tip
Of ear. While they are in alarm the shaft
Through both of Tagus' temples hissing
  passed,
And, heated, to his piercèd brain it cleaved.
Fell Volscens storms, nor anywhere descries
The sender of the lance, nor whither he,
Should throw him all aglow. " Still, thou
  meanwhile
With thy hot blood to me the penalties
Shalt pay for both," he cries: at once
  with sword   600
Unsheathed upon Euryalus he rushed.
Then sooth affrighted, wildly Nisus shrieks;
Nor could he any longer shroud himself
Within the gloom, or bear so sore a pang:
"Me, me!—I'm here!—[the man] who did
  the deed;
On me the falchion turn, O Rutuli!
Mine own is all the stratagem; that [youth]
Naught either dared or could; this firma-
  ment
And conscious stars to witness do I call.
He only loved too well his hapless friend."
Such like the words he uttered: but the
  sword,   611
Thrust home with power, grided through
  his ribs,
And brasts his snowy breast. Euryalus

---

605. Eve says:
  ' And to the place of judgment will return,
  There with my cries importune Heaven, that all
  The sentence, from thy head removed, may light
  On me, sole cause to thee of all this woe,
  Me, me only, first object of his ire."
                        Milton, *P. L.*, b. x.
                       " Stop, O stop!
  Hold your accursed hands! On me, on me
  Pour all your torments."
                        Brown, *Barbarossa*, v. 2.

610. So Othello:
  " Speak of me as I am; nothing extenuate,
  Nor set down aught in malice: then must you
    speak
  Of one, that lov'd not wisely, but too well."
                        Shakespeare, *Othello*, end.

613. "Which when that warriour heard, dismount-
  ing straict
  From his tall steed, he rusht into the thick,
  And soone arrived where that sad portraict
  Of death and dolour lay, halfe dead, halfe quick;
  In whose white alabaster brest did stick
  A cruell knife that made a griesly wownd,
  From which forth gusht a stream of gore blood
    thick,
  That all her goodly garments staind arownd,
  And into a deepe sanguine dide the grassy grownd."
                        Spenser, *F. Q.*, ii. 1, 39.

Is rolled in death, and o'er his comely limbs
Gore gushes, and upon his shoulders sinks
His fainting neck: as when a gaudy flower,
Cut under by the plough, in dying flags;
Or poppies with a weary neck droop head,
When haply they are cumbered by the rain.
But Nisus hurtles on the midmost [foes],
And singly through them all he Volscens
  seeks;   621

---

614. The same great poet, on Belphœbe's seeing
the wounded Timias:
  " Shortly she came whereas that woefull squire
  With blood deformed lay in deadly swownd:
  In whose faire eyes, like lamps of quenched fire,
  The christall humour stood congealed rownd;
  His locks, like faded leaves fallen to grownd,
  Knotted with blood in bounches rudely ran;
  And his sweete lips, on which before that stownd
  The bud of youth to blossome faire began,
  Spoild of their rosy red were woxen pale and wan."
                            F. Q., iii. 5, 29.

614, 15. " See, his rich blood in purple torrents
flows,
  And Nature sallies in unbidden groans;
  Now mortal pangs distort his lovely form;
  His rosy beauty fades, his starry eyes
  Now darkling swim, and fix their closing beams;
  Now in short gasps his labouring spirit heaves,
  And weakly flutters on his faultering tongue,
  And struggles into sound."
                    Smith, *Phædra and Hippolytus*, act v.

616. This beautiful figure is employed by the
author of the elegy on the death of Sir Philip
Sidney, entitled *The Mourning Muse of Thestylis*.
It was not written by Spenser, but is appended by
him to his own charming *Astrophel*.
  " His lips waxt pale and wan, like damaske roses
    bud
  Cast from the stalke, or like in field to purple
    flowre,
  Which languisheth being shred by culter as it
    past." Lodowick *Bryskett*, in Spenser's Works.

618. *Demisere*, v. 437, is plainly an aorist.
  " Yet in her side deep was the wound in fight:
  Her flowing life the shining armour stains:
  From that wide spring long rivers took their flight,
  With purple streams drowning the silver plains:
  Her cheerful colour now grows wan and pale,
  Which oft she strives with courage to recal,
  And rouse her fainting head, which down as oft
    would fall.
  All so a lily press'd with heavy rain,
  Which fills her cup with show'rs up to the
    . brinks:
  The weary stalk no longer can sustain
  The head, but low beneath the burden sinks.
  Or as a virgin rose her leaves displays,
  Whom too hot scorching beams quite dis-
    arrays:
  Down flags her double ruff, and all her sweet
  decays." P. Fletcher, *Purple Island*, xi. 29, 30.

  " Thus the fair lily, when the sky's o'ercast,
  At first but shudders in the feeble blast;
  But when the winds and weighty rains descend,
  The fair and upright stem is forc'd to bend;
  Till broke at length, its snowy leaves are shed
  And strew world with dying sweets their native bed."
                    Young, *Force of Religion*, b. ii. end.

On Volscens singly fixes thought. Whom
  round
The clustered foes this side and that repulse
With sword in hand. He presses none
  the less,
And whirls his blade of lightning; till
  within
The yelling Rutulan's confronted mouth
He buried it, and, as he dies, his foe
Bereft of life. Then o'er his lifeless friend
He forward flung himself, pierced through
  and through,
And there at length in calm of death reposed.
O happy pair! If aught my lays can do,
No day shall ever from a mindful age 632
Erase you, long as shall Æneas' house
Inhabit Capitolium's moveless rock,
And sovereignty the Roman father hold.
  The conqu'ring Rutuli, of prey and spoils
The masters, breathless Volscens to the
  camp
A-weeping bare. Nor less in camp the woe,
On Rhamnes being found deprived of life,
And chiefs so many slain in common death,
Serranus too, and Nyma. Vast the throng
E'en at the corses and the men half-dead,

And at the spot, with milkwarm slaughter
  fresh, 643
And runnels brimming with their foaming
  blood.
They recognise the spoils among themselves,
Alike the shining helmet of Messapus,
And trappings with a flood of sweat regained.
  And now first sprent the lands with
  virgin light
Aurora, leaving Tithon's saffron bed,
The sun now shed upon them, objects now
In light uncurtained. Turnus to their arms,
In arms arrayed himself, his men awakes;
And musters each the bronzen lines his own,
For battle, and with manifold reports 654
They whet their wrath. Yea,—piteous to
  be seen,—
Impale they on the points of hoisted spears
Euryalus' and Nisus' very heads,
And follow in full shout. The sturdy
  Æneadæ
Within the left-hand quarter of the walls
Arrayed their line against them,—for the
  right 660
Is girdled by the stream,—and occupy
Their trenches vast, and on the lofty towers
In melancholy do they stand; at once
The heroes' heads impaled [their spirit]
  roused,
But too familiar to their wretched [friends],
And dripping with a sable gore. Meanwhile,
Throughout the quaking city flitting round,
The wingèd courier Rumor posts, and glides
On to Euryalus's mother's ears.
But suddenly the wretched [lady's] bones
Their heat forsook; the shuttle from her
  hands 671

---

625.   " I ne'er saw
A lightning shoot so, as my servant did:
His rapier was a meteor, and he waved it
Over them, like a comet, as they fled him.
I mark'd his manhood! Every stoop he made
Was like an eagle's at a flight of cranes."
                Ben Jonson, *The New Inn*, iv. 3.

628, 9. " Suffolk first died, and York, all haggled
  over,
Comes to him, where in gore he lay insteep'd,
And takes him by the beard: kisses the gashes,
That bloodily did yawn upon his face;
And cries aloud: 'Tarry, dear cousin Suffolk!
My soul shall thine keep company to heaven:
Tarry, sweet soul, for mine, then fly abreast;
As in this glorious and well-foughten field
We kept together in our chivalry!'
Upon these words I came, and cheer'd him up:
He smil'd me in the face, raught me his hand,
And, with a feeble gripe, says: 'Dear my lord,
Commend my service to my sovereign.'
So did he turn, and over Suffolk's neck
He threw his wounded arm, and kiss'd his lips;
And so, espous'd to death, with blood he seal'd
A testament of noble-ending love."
                Shakespeare, *K. Henry V.*, iv. 6.
To the poet himself may be applied the praise
bestowed on Colin by Alexis.
" By wondring at thy Cynthiaes praise,
Colin, thyselfe thou mak'st us more to wonder,
And her upraising doest thyselfe upraise."
                Spenser, *Colin Clouts Come Home Again*.

632, 3. " You may sooner part the billows of the sea,
And put a bar betwixt their fellowships,
Than blot out my remembrance; sooner shut
Old Time into a den, and stay his motion;
Wash off the swift hours from his downy wings,
Or steal eternity to stop his glass,
Than shut the sweet idea I have in me."
                Fletcher, *The Elder Brother*, iii. 5.

649. " Aurora from old Tithon's frosty bed
  (Cold, wint'ry, wither'd Tithon) early creeps,
Her cheek with grief was pale, with anger red,
  Out of her window close she blushing peeps;
Her weeping eyes in pearled dew she steeps."
                P. Fletcher, *Piscatory Eclogues*, vii. 1.

657. So the Picts are said to have treated King
  Alpin:
          " That sacred head,
Where late the Graces dwelt, and wisdom mild
Subdued attention, ghastly, pale, deform'd,
Of royalty despoil'd, by ruthless hands
Fixt on a spear, the scoff of gazing crowds,
Mean triumph, borne."
                Hamilton, *Episode of the Thistle*.

668. " This tattling gossip hath a thousand eyes:
Her airy body hath as many wings;
Now about Earth, now up to Heav'n she flies,
And here and there with every breath she flings
Hither and thither lies and tales she brings."
                Drayton, *Legend of Matilda the Fair*, 14.
" For evil news rides post, while good news baits."
                Milton, *Samson Agonistes*.

671. " Too trew the famous Marinell it fownd:
Who, through late triall, on that wealthy strond
Inglorious now lies in sencelesse swownd
Through heavy stroke of Britomartis hond.

Was shaken out, the web, too, tumbled o'er.
Forth flies she hapless, and, with woman's shriek,
With tattered hair, the walls and foremost bands
She wildly seeks with speed: not she of men,
Not she of risk and weapons, heedful; heaven
Thereon with her complainings does she fill:
"Is't thus, Euryalus, I thee behold?
Couldst thou, that one, who wert the late repose
Of my old age, O heartless, leave me lorn?
Neither to thee, upon such grievous risks

Sent secretly, t'address her latest word,
To thy sad mother were the means vouchsafed? 683
Ah! thou upon a land unknown, consigned
A prey to Latin dogs and birds, dost lie!
Nor I thy mother, at thine obsequies
Have led thee forth, or have I closed thine eyes,
Or bathed thy wounds; shrouding thee with the robe,
Which I for thee quick hastened night and day,
And with the loom an agèd woman's cares
Would comfort. Whither shall I follow thee? 691
Or now what land thy joints, and wrenchèd limbs,
And mangled carcass holds? Is't this that thou
Returnest to me of thyself, my son?
Is't this I've followed both by land and sea?
Pierce me, if ye have any duteousness;
On me launch all your darts, O Rutulans;
Me first annihilate ye with the sword;

"Which when his mother dear did understand,
And heavy tidings heard, whereas she playd
Amongst her watry sisters by a pond,
Gathering sweete daffadillyes, to have made
Gay girlonds, from the Sun their forheads fayr to shade;
"Eftsoones both flowres and girlands far away
She flong, and her faire deawy lockes yrent;
To sorrow huge she turnd her former play,
And gamesom merth to grievous dreriment:
She threw herself down on the continent,
Ne word did speake, but lay as in a swowne,
Whiles all her sisters did for her lament
With yelling outcries, and with shrieking sowne;
And every one did tear hir girlond from her crowne."
Spenser, *F. Q.*, iii. 4, 29, 30.

674. "Her yellow locks that shone so bright and long,
As sunny beames in fairest somers day,
She fiersly tore, and with outragious wrong
From her red cheeks the roses rent away:
And her faire brest, the thresaury of ioy,
She spoyld thereof, and filled with annoy."
Spenser, *Astrophel*, 27.

"Th' inexorable hand of Fate
Weighs down his eyelids, and the gloom of death
His fleeting light eternally o'ershades.
Him on Choaspes o'er the blooming verge
A frantic mother shall bewail; shall strew
Her silver tresses in the crystal wave:
While all the shores re-echo to the name
Of Teribazus lost." Glover, *Leonidas*, b. viii.

680. "My boy, my Arthur, my fair son!
My life, my joy, my food, my all the world!
My widow-comfort, and my sorrow's cure!"
Shakespeare, *K. John*, iii. 4.

"Does the kind root bleed out his livelihood
In parent distribution to his branches,
Adorning them with all his glorious fruits,
Proud that his pride is seen when he's unseen:
And must not gratitude descend again
To comfort his old limbs in fruitless winter?"
Massinger, *The Old Law*, i. 1.

"Thou art the only comfort of my age;
Like an old tree I stand among the storms;
Thou art the only limb that I have left me,
My dear green branch; and how I prize thee, child,
Heaven only knows." Lee, *Theodosius*, ii. 1.

685. "O parents ruthful, and heart-renting sight!
To see that son, that your soft bosoms fed,
His mother's joy, his father's sole delight,
That with much cost, yet with more care, was bred,
A spectacle, ev'n able to affright
A senseless thing, and terrify the dead!
His dear, dear blood upon the cold earth pour'd,
His quarter'd corse of crows and kites devour'd."
Drayton, *Barons' Wars*, ii. 67.

"Besides remember this in chief:
That, being executed, you deny
To all his friends the rites of funeral,
And cast his carcase out to dogs and fowls."
J. Fletcher, *The Bloody Brother*, iii. 1.

687. "Ah, too, the lustre of the eyes is fled!
Heavy and dull, their orbs neglect to roll,
In motionless distortion stiff and fixed:
Till by the trembling hand of watchful age ....
Clos'd; and, perhaps for ever! ne'er again
To open on the sphere, to drink the day."
W. Thompson, *Sickness*, b. iii.

692. "This country here hath bred me, brought me up,
And shall I now refuse a grave in her?
I am in my second infancy, and children
Ne'er sleep so sweetly in their nurse's cradle
As in their natural mother's."
Massinger, *The Old Law*, i. 1.

694. *Gustavus*; as *Arvida* dies:
"Friend! brother! speak.—He's gone;—and here is all
That's left of him, who was my life's best treasure.
How art thou fall'n, thou greatly valiant man!
In ruin graceful, like the warrior spear,
Tho' shiver'd in the dust."
Brooke, *Gustavus Vasa*, v. 7.

697, 8. "'Why do I overlive?
Why am I mock'd with death, and lengthen'd out
To deathless pain? How gladly would I meet
Mortality, my sentence, and be earth
Insensible! How glad would lay me down

Or thou, great sire of gods, compassion take,
And with thy bolt thrust down this hated head   700
Beneath th' infernal realms; since otherwise
I cannot burst away a ruthless life."
By this her weeping are their spirits shocked,
And mournful wailing spreads among them all:
Their shattered pow'rs are listless for the frays.
Her, as their sorrows she inflames, Idæus
And Actor, by direction of Ilioneus,
And of Iulus, weeping sorely, grasp,
And 'tween their hands replace beneath her roof.

As in my mother's lap! There I should rest,
And sleep secure. . . . . Why comes not death,'
Said he, ' with one thrice-acceptable stroke
To end me?'"   Milton, *P. L.*, b. x.

" O amiable lovely death! . . . .
Arise forth from the couch of lasting night,
Thou hate and terror to prosperity,
And I will kiss thy detestable bones ;
And put my eye-balls in thy vaulty brows:
And ring these fingers with thy household worms:
And stop this gap of breath with fulsome dust,
And be a carrion monster like thyself."
                        Shakespeare, *K. John*, iii. 4.

703. Grief is the greater suffering for the *want* of tears :
" Is it at last then so? Is he then dead?
What! dead at last? quite, quite, for ever dead?
There, there, I see him : there he lies, the blood
Yet bubbling from his wounds. Oh, more than savage!
Had they or hearts or eyes that did this deed ?
Could eyes endure to guide such cruel hands ?
Are not my eyes guilty alike with theirs,
That this can gaze, and yet not turn to stone ?—
I do not weep! The springs of tears are dried ;
And of a sudden I am calm, as if
All things were well;—and yet my husband's murdered!
Yes, yes, I know to mourn! I'll sluice this heart,
The source of woe, and let the torrent loose."
                  Congreve, *Mourning Bride*, end.

705. " This melancholy flatters, but unmans you ;
What is it else but penury of soul ;
A lazy frost, a numbness of the mind,
That locks up all the vigour to attempt?"
                        Dryden, *Cleomenes*, i. 1.

Glover attributes the same effect to tender music, and beautifully illustrates it:
            " In admiration mute,
With nerves unbrac'd by rapture, he, entranc'd,
Stands like an eagle, when his parting plumes
The balm of sleep relaxes, and his wings
Fall from his languid side."   *Leonidas*, b. vi.

709. They might have said to her :
" Weep no more, nor sigh, nor groan ;
  Sorrow calls no time's that gone :
  Violets pluck'd the sweetest rain
  Makes not fresh, nor grow again.
  Trim thy locks, look cheerfully ;
  Fate's hid ends eyes cannot see :
  Joys as winged dreams fly fast!
  Why should sadness longer last?

But fearful din the trumpet from afar
Clanged forth from ringing bronze : a shout ensues,   711
And back the welkin roars. The Volsci haste
At even pace, a vault of bucklers formed ;
And they the trenches to fill up prepare,
And root away the palisade. Some seek
An entrance, and with scaling-gear to climb
The ramparts, where the line is thin, and light
The ring lets through, not so compact with men.
On th' other hand the Teucri shower forth
All sort[s] of weaponry, and thrust them down   720
With sturdy poles, inured to guard their walls
In their long war. Stones, too, with troublous weight
They rolled, if they could any way break through
The shielded line : while still it is their joy
Beneath the serried vault of shields to bear
All hazards. Neither do they now hold out :
For, where th' enormous phalanx edges nigh,
The Trojans roll alike and force along
A monster pile, which whelmed the Rutuli
Far-wide, and broke their canopy of arms.
Nor further do the bold Rutulians seek   731
In blind encounter to engage, but strive
To drive them from the palisade with darts.
Elsewhere Mezentius, fearful to be viewed,
Swayed an Etruscan pine, and on them flings
Smoke-yielding fires. Moreo'er Messapus,
Steed-tamer, Neptune's son, the palisade
Tears down, and calls for ladders 'gainst the walls.
You, O Calliope, do I entreat,
Breathe on me as I sing what massacres
There then with steel, what deaths, did Turnus cause ;   741
What hero each despatched adown to hell ;
And the great outlines of the war with me
Do ye unfold : for ye, O goddesses,
Alike remember, and ye can record.
There was a tower of colossal height
And [flanked] with lofty bridges, by its place

Grief is but a wound to woe :
Gentlest fair, mourn, mourn no mo."
        Fletcher, *The Queen of Corinth*, iii. 2.

717. " And now reduc'd on equal terms to fight,
Their ships like wasted patrimonies show ;
Where the thin scattering trees admit the light,
And shun each other's shadows as they grow."
          Dryden, *Annus Mirabilis*, 126.

746. " And lifted up his loftie towres thereby,
That they began to threat the neighbour sky."
          Spenser, *Mother Hubberd's Tale*.

Of vantage ; which to th' utmost of their strength '
Th' Italians struggled all to take by storm,
And raze with fullest effort of their powers.
The Trojans, on the other hand, with stones
Protect it, and through hollow loopholes, close, 752
Their weapons launch upon them. In the van
A flaring firebrand Turnus hurled amain,
And to its side a blaze he fastened ; which
All-potent through the wind, the plankings seized,
And grappled to the uprights, inly gnawed.
They, in confusion, are alarmed inside,
And vainly from their evils wish escape.
While they together crowd, and settle back
Upon that side, which from the plague is free ; 761
Then with the sudden weight down fell the tower,
And all the welkin thunders with the crash.
To earth half-lifeless, with a monster mass
Pursuing them, and stabbed by their own darts,
And through their breasts with rigid wood transpierced,
They swoop. With difficulty one, Helenor
And Lycus 'scaped : of whom the tender-aged
Helenor,—whom to the Mæonian king
The slave Licymnia covertly had borne,
And in forbidden armor sent to Troy,—
Was light [accoutred] with a naked sword,
And with a blank escutcheon unrenowned.
And he,—when he perceived himself amid
The heart of Turnus' thousands, Latin troops 775
On this side standing by, and troops on that ;—
As [some] wild beast, which by a massive ring
Of hunters pent, against their weapons storms,
And flings her, not unknowing, on her death,
And with a spring is borne beyond their spears :— 780
Not otherwise the stripling, doomed to die,
Hurtles upon the centre of his foes,
And, where he sees the weapons thickest, darts.
But Lycus, far superior with his feet,
Alike amid the foes, and 'mid their arms,
In flight is holding on the walls, and strives
To clutch the lofty copings with his hand,
And reach the right hands of his comrades : whom
Turnus, at once pursuing with full speed
And dart, upbraids triumphant in these [terms]: 790
" Hast hoped, O madman, that thou couldst escape
Our hands ?" At once he grasps him as he hangs,
And with a mighty portion of the wall
He tears him down : as when or hare, or swan
Of snowy figure, hath the squire of Jove,
Seeking the heights, upborne with hooky claws ;
Or, by its mother sought with many a bleat, a lamb
The wolf of Mars hath ravished from the cotes.
In every quarter is a shout upraised.
On rush they, and with rubbish fill the dykes : 800
Some volley blazing torches to the heights.
Ilioneus [lays prostrate] with a rock,
E'en a stupendous fragment of a mount,
Lucetius, as he closes on the gate,
And carries fires ; Liger Emathion fells,
Asilas Corynæus ;—one adept
In javelin, in the far-deceiving bolt
The other. Cæneus [kills] Ortygius,
Turnus the conqu'ring Cæneus ; Turnus [slays]
Itys, and Clonius, Dioxippus, 810
And Promolus, and Sagaris, and Idas,
As he is standing for the tower tops ;
Capys Privernus. Him Themilla's nimble spear
At first had grazed : he,—buckler cast away,—
A hand in madness to the wound applied :
So towards him flew the arrow on its wings,
And to his left side fast the hand was nailed,
And, inly buried, with a deathful wound
The spirit's breathing passages it burst.
In peerless arms the son of Arcens stood,

794. Spenser thus describes the whiteness of the swan:

" With that I saw two swannes of goodly hewe
Come softly swimming downe along the lee ;
Two fairer birds I yet did never see :
The snow, which doth the top of Pindus strew,
Did never whiter shew,
Nor Jove himselfe, when he a swan would be
For love of Leda, whiter did appeare :
Yet Leda was (they say) as white as he,
Yet not so white as these, nor nothing near
So purely white they were,
That even the gentle stream, the which them bare,
Seem'd foule to them, and bad his billowes spare
To wet their silken feathers, least they might
Soyle their fayre plumes with water not so fayre ;
And marre their beauties bright,
That shone as Heavens light."
Prothalamion, st. 3.

With needled cloak, and bright in dusky
dye 821
Of Spain, distinguished in appearance;
whom
His father Arcens had despatched, brought
up
Within his mother's grove, about the streams
Of the Symæthus, where Palicus' altar
[stands],
Rich and appeasable. His whizzing sling,—
Spears laid aside,—Mezentius e'en himself,
Its thong indrawn thrice round his head,
discharged,
And in the centre clove apart his brows,
As he confronted him, with molten lead,
And stretched him prostrate on the plen-
teous sand. 831
Then first in battle is Ascanius said
T' have aimed the nimble arrow, (hereto-
fore
Accustomed to alarm the flying beasts,)
And with his hand t' have overthrown the
brave
Numanus, who had Remulus for surname;
And, lately wedded in the marriage bond,
Had Turnus' younger sister [to his bride].
He, yelling out before the leading line
[Words] seemly and unseemly to be named,
And puffed in heart with novel kingship,
stalked, 841
And moved him on, a giant, with the cry:
"Doth it not shame you to be closed again
By siege and trench, ye Phrygians, cap-
tived twice,
And in the front of death to stretch your
walls?
Lo! [fools,] who matches with us claim to
them
By war! What god, what madness, drove
you on
To Italy? No sons of Atreus here,
No, nor Ulysses, liar in his speech.
Hardy from its original our race, 850
Our children to the rivers from the first
We carry down, and in the felon frost,
And in the waves we steel them; for the
chase
Our boys are wakeful, and they tire the
woods;

---

852. "Heaven's arch is oft their roof, the pleasant
shed
Of oak and plane oft serves them for a bed.
To suffer want, soft pleasure to despise,
Run over panting mountains crown'd with ice,
Rivers o'ercome, the wasted lakes appal,
(Being to themselves oars, steerers, ships and all,)
Is their renown: a brave all-daring race,
Courageous, prudent, doth this climate grace."
Drummond, *The Speech of Caledonia*.

854. "Let Sloth lie softening till high noon in down,
Or lolling fan her in the sultry town,

Their pastime is to manage steeds, and
shafts
To aim from bow. Yea, tolerant of toils,
And used to scantness, either doth our
youth
Tame earth with harrows, or thrill towns
with war.
With iron every stage of life is worn,

Unnerv'd with rest: and turn her own disease,
Or foster others in luxurious ease:
I mount the courser, call the deep-mouth'd hounds,
The fox unkennell'd flies to covert grounds;
I lead where stags through tangled thickets tread,
And shake the saplings with their branching head:
I make the faulcons wing their airy way,
And soar to seize, or stooping strike their prey;
To snare the fish I fix the luring bait:
To wound the fowl I load the gun with fate."
Parnell, *Health*.

855. "Oh! he's all hero, scorns th' inglorious ease
Of lazy Crete, delights to shine in arms,
To wield the sword, and lanch the pointed spear:
To tame the generous horse, that nobly wild
Neighs on the hills, and dares the angry lion:
To join the struggling coursers to his chariot,
To make their stubborn necks the reins obey,
To turn, to stop, or stretch along the plain."
Smith, *Phædra and Hippolytus*, i. 1.

857. "To dare boldly,
In a fair cause, and, for their country's safety,
To run upon the cannon's mouth undaunted;
To obey their leaders, and shun mutinies;
To bear with patience the winter's cold,
And summer's scorching heat, and not to faint,
When plenty of provision fails, with hunger;—
Are the essential parts make up a soldier."
Massinger, *A New Way to Pay Old Debts*, i.

"Yet still, e'en here, content can spread a charm,
Redress the clime, and all its rage disarm.
Though poor the peasant's hut, his feasts though
small,
He sees his little lot the lot of all;
Sees no contiguous palace rear its head,
To shame the meanness of his humble shed;
No costly lord the sumptuous banquet deal,
To make him loathe his vegetable meal;
But calm, and bred in ignorance and toil,
Each wish contracting, fits him to the soil.
Cheerful at morn, he wakes from short repose,
Breathes the keen air, and carols as he goes;
With patient angle trolls the finny deep,
Or drives his vent'rous ploughshare to the steep;
Or seeks the den where snow-tracks mark the
way,
And drags the struggling savage into day.
At night returning, ev'ry labour sped,
He sits him down the monarch of a shed;
Smiles by his cheerful fire, and round surveys
His children's looks, that brighten at the blaze
While his lov'd partner, boastful of her hoard,
Displays her cleanly platter on the board:
And haply too some pilgrim, thither led,
With many a tale repays the nightly bed."
Goldsmith, *Traveller*.

859. "Nature, a mother kind alike to all,
Still grants her bliss at labour's earnest call;
With food as well the peasant is supply'd
On Idra's cliff as Arno's shelvy side;
And though the rocky-crested summits frown,
These rocks, by custom, turn to beds of down."
Ibid.

S

And with the spear reversed our bullocks'
  backs   860
We harass ; nor doth sluggish eld impair
The powers of our mind, and change their
  force.
Hoar hairs with helm we press, and 'tis
  our joy
To bring together booty ever fresh,
And live by plunder. Broidered is your dress
With saffron hue and shining purple dye ;
Sloth is your heart['s delight] ; your joy it is
To revel in the dance ; your tunics, too,
Have sleeves, and lappets have your caps.
  O sooth
Ye Phrygian *girls*, for you're no Phrygian
  men,   870
Go through the lofty tops of Dindymus,
Where gives the pipe to you, thereto inured,
A melody [that rings] from double mouth.
The timbrels, and the Berecynthian flute
Of the Idæan mother summon *you ;*
Leave arms to *men*, and from the sword
  withdraw."

868. " Thee the voice, the dance, obey,
    Temper'd to thy warbled lay,
    O'er Idalia's velvet-green
    The rosy-crowned Loves are seen
    On Cytherea's day,
    With antic sports and blue-ey'd pleasures,
    Frisking light in frolic measures ;
    Now pursuing, now retreating,
    Now in circling troops they meet :
    To brisk notes in cadence beating,
    Glance their many-twinkling feet."
        Gray, *The Progress of Poesy.*
870. " Where hast thou been since first the fight
        began,
    Thou less than woman in the shape of man ?"
        Dryden, *The Indian Emperor*, i. 2.
873.   " Lycis dies,
    For boist'rous war ill-chosen. He was skill'd
    To tune the lolling flute, and melt the heart ;
    Or with his pipe's awak'ning strain allure
    The lovely dames of Lydia to the dance.
    They on the verdant level graceful mov'd
    In vary'd measures ; while the cooling breeze
    Beneath their swelling garments wanton'd o'er
    Their snowy breasts, and smooth Caÿster's
        stream,
    Soft-gliding, murmur'd by."
        Glover, *Leonidas*, b. viii.
876. " Remember whom you are to cope withal :
    A sort of vagabonds, rascals, run-aways,
    A scum of Bretagnes, and base lackey peasants,
    Whom their o'er-cloyed country vomits forth
    To desp'rate ventures, and assur'd destruction.
    You sleeping safe, they bring you to unrest ;
    You having lands, and bless'd with beauteous
        wives,
    They would distrain the one, distain the other.
    And who doth lead them, but a paltry fellow,
    Long kept in Bretagne at our mother's cost ;
    A milksop, one that never in his life
    Felt so much cold as over shoes in snow ?
    Let's whip these stragglers o'er the seas again ;
    Lash hence these over-weening rags of France,
    These famish'd beggars, weary of their lives ;
    Who, but for dreaming on this fond exploit,

The like as brags he in his speech, and
  chants
His awful taunts, Ascanius brooked him not ;
And, right in front, upon the horse-hair
  string
He stretched the bolt, and, drawing out
  his arms   880
In opposite directions, took his stand,
First humbly supplicating Jove by vows :
" Almighty Jove, assist my bold emprise.
Myself will, in thy honor, to thy fanes
Bring yearly gifts, and 'fore thy altars place
A snowy bullock with a gilded brow,
And bearing on a level with the dam
His head, who butts already with his horn,
And tosses with his feet the sand." The
  father heard,
And from a cloudless quarter of the sky
He thundered on the left : the doom-fraught
  bow   891
At the same instant gives a twang. Forth
  flies,
As fearfully it whirrs, the indrawn shaft,
And pierces through the head of Remulus,
And with the steel bores through his hollow
  brows.
" Go, mock our valor with thy haughty prate !
Twice-captived Phrygians these replies
  return
To Rutulans." Ascanius this alone.
The Teucri follow with acclaim, and shout
With joy, and raise his courage to the stars.
In the celestial region then by chance   901
The tressed Apollo from above beheld
The squadrons of Ausonia, and their town,—
Sitting upon a cloud,—and in these [words]
The conquering Iulus he bespeaks :
" Heav'n bless thee in thy virgin valor, boy ;

    For want of means, poor rats, had hang'd them-
        selves :
    If we be conquer'd, let men conquer us."
        Shakespeare, *K. Richard III.*, v. iii.
900. " A valiant gentleman, whate'er thou art !
    And, by mine honour, very nobly fought
    I have not seen, in all my life before,
    So young, and tender, and effeminate a face
    Father such rough and manly fortitude."
    Webster, *The Weakest goeth to the Wall*, v. 1.
902.   " When good men pursue
    The path mark'd out by virtue, the blest saints
    With joy look on it, and seraphick angels
    Clap their celestial wings in heavenly plaudits,
    To see a scene of grace so well presented,
    The fiends, and men made up of envy, mourn-
        ing."   Massinger, *The Maid of Honour*, v. 1.
                    " He is like
    Nothing that we have seen, yet doth resemble
    Apollo, as I oft have fancied him,
    When, rising from his bed, he stirs himself
    And shakes day from his hair."
        Beaumont and Fletcher, *Cupid's Revenge*, i. 3.
906.   " This brave youth,
    This bud of Mars, (for yet he is no riper,)

Thus to the stars advance is made, O thou
By gods engendered, and to gender gods.
All wars, which are by fate to come, beneath
The line of Assarac shall duly sink   910
To rest; nor thee doth Troy confine." At once
These having spoken forth, from heav'n on high
He throws himself, disparts the breathing gales,
And seek Ascanius.   Then in shape of face
Is metamorphosed into Butes aged.
He to the Dardan[-sprung] Anchises erst
Was squire, and trusty warder at his gates:
His sire then to Ascanius as his mate
Consigned him.   Paced Apollo, 'like in all
The agèd [man], both in his voice and hue,
And hoary locks, and armor, fell with din;
And in these words the hot Iulus he   922
Accosts: "Be it enough, Æneas-born,
That by thy weapons hath Numanus fallen,
With mischief none [to thee]: this maiden praise
The great Apollo doth to thee allow,
And grudgeth not equality in arms.
For what remains, desist, O boy, from war."
Thus saying, in the midst of his discourse
Apollo quitted mortal ken, and far   930
To filmy air he vanished from his eyes.
The Dardan chieftains recognised the god,
And heav'nly shafts, and in his flight they heard
His quiver rattling.   Therefore at the words
And will divine of Phœbus they restrain
Ascanius, greedy of the fight: themselves
Into the battle-strife once more advance,
And on unhidden dangers fling their lives.

When once he had drawn blood, and fleshed his sword,
Fitted his manly metal to his spirit,
How he bestirred him! What a lane he made,
And through their fiery bullets thrust securely,
The hardened villains wondering at his confidence!"
J. Fletcher, *The Lover's Progress*, i. 2.

Ascanius might have said, with Melantius in *The Maid's Tragedy*, by Beaumont and Fletcher, iv. 2:
"When I was a boy,
I thrust myself into my country's cause,
And did a deed that pluck'd five years from time,
And styl'd me man then."

"Come, brother John; full bravely hast thou flesh'd
Thy maiden sword."
Shakespeare, 1 *K. Henry IV.*, v. 4.

928. Ascanius was probably inclined enough to quarrel with the inhibition.

"*K. James.* And whither art thou going, pretty Ned?
Ned. To seek some birds, and kill them, if I can:
And now my schoolmaster is also gone,
So have I liberty to ply my bow:
For, when he comes, I stir not from my book."
R. Greene, *George-a-Greene*.

A shout careers along the battlements
Throughout the walls; they briskly bend the bows,   940
And whirl the thong: with weapons all the ground
Is strewed.   Then bucklers and the hollow helms
Give forth a ringing with the clash. A fight
Fierce rises, fierce as, swooping from the west,
Through [influence] of the rainy Kids, a shower
Lashes the ground; as storms, with plenteous hail,
Dash headlong on the floods, when Jupiter,
With Austers dread, a wat'ry tempest hurls,
And in the welkin brasts the hollow clouds.
Pand'rus and Bitias, sprung from Ida-born
Alcanor, whom within the holy wood   951
Of Jove the sylvan [nymph] Iæra reared,—
Youths on a level with their native firs
And mounts,—the gate, which at the chief's command
Was given to their charge, they open throw,
Relying on their arms, and freely court
The foe inside their walls.   Themselves within
Upon the right and left, before the towers
Stand armed in steel, and glist'ring with their plumes
Upon their stately heads: as, heaven-high,
By rilling streams, or on the banks of Po,
Or near sweet Athesis, in union mount
A pair of oaks, and lift their heads unshorn   963
Up to the sky, and nod with tow'ring crest.
The Rutuli burst in, when they beheld
A passage lying open.   Quercens straight,
And, beauteous in his arms, Aquicolus,
And Tmarus, rash of soul, and warlike Hæmon,
With all their troops, or, routed, turned their backs,
Or in the very threshold of the gate   970
Laid down their life.   Then passion more and more
Is waxing greater in their hostile souls;
And now, together massed, the Trojans crowd
To the same point, and dare with hand to hand
T' encounter, and to sally farther forth.
To chieftain Turnus, at a diff'rent side
While storming, and confounding troops, is brought
The tidings, that the foe is all afire
With slaughter fresh, and proffers open gates.

963. "Having their tops familiar with the sky."
Drayton, *Polyolbion*, vii.

He quits his enterprise, and, roused by wrath
Ferocious, dashes to the Dardan gate, 981
And the proud brothers ; and Antiphates
The first, (for he himself presented first,)
The bastard issue from a Theban dame
Of high Sarpedon, with a jav'lin hurled
Does he lay low : th' Italian cornel wings
Through balmy air, and, in the gorget stuck,
It penetrates beneath his bosom deep :
The cavern of the sable wound returns
A frothing wave, and in his piercèd lung
The iron heats. Then Merops with his hand
He fells, and Erymas, Aphidnus then ; 992
Then Bitias, as he flashes with his eyes,
And rages in his spirit,—not with dart :
For not to dart would he have life resigned ;
But, hissing loud, the whirled phalaric
  swooped,
Shot like the levin ; which nor twain bull-
  hides,
Nor trusty coat of mail, with double plate
And gold withstood : together sinking fall
His giant limbs. The earth gives forth a
  groan, 1000
And o'er him thunders his colossal shield.
Suchlike at times on the Eubœan strand
Of Baiæ doth a stony structure sink,
Which, whilom built of mountain piles,
  they fling
In ocean : thus it headlong trails a wreck,
And, dashed upon the shoals, sinks quite to
  rest ;
The seas embroil them and the swarthy sands
Are heaved. Then quakes with din high
  Prochyta,
And,—flinty couching-place,—Inarime,
By Jove's commands upon Typhœus placed.
Here armor-puissant Mars imparted soul

And vigor to the Latins, and he turned
His pungent goads beneath their breast,
  and sent 1013
Upon the Trojans Flight and gloomy Fear.
From ev'ry quarter they together flock,
Since opportunity of fight is given,
And on their spirit falls the warrior-god.
As soon as Pandarus his brother sees
With outstretched carcass, and in what estate
Their fortune stands, what chance directs
  affairs : 1020
The gate upon its veering hinge he wheels
With force prodigious, with his shoulders
  broad
Against it bearing, and leaves many of his
  [friends]
In the sore contest from the walls shut out ;
But others of them with himself shuts in,
And as they rush along admits them : fool !
Who could not see in centre of the troop
The king of the Rutulians hurtling on,
But pent him in the town by his own act,
Like [some] huge tiger 'mong the passive
  flocks. 1030
Straight from his eyes beamed forth un-
  wonted light,
And fearfully his armor clanged ; his plumes
Of bloody color quiver on his head,
And flashing levins from his shield he darts.
The Æneads, troubled on a sudden, know
His hated visage and his giant limbs.
Then Pandarus, the mighty, forward springs,
And, hot with choler at a brother's death,
Speaks forth : " This is not, of thy dowry
  [share],
Amata's palace ; nor doth Ardea's heart
Incloister Turnus in his native walls. 1041
Hostile encampments thou beholdest : hence
There is no power to escape." To him
The smiling Turnus with a breast composed :
" Begin, if any prowess in thy soul
[There dwelleth], and thy right hand close
  engage ;
To Priam thou shalt say, that here as well
There hath been an Achilles found :" he said.
The other, straining with his utmost strength,
A spear hurls forth upon him, rough with
  knots,
And bark untrimmed. The gales caught
  up the wound ; 1051
Saturnian Juno coming turned it off,
And on the gate the spear is stuck. " But not
This weapon, which with pow'r wields *my*
  right hand,
Shalt thou escape : for no such [warrior] he,
The sender of the weapon and the wound."

---

989. If "cavern" be thought too strong for English usage, it is easy to substitute "hollow" or "opening."

1000, 1. Spenser speaks similarly of the fall of the giant's club, in the duel with Arthure :

"Therewith the gyaunt buckled him to fight,
Inflamd with scornefull wrath and high disdaine,
And lifting up his dreadfull club on hight,
All armd with ragged snubbes and knottie graine,
Him thought at first encounter to have slaine.
But wise and wary was that noble pere ;
And, lightly leaping from so monstrous maine,
Did fayre avoide the violence him nere ;
It booted nought to thinke such thunderbolts to beare ;

" Ne shame he thought to shonne so hideous might :
The ydle stroke, enforcing furious way,
Missing the marke of his misaymed sight,
Did fall to ground, and with his heavy sway
So deepely dinted in the driven clay,
That three yardes deepe a furrow up did throw :
The sad earth, wounded with so sore assay,
Did grone full grievous underneath the blow ;
And, trembling with strange feare, did like an erthquake show." F. Q., i. 8, 7, 8.

1029. *Que*, if rendered "and," would make the passage unintelligible.

Thus speaks he, and he rises up aloft
On his uplifted sword, and with the steel
His middle brow, betwixt the temples twain,
He rives asunder, and the hairless cheeks,
With an enormous wound. A crash is raised:
The earth is with the giant load convulsed.
His sinking limbs and arms, blood-stained
  with brains, 1063
He stretches as he dies upon the ground;
And down his head on this side and on that
In equal parts from either shoulder hung.
The Trojans, wheeled around with quaking
  dread,
In all directions fly, and if that thought
Had straightway to the conqueror oc-
  curred,—
To burst the bolts asunder with his hand,
And through the gates to let his comrades
  in,— 1071
That day would to the war and race have
  proved
Their last. But frenzy, and the madding lust
Of slaughter, drove him burning on his foes
In front. First Phalaris he overtakes,
And hamstrung Gyges; then he flings the
  spears,
Reft from them, on the fliers on their back:
Juno the powers and the soul supplies.
He Halys adds their comrade, Phegeus too,
With shield transpierced; then wareless on
  the walls, 1080
And rousing Mars, Alcander e'en and
  Halius,
Noëmon too and Prytanis,
Lynceus, against him moving in advance,
And calling on his mates, with waving sword
He, straining ev'ry effort, from the mound
Deftly anticipates; his head, struck off
In close encounter at a single blow,
Lay far away together with his helm.
Next Amycus, destroyer of wild-beasts,
Than whom none other was more fortunate
In ointing jav'lins, and in arming steel
With poison; Clytius, too, of Æolus 1092
The son, and Cretheus, of the Muses friend,

Cretheus, the Muses' comrade, in whose
  heart
Songs ever [dwell], and citherns, and [the
  love] to strain
His numbers on the strings: he ever used,
Horses, and heroes' arms, and fights, to
  chant.
At length, [when now] the slaughter of
  their men
Is heard, the Trojan chiefs in conclave meet,
Mnestheus and keen Serestus, and they see
Their comrades flying and a foe let in.
And Mnestheus: "Whither, whither next
  do ye 1102
Your flight advance?" he cries; "what
  other walls,
What buildings, now beyond do ye possess?
Shall one man,—[he] too, O my citizens,
Walled by your ramparts in on ev'ry side,
Such fearful massacres have, unamerced,
Throughout the city dealt? So many chiefs
Of youths despatched to Orcus? Do ye not
For your unhappy land, and ancient gods,
And great Æneas, dastard [as ye be],
Both pity feel and shame?" They, fired by
  such, 1112
Are reassured, and stand in serried host.
By slow degrees 'gan Turnus to retreat

> Crown'd with the rich traditions of a soul,
> That hates to have her dignity prophaned
> With any relish of an earthly thought:—
> Oh then how proud a presence doth she bear!
> Then is she like herself, fit to be seen
> Of none but grave and consecrated eyes.
> Nor is it any blemish to her fame
> That such lean, ignorant, and blasted wits,
> Such brainless gulls, should utter their stolen
>   wares
> With such applauses in our vulgar ears;
> Or that their slubber'd lines have current pass
> From the fat judgments of the multitude;
> But that this barren and infected age,
> Should set no difference 'twixt these empty spirits,
> And a true poet; than which reverend name
> Nothing can more adorn humanity:"
> *Every Man in his Humour*, v. 1, Gifford's
>   note, p. 157, ed. 1816.

1102–12. "He call'd so loud, that all the hollow deep
Of Hell resounded. 'Princes, potentates,
Warriors, the flower of Heaven! once yours, now
  lost;
If such astonishment as this can seize
Eternal spirits: or have ye chosen this place
After the toil of battle to repose
Your wearied virtue, for the ease you find
To slumber here, as in the vales of Heaven?
Or in this abject posture have ye sworn
To adore the conqueror, who now beholds
Cherub and seraph rolling in the flood,
With scatter'd arms and ensigns; till anon
His swift pursuers from Heaven-gates discern
The advantage, and, descending, tread us down
Thus drooping, or with linked thunderbolts
Transfix us to the bottom of this gulf?
Awake, arise, or be for ever fallen!'"
  Milton, *P. L.*, b. i.

1073. See note on l. 501, 2.

1093–6. Ben Jonson has a noble passage, in
which he contrasts the good poet with the bad:
"I can refell opinion, and approve
The state of poesy, such as it is,
Blessed, eternal, and most true divine:
Indeed, if you will look on poesy,
As she appears in many, poor and lame,
Patch'd up in remnants and old worn-out rags,
Half starv'd for want of her peculiar food,
Sacred invention; then, I must confirm
Both your conceit and censure of her merit:
But view her in her glorious ornaments,
Attired in the majesty of art,
Set high in spirit with the precious taste
Of sweet philosophy; and, which is most,

From the engagement, and to seek the stream,
And quarter which is skirted by its wave.
Thereby more keenly, with a mighty shout,
The Trojans ply them, and compact their band:
As when a troop with hostile weapons galls
A furious lion; but affrighted he, 1120
Fell, grimly scowling, backward draws away;
And neither rage nor prowess him allow
To turn his back, nor,—sooth desiring this,—
Is he against it able to advance,
For weaponry and men. Not otherwise,
The doubting Turnus back withdraws his steps,
Not hurried, and his soul boils up with wrath.
Moreo'er he even then had twice assailed
The centre of his foes; he turns their troops
Along the ramparts routed twice in flight.
But all the host in hurry from the camp
Collects in one; nor strength against him dares 1132
Saturnian Juno to supply; for Jove
Sent down the airy Iris from the sky,
Bearing his sister no silk-soft behests
If Turnus from the Teucri's lofty walls

Should not retire. So, neither with his shield,
Nor his right hand, the youth so rude [a shock]
Is able to withstand: he thus with darts,
From all sides showered down, is overwhelmed. 1140
Rings with unceasing clank the casque around
His hollow brows, and with the stones [its plates]
Of massive bronze gape open, and its plumes
Are torn from off his head; nor boss avails
Against their dints: redouble with their spears
Both Trojans, and e'en thundering Mnestheus. Then
All o'er his body perspiration drips,
And drives,—nor pow'r to breathe,—a swarthy tide;
A sickly panting shakes his jaded joints.
He then at length head foremost with a spring
In all his armor flung him on the flood.
This caught the comer with its yellow gulf,
And bore him up on gentle waves, and blithe, 1153
The blood washed off, restored him to his mates.

BOOK X.

MEANWHILE all-powerful Olympus' dome
Is opened, and the father of the gods,
And monarch of mankind, a congress calls
To his star-gemmed abode, wherefrom aloft
On all the lands he gazes, and the camp
Of the Dardanians, and the Latin tribes.
They take their seats in double-gated halls.
Himself begins: "Great denizens of heaven,
Pray why is your decision backward turned,

And ye so fiercely strive with hostile souls?
I had refused that Italy in war 11
Should clash with Teucer's sons; what variance this

---

10. "Ay me! what thing on Earth, that all thing breeds,
Might be the cause of so impatient plight?
What furie, or what feend, with felon deeds
Hath stirred up so mischievous despight?
Can griefe then enter into heavenly harts,
And pierce immortall breasts with mortall smarts?"
Spenser, *Teares of the Muses*, 8.

12. The evil effects of dissension are charmingly described by Shakespeare, who makes *Titania* say to *Oberon*:

"These are the forgeries of jealousy;
And never, since the middle summer's spring,
Met we on hill, in dale, forest, or mead,
By paved fountain, or by rushy brook,
Or on the beached margent of the sea,
To dance our ringlets to the whistling wind,
But with thy brawls thou hast disturb'd our sport.
Therefore the winds, piping to us in vain,
As in revenge, have suck'd up from the sea
Contagious fogs; which, falling in the land,
Have every pelting river made so proud,
That they have overborne their continents:

Line 6. "The great seraphic lords and cherubim
In close recess and secret conclave sat;
A thousand demigods on golden seats,
Frequent and full." Milton, *P. L.*, b. i.
Olympus' gates unfold; in heaven's high towers
Appear in council all th' immortal powers.
Great Jove above the rest exalted sate,
And in his mind revolved succeeding fate;
His awful eye with ray superior shone,
The thunder-grasping eagle guards his throne;
On silver clouds the great assembly laid,
The great creation at one view surveyed."
Gay, *The Fan*, ii. 1-8.

BOOK X. 263

Against my inhibition? What alarm
Or these, or those, hath moved to follow
   arms,
And to provoke the sword? The proper
   time,—
Forestall it not,—for conflict will arrive,
When fierce Carthago on the Roman
   heights
One day gigantic ruin, and the Alps,
Unlocked, shall loose. It then will be
   allowed
To strive in hatred, then to force events.
Now cease, and glad adjust a league
   agreed."   21
These Jupiter in few; but not a few
The golden Venus in reply returns:
"O father, O thou everlasting power
O'er men and things,—for now what is
   there else
We can entreat?—dost thou perceive how
   mock
The Rutuli, and Turnus through the midst
Is borne along, conspicuous in steeds,
And dashes forward, puffed with fav'ring
   Mars?
Their fencèd works screen not the Teucri
   now;   30
Moreo'er, they battle join inside the gates,
And in the very bulwarks of the walls;
And overflow the trenches with their blood.
Æneas, wareless of it, is away.
Wilt thou ne'er let them be relieved from
   siege?
Once more upon the walls of infant Troy

The ox hath therefore stretch'd his yoke in vain,
The ploughman lost his sweat; and the green corn
Hath rotted, ere his youth attained a beard:
The fold stands empty in the drowned field,
And crows are fatted with the murrain flock:
The nine men's morris is fill'd up with mud;
And the quaint mazes in the wanton green,
For lack of tread are undistinguishable.
The human mortals want their winter cheer;
No night is now with hymn or carol blest:—
Therefore the moon, the governess of floods,
Pale in her anger, washes all the air,
That rheumatic diseases do abound.
And thorough this distemperature, we see
The seasons alter: hoary-headed frosts
Fall in the fresh lap of the crimson rose;
And on old Hyems' chin, and icy crown,
An odorous chaplet of sweet summer buds
Is, as in mockery, set. The spring, the summer,
The childing autumn, angry winter, change
Their wonted liveries; and the mazed world,
By their increase, now knows not which is which:
And this same progeny of evil comes
From our debate, from our dissension:
We are their parents and original."
   Midsummer Night's Dream, ii. 2.

20. Does it not seem more natural to apply *res rapuisse* to the gods, whom Jupiter is addressing, and more dignified to make them anxious rather for activity than for plunder?

The foeman hangs, aye e'en another host;
Once more, too, 'gainst the Trojans rises
   up
From the Ætolian Arpi Tydeus' son.
I sooth believe that wounds remain for me,
And I, thy offspring, human arms await!
If without thy permission, and despite 42
Thy heav'nly will, the Trojans Italy
Have sought,—their errors let them ex-
   piate;
Neither do thou assist them with thy aid:
But if, in their pursuance of replies
So many, which the deities on high,
And Manes, deigned; why now can any
   one
Upset thy laws, or why new fates devise?
For what should I recall the ships burnt up
On Eryx's strand? For what the king of
   storms   51
And blasts of fury, from Æolia roused?
Or Iris, from the clouds despatched? Now
   e'en
The Manes,—this department of the world
Remained untried,—she stirs, and, on the
   upper realms
Let loose upon a sudden, hath throughout
The central cities of the Itali
Allecto revelled. Not a whit concerned
For universal sway am I: those hopes
We cherished while our fortune stood: let
   those   60
Prevail, whom thou would'st rather should
   prevail.
If lies no district, which to Teucer's sons
Thy flinty consort may vouchsafe,—O sire,
By ruined Troja's smoking wreck I crave,
Be it allowed [to me] from arms to send
Ascanius safe away; be it allowed
My grandson may survive. Let,—if you
   will,—
Æneas be on unknown billows tossed,
And whatsoever path shall Fortune deign,
Let him pursue: this [boy] may I have
   power   70
To screen, and steal him from the awful
   fight.
Amath is [mine, mine] lofty Paphus is,
And high Cythera, and Idalia's home:
Arms laid aside, here let him pass unfamed
His life. With sovereign sway Carthago
   bid
To gall Ausonia: naught to Tyrian towns
Shall from this quarter in resistance rise.
What boots it to escape the plague of war,
And midway to have fled through Grecian
   fires,
And that so many dangers of the sea, 80

---

80. See note on *Æn.* v. 854.

And land unbounded, to their dregs are drained,
While Latium and a re-arising Pergamus
The Teucri seek? Had it not better proved
On the last ashes of their native land
T" have settled down, and on the ground whereon
Troy stood? The Xanthus and the Simoïs,
I pray, restore them [in their] wretched [plight];
And Ilian's haps once more to undergo,
O father, to the Teucer-race vouchsafe."
Then royal Juno, spurred by heavy rage:
" Why dost thou drive me silence deep to break,   91
And blaze abroad in words a smothered grief?
Hath any one of men and gods compelled
Æneas wars to follow, or himself
A foe on king Latinus to inflict?
Italia, fates the movers, he hath sought :—
Be it so ;—by Cassandra's frenzies driven :
Have we advised him to forsake his camp,
Or trust his life to winds? Or to a boy
The head administration of a war,   100
Or ramparts, to confide? and agitate
A Tyrrhene covenant, or tribes at peace?
What deity, what rigid force of ours,
Hath driven him to the blunder? Where is here
Juno, or Iris, from the clouds sent down?
A scandal is it that the Itali
Your baby Troy with blazes should invest,
And Turnus settle in his native land,
Who had Pilumnus for his father's sire,
Whose mother was Venilia the divine :—
What! are the Trojans with a murky torch
Upon the Latins violence to bring?   112
The fields of others 'neath their yoke to gall,
And carry off the plunder? What! to cheat

Brides' fathers, and from [people's] laps to filch
Betrothèd [maids]? With hand to sue for peace,
Ahead upon their ships to fasten arms?
Æneas thou art able to withdraw
From hands of Greeks, and in a hero's stead
To spread in front a cloud and empty gales ;
And thou art able to transshape his fleet
Into as many nymphs :—that we, on th' other side,   122
In aught should aid Rutulians,—is 't a crime?
Æneas, wareless of it, is away,—
And *let* him, wareless of it, *be* away.
Paphus belongs to thee, Idalium too,
And high Cythera : wherefore dost thou goad
A city big with wars, and rugged hearts?
Are we 'gainst thee thy Phrygia's frail estate
Attempting from its base to overthrow?
We? or [the hero] who to Greeks exposed
The wretched sons of Troy? What was the ground   132
That Europe e'en and Asia rose at once
To arms, and broke the treaties by intrigue?
With me for captain did th' adulterer
[Of] Dardan [line] on Sparta make assault?
Or was it I that furnished him with arms?
Or have I fostered wars by means of lust?
It then became thee to have feared for thine;
Thou, now too late, with thy unrighteous plaints   140
Art rising up, and flinging bootless brawls."
In such did Juno plead; and murmured all
The denizens of heaven with assent
Diversified : as first[-arising] gales,
When intercepted, murmur in the woods,
And roll the smothered whisperings along,
To mariners disclosing blasts to come.
Then the almighty father, [he], to whom
The sovereign power o'er the universe
[Belongs], commences. As he speaks,   150
The gods' exalted mansion drops to rest,

---

84. " Wasted it is, as if it never were ;
And all the rest, that me so honord made,
And of the world admired ev'rie where,
Is turnd to smoake, that doth to nothing fade ;
And of that brightnes now appears no shade,
But grieslie shades, such as doo haunt in hell
With fearfull fiends, that in deep darknes dwell.

" Where my high steeples whilom usde to stand,
On which the lordly faulcon wont to towre,
There now is but an heap of lyme and sand
For the shriche-owle to build her balefull bowre :
And where the nightingale wont forth to powre
Her restles plaints, to comfort wakefull lovers,
There now haunt yelling mewes and whining plovers." Spenser, *The Ruines of Time*, 18, 19.

89. " Didst thou to Heaven address the forceful prayer,
Fold thy fair hands, and raise the mournful eye,
Implore each power benevolent to spare,
And call down Pity from the golden sky?"
Langhorne, *To Miss Cracroft*, 1763.

142, 3. " He scarce had finish'd, when such murmur fill'd
Th' assembly, as when hollow rocks retain
The sound of blustering winds, which all night long
Had roused the sea, now with hoarse cadence hull
Seafaring men o'er-watch'd, whose bark by chance,
Or pinnace, anchors in a craggy bay
After the tempest: such applause was heard
As Mammon ended." Milton, *P. L.*, b. ii.

151. " But as the Colchian sorceress, renown'd
In legends old, or Circe, when they fram'd
A potent spell, to smoothness charm'd the main,

And earth, compelled to quiver to its base ;
The lofty sky is hushed ; then Zephyrs lulled ;
The ocean quells to calm his surface-waves.
"Receive then in your minds, and these my words
Imprint ye. Since that Ausons should be yoked
In league with Teucer's sons 'tis not allowed,
Nor your disunion of a close admits,
Whatever fortune doth to each belong
This day, whatever hope may each carve out,   160
Whether he Trojan or Rutulian be,
Without distinction I shall [all] regard :
Whether through fates their camp is held by siege
Of Itali, or through the ill mistake,
And inauspicious oracles of Troy.
Neither do I the Rutulans release.
To each shall his own enterprises bring
Or suff'ring, or success : king Jupiter
To all the same : the Fates a path shall find."
He by his Stygian brother's floods, by banks,   170
That seethe with pitch and sooty whirlpool, nods,
And by the nod made all Olympus quake.
This th' end of speaking. From his throne of gold
Then Jove arises, whom the denizens
Of heav'n amidst them to the doors escort.

Meanwhile the Rutuli at all the gates
Press round to lay the men in slaughter low,
And wrap the walls in flames. But th' Æneads' host
Within their trenches by blockade are kept ;
Nor any hope of their escape. Distressed,
They stand upon the lofty tow'rs in vain,
And with a scanty ring beset the walls.
Asius Imbrasides, and Hicetaon-sprung
Thymœtes, and the twain Assaraci,   184
And Thymbris aged, with Castor—the front line.
These both Sarpedon's brothers, Clarus e'en
And Themon, company from Lycia high.
With his whole body straining, brings a stone,
Immense, no trifling portion of a mount,
Lyrnesian Acmon, neither to his sire   190
Clytius inferior, neither to his brother
Menestheus. These with javelins, those with stones,
Endeavor at defence, and fire to wield,
And fit them arrows to the string. Himself,
Among the midmost the all-righteous care
Of Venus, the Dardanian boy, behold !
Upon his comely head uncovered, gleams
As doth a jewel, which the yellow gold
Disparts, a grace to either neck or head ;
Or as, through skilfulness inlaid in box,
Or ebony Orician, iv'ry shines :—   201
Whose streaming locks his milk-white neck receives,
And band that ties them up with yielding gold.
Thee also, Ism'rus, high-souled nations saw
Wounds aiming, and with poison-arming bolts,
O gentle scion from a Lydian house :
Where tilths of richness work alike the swains,
And waters them Pactolus with his gold.
There, too, was Mnestheus, whom the late renown
Of Turnus, from the bulwark of the walls
Forced back, on high upraises ; Capys, too :

And lull'd Æolian rage by mystic song,
Till not a billow heav'd against the shore,
Nor ev'n the wanton-winged Zephyr breath'd
The lightest whisper through the magic air :
So, when thy voice, Leonidas, is heard,
Confusion listens ; ire in silent awe
Subsides."   Glover, *Leonidas*, b. ix.

174, 5.   " Thus saying rose
The Monarch, and prevented all reply.
   *   *   *   But they
Dreaded not more th' adventure than his voice
Forbidding ; and at once with him they rose :
Their rising all at once was as the sound
Of thunder heard remote. Towards him they bend
With awful reverence prone.
   " The Stygian council thus dissolved : and forth
In order came the grand infernal Peers.
Midst came their mighty Paramount, and seem'd
Alone th' antagonist of Heaven, nor less
Than Hell's dread emperor, with pomp supreme
And godlike imitated state : him round
A globe of fiery Seraphim enclosed
With bright emblazonry and horrid arms.
Then of their session ended they bid cry
With trumpets' regal sound the great result.
Towards the four winds four speedy Cherubim
Put to their mouths the sounding alchemy,
By heralds' voice explain'd : the hollow abyss
Heard far and wide, and all the host of Hell
With deafening shout return'd them loud acclaim."
                              Milton, *P. L.*, b. ii.

207, 8. " Where palaces, and fanes, and villas rise,
And gardens smile around, and cultur'd fields,
And fountains gush ; and careless herds and flocks
Securely stray ; a world within itself,
Disdaining all assault. There let me draw
Ethereal soul, there drink reviving gales,
Profusely breathing from the spicy groves,
And vales of fragrance ; there at distance hear
The roaring floods, and cataracts, that sweep
From disembowel'd Earth the virgin gold."
                              Thomson, *Summer*.

Hence is derived the Campan city's name.
These 'tween them had the frays of rugged
  war   213
Encountered : in the middle of the night
The narrows was Æneas cutting through.
For when he, ent'ring the Etrurian camp,
[Come] from Evander, to the king repairs,
And tells the king alike his name and race ;
E'en what he seeks, and what he brings
  himself ;
What arms Mezentius to his party wins,
And Turnus' furious passions, deep ex-
  plains ;   221
Reminds him what should be the trust in
  human things ;
And blends entreaties :—there is no delay:
Tarcho unites his pow'rs, and strikes a
  league.
Then uncontrolled by fate, on board their
  fleet
Embarks the Lydian nation, by behests
Of gods entrusted to a foreign chief.
The galley of Æneas keeps the van,
With Phrygian lions yoked beneath her
  beak ;
An Ida overhangs them from above,   230
All-pleasing to the wand'ring Teucri. Here
The great Æneas sits, and with himself
Revolves the diff'rent issues of the war ;
And Pallas, to his side upon the left
Attached, now questions him about the
  stars,
[Guides of] their voyage through the dark-
  some night ;
Now what he bore alike by land and sea.
  Now open Helicon, O goddesses,
And stir ye up my lays ;—what host mean-
  while
Attends Æneas from the Tuscan coasts,
And mans his ships, and o'er the deep is
  borne.   241
  First, in the bronze-beaked " Tigress "
  Massicus
Cuts through the surface-waters, under
  whom
There is a brigad of a thousand youths,

228-30. The commentators here find a difficulty
in explaining how, in the short space of a single
day, a ship should be provided with a figure-head,
embodying Trojan traditions. Forbiger seems to
think that it is easily got rid of, by the plea, that
Virgil writes as a poet, rather than as a historian ;
and that, if he succeed in pleasing his readers, he
has done all that can well be expected of him. Yet
this seems but sorry argument, when an author
outrages probability without the slightest necessity
to justify it. Indeed it is quite amusing to see how
the admirers of Virgil defend him on all occasions,
no matter what he says. In the present instance it
is evident enough that he has been guilty of an
oversight, though he is allowed to be one of the
most correct writers that ever wrote.

Who Clusium's walls, and who the city
  Cosæ, left :
Whose weapons arrows be, and quivers
  light
Upon their shoulders, and the deathful bow:
Along with him the grisly Abas sailed :
His squadron wholly in distinguished arms,
And with a gilt Apollo gleamed the stern.
His native Populonia had to him   251
Six hundred youths vouchsafed, adepts in
  war ;
But Ilva thrice a hundred men, an isle
Bounteous in Chalybs' inexhausted mines.
The third, Asylas, of mankind and gods
That famous seer, whom entrails of the
  flocks,
Whom stars of heav'n, obey, and tongues
  · of birds,
And fires of flash foresightful, hurries on
His thousand, close in line and bristling
  spears.
These orders to be subject [to his sway]
Pisa, Alphæan from its origin,   261
A town in site Etruscan. Follows on
All-beauteous Astur, Astur on his steed
Relying, and in arms of motley hue.
Three hundred,—in them all the one re-
  solve
Of following him,—contribute they, who
  dwell
In Cære's home, they who in Minio's fields :
And ancient Pyrgi, and Graviscæ healthless.
I could not pass thee o'er, O Cinyra,
The Ligurs' chief, all-chivalrous in war,
And [thee,] Cupavo, companied by few,
From crest of whom swan's plumes arise.
  Your fault   272
Was love, and th' emblem of your father's
  shape.

254. Garth describes other mines :
" Now those profounder regions they explore,
Where metals ripen in vast cakes of ore.
Here, sullen to the sight, at large is spread
The dull unwieldy mass of lumpish lead,
There, glimmering in their dawning beds, are seen
The light aspiring seeds of sprightly tin.
The copper sparkles next in ruddy streaks,
And in the gloom betrays its glowing cheeks.
The silver then, with bright and burnish'd grace,
Youth and a blooming lustre in his face,
To th' arms of those more yielding metals flies,
And in the folds of their embraces lies."
             Dispensary, c. vi. 71-82.
Perhaps the line in the version ought to be ren-
dered :
" Bounteous in Chalybes' exhaustless mines :"
that is, viewing *inexhaustis*, v. 174, as if an adjec-
tive in *bilis*; which principle must certainly be fol-
lowed in the case of *invictum*, v. 243.
  Marston and Milton have both " unvalued " for
" invaluable."

For they report that Cycnus, in his woe
For his belovèd Phaeton, among
The leaves of poplar and his sisters' shade,
The while he chants, and comforts with his
  Muse
His mournful love, old age brought on him,
  silv'ring o'er
With downy feather, as he leaves the lands,
And follows with his note the stars. His
  son, 280
Attending in the fleet his fellow troops,
The mighty "Centaur" forces on with oars:
It stands upon the water, and, a rock
Stupendous on the billows, threats aloft,
And furrows seas profound with lengthful
  keel.
  Famed Ocnus, also, from his native coasts
His host awakens, of prophetic Manto
And of the Tuscan stream the son, who gave
Thy walls, O Mantua, and his mother's
  name
To thee, in ancestry, O Mantua, rich: 290
But not the same the pedigree of all.
A threefold race is her's; quadruple tribes
Under each race; herself of tribes the head;
From Tuscan blood her strength [derived].
  Here too
Five hundred 'gainst himself Mezentius
  arms,
Whom Mincius, from his sire Benacus
  [sprung],
Encircled with a reed of ocean-green,
Brought in a hostile galley to the seas.
Unwieldy moves Aulestes, and the waves,
Uprising, lashes with a hundred trees: 300
The waters foam, their surface swept.
  Bears him
The monster "Triton," e'en the sea-green
  floods
Affrighting with his shell; whose shaggy
  front,
In swimming, to the waist the human shape
Displays, the belly in a *pristis* ends;
In foam, below his semi-savage chest,
The billow brawls. So many chosen chiefs
Advanced in thrice ten vessels, for support

---

274. In this difficult passage, which is either corrupted by the scribes, or discreditable to the poet, Trapp seems to take a sounder view than Wagner and Forbiger. It seems preferable to look upon *vestrum*, v. 188, as applying to Cinyra and Cupavo, regarding them as brothers.

The *que* in *formæque* seems fatal to Wagner's interpretation; while the main objection to Trapp's is the singular *filius*; which may yet be well confined to Cinyra, who was evidently a person of greater consequence than the other.

308. "Suppose that you have seen
The well-appointed king at Hampton Pier
Embark his royalty; and his brave fleet
With silken streamers the young Phœbus fanning

Of Troy, and cut with bronze the plains of
  salt.
And now had day retreated from the sky,
And, bounteous, in her car that strays by
  night, 311
Was Phœbe striking the meridian heaven:
Æneas,—for anxiety vouchsafes

Play with your fancies, and in them behold
Upon the hempen tackle ship-boys climbing;
Hear the shrill whistle, which doth order give
To sounds confus'd; behold the threaden sails,
Borne with th' invisible and creeping wind,
Draw the huge bottoms through the furrow'd sea,
Breasting the lofty surge. O! do but think
You stand upon the rivage, and behold
A city on th' inconstant billows dancing;
For so appears this fleet majestical,
Holding due course to Harfleur."
      Shakespeare, *K. Henry V.*, iii. chorus.

313, 314. "Soft pow'r of slumbers, dewy-feather'd
  Sleep,
Kind nurse of nature! whither art thou fled,
A stranger to my senses, weary'd out
With pain, and aching for thy presence? Come,
O come! embrace me in thy liquid arms:
Exert thy drowsy virtue; wrap my limbs
In downy indolence, and bathe in balm."

      " Indulgent quit
Thy couch of poppies! steal thyself on me,
(In rory mists suffus'd and clouds of gold)
On me, thou mildest cordial of the world!

" The shield his pillow in the tented field,
By thee the soldier, bred in iron war,
Forgets the mimic thunders of the day,
Nor envies Luxury her bed of down.
Rock'd by the blast, and cabin'd in the storm,
The sailor hugs thee to the doddering mast,
Of shipwreck negligent while thou art kind.
The captive's freedom, thou! the labourer's hire;
The beggar's store; the miser's better gold;
The health of sickness, and the youth of age!
At thy approach the wrinkled front of Care
Subsides into the smooth expanse of smiles;
And, stranger far! the monarch, crowned by thee,
Beneath his weight of glory gains repose.

" What guilt is mine, that I alone am wake,
Ev'n though my eyes are seal'd, am wake alone?
Ah! seal'd, but not by thee."
          W. Thompson, *Sickness*, b. iv.

" *Thierry.*   One of you sleep;
Lie down and sleep here, that I may behold
What blessed rest it is my eyes are robb'd of.
    [*An Attendant lies down.*
See, he can sleep, sleep any where, sleep now,
When he that wakes for him can never slumber!
Is't not a dainty ease?
  Second Doctor. Your grace shall feel it.
  Thierry. Oh, never I, never. The eyes of heaven
See but their certain motions, and then sleep;
The rages of the ocean have their slumbers
And quiet silver calms; each violence
Crowns in his end a peace; but my fix'd fires
Shall never, never set!"
          Beaumont and Fletcher, *Thierry and
              Theodoret,* v. 2.

Malevole cannot sleep from discontent:
" I cannot sleep; my eyes' ill-neighbouring lids
Will hold no fellowship. O thou pale sober night,
Thou that in sluggish fumes all sense dost steep;
Thou that giv'st all the world full leave to play,

His limbs no rest,—himself e'en, sitting down,
Both guides the tiller, and attends the sails.
And lo! there meets him in his middle course
A choir of his companion [maid]s: the Nymphs,
Whom had the boon Cybebe bid enjoy
The godship of the sea, and Nymphs become
From ships, with even motion swam along,
And cut the surges, many as erewhile 321
Bronze-beakèd stems had rested by the shore.
They at a distance recognise the king,
And in their circling dances course around.
Of whom the one, who was most learned in speech,
Cymodocea, following in his wake,
With right hand grasps the stern, and with her back
Herself o'ertops [the deep], and with the left
Behind him sculls upon the quiet waves.
Then him, unknowing, thus doth she accost:
" Art thou awake, Æneas, child of gods?
Be wakeful, and to sails let loose the sheets.

Unbend'st the feeble veins of sweaty labour!
The galley-slave, that all the toilsome day
Tugs at the oar against the stubborn wave,
Straining his rugged veins, snores fast;
The stooping scythe-man, that doth barb the field,
Thou mak'st wink sure. In night all creatures sleep;
Only the malcontent, that 'gainst his fate
Repines and quarrels; alas, he's goodman tell-clock;
His sallow jaw-bones sink with wasting moan;
Whilst other beds are down, his pillow's stone."
Marston, *The Malcontent*, iii. 2.

315. Perhaps some such thoughts occurred to Æneas as those which Ferdinand expresses, when carrying firewood for Prospero's cell:
"There be some sports are painful, and their labour
Delight in them sets off: some kinds of baseness
Are nobly undergone; and most poor matters
Point to rich ends. This my mean task
Would be as heavy to me, as odious; but
The mistress which I serve quickens what's dead,
And makes my labours pleasures."
Shakespeare, *Tempest*, iii. 1.

324. Like the dolphins seen by Falconer:
"But now, beneath the lofty vessel's stern,
A shoal of sportive dolphins they discern,
Beaming from burnish'd scales refulgent rays,
Till all the glowing ocean seems to blaze.
In curling wreaths they wanton on the tide,
Now bound aloft, now downward swiftly glide;
Awhile beneath the waves their tracks remain,
And burn in silver streams along the liquid plain."
Shipwreck, ii. 2.

328. *Ipsa*, v. 226, evidently means the nymph, excluding her right hand; the greatest portion of her form,—the nymph herself. But it is hard to render the word, so as to bring out its whole signification, without an objectionable paraphrase.

We, pines of Ida from its holy brow, 333
Are Nymphs of ocean now, thy fleet. When us,
On ruin's brink, with falchion and with fire,
The traitorous Rutulian pressed, we, loth,
Thy cables burst, and seek thee through the sea.
This shape in ruth the Mother framed anew,
And gave us to be goddesses, and life
To pass below the surges. But thy boy 340
Ascanius is by wall and trenches pent,
Amid the midst of arms, and Latin [band]s,
Bristling with Mars. Now holds appointed posts,
With brave Etruscan joined, the Arcad horse.
To range against them intercepting troops,
Lest they should with the camp unite, the mind
Of Turnus is resolved. Come then, arise!
And on the coming dawn forthwith command
Thy comrades to be called to arms, and take
The buckler, which the lord of fire himself
Vouchsafed, unconquerable, and with gold
Its edges bordered round. To-morrow's light, 352
If mine thou shouldest deem no idle words,
Of Rutulan destruction mountain heaps
Shall view." She said; and as she drew away
With right hand urged,—not unaware of means,—
The lofty stern. It flies along the waves,
E'en fleeter than the jav'lin, and the bolt,
That mates the winds. Thereon the others speed
Their course. Anchises' Trojan son himself
In ignorance is lost; yet animates 361
His spirit with the token. Then in brief,

334, 5. It would bring out the meaning of v. 231 with greater distinctness to render it thus:
"Are nymphs of ocean now, thy navy [erst]
When us, on ruin's brink, with sword and blaze," &c.

351. *Invictum*, v. 243, is evidently the same as *invincibilis*. To say that a shield, which had never been tried in action, was "unconquered," would be absurd. See note on l. 254.

356. Heyne, Wagner, and Forbiger approve of the comment of Servius on *Haud ignara modi*, v. 247; who says that *modi* here means *moderation*, inasmuch as *method* would be a weak sense. Now, in the first place, it does not quite follow that, because an idea is weak, it cannot be Virgil's; in the second place, the expression is weak according to either interpretation; and in the third place, an examination of the context will show that there was no moderation about the matter. Under the impulsive hand of the nymph the ship absolutely *flew*;—nay, flew more swiftly than a javelin, or even than the winds themselves. The view in the version is that generally taken by the translators.

While gazing on the vault above, he prays:
"O boon Idæan mother of the gods,
T' whose heart the heights of Dindymus
  [are dear],
And cities crowned with turrets, lions, too,
In couples harnessed for the reins; do thou
For me be now the leader of the fight;
Do thou the omened issue duly haste,   369
And for the Phrygians, goddess, be at hand
With step of favor." He but uttered [this];
And in the mean time, wheeled around, the day
Was posting on with now a mellow light,
And night had chased aloof. He firstly gives
His mates commands, the signals to obey,
And fit their souls for warfare, and for fight
Prepare themselves. And now he holds in view
The Teucri and the camp his own, as he
Is standing on the lofty stern: when straight
In his left hand his shield he lifted up   380
Ablazing. Raise an outcry to the stars
The Dardans from the walls: imparted hope
Awakes resentments; weapons with the hand
They fling: as underneath the sullen clouds
Strymonian cranes give signals, and athwart
The welkin with a din they scud, and flee
The southern breezes with a happy cry.
  But these seemed wondrous to Rutulia's king
And Auson chiefs, until they spy behind
The galleys veered to shore, and all the main   390

373. "As the morning steals upon the night,
Melting the darkness."
    Shakespeare, *Tempest*, v. 1.

381, 2. Similar effects are attributed to Satan's voice:
"So Satan spake, and him Beelzebub
Thus answer'd. Leader of those armies bright,
Which but the Omnipotent none could have foil'd!
If once they hear that voice, their liveliest pledge
Of hope in fears and dangers, heard so oft
In worst extremes, and on the perilous edge
Of battle when it raged, in all assaults
Their surest signal, they will soon resume
New courage and revive."   Milton, *P. L.*, b. i.

383. "Go show thyself to them, wave but thy sword,
And bid them follow thee; not one of them
But shall in speed and reckless fury mock
The tyger of the desert. Where thou lead'st
Shouting around thee they will sweep the plain,
Spurning at opposition. . . . Away, Sicardo!
Our pledge of certain victory we possess
In this beloved, this noble youth, whose presence
Inspires the warrior's heart with martial fire,
As the enlivening sun all nature warms.
Shaded awhile in dim eclipse he left us,
And clouds of pale dismay began to lour;
But now returning with recovered splendour,
He in the sky of glory beams supreme,
And we, in his bright influence exulting,
Resume our ardour, and our foes defy."
    Macdonald, *Fair Apostate*, iv. 2.

With vessels gliding on. His helmet glows
Above his head, and from the crest a blaze
Is darted through its plumes, and monstrous
  flames
The golden boss spews forth: not otherwise
Than if at times in some translucent night
Blood-tinted comets show a dismal red;
Or heat of Sirius,—he that carries drought

396.   "On the other side,
Incensed with indignation, Satan stood
Unterrified, and like a comet burn'd,
That fires the length of Ophiuchus huge
In th' Arctic sky, and from his horrid hair
Shakes pestilence and war."
            Milton, *P. L.*, b. ii.

397. "And now the Sunne hath reared upp
  His fierie-footed teme,
Making his way between the cupp
  And golden diademe;
The rampant lyon hunts he fast,
  With dogges of noisome breath,
Whose baleful barking bringes in hast
  Pyne, plagues, and dreerie death."
      Spenser, *Shepheards Calender*, July.

"Whose often prostitution hath begot
More foul diseases than e'er yet the hot
Sun bred thorough his burnings, whilst the Dog
Pursues the raging Lion, throwing fog
And deadly vapour from his angry breath,
Filling the lower world with plague and death."
    J. Fletcher, *The Faithful Shepherdess*, i. 2.

See Dyce's note on the passage.

            "Ha! 'twas the king!
The king that parted hence! frowning he went;
His eyes like meteors roll'd, then darted down
Their red and angry beams: as if his sight
Would, like the raging Dog-star, scorch the earth,
And kindle ruin in its course."
    Congreve, *The Mourning Bride*, v. 3.

"All is not well; the pale-ey'd moon
Curtains her head in clouds, the stars retire,
Save from the sultry south alone
The swart star flings his pestilential fires."
    Mason, *Caractacus*, Ode.

The following description of thirst and heat, not, indeed, owing to the influence of Sirius, but to the operation of poison, is from Fletcher's *A Wife for a Month*:

"[*Alphonso is brought in on a couch by two Friars.*]

Alphonso. Give me more air, air, more air!
  Blow, blow!
Open, thou eastern gate, and blow upon me!
Distil thy cold dews, oh, thou icy moon!
And, rivers, run through my afflicted spirit!
I am all fire, fire, fire! The raging Dog-star
Reigns in my blood! Oh! which way shall I turn
  me?
Ætna, and all his flames, burn in my head!
Fling me into the ocean, or I perish!
Dig, dig, dig, till the springs fly up,
The cold, cold springs, that I may leap into 'em,
And bathe my scorch'd limbs in their purling pleasures!
Or shoot me up into the higher region,
Where treasures of delicious snow are nourish'd,
And banquets of sweet hail!
  Rugio.   Hold him fast, friar:
Oh, how he burns!

And sicknesses to ailing mortals,—rises up,
And with disastrous light beglooms the sky.
    Howe'er his confidence did not forsake
Bold Turnus, to preoccupy the shores, 401
And as they come to drive them from the
    land.
He e'en their spirits raises by his words,
And e'en he chides them : " That, which
    ye in vows
Have yearnèd after, is arrived,—[the foe]
With your right hand to shatter. Mars
    himself
Is in your hands, my heroes. Now let each
Of his own spouse and home be mindful; now
Grand feats repeat, the praises of his sires.
Unchallenged let us meet them at the wave,
While in disorder, and, as they debark,
Their first steps stagger. Fortune aids the
    bold."   412

    Alph.   What, will ye sacrifice me ?
Upon the altar lay my willing body,
And pile your wood up, fling your holy incense ;
And, as I turn me, you shall see all flame,
Consuming flame. Stand off me, or you are ashes !
    Rug. and Marco. Most miserable wretches !
    Alph.   Bring hither Charity,
And let me hug her, friar ; they say she's cold,
Infinite cold ; devotion cannot warm her.
Draw me a river of false lovers' tears
Clean through my breast ; they are dull, cold, and
    forgetful,
And will give ease. Let virgins sigh upon me,
Forsaken souls ; their sighs are precious ;
Let them all sigh. Oh hell, hell, hell ! O horror !
    Marco. To bed, good sir.
    Alph.   My bed will burn about me :
Like Phaeton in all-consuming flashes
I am enclos'd. Let me fly, let me fly, give room !
Betwixt the cold Bear and the raging Lion
Lies my safe way. Oh, for a cake of ice now
To clap unto my heart to comfort me !
Decrepit Winter, hang upon my shoulders,
And let me wear thy frozen icicles,
Like jewels round about my head, to cool me !
My eyes burn out, and sink into their sockets,
And my infected brain like brimstone boils !
I live in hell, and several Furies vex me !
Oh, carry me where no sun ever show'd yet
A face of comfort, where the earth is crystal,
Never to be dissolv'd ! Where nought inhabits
But night and cold, and nipping frosts, and winds,
That cut the stubborn rocks, and make them
    shiver !
Set me there, friends !"   Act iv. 4.
    412. "Lo! sluggish knight, the victor's happie
    pray !
So fortune friends the bold."
            Spenser, *F. Q.*, iv. 2, 7.
Yet she is not always so considerate :
" He is the scorn of Fortune. But you'll say
That she forsook him for his want of courage,
But never leaves the bold : now by my hopes
Of peace and quiet here, I never met
A braver enemy."
        J. Fletcher, *The Prophetess*, iv. 5.
" Let thy great deeds force Fate to change her
    mind ;
He that courts Fortune boldly makes her kind."
        Dryden, *The Indian Queen*, i. 1.

These [words] he speaks, and ponders with
    himself
Whom he can lead against them, or to whom
He's able to intrust the leaguered walls.
    Meanwhile Æneas from the lofty ships
His comrades lands by bridges. Many watch
The ebbing motions of the slacking sea,
And with a spring commit them to the
    flats ;
By oars the others. Tarchon having scanned
    the shores,   420
Where shallows pant not, nor the broken
    surge
Booms back, but unimpeded glides the main
With rising tide, veers towards them sud-
    denly
His prows, and he entreats his comrades :
    " Now,
O chosen squadron, to your lusty oars
Bend ye ! lift, drive your galleys ! with
    their beaks
This hostile region cleave, and for itself
A furrow let the very keel imprint.
In such a roadstead do I not decline
To break my vessel, once the land secured."
The like whereof when once had Tarchon
    said,   431
His comrades to their oars together rise,
And to the Latin fields their foaming ships
Force onward, till the beaks dry [land]
    possess,
And all the keels uninjured came to rest :
But, Tarcho, not thy craft. For, dashed
    on shoals,
Upon a ridge unrighteous while it hangs,
Long in suspense upheld, and tires the
    waves,
'Tis broken up, and out it casts the crew
Amid the waves ; whom shattered bits of
    oars   440
And swimming benches hamper, and at
    once
Their footing the withdrawing surge sup-
    plants.
    Nor Turnus does a slack delay restrain ;
But hurries he in vigor his whole host
Against the Teucri, and upon the beach
Afront them marshals it. The signals sound.
Æneas first assailed the rustic troops,—
An omen of the fray,—and prostrate laid
The Latins, Thero being slaughtered, who,
The tallest of their men, of free accord 450

417. "They have alreadie plough'd th' unruly seas,
And with their breasts, proofe 'gainst the battering
    waves,
Dasht the bigge billowes into angry froth,
And, spight of the contentious full-mouth'd gods
Of sea and wind, have reacht the city frontiers,
And begirt her navigable skirts."
        Rawlins, *The Rebellion*, ii. 1.

Attacks Æneas: with the sword he drains
His side laid open, e'en through folds of
  bronze,
Through gold-crisp tunic. Lichas next he
  smites,
Ripped from a now dead mother, and to
  thee,
Devote, O Phœbus, seeing 'twas allowed
To him, a babe, to 'scape the risks of steel.
Not far, firm Cisseus, giant Gyas too,
Troops felling with his club, he stretched
  in death :   458
Naught booted them the arms of Hercules,
Nor able hands, nor yet their sire Melampus,
Alcides' comrade, long as earth supplied
Her toilsome travails. Lo! on Pharus, whilst
He flings his idle pratings, hurling forth
A dart, he plants it in the shouter's mouth.
Thou also, whilst, ill-starred, thou followest
Thy Clytius, yellowing o'er with virgin down
His cheeks,—thy fresh delight,—O Cydon,
By the Dardanian right hand overthrown,
Set free from [pain] of loves, which aye
  hadst thou
For striplings, wouldest, pitiable [youth],
Have lain ; had not thy brethren's serried
  band   471
Opposed it,—Phorcus' race, in number
  seven,
And sev'nfold darts they launch. Some
  from his helm
And from his shield rebound effectless ;
  some
Boon Venus, as they graze his body, turned
Aside. Æneas stanch Achates speaks :
"Supply me weapons ! None shall my
  right hand
In vain on Rutuli have hurled, [of those,]
Which stood in corse of Greeks upon the
  plains
Of Ilium." Then a mighty spear he grasps,
And launches it. Upon the wing it smites
Right through the bronze[n plate]s of Mæon's
  shield,   482
And habergeon together with the breast
It bursts. A brother to his succor comes,
Alcanor, and his falling brother props
With his right hand. Shot through his
  arm transpierced,
Straight flies a spear, and, bloody, holds
  its course ;

And his right hand, in dying, by the thews
Down from the shoulder hung. Then
  Numitor,—   489
A jav'lin from his brother's body reft,—
Æneas sought : but not to pierce as well
Is it in turn allowed him, but it grazed
The thigh of great Achates. Clausus here,
Of Cures, trusting in his youthful frame,
Comes up, and Dryops from afar he smites
With lance unbending, underneath the chin
Deep driven ; and at once the speaker's
  voice
And life he reaves away, his throat trans-
  pierced :
But th' other with his forehead strikes the
  earth,   499
And clotted gore disgorges from his mouth.
Three Thracians, also, of the highest strain
Of Boreas, and three, whom doth their sire,
Idas, and native [crests of] Ismarus,
Despatch, by sundry fates he overthrows.
Up runs Halesus, and Auruncan bands ;
To aid them e'en the son of Neptune comes,
Messapus, striking in his steeds. Now
  these,
Now those, endeavor to drive out [the rest] :
The contest at Ausonia's very door
Is waged : as in the vasty firmament   510
The jarring winds encounters raise, with
  heart
And powers balanced : nor do they them-
  selves
Among them,—neither clouds nor ocean,—
  yield ;
The fray long doubtful ; all in struggle
  stand,
Against [each other ranged] : not otherwise
The Trojan lines and lines of Latium clash :

---

v. 340, being a second spear. One spear, after
passing through a man, may hold its course as well
as another : for where a hero is invested with fabu-
lous strength, shield and breastplate are but slight
additional difficulties.

516.   " Now storming fury rose
And clamour such as heard in Heaven till now
Was never ; arms on armour clashing bray'd
Horrible discord, and the madding wheels
Of brazen chariots raged : dire was the noise
Of conflict ; overhead the dismal hiss
Of fiery darts in flaming volleys flew,
And flying vaulted either host with fire.
So under fiery cope together rush'd
Both battles main, with ruinous assault
And inextinguishable rage. All heaven
Resounded : and had earth been then, all earth
Had to her centre shook." Milton, *P. L.*, b. vi.

Fletcher has a spirited battle-scene in a song in
The Mad Lover:
" Arm, arm, arm, arm ! the scouts are all come in :
Keep your ranks close, and now your honours
  win.
Behold from yonder hill the foe appears ;
Bows, bills, glaves, arrows, shields, and spears !

---

460. The English idiom will not allow of *que*, v.
320, being rendered in the ordinary way.

466. " And on his tender lips the downy heare
Did now but freshly spring, and silken blossoms
beare."   Spenser, *F. Q.*, ii. 12, 79.

487. Dr. Trapp has a good note upon this passage. However, it would not seem that *servatque
tenorem* is any objection to the idea of the *hasta*,

Foot links with foot, and man close set with man.
But in another quarter, where, far-wide
The flood had forced along the rolling rocks,
And bushes, torn asunder from its banks,
The Arcads, unaccustomed to advance   521
Their lines on foot, as soon as Pallas saw
Turning their backs to Latium in pursuit ;
Whom since the rugged nature of the spot
Induced to let their horses go ;—[a course,]
Which only in the case of need remained ;—
Now by entreaty, now by bitter words,
He fires their valor : " Whither do ye fly,
O comrades ? E'en by your heroic deeds
[Do I conjure] you, by Evander's name,
Your chief, and battles battled to the last,
And my own hope, which of my father's praise   532
Now emulous arises, trust not feet :
With sword a way must through the foes be burst.
Where thickest closes on that knot of men,
By this your noble land claims you again,
And Pallas your commander. 'Tis no gods pursue !
We, mortals, by a mortal foe are pressed ;
With us alike as many lives and hands.
Behold ! with huge sea-barrier pens us in
The deep ; land now is lacking for a flight.   541
Is it the main or Troy we are to seek ?"
These words he speaks, and in the centre he
Upon the serried foemen flings him forth.
First Lagus meets him, lured by fates unkind :
Him, whilst he plucks a rock of mighty weight,

Like a dark wood he comes, or tempest pouring,
Oh ! view the wings of horse the meadows scouring !
The vanguard marches bravely : hark the drums !
They meet, they meet, and now the battle comes :
See how the arrows fly,
That darken all the sky !
Hark how the trumpets sound !
Hark how the hills rebound !
Hark how the horses charge ! in, boys, boys in !
The battle totters ; now the wounds begin :
Oh, how they cry !
Oh, how they die !
Room for the valiant Memnon, arm'd with thunder !
See how he breaks the ranks asunder :
They fly, they fly ! Eumenes has the chase,
And brave Polybius makes good his place,
To the plains, to the woods,
To the rocks, to the floods,
Then fly for succour. Follow, follow, follow !
Hark how the soldiers hollow !
Brave Diocles is dead,
And all his soldiers fled :
The battle's won, and lost,
That many a life hath cost."
Song by Stremon, v. 4.

He spears with whirlèd weapon, where the chine
Along the middle caused a sev'rance, and the lance
Recovers he while clinging to the bones.
Whom Hisbo from above forestalls not,—he
In sooth expecting this ; for Pallas first,
As he is dashing on, the while he storms,
Unwary through a comrade's ruthless death,
Receives him, and his sword in his swoln lung   554
He buries. Sthenelus he next assails,
And Anchemol, from Rhætus' ancient race,
Who dared to stain a stepdame's bed. Ye, too,
Twin [brother]s, fell upon Rutulian fields,
O progeny of Daucus, most alike,
Laride and Thymber, past distinguishment
By their own parents, e'en their fond mistake.   561
But Pallas now stern marks of difference
Bestowed upon you : for from thee, O Thymber,
Thy head Evander's falchion reft away ;
Thee, O Laride, its owner, thy right hand,
Lopped off, is seeking, and, half-living, twitch
The fingers, and the weapon grasp again.
Arm mingled pain and shame against the foes,
Th' Arcadians, by his warning set afire,
And gazing on the hero's brilliant deeds.
Then Pallas pierces Rhæteus through and through,   571
While flying past him in his two-horse car.
This—interval and so much respite proved
To Ilus ; for at Ilus he from far
A lusty spear had aimed, which, as he intervenes,
Does Rhœteus intercept, best Teuthras, thee
Avoiding and thy brother Tyre ; and, rolled
From forth his chariot, smites he, half-alive,
The fields of the Rutulians with his heels.
And as, when gales are in the summer-tide
Arisen to his wish, the shepherd sets   581
Abroach upon the stubbles scattered fires ;
Those in the centre on a sudden seized,
Vulcan's dread battle-line at once is spread
Throughout the spacious plains : he, while he sits,
Looks down in triumph on th' exulting flames :
Not elsewise all the prowess of thy mates
Combines in one, and thee, O Pallas, aids.
But, keen in wars, Halesus, on the foes
Moves on, and gathers him within his arms.
He here despatches Ladon, Pheres too,
Demodocus too ; from Strymonius he   592

Strikes off his right hand with his gleaming sword,
Against his throat uplifted ; with a stone
The face of Thoas batters, and his bones
He scattered, blent with gory brains.
Chanting his fates, his father in the woods
Had hid Halesus : when the agèd [sire]
His eyeballs, filming white in death, relaxed,
Their hand upon him did the Parcæ lay,
And dedicated him t' Evander's darts. 601
Whom Pallas seeks, thus having prayed before :
"Grant now, O father Tiber, to the steel,
Which, ready to be hurled, I poise, success
And passage through the stern Halesus' breast :
These arms and th' hero's spoils thy oak shall own."
The god he heard it : while Halesus screened
Imaon, he unhappily presents
A breast unguarded to th' Arcadian dart.
But Lausus,—mighty portion of the war,—
Does not allow the troops to be dismayed
By such great carnage on the hero's side. 612
First, Abas, placed against him, he destroys,
Alike the knot and lengthening of the fight.
The offspring of Arcadia low is laid,
The Tuscans are laid low, and, Teucri, ye,
O bodies undestroyed by Greeks. The hosts
Engage them e'en with balanced chiefs and powers.
Close crowd the furthest lines; nor does the throng
Their arms and hands allow of being stirred.
Here Pallas closes in and spurs them on ;
Against him Lausus *there;* nor differs much
Their age ; in beauty peerless ; yet to whom
Return to native land had Fate denied. 624
Howe'er, the ruler of the mighty heaven
With one another let them not engage :
Their deaths soon wait them 'neath a nobler foe.
Meanwhile his kindly sister warns to take
The place of Lausus,—Turnus, who disparts
The central squadron in his flying car. 630
As soon as he his comrades viewed : "'Tis time
To cease from fight ; 'gainst Pallas I alone
Am borne ; to me alone is Pallas due :
I would his sire himself were witness here."
These saith he ; and his comrades from the plain,
The subject of his order, have withdrawn.

---

610. Manoah says of Samson :
"Himself an army."
Milton, *Samson Agonistes.*

But on the Rutulans' retirement, then
The youth, astounded at his haught commands,
At Turnus is in wonder lost, and o'er
His giant body rolls around his eyes, 640
And all surveys aloof with grim regard ;
And with such words against the monarch's words
Replies : "Or through the chiefest spoils, now seized,
Or death distinguished, I shall be extolled :
To either lot indiff'rent is my sire :
Away thou with thy threats !" He, having said,
Advances on the centre of the field.
A cold around th' Arcadians' hearts their blood
Congeals. Down Turnus from his chariot leaped ;
Afoot prepares to meet him hand to hand.
And as a lion, when he hath perceived 651
From his high watch-post, far upon the plains,
A bull to stand preparing for the frays,
Flies up to him : no different the pictur: is
Of Turnus swooping on. When him he deemed
Within the compass of his vollied spear,
Pallas was first to move, if any chance
Would aid him, venturing with unequal powers ;
And thus addresses he the mighty heaven :
"By th' hospitage and table; of my sire, 66)
Which thou a stranger hast approached, I thee
Entreat, Alcides, aid my grand emprise.
From him half-dead may he perceive me seize
His bloody arms ; and may the dying eyes
Of Turnus brook a conqueror !" Alcides heard
The youth, and 'neath his deep of heart he checks
A heavy groan, and idle tears outpours.
The sire then speaks his son in kindly words :
"To each his day is fixed ; the term of life

667. "Then like a torrent had been stopt before,
Tears, sighs, and words, doubled together flow ;
Confus'dly striving whether should do more,
The true intelligence of grief to show.
Sighs hinder'd words : words perish'd in their store ;
Both, intermix'd in one, together grow."
Daniell, *Civil War,* b. ii. 81.

669. "Thou glimm'ring taper? by whose feeble ray
In thoughtful solitude the night I waste,
How dost thou warn me by thy swift decay,
That equal to oblivion both we haste !
The vital oil that should our strength supply,
Consuming wastes, and bids us learn to die."

T

Is short and irretrievable to all ; 670

"Touch'd by my hand, thy swift reviving light
  With new-gain'd force again is taught to glow :
  Lo, rising from surrounding troubles bright,
  My conscious soul begins herself to know ;
And, from the ills of life emerging forth,
Learns the just standard of her native worth.
"But see, in mists, thy fading lustre veil'd,
  Around thy head the dusky vapours play :
So, by opposing fortune's clouds conceal'd,
  In vain to force a passage I essay :
While round me, gathering thick, they daily spread,
And living, I am number'd with the dead !
"But now thy flame diminish'd quick subsides,
  Too sure a presage that thy date is run :
Alike I feel my life's decreasing tides,
  Soon will like thine my transient blaze be gone !
Instructive emblem !—How our fates agree !
I haste to darkness, and resemble thee."
                Boyse, *Stanzas to a Candle.*

670. " Like to the falling of a star,
Or as the flights of eagles are,
Or like the fresh spring's gaudy hue,
Or silver drops of morning dew,
Or like a wind that chafes the flood,
Or bubbles which on water stood :
Even such is man, whose borrowed light
Is straight called in and paid to night :
The wind blows out, the bubble dies,
The spring intombed in autumn lies :
The dew's dry'd up, the star is shot,
The flight is past, and man forgot."
          F. Beaumont, *On the Life of Man.*
Milton makes Satan say in his address to Sin,
P. L., b. ii. :
              " Be this, or aught
Than this more secret, now design'd, I haste
To know ; and this once known, shall soon return
And bring ye to the place where thou and Death
Shall dwell at ease, and up and down unseen
Wing silently the buxom air, embalm'd
With odours ; there ye shall be fed and fill'd
Immeasurably, all things shall be your prey."

" O gentlemen ! the time of life is short !
To spend that shortness basely were too long,
If life did ride upon a dial's point,
Still ending at th' arrival of an hour."
        Shakespeare, 1 *King Henry IV.*, v. 2.
" To-morrow, and to-morrow, and to-morrow,
Creeps in this petty pace from day to day,
To the last syllable of recorded time :
And all our yesterdays have lighted fools
The way to dusty death. Out, out, brief candle !
Life's but a walking shadow ; a poor player,
That struts and frets his hour upon the stage,
And then is heard no more." *Macbeth*, v. 5.
" Life ! What is life ? A shadow !
Its date is but th' immediate breath we draw :
Nor have we surety for a second gale :
Ten thousand accidents in ambush lie
For the embodied dream.
A frail and fickle tenement it is,
Which, like the brittle glass, that measures time,
Is often broke, ere half its sands are run."
          Jones, *The Earl of Essex*, v. 3.
" Time's but a hinge, whereon mortality,
A narrow portal, turns : behind, before,
Lies the wide main of being."
          Brooke, *The Impostor*, iv. 12.

But fame to lengthen by achievements,—this
Is virtue's work. 'Neath Troja's stately walls
So many children of the gods have fallen ;
E'en fell with them Sarpedon, offspring mine.
His destinies are calling Turnus too,
And he hath reached the bounds of granted life."
So speaks he, and turns off his eyes from fields
Of Rutuli. But Pallas shoots a lance
With lusty pow'rs, and from its hollow sheath
Tears forth his gleaming sword. This,
  flying, where   680
The highest screenings of his shoulder rise,
Alights, and having worked a passage through
The edges of his buckler, at the last
E'en grazed [a part] of Turnus' giant frame.
Here Turnus, poising long the timber, tipped
With sharpened iron, [this] at Pallas flings,
And thus he speaks : " Look, whether ours may prove
A still more trenchant weapon." He had said ;
But through the shield,—so many plates of steel,
Of bronze so many,—though so many times
The bull-hide span it, spread around, the point   691
Strikes through its centre with a quiv'ring blow,
And bores the mail's obstructions, and his giant chest.
He tears the heated weapon from the wound
All vainly : by the one and selfsame path
The blood and spirit follow. Down he sinks
Upon the wound : a clang above him gave
His arms ; and as he dies he seeks the earth,
His foeman, with a gory mouth. O'er whom,
While standing by him, Turnus cries :
        " These words   700
Of mine, Arcadians, mindfully report
To your Evander : ' Such as he deserved
I send him Pallas back. Whatever be

671. " Our life is short, but to extend that span
          To vast eternity, is Virtue's work."
          Dryden, *Troilus and Cressida*, v. 1.

675, 6.   " For within the hollow crown,
That rounds the mortal temples of a king,
Keeps Death his court, and there the antic sits,
Scoffing his state, and grinning at his pomp ;
Allowing him a breath, a little scene,
To monarchise, be fear'd, and kill with looks ;
Infusing him with self and vain conceit,
As if this flesh, which walls about our life,
Were brass impregnable ; and, humour'd thus,
Comes at the last, and with a little pin
Bores through his castle wall, and—farewell king !" Shakespeare, *K. Richard II.*, iii. 2.

The honor of a sepulchre, whate'er
The comfort of a burial, I bestow.
The hospitality t' Æneas [shown]
Shall stand him in no trifle.'" And the like
He having spoken pressed with his left foot
The lifeless [stripling], as he tears away
The belt's enormous weight, and graven
    guilt :— 710
A band of youths within one wedding night
Slain foully, and their marriage-beds in
    blood :
Which Clonus, son of Eurytus, had carved
In plenteous gold ;—in which, his trophy,
    now
Turnus exults, and in possession joys.
O mind of human beings, unaware
Of fate and lot to come, and how to keep

---

716. "Ah! gentle pair, ye little think how nigh
Your change approaches, when all these delights
Will vanish, and deliver ye to woe ;
More woe, the more your taste is now of joy ;
Happy, but for so happy ill secured
Long to continue." Milton, *P. L.*, b. iv.

"O fleeting joys
Of Paradise, dear bought with lasting woes!"
    Ibid., b. x.

"Short is, alas! the reign
Of mortal pride: we play our parts awhile,
And strut upon the stage ; the scene is chang'd,
And offers us a dungeon for a throne.
Wretched vicissitude! for, after all
His tinsel dreams of empire and renown,
Fortune, capricious dame, withdraws at once
The goodly prospect."
    Somerville, *Hobbinol*, c. iii.

"Frail man, how various is thy lot below!
To-day though gales propitious blow,
And Peace, soft gliding down the sky,
Lead Love along and Harmony,
To-morrow the gay scene deforms ;
Then all around
The thunder's sound
Rolls rattling on through heaven's profound,
And down rush all the storms."
    Beattie, *Ode to Hope*, ii. 3.

"O, momentary grace of mortal men!
Which we more hunt for than the grace of God.
Who builds his hope in air of your good looks
Lives like a drunken sailor on a mast,
Ready with every nod to tumble down
Into the fatal bowels of the deep."
    Shakespeare, *K. Richard III.*, iii. 4.

717. "The withered primrose by the mourning river,
The faded summers-sunne from weeping fountaines,
The light-blowne bubble, vanished for euer,
The molten snow vpon the naked mountaines,—
Are emblems that the treasures we vp-lay,
Soone wither, vanish, fade, and melt away.

"For as the snow, whose lawne did ouer-spread
Th' ambitious hils, which giant-like did threat
To pierce the heauen with their aspiring head,
Naked and bare doth leaue their craggie seat,
Whenas the bubble, which did empty flie
The dalliance of the vndiscerned winde,
On whose calme rowling waues it did relie,
Hath shipwrack made, where it did dalliance finde:

[Due] measure, when uplifted by success !
To Turnus there shall come a time, when he
Will wish were purchased at a costly price,

And when the sun-shine which dissolu'd the snow,
Coloured the bubble with a pleasant varie,
And made the rathe and timely primrose grow,
Swarth clouds with-drawne (which longer time do
    tarie)
—Oh what is praise, pompe, glory, ioy, but so
As shine by fountaines, bubbles, flowers, or
    snow?"
Palinode, by E. Bolton, in *England's Helicon*.

"Have you never
Look'd from the prospect of your palace window,
When some fair sky courted your eye to read
The beauties of a day ; the glorious sun
Enriching so the bosom of the earth,
That trees and flowers appear'd but like so much
Enamel upon gold ; the wanton birds,
And every creature but the drudging ant,
Despising providence, and at play ; and all
That world you measure with your eye, so gay
And proud, as winter were no more to shake
His icy locks upon them, but the breath
Of gentle zephyr to perfume their growth,
And walk eternally upon the spring !
When, from a coast you see not, comes a cloud,
Creeping as overladen with a storm,
Dark as the womb of night, and with her wings
Surprising all the glories you beheld,
Leaves not your frighted eyes a light to see
The ruins of that flattering day?"
    Shirley, *The Royal Master*, ii. 2.

718. "O how portentous is prosperity!
How, comet-like, it threatens while it shines !!
Few years but yield us proof of *Death's* ambition,
To cull his victims from the fairest fold,
And sheath his shafts in all the pride of life.
When flooded with abundance, purpled o'er
With recent honours, bloom'd with every bliss,
Set up in ostentation, made the gaze,
The gaudy centre, of the public eye ;
When *Fortune* thus has toss'd her child in air,
Snatcht from the covert of an humble state,
How often have I seen him dropt at once,
Our morning's envy, and our evening's sigh !
As if her bounties were the signal given,
The flowery wreath to mark the sacrifice,
And call Death's arrows on the destin'd prey."
    Young, *Complaint*, N. v.

719, 20. "While music flows around,
Perfumes, and oils, and wine, and wanton hours,
Amid the roses fierce Repentance rears
Her snaky crest : a quick-returning pang
Shoots through the conscious heart."
    Thomson, *Spring*, 997-1001.

"When you awake from this lascivious dream,
Repentance then will follow, like the sting
Plac'd in the adder's tail."
    Webster, *Vittoria Corombona*, act ii.

Wolsey's good wishes, like those of Turnus, came
too late:
"Farewell! a long farewell to all my greatness!
This is the state of man : to-day he puts forth
The tender leaves of hope, to-morrow blossoms
And bears his blushing honours thick upon him :
The third day comes a frost, a killing frost ;
And,—when he thinks, good easy man, full surely
His greatness is a ripening,—nips his root,
And then he falls, as I do. I have ventur'd
Like little wanton boys that swim on bladders,

Pallas untouched; and when these spoils and day 721
He will regard with loathing. But his mates,
With many a moan and tear, in crowds bring back
Their Pallas on his buckler laid. O [thou],
Doomed to thy parent to return, a pang
And lofty honor! this, thy op'ning day,
Vouchsafed thee to the battle; this, the same
Away doth sweep thee, when thou, ne'ertheless,
Colossal heaps of Rutuli dost leave!
 Nor now [mere] rumor of calamity 730
So grievous, but a surer voucher wings
Its way t' Æneas,—that his [comrades] stood
In death's strait crisis; that [high] time it was
To aid the routed Teucri. Down he mows

Each nearest [object] with his sword, and through
The wide-spread army forces, [all] afire,
A passage with the steel, in quest of thee,
O Turnus, of thy recent slaughter proud.
Pallas, Evander,—in his very eyes
Are all,—the boards which first, a stranger, he 740
Just then approached, and right hands granted. Here,
In Sulmo sired, four youths, as many more,
Which Ufens rears, he grasps alive, whom he
May butcher, off'rings to his shades, and drench
With captive blood the blazes of his pyre.
He next at Magus from afar had launched
A hostile spear. In craft the other stoops;
But, quiv'ring over him, the javelin flies;
And he, his knees embracing, utters such
Right humbly: " By the Manes of thy sire
And rising Iulus' hopes, I thee entreat, 751
This life preserve alike for son and sire.
A stately house I own; there lie within
Of graven silver talents buried deep;

This many summers in a sea of glory,
But far beyond my depth: my high-blown pride
At length broke under me; and now has left me,
Weary, and old with service, to the mercy
Of a rude stream, that must for ever hide me.
Vain pomp and glory of this world, I hate ye!
I feel my heart new open'd. Oh! how wretched
Is that poor man, that hangs on princes' favours.
There is, betwixt that smile we would aspire to,
That sweet aspect of princes, and their ruin,
More pangs and fears than wars or women have;
And when he falls, he falls like Lucifer,
Never to hope again."
 Shakespeare, *K. Henry VIII.*, iii. 2.

But Fletcher makes Dioclesian wiser:

Suppose this done, or were it possible
I could rise higher still, I am a man;
And all these glories, empires heap'd upon me,
Confirm'd by constant friends and faithful guards,
Cannot defend me from a shaking fever,
Or bribe the uncorrupted dart of Death
To spare me one short minute. Thus adorn'd
In these triumphant robes, my body yields not
A greater shadow than it did when I
Liv'd both poor and obscure; a sword's sharp point
Enters my flesh as far; dreams break my sleep,
As when I was a private man; my passions
Are stronger tyrants on me; nor is greatness
A saving antidote to keep me from
A traitor's poison. Shall I praise Fortune,
Or raise the building of my happiness
On her uncertain favour? or presume
She is my own, and sure, that yet was never
Constant to any?" *The Prophetess*, iv. 5.

" Prosperity!—a harlot,
That smiles but to betray! O shining ruin!
Thou nurse of passions, and thou bane of virtue!
O self-destroying monster! that art blind,
Yet putt'st out Reason's eye, that still should guide thee,—
Then plungeth down some precipice unseen,
And art no more! Hear me, all-gracious Heaven!
Let me wear out my small remains of life;
Obscure, content with humble poverty,
Or in Affliction's hard but wholesome school,
If it must be:—I'll learn to know myself,
And that's more worth than empire. But, O Heaven,
Curse me no more with proud prosperity."
 Hughes, *The Siege of Damascus*, v. 2.

744. " They come like sacrifices in their trim,
And to the fire-ey'd maid of smoky war,
All hot, and bleeding, will we offer them:
The mailed Mars shall on his altar sit,
Up to the ears in blood."
 Shakespeare, 1 *K. Henry IV.*, iv. 1.

754. " Would you corrupt our valour with your coin?
Or do you think the Spaniard is so poor,
A little gold can make him sell his honour?
No! were your streets through stoned with diamonds,
And you should dig them up to bring them hither;
Or were your houses, in the stead of slate,
Covered with silver, and yourselves prepared
To tear it off, and give it unto us:
Nay, were your walls of purest chrysolite,
And pulled beside their bounds for our own use,
Yet would we scorn all this, and ten times more;
For we count honour sweetness of dominion:
'Tis lordship that we come for, and to rule,
More worth than millions."
 Webster, *The Weakest goeth to the Wall*, ii. 1.

" Say, though thy heart be rock of adamant,
Yet rocks are not impregnable to bribes:
Instruct me how to bribe thee."
 Dryden, *Don Sebastian*, iii. 1.

" When now the thunder roars, the lightning flies,
And all the warring winds tumultuous rise;
When now the foaming surges, tost on high,
Disclose the sands beneath, and touch the sky;
When Death draws near, the mariners aghast
Look back with terror on their actions past;
Their courage sickens into deep dismay,
Their hearts, through fear and anguish, melt away.
Nor tears, nor prayers, the tempest can appease;
Now they devote their treasure to the seas;
Unload their shatter'd bark, though richly fraught,
And think the hopes of life are cheaply bought
With gems and gold: but oh, the storm so high!
Nor gems nor gold the hopes of life can buy."
 Young, *Last Day*, b. i.

Burdens of wrought and unwrought gold
are mine.
The Teucri's conquest does not hinge on this ;
Nor will one life so wide a diff'rence cause."
He spoke. To whom Æneas in reply
Such-like returns : " Of silver and of gold
The many talents, which thou namest, spare
For thy own sons. These bargainings of war
Hath Turnus been the first to abrogate, 762
From th' instant of my Pallas being slain.
The Manes of my sire Anchises this,
This thinks Iulus." Having spoken thus,
The helmet he engrasps in his left hand,
And in his neck bowed backward, as he sues,
His falchion plunges to the hilt. Not far
Hæmonides, of Phœbus and of Trivia priest,
Whose brows a fillet with its holy band 770
Environed, all in glitter with his robe
And with distinguished arms : encount'ring
  whom,
He drives him through the plain, and
  standing o'er
The fallen, offers him a sacrifice,
And shrouds him in vast shade ; his gathered
  arms
Serestus on his shoulders carries back,
A trophy, king Gradivus, [gift] to thee.
From Vulcan's stock begotten, Cæculus,
And Umbro, coming from the Marsi's
  mounts,
Rally the ranks. The son of Dardanus 780
Against them rages. He had with the sword
Anxur's left hand, and, wholly with its steel,
His buckler's rim, struck off :—he some-
  thing big
Had uttered, and supposed that in the
  speech
There lay [some] virtue, and to heav'n his
  soul
Was haply lifting up, and hoary hairs
And length of years t' himself had guaran-
  teed :
Tarquitus, leaping out on th' other side
In sparkling arms, whom Dryope, the
  nymph,
Had borne to Faunus, haunter of the
  woods, 790
Exposed himself to meet the fiery [chief] :
The other hampers with his indrawn lance
His coat of mail, and buckler's mountain
  load.

His head, then, as he begs in vain, and
  many a word
Prepares to say, he tumbles to the ground,
And, rolling on the blood-warm trunk, he
  these
Above it from a hostile bosom speaks :
" Lie there now, O redoubtable ! Not thee
Shall thy most worthy mother hearse in
  earth,
And with a barrow of thy native land 800
Thy limbs encumber. To the savage fowls
Shalt thou be left ; or, sunken in the gulf,
The surge shall sweep thee off, and fish,
  unfed,
Thy wounds shall lick." Antæus straight,
  and Lucas,
Head champion-men of Turnus, he pur-
  sues ;
Brave Numa, too, and Camers yellow
  [-haired],
From high-souled Volscens sprung, who
  was in land
The richest of Ausonia's sons, and reigned
O'er still Amyclæ. Like Ægeon, who,
They tell us, had a hundred arms, and
  hands 810
A hundred, and that from his fifty mouths
And bosoms blazed there forth a flame,
  what time
Against Jove's levins he with equal shields
So many clanged, unsheathed so many
  swords.
Thus o'er the plain thro'out Æneas storms,
A conqueror, when once his sword-point
  warmed.
Lo ! e'en against Niphæus' four-yoked
  steeds,
And their confronted chests, he marches
  on ;
And when they saw him taking lengthful
  strides,
And raging awfully, wheeled round with
  fright, 820
And dashing back, e'en fling they out the
  chief,
And hurry off the chariot to the shores.

---

768. This is an uncommon, if not a solitary, example of *applico* (v. 536) being joined with an
ablative. Some translators consider *cervice* to be
in the absolute case ; and perhaps it may be so ;
but then an ellipse must be the consequence, which
they differ in supplying. If this view of the construction be preferred, the passage must be otherwise rendered :
" And as the suitor's neck is backward bent," &c.

794. "Yet loe! the seas I see by often beating
Doe pearce the rockes ; and hardest marble weares ;
But his hard rocky hart for no entreating
Will yield, but, when my piteous plaints he heares,
Is hardned more with my aboundant teares."
,Spenser, *F. Q.*, iv. 12, 7.

But Marinell was only obdurate ; Æneas was
simply brutal.

801. Spenser represents the birds as looking out
for the future corpse !
" Loe ! loe already how the fowles in aire
Doe flocke, awaiting shortly to obtayn
Thy carcas for their pray, the guerdon of thy
payn."
F. Q., ii. 6, 28.

Meanwhile in car, with twain white coursers
  yoked,
Leucagus on the midmost bears him down;
His brother Liger too; but with the reins
His brother sways the steeds, keen Leu-
  cagus
His unsheathed falchion brandishes around.
As they are fuming with such fiery heat,
Æneas brooked them not : he rushes on,
And loomed a giant with a hostile spear.
T' whom Liger [cries] : "Not steeds of
  Diomede,   831
Nor chariot of Achilles, thou dost see,
Or plains of Phrygia : now shall on these
  grounds
The war's conclusion and thy life's be
  deigned."
Such words from raving Liger widely fly :
But 'tis not words Troy's hero e'en prepares
In answer ; for a javelin on the foe
He hurls. As Leucagus, while o'er the
  strokes
He's stooping forward, with his weapon
  warned
His twain-yoked steeds; while with left
  foot advanced   840
He fits him for the fight ; the spear runs
  through
The lowest borders of his beaming shield ;
Then pierces his left groin : flung from his
  car,
About to die, he o'er the fields is rolled.
Whom good Æneas speaks in bitter terms :
"O Leucagus, no plodding flight of steeds
Thy car betrayed, or it have overturned
Unreal phantoms from thy foes. Thyself
Dost leave the chariot, vaulting from the
  wheels."
These having spoken thus, the steeds he
  seized.   850
His hapless brother stretched his feeble
  hands,
Fall'n from the selfsame chariot : "By
  thyself,
By parents thine, who such have thee
  begot,
O Trojan hero, leave to me this life,
And pity one who supplicates." To him
Æneas, as he pleads in further [terms] :
"Not such-like words thou late didst utter :
  die !"

And do not thou a brother, brother quit."
Then with the sword-point he unlocks his
  breast,
The spirit's shroud. Such deaths through-
  out the plains   860
The Dardan leader dealt, while raging on
In fashion of a sweeping stream, or inky
  storm.
At last the boy Ascanius and the youth,
Besieged in vain, burst forth and leave the
  camp.
Jove in the meanwhile Juno unaddressed
Accosts : "O sister mine, and thou the same
My dearest consort, as thou didst suppose,
Venus,—nor doth thy judgment thee mis-
  lead,—
Upholds the Trojan powers ; with her
  men
No right hand is there quick for war, and
  soul   870
Of chivalry, and tolerant of risk."
T' whom crest-fall'n Juno : "Why, O fairest
  spouse,
Dost vex me, sick at heart, and fearing thy
  keen taunts ?
Would heav'n there were that power in my
  love,
Which there was once, and which 'twas
  right there was !
For this to me thou wouldest not deny,
O thou almighty, but that from the fray
I might be able Turnus to withdraw,
And keep him for his father Daunus safe.
Now let him perish, and to Teucer's sons
Discharge amercements with his duteous
  blood.   881
Still he from our original derives
His title, and [within] the fourth [degree]
Pilumnus is his sire ; and often has he
  heaped
Thy courts with lavish hand and many a
  gift."
To whom the monarch of empyreal
  heaven
Thus shortly spake : "If from immediate
  death
Reprieve and respite for the falling youth
Be craved, and thou conceivest that I this
Should thus ordain : bear Turnus off in
  flight,   890
And rescue him from his impending fates.
Thus far it is my pleasure thee t' indulge.
But if there any higher favor lurks
'Neath those entreaties, and the whole
  campaign
Thou deemest can be shifted or be
  changed ;—
Thou feedest idle hopes." And Juno [at
  the speech]

---

845. Say what the commentators please, *pius* (v. 591) is an unhappy term to apply to this hard-hearted man ; at least, in the present instance. Leucagus would have said no more than the truth, if he had addressed him in the language of Gloucester to the two murderers :

"Your eyes drop millstones, when fools' eyes fall tears." Shakespeare, *K. Richard III.*, i. 4.

Tears shedding : " What if thou in *mind* shouldst grant
What thou in *voice* declinest ; and, confirmed
To Turnus, should this life abide? Now waits
The guiltless [youth] a galling end ; or I, Mistaken in the truth, am swept along.
Wherein, Oh ! would that I were rather mocked 902
By groundless dread, and for the better thou,
Who 'rt able, would'st thy course begun reverse !"
When uttered she these words, from heav'n on high
Forthwith she flung her, driving through the air
A tempest, girdled with a cloud ; and sought
The Ilian army and Laurentine camp.
Then doth the goddess, of a hollow mist
A ghost, thin, strengthless, in Æneas' guise,— 910
A prodigy astounding to be seen !—
Trick out in Dardan arms ; and counterfeits
His shield, and helm-crests of his god-like head ;
Gives empty words, gives sound without a soul,
And represents the gait of one that walks :
Such as the shapes, when death is undergone,—
The legend goes,—flit to and fro ; or dreams,

Which drowsèd senses mock. But frisks about
The blithesome sprite before the leading lines,
And chafes with arms the hero, and with voice 920
Exasperates. On whom does Turnus press,
And from a distance hurls a hissing spear :
It, with its back presented, wheels its steps.
Then sooth as soon as ever Turnus thought
That, being turned away, Æneas yields,
And, [all] in tumult in his soul, vain hope
Drank in : " Æneas, whither dost thou fly?

919. It is well known that there are in reality as treacherous phenomena as the phantom which deluded Turnus, though not quite of the same kind.
" Perhaps, impatient as he stumbles on,
Struck from the root of slimy rushes, blue,
The wild-fire scatters round, or gather'd trails
A length of flame deceitful o'er the moss ;
Whither decoy'd by the fantastic blaze,
Now lost, and now renew'd, he sinks absorpt,
Rider and horse, amid the miry gulf :
While still, from day to day, his pining wife
And plaintive children his return await,
In wild conjecture lost. At other times,
Sent by the *better genius* of the night,
Innoxious, gleaming on the horse's mane,
The meteor sits ; and shows the narrow path
That winding leads through pits of death, or else
Instructs him how to take the dangerous ford."
Thomson, *Autumn*.
Collins is more particular ; but it would seem that he drew his ideas from the poem of his friend just quoted :
" Let not dank Will mislead you to the heath ;
Dancing in mirky night, o'er fen and lake,
He glows, to draw you downward to your death,
In his bewitch'd, low, marshy willow brake !
What though far off, from some dark dell espied,
His glimmering mazes cheer th' excursive sight,
Yet turn, ye wanderers, turn your steps aside,
Nor trust the guidance of that faithless light.
For watchful, lurking, 'mid the unrustling reed,
At those mirk hours the wily monster lies,
And listens oft to hear the passing steed,
And frequent round him rolls his sullen eyes,
If chance his savage wrath may some weak wretch surprise."
Ode on the Superstitions of the Highlands.

897. Juno wished Jupiter to answer pretty much as the Groom replied to King Richard II. (Act v. 2) :
" What my tongue dares not, that my heart shall say ;"
holding, perhaps, with Suffolk, that
" Things are often spoke, and seldom meant."
2 *K. Henry VI*., iii. 1.
916. " Such are those thick and gloomy shadows damp,
Oft seen in charnel vaults and sepulchres
Lingering, and sitting by a new-made grave,
As loth to leave the body that it loved."
Milton, *Comus*.
Ford employs the notion with effect :
" Peace and sweet rest sleep here ! Let not the touch
Of this my impious hand profane the shrine
Of fairest purity, which hovers yet
About these blessed bones inhears'd within.
If in the bosom of this sacred tomb,
Bianca, thy disturbed ghost doth range,
Behold, I offer up the sacrifice
Of bleeding tears, shed from a faithful spring ;
Pouring oblations of a mourning heart
To thee, offended spirit." *Love's Sacrifice*, v. 4.
917. See note on *Æn*. vi. *l*. 398.

927. "*Demetrius*. Lysander, speak again.
Thou runaway, thou coward, art thou fled?
Speak ! In some bush ? Where dost thou hide thy head?
Puck. Thou coward ! art thou bragging to the stars,
Telling the bushes that thou look'st for wars,
And wilt not come ? Come, recreant ; come, thou child ;
I'll whip thee with a rod : he is defil'd
That draws a sword on thee.
Demetrius.   Yea ; art thou there?
Puck. Follow my voice : we'll try no manhood here.
Lysander. He goes before me, and still dares me on |
When I come where he calls, then he is gone.
The villain is much lighter heel'd than I :
I follow'd fast, but faster he did fly."
Shakespeare, *Midsummer Night's Dream*, lii. 2.

Abandon not the plighted marriage-beds !
With this right hand shall be vouchsafed
  the soil
Sought o'er the waves." He, shouting
  such, pursues,   930
And brandishes his falchion-blade un-
  sheathed ;
Nor sees the breezes bear away his joys.
By chance a galley, moored to th' eminence
Of steepy rock, with stretched-out ladders,
  stood,
And gangway ready laid ; wherein the king
Osinius was conveyed from Clusium's coasts.
Hither, within its lurking-places, throws
  itself
The flurried phantom of Æneas taking
  flight.
Nor Turnus more inactive presses on,
And obstacles surmounts, and springs across
The lofty gangways. Scarce the prow he'd
  reached :—   941
Saturnia snaps the rope, and tows away
The wrenchèd vessel o'er the rolling seas.
Then the light phantom now no further
  seeks
The lurking spots, but, soaring up aloft,
Itself it blended with a pitchy cloud.
But him, not present [there], Æneas calls
To combat : he despatches down to death
The many hero-bodies in his way.
When, in the meantime, on the midst of sea
A storm sweeps Turnus off, he looks behind,
Unconscious of events, and for escape 952
Unthankful, and both hands, along with
  voice,
He stretches to the stars : " Almighty sire,
Hast deemed me worthy of so grave a
  charge,
And willed that I such penalties should
  pay ?
Whither am I borne on ? Whence have I
  come ?
What speed shall bring me back, or [bring
  me] what [in fame] ?
Shall I once more Laurentum's walls and
  camp
Behold ? What of that band of heroes, who
Me and my arms have followed ? all of
  whom—   961
O guilt !—in cursèd death have I forsook ?
And now I see them straggling, and I hear

958.   "My dear, dear lord,
  The purest treasure mortal times afford
Is spotless reputation : that away,
Men are but gilded loam, or painted clay.
A jewel in a ten times barr'd-up chest
Is a bold spirit in a loyal breast.
Mine honour is my life ; both grow in one :
Take honour from me, and my life is done."
                Shakespeare, *K. Richard II.*, i. 1.

The groan of those that fall. What is 't I
  do ?
Or now what deep of earth can wide
  enough
Gape ope for me ? Ye rather, O ye winds,
Have pity on me ! On the cliffs, on
  rocks,—
I, Turnus, heartily do you beseech,—
My vessel force along, and let it drive
Upon the felon shallows of the Syrt,   970
Whither nor Rutuli, nor conscious Rumor,
May follow me." As he these [words]
  repeats,
Now hither does he waver in his mind,
Now thither :—whether he with point of
  sword
Should wildly stab himself, because of such
His deep disgrace, and through his ribs
  drive home
The ruthless falchion ; or should fling him-
  self
Upon the centre of the waves, and seek
The winding shores by swimming, and
  again
Return against the Teucri's arms. Three
  times   980
Either expedient he essayed ; three times
The highest Juno checked him, and, the
  youth
Compassionating from her soul, restrained.

966.   " On the ground
Outstretch'd he lay, on the cold ground ; and oft
Cursed his creation : Death as oft accused
Of tardy execution, since denounced
The day of his offence. 'Why comes not Death,'
Said he, 'with one thrice-acceptable stroke
To end me ? Shall Truth fail to keep her word ?
Justice divine not hasten to be just ?
But Death comes not at call ; Justice divine
Mends nor her slowest pace for prayers or cries.
O woods, O fountains, hillocks, dales, and bowers !
With other echo late I taught your shades
To answer, and resound far other song.'"
                Milton, *P. L.*, b. x.

" Then hear me, Heaven, to whom I call for right,
And you, fair twinkling stars, that crown the
  night ;
And hear me, woods, and silence of this place,
And ye, sad hours, that move a sullen pace ;
Hear me, ye shadows, that delight to dwell
In horrid darkness, and ye powers of hell,
Whilst I breathe out my last."
          J. Fletcher, *The Faithful Shepherdess*, iv. 4.

The misery of Turnus may call to mind the exclamation of the unhappy Richard :

          " O ! that I were as great
As is my grief, or lesser than my name,
Or that I could forget what I have been,
Or not remember what I must be now."
          Shakespeare, *K. Richard II.*, iii. 3.

973. " *Talbot.* My thoughts are whirled like a
  potter's wheel ;
I know not where I am, or what I do."
          Shakespeare, 1 *K. Henry VI.*, i. 5.

He glides, the sea-depths sundering, alike
With surge and tide of favor, and is borne
On to his father Daunus' ancient town.
But meanwhile, by the impulses of Jove,
Mezentius, burning, to the fight succeeds,
And on the Teucrians, as they exult,
He charges. Run in mass the Tuscan
  troops, 990
And with all hate and crowding darts
Upon one hero, [yea] on one, they rush.
He,—like a cliff, which into ocean vast
Juts out, exposed to frenzies of the winds,
And open to the deep, bears all the brunt
And threats alike of heav'n and of the sea,
Itself abiding moveless :—Hebrus, son
Of Dolichaon, fells to earth, with whom
[He] Latagus and flying Palmus [slays] :
But Latagus he with a rock, aye e'en 1000
The mighty fragment of a mount, forestalls
Upon the mouth and his confronted face :
Palmus, with severed ham-string he allows
Inactive to be tumbled, and his arms
To Lausus on his shoulders grants to wear,
And on his crest to plant his plumes.
  Moreo'er,
He fells Evanth the Phrygian, Mimas too,
[Of] equal [age] with Paris, and his mate,
Whom in one night Theano brought to light
For Amycus his sire, and, pregnant with a
  torch, 1010
The queen Cisseis Paris : Paris rests
[Tombed] in the city of his ancestors :
Mimas, unknown, Laurentum's coast con-
  tains.
And like as, hounded by the fang of dogs
From lofty mountains down, some famous
  boar,
Whom piny Vesulus for many a year
Bescreens, for many, too, the Laurent
  marsh,
Fed in the reedy forest, when he once
Among the nets is come, has ta'en his
  stand,
And bellowed in his rage, and bristled up
His shoulders ; nor has one the hardi-
  hood 1021
To show his wrath, and nearer to ap-
  proach ;
But him with darts and shoutings safe afar
They ply : still he, undaunted, slowly turns
Towards ev'ry quarter, gnashing with his
  tusks,
And from his side he shakes the lances
  down :
No otherwise, not one of those, to whom
Mezentius was the cause of righteous wrath,
Has courage to engage with sword un-
  sheathed ;
With missiles from afar and lusty shout

They worry him. From Coryth's ancient
  bourns 1031
Had Acron come, a man [of] Grecian [line],
An exile, leaving incomplete the rites
Of marriage. Him when from afar he saw
Discomfiting the central squadrons, gay
In plumes and purple of his plighted bride :
As oft a foodless lion, ranging o'er
The lofty stalls, (for madding hunger
  prompts,)
If haply he hath spied a flitting roe,
Or hart with antlers tow'ring high, exults
Hideously yawning, and hath raised his
  mane, 1041
And to the entrails, couching o'er them,
  clings ;
The noisome gore bewets his felon jaws :
So, eager hurtles on his serried foes
Mezentius. Hapless Acron low is laid,
And, dying, with his heels the murky ground
He smites, and smears with blood the shat-
  tered darts.
And he, the same, deigned not to overthrow
Orodes, as he's flying, nor to deal
A wound invisible with darted lance : 1050
He meets him in his path and to his face,
And fell to the encounter man to man,
Superior, not in guile, but gallant arms.
Then with his foot placed o'er him, stricken
  down,
And leaning on his spear : "Lies, warriors !
  [here]
No despicable portion of the war,
The high Orodes." Following him, his
  mates

1036. Acron, though not deficient in bravery, would not have been quite to the taste of the poor Captain in Ford's *Unnatural Combat*. Speaking of his armor, he says:
  " This hath past through
A wood of pikes, and every one aimed at it,
Yet scorn'd to take impression from their fury :
With this, as still you see it, fresh and new,
I've charg'd through fire that would have sing'd
  your sables,
Black fox, and ermines, and changed the proud
  colour
Of scarlet, though of the right Tyrian die.—
But now, *as if the trappings made the man,*
Such only are admir'd that come adorn'd
With what's no part of them." Act iii. 3.

1037. " What if the lion in his rage I meet !—
Oft in the dust I view his printed feet :
And, fearful ! oft when Day's declining light
Yields her pale empire to the mourner Night,
By hunger rous'd, he scours the groaning plain,
Gaunt wolves and sullen tigers in his train :
Before them Death with shrieks directs their way,
Fills the wild yell, and leads them to their prey."
  Collins, *Oriental Eclogues*, ii.

1052. " Blood hath bought blood, and blows have answer'd blows :
Strength match'd with strength, and power confronted power." Shakespeare, *K. John*, ii. 2.

A joyful pæan in a chorus shout.
But, dying, he: "Not over me, unwreaked,
Nor long, shalt thou, whoe'er thou art, exult
In conquest: equal destinies await   1061
Thee, too, and soon thou'lt gripe the self-
same fields."
To whom Mezentius, smiling with mixt rage:
"Now perish! But the father of the gods
And king of men will see to me." As this
He speaks, he wrenched the weapon from
the corpse:
Stern rest and steely slumber press his'orbs;
His eyes are shut in everlasting night.

1067.   "Death is an equall doome
        To good and bad, the common in of rest."
                        Spenser, *F. Q.*, ii. 1, 45.
Beautifully of sleep in life and health:
" The whyles his lord in silver slomber lay,
  Like to the evening starre adorn'd with deawy
  ray."   *F. Q.*, vi. 7, 19.
Shakespeare, differently:
" Till o'er their brows death-counterfeiting sleep,
  With leaden legs and batty wings, doth creep."
                Midsummer Night's Dream, iii. 2.
Dryden, of Charles II.:
" An iron slumber sat on his majestic eyes."
                        Threnodia Augustalis.

1068. Perhaps *in*, v. 746, should be rendered by
for.
" And when those pallid cheekes and ashe hew,
  In which sad Death his pourtraiture had writ,
  And when those hollow eyes and deadly view,
  On which the cloud of ghastly night did sit," &c.
                Spenser, *Daphnaida*, iii. 2.
" Then going forth, and finding in his way
  A souldier of the watch, who sleeping lay,
  Enrag'd to see the wretch neglect his part,
  He strikes his sword into his trembling heart:
  The hand of death, and iron dulnesse, takes
  Those leaden eyes, which nat'rall ease forsakes."
        Sir John Beaumont, *Bosworth Field.*
" See, while I speak, high on her sable wheel
  Old Night advancing climbs the eastern hill:
  Troops of dark clouds prepare her way; behold
  How their brown pinions, edg'd with evening
  gold,
  Spread shadowing o'er the house, and glide away,
  Slowly pursuing the declining day;
  O'er the broad roof they fly their circuit still,
  Thus days before they did, and days to come
  they will;
  But the black cloud, that shadows o'er his eyes,
  Hangs there immoveable, and never flies:
  Fain would I bid the envious gloom be gone;
  Ah, fruitless wish! how are his curtains drawn
  For a long evening that despairs the dawn!"
  Watts, *Lyric Poems*, b. iii. To the Memory
  of Gunston.
Gray uses the expression of Milton's blindness:
" The living throne, the sapphire-blaze
  Where angels tremble while they gaze,
  He saw! but, blasted with excess of light,
  Clos'd his eyes in endless night."
                The Progress of Poesy, iii. 2.

Cædicus puts Alcathous to death,
Sacrator [kills] Hydaspes; Rapo, too,   1070
Parthenius; also, passing strong in might,
Orses; Messapus also Clonius [slays],
And Ericetes of Lycaon['s line];
That,—by the fall of his unruly steed,
Lying on earth;—a footman *this*,—on foot.
And Lycian Agis had advanced in front:
Whom, yet, not lacking of the bravery
Of ancestors, doth Valerus o'erthrow;
While Salius Thronius [puts to death],
Likewise Nealces Salius, in the dart   1080
Distinguished, and the far deceiving bolt.
Now grisly Mars was balancing their
    woes
And mutual slaught'rings: slew alike and
    fell alike
The conq'rors and the conquered: flight
    was known
Neither to these, nor those. The deities
Within the courts of Jove compassion feel
For th' idle wrath of both, and that such
    deep
Distresses were [the lot] of mortal men:
To this side Venus, on the other hand,
To that, Saturnian Juno pays regard;   1090
The wan Tisiphone, among the midst
Of thousands, is in fury. But, in sooth,
Mezentius, shaking his prodigious spear,
[All] in a tumult, marches on the field:
As great Orion, when afoot he walks
Through central Nereus' vasty floods, his
    path
Disparting, by his shoulder overtops
The waves; or, bringing down from moun-
    tain crests
An agèd ash, both stalks upon the ground,
And hides his head among the clouds:
    such-like   1100

            " The torpid pow'rs
Of heaviness weigh'd down my beamless eyes,
And pressed them into night."
                W. Thompson, *Sickness*, b. i.
        " What mist weighs down
My eyes already! Oh, 'tis death; I see,
In a long robe of darkness, is preparing
To seal them up for ever."
                Shirley, *Love's Cruelty*, v. 2.
" A mist hangs o'er mine eyes; the sun's bright
    splendour
Is clouded in an everlasting shadow."
                Ford, *The Broken Heart*, v. 3.
1095. See note on *Æn*. iii. *l.* 931.
1096. " Forthwith upright he rears from off the
    pool
His mighty stature; on each hand the flames,
Driven backward, slope their pointing spires, and,
    roll'd
In billows, leave i' the midst a horrid vale."
                Milton, *P. L.*, b. i.

Mezentius bears him on in giant arms.
Æneas, on the other hand, prepares
To meet him in advance, as him he spied
In the long line. He undismayed remains,
His high-souled foe awaiting, and he stands
In his own bulk, and meting with his eyes
A range, far as sufficient for his spear:
"May my right hand, a deity to me,
And dart, which, ready to be launched, I
  poise, 1109
Stand by me now! 'Tis thee thyself that I,
O Lausus, hallow, mantled in the spoils,
Reft from the carcass of a pirate-knave,
A trophy of Æneas." [Thus] he spake,
And from a distance flung the hissing lance:
But, flying, 'tis from off his buckler shot,
And far the excellent Antores spears
Between the side and loins; Antores, mate
Of Hercules, who had, from Argi sent,
Held to Evander, and had settled down
In his Italian city. He is felled, 1120
Of evil fortune, by another's wound,
And casts a look to heav'n, and, as he dies,
Recalls the charming Argi to his soul.
Then does the good Æneas throw his spear:
It through the hollow disk with triple bronze,
Through folds of canvas, and the work, in-
  wove
With three bull[-hide]s, careered, and came
  to rest
Deep in the groin: but carried on its force
No further. Quick his sword Æneas, blithe
At sight of Tuscan blood, tears from his
  thigh, 1130
And hotly presses on his wildered [foe].
Lausus, when he beheld it, deeply groaned,
In his affection for his darling sire,

And tears came o'er his features coursing
  down.
Here, the disaster of thy grievous death,
And thy most glorious deeds, if any age
Will credit to so great a work extend,
I shall not sooth, nor thee shall I, O youth,
Deserving record, pass in silence by.
He, drawing back his foot, disabled e'en,
And hampered, was retreating, and the
  hostile shaft 1141
Was trailing in his shield. Forth sprang
  the youth,
And mingled him among their arms. And
  now
He passed beneath Æneas' falchion-point,
As with his right hand rises he on high,
And deals a blow, and him by checking
  bore.
His comrades second him with lusty cheer,
While, guarded by the buckler of the son,
The sire withdrew; and darts together hurl,
And from afar with missiles drive away 1150
The foe. Æneas fumes, and keeps himself
Ensconced. And as, if storms at times
With drifted hail swoop downward, from
  the plains
Hath ev'ry ploughman 'scaped, and ev'ry
  swain;
And in a safe retreat the traveller hides,
Or by a river's banks, or by a vault
Of tow'ring rock, while on the lands it rains,
That they may, on returning of the sun,
Be able to employ the day in toil:

1101. " Disdayne he called was, and did disdayne
To be so cald, and who so did him call:
Sterne was his looke, and full of stomacke vayne;
His portaunce terrible, and stature tall,
Far passing th' hight of men terrestriall;
Like an huge gyant of the Titans race ;
That made him scorne all creatures great and
  small,
And with his pride all others powre deface:
More fitt emongst black fiendes then men to have
  his place." Spenser, F. Q., ii. 7, 41.

" On th' other side, Satan, alarm'd,
Collecting all his might, dilated stood,
Like Teneriff or Atlas, unremoved :
His stature reach'd the sky, and on his crest
Sat Horror plum'd ; nor wanted in his grasp
What seem'd both spear and shield."
  Milton, P. L., b. iv.

1108. Mezentius was like Sansfoy :
" At last him chaunst to meete upon the way
A faithlesse Sarazin, all armde to point,
In whose great shield was writ with letters gay
Sans foy; full large of limbe and every ioint
He was, and cared not for God or man a point."
  Spenser, F. Q., i. 2, 12.

1134. If attention to voice be insisted on, v. 790
may be rendered thus:
"And tears were forced in courses o'er his cheeks."

1137. Tanto operi may fairly be looked upon as
a reference to the poem itself. It is like Virgil,
who, on the occasion of recording the feats of Nisus
and Euryalus, uses a similar expression: si quid
mea carmina possunt.

1149. Guyomar says to his father Montezuma, in
Dryden's Indian Emperor :
" Fly, sir, while I give back that life you gave,
Mine is well lost, if I your life can save."
  Act i. 2.
1153. " The sulphurous hail
Shot after us in storm, o'erblown, hath laid
The fiery surge that from the precipice
Of Heaven received us falling : and the thunder,
Wing'd with red lightning, and impetuous rage,
Perhaps hath spent his shafts, and ceases now
To bellow through the vast and boundless deep."
  Milton, P. L., b. i.
1158. " As when from mountain tops the dusky
  clouds
Ascending, while the north wind sleeps, o'erspread
Heaven's cheerful face, the lowering element
Scowls o'er the darken'd landskip snow, or shower :
If chance the radiant sun with farewell sweet
Extend his evening beam, the fields revive,
The birds their notes renew, and bleating herds
Attest their joy, that hill and valley rings."
  Ibid., b. ii.

Thus, overwhelmed by darts on ev'ry side,
Æneas bears the battle-storm, until 1161
All thunder clears away; and Lausus chides,
And Lausus threatens: "Whither, doomed
to die,
Dost rush, and darest [deeds] above thy
strength?
Thee, heedless [youth], thy piety misleads."
Nor doth the other madly triumph less.
And higher rises now the felon rage
Of the Dardanian leader, and the Weirds
For Lausus gather up the last of threads.
For home Æneas drives his lusty sword
Through the youth's midriff, and deep hides
the whole. 1171
The falchion-point both traversed through
his shield,
The threat'ning [youth's] light armor, and
the frock
Which had his mother spun with ductile
gold;
And blood his bosom filled: then life
through air
Fled rueful to the Ghosts, and left the corse.

1169. See note on *Ecl.* iv. *l.* 62.
" But grant man happy; grant him happy long;
Add to life's prize her latest hour;
That hour, so late, is nimble in approach,
That, like a post, comes on in full career:
How swift the shuttle flies, that weaves thy
shroud!"
Gascoigne's *Greene Knight* would have wished
it had in his case:
" The fatal Sisters three,
Which spun my slender twine,
Knew wel how rotten was the yarne,
Frō whence they drew their line:
Yet haue they wouen the web,
With care so manifolde,
(Alas I woful wretch the while)
As any cloth can holde:
Yea though the threeds be cowrse,
And such as others lothe,
Yet must I wrap alwayes therin
My bones and body both;
And weare it out at length,
Which lasteth but too long:
O weauer, weauer, work no more;
Thy warp hath done me wrong."
Weedes: Complaint of the Greene Knight.
Chaucer has a different image:
" For sikerly, whan I was borne, anon
Deth drow the tappe of lif, and let it gon:
And ever sith hath so the tappe yronne,
Till that almost all empty is the tonne."
Canterbury Tales; the Reve's Prologue.
Shakespeare makes King John say:
" The tackle of my heart is crack'd and burn'd;
And all the shrouds, wherewith my life should sail,
Are turned to one thread, one little hair:
My heart hath one poor string to stay it by,
Which holds but till thy news be uttered,
And then all this thou seest is but a clod,
And model of confounded royalty." Act. v. 7.

But when, in sooth, Anchises' offspring
saw
The face and features of the dying youth,—
Features in wondrous fashion waxing wan;
Compassionating him he deeply groaned,
And stretched his right hand forth, and to
his mind 1181
The picture of a father's love occurred.
" What now to thee, O piteous youth, for
these
Thy merits, what can good Æneas grant,
Worthy of such a noble nature? [These]
the arms
Wherein thou hast rejoiced, keep thine,
and thee
I to the ghosts and ashes of thy sires,—
If that have any interest,—resign.
Yet thou herewith, ill-starred, sad death
shalt cheer:—
By great Æneas' right hand thou dost fall."
Thereon he chides his loit'ring mates, and
lifts 1191
Him up from earth, defiling with his blood
His tresses, trimmed in customary form.
Meanwhile his sire at Tiber's river-wave
His wounds was stanching with its crystal-
streams,
And, leaning on a tree-bole, rested he his
frame.
Hangs from the boughs apart his helm of
bronze,
And on the mead his cumbrous arms repose.
Choice youths around him stand; he, faint
himself,
Gasping for breath, supports his neck, his
beard 1200
In forward culture flowing on his breast.
Of Lausus many a question does he ask,
And many a one he sends, to call him back
And bear the orders of his mourning sire.
But Lausus lifeless his companions bore
Upon his arms, in tears,—a mighty [youth],
And conquered by a mighty wound. A mind,
Of ill foresightful, understood afar
Their groan. His hoary hairs with plen-
teous dust
He mars, and stretches both his hands to
heaven, 1210
And fastens on the body: " O my son,
Hath such a whelming appetite for life
Held me, that I should in my stead allow
To take my place beneath the foe's right
hand

1190. So Olivia says:
" If one should be a prey, how much the better
To fall before the lion than the wolf!"
Shakespeare, *Twelfth Night*, iii. 1.
1202. " Stay, you imperfect speakers, tell me
more." Shakespeare, *Macbeth*, i. 3.

v. 848—869. BOOK X. v. 869—882. 285

Him whom I've sired? By these thy wounds am I,
Thy father, rescued, living by thy death?
Now, welaway! to wretched me at length
A hapless end!—A wound now driven deep!
I, son, the same, have stained thy name by guilt, 1219
From throne and sceptre of my fathers driven
Through infamy. Had I a forfeit owed
To native country and my [people's] hate,
By every death would I myself had given
My guilty spirit! Now I live, nor yet
Mankind and light I leave!—but leave I will."
At once, while saying this, he lifts him up
Upon his sickly thigh, and, though his strength
Foreslows him, owing to his deepsome wound,
He, not cast down, his charger bids be brought.
This was his pride, his comfort this; with this 1230
He issued conqueror from ev'ry war.
He speaks the mourning [steed], and in the like
Begins: "O Rhœbus, long,—if any thing
Is long for mortal beings,—have we lived.
Thou either conq'ror shalt to-day bring back
Those bloody trophies and Æneas' head,
And of the pangs of Lausus venger be
With me; or, if no pow'r disclose a way,
Along with me shalt die. For deem not I,
O thou most gallant [horse], that thou wilt deign 1240
To brook outlandish rules and Trojan lords."
He said; and, on his back received, [there] placed
His wonted limbs, and laded both his hands
With pointed jav'lins, glitt'ring on his head

1216. "No tomb shall hold thee
But these two arms, no trickments but my tears;
Over thy hearse my sorrows, like sad arms,
Shall hang for ever; on the toughest marble
Mine eyes shall weep thee out an epitaph:
Love at thy feet shall kneel, his smart bow broken,
Faith at thy head, Youth and the Graces mourners:
Oh, sweet young man!"
Fletcher, *The Mad Lover*, v. 4.

1232. See note on *Æn.* iv. *l.* 101, and xi. *l.* 127.

1242. Only for his wound, the following quotation might be appropriate:

"I saw young Harry, with his beaver on,
His cuisses on his thighs, gallantly arm'd,
Rise from the ground like feathered Mercury,
And vaulted with such ease into his seat,
As if an angel dropp'd down from the clouds,
To turn and wind a fiery Pegasus,
And witch the world with noble horsemanship."
Shakespeare, 1 *K. Henry IV.*, iv. 1.

With bronze, and bristling with a horse-hair plume.
Thus on the midmost, fleet, he sped his course.
Seethes mighty shame within a single heart,
And a deliriousness with mingled woe,
And love by Furies racked, and conscious worth.
And here Æneas thrice with lusty voice
He called. Him sooth Æneas knew, and glad 1251
He prays: "So grant that mighty sire of gods!
So high Apollo! To engage the hand
Do thou begin." He uttered only this;
And goes to meet him with a hostile spear.
But he: "How scare you me, thrice-brutal [wretch],
My son reft from me? This was th' only way,
Whereby you could destroy. Nor dread we death,
Nor any of the deities we spare.
Surcease! I now am coming, doomed to die,
And these my gifts to thee I carry first."

1256. What Caraza says to Irene might have been applied to Mezentius:
"While unavailing anger crowds thy tongue
With idle threats and fruitless exclamation,
The fraudful moments ply their silent wings,
And steal thy life away. Death's horrid angel
Already shakes his bloody sabre o'er thee."
Johnson, *Irene*, v. 9.

1258. "And why not death, rather than living torment?
To die is to be banished from myself,
And Silvia is myself: banish'd from her,
Is self from self; a deadly banishment.
What light is light, if Silvia be not seen?
What joy is joy, if Silvia be not by?
Unless it be to think that she is by,
And feed upon the shadow of perfection.
Except I be by Silvia in the night,
There is no music in the nightingale;
Unless I look on Silvia in the day,
There is no day for me to look upon.
She is my essence; and I leave to be,
If I be not by her fair influence
Foster'd, illumin'd, cherish'd, kept alive.
I fly not death, to fly his deadly doom:
Tarry I here, I but attend on death;
But, fly I hence, I fly away from life."
Shakespeare, *Two Gentlemen of Verona*, iii. 1.

"Why stare ye on me?
You cannot put on faces to affright me:
In death I am a king still, and contemn ye.
Where is that governor? Methinks his manhood
Should be well pleas'd to see my tragedy,
And come to bathe his stern eyes in my sorrows:
I dare him to the fight; bring his scorns with him,
And all his rugged threats."
Fletcher, *The Island Princess*, ii. 5.

"The sense of death is most in apprehension,
And the poor beetle, that we tread upon,
In corporal sufferance finds a pang, as great
As when a giant dies."
Shakespeare, *Measure for Measure*, iii. 1.

He said, and whirled a jav'lin on the foe;
And after that moreover fastens firm 1263
Another, and another, and he flies
In spacious circuit : but the golden boss
Supports them. Thrice around him, as he
    stands,
He rode in circles to the left, his darts
Forth launching from his hand; thrice with
    himself
The Trojan hero a prodigious wood
Bears round upon his canopy of bronze.
Then, when it irks him to have eked delays
So many, darts so many to uproot,   1272
And, being in unequal fight engaged,
Is harassed : stirring many [a thought] in
    mind,
Now bursts he forth at last, and [right] be-
    tween
The war-steed's hollow brows he hurls a
    spear.
The quadruped rears upright, and the air
Smites with its heels, and, following itself
Upon the top of th' horseman, pitched
    abroad,   1279
Encumbers him, and, falling on its face,
On him, unseated, with its shoulder lies.
Trojans alike and Latins with a yell

1267. *"Alexander.* Was I a woman, when, like
Mercury,
I left the walls to fly amongst my foes,
And, like a baited lion, dyed myself
All over with the blood of those bold hunters ;
Till, spent with toil, I battled on my knees,
Plucked forth the darts, that made my shield a
forest,
And hurled them back with most unconquered
fury !"   Lee, *The Rival Queens,* iv. 2.

Set heav'n afire. Æneas to him flies,
And from its scabbard draws his falchion
    forth,
And o'er him these : "Where now Me-
    zentius fierce,
And that wild force of soul ?" On th' other
    hand,
The Tuscan, when, upgazing to the air,
He drank in heaven, and recovered thought :
"O bitter foeman, why dost thou upbraid
And threaten death ? In shedding of my
    blood—   1290
No crime ; nor have I on these terms
To battle come ; nor hath my Lausus struck
These covenants on my behalf with thee.
This one thing by [the grace],—if any grace
There is for conquered enemies,—I crave :
That thou would'st let my corse be hearsed
    in earth.
I know my [subjects'] bitter hate besets :
This rage, I pray, ward off, and grant that I
May be my son's co-partner in the grave."
These speaks he, and, not unaware, receives
Within his throat the falchion, and his life
Spurts forth upon his arms with waving
    gore.   1302

1296.   " O, father abbot !
An old man, broken with the storms of state,
Is come to lay his weary bones among ye ;
Give him a little earth for charity."
          Shakespeare, *K. Henry VIII.,* iv. 2.

1302. There were some redeeming points in the
character of Mezentius ; so that, if he had not been
so irreligious and cruel, he might have deserved the
wish of Queen Katherine for Wolsey :
"So may he rest : his faults lie gently on him !"

BOOK XI.

MEANWHILE Aurora rising ocean left.
Æneas, though alike solicitudes
Hurry him forward to devote the time
To burying his comrades, and his mind
Is troubled at their death, the off'rings due
To deities, as conqueror, he paid
At th 'infant Dawn. A giant oak, its boughs
On all sides lopped away, upon a knoll
He reared, and tricks it out in gleaming
    arms,
Spoils from the general Mezentius stript,
To thee a trophy, puissant lord of war.   11

Line 11. Glover well describes the erection of a trophy :
          "Green Psittalia there
Full opposite exhibits, high and large,
A new erected trophy. Twenty masts

Thereto does he adjust the hero's plumes,
With blood distilling, and his shattered
    darts,

Appear, the tallest of Phœnician pines,
In circular position. Round their base
Are massive anchors, rudders, yards, and oars,
Irregularly pil'd, with beaks of brass,
And naval sculpture from barbarian sterns,
Stupendous by confusion. Crested helms
Above, bright mail, habergeons scal'd in gold
And figur'd shields along the spiry wood,
Up to th' aerial heads in order wind,
Tremendous emblems of gigantic Mars.
Spears, bristling through the intervals, uprear
Their points obliquely ; gilded staves project
Embroider'd colors ; darts and arrows hang
In glitt'ring clusters. On the topmost height
Th' imperial standard broad, from Asia won,
Blaz'd in the sun, and floated in the wind."
                              Athenaid, b. xvii.

His cuirass also, point of aim, and pierced
In twice six places, and his targe of bronze
He fastens to the left side underneath,
And hangs his sword of iv'ry from the neck.
His comrades then,—for all the crowded staff
Of chieftains closed him in,—beginning thus,
He heartens in their triumph : " An event
Of deepest moment is, O warriors, brought
   to pass ;   21
All fear avaunt in what remains ! these be
The spoils and first-fruits of a haughty prince ;
And in my hands here stands Mezentius. Now
There is a passage for us to the king
And walls of Latium. Get ye ready arms ;
With courage and with hope forestall the war ;
Lest any obstacle, while unaware,
When first the heav'nly powers shall allow
To pluck the standards up, and march the youth   30
From out th' encampment, may embarrass you ;
Or purpose stay you, listless through alarm.
Meanwhile let us to earth commit our mates,
And their unburied corses, which alone
The honor is 'neath lowest Acheron.
Go ye," saith he ; " the passing noble souls,
Who have by their own blood this country won
For us, do ye with latest duties grace ;
And to Evander's mourning city first
Let Pallas be conveyed, whom lacking not
Of prowess, hath a day of darkness reft,   41
And in untimely dissolution plunged."
Thus speaks he weeping, and withdraws
   his step

To [his own] thresholds, where, laid out, the corse
Of lifeless Pallas old Acœtes watched ;
Who to Evander of Parrhasia erst
Was armor-bearer ; but with auspices,
Not equally propitious, then assigned   48
The guardian to a darling son, he marched.
Around e'en all the band of servants [stood],
And throng of Trojans, and the Ilian dames,
With mourning locks, in customary form
Let loose. But when Æneas passed inside
The stately gates, a mighty groan do they
With smitten bosoms to the stars upraise,
And with a wail of woe the palace rang.
Himself, when snow-like Pallas' cushioned head
And face he saw, and in his glossy breast
The yawning wound of the Ausonian lance,
On this wise speaks with springing tears :
   " Hath thee,"   60
He cries, " O pitiable youth, what time
She came propitious, Fortune grudged to me ;
That thou our kingdoms mightest not behold,
Nor conq'ror to thy father's seat be borne ?
'Twas not these pledges of thee to thy sire,
Evander, at departing I had given,
When, me embracing as I went away,
He sent me to acquire a mighty rule,

---

40. " Let us go find the body where it lies,
    Soak'd in his enemies' blood ; and from the stream
    With lavers pure, and cleansing herbs, wash off
    The clotted gore. I, with what speed the while,
    (Gaza is not in plight to say us nay,)
    Will send for all my kindred, all my friends,
    To fetch him hence, and solemnly attend
    With silent obsequy, and funeral train,
    Home to his father's house."
                            Milton, *Samson*, end.

41. " O grief ! and could one day
    Have force such excellence to take away?
    Could a swift flying moment, ah ! deface
    Those matchless gifts, that grace,
    Which art and nature had in thee combin'd
    To make thy body paragon thy mind ?
    Hath all pass'd like a cloud,
    And doth eternal silence now them shroud ?
    Is that, so much admir'd, now naught but dust,
    Of which a stone hath trust ?
    O change ! O cruel change ! thou to our sight
    Show'st the Fates' rigour equal to their might ?"
        • Drummond, *Sonnets, &c.*, ii. 13, 4.

51. " Infinite ben the sorwes and the teres
    Of olde folk, and folk of tendre yeres,
    In all the toun for deth of this Theban :
    For him ther wepeth bothe childe and man.
    So gret a weping was ther now certain,
    Whan Hector was ybrought, all fresh yslain
    To Troy, alas ! the pitee that was there,
    Cratching of chekes, rending eke of here."
                    Chaucer, *The Knightes Tale*.

60.   " And she believes . . . . . .
    That you are dead ; and as she now scorn'd life,
    Death lends her cheeks his paleness, and her eyes
    Tell down their drops of silver to the earth,
    Wishing her tears might rain upon your grave,
    To make the gentle earth produce some flower
    Should bear your names and memories."
        Shirley, *The Grateful Servant*, iii. 3.

62. " But what we couet most
        or chiefest holde in price,
    With greedie gripe of darting death
        is reaved with a trice.
    " The cruell Sisters three
        were all in one agreede,
    To let the spindle runne no more
        but shrid the fatall threede.
    " And Fortune, (to expresse
        What swing and sway she bare,)
    Allowde them leaue to vse their force
        vpon this Jewell rare.
    " Thus hath the Welkin wunne,
        and we a losse sustainde :
    Thus hath hir corse a Vaute found out,
        hir sprite the Heauens gainde."
    Turberville, *On the Death of Elisabeth Arhundle*.

And, fearing, warned me that the men were fierce ;
That with a hardy nation were the frays.
And now he, sooth, deep-duped by idle hope, 71
Is peradventure e'en discharging vows,
And piling up high altars with his gifts :
We [this] unbreathing youth, and one that now
Owes naught to any of the heav'nly powers,
Attend in sorrow with a fruitless pomp.
Ill-starred ! Thy son's heart-rending funeral
Shalt thou behold ! Can these be our returns,
And looked-for triumphs ? This my lofty trust ?
But thou, Evander, shalt not look on him,
[As one] discomfited by shameful wounds ;
Nor thou a father for a son unhurt 82
A death accursèd shalt desire. Ah me !
How great a bulwark, O Ausonia [thou],
How great dost thou, too, O Iulus, lose !"
  When these in tears he ended, he commands
The piteous corse to be upraised, and sends
A thousand men from all the army culled,
The closing ceremony to attend,
And in his father's tears to bear a part : 90
A scanty comfort for a mighty grief,
But to a wretched father due. Not slow
Weave hurdles others, and a pliant bier,
Of arbute switches and of oaken twig,
And with a canopy of leaf o'ershade

---

84. " So have I seen some tender slip
    Saved with care from winter's nip,
    The pride of her carnation train,
    Plucked up by some unheedy swain,
    Who only thought to crop the flower
    New shot up from vernal shower :
    But the fair blossom hangs the head
    Sideways, as on a dying bed,
    And those pearls of dew, she wears,
    Prove to be presaging tears,
    Which the sad morn had let fall,
    On her hastening funeral." Milton, *Odes*.

" Young Damon of the vale is dead,
  Ye lowland hamlets, moan ;
  A dewy turf lies o'er his head,
  And at his feet a stone.

" His shroud, which Death's cold damps destroy,
  Of snow-white threads was made :
  All mourn'd to see so sweet a boy
  In earth for ever laid.

" Pale pansies o'er his corpse were plac'd,
  Which, pluck'd before their time,
  Bestrew'd the boy, like him to waste,
  And wither in their prime.

" But will he ne'er return, whose tongue
  Could tune the rural lay ?
  Ah, no ! his bell of peace is rung,
  His lips are cold as clay."
                    Collins, *Song*, end of Poems.

The high-raised couch. On rustic litter here
The youth they lay aloft : just like a flower,
Dissevered by the finger of a maid,
Either of violet soft, or drooping martagon,
Whose brilliance not as yet hath passed away,
Nor yet its beauteousness : no more does earth, 101
Its mother, foster it and strength purvey.
Then vestures twain, stiff both with gold and dye
Of purple, forth Æneas brought, the which for him,
Blithe at her travails, had with her own hands,
Herself Sidonian Dido whilom made,
And with thin gold diversified the web.
In one of these the youth in sorrow he
Arrays, the closing honor ; and his hair,
About to burn, he muffles in a veil ; 110
And many a prize of the Laurentine war
Moreo'er he piles, and orders that the spoil
In lengthful train be led. He adds the steeds
And arms, which he had from the foeman stript.
And he had bound behind their backs their hands,
Whom he might send as off'rings to his shades,
With butchered blood about to dew the flame ;
He orders, too, the chiefs themselves to bring
Tree-boles, in armor of their foes arrayed,
And that their hostile names should be engraved. 120
Ill-starred Acœtes, spent with age, is led,
His breasts now marring with closed hands, his face
Now with his nails ; and he is prostrate laid,
Full length flung forward on the earth.
  And they
Lead on the chariots, with Rutulian blood
Bespattered. Next, its trappings laid aside,
His war-steed Æthon weeping goes, and wets

---

98. Spenser introduces a less merciful despoiler of floral beauties :

" Great enimy to it, and t' all the rest
  That in the Garden of Adonis springs,
  Is wicked Time ; who with his scyth addrest
  Does mow the flowring herbes and goodly things,
  And all their glory to the grownd downe flings,
  Where they do wither and are fowly mard :.
  Ne flyes about, and with his flaggy wings
  Beates downe both leaves and buds without regard,
  Ne ever pitty may relent his malice hard."
              Faerie Queene, iii. 6, 39.

127, 8. It is well known that some animals shed tears in distress ; but who ever heard of a weeping

With bulky drops its cheeks. His spear and helm
Bear others ; for the conq'ring Turnus holds the rest.
A mournful squadron then, both Teucrians, And Tyrrhenes, and Arcadians, follow, all
With arms inverted. After all the train
Of the attendants far ahead had marched,
Æneas halted, and these [words] subjoined
With groaning deep : " To tears for others, hence 135
The same dread fates of battle call us off.
Most noble Pallas ! fare thee well, to me

---

horse ? The British poets continually allude to the dying sorrows of the stag :
" His once so vivid nerves,
So full of buoyant spirit, now no more
Inspire the course ; but fainting breathless toil,
Sick, seizes on his heart : he stands at bay ;
And puts his last weak refuge in despair.
The big round tears run down his dappled face ;
He groans in anguish : while the growling pack,
Blood-happy, hang at his fair jutting chest,
And mark his beauteous checker'd sides with gore."
    Thomson, *Autumn*.
" Rouse ye the lofty stag, and with my bell-horn
Ring him a knell, that all the woods shall mourn him,
Till, in his funeral tears, he fall before me."
    J. Fletcher, *Beggar's Bush*, iii. 4.
135.   " Oh, my heart
Is witness how I lov'd him ! Would he had not
Led me unto his grave, but sacrific'd
His sorrows upon mine ! He was my friend,
My noble friend ; I will bewail his ashes :
His fortunes and poor mine were born together,
And I will weep 'em both : I will kneel by him,
And on his hallow'd earth do my last duties ;
I'll gather all the pride of spring to deck him ;
Woodbines shall grow upon his honour'd grave,
And, as they prosper, clasp to show our friendship,
And, when they wither, I'll die too."
    J. Fletcher, *The Lovers' Progress*, iv. 3.
137. Tickell, in his beautiful poem *On the Death of Addison*, says :
" Can I forget the dismal night that gave
My soul's best part for ever to the grave ?
How silent did his old companions tread,
By midnight lamps, the mansions of the dead,
Through breathing statues, then unheeded things,
Through rows of warriors, and through walks of kings !
What awe did the slow solemn knell inspire,
The pealing organ, and the pausing choir ;
The duties by the lawn-rob'd prelate paid ;
And the last words that dust to dust convey'd !
While speechless o'er thy closing grave we bend,
Accept these tears, thou dear departed friend.
    , gone for ever ! take this long adieu ;
And sleep in peace next thy lov'd Montague.

    " Farewell the hopes of Britain !
Thou royal graft, farewell for ever ! Time and Death,
Ye have done your worst. Fortune, now see, now proudly
Pluck off thy veil, and view thy triumph ! Look,
Look what thou hast brought this land to ! O, fair flower,

For ever, and for ever fare thee well !"
Nor further speaking, to the lofty walls
He marched, and moved his footstep to the camp.   140
And now came envoys from the Latin town,
With boughs of olive decked, and craving grace :—
That he the bodies, which along the plains
Lay scattered by the falchion, would restore,
And let them pass beneath a mound of earth:
That strife there could be none with conquered men,
And those devoid of breath : that he would spare
Who once were titled hosts and sires of brides.
Whom, suing in no despicable prayers,
The good Æneas with the grace presents,
And these in words moreover he subjoins :
" Pray what unworthy chance hath you involved,   152
O ye Latini, in so sharp a war,
Who us decline as friends ? Crave ye of me
Peace for the dead, and slain by chance of Mars ?
I sooth would grant it to the living too ;
Nor had I come, save fates a place and home
Had deigned. Nor is it with your race that I
Am waging war : the king hath hospitage
With us forsook, and rather placed his trust
On arms of Turnus. Fairer had it been
For Turnus to expose him to this death.
If with his hand to terminate the war, 163
If to eject the Teucri, he prepares,
It had been meet that in these arms with me
He should engage : he would have lived, to whom
The god or his right hand had granted life.

How lovely yet thy ruins show, how sweetly
Even Death embraces thee ! The peace of Heaven,
The fellowship of all great souls, be with thee !"
    Beaumont and Fletcher, *Bonduca*, v. 5.
145.   " No, great king :
I come to thee for charitable license,
That we may wander o'er this bloody field,
To look our dead, and then to bury them ;
To sort our nobles from our common men ;
For many of our princes,—woe the while !
Lie drown'd and soak'd in mercenary blood :
So do our vulgar drench their peasant limbs
In blood of princes, and their wounded steeds
Fret fetlock deep in gore, and with wild rage
Yerk out their armed heels at their dead masters
Killing them twice. O ! give us leave, great king
To view the field in safety, and dispose
Of their dead bodies."
    Shakespeare, *K. Henry V.*, iv. 7.
157. The perfect here, v. 112, would be intolerable.

U

Now go, and fire do ye apply beneath
Your hapless countrymen." Æneas said.
In wonder were they stricken dumb, and
 kept 170
Their eyes and faces on each other turned.
Then Drances aged, and aye with hate and
 charge
To youthful Turnus hostile, thus in turn
[These] op'ning accents utters with his lips:
" O great by rumor, greater by thine arms,
Thou Trojan hero, by what lauds should I
Thee level bring with heaven ? Or at thee
Should marvel rather for thy righteousness,
Or toils of war? We sooth will these
 [replies]
T' our native city thankfully take home,
And thee, if any fortune shall vouchsafe
The path, to king Latinus will unite: 182
Let Turnus look for treaties for himself !
Yea too, thy walls' predestinated piles
To raise, and on our shoulders to upbear
The stones of Troja, will be our delight."
These spake he, and they all with single
 voice
Shouted assent. [An armistice] they framed
For twice six days, and in the mediate
 truce,
Thro'out the forests on the mountain brows,
The Teucri and the Latins, mingled, ranged

Without disturbance. Rings with two-
 edged steel 192
The stately ash ; they overthrow the pines,
Projected to the stars ; nor hearts of oak,
And cedar sweet, with wedges do they cease
To split, and carry elms on groaning drays.
 And Rumor flying now, of woe so great
The harbinger, Evander and the courts
And city of Evander fills, who late
To Latium Pallas conqueror announced.
Th' Arcadians hurry to the gates, and seized,
After the olden fashion, fun'ral brands.
The pathway gleams with lengthful train
 of fires, 203
And far and near distinctly marks the fields.
In the reverse direction coming on,
A band of Phrygians joins the wailing hosts.
Whom when the dames once saw approach
 their homes,
They fire the sorrowed city with their
 shrieks.
Yet power none is able to restrain
Evander ; but he rushes on the midst. 210
The bier deposited, he forward fell
O'er Pallas, and he clings, both shedding
 tears,
And groaning, and a passage for his voice
At last was scarcely loosened through his
 grief :

---

172. " Man, hard of heart to man! Of horrid
 things
Most horrid ! 'Mid stupendous, highly strange !
Yet oft his courtesies are smoother wrongs ;
Pride brandishes the favour he confers,
And contumelious his humanity :
What then his vengeance? Hear it not, ye stars !
And thou, pale moon ! turn paler at the sound ;
Man is to man the sorest, surest ill.
A previous blast foretells the rising storm ;
O'erwhelming turrets threaten ere they fall ;
Volcanoes bellow ere they disembogue ;
Earth trembles ere her yawning jaws devour ;
And smoke betrays the wide-consuming fire :
Ruin from man is most conceal'd when near,
And sends the dreadful tidings in the blow."
 Young, *The Complaint*, N. iii.

" Or wouldst thou change the scene, and quit the
 den,
Behold the Heav'n-deserted fen,
Where spleen, by vapours dense begot and bred,
Hardness of heart and heaviness of head,
Have raised their darksome walls, and placed
 their thorny bed ;
There may'st thou all thy bitterness unload,
There may'st thou croak in concert with the toad.
With thee the hollow howling winds shall join,
 Nor shall the bittern her base throat deny,
The querulous frogs shall mix their dirge with
 thine,
Th' ear-piercing hern, the plovers screaming
 high,
Millions of humming gnats fit œstrum shall
 supply." Smart, Ode vi. *On Ill-Nature*.

188. " Assent." To translate *eadem*, v. 132,
literally, would involve a great awkwardness.

197, &c. Far finer is Dryden. Speaking of
Charles II.'s death :
" Soon as the ill-omen'd rumour reach'd his ear,
 (Ill news is wing'd with fate, and flies apace ;)
 Who can describe the amazement of his face ?
Horror in all his pomp was there,
Mute and magnificent without a tear."
 Threnodia Augustalis.

211. Henry VI. shrank from contact with his
uncle Humphrey's corpse:
" Fain would I go to chafe his paly lips
With twenty thousand kisses, and to rain
Upon his face an ocean of salt-tears,
To tell my love unto his dumb deaf trunk,
And with my fingers feel his mad unfeeling ;
But all in vain are these mean obsequies,
And to survey his dead and earthy image,
What were it but to make my sorrow greater ?"
 Shakespeare, 2 *K. Henry VI.*, iii. 2.

212. " These arms of mine shall be thy winding-
 sheet ;
My heart, sweet boy, shall be thy sepulchre,
For from my heart thy image ne'er shall go ;
My sighing breast shall be thy funeral bell."
 Shakespeare, 3 *K. Henry VI.*, ii. 5.
 " But chiefly
Him that you term'd the good old lord Gonzalo :
The tears run down his beard, like winter's drops
From eaves of reeds." *Tempest*, v. i.

214. " Who, when he saw his sonne so ill bedight
With bleeding wounds, brought home upon a
 beare
By a faire lady and a straunger knight,
Was inly touched with compassion deare,

"Not these engagements, O my Pallas,
 thou
Hadst given to thy parent. Would to
 heaven
That thou more circumspectly hadst de-
 sired
To trust thyself to unrelenting Mars!
Not unaware was I, how great a power
Had new renown in arms, and, passing
 sweet,   220
The glory in a maiden combat. Sad
Youth's budding feats, and sore th' essays
Of war at hand, and vows and prayers of
 mine,
Regarded by not one of gods! And thou,
O holiest consort, blessèd in thy death,
Nor to this anguish kept! On th' other
 hand,
By living I have overpassed my fates,—
That a surviving father I abide.
[Him,] who has followed Trojans' fed'rate
 arms,
Would heav'n the Rutuli with darts had
 whelmed!   230
I freely would have given up my life,
And back this pageant should have brought
 home *me*,
Not Pallas. Trojans, I could blame nor
 you,
Nor leagues, nor right hands, which in
 hospitage
We've linked; that lot to our old age was
 due.
But if a timeless death my son awaited, .

And deare affection of so dolefull dreare,
And he these words burst forth: 'Ah! sory boy!
Is this the hope that to my hoary heare
Thou brings? aie me! is this the timely ioy
Which I expected long, now turnd to sad annoy?"
                        Spenser, *F. Q.*, vi. 3, 4.
217. As if he had thought:
"You may as well spread out the unsunn'd heaps
Of miser's treasure by an outlaw's den,
And tell me it is safe, as bid me hope
Danger will wink on Opportunity."
                        Milton, *Comus*.

219. Morton's address to the Earl of Northum-
berland on Percy's death would have been equally
applicable to Evander:
     "It was your pre-surmise,
That, ' i the dole of blows your son might drop;
You k .ew he walk'd o'er perils, on an edge,
More likely to fall in than to get o'er;
You were advis'd his flesh was capable
Of wounds and scars, and that his forward spirit
Would lift him where most trade of danger rang'd:
Yet did you say: Go forth; and none of this,
Though strongly apprehended, could restrain
The stiff-borne action. What hath then befallen,
Or what hath this bold enterprise brought forth,
More than that being which was like to be?"
                Shakespeare, *2 K. Henry IV.*, i. 1.
236. "Untimely issue for a timeless grave."
                        Drayton, *Moses*.

With thousands of the Volsci slaughtered
 first,
'Twould be a happiness that he had fallen,
The Teucri leading into Latium. Yet
I could not thee, O Pallas, worthy deem
Of other fun'ral than the good Æneas
 [deems],   241
And [deem] the mighty Phrygians, aye
 and [deem]
The Tyrrhene chieftains, all the Tyrrhenes'
 host.
They bear grand trophies, which thy right
 hand gave
To death. Thou also wouldst be standing
 now
A giant trunk in arms, had equal been
My age, and from my years my strength the
 same,
O Turnus. But ill-fortuned, why should I
The Teucri stay from arms? Go ye, and
 these
My orders mindful to your king take back:
'That I a hated life am ling'ring out,—
My Pallas slain,—thy right hand is the
 cause;   252
Which thou dost see it Turnus owes alike
To son and sire. This place alone is void
For thy deserts and fortune. Joys for life
I do not seek, nor is it lawful; but [this news]
To bring my son beneath the lowest shades.'"

"Him while fresh and fragrant Time
 Cherish'd in his golden prime;
Ere Hebe's hand had overlaid
 His smooth cheeks with a downy shade;
The rush of Death's unruly wave
 Swept him off into his grave."
                Crashaw, *Epitaph on Herrys*.

241. It is impossible to translate the thrice-
repeated *quam*, v. 170, without a weakness.
251. "To mourn thy fall, I'll fly the hated light,
And hide my head in shades of endless night:
For thou wert light, and life, and health, to me:
The sun but thankless shines, that shows not thee.
Wert thou not lovely, graceful, good, and young?
The joy of sight, the talk of every tongue?
Did ever branch so sweet a blossom bear?
Or ever early fruit appear so fair?
Did ever youth so far his years transcend?
Did ever life so prematurely end? . . . .
There let me fall, there, there lamenting lie,
There grieving grow to earth, despair, and die."
                Congreve, *Tears of Amaryllis*.
"Now my soul's palace is become a prison:
Ah! would she break from hence, that this my
 body
Might in the ground be closed up in rest;
For never henceforth shall I joy ag in."
                Shakespeare, *3 K. Henry VI.*, ii. 1.
255. "For which I mourn, and will for ever mourn;
Nor will I change these black and dismal robes,
Or ever dry these swollen and watery eyes,
Or ever taste content, or peace of heart,
While I have life, and thought of my Alphonso."
                Congreve, *Mourning Bride*, i. 1.

Meanwhile Aurore had bounteous light
  brought forth
To wretched mortals, bringing back their
  tasks
And toils. Now sire Æneas, Tarchon now,
Upon the winding strand constructed pyres.
They hither each the bodies of their
  [friends], 262
In fashion of their ancestors, conveyed ;
And,—sooty fires beneath them laid,—
  high heaven
Is shrouded into darkness with the murk.
Three times around the kindled fun'ral
  piles,

The whole passage from v. 177-181, owing to its brevity, is somewhat obscure, but a little examination will make the meaning tolerably plain. This would seem to be its significance : Go, and carefully report these my charges to your Prince. Tell him that life has become hateful to me, now that Pallas is no more ; and that there is but one reason why I do not lay violent hands upon myself, and put an end to it at once. The sole cause of my delaying the suicidal act lies in himself alone ; for to him alone can I look for that vengeance upon my enemy, which I must see exacted before I die. I live, because Turnus lives ; and I must continue to live, until the right hand of Æneas shall accomplish the destruction of the man who has destroyed my child. That that right hand owes this debt both to my son and to me, must be evident, even to himself. Great as are his merits and his fortune ; many as are the obligations under which he has already laid me ; yet there is one act, —though *but* one,—which still remains for him to perform, in order to crown his own career, and to complete his services to me.—Turnus must fall. I desire no enjoyments for myself as a living man ; nor, were I so inclined, would it be decorous in me, after the irreparable loss that I have sustained. It is of Pallas that I am thinking, and not of myself ; of his happiness below, and not of my own above. In this life I seek for nothing now, but the power of carrying down to my son, in the infernal realms, the happy intelligence, that the man who slew him, has himself been slain.

258. " Hail to thy living light,
  Ambrosial morn ! all hail thy roseat ray !
That bids young Nature all her charms display.
  In varied beauty bright ;
That bids each dewy-spangled flowret rise,
And dart around its vermeil dyes ;
Bids silver lustre grace yon sparkling tide,
That winding warbles down the mountain's side.
  Away ! ye goblins all,
Wont the bewilder'd traveller to daunt,
Whose vagrant feet have traced your secret haunt
  Beside some lonely wall,
Or shatter'd ruin of some moss-grown tow'r,
Where, at pale mid ight's stillest hour,
Through each rough chink the solemn orb of night
Pours momentary gleams of trembling light.
  Away ! ye elves, away !
  Shrink at ambrosial morning's living ray ;
That living ray, whose pow'r benign   .
  Unfolds the scene of glory to our eye,
  Where, thron'd in artless majesty,
The cherub Beauty sits on Nature's rustic shrine."
    Mason, *Elfrida*, 1st Ode.

Arrayed in gleaming arms, they marched;
  three times
The fun'ral's doleful fire they compassed
  round
On steeds, and shriekings uttered from their
  lips.
E'en earth is sprent with tears, and sprent
  are arms; 270
Scales heav'n both cry of men and din of
  trumps.
Then some—the spoils, from slaughtered
  Latins reft,
Fling on the fire, their helmets, and their
  swords
Of beauty, bridles too, and glowing
  wheels ;—
Some—well known off'rings, bucklers of
  their own,
And not successful darts. Of oxen round
Are many bodies sacrificed to Death,
And bristly boars, and, seized from all the
  fields,
Sheep for the flame they butcher. Then
  throughout
The strand they gaze upon their burning
  , mates, 280
And pyres half-burnt are watching ; nor
  can they
Be torn away, until the moistful night
Inverts the heav'n, enchased with blazing
  stars.
No less the miserable Latins too,

---

267. The tutor will of course point out the technical use of *decurro*, v. 189.

282, 3. " Now came still Evening on, and Twilight
  gray
Had in her sober livery all things clad.
Silence accompanied : for beast and bird,
They to their grassy couch, these to their nests,
Were slunk, all but the wakeful nightingale :
She all night long her amorous descant sung.
Silence was pleas'd. Now glow'd the firmament
With living sapphires: Hesperus, that led
The starry host, rode brightest, till the Moon,
Rising in clouded majesty, at length
Apparent queen unveil'd her peerless light,
And o'er the dark her silver mantle threw."
    Milton, *P. L.*, b. iv.

" How, like a widow in her weeds, the Night,
Amid her glimmering tapers, silent sits !
How sorrowful, how desolate, she weeps
Perpetual dews, and saddens Nature's scene !
    . . . . O majestic Night !
Nature's great ancestor, Day's elder-born !
And fated to survive the transient Sun !
By mortals and immortals seen with awe !
A starry crown thy raven brow adorns,
An azure zone thy waist: clouds, in Heaven's loom
Wrought through varieties of shape and shade,
In ample folds of drapery divine,
Thy flowing mantle form ; and Heaven throughout
Voluminously pour thy pompous train."
    Young, *The Complaint*, N. 9.

Reared in a diff'rent quarter countless pyres,
And many a corse of heroes in the earth
Partly inter, and partly raise them up,
And cart them off upon the neighb'ring fields,
And send them to their city home. The rest,
Of huddled slaughter e'en a mountain heap,
With neither count nor compliment, they burn ; 291
In all directions then the spacious fields
Shine out in rivalry with frequent fires.
Third light [of day] the icy shade from heaven
Had chased aloof : a-mourning, th' ashes deep
And jumbled bones they ransacked on the hearths,
And laded with a milk-warm mound of earth.
But now within the dwellings, in the town
Of passing rich Latinus, chief the din,
And greatest portion of the lengthful woe.
Here mothers, and their sons' unhappy wives, 301
Here grieving sisters' loving breasts, and boys,
Of parents orphaned, curse the awful war,
And Turnus' nuptials. They insist that he,
Himself, the quarrel should decide by arms,
Aye by the sword himself, who claims t' himself
Italia's realm and dignities the first.
These [feelings] bitter Drances aggravates,
And witnesses that he alone is called,
Alone is Turnus challenged to the frays.
At the same time, upon the other hand,
Extensive suffrage with diverse debates
[Lies] on the side of Turnus, and the queen's 313
High name o'ershades him ; much of fame supports
The hero with his trophies, duly earned.
'Mid these excitements, 'mid the burning coil,

Behold, moreo'er, in woe, th' ambassadors
From Diomed's great city bring replies :
" With all the cost of toil so great—naught done ;
Naught gifts, nor gold, nor earnest prayers, availed ; 320
Arms other by the Latins should be sought,
Or peace entreated from the Trojan prince."
In anguish deep sinks e'en the king himself
Latinus. That Æneas, [child] of fate,
Was carried on by potent will divine,—
Warns him the wrath of gods, and graves [still] fresh
Before his eyes. Accordingly
A grave assembly, and the leading men
Of his own people, summoned to the throne,
Inside his lofty portals he convenes. 330
They flocked together, and from brimming roads
Flow to the royal courts. Amidst them sits
E'en most advanced in age, and first in sway,
Latinus, with no blithesome brow. And here,
The envoys, from th' Ætolian towns sent back,
He bids announce what [tidings] they report,
And in their order all replies demands.
Thereon was silence with their tongues observed,
And Venulus, his word obeying, thus
Begins to speak : " We have, O citizens,
Seen Diomedes and the Argive camp ; 341
And, meting out the journey, overpassed
All hazards, and have touched the hand, whereby
Fell Ilium's region. He Argyripa,
His city, from his native city's name,
A conqueror, was founding in the fields
Of Iapygian Garganus. When once
Entered within, and means of speaking deigned,
Before him we our gifts present, and tell
Our name and country ; who have brought the war 350
On us ; what cause hath us to Arpi drawn.
To these, when heard, he thus with gentle lip
These [words] returned : ' O nations, happy starred,
Saturnian realms, Ausonians dating high,
What fortune is it rouses you at rest,
And prompts you unknown battles to provoke ?

---

290. " A thousand glorious actions, that might claim
Triumphant laurels and immortal fame,
Confus'd in crowds of glorious actions lie,
And troops of heroes undistinguish'd die."
Addison, *The Campaign.*

308. " The specious shield, which private malice bears,
Is ever blazon'd with some public good :
Behind that artful fence skulk low, conceal'd,
The bloody purpose and the poison'd shaft.
Ambition there and envy nestle close,
From whence they take their fatal aim unseen,
And honest merit is their destin'd mark."
Jones, *The Earl of Essex,* i. 1.

316. Or: "Amid these stirs, amid the burning broil."

356. " And who would run, that's moderately wise,
A certain danger for a doubtful prize ? . . . .
You draw, insensibly, destruction near,
And love the danger, which you ought to fear."
Pomfret, *Love Triumphant over Reason.*

Whoe'er of us have outraged with the sword
The fields of Ilium,—I those [woes of ours]
Pass by, which to the very dregs were
    drained,
In battling underneath her stately walls;
What heroes that their Simois confines;—
We all, unutterable punishments   362
Throughout the globe, and pains of crimes,
    have paid,
A band, that pity e'en at Priam's hands
Deserves; [this] knows Minerva's plagueful
    star,
And the Eubœan rocks, Caphareus too,
Avenger. Since that warfare to a varied
    coast
Forth driven, Menelaus, Atreus' son,
As far as Proteus' pillars homeless roams;
Th' Ætnean Cyclops hath Ulysses seen.
Should I the realms of Neoptolemus   371
Relate, Idomeneus' Penates, too,
O'erthrown? Or Locri, dwelling on the
    shore
Of Libya? E'en himself the Mycene chief
Of mighty Greeks, by right hand of his
    spouse,
Accursed, within his foremost thresholds
    died;
Crushed Asia the adulterer forelaid.
[Why tell] that gods begrudged me, that,
    restored
To altars of my country I should see
My longed-for spouse, and Calydon the fair?
Now too, of frightful aspect, monster forms
Pursue me, and my comrades, lost, have
    sought
The air with wings, and wander o'er the
    floods   383
As birds,—ah! awful vengeance on my
    [friends]—

And with their tearful voices fill the cliffs.
These [ills], indeed, thenceforward were by
    me
Anticipated, when a madman I
Desired the heav'nly bodies for my sword,
And Venus' right hand with a wound pro-
    faned.
Sooth do not, do not drive me to such frays.
Nor have I with the Trojans any war   391
Since Pergamus was ruined; nor do I
Their ancient woes remember, nor [therein]
Rejoice. The presents, which ye bring to
    me
From your paternal coasts, do ye transfer
T' Æneas. We have stood against his arms
Of fierceness, and have hand with hand
    engaged:
Trust one who has tried,—how grand he
    rises to his shield!
With what a whirlwind does he fling his
    lance!
If two such heroes the Idæan land   400
Had borne besides, unchallenged would
    have come
The Dardan to the towns of Inachus,
And Greece would mourn her destinies re-
    versed.
Whate'er delay was caused before the walls
Of iron Troy, the conquest by the Greeks
Halted through Hector's and Æneas' hand,
And till the tenth year backward traced its
    steps:
Both marked for courage, both for peerless
    arms;
This in his piety superior. Let right hands
Unite for leagues, as far as 'tis vouch-
    safed: 410
But have a care lest arms with arms may
    clash.'
At once both what are th' answers of the
    king,
O king most worthy, thou hast heard, and
    what
Is his decision on the mighty war."
These scarce the envoys; when a varied
    buzz
Throughout the Ausons' troubled lips there
    ran:

---

364. Even Shore pitied his erring wife:
And can she bear it? Can that delicate frame
Endure the beating of a storm so rude?
Can she, for whom the various seasons chang'd,
To court her appetite, and crown her board,
For whom the foreign vintages were press'd,
For whom the merchant spread his silken stores,
Can she—
Intreat for bread, and want the needful raiment
To wrap her shiv'ring bosom from the weather?
When she was mine, no care came ever nigh her.
I thought the gentlest breeze that wakes the
    spring
Too rough to breathe upon her; cheerfulness
Dane'd all the day before her; and at night
Soft slumber waited on her downy pillow:—
Now sad and shelterless, perhaps, she lies,
Where piercing winds blow sharp, and the chill
    rain
Drops from some pent-house on her wretched
    head,
Drenches her locks, and kills her with the cold.
It is too much;—hence with her past offences;
They are aton'd at full."
                Rowe, *Jane Shore*, act v.

---

398. So Abdalla of Demetrius:
" Too well I know him, since on Thracia's plains
I felt the force of his tempestuous arm,
And saw my scattered squadrons fly before him."
                        Johnson, *Irene*, iv. 4.

400.   " Two more such women
    Would save their sex."
            J. Fletcher, *Thierry and Theodoret*, iv. 1.

414. Surely *responsa* and *sententia*, vv. 294; 5,
refer to the same person,—Diomed. Virgil frequently omits his prepositions; and to make *bello* a person seems very forced.

As when the rocks delay the sweepy streams,
A din arises from the prisoned gulf,
And boom the neighb'ring banks with brawling waves.
As soon as minds were calmed, and troublous tongues   420
Were silent, having first addressed the gods,
The king commences from his lofty throne :
" Erenow, in sooth, that of our highest weal
We had determined, Latins, I could both
Desire, and it had been the better [course],
At such an hour not council to convene,
What time the foe is leaguering our walls.
O citizens, unfitting warfare with a race
Of gods, and with unconquered heroes, we
Are waging, whom no battles weary out,
Nor can they, vanquished, from the sword refrain.   431
If any hope in the Ætolians' arms,
Invited to us, ye have had, lay [this]
Aside : a hope must each be to himself :
But this, how spare, ye see. In what a wreck
The rest of your affairs lie overwhelmed,
Is all before your eyes and in your hands :
Nor do I any one upbraid. What could
The fullest valor be, has been ; the strife
With the whole kingdom's force has been maintained.   440
Now then, what be the notion of my wav'ring mind
Will I unfold, and—your attention give—
In [words] a few will teach. To me belongs
An ancient region, next the Tuscan tide,
Extended westward, far as and beyond
The bourns of the Sicanians ; the Aurunci
And the Rutulians sow, and work with share
The churlish hills, and graze their wildest [spots].

Let all this district, and the piny tract
Of lofty mountain be surrendered up   450
To friendship with the Trojans ; and let us
Impartial terms of covenant pronounce,
And woo them to our kingdom as allies.
Let them, if such a strong desire there be,
Take up a settlement, and cities build.
But if it is their mind, of other bourns to take
Possession, and another nation['s land],
And from our ground they can depart : let us
Build twice ten vessels of Italian oak,
Or more, if they can man them : by the wave   460
Lies all material ; let themselves prescribe
Both number and the model for the barks ;
Give we the bronze, the hands, the naval stores.
Moreo'er, to bear our message, and cement
The leagues, it is our pleasure there should go
A hundred Latin envoys from our chiefest tribe,
And in their hand outstretch the boughs of peace ;
Our presents bearing, talents e'en of gold
And iv'ry, and the badges of our realm,
The chair and trabea. For the commonweal   470
Deliberate, and aid our weakly state."
Then the same hostile Drances, whom the fame
Of Turnus spurred with crooked jealousy,

434.
    " No thought of flight,
None of retreat, no unbecoming deed,
That argued fear ; ' u.ch on himself relied,
As only on his arm the moment lay
Of victory."   Milton, *P. L.*, b. vi.
    " We are circled round
With danger ; o'er our heads, with sail-stretch'd wings,
Destruction hovers, and a cloud of mischief
Ready to break on us ; no hope left us
That may divert it, but our sleeping virtue,
Roused up by brave Timoleon."
    Massinger, *The Bondman*, i. 3.
    " I'll tell thee, my Tamira,
Even at my falling fortune's deepest ebb,
While all my outward state was most forlorn,
Within I was a king."
    Macdonald, *Fair Apostate*, iii. end.
448. " My soul, turn from them, turn we to survey
Where rougher climes a nobler race display,

Where the bleak Swiss their stormy mansions tread,
And force a churlish soil for scanty bread.
No product here the barren hills afford
But man and steel, the soldier and his sword.
No vernal blooms their torpid rocks array,
But Winter ling'ring chills the lap of May ;
No Zephyr fondly sues the mountain's breast,
But meteors glare, and stormy glooms invest."
    Goldsmith, *The Traveller*.

472, &c. Drances could not have said with Iden :
" I seek not to wax great by others waning."
    Shakespeare, 2 *K. Henry VI.*, iv. 10.
He was more like Belial, as Milton describes him :
    " On the other side uprose
Belial, in act more graceful and humane :
A fairer person lost not Heaven ; he seem'd
For dignity compos'd, and high exploit :
But all was false and hollow. Though his tongue
Dropp'd manna, and could make the worse appear
The better reason, to perplex and dash
Maturest counsels : for his thoughts were low ;
To vice industrious, but to nobler deeds
Timorous and slothful."   *P. L.*, b. ii.
473. " Envy the next, Envy with squinted eyes :
    Sick of a strange disease, his neighbour's health :
Best lives he then, when any better dies ;
Is never poor but in another's wealth.

And bitter stings, wealth-rife, and in his
    tongue
Superior, but his right hand chill in war;
In counsels deemed no weak authority;
In faction strong ; his mother's noble rank
Proud birth bestowed him ; from his father
    he
A questionable one maintained ;—gets up
And loads him with these taunts, and swells
    their wrath :   480
" Upon a matter, that is dark to none,
Nor needing voice of ours, thou seek'st
    advice,
O gracious sovereign. All allow they know
What may the welfare of the nation claim ;
But hesitate to say. Let him vouchsafe
Freedom of speech, and arrogance abate,
Because of whose ill-omened management,
And evil dealings,—truly I will speak,
Though he may threaten me with arms and
    death,—
So many lights of leaders see we set,   490
And all the city sitting down in woe,
The while he tempts the Trojan camp, on
    flight

On best men's harms and griefs he feeds his fill :
Else his own maw doth eat with spiteful will :
Ill must the temper be, where diet is so ill.
" Each eye through divers optics slily leers,
    Which both his sight and objects self bely ;
So greatest virtue as a moat appears,
    And molehill faults to mountains multiply.
When needs he must, yet faintly then he praises ;
Somewhat the deed, much more the means he
    raises :
So marreth what he makes, and, praising most,
    dispraises."
        P. Fletcher, *The Purple Island*, vii. 66, 7.

                " Accursed jealousy !
O merciless, wild and unforgiving fiend !
Blindfold it runs to undistinguish'd mischief,
And murders all it meets. Curst be its rage,
For there is none so deadly ; doubly curs'd
Be all those easy fools who give it harbour ;
Who turn a monster on mankind,
Fiercer than famine, war, or spotted pestilence ;
Baneful as death, and horrible as hell."
            Rowe, *Jane Shore*, act iv.
" Peace, slave ; he is my noble friend, of noble
    blood,
Whose fame's above the level of those tongues,
That bark by custom at the brightest virtues,
As dogs do at the moon."
    Tuke, *The Adventures of Five Hours*, act v.

474. 5. So Queen Katherine says of Wolsey :
                " Your words,
Domestics to you, serve your will, as 't please
Yourself pronounce their office."
            Shakespeare, *K. Henry VIII.*, ii. 4.
480.   " And yet there may
Be malice in complaints. The flourishing oak,
For his extent of branches, stature, growth,
The darling, and the idol of the wood,
Whose awful nod the under trees adore,

Depending, and the sky affrights with arms.
One also to those gifts, which thou dost bid,
Full many, to the Dardans to be sent
And gaged, thou, best of monarchs, one
    shouldst add ;
Nor let the violence of any man
O'erpow'r thee, that, a sire, thou shouldst
    not give
Thy daughter to a peerless son-in-law,
And worthy match, and by an endless
    league   500
This peace cement. But if so great a dread
Our minds and breasts there holds, let us
    beseech
Himself, and crave the favor from himself :
That he would yield ;—their proper right
    resign
To king and country. Why so many times
On open dangers dost thou send adrift
Thy wretched citizens, O thou to Latium
Of these calamities the head and source ?
No safety [lies] in war ; a peace of thee
We all, O Turnus, beg,—along with [this]
The one inviolable pledge of peace.   511
I first, whom thou imaginest thy foe,—
And I at being so am naught concerned,—
Lo ! suitor, come. Compassionate thine
    own ;
Lay wrath aside, and, routed, go thy way.
We deaths enough, discomfited, have seen,
And made a wilderness of spacious fields.
Or if renown hath influence, if thou
Enwombest such high courage in thy breast,
And if a palace, as thy dower, be   520
So in thine heart ;—dare thou, and trust-
    fully
Thy bosom bear confronted on the foe.
Aye that indeed to Turnus there may fall
A royal bride, we, despicable souls,
A rout unsepulchred and undeplored,
Are prostrate to be tumbled on the plains !
And now do thou, if any might be thine,

Shook by a tempest, and thrown down, must
    needs
Submit his curled head, and full-grown limbs.
To every common axe ; be patient, while
The torture's put to every joint, the saws
And engines making, with their very noise,
The forests groan and tremble : but not one,
When it was in its strength and state, revil'd it,
Whom poverty of soul, and envy, sends
To gather sticks from the tree's wish'd-for ruin,
The great man's emblem !"
            Shirley, *The Royal Master*, v. 2.
505.   " But, above all,
Avoid the politic, the factious fool,
The busy, buzzing, taking, hardened knave,
The quaint smooth rogue, that sins against his
    reason,
Calls saucy loud suspicion public zeal,
And mutiny the dictates of his spirit."
            Otway, *The Orphan*, iii. 1.

If thou hast any of thy native Mars,
Look him, who challenges thee, in the
   face."
   Up kindled Turnus' passion at such
      words :   530
He gives a groan, and from his bosom's
   depth
These accents forces forth : " O Drances,
   sooth,
Thou ever hast a plenteous store of prate
Then, when the battles call for deeds ; and
   thou
Art with the summoned fathers present first.
But with thy words the court must not be
   palled,
Which safely fly magnific from thee, whilst
The ramparts' mound is holding back the
   foe,
Nor are the trenches flowing o'er with blood.
Then thunder on in eloquence, thy wont,
And me with cowardice, thou Drances,
   charge,
Since thy right hand hath caused so many
   heaps   542
Of Trojans' slaughter, and eachwhere thou
   mark'st

530. " See, see ! King Richard doth himself appear,
  As doth the blushing discontented sun
  From out the fiery portal of the east,
  When he perceives the envious clouds are bent
  To dim his glory, and to stain the track
  Of his bright passage to the occident."
            Shakespeare, *K. Richard II.*, iii. 3.
531. A bystander might have exclaimed :
" Look down, ye spirits above ; for if there be
  A sight on earth worthy of you to see,
  'Tis a brave man, pursu'd by unjust hate,
  Bravely contending with his adverse fate."
        Tuke, *The Adventures of Five Hours*, act v.
534. " There is no vice so simple, but assumes
  Some mark of virtue on his outward parts.
  How many cowards, whose hearts are all as false
  As stairs of sand, wear yet upon their chins
  The beards of Hercules and frowning Mars,
  Who, inward search'd, have livers white as milk !"
            Shakespeare, *Merchant of Venice*, iii. 2.
540. " Thence on maturer judgment's anvil wrought,
  The polish'd falsehood" into public brought:
  Quick circulating slanders mirth afford,
  And reputation bleeds in ev'ry word."
                      Churchill, *The Apology*.
Goldsmith's village schoolmaster was likewise an
egregious talker : though the comparison does
Drances too much honour :
" In arguing, too, the parson own'd his skill,
  For ev'n though vanquish'd he could argue still ;
  While words of learned length, and thund'ring
      sound,
  Amaz'd the gazing rustics rang'd around ;
  And still they gaz'd, and still the wonder grew,
  That one small head should carry all he knew."
                              Deserted Village.
Yet Drances was not to be despised :
    " Throw but a stone, the giant dies."
                      Matthew Green, *The Spleen*.

The fields with trophies. What thy lively
   valor may
Avail, thou mayest put to proof : not far,
In sooth, have foemen to be sought by us :
On every side do they beset the walls.
March we against our enemies ? Why pause ?
Shall aye thy Mars be in thy empty tongue,
And in those feet [of thine] that run away ?
' *I* routed ?' Or can fairly any man,   551
Thou scum, tax me with being routed, who
Shall see swoln Tiber rise with Ilian blood,
And, root and branch, Evander's family
Fall'n prostrate, and the Arcads stript of
   arms ?
Not so have Bitias and huge Pandarus
Found me on trial, and the thousand, whom
I, conq'ror, in a day 'neath Tart'rus sent,

549.   " True courage scorns
  To vent her prowess in a storm of words ;
  And to the valiant actions speak alone :
  Then let my deeds approve me."
                  Smollett, *The Regicide*, ii. 7.
Ulysses says the opposite of Troilus :
" Speaking in deeds, and deedless in his tongue."
          Shakespeare, *Troilus and Cressida*, iv. 5.
" You cannot blast me with your tongue, and that's
  The strongest part you have about you."
    Beaumont and Fletcher, *The Maid's Tragedy*,
                                          iv. 2.
550. " The grim logician puts them in a fright :
  'Tis easier far to flourish than to fight."
              Dryden, *Hind and Panther*, P. iii.
" Where was your soldiership ? Why went not you
      out ?
  Why met you not the Tartar, and defied him ?
  Drew your dead-doing sword, and buckled with
      him ?
  Shot through his squadrons like a fiery meteor ?
  And, as we see a dreadful clap of thunder
  Rend the stiff-hearted oaks and toss their roots up,
  Why did not you so charge him ? You were sick
      then ;
  You, that dare taint my credit, slipp'd to bed then,
  Stewing and fainting with the fears you had."
                  J. Fletcher, *The Loyal Subject*, iv. 5.
The first two lines are quoted *Æn.* ii. *l.* 533.
558.   " I know no court but martial ;
  No oily language but the shock of arms ;
  No dalliance but with death ; no lofty measures,
  But weary and sad marches, cold and hunger,
  'Larums at midnight Valour's self would shake at :
  Yet I ne'er shrunk. Balls of consuming wildfire,
  That lick'd men up like lightning, have I laugh'd at,
  And toss'd 'em back again like children's trifles ;
  Upon the edges of my enemies' swords
  I have march'd like whirlwinds. Fury at this hand
      waiting,
  Death at my right ; Fortune my forlorn hope,
  When I have grappled with Destruction,
  And tugg'd with pale-fac'd Ruin, Night, and Mis-
      chief,
  Frighted to see a new day break in blood :
  And every where I conquer'd,—and for you, sir."
                        J. Fletcher, *The Mad Lover*, i. 1.
Turnus might have exclaimed with the exiled
Duke :

Cooped in their walls, and by a hostile trench
Enclosed. 'No safety [lies] in war!' Chant
thou   560
The like, O madman, to the Dardan chief,
And thine own int'rest. Then with whelming fear
Cease not to trouble all, and raise on high
The powers of a nation conquered twice;
On th' other hand to sink Latinus' arms.
Now e'en the chiefs of Myrmidonians quail
At Phrygian arms; now even Tydeus' son,
Achilles, too, of Larissæan [birth];
And backward from the Hadriatic waves
The river Aufidus retreats. Aye when 570

The villain of a hypocrite pretends
That he is frighted at his brawls with me,
And aggravates his charge with his alarm,—
Thou never such a soul by this right hand,—
Cease to be discomposed,—shalt lose; with thee
It may abide, and in that bosom rest.
Now I to thee and to thy grand debates,
O sire, return. If in our arms no hope
Thou any further dost repose; if we
Are so forlorn, and with the army once
Discomfited are utterly undone,   581
Nor backward step hath Fortune; peace let us
Entreat, and slack right hands stretch forth.
   Yet, oh!
If aught we had of our accustomed worth,
Before all others in my view is he
Both blest in travails, and of spirit rare,
Who, lest he aught the like should see, hath fallen
In death, and with his mouth once champed the earth.
But if with us there e'en resources [rest],
And youth as yet uninjured, and for aid
Cities and clans of Italy abound;—   591
But if, too, fame hath to the Trojans come
With plenteous blood—their funerals have they,
And o'er us all alike the storm [hath swept];—
Why is it we disreputably faint
In the first entrance? Why before the trump
Does quaking seize our limbs? A length of time,
And changeful travail of a chequered life

"Blow, blow, thou winter wind,
   Thou art not so unkind
As man's ingratitude;
Thy tooth is not so keen,
Because thou art not seen,
   Although thy breath be rude.

"Freeze, freeze, thou bitter sky,
That dost not bite so nigh
   As benefits forgot:
Though thou the waters warp,
Thy sting is not so sharp
   As friend remember'd not."
         Shakespeare, *As You Like It*, ii. 7.

560.   "Yes, peace hath sweets
That Hybla never knew; it sleeps on down,
Cull'd gently from beneath the cherub's wing:—
No bed for mortals; man is warfare; all
A hurricane within."
         Brooke, *Gustavus Vasa*, ii. 8.

562. "For public good to bellow all abroad
Serves well the purposes of private fraud.
Prudence by public good intends her own;
If you mean otherwise, you stand alone."
         Churchill, *The Conference*.

570. The commentators tell us that Quintilian has praised some archaism in v. 406; but, as he has not informed us whereabouts it lies, why should we fasten it upon *vel quum*, when the words, in their ordinary use, supply an excellent sense? *Vel* is plainly a particle of transition; and though the whole construction of the sentence which it introduces is different from that which precedes, yet it is just what might have been expected from a speaker who was in a state of great excitement. The bravery of Turnus had been impugned, and so he is naturally angry, and therefore abrupt. The meaning of the passage seems to be this: Turnus being most anxious for the war to proceed, seeks to weaken all the arguments which Drances had urged against it, by showing that they proceeded from sheer cowardice on the part of his adversary. First addressing Drances, he says: "Go on throwing everything into confusion by exciting the alarms of the weak; magnify the powers of a race who have already been beaten twice,—once by Hercules, and the other day by the Greeks; detract from the prowess of your own nation, and the army of your prince; tell us that Grecian chiefs are now obliged to quake at Trojan arms; that Diomed is in dread, and Achilles panic-stricken; and that such a horror has been raised by the very name of Æneas, that even the rivers of Italy recoil in their courses, and fly backward from the sea. Do all this, and continue to do it,—because you are a coward.

"Aye, even when" (turning to the audience) "this hypocritical knave affects to feel afraid of violence at my hands, and magnifies the miserable grounds, which he may plead for the apprehension, by his own assumed terror; though he speaks false, and knows it, yet he has counterfeited the fear,—only because he is a coward. But," (turning to Drances,) "you need not be afraid; for do not flatter yourself that I ever could condescend to sully my sword with the blood of such a dastard as you. Keep that pitiful spirit of yours, for all you need fear from me; it may dwell with you for ever, for ever continue to animate that wretched breast, before I could stoop to disturb you in so contemptible a possession."

574. "He, when the nipping blasts of envy rise,
Its guilt can pity, and its rage despise."
         Young, *The Instalment*.

"Away, lewd railer! Not thy slanderous throat,
So fruitful of invectives, shall provoke me
To wreak unworthy vengeance on thee."
         Smollett, *The Regicide*, ii. 7.

Though an inferior spirit to Turnus might have counselled with Gloster:

"Why should he live? to fill the world with words?"   Shakespeare, 3 *K. Henry VI.*, v. 5.

588. See note on *Æn.* x. *l.* 670, &c.

Hath matters to a better [state] restored;
Her visits paying o'er again by turns, 600
Hath Fortune many mocked, and on firm ground
Once more hath placed them. The Ætolian [prince]
And Arpi will not stand to us for aid:
But [yet] Messapus will, Tolumnius, too,
The blest, and leaders whom so many tribes
Have sent; nor shall a scant renown attend
The chos'n from Latium and Laurentine fields.
With us, too, is, from Volscians' noble race,
Camilla, leading on her troop of horse,
And her battalions, blossoming in bronze.
But if the Teucri for the contests me 611
Alone demand, and that your pleasure proves,
And I so much withstand the common good:
Not so hath Conquest in aversion fled
These hands, that I for such a glorious hope
Should any thing to enterprise decline.
With courage I against him will advance;
Though e'en the great Achilles he surpass,
And don like armor, forged by Vulcan's hands.
To you and to my consort's sire, Latinus,
This life I, Turnus, second not to one 621
Of those of olden days in bravery,
Have hallowed. Me Æneas challenges
Alone: and may he challenge me! I pray.
Nor Drances let the rather,—whether this
Be wrath of gods,—atone for it by death;
Or prowess be and fame,—bear off [the palm]."
They these [discussions] on their doubtful state
With one another in contention held:
Æneas was advancing camp and line. 630
A courier through the courts of royalty
In mighty agitation, lo! darts on,
And with immense alarms the city fills:—

614.   "Grant me license
To answer this defiance. What intelligence
Holds your proud master with the will of Heaven,
That, ere the uncertain die of war be thrown,
He dares assure himself the victory?
Are his unjust invading arms of fire?
Or those we put on, in defence of right,
Like chaff, to be consumed in the encounter?
I look on your dimensions, and find not
Mine own of lesser size; the blood, that fills
My veins, as hot as yours; my sword as sharp,
My nerves of equal strength, my heart as good;
And, confident we have the better cause,
Why should we fear the trial?"
                Massinger, *The Bashful Lover*, i. 2.

624.   " Neither are we
So unprovided as you think, my lord:
He shall not need to seek us; we will meet him,
And prove the fortune of a day, perhaps
Sooner than he expects."   *Ibid.*

That, in array embattled, from the flood
Of Tiber Trojans and the Tyrrhene band
Were swooping down throughout the plains,
   Forthwith
Their minds were troubled, and the commons' breasts
Convulsed, and wrath by no soft stimulants
Uproused. They, flurried, call for arms in hand;
" Arms!" yell the youth. The mourning fathers weep   640
And mutter. Here on every side a cry,
With changeful discord, rises loud to air:
Not otherwise than in a lofty grove
When flocks of birds by chance have lighted down,
Or in Padusa's fishful stream hoarse swans
Give forth a noise throughout the babbling pools.
" Aye sooth!" cries Turnus, "O ye citizens,
Seizing your opportunity, convene
A council, and, ye sitters, praise a peace:
Let them in arms upon the kingdom rush."
Nor speaking more he tore himself away,
And from the stately chamber quick withdrew.
" Do thou, Volusus, to the Volscians' bands
Give orders to be armed; and lead," saith he,
" The Rutuli. The cavalry in arms,   655
Messapus, Coras with thy brother, too,
Spread o'er the spacious plains. Let some secure

640.   " Peace is despair'd:
For who can think submission? War, then, war,
Open or understood, must be resolved."
                    Milton, *P. L.*, b. i.

649. Of course Turnus meant:
              " Shame on that friend,
Who in the hour of danger can deliberate,
And sit at ease, debating with Dame Counsel,
While Action frowns and beckons him away."
              Macdonald, *The Fair Apostate*, i. 2.

653. This activity on the part of Turnus, in spite of all that Drances had said, no doubt proceeded upon the principle, which Wolsey justifies to the king:
                    " If I am
Traduc'd by ignorant tongues, which neither know
My faculties, nor person, yet will be
The chronicles of my doing, let me say,
'Tis but the fate of place, and the rough brake
That virtue must go through. We must not stint
Our necessary actions, in the fear
To cope malicious censurers; which ever,
As ravenous fishes, do a vessel follow
That is new trimm'd, but benefit no farther
Than vainly longing, what we oft do best,
By sick interpreters, (once weak ones,) is
Not ours, nor allow'd; what worst, as oft,
Hitting a grosser quality, is cried up
For our best act. If we shall stand still,
In fear our motion will be mock'd or carp'd at,
We should take root here, where we sit, or sit
State statues only."
        . Shakespeare, *K. Henry VIII.*, i. 2.

The city avenues, and man the towers;
Let the remainder of the force with me
Bring arms to bear, where'er shall I com-
   mand."   660
They straight thro'out the city to the walls
Run to and fro. The council and his grand
      designs
Does he himself, the sire Latinus, quit,
And, troubled at the dismal crisis, he
Adjourns them, and heaps many a reproach
Upon himself, that he had not received
Dardan Æneas of his own accord,
And to the city as his daughter's spouse
Admitted him. Some delve before the gates,
Or carry stones and stakes. The trumpet
      hoarse   670
The bloody signal for the battle gives.
Mothers and boys then crowned with motley
      ring
The walls; their latest travail summons all.
Moreover, to the fane and highest towers
Of Pallas, with a bevy vast of dames,
The queen is carried up, presenting gifts,
And her companion by her side, the maid
Lavinia, fountain of calamity
So grievous, downcast in her lovely eyes.
Pass in the matrons, and with incense fume
The fane, and from the lofty gate outpour
Sad words: "Arms-puissant, patroness of
      war,   682
Tritonian maiden, shatter with thy hand
The Phrygian pirate's weapon, and himself
Do thou lay prostrate headlong on the earth,
And fling him forth beneath the lofty gates."
In emulation storming, Turnus' self
Is girded for the conflicts. And so now

In his Rutulian habergeon bedight,
In scales of bronze he bristled, and his legs
Had cased in gold, still bare upon his brows,
And to his side had buckled on his sword,
And, from the lofty fortress posting down,
[All] gold he sparkled, and in spirit bounds,
And now in hope anticipates the foe: 695
As when, his fetters burst, the racks hath fled
The courser, free at last, and having gained
The open field, he either bends [his way]
To feeding grounds, and to the herds of
      mares,
Or, in the water's well-known rivulet   700
Accustomed to be bathed, he sallies forth,
And, wantoning with crest high lifted,
      neighs,
And o'er his neck, o'er shoulders, plays his
      mane.
Whom coming in his path Camilla meets,
A squadron of the Volsci in her train,
And from her charger, 'neath the very gates,
Down sprang the queen, whom copying,
      all the troop,
With horses left, dropped down upon the
      ground :
Then such she speaks: "If, Turnus, any
      trust
Of self dwells justly in the brave, I dare,
And I engage to meet the Æneads' band,
And march alone against the Tuscan horse.
Let me with hand essay war's op'ning risks;
Do thou on foot continue by the walls, 714
And guard the city." Turnus [saith] to
      these,
On the dread maiden riveting his eyes:
"O maid, Italia's pride, what thanks to
      speak,

---

679. So Davenant represents Gartha :

"Thro' all the camp she moves with fun'ral pace,
   And still bowes meekly down to all she saw ;
Her grief gave speaking beauty to her face,
   Which lowly look'd, that it might pitty draw."
                              Gondibert, ii. 3, 51.

"When graceful Sorrow in her pomp appears,
Sure she is dress'd in Melesinda's tears.
Your head reclin'd, (as hiding grief from view,)
Droops like a rose surcharg'd with morning dew."
          Dryden, *Aurungzebe*, iii. 1.

683. So Nennius, at the temple of the Druids :

"Thou great Tiranes, whom our sacred priests,
Armed with dreadful thunder, place on high
Above the rest of the immortal gods,
Send thy consuming fires and deadly bolts,
And shoot 'em home; stick in each Roman heart
A fear fit for confusion ; blast their spirits,
Dwell in 'em to destruction; thorough their
      phalanx
Strike, as thou strik'st a proud tree ; shake their
      bodies,
Make their strengths totter, and their topless
      fortunes
Unroot, and reel to ruin."
     Beaumont and Fletcher, *Bonduca*, lii. 1.

---

697. "Where, fearless of the hunt, the hart se-
      curely stood,
And every where walk'd free, a burgess of the
      wood."   Drayton, *Polyolbion*, s. 18.

"The exile feels
Returning warmth, like some neglected steed
Of noblest temper, from his wonted haunts
Who long hath languish'd in the lazy stall ;
Call'd forth, he paws, he snuffs th' enliv'ning air ;
His strength he proffers in a cheerful neigh
To scour the vale, to mount the shelving hill,
Or dash from thickets close the sprinkling dew."
                    Glover, *Athenaid*, b. v.

"Nature imprints upon whate'er we see,
That has a heart and life in it, Be free.
The beasts are charter'd : neither age nor force
Can quell the love of freedom in a horse :
He breaks the cord, that held him at the rack :
And, conscious of an unincumber'd back,
Snuffs up the morning air, forgets the rein ;
Loose fly his forelock and his ample mane ;
Responsive to the distant neigh he neighs ;
Nor stops, till, overcoming all delays,
He finds the pasture where his fellows graze."
                        Cowper, *Charity*.

Or what to recompense, can I prepare?
But now, since stands that soul above all
  [risks]
Do thou along with me partake the toil.
Æneas, as report and scouts despatched
Assurance bring, light weaponed cavalry
Hath in advance unscrupulously sent, 723
That they may scour the champaign; he
  himself
Along a mountain's unfrequented heights,
Its brow o'erpassing, nigh the city draws.
I in a winding pathway of the wood
Plan crafts of war,—with soldiery in arms
To block the entrance with its twain defiles.
Do thou the Tyrrhene horsemen, standards
  joined, 730
Engage; with thee will be Messapus fierce,
And Latium's brigads, and Tiburtus' bands:
Do thou as well the gen'ral's charge assume."
On this wise speaks he, and with like address
Cheers on Messapus and the fed'rate chiefs
To battle, and advances on the foe.
A glen there is with serpentizing bend,
Suited for ambush and the wiles of war;
Which either side dark hems with clustered
  leaves;
Whither a scanty path conducts, and lead
Confined defiles and jealous avenues. 741
Above this [glen], upon the mountain-heights
And topmost crest, there lies a flat unknown,
And safe retreats; or if upon the right
And on the left you list to meet the fray,
Or from the brows attack, and roll huge
  stones.
Hither along the path's familiar line
The youth is borne, and on the post he
  seized,
And couched in ambush in unrighteous
  woods.
Meanwhile Latonia in the seats above
Fleet Opis, one of her companion maids,
And of her holy retinue, addressed, 752
And these sad accents uttered from her lip:
"Camilla marches to the murd'rous war,
O maid, and in our arms is girt in vain,
To me beyond [all] other [virgins] dear;
For not to Dian fresh this love hath come,
And stirred her spirit with a sudden charm.

---

737. "O'erbreath'd we come where, 'twixt impend-
  ing hills,
Ran the joint current of two gurgling rills;
On either hand, adown each fearful steep,
Hung forth the shaggy horrors, dark and deep:
Here, thro' brown umbrage, glow'd the vivid green,
And headlong slopes, and winding paths between;
Growth above growth, tall trees arose,
The tops of these scarce veil'd the roots of those:
A winding court where wandering Fancy walk'd,
And to herself responsive Echo talk'd."
                    Brooke, *The Fox-Chase*.

Forced from his realm through [popular]
  dislike, 759
And his haught violence, when Metabus
Departed from Privernum['s] ancient town,
He flying right amid the frays of war,
The babe, the partner in his banishment,
Bore off, and from its mother's name, 'Cas-
  milla,'
He called her,—by a portion of it changed,—
'Camilla.' In his bosom he himself
Before him carrying [the infant], sought
The distant summit of the lonely woods.
Fell weapons harassed him on every side,
And, with their soldiery dispread around,
[About him] did the Volsci hover. Lo!
Amid his flight, upon its highest banks 772
The Amasenus overflowing foamed;
So great a shower from the clouds had burst.
He, as to swim it he prepares, is stayed
By his affection for the babe, and fears
For his belovèd burden. In a trice,
In him, revolving all within himself,
Scarce settled this resolve:—a weapon huge,
Which in his stalwart hand the warrior
  chanced 780
To carry, hard with knots and fire-dried
  oak:—
To this his child, in bark and wild-wood
  cork
Encased, he binds, and deftly fitted, round
He ties her to the centre of the lance;
Whom poising in his giant right hand, thus
He speaks to heav'n: 'Boon patroness of
  woods,
To thee this [babe], Latonian maid, do I,
Her sire, myself thy servant dedicate;
Thine arms, her first, she grasping, through
  the air
Is in submission flying from her foe. 790

---

759. "Thus kings, by grasping more than they
  could hold,
First made their subjects by oppression bold;
And popular sway, by forcing kings to give
More than was fit for subjects to receive,
Ran to the same extremes; and one excess
Made both, by striving to be greater, less."
              Sir John Denham, *Cooper's Hill*.

766. Chaucer has a touching instance of parental
tenderness; in which the following occurs:
  "Hire litel child lay weping in hire arm,
  And kneling pitously to him she said:
  Pees, litel sone, I wol do thee no harm.
  With that hire couverchief of hire hed she braid,
  And over his litel eyen she it laid,
  And in hire arme she lulleth it ful fast,
  And into the heven hire eyen up she cast."
                  The Man of Lawes Tale.

769. "The sword behind him flash'd; before him
  roar'd,
Deaf to his woes, the deep. Forlorn, around
He roll'd his eye."
                Thomson, *Liberty*, P. iv. 662-5.

Receive, O goddess, I entreat, thine own,
Who now is trusted to uncertain winds.'
He said, and with his indrawn arm he flings
The spear-shaft whirled around; the billows
   boomed;
Ill-starred Camilla o'er the sweepy tide
On whizzing jav'lin flies. But Metabus,—
Now nearer closing him a mighty troop,—
Resigns him to the flood, and, in success,
The jav'lin with the maid he tears away,
A gift to Trivia from the grassy turf. 800
Him not within their dwellings, nor their
   walls,
Admitted any cities: nor would he
Have stooped to them himself through
   fierceness: e'en
In lonely mounts he passed a shepherd's life.
His daughter here in brakes, and 'mid dread
   haunts,
Upon the dugs and wild milk of a mare,
Belonging to the herd, he nourished up,
Milking its nipples in her tender lips.
And soon as ever with her footsoles first
The babe her steps had planted [on the
   ground],   810
With pointed javelin did he arm her hands,
And from the shoulder of the tiny [maid]
Hung arrows and a bow. For hairy gold,
For the investment of a trailing robe,
Along her back down wimples from her neck
A tiger's hide. E'en then her babish darts
From dainty hand she flung, and round her
   head
A sling she flourished with a rounded thong,
And Strymon's crane, or snowy swan, struck
   down.
Her many a mother through the Tuscan
   towns   820
Desired for their daughter-in-law in vain:

796. *Telum, hasta, hastile,* and *jaculum* (v. 545-563) are all used of the same weapon, unless *hastile* means the *shaft;* which is doubtful.

805. Camilla might have said with Comus:
" I know each lane, and every alley green,
Dingle, or bushy dell of this wild wood,
And every bosky bourn from side to side,
My daily walks and ancient neighbourhood."
                                Milton, *Comus.*
" What art thou, that into this dismal place,
Which nothing could find out but misery,
Thus boldly step'st? Comfort was never here;
Here is no food, nor beds, nor any house
Built by a better architect than beasts;
And ere you get a dwelling from one of them,
You must fight for it."
   Beaumont and Fletcher, *Cupid's Revenge,* v. 4.
807. How *armentalis equæ* can be tortured into " brood-mare," is hard to comprehend. Is not the expression exactly equivalent to Homer's βοῦς ἀγελαία (*Iliad,* 11, 728), which means, " still in the herd," *i. e.,* "wild"?

821. Or: "In vain desired as partner for a son."

She, only with Diana satisfied,
The deathless love of darts and maidenhood
Unsullied cherishes. I [fain] could wish
She had not been by such a warfare seized,
The Teucer-race essaying to attack:
How precious would she be to me, and one
Of my attendant maids! But come, since she
Is pressed by bitter destinies, glide down,
O Nymph, from heav'n, and visit Latium's
   bours,   830
Where is with luckless omen set abroach
The rueful fray. Take these, and from its
   sheath
Draw forth a vengeful bolt: herewith,
   whoe'er
Her hallowed body shall have by a wound
Profaned,—a Trojan or Italian,—he
To me in equal sort shall by his blood
Pay forfeit. I then in a hollow cloud
The pitiable [virgin's] corse, and arms
Unplundered, to the sepulchre will bear,

822. So Chaucer, of Zenobia:
" From hire childhode I finde that she fledde
Office of woman, and to wode she went;
And many a wilde harte's blood she shedde
With arwes brode, that she to hem sent;
She was so swift, that she anon hem hent.
And whan that she was elder, she wold kille
Leons, lepards, and beres al to-rent,
And in hire armes weld hem at hire wille.
" She dorst the wilde bestes dennes seke
And rennen in the mountaignes all the night,
And sleep under the bush."   *The Monkes Tale.*

823. Perhaps she might have been less resolute, had her shepherd-wooers learned the art of courtship from Marlow's exquisite song:
" Come liue with me, and be my loue,
And we will all the pleasures proue,
That vallies, groues, hills, and fields,
Woods, or steepie mountaine yeelds.

" And we will sit vpon the rockes,
Seeing the shepheards feede their flockes
By shallow riuers, to whose falls
Melodious birds sing madrigalls.

" And I will make thee beds of roses,
And a thousand fragrant poesies,
A cap of flowers, and a kirtle
Imbroydered all with leaues of mirtle.

" A gowne made of the finest wooll,
Which from our pretty lambs we pull;
Faire lined slippers for the cold,
With buckles of the purest gold.

" A belt of straw, and iuie buds,
With coral clasps and amber studs:
And if these pleasures may thee moue,
Then liue with me, and be my loue.

" The shephard swaines shall dance and sing,
For thy delight each May-morning:
If these delights thy minde may moue,
Then liue with me and be my loue."
   *England's Helicon, The Passionate Shepheard
   to his Loue.*

And reinstate them in her native land."
She said; but through the buoyant gales
of heaven   841
The other swooping down gave forth a sound,
In murky whirlwind vested round her form.
But meanwhile to the walls the Trojan
band
Draws near, and Tuscan chiefs, and all the
host
Of horsemen ranged by number into troops.
Through the whole champaign neighs the
prancing steed,
And fights against the tightened reins,
whirled round
To this side and to that. Then far and wide
A field of iron bristles with their spears,
And glow the plains with arms on high.
Messapus, too,   851
Upon the other side, and Latins fleet,
And, with his brother, Coras, and the maid
Camilla's wing, confronted on the field,
Appear, and, with their right hands drawn
aback,
Their lances to a distance they outstretch,
And whirl their missiles; and th' approach
of men,
And snort of horses waxes louder still.
And now, within a javelin-cast advanced,
Each [host] had halted: with a sudden shout
They burst away, and cheer their fuming
steeds.   861
They pour at once on every side their darts,
Thick in the guise of snow, and heav'n is
veiled
In shade. Straight, forcing with confronted
spears,
Hurtle Tyrrhenus and Aconteus keen,
And are the first to cause a crash, with din
Prodigious, and their horses' battered chests
To chests they dash. Aconteus, pitched
abroad,
In fashion of a thunderbolt, or charge,
Shot from an engine, headlong flings [him-
self]   870
Afar, and life he scatters to the gales.
The lines are straight discomfited, and back

---

840. If the reader should wish to be introduced into the kind of scene, which the poet briefly describes in the foregoing passage, let him read the 6th canto of the 3rd book of the *Faerie Queene*; and he will be charmed.

841. " I see His ministers; I see, diffus'd
In radiant orders, essences sublime,
Of various offices, of various plume,
In heavenly liveries, distinctly clad,
Azure, green, purple, pearl, or downy gold,
Or all commix'd. They stand, with wings outspread,
Listening to catch the Master's least command,
And fly through Nature, ere the moment ends;
Numbers innumerable."
                Young, *The Complaint*, N. ix.

The routed Latins throw away their shields,
And towards the city wheel around their
steeds.
The Trojans hunt them: at their head the
troops
Leads on Asilas. And they now approached
The portals, and the Latins raise again
A shout, and pliant necks turn round: these
fly,
And with full granted reins are carried back:
As when, advancing with alternate flood,
The ocean now swoops onward to the lands,
And with its surge the rocks o'erlays, in
foam,   882
And drenches with its curve the farthest
sand;
Now backwards swift, and sucking in again
The shingle by the tide rolled back, it flies,
And with retreating shallow quits the shore.
Twice did the Tuscans to their walls pursue
The routed Rutuli: they, twice rebuffed,
Face towards them as they screen their
backs with arms.
But when they for the third encounters met,
They mutually entangled their whole lines,
And singled man his man. Then sooth
[ensues]   892
E'en groan of those in death, and in deep
blood
Both arms, and corses, and half-living steeds,
With heroes' carnage blent, are rolled along.
A battle fierce springs up. Orsilochus
On Remulus's charger, since himself
He dreaded to assail, hurled forth a lance,
And left the steel behind, beneath its ear;
With which its stroke the charger fumes aloft,
And, of the wound impatient, tosses high
Its legs, with chest uplifted. He, unhorsed,
Is rolled along the ground. Catillus [fells]
Iollas, and, a giant in his soul,
A giant in his body and in arms,
Herminius overthrows: on whose bare head
[Wave] yellow locks; his shoulders, too,
are bare;
Nor him do wounds alarm: so much he lies
Exposed to weapons. Through his shoulders
broad
The driven spear stands quiv'ring, and, shot
through,   910
It doubles up the warrior with the pang.
In every quarter sable gore is shed;
They, vying, deal destruction with the sword,
And seek by wounds an honorable death.
But 'mid the centre of the slaughtered
heaps,
Forth prances an Amazon, on one breast

---

916. In the face of *exsultat Amazon*, v. 648, is one to write: "An Amazon forth prances," &c. ?

Stript for the fight, Camilla, quiver-armed,
And, scatt'ring with her hand, now showers
  thick
The limber jav'lins; now with her right
  hand
A sturdy battle-axe with double edge 920
Unwearied seizes. From her shoulder rings
A golden bow, and Dian's armory.
She, too, if ever, driven rearward, she
Retired, aims arrows flying from a bow
Reversed. But round [her stood] choice
  virgin-mates,
Alike the maid Larine, and Tulla [too],
Tarpeia, also, swaying axe of bronze,
Italian ladies; whom t' herself a grace,
Herself divine Camilla singled out,
Her worthy handmaids both in peace and
  war.   930
Such as when Thracian Amazonians strike
Thermodon's floods, and fight in painted
  arms;
Or round Hippolyte, or when returns
Mars-sired Penthesilea in her car,
And with loud yelling uproar women-troops
Bound forth with moony shields. Whom
  first with dart,
Whom last, fierce damsel, dost thou over-
  throw?
Or what the count of dying bodies thou
Upon the ground dost prostrate lay? The
  first,
Eunæus, of his father Clytius [sired],   940
Whose opened bosom, as he stands in front,
She with a lengthful fir[-shaft] pierces thro'.
He, rivulets of blood disgorging, falls,
And bites the gory ground, and as he dies
He writhes himself about upon his wound.
Then Liris [she destroys], and Pagasus be-
  sides:
Of whom the one, rolled backward from his
  horse,
Beneath him wounded, while he gathers up
The reins; the other, while he comes in aid,
And towards him, as he sinks, a weak right
  hand   950
Outstretches;—headlong and at once they
  fall.
To these Amaster, son of Hippotas,
She adds, and, plying with her spear afar,
Pursues both Tereus, and Harpalycus, .
Alike Demophoon and Chromis; and as
  many darts
As, from her hand discharged, the maiden
  launched,
So many Phrygian heroes fell.   Far off,
The hunter Ornytus, in armor strange,
And on an Iapygian steed, is borne,
Whose shoulders broad, a warrior, palls a
  hide   960

Reft from a steer; a wolf's huge grinning
  mouth,
And jaws with snowy grinders, screened
  his head;
And arms his hands a clownish truncheon; he
Is in continued motion 'mid the troops,
And by a head entire above them stands.
Him, intercepted,—for it was no toil,
His troop discomfited,—she pierces through.
And these, moreover, speaks with hostile
  breast:
"Didst thou imagine, Tuscan, thou didst
  chase
Wild animals in woods? The day hath come,
Which by a woman's arms will have dis-
  proved   971
Your words. Still this, no light distinc-
  tion, thou
Shalt carry to the Manes of thy sires,—
That thou hast fallen by Camilla's dart."
She next Orsilochus and Butes [slays],
Of Teucer's sons the twain most bulky frames:
But Butes, turned away, with point of spear
Between the corselet and the casque she
  pierced,
Where, as he sits, conspicuous is his neck,
And from his left arm down his buckler
  hangs: 980
Fleeing, and hunted thro' a spacious ring,
In circle narrower, Orsilochus
She mocks, and her pursuer she pursues.
Then her stout axe both thro' the hero's arms,
And thro' his bones, uprising higher, whilst
He's suing, and outpouring many a prayer,
She drives and drives again: with his hot
  brains
The wound bedews his face. Across her
  came,
And halted, at the sudden sight appalled,
Haunter of Apennine, the warrior-son 990
Of Aunus, of Ligurians not the last,
While destinies permitted him to cheat.
He too, when now he sees that by no flight
He can escape the fray, nor turn aside
The pressing queen:—essaying to contrive
His stratagems with policy and craft,
Begins these [words]: "What so surpassing
  [feat], if thou,
A woman, trustest to a gallant steed?
Forego thy [means of] flight, and hand to
  hand
With me commit thee to the righteous
  ground,   1000
And gird thee for a fight on foot; thou soon
Shalt know to whom vain bragging brings
  the praise."

998. That is, though a woman; for it weakens
the passage to make *femina*, v. 705, the vocative
case.

He said; but she in fury, and afire
With keen vexation, to a comrade hands
   her horse,
And stands opposed to him in even arms,
Afoot with naked falchion, and unawed
With spotless buckler. But the youth
   himself,
Supposing he had triumphed by his trick,
Flies off,—there's no delay,—and with the
   reins
Shifted around, a runagate, is borne away,
And tires his nimble steed with ironed heel.
"False Ligur, and in vain with haughty soul
Uplifted, idly thou, a slipp'ry [knave],
Thy country's crafts hast tried, nor shall thy
   guile   1014
To lying Aunus thee in safety bear."
These speaks the maiden, and with nimble
   soles,
Flame-like, outstrips him with the pace of
   steeds;
And, bridle seized, she meets him to his
   face,
And takes her vengeance on his hostile
   blood:
As readily a falcon, hallowed bird,   1020
Pursues with pinions from a lofty rock,
A dove high poised in cloud, and gripes her
   clutched,
And disembowels her with hooky claws;
Then blood and rifled feathers drop from
   heaven.
But, watching these with not unheedful
   eyes,
The sire of men and gods sits on the crest
Of heav'n aloft. The father rouses up
Tyrrhenian Tarcho to the felon fights,
And with no mild incentives wrath instils.
So Tarcho 'mid the slaughter, and the
   yielding troops,   1030
Is borne upon his steed, and goads the wings
In sundry accents, calling each by name,
And rallies to the frays his routed men.

1032. So Talbot was equally horrified by his countryman's behaviour, on the attack by Joan of Arc:
"My thoughts are whirled like a potter's wheel;
   I know not where I am, or what I do.
A witch by fear, not force, like Hannibal,
Drives back our troops, and conquers as she lists:
So bees with smoke, and doves with noisome
   stench,
Are from their hives and houses driven away.
They call'd us for our fierceness English dogs;
Now, like to whelps, we crying run away.
Hark, countrymen! either renew the fight,
Or tear the lions out of England's coat;
Renounce your soil, give sheep in lions' stead:
Sheep run not half so timorous from the wolf,
Or horse, or oxen, from the leopard,
As you fly from your oft-subdued slaves."
         Shakespeare, 1 *K. Henry VI.*, i. 5.

"What fear, O ye who ne'er will feel
   aggrieved,
O ever mopish Tuscans, what such gross
Poltroonery within your souls hath come?
You rovers doth a woman hound, and turns
These your battalions? Wherefore sword,
   or why
These unavailing weapons, do we bear
In our right hands? But not for Venus slow
And nightly brawls, or, when the bending
   pipe   1041
Of Bacchus hath proclaimed the choirs, to
   wait
The cates and goblets of the plenteous
   board,—
This is your passion, this your aim,—the
   while
Auspicious seer his holy tidings tells,
And fatted victim calls to lofty groves."
These having uttered, on the midmost he,
That e'en would die himself, his charger
   spurs,
And, chafing, bears him against Venulus,
And, torn from off his horse, he grasps the foe
With his right hand, and with prodigious
   force   1051
Before his bosom quickly bears him off.
A shouting to the welkin is upraised,
And all the Latins turned about their eyes.
The fiery Tarcho flies along the plain,
His arms and hero bearing; then from off
His own lance-tip he snaps away the steel,
And ransacks the uncovered parts, where he
May deal the deathful wound; on th' other
   hand,
Against him th' other fighting, from his throat
His right hand stays, and parries force by
   force.
And as what time the golden eagless, high
Upon the wing, bears off a serpent clutched,
And into him hath doubled in her claws,
And fastened with her pounces; but the
   snake,   1065
Wound-stricken, writhes about his coiling
   folds,
And bristles with his elevated scales,
And hisses with his mouth, uprising tall;
Him, as he struggles, none the less she plies
With hooky beak; she at the same time flaps
The welkin with her wings: not otherwise,
His booty from the men of Tibur's troop,
Off Tarcho bears in triumph. Following
The pattern and the fortune of their chief,
Mæonia's sons rush on. Then Arruns, due

1074. "But those fears,
Feeling but once the fires of nobler thoughts,
Fly, like the shapes of clouds we form, to nothing."
         Beaumont and Fletcher, *Thierry and Theodoret*, iv. 1.

x

To fates, with jav'lin, and with ample skill,
Carcers round fleet Camilla in advance, 1077
And what may be his readiest chance essays.
Where'er herself the chafing maiden threw
In centre of the host, there Arruns comes
Hard by, and silently surveys her steps:
Where conq'ress she returns, and from the
  foe 1082
Withdraws her foot, here stealthily the youth
Turns off the hasty reins. Approaches these,
And now approaches those, he traverses,
And every circling range on every side;
And shakes the caitiff his unerring spear.
By chance Chloreus, to Cybele devote,
And erst her priest, distinguished shone afar
In Phrygian arms, and urged his foaming
  steed, 1090
Which a gold-buckled skin with scales of
  bronze,
In feather-fashion palled. Himself, all-
  bright
In foreign steely-blue and purple dye,
Shot Cretan arrows from a Lycian bow;
Forth from his shoulders rings the bow of
  gold,
And golden was the prophet's helm; he next
Both saffron cloak, and rustling folds of
  lawn,
With tawny gold had gathered into knot;
His tunic, and his legs' outlandish greaves,
With needle broidered. Him the huntress-
  maid,— 1100
Whether that she might on the temples'front
His Trojan weapons fasten, or that she
Might figure in his captured gold,—alone
From all the battle's contest blind pursued,
And heedlessly through all the army burned
With woman's love of booty and of spoils:
When Arruns,—his occasion seized at last,—
A weapon from his ambush shoots, and thus
The heav'nly pow'rs beseeches with his
  voice:
"Most high of gods, divine Soracte's guard,
Apollo, whom we foremost venerate, 1111
Whose blaze of fir is fuelled by a pile,
And we, thy vot'ries, on our holiness
Relying, through the centre of the fire
Our footsteps plant on plenteous living coal;
Vouchsafe, almighty sire, that this disgrace
Be from our arms expunged! Not stript-off
  gear
Or trophy of a vanquished maid, or aught
Of plunder do I seek. My other feats
Shall bring me credit. So that this dread
  plague, 1120
Struck by a wound from me, may fall, un-
  famed
I to my native city shall return."
Apollo heard, and granted in his soul

That of the prayer a part should reach its
  end;
A part he scattered to the wingy gales.
That he should fell by sudden death the
  mazed
Camilla, to the suitor he vouchsafes;
That him, returned, his glorious native land
Should see,—he granted not; and [this]
  request
The tempests turned away upon the winds.
Accordingly, when, from his hand dis-
  charged, 1131
The lance along the breezes gave a sound,
The Volsci all their keen attention bent,
And carried towards the queen their eyes.
  She naught
Regardful, neither of the breeze, nor sound,
Nor of the weapon swooping from the sky;
Till, plunged beneath her bosom bared, the
  lance
It stuck, and, driven home, deep drank her
  maiden blood.
Her wildered retinue together haste,
And raise their fallen mistress. Arruns flies,
Stunned above all with joy and mingled
  fright; 1141
Nor dares he venture any more to trust
His spear, nor meet the weapons of the maid.
And as, before the hostile darts pursue,
Some famous wolf hath straight to lofty
  mounts,
From path aloof, retired,—a shepherd slain
Or stately steer,—aware of his bold deed,
And, drawing in his tail, that shakes with
  fear,
Hath laid it 'neath his paunch, and sought
  the woods:
Not otherwise, wild Arruns from their view
Removed himself, and satisfied with flight,
He mixed him up among the central arms.
She, dying, with her hand the bolt with-
  draws; 1153
But in her ribs, among the bones, stands
  [fixed]
The steely spear-point in the deepsome
  wound.
She bloodless sinks; sink cold in death her
  eyes,

1125. Milton alludes to the same idea:
    "To Heaven their prayers
Flew up, nor miss'd the way, by envious winds
Blown vagabond or frustrate."
        P. L., b. xi. 14-16.

1129. Or: "his voice."

1140. "But hollow men, like horses hot at hand,
Make gallant show and promise of their mettle;
But when they should endure the bloody spur,
They fall their crests, and, like deceitful jades,
Sink in the trial."
        Shakespeare, *Julius Cæsar*, iv. 2.

The hue, once rosy, hath her features left.
Then, as she dies, she Acca thus accosts,
One of her fellows, who before the rest
Alone was to Camilla true, with whom
She used to share her cares ; and these thus
    speaks : 1161
"Thus far I, sister Acca, have availed ;
A bitter wound now brings me to my end,
And all in murk is waxing dark around.
Fly off, and carry these my last behests
To Turnus : to the fight t'advance, and drive
The Trojans from the town. And now farewell !"
At the same instant with these words she loosed
The reins, as she is sinking to the earth ·
Not of her own free will. Then, cold, by
    slow degrees 1170
From her whole body she herself released,
And her lithe neck and death-caught head
    laid down,
Her arms abandoning ; and with a groan
The life disdainful flies beneath the shades.
Then of a truth past measure, does a cry
Arising, strike the golden stars ; the fray
More bloody grows, Camilla overthrown ;
At once close hurtle all the Teucri's host,
And Tuscan chieftains, and Evander's
    Arcad wings.
But long since Opis, Trivia's sentinel,
Aloft is sitting on the mountain-tops, 1181
And gazing on their tourneys unalarmed.
And when afar, amid the yell of youths
In frenzy, she Camilla spied, amerced
In rueful death, she both gave forth a groan,
And heaved these accents from her lowest
    breast:
"Ah ! too, too barbarous a penalty,
O maiden, thou hast paid, for having tried
The Teucri to provoke in war ! Nor thee,
All lonely in the brakes, hath it bestead
Diana to have worshipped, or have worn
Our quivers on thy shoulder. Still, thy queen
Hath not forsaken thee, dishonored, now
In death's extremity ; nor this thy end
Shall thro' the nations be without renown,
Or shalt thou bear the scandal of a maid,
Unwreaked ; for whosoe'er by wound pro-
    faned 1197
Thy body, shall atone by death condign."
Beneath a lofty mountain lay immense,
The sepulchre of th' old Laurentine king,
Dercennus, [fashioned] of a mound of earth,
And bowered by a shady holm. Here first
The passing lovely goddess plants herself
With effort quick, and from the stately tomb
Observes she Arruns. When she him
    beheld 1205
Joying in soul, and venting idle vaunts :
"Why," cries she, "goest thou off a different way ?
Direct thy footstep hither ; hither come,
O [thou who 'rt] doomed to die, that
    guerdons thou
Deserving of Camilla may'st receive. 1210
Shalt thou, too, perish by Diana's shafts ?"
She said, and from her quiver, trimmed
    with gold,
The Thracian [nymph] drew forth a wingy
    bolt,
And, angered, strained the bow, and drew
    it far,
Until the ends imbowed together met ;
And now with [both] her hands alike she
    touched,—
The sharpened point of th' iron with her
    left,—
Her bosom with her right and with the
    string.
Forthwith the weapon's whirr and whizzing
    air
Together Arruns heard, and in his frame
The iron stuck. Him, breathing out [his
    soul], 1221
And heaving forth his latest groans, his
    mates,
Regardless, on the champaign's unknown dust
Abandon : Opis on her wings away
Is wafted to the empyrean heaven.
First flies, their mistress lost, Camilla's
    wing
Light[-armed] ; the Rutulans disordered fly ;
Flies fierce Atinas ; and the routed chiefs
And companies forlorn seek safe [retreats],
And, turned aloof, upon their chargers they
Speed to the city. Nor hath one the power
With darts to bear the Teucri pressing on,
And dealing death, or 'gainst them make a
    stand ; 1233
But on their feeble shoulders bear they off
Their bows unstraitened ; and in their career
The hoof of horses shakes the mould'ring
    plain.
The agitated dust in pitchy gloom
Is volumed to the walls, and from the heights
The bosom-strickened dames their woman's
    shout
Raise to the stars of heaven. Who in flight
Dashed forward first to open gates,—on
    these 1241
A hostile multitude in jumbled host
Is closing : nor escape they dismal death :

1157. "Such ruby lips, and such a lovely bloom,
    Disdaining all adult'rate aids of art,
    Kept a perpetual spring upon her face,
    As Death himself lamented, being forced
    To blast it with his paleness."
        Massinger, *The Unnatural Combat*, i. 3.

X 2

But in the very threshold, by their native walls,
And 'mid the shelter of their homes, they, pierced,
Breathe forth their spirits. Some begin to shut the gates;
Nor for their comrades dare to ope a way,
Nor take them, craving it, inside the walls;
And slaughter most deplorable begins
Of those that guard the passes with their arms, 1250
And those upon [these] arms who rush. [The men,]
Barred out before their weeping parents' eyes
And faces, some,—destruction driving on,—
Into the steepy dykes are rolled; some, blind and quick,
With slackened bridles batter on the gates
And gate-posts, sturdy through a barricade.
In utmost rivalry the very dames,
From off the walls, (true love of country guides,)
Like as they saw Camilla, from their hand
Throw weapons, flurried, and with stubborn oak, 1260
With stakes, and bludgeons, hardened in the fire,

1259. It is by no means easy to see what is the exact force of *ut videre Camillam*, v. 892. Of all the views which have been put forward, that is adopted which seems to be the least unsatisfactory; though *ut*, in the sense of "like as," would appear to require *viderant*. Yet Virgil at times employs an unexpected tense. The passage, taken by itself, would at once suggest that *Camillam* meant the *body* of Camilla; but, unfortunately for this view, Diana had already declared to Opis, that she would convey it away on her death. Trapp's answer to this objection is not tenable for a moment. It cannot be imagined that the goddess would have allowed the corpse to be carried to the town, before she removed it from public gaze. She declares that after the death of Arruns—*post*—she would bear it to the sepulchre.

In headlong hurry do they mimic steel,
And foremost for their city burn to die.
Meanwhile the cruellest intelligence
Fills Turnus in the woods, and to the youth
Acca announces the prodigious coil :—
"Annihilated were the Volscians' lines,
Camilla fall'n, the furious foe rush on,
And with Mars fav'ring, every [spot] had seized ;
That terror now was carried to the town."
He, frantic,—even thus Jove's fell decrees
Require,—abandons the beleaguered hills,
Quits the rough woods. He'd scarce gone out of sight, 1273
And gained the plain, when sire Æneas,
On open passes entered, both surmounts
The ridge, and issues from the gloomy grove.
Thus both, impetuous, and with all their host,
Are hurried to the walls, nor stand apart
By paces long between them. And as soon
As from afar Æneas spied the plains, 1280
Smoking with dust, and saw Laurentum's bands,
And Turnus fell Æneas knew in arms,
And heard th' approach of foot and snorts of steeds:—
They even instantly upon the fights
Would enter, and essay encounters, did not now
His jaded coursers rosy Phœbus dip
Within Iberia's gulf, and night restore,
The day declining. In their camp they rest
Before the city, and the walls invest.

1287. "The gaudy, blabbing, and remorseful day
Is crept into the bosom of the sea,
And now loud-howling wolves arouse the jades,
That drag the tragic melancholy night;
Who with their drowsy, slow, and flagging wings
Clip dead men's graves, and from their misty jaws
Breathe foul contagious darkness in the air."
Shakespeare, 2 *K. Henry VI.*, iv. 1, 1-7.

BOOK XII.

As soon as Turnus sees that, broken down
By hostile Mars, the Latins heart had lost;
That his own pledges were exacted now;
That he himself was marked by every eye;—
Of his own motion, not to be appeased,
He blazes, and his courage raises high.
Such-like, as in the Carthaginians' fields

Line 4. Or, more literally: "marked out by their eyes."

Some famous lion, by a heavy wound 8
From hunters in the bosom stricken, then
At length prepares for battle, and delights,
Shaking the manèd thews upon his neck,
And fearless breaks the robber's bolt infixed,
And roars with gory mouth : not otherwise

8, 9. The genitive case is not always possessive in the ordinary sense. Compare *venantum vulnere*, v. 5, with *dona Minervæ*. Æn. ii. 189.
10. *Movet arma*, v. 6, is too technical an expression to bear a literal version.

In Turnus, set afire, does fury swell.
Then thus he speaks the king, and so begins
In agitation : " There is no delay
In Turnus ; naught [of pretext] is there why
The dastard Æneads should revoke their
    words,
Nor what they've covenanted should decline.
To combat do I march. O father bring
The holy off'rings, and do thou draw up
The league. I either will with this right hand
The Dardan renegade of Asia send
'Neath Tart'rus,—let the Latins sit and
    see !—
And singly with the sword will I rebut
The universal charge : or let him hold
Us conquered ; let Lavinia yield, his bride."
    To him Latinus with a heart composed
Replied : " O youth of spirit rare, as much
As in fierce gallantry thou dost excel, 30
So much the more devotedly 'tis right
That I take thought for thee, and that in fear
I weigh all risks. Thy father Daunus' realms
Are thine ; towns many, taken by thy hand,
Are [thine]: yea, too, both gold and [kindly]
    mind
Latinus owneth : other spouseless maids
In Latium be, and in Laurentine fields,
Nor they unnoble in their pedigree.
Allow me, reservations laid aside,
To open these, not balmy to be told ; 40
This at the same time in thy mind imbibe.
To none of former suitors was it right
That I my daughter should espouse, and this
Did all, both gods and men, pronounce.
O'erwhelmed by love of thee, by kindred
    blood
O'erwhelmed, and by my mourning consort's
    tears,
All ties I burst ; reft from my daughter's
    spouse
His fianced [bride] ; ungodly arms took up.
What misadventures from that [hour], what
    wars,
Pursue me, thou, O Turnus, dost behold ;
What grievous travails thou in chief dost
    bear. 51
Twice conquered in the mighty fray, we
    scarce
Italia's hopes within the city guard ;
With blood of ours still warm are Tiber's
    streams,
And spacious plains are bleaching with our
    bones.
Whither am I so often driven back?
What frenzy shifts my mind? If, Turnus
    dead,
I'm ready to invite them as allies,
Why do I not the rather, while he's safe,
Remove disputes? What will the Rutulans,

My kinsfolk, what the rest of Italy say, 61
Should I,—may Fortune give my words the
    lie !—
Have thee betrayed to death, while thou
    dost woo
My daughter and the nuptial link with us?
Reflect upon the diverse haps in war ;
Have pity on thy agèd sire, whom now,
In woe, his native Ardea severs far
[From us]." In no wise is the vehemence
Of Turnus by his language swayed : he
    swells
The more, and in the curing waxes sick. 70
As soon as he could speak, he thus began
From out his lip: "What care on my account
Thou entertainest, this, most worthy [prince]
For my sake, I beseech thee, lay aside,
And suffer me to barter death for praise.
We, too, O father, darts and no weak steel
Scatter from our right hand, and from the
    wound
Of our [infliction] follows blood. From him
His goddess-mother will be far, who screens
A runagate within a woman-cloud, 80
And shrouds him over with her empty
    shades."
    But, at the novel posture of the fray
The queen affrighted wept, and, death-pre-
    pared,
Her daughter's fiery spouse she held : " O
    Turnus, I
Of thee, by these my tears, by reverence

75. " Behold in awful march, and dread array,
The long-extended squadrons shape their way !
Death, in approaching terrible, imparts
An anxious horror to the bravest hearts ;
Yet do their beating breasts demand the strife,
And thirst of glory quells the love of life."
            Addison, *The Campaign.*

79. Wagner considers that the clause *quæ* . . . .
umbris, refers to the thoughts of Æneas ; which is,
no doubt, true in the main : but it is evident that
some of the terms express the feelings of the speaker
himself. If the view taken in the version is right,
the passage may be thus paraphrased :
    We too, my father, can wield weapons, and
launch no puny darts ; our swords can draw blood
as well as theirs. As to this goddess-mother, (of
whom Æneas prates,) we need be under no apprehension from her,—she will be far enough away
from him (—for his mother is no goddess at all : the
whole story is a mere fable). We need not be
alarmed (whether he fancies or affects) that she
will protect him (—runaway that he is !) by a cloud,
(—shame upon the soldier that looks to a female
for aid in war !—) and muffle him up in shades
(which, we know full well, are all fictitious).

85. " Oh, I can't bear this cold contempt of death !
This rigid virtue, that prefers your glory
To liberty or life. O cruel man !
By these sad sighs, by these poor streaming eyes,
By that dear love that makes us now unhappy,
By the near danger of that precious life,
Heaven knows I value much above my own :—

For thy Amata, if doth any touch
Thy spirit,—thou art now the single hope,
Thou art the peace, of my unhappy eld ;
Latinus' dignity and sovereign sway
Are in thy hands ; our falling house on thee
All leans :—this single [favor] do I crave :
Forbear with Trojans to engage thy hand.
Whatever chances in that strife wait thee,
Wait me, too, Turnus. I with thee will leave
These hated lights, nor consort of my child
Will I, a captived [dame], Æneas see." 96
Lavinia listened to her mother's voice,
With tears besprinkled o'er her glowing
   cheeks ;
In whom a plenteous blushing raised a fire,
And through her heated lineaments careered.
As if with ruddy purple should some [hand]

"What! Not yet mov'd! Are you resolv'd on death?
Then, ere 'tis night, I swear by all the powers,
This steel shall end my fears and life together."
     Smith, *Phædra and Hippolytus*, act ii.

92. " Forbear, Demetrius, 'tis Aspasia calls thee ;
Thy love, Aspasia, calls ; restrain thy sword ;
Nor rush on useless wounds with idle courage."
     Johnson, *Irene*, v. 4.

98. " With that adowne out of her christall eyne
New trickling teares she softly forth let fall,
That like two orient perles did purely shyne
Upon her snowy cheeke."
     Spenser, of Florimell, *F. Q.*, iii. 7, 9.

" The godlike maid, awhile all silent stood,
And down to th' earth let fall her humble eyes ;
While modest thoughts shot up the flaming blood,
Which fir'd her scarlet cheek with rosy dyes :
But soon to quench the heat, that lordly reigns,
From her fair eye a show'r of crystal rains,
Which with his silver streams o'erruns the beau-
teous plains." P. Fletcher, *Purple Island*, xi. 10.

The following extract but partly applies to the
case of the unhappy Lavinia ; but it is altogether a
most beautiful passage :

" Her eye did seem to labour with a tear,
 Which suddenly took birth, but, overweigh'd
With its own swelling, dropp'd upon her bosom,
Which, by reflection of her light, appear'd
As nature meant her sorrow for an ornament.
After, her looks grew cheerful, and I saw
A smile shoot graceful upward from her eyes,
As they had gain'd a victory o'er grief,
And with it many beams twisted themselves,
Upon whose golden threads the angels walk
To and again from heaven."
     Shirley, *The Brothers*, i. 1.

" In tears your beauteous daughter drowns her
   sight,
Silent as dews that fall in dead of night."
     Dryden, *The Indian Emperor*, iii. 3.

99. " The bashfull blood her snowy cheekes did
   dye,
That her became, as polisht yvory,
Which cunning craftesman hand hath overlayd
With fayre vermillion or pure castory."
     Spenser, *F. Q.*, ii. 9, 41.

"'Tis beauty truly blent, whose red and white
Nature's own sweet and cunning hand laid on."
     Shakespeare, *Twelfth Night*, i. 5.

Have stained the ivory of Ind ; or when
Blush snowy lilies, blent with many a rose :
Such hues the damsel on her visage raised.
Him love confounds, and fastens he his looks
Upon the maid ; he burns for arms the more,
And speaks in few Amata : " Do not, pray,
Do not with tears, nor such a grave presage,
Attend me, O my mother, as I go
To the encounters of relentless Mars ;   110

103. " The lilly in the field,
   That glories in his white,
For purenesse now must yeeld,
   And render up his right.
Heauen, pictur'd in her face,
   Doth promise ioy and grace.

" Faire Cynthiaes siluer light,
   That beates on running streames,
Compares not with her white,
   Whose haires are all sun-beames.
So bright my Nimph doth shine,
   As day unto my eyne.

" With this there is a red
   Exceedes the damaske-rose,
Which in her cheekes is spred,
   Whence euery fauor growes.
In skie there is no starre,
   But she surmounts it farre.

" When Phœbus from the bed
   Of Thetis doth arise,
The morning blushing red,
   In faire carnation wise,
He shewes in my Nimphs face
   As queene of euery grace.

" This pleasant lilly white,
   This taint of roseate red,
This Cynthiaes siluer light,
   This sweet faire Dea spred,
These sun-beames in mine eye,—
   These beauties make me die."
Earle of Oxenforde, in *England's Helicon*.

" O ruddier than the cherry !
O sweeter than the berry !
O Nymph more bright
   Than moonshine night,
Like kidlings blithe and merry !
Ripe as the melting cluster,
   No lily has such lustre."
     Gay, *Acis and Galatea*.

105. " O do not wanton with those eyes,
   Lest I be sick of seeing ;
Nor cast them down, but let them rise,
   Lest shame destroy their being.

" O be not angry with those fires,
   For then their threats will kill me :
Nor look too kind on my desires,
   For then my hopes will spill me.

" O do not steep them in thy tears,
   For so will sorrow slay me :
Nor spread them as distract with fears :
   Mine own enough betray me."
     Ben Jonson, *Underwoods, Miscellaneous
     Poems*, ii.

" Who can but doat on this humility,
That sweetens, — Lovely in her tears ! — The
   fetters,
That seem'd to lessen in their weight but now,
By this grow heavier on me."
     Massinger, *The Unnatural Combat*, iv. 1.

For death's delay is not to Turnus free.
Do thou, O herald Idmon, carry forth
Unto the Phrygian despot these my words,
That are not doomed to please : 'When first,
In heaven of to-morrow wafted on
Upon her purplish wheels, Aurore shall blush,
'Gainst Rutulans let him not Teucri lead ;
Let Trojans' arms, and Rutuli repose ;
By our own blood the war let us decide ;
The bride Lavinia on that plain be sought.' "
These words when uttered he, and quick withdrew   121
Within the palace, he demands his steeds,
And joys in gazing on them as they neigh
Before his eyes ; which Orithyia's self
Presented as an honorable gift
To [sire] Pilumnus, such as might surpass
The snows in whiteness, in career the gales.
Round stand officious grooms, and stimulate
Their bosoms, patted with their hollow hands,
And comb their manèd necks. Then he himself   130
Around his shoulders dons his coat of mail,
With gold and sheeny orichalcum crisp ;
At the same time for service does he fit
His falchion e'en, and buckler, and the cones
Of his encrimsoned plume ; the falchion, which
The deity, [who reigns] the lord of fire,
Himself had for his father Daunus forged,
And plunged it, glowing, in the Stygian wave.
Next seizes he with force his sturdy spear,
Which, resting on a giant pillar, stood   140
Amid the dome, Auruncan Actor's spoil,
And shakes it quiv'ring, lifting up his voice :

"Now, O thou spear, that never balked my calls,
The time is now at hand ; thee [wielded] once
Thrice gallant Actor ; wields thee the right hand
Of Turnus now : vouchsafe me low to lay
The body of this Phrygian, half a man,
And rend with stalwart hand his wrenchèd mail,
And in the dust his tresses to defile,
With heated iron curled, and soaked in myrrh."   150
By these his frenzies he is hounded on ;
And from the burning [warrior's] face throughout
Sparks fly ; fire flashes from his furious eyes.
As when tremendous bellowings the bull
Wakes for the first encounters, and essays
His anger to concentrate in his horns,
Against some tree-bole butting, and the winds
Provokes with thrusts, and with the scattered sand
Beforehand practises against the fray.
Nor less, meanwhile in his maternal arms
Ferocious does Æneas sharpen Mars,   161
And rouse himself with wrath, rejoicing o'er
The war's adjustment through the proffered league.
His comrades then, and sad Iulus' fear,
He comforts, teaching them the fates ; and bids
To king Latinus envoys to return
His sure replies, and name the terms of peace.
Next Dawn arisen scarce besprent with light
The mountain-tops, when first upraise their forms

---

122. Glover, of Xerxes' chariot and horses :
" The monarch will'd ; and suddenly he heard
His trampling horses. High on silver wheels
The iv'ry car with azure sapphires shone,
Cerulean beryls, and the jasper green,
The emerald, the ruby's glowing blush,
The flaming topaz with its golden beam,
The pearl, th' empurpled amethyst, and all
The various gems, which India's mines afford
To deck the pomp of kings. In burnish'd gold
A sculptur'd eagle from behind display'd
His stately neck, and o'er the royal head
Outstretch'd his dazzling wings. Eight gen'rous steeds,
Which on the fam'd Nisæan plain were nurs'd
In wintry Media, drew the radiant car."
        Leonidas, b. iv.
134, 5.   " Diomedon
Led on the slaughter. From his nodding crest
The sable plumes shook terrour. Asia's host
Shrunk back, as blasted by the piercing beams
Of that unconquerable sword, which fell
With lightning's swiftness on dissever'd helms."
        Ibid., b. v.

153. " Dauntless on his native sands
The dragon-son of Mona stands ;
In glittering arms and glory drest,
High he rears his ruby crest.
There the thundering strokes begin,
There the press, and there the din ;
Talymafra's rocky shore
Echoing to the battle's roar ;
Where his glowing eye-balls turn,
Thousand banners round him burn."
        Gray, *The Triumphs of Owen*.

168, 9. " And now the taller sons (whom Titan warns)
Of unshorn mountains, blown with easy winds,
Dandled the morning's childhood in their arms."
        Giles Fletcher, *Christ's Triumph after Death*, st. 3.

" The Summer Sunne hath guilded faire
    With morning rayes the mountaines ;
The birds doe caroll in the ayre,
    And naked Nimphs in fountaines."
Theorello, by E. Bolton, in *England's Helicon*.

From the deep gulf the horses of the Sun,
And forth from lifted nostrils breathe
  the light :—   171
A field for their encounter, underneath
The stately city's walls, both Rutulan
And Trojan warriors having meted out,
Arranged it ; and, within the centre, hearths
And turfy altars to their common gods.
Others alike spring-water brought and fire,
In apron mantled, and upon their brows
With vervain garlanded. There marches
  forth
A legion of Ausonia's denizens,   180
And javelined brigads pour from crowded
  gates.
Here all the Trojan and Tyrrhenian host
Swoops on in motley arms, equipped in steel,
Not otherwise than if the cruel fight
Of Mars should call. Moreover, in the midst
Of thousands do the generals themselves
Flit to and fro, in gold and purple graced ;—
E'en Mnestheus, offspring of Assaracus,
And brave Asylas, and Messapus [too],
Of steeds the tamer, Neptune's son. And
  when,   190

" From the red wave rising bright,
  Lift on high thy golden head ;
  O'er the misty mountains spread
  Thy smiling rays of orient light !"
        Langhorne, *Hymn to the Rising Sun.*

170, &c. " Hark ! hark ! the watchful chanticler
  Tells us the day's bright harbinger
  Peeps o'er the eastern hills, to awe,
  And warn night's sovereign to withdraw.

" The morning curtains now are drawn,
  And now appears the blushing dawn ;
  Aurora has her roses shed,
  To strew the way Sol's steeds must tread.

" Xanthus and Æthon harness'd are,
  To roll away the burning car,
  And, snorting flame, impatient bear
  The dressing of the charioteer."
        Charles Cotton, *The Morning Quatrains,* 4–6.

" Till, as a giant strong, a bridegroom gay,
  The Sun springs dancing thro' the gates of day ;
  He shakes his dewy locks, and hurls his beams
  O'er the proud hills, and down the glowing
    streams.
  His fiery coursers bound above the main,
  And whirl the car along th' ethereal plain :
  The fiery coursers and the car display
  A stream of glory, and a flood of day."
        Broome, *Paraphrase on Job.*

" For see, fair Thetis hath undone the bars
  To Phœbus' team ; and his unrivall'd light
  Hath chas'd the morning's modest blush away."
        J. Fletcher, *The Woman-Hater,* i. 1.

187.   ." All furnish'd, all in arms,
  All plum'd like estridges that wing the wind,
  Bated like eagles having lately bath'd ;
  Glittering in golden coats like images ;
  As full of spirit as the month of May,
  And gorgeous as the sun at midsummer."
        Shakespeare, 1 *K. Henry IV.,* iv. 1.

The signal given, to their posts hath each
Withdrawn, down plunge they in the earth
  their spears,
And rest their shields. Then, pouring forth
  in zeal,
Dames, and th' unweaponed rout, and weak
  old men,
Of tow'rs and houses' roofs possession seized :
The others by the stately portals take their
  stand.
But Juno from the eminence, which now
Is Alban called,—then neither name at-
  tached,
Nor dignity, or glory, to the mount ;—
Gazing abroad, was poring on the field, 200
And both Laurentines' and the Trojans' lines,
And city of Latinus. In a trice
On this wise Turnus' sister she addressed,—
The deity—a goddess, who presides
O'er standing waters and the booming
  floods :—
This dignity on her the lofty king
Of th' Empyrean, Jove, for maidhood reft
Bestowed :—" Nymph, pride of rivers, of
  my soul
Chief favorite, thou know'st that thee alone
To all [the maids], whoe'er of Latian [birth]
Have mounted high-souled Jove's offensive
  bed,   211
I have preferred, and in a share of heaven
Have freely placed thee : O Juturna, learn,—
That thou mayst not upbraid me,—thy own
  woe.
Where Fortune seemed to suffer it, and
  Fates
Allowed affairs with Latium to advance,
I Turnus and thy city have bescreened.
The youth now see I with unequal fates
Engaging, and the day and hostile power
Of Fates approaches. Not this fight, not
  leagues,   220
View can I with mine eyes. Do thou, if thou
Dost aught more ready for thy brother's sake
Adventure, go ; it thee beseems : perchance
Th' unfortunate will better [fates] attend."
She scarcely these, when eye-drops from her
  eyes
Outpoured Juturna, and three times and four
She smote her dainty bosom with her hand.
" This," cries Saturnian Juno, " is no time
For tears : haste, and, if any means there be,
Thy brother snatch from death ; or wars do
  thou   230
Awake, and shatter their concerted league :
The instigator of thy daring I."
Thus having urged, she left her in suspense,
And troubled by a woeful wound of soul.
  Meanwhile the kings,—Latinus, of a frame
Gigantic, in a four-horse car is borne,

Whose sheeny brows around twice six gilt beams,
The token of his ancestor the Sun,
Encircle ;—Turnus in a chariot goes,
With twain white coursers, swaying in his hand   240
Two javelins with broad steel. From th' other side
The sire Æneas, source of Roma's race,
Blazing in starry shield and heav'nly arms,
And by his side Ascanius, second hope
Of mighty Rome, march forward from the camp ;
And in a spotless garment did the priest
Bring up the youngling of a bristly swine,
A ewe-lamb too unshorn, of two years old,
And to the flaring altars led the beasts.
They, with their eyes turned towards the rising sun,   250
Present the salted meal within their hands,
And with the steel the victims' temple-tips
They mark, and drench the altars from the bowls.
Then good Æneas, with his falchion drawn,
Thus prays : " Be witness now, O Sun, for me,
Who call upon thee, and this Land, for whom
Such grievous toils have I availed to bear ;
And, O almighty father, and O thou Saturnian consort, now more placable,
Now, goddess, I entreat ; and thou, famed Mars,   260
Who every war, O sire, 'neath thy decree
Dost bend ; on Springs, too, and on Floods I call ;
And what the Sanctity in Air aloft,
And what the Pow'rs be in the azure Deep :—
If conquest shall to Auson Turnus chance
To fall, it is agreed the conquered [side]
Shall to Evander's city draw away ;
Iulus from [these] regions shall retire ;
Nor shall thereafter the Æneans sons,
Renewing warfare, any arms repeat,   270
Or vex these realms with steel. But if to us
Shall Conquest signify that Mars is ours,—
As I the rather deem, and may the gods
The rather stablish it by their decree !—
I will not either on Italians call
The Trojans to obey, nor do I seek
Their kingdoms for myself. On equal terms
Let both unconquered nations meet for leagues,

Unending. Holy rites and gods I'll give ;
Arms let my consort's sire Latinus hold ;
My consort's sire his customary rule.   281
For me the Teucri shall my walls construct,
And to my town Lavinia deign her name."
Æneas thus the foremost [spake] ; thus next
Latinus follows, looking up to heaven,
And stretches forth his right hand to the stars :
" Æneas, by these same, Land, Ocean, Stars,
I swear, and by Latona's twin descent,
And Janus double-faced, and hellish power
Of deities, and by the hallowed courts   290
Of ruthless Dis ; may these the father hear,
Who with his levin ratifieth leagues !
I touch the altars ; I the central fires
And deities to witness take ; no day,
Upon th' Italians' part, this peace, or league
Shall rupture, howsoc'er events shall fall ;
Nor shall there any force with my consent
Warp me ;—no, if it should outpour the land
Upon the waves, in deluge blending it,
And crumble into Tartarus the heaven.   300
As this my sceptre," (for in his right hand
His sceptre wielded he by chance,) " shall ne'er
Shoot forth with filmy leafage sprays nor shades,
Since once within the forests, lopped away
From lowest stem, its parent [tree] it lacks,
And down hath laid through steel its leaves and sprigs ;
Erstwhile a sapling ; now the craftsman's hand
Hath prisoned it in ornamental bronze,
And giv'n it to the Latin sires to bear."
In suchlike words between them they the leagues   310
Established 'mid the nobles' presence. Then,
Duly devote, beasts stab they for the blaze,

253. It is very doubtful that the poet contemplated any difference between *aris*, v. 171, and *altaria*, v. 174, though he unquestionably contrasts the terms in *Ecl.* v. 36.

279. The poet intends his hero to be distinguished for religion : how far the man, who treated the unfortunate Dido as he did, was suited for an apostle, or a model, is another consideration.

292. This mention of Jove's thunder may refer to the vengeance he would take on perjury : so the Queen in Fletcher's *Queen of Corinth* :

" May the gods,
That look into king's actions, smile upon
The league we have concluded ; and their justice
Find me out to revenge it, if I break
One article."   Act i. 3.

299. " Hence, in old dusky time, a deluge came :
When the deep-cleft disparting orb, that arch'd
The central waters round, impetuous rush'd,
With universal burst, into the gulph,
And o'er the high-pil'd hills of fractur'd earth
Wide dash'd the waves, in undulation vast ;
Till, from the centre to the streaming clouds,
A shoreless ocean tumbled round the globe. "
    Thomson, *Spring*.

And draw the bowels from them while alive,
And pile the altars with the chargers heaped.
But to the Rutuli, sooth, long erewhile
Unfair appeared that combat, and their breasts
With changeable emotion are turmoiled;
The more so then, when closer they contend
With pow'rs unequal. Helps [this state of soul]
Turnus advancing with a silent gait,   320
And th' altar worshipping with downcast eye
In prayerful posture; and his sunken cheeks,
The wanness, too, throughout his youthful frame.
Which disputation soon as e'er Juturn,
His sister, saw gain ground, and wavering
The populace's fluctuating hearts:
Upon the centre of the troops, in shape
To Camers likened;—[one,] to whom belonged
A noble lineage from his ancestors,
And, from the valor of a father [gained],
A brilliant name, and he himself in arms 331
Thrice-gallant;—on the centre of the troops
She flings her, of their state not unaware,
And sundry rumors sows, and speaks the like:
" Doth it not shame you, O ye Rutuli,
For all, his like, a single life t' expose !
In count or powers are we not their peers ?
Lo! these are all,—as well the men of Troy,
As the Arcadians, and the fateful band,
Etruria,—in hostility to Turnus. If   340
We should, each second man of us, engage,
Scarce an antagonist have we. He, sooth,
To heav'nly powers, for whose altars he
Devotes himself, shall in renown advance,
And deathless through the mouths [of men] be noised:
We,—country lost,—shall haughty lords be forced
T' obey, [we,] who are idly seated now
Upon the fields." The feeling of the youths
By suchlike words is fired now more and more,
And through the troops a murmur creeps: e'en changed   350
Are the Laurentines, e'en the Latins too.
Those, who erewhile were hoping for themselves
Repose from fight, and safety for the state,
Now wish for arms, and pray the league unmade,
And feel compassion at th' unrighteous lot
Of Turnus. To these [thoughts] Juturna adds
Another greater [stimulant], and gives
A signal from the height of heav'n, than which

None troubled more effectively the minds
Of th' Itali, and by its ill portent   360
Deceived. For, flying in the ruddy sky,
Jove's tawny bird was chasing fowls of shore,
And noisy bevy of the wingèd host ;
When, swooping in a trice upon the waves,
The felon trusses with his hooky claws
A peerless swan. Th' Italians roused their souls,
And all the birds with screaming wheel their flight,—
A marvel to be seen !—and with their wings
Bedim the sky, and, forming in a cloud,
The foe they harass thro' the air, until   370
O'erwhelmed by force and by his very load,
The bird gave way, and from his talons dashed
His quarry in the stream, and flew afar
Into the clouds. Then sooth Rutulians greet
The omen with a cheer, and hands prepare ;
And first Tolumnius the augur cries :
" 'Twas this, this, what with prayers I often sought :
I welcome it, and recognise the gods.
With me, with me, your leader, seize the sword,
O wretched, whom a felon foreigner   380
Thro' battle strikes with fear, as weakly birds,
And ravages with violence your coasts.
To flight shall he resort, and set his sails
Afar upon the deep. With one consent
Do ye compact your squadrons, and your king,

365. " A cast of haggard falcons, by me mann'd,
Eying the prey at first, appear as if
They did turn tail ; but with their labouring wings
Getting above her, with a thought their pinions
Cleaving the purer element, make in,
And by turns bind with her ;* the frighted fowl,
Lying at her defence upon her back,
With her dreadful beak, awhile defers her death."
                           Massinger, *The Guardian.*

370. " Have you not seen, when, whistled from the fist,
Some falcon stoops at what her eye design'd,
And with her eagerness the quarry miss'd,
Straight flies at check, and clips it down the wind?
" The dastard crow, that to the wood made wing,
And sees the groves no shelter can afford,
With her loud kaws her craven kind does bring,
Who safe in numbers cuff the noble bird."
                      Dryden, *Annus Mirabilis,* 86, 7.

Spenser somewhat differently :
" Like as a goshauke, that in foote doth beare
A trembling culver, having spide on hight
An eagle that with plumy wings doth sheare
The subtile ayre stouping with all his might,
The quarrey throwes to ground with fell despight."
                           F. Q., iii. 7, 39.

* " Bind with her ;" a term in falconry, meaning to *seize.* See Gifford's note.

Reft from you, in the battle guard." He said,
And on the foes confronted to him hurled
A javelin, as he forward runs. A twang
Emits the whirring corneil, and the air 389
Unerring cuts. At once this [feat is done],
At once a mighty shout,—and all the rows
Are troubled, and with turmoil heated be
Their hearts. The flying spear, as by a chance
Nine brothers' fairest forms against it stood,—
Whom had, so many, one true Tyrrhene wife
Borne to Gylippus [of] Arcadian [line];—
Of these, one at the midriff, where the belt,
With stitches joined, is by his stomach chafed,
And gripes a brooch the meetings of its ends,—
A youth preeminent in comeliness, 400
And beaming arms;—transpierces in the ribs,
And flings him forward on the golden sand.
Yet do the brotherhood,—a mettled troop,
And fired by grief,—with hands some draw their swords,
Some clutch the missive steel, and blindly rush :
'Gainst whom the bands of the Laurentines dash
Amain. Next Trojans overflow in crowds
Once more, and Agyllini, Arcads too,
With their bepainted arms. Thus one desire
Holds all,—the strife to settle with the steel.
They've sacked the altars ; all through heav'n there shoots 411
A rageful hurricane of darts, and down
An iron shower sluices ; bowls alike
And hearths they carry off. Latinus' self
Decamps, conveying back his outraged gods,
The league dissolved. Their chariots others yoke,
Or mount them with a vault upon their steeds,
And with their falchions drawn do they appear.
Messapus, eager to upset the league,
With his confronted charger scares away
A king, and wearing th' emblem of a king,
Tyrrhene Aulestes : he retreating falls,
And on the altars, planted in his way 423
Behind him, he, the pitiable [man]
Is on his head and shoulders tossed abroad.
But hot flies up Messapus with a lance,
And with his beamy weapon from above,
Aloft upon his horse, as many a prayer
He offers, sorely smites him, and thus speaks:
" He has it ! to the mighty gods is given
This richer sacrifice." Together run 431
The Itali, and strip his tepid limbs.
To meet [the foeman] Corynæus grasps

A brand from off the altar partly burnt,
And with the flames the face of Ebusus
Assails he, as he comes and aims a blow.
Gleamed his huge beard, and, singed, gave forth a scent.
The other, following on, with his left hand
The tresses of the wildered foeman grasps,
And, leaning on him with imbedded knee,
He rivets him to earth : in such a plight
He smites his side with his unbending blade.
On Alsus, shepherd, and in foremost line
While dashing through the darts, with naked sword 444
Does Podalirius, dogging him, o'erhang :
With axe drawn back the middle brow and chin
Of his antagonist he rives apart,
And wide his armor dews with spattered gore.
Stern rest and steely slumber press his eyes ;
Their orbs are sealed for everlasting night.
But good Æneas stretched out his right hand, 451
Unweaponed, with uncovered head, and called
His [comrades] with the outcry : " Whither rush ?
Or what that sudden strife that rises up ?
O curb your anger ! Now the league is struck,
And all its terms arranged. The right t' engage
Is mine alone : let me ; and banish fears.
The leagues will I make stable with my hand ;
These holy rites now Turnus owe to me."
Amid these accents, right amid such words,
Lo ! to the hero whizzing on its wings 461
There flew an arrow ;—doubtful by what hand
'Twas driven, by what whirling power shot ;
What,—whether accident or god,—renown
So high may to the Rutulans have brought

---

449. Gray uses the same metaphor :
" Hie thee hence, and boast at home,
That never shall inquirer come
To break my iron sleep again
Till Lok has burst his tenfold chain."
The Descent of Odin, end.

450. " The sun sets on my fortune, red and bloody,
And everlasting night begins to close me :
'Tis time to die."
J. Fletcher, *The Double Marriage*, iv. 3.

452. " Anone one sent out of the thicket neare
A cruell shaft headed with deadly ill,
And fethered with an unlucky quill :
The wicked steele stayd not till it did light
In his left thigh, and deepely did it thrill.
Exceeding griefe that wound in him empight,
But more that with his foes he could not come to fight."
Spenser, *F. Q.*, iii. 5, 20.

The credit of the noted deed is sunk ;
Nor vaunted any in Æneas' wound.
Turnus, as soon as he Æneas saw
Withdrawing from the army, and the chiefs
Confounded, glowing burns with sudden
    hope. 470
He calls at once for horses and for arms,
And with a bound proud springs upon his
    car,
And manages the reins in his own hands.
Hov'ring around, he many a gallant frame
Of heroes gives to death ; rolls many o'er
Half-dead, or 'neath his chariot grinds the
    troops,
Or lances, seized, pours on them as they flee.
As when, aroused by icy Hebrus' streams,
The bloody Mavors clatters with his shield,
And, kindling wars, lets loose his fuming
    steeds : 480
They on the open champaign Southern gales
And Western breeze outfly : the farthest
    Thrace
Groans with the tramping of their feet ;
    and round
The features of grim Fear, and Wrath, and
    Stratagem,

469. Turnus was unfortunately too sanguine.
Glover beautifully illustrates Artemisia's retreat :
" With her last effort whelming, as she steer'd,
One Grecian more beneath devouring waves,
Retreats illustrious. So in trails of light
To Night's embrace departs the golden Sun,
Still in remembrance shining ; none believe
His rays impair'd, none doubt his rise again
In wonted splendour to emblaze the sky."
    Athenaid, b. vi.

479. " Devouring War, imprison'd in the North,
Shall at our call in horrid pomp break forth,
And when, his chariot wheels with thunder hung,
Fell Discord braying with her brazen tongue,
Death in the van, with Anger, Hate, and Fear,
And Desolation stalking in the rear,
Revenge, by Justice guided, in his train,
He drives impetuous o'er the trembling plain," &c.
    Collins, *The Prophecy of Famine.*

484. " Thou, to whom the world unknown
With all its shadowy shapes is shown ;
Who seest appall'd th' unreal scene,
While Fancy lifts the veil between :
    Ah, Fear ! ah, frantic Fear !
    I see, I see thee near.
I know thy hurried step, thy haggard eye !
Like thee I start, like thee disorder'd fly ;
For, lo ! what monsters in thy train appear !
Danger, whose limbs of giant mould
What mortal eye can fixt behold ?
Who stalks his round, a hideous form,
Howling amidst the midnight storm,
Or throws him on the ridgy steep
Of some loose hanging rock to sleep ;
And with him thousand phantoms join'd,
Who prompt to deeds accurs'd the mind :
And those, the fiends, who, near allied,
O'er Nature's wounds and wrecks preside :
While Vengeance, in the lurid air,
Lifts her red arm, expos'd and bare :

The escort of the god, are hurried on.
Like eager, Turnus 'mid the central fights
His coursers urges, reeking in their sweat,
Trampling upon his sadly slaughtered foes ;
The nimble hoof bescatters dews of blood,
And gore is trodden down with blended
    sand. 490
And now to death he gave both Sthenelus,
And Thamyris, and Pholus, this and that
Engaging close,—the other, from afar ;
[E'en] from afar both sons of Imbrasus,
Glaucus and Lades, whom had Imbrasus
Himself brought up in Lycia, and arrayed
In arms alike, or hand to hand to fight,
Or on the charger to outstrip the winds.
In other quarter on the midmost frays
Is borne Eumedes, ancient Dolon's son, 500
Illustrious in battle, by his name
His grandsire representing, by his soul
And deeds his sire, who whilom, when a spy
He sallied to th' encampment of the Greeks,
Pelides' car his guerdon dared to claim.
Him with another guerdon did the son
Of Tydeus treat for such his bold attempts ;
Nor does he to Achilles' steeds aspire.
When Turnus at a distance him espied
On th' open champaign, first with javelin light
Pursuing him throughout the stretching void,
He brings his twain-yoked coursers to a
    stand, 512

On whom that ravening brood of Fate,
Who lap the blood of Sorrow, wait ;
Who, Fear, this ghastly train can see,
And look not madly wild like thee ?"
    Collins, *Ode to Fear.*

" And him beside rides fierce revenging Wrath,
Upon a lion, loth for to be led ;
And in his hand a burning brond he hath,
The which he brandisheth about his hed :
His eies did hurle forth sparcles fiery red,
And stared sterne on all that him beheld ;
As ashes pale of hew, and seeming ded ;
And on his dagger still his hand he held,
Trembling through hasty rage, when choler in him
    sweld.

" Full many mischiefes follow cruell Wrath :
Abhorred Bloodshed, and tumultuous Strife,
Unmanly Murder, and unthrifty Scath,
Bitter Despight with Rancours rusty Knife :
And fretting Griefe, the enemy of life :
All these, and many moe haunt Ire
The swelling Splene, and Frenzy raging rife,
The shaking Palsey, and Saint Fraunces fire :
Such one was Wrath, the last of this ungodly tire."
    Spenser, *F. Q.,* i. 4, 33, 35.

Fletcher calls " Anger the twin of Sorrow."
    The Bloody Brother, iv. 3.

Ben Jonson has a magnificent description of
bloodshed in war ; *Catiline,* i. 1 :
" Slaughter bestrid the streets, and stretch'd himself
To seem more huge ; whilst to his stained thighs
The gore he drew flow'd up, and carried down
Whole heaps of limbs and bodies through his
    arch."

And from his chariot down he springs, and comes
Upon him half-alive and fall'n along,
And, with his foot imbedded in his neck,
The falchion wrenches out of his right hand,
And bathes it glitt'ring in his deep of throat,
And these withal subjoins : " Behold the fields,
And, [that] which in the war, O Trojan, thou
Hast sought, Hesperia measure as thou liest:
These guerdons they, who with the sword have dared   521
T' assail me, reap ; they thus construct their walls."
As his companion, with a hurtled lance
He sends Asbutes, Chloreus too, and Sybaris,
And Dares, and Thersilochus ; Thymœtes too,
Fall'n from his rider-flinging horse's neck.
And as, what time Edonian Boreas' blast
Roars on th' Ægean deep, and hunts to shore
The billows ; where the winds have plied [their force],
Clouds speed their flight from heav'n : to Turnus thus,   530
Where'er he cuts his way, the squadrons yield,
And, wheeled about, off dash the lines ; himself
His ardor hurries onward, and the gale,—
The car confronted,—shakes his flutt'ring plume.
Him, bearing on, and gnashing in his rage,
Phegeus did not endure ; himself he flung
Before the chariot, and with his right hand
Twisted aside the speeding coursers' mouths,
While frothing on their bits. Whilst he is dragged,
And hangs upon their collars, a broad spear
Him, undefended, reaches, and, infixed,
The mail twain-tissued brasts, and with a wound   542
The surface of his body grazes. Yet
He, turned upon the foe, with shield opposed
Advanced, and succor sought from his drawn blade :
When wheel and axle, urged in their career,
Him headlong drove, and pitches him on earth ;
And Turnus following, 'tween his helmet's base
And edges of his corselet-top, with sword cut off
His head, and left the trunk upon the sand.
Now, whilst deals conq'ring Turnus on the plains   551
These deaths, meanwhile have Mnestheus, and the stanch

Achates, and Ascanius their companion,
Within the camp Æneas placed, blood-stained,
Supporting with a long spear-end his steps
Alternately. He rages, and,—the shaft snapped off,—
Strains to out-wrest the weapon, and the path
To succor, which the nearest [lies], demands :—
That with the broad sword they would cut the wound,
And deep within lay ope the missile's shroud,
And send him to the battles back. And now
Stood by, of Phœbus loved before all else,
Iapis, son of Iasus ; to whom   563
By violent affection erst enslaved,
Apollo's self glad proffered his own crafts,
His favors,—augury, and lyre, and nimble bolts.
He, that his laid out father's destinies
He might protract, to know the pow'rs of herbs,

554. " Support your master, legges, a little further ;
Faint not, bolde heart, with anguish of my wound ;
Try further yet : can bloud weigh down my soul ?"
        Marston, *The Insatiate Countesse*, iii.

556. " Whom so dismayd when Cambell had espide,
Againe he drove at him with double might,
That nought mote stay the steele, till in his side
The mortale point most cruelly empight ;
Where fast infixed, whilest he sought by slight
It forth to wrest, the staffe asunder brake,
And left the head behinde : with which despight
He all enrag'd his shivering speare did shake."
        Spenser, *F. Q.*, iv. 3, 10.

562. Spenser adds the charm of music to the physician's care :
" Home is brought, and layd in sumptuous bed ;
Where many skilfull leaches him abide
To salve his hurts, that yet still freshly bled.
In wine and oyle they wash his woundes wide,
And softly gan embalme on everie side.
And all the while most heavenly melody
About the bed sweet musicke did divide,
Him to beguile of grief and agony."
        F. Q., i. 5, 17.

568. " From creeping moss to soaring cedar thou
Dost all the powers and several portions know,
Which father—Sun, and mother—Earth below,
On their green infants here bestow :
Canst all those magic virtues from them draw,
That keep Disease and Death in awe."
        Cowley, *To Dr. Scarborough*.

" Care and utmost shifts,
How to secure the Lady from surprisal,
Brought to my mind a certain shepherd lad,
Of small regard to see to, yet well skill'd
In every virtuous plant, and healing herb,
That spreads her verdant leaf to the morning ray.
He loved me well, and oft would beg me sing ;
Which when I did, he on the tender grass
Would sit and hearken even to ecstasy,
And in requital ope his leathern scrip,
And show me simples of a thousand names,
Telling their strange and vigorous faculties."
        Milton, *Comus*.

The practice too of healing, rather chose,
And fameless exercise the silent arts. 570
Bitterly chafing did Æneas stand,
While leaning on a mighty spear, with
   flocking vast
Of youths and of Iulus sad [at heart],—
By tears immovable. The famed old man,
In garb drawn back, tucked up in Pæon mode,
With healing palm, and Phœbus' sovereign
   plants,
Makes many an anxious effort all in vain;
In vain the barbs with his right hand he
   shakes,
And with his griping pincers grasps the steel.
No Fortune indicates the course, naught aids
His guide Apollo; spreads, too, more and
   more 581
Fierce terror on the field, and nigher lies
The evil. Heav'n now see they stand in
   dust;
And cavalry advance, and thick the darts
Amid th' encampment drop. A dismal cry
Ascends to ether of the battling youths,
And those that fall beneath remorseless
   Mars.
Here, by th' unrightful suff'ring of her son,
His mother Venus, shocked, culls dittany
From Cretan Ida, stalk with downy leaves,
And tufting with a purple flow'r: those
   herbs 591
To the wild goats are not unknown, what
   time
Have wingy arrows fastened in their back.
This Venus, compassed with a darkling cloud
About her face, brought down; with this
   the stream,
Poured out in sheeny basins, she impregns,
In secret healing it; and sprinkles o'er

The juices of Ambrosia fraught with health,
And perfumed panacee. With lotion this
Iapis aged, unknowing, stuped the wound,
And in a trice sooth vanished from his frame
All smart; at the wound's root stanched
   all the blood. 602
And now the arrow, as it tracks the hand,
None forcing it, drops out, and fresh re-
   turned
His powers to their former state. "His arms
Quick hasten for the hero! Wherefore
   stand?"
Iapis shouts, and first their souls he fires
Against the foe: "Not these by mortal
   might,
Nor by the mastership of skill, accrue;
Nor thee doth my right hand, Æneas, save:
A god more puissant acts, and sends thee back
To grander feats." He, eager for the fight,
His legs had cased in gold this side and that,
And loathes delays, and brandishes his lance.
When once his shield is fitted 'to his side,
And corselet to his back, with arms out-
   spread 616
He clasps Ascanius round, and, through his
   casque
The surface of his lips bekissing, speaks:
"Learn valor and true hardness, child,
   from me,

---

573. Iulus felt with Aminta:
      "Oh! but your wounds
How fearfully they gape! and every one
To me is a sepulchre: if I lov'd truly,
(Wise men affirm that true love can do wonders,)
These bath'd in my warm tears would soon be cur'd,
And leave no orifice behind. Pray, give me leave
To play the surgeon, and bind 'em up;
The raw air rankles 'em."
      J. Fletcher, *The Sea-Voyage*, ii. 1.

577. "What has been left untried that art can do?
The hoary wrinkled leech has watch'd and toil'd,
Tried every health-restoring herb and gum,
And wearied out his painful skill in vain."
      Rowe, *Lady Jane Gray*, act i.

594. "Here lights Hygeia, ardent to fulfill
Mercy's behest. Light she sprung
Along th' empyreal road: her locks distill'd
Salubrious spirit on the stars. Full soon
She pass'd the gate of pearl, and down the sky,
Precipitant, upon the ev'ning-wing
Cleaves the live ether, and with healthy balm
Impregnates, and fecundity of sweets."
      W. Thompson, *Sickness*, b. iv.

604. This whole scene may remind Spenser's readers of Belphœbe's curing Prince Arthur:
"Unto the woods thenceforth in haste shee went,
  To seeke for herbes that mote him remedy;
For shee of herbes had great intendiment,
  Taught of the nymphe, which from her infancy
  Her nourced had in trew nobility:
There, whether yt divine tobacco were,
  Or panachæa, or polygony,
She fownd, and brought it to her patient deare,
Who al this while lay bleding out his hart-blood
  neare.

"The soveraine weede betwixt two marbles plaine
  Shee pownded small, and did in peeces bruze;
And then atweene her lilly handës twaine
  Into his wound the juice thereof did scruze;
  And round about, as she could well it uze,
The flesh therewith she suppled and did steepe,
  T' abate all spasme and soke the swelling bruze;
And, after having searcht the intuse deepe,
She with her scarf did bind the wound, from cold
  to keepe."   *F. Q.*, iii. 5, 32, 33.

616. Glover has a fine passage, describing the parting scene between Leonidas and his family; at the end of which the following occurs:
      "On ev'ry side his children press,
Hang on his knees, and kiss his honour'd hand,
His soul no longer struggles to confine
Her agitation. Down the hero's cheek,
Down flows the manly sorrow. Great in woe
Amid his children, who enclose him round,
He stands, indulging tenderness and love
In graceful tears."   *Leonidas*, b. i.

619. "Ev'n present, in the very lap of love
Inglorious laid: while music flows around,

Success from others. Now shall my right hand, 620
By means of battle, render thee secure,
And lead thee through my noble guerdons. See
That thou [thereof] be mindful, when erelong
Thy age shall have advanced [to] ripe [estate],
And thee, as thou recallest in thy mind
Thy [fathers'] patterns, let alike thy sire
Æneas and thy uncle Hector rouse."
These words when he delivered, from the gates

Perfumes, and oils, and wine, and wanton hours;
Amid the roses fierce Repentance rears
Her snaky crest: a quick returning pang
Shoots through the conscious heart, where honour still,
And great design, against the oppressive load
Of luxury, by fits, impatient heave."
    Thomson, *Spring*.

" But happen what there can, I will be just;
My fortune may forsake me, but not my virtue."
   Ben Jonson, *Catiline*, iv. 6, end.

" Have a full man within you : . . .
Perfumes, the more they are chafed, the more they render
Their pleasing scents; and so affliction
Expresseth virtue fully, whether true,
Or else adulterate."
   Webster, *Vittoria Corombona*, act i.

" Who trained thee up in arms but I? Who taught thee,
Men were men only when they durst look down
With scorn on death and danger, and contemned
All opposition, till plumed Victory
Had made her constant stand upon their helmets?
Under my shield thou hast fought as securely
As the young eaglet, covered with the wings
Of her fierce dam, learns how and where to prey."
   Massinger, *The Unnatural Combat*, ii. 1.

620. " Without misfortune Vertue hath no glory."
   Marston, *Sophonisba*, ii. 1.

621. " Young Ned, for thee, thine uncles and myself
Have in our armours watch'd the winter's night;
Went all a-foot in summer's scalding heat,
That thou might'st repossess the crown in peace;
And of our labours thou shalt reap the gain."
   Shakespeare, 3 *K. Henry VI.*, v. 7.

626. " Hang all your rooms with one large pedigree;
'Tis virtue alone is true nobility :
Which virtue from your father, ripe, will fall;
Study illustrious him, and you have all."
   Ben Jonson, *Underwoods*, cix. 8.

Arcite laments to Palamon:
   " No issue know us,
No figure of ourselves shall we e'er see,
To glad our age, and like young eagles teach 'em
Boldly to gaze against bright arms, and say,
' Remember what your fathers were, and conquer!' "
   Shakespeare and Fletcher, *The Two Noble Kinsmen*, ii. 1.

He sallied forth, a giant, swaying in his hand
A javelin huge : at once in serried troop 630
Antheus alike, and Mnestheus, dash amain,
And from the quitted camp tides all the throng.
The field is then with dingy dust turmoiled,
And quakes with tramp of feet the startled earth.
Turnus beheld them, coming from the mound
In front; Ausons beheld them ; and a thrill,
Ice-cold, careered throughout their inmost bones.
Juturna first 'fore all the Latins heard,
And knew the noise, and frightened fled away.
He flies, and hurries through the open plain
His dusky brigad: as when towards the lands, 641
From constellation burst, a storm-cloud swoops
Along 'mid ocean ; ah ! in wretched swains
Their far foresightful hearts begin to dread :
'Twill downfall deal to trees, and overthrow
To standing corn ; all far and wide 'twill wreck :
Winds fly ahead, and waft a din to shore.
Such the Rhœtean chieftain leads his troop
Against the fronting foes ; they mass them close
All in compacted wedges. With the sword
Thymbræus ponderous Osiris smites, 651
Mnestheus Archetius, slays Achates Epulo,
And Gyas Ufens ; falls the augur's self,
Tolumnius, who first a dart had hurled
Against the fronting foes. A shout is raised
To heav'n, and, routed in their turn, the Rutuli
Show dusty backs in flight thro'out the fields.
Himself nor deigns to overthrow for death
Those turned away ; nor those with even foot
Closely engaged, nor those, who hurtle darts,

629. " In peace, there's nothing so becomes a man,
As modest stillness and humility;
But when the blast of war blows in our ears,
Then imitate the action of the tiger:
Stiffen the sinews, summon up the blood,
Disguise fair nature with hard-favour'd rage :
Then lend the eye a terrible aspect ;
Let it pry through the portage of the head,
Like the brass cannon ; let the brow o'erwhelm it,
As fearfully as doth a galled rock
O'erhang and jutty his confounded base,
Swill'd with the wild and wasteful ocean.
Now set the teeth, and stretch the nostril wide;
Hold hard the breath, and bend up every spirit
To his full height !"
   Shakespeare, *K. Henry V.*, iii. 1.

658.   " Merciful heaven!
Thou rather with thy sharp and sulphurous bolt
Split'st the unwedgeable and gnarled oak,
Than the soft myrtle."
   Shakespeare, *Measure for Measure*, ii. 2.

Pursues: he, searching, Turnus tracks alone
In the thick cloud; claims him alone for fight.
Shocked by this apprehension in her soul,
Juturna, manly maid, amid the reins   664
Metiscus, Turnus' charioteer, unseats,
And leaves him fallen from the pole afar.
She takes his place herself, and with her
    hands
The waving reins she guides, assuming all,
Alike Metiscus' voice, and form, and arms.
As when the dusky swallow wings her way
Through noble mansions of a wealthy lord,
And on her pinions round the lofty courts,
Her scanty diet culling, and the food   673
For babbling nests; and now in void arcades,
Now round the moistful pools, she twit-
    ters :—like
[To her] Juturna on the midmost foes
Is carried by the steeds, and, flying on,
Through all she passes in the speeding car ;
And here now, and now there, her brother
    shows
Exulting; neither does she him allow   680
T' engage his hand ; far flies she from the
    paths.
No less, to meet him, does Æneas thread
The writhing circuits, and the hero tracks,
And calls through scattered troops with
    thund'ring voice.
As oft as on the foe he cast his eyes,
And the wing-footed coursers' flight essayed
In his career,—the chariot, veered away,
So oft Juturna wheeled aside. Alas!
What could he do?   Upon a shifting tide
He vainly wavers, and discordant cares
Invite his spirit to opposing [plans].   691
At him Messapus, as in his left hand
By chance he wielded, fleet in his career,
Two lithe spear-handles, tipped with steel ;
    of these
One launching, aims it with unerring blow.
Æneas halted, and within his arms
His form he gathered sinking on his knee :
Yet swift the lance his helm-top bore away,
And from his head struck off the topmost
    plumes.
Then, sooth, upstarts his wrath and, over-
    matched   700
By stratagem, when feels he that the steeds,
Turned from him, and the car were driven
    back,
In many a word to witness calling Jove,
And altars of the violated league,

He now at length upon the midmost swoops,
And, dreadful through a favorable Mars,
Without distinction hideous slaughter wakes,
And all the reins of anger flings adrift.
What god can now to me so many scenes
Of bitterness, what [god] can in the song
The varied havoc, and the death of chiefs,
Whom all thro'out the plain, and in his turn,
Now Turnus, now the Trojan hero, hunts,—
Develop?   Was it thy decree, O Jove, 714
That in such fierce excitement should engage
The nations, doomed to live in endless peace?
Æneas Sucro of Rutulia[n birth],
This combat first the hurtling Teucri fixed
In [one] position,—causing him no great
    delay,
Receives upon his side, and where the fates
Are speediest, drives home the ruthless blade
Right thro' his ribs and fences of his breast.
Turnus, on foot encount'ring Amycus, 723
Down from his charger flung, Diores too,
His brother, smites the one with lengthful
    spear,
As up he comes, the other with the sword ;
And in his car the severed heads of both
Hangs up, and bears them stilling with their
    blood.
The other Talos to his death, and Tanais,
And brave Cethegus, three in one assault,
And sad Onytes sends, Echion's name,
And of his mother Peridia son ;   732
This [slays] the brotherhood, from Lycia
    sent
And from Apollo's fields ; Menœtes too,
An Arcad youth, detesting wars in vain,
Whose handicraft and indigent abode
Had been about the fishful Lerna's streams:
Nor were th' employments of the pow'rful
    known ;
And in a rented land his father sowed.
And like as fires, from diff'rent quarters
    loosed   740
Upon the parching wood, and coppices,
That crack with bay ; or when in swift
    descent

707. " Stand out, and witness this, unhappy Spain !
Lift up to view the mountains of thy slain :
Tell how thy heroes yielded to their fear,
When Stanhope rous'd the thunder of the war;
With what fierce tumults of severe delight
Th' impetuous hero plung'd into the fight.
How he the dreadful front of Death defac'd,
Pour'd on the foe, and laid the battle waste.
Did not his arm the ranks of war deform,
And point the hovering tumult where to storm ?
Did not his sword through legions cleave his way,
Break their dark squadrons, and let in the day?
Did not he lead the terrible attack,
Push Conquest on, and bring her bleeding back?
Throw wide the scenes of horrour and despair,
The tide of conflict, and the stream of war?"
    Pitt, *On the Death of Earl Stanhope.*

674.   " Her young meanwhile,
Callow and cold, from their moss-woven nest
Peep forth ; they stretch their little eager throats
Broad to the wind, and plead to the lone spray
Their famish'd plaint importunately shrill."
    Mason, *English Garden,* b. iii.

Adown from lofty mounts the foamy floods
Give forth a din, and hurry to the seas,
Each turning his own passage into waste :—
No slower Turnus and Æneas, both,
Dash through th' [em]battle[d line]s ; now,
    now their wrath
Surges within; their breasts are being burst,
Unknowing to be overpowered ; now
On wounds they rush with all their might
    and main.   750
The one—Murranus, vaunting ancestry,
And ancient titles of his father's sires,
And pedigree, all traced through Latin
    kings,
Headforemost with a rock, and whirling-cast
Of monstrous stone, o'erthrows, and flings
    him out
Upon the ground. Him 'neath the reins
    and yokes
The car rolled forward; with repeated blow
Down tramples him, above, the hurried hoof
Of horses, not regardful of their lord.
The other—Hyllus, as he hurtles on,
And rages hideously with passion, meets,
And whirls a javelin at his gilded brows ;
Stood in his brain, through helmet pierced,
    the spear.   763
Nor did thy right hand thee, most brave of
    Greeks,
O Cretheus, save from Turnus ; nor his gods
Bescreen Cupencus, when Æneas comes :
His bosom proffered he to meet the steel;
Nor did reprieve of bronzen shield bestead
The wretched man. Thee, Æolus, as well,
Laurentine fields saw perish, and the earth
Wide cov'ring over with thy back. Thou
    diest,   771
Whom could not Argive phalanxes lay low,
Nor the demolisher of Priam's realms,
Achilles : here for thee were goals of death;
A stately mansion under Ida [stands],
A stately mansion at Lyrnese [for thee],
In the Laurentine ground thy grave. So
    much

---

744. " Smooth to the shelving brink a copious flood
Rolls fair, and placid ; where, collected all
In one impetuous torrent, down the steep
It thundering shoots, and shakes the country round.
At first, an azure sheet, it rushes broad ;
Then whitening by degrees, as prone it falls,
And from the loud resounding rocks below
Dash'd in a cloud of foam, it sends aloft
A hoary mist, and forms a ceaseless shower.
Nor can the tortur'd wave here find repose :
But, raging still amid the shaggy rocks,
Now flashes o'er the scatter'd fragments, now
Aslant the hollow channel rapid darts ;
And, falling fast from gradual slope to slope,
With wild infracted course, and lessen'd roar,
It gains a safer bed, and steals at last
Along the mazes of the quiet vale."
                           Thomson, *Summer*.

The hosts are wholly on each other turned,
E'en all the Latins, all the Dardan sons :
Mnestheus, and keen Serestus, and Mes-
    sapus,   780
Steeds-tamer, and Asilas brave, and band
Of Tuscans, and Evander's Arcad wings.
According to their strength the warriors each
Strive with the utmost effort of their powers:
Nor stay, nor rest ; in struggle vast they
    strain.
   Here did his fairest mother send the
    thought
T' Æneas, to the walls to march, and turn
His army to the city with despatch,
And with a sudden slaughter to confound
The Latins. He, when through the diff'rent
    ranks   790
In tracking Turnus, he this side and that
His eyes turned round, the city sees exempt
From war so sore, and unchastised at ease.
Forthwith the notion of a grander fray
Inflames him. Mnestheus and Sergestus he
Calls up, and brave Serestus, chiefs, and takes
Possession of a knoll ; to which [resort]
Flocks the remaining host of Teucer's sons;
Neither their bucklers or their darts do they,
Close[-filed], lay down. Upon the lofty
    mound   800
He, standing central, speaks : "Be no demur
To my injunctions ; Jove on this side stands:
Nor may there any, from the suddenness
Of my emprise, for me the slower move.
To-day the city, of the war the cause,
Latinus' very realm, unless they pledge
    themselves
To take the bit, and conquered to succumb,
Will I uproot, and even with the earth
Their smoking roof-tops lay. Am I, for-
    sooth,
To wait till please it Turnus to endure 810
Our fight, and he again may choose t' en-
    gage,
[Though] conquered? This the head, O
    citizens,
This is the front of the accursèd war.
Bring torches quick, and redemand the
    league
With blazes." He had said, and they at
    once
With emulating souls all form a wedge,
And in a mass compacted, to the walls
Are hurried forward. Unexpectedly
Have ladders and a sudden fire appeared.
Some run from diff'rent quarters to the gates
And massacre the first ; some whirl the steel,
And overshade the welkin with their darts.
Himself Æneas, 'mid the foremost ranks,
His right hand stretches forth below the
    walls,   824

And chides Latinus with a thund'ring voice;
And calls the gods to witness, that again
To battles is he driven; that now twice
Th' Italians were become his foes; that this
Was now the second league which had been
broke.
Up springs among the quaking citizens 830
A strife. Some bid the city to unbar,
And ope the portals to the Dardan sons,
And to the ramparts drag their very king;
Arms others bear, and march to guard the
walls.
As when, within a shroudy pumice-rock
Ensconced, a shepherd hath [a swarm of]
bees
Traced out, and filled it up with pungent
smoke;
They in the inside, trembling for the state,
Throughout their camp of wax run to and fro,
And with their lusty buzzings whet their
wrath; 840
A sooty stench is volumed to the roofs:
Then with mysterious humming ring the
rocks
Within; smoke rises to the empty air.
  This hap the harassed Latins too befell,
Which the whole city from its base convulsed

---

835.   " Through subterranean cells,
Where searching sunbeams scarce can find a way,
Earth animated heaves. The flowery leaf
Wants not its soft inhabitants. Secure
Within its winding citadel, the stone
Holds multitudes."   Thomson, *Summer*.

837. Or, more clearly:
" And filled [their home] with pungent smoke."

" Ah! see, where robb'd and murder'd, in that pit
Lies the still heaving hive! At evening snatch'd
Beneath the cloud of guilt-concealing night,
And fix'd o'er sulphur: while, not dreaming ill,
The happy people, in their waxen cells,
Sat tending public cares, and planning schemes
Of temperance, for Winter poor; rejoic'd
To mark, full flowing round, their copious stores.
Sudden the dark oppressive steam ascends;
And, us'd to milder scents, the tender race,
By thousands, tumble from their honey'd domes,
Convolv'd, and agonising in the dust.
And was it then for this you roam'd the Spring,
Intent from flower to flower? for this you toil'd
Ceaseless the burning Summer-heats away?
For this in Autumn search'd the blooming waste,
Nor lost one sunny gleam? for this sad fate?
O, man! tyrannic lord! how long, how long,
Shall prostrate Nature groan beneath your rage,
Awaiting renovation? When oblig'd,
Must you destroy? Of their ambrosial food
Can you not borrow; and, in just return,
Afford them shelter from the wintry winds?
Or, as the sharp year pinches, with their own
Again regale them on some smiling day?
See where the stony bottom of their town
Looks desolate and wild; with here and there
A helpless number, who the ruin'd state,
Survive, lamenting weak, cast out to death."
                              Thomson, *Autumn*.

With woe. The queen, when she the foe-
man spies
Advancing on the town, the walls assailed,
Fires flying to the roofs; on th' other side
Nowhere Rutulian bands, not any troops
Of Turnus;—evil-starred, believes the youth
In strife of battle quenched, and in her mind
Bewildered with the sudden pang, cries out
That she is source, and guilty cause, and
head 853
Of their mishaps; and, venting many a
word,
Distraught, in rueful frenzy, with her hand
Her purple garments she, about to die,
Asunder rends, and from a beam aloft
Inweaves the noose of an unsightly death.
The which calamity when once, in woe,
The Latin ladies learnt, her daughter first,
Lavinia, lacerated by her hand 861
In amber tresses, and in rosy cheeks,
Then the remaining throng around her,
raves:
Wide rings again the palace with their wails.
The wretched rumor hence is noised abroad
Through the whole city. They their souls
depress;
Latinus paces with his raiment rent,
Stunned by his consort's fates and city's
wreck,
His hoary hairs, besprent with dust unclean,
Defiling; and himself he much upbraids,
For that he had not heretofore received
Æneas [of] Dardanian [line], and him 872
Admitted freely as his daughter's spouse.
  Meanwhile upon the plain['s] remotest
[part]
The warrior Turnus hunts a straggling few,
Now more inactive, and now less and less
Delighting in his coursers' blest career.
The breeze this outcry wafted to him, blent

---

866. Shakespeare gives the following graphic
picture of a disheartened host:
" Why do you stay so long, my lords of France?
Yond' island carrions, desperate of their bones,
Ill-favour'dly become the morning field:
Their ragged curtains poorly are let loose,
And our air shakes them passing scornfully.
Big Mars seems bankrupt in their beggar'd host,
And faintly through a rusty beaver peeps.
The horsemen sit like fixed candlesticks,
With torch-staves in their hand; and their poor
jades
Lob down their heads, dropping the hides and
hips,
The gum down-roping from their pale-dead eyes,
And in their pale dull mouths the gimmal bit
Lies foul with chew'd grass, still and motionless;
And their executors, the knavish crows,
Fly o'er them, all impatient for their hour.
Description cannot suit itself in words,
To demonstrate the life of such a battle,
In life so lifeless as it shows itself."
                              K. Henry V., iv. 2.

With dark alarms, and struck his ears up-
  roused
The wildered city's noise and joyless din.
"Ah me! why be the bulwarks with a wail
So sore turmoiled? Or what such grievous cry
Bursts from the city on a diff'rent side?"
So speaks he, and distraught, with reins
  indrawn, 884
Stood still. And him his sister, as, trans-
  shaped
Into his charioteer Metiscus' guise,
Alike the car, and steeds, and reins she ruled,
Meets with such accents: "Turnus, by this
  [path]
Let us pursue the sons of Troy, where first
A passage conquest opes; there others be,
Who by their valor can protect their homes.
Æneas swoops upon the Itali, 892
And blends the frays; let us, too, with the
  hand
Upon the Teucri send remorseless deaths.
Inferior neither in the tale [of slain],
Nor glory of the fight, shalt thou retire."
Turnus to these: "O sister, e'en long since
I knew thee, when at first thou didst by craft
Unhinge the leagues, and gav'st thee for
  these wars;
And now, [though] goddess, thou deceiv'st
  in vain. 900
But who hath willed that thou, sent down
  from heaven,
Shouldst bear such grievous suff'rings?
  Is't that thou
Thy wretched brother's ruthless death
  shouldst see?
For what am I to do? Or Fortune what
Now pledges safety? I myself beheld
Before my eyes, calling me with his voice,
Murranus, [one,] than whom more dear to me
Survives no other, die, a mighty man,
And by a mighty wound subdued. Hath
  fallen
The luckless Ufens, lest he our disgrace 910
Should view; the Teucri hold his corpse
  and arms.
Our houses to be razed (this single [woe]
Was lacking to our state;) shall I endure?
Neither shall I with [this] right hand rebut
The taunts of Drances? Shall I turn my
  back?
And Turnus flying shall this land behold?
Is it so very sad a thing to die?
Ye, O ye gods below, to me be kind,

Since hostile is the will of gods above.
To you, a holy soul, and of that fault 920
Unknowing, shall I downward go, not e'er
Unworthy of my mighty ancestors."
  Scarce these he'd said,—lo! through the
    midst of foes
Flies Saces, carried on a foaming steed,
By hostile arrow wounded in the face,
And rushes forward, Turnus by his name
Beseeching: "Turnus, [resting is] on thee
Our last relief; have pity on thine own!
Thunders Æneas in his arms, and threats
That he will overthrow the topmost towers
Of Itali, and [these] consign to wreck; 931
E'en now the brands are flying to the roofs.
On thee their faces do the Latins turn,
On thee their eyes: the king Latinus' self
Is musing, whom his sons-in-law to call,
Or to which covenants himself to bend.
Moreo'er the queen, all-faithful [she] to thee,
Herself hath fallen by her own right hand,
And, frighted, fled the light. Before the
  gates
Alone Messapus and Atinas brave 940
Support the fight. Round these on either side
The phalanxes stand close, and with drawn
  blades
A crop of iron bristles; thou thy car
Art wheeling round upon a waste of grass."
  Mazed by the chequered picture of their
    state,
Was Turnus stunned, and stood in silent
  gaze.
Seethes mighty in a single heart a shame,
And madness with a mingled grief, and love,
By Furies racked, and conscious worth.
  When first
Were shades dispersed, and light was to his
  mind 950
Restored, his flaming eyeballs to the walls
He wildly rolled around, and from the
  car
Towards the great city cast a look behind.
But lo! with blazes volumed through the
  floors,
To heav'n there waved a crest, and seized a
  tower,—
The tow'r, which he himself with jointed
  beams
Had reared, and underneath applied the
  wheels,
And overlaid with bridges high. "Now,
  now,
O sister, do the Destinies prevail;

---

883. "What meanes this capering eccho? Or from
  whence
Did this so lively counterfeit of thunder
Breake out to liberty?
    "Tis from the city."
        Rawlins, *The Rebellion*, act ii.

920. "Then free from fear or guilt, I'll wait my
  doom:
Whate'er 's my fault, no stain shall blot my glory.
I'll guard my honour, you dispose my life."
        Smith, *Phædra and Hippolytus*, act ii.

Y 2

Forbear to stay me; whither calls a god,
And whither rigid Fortune, follow we. 961
'Tis fixed that with Æneas I engage
My hand; 'tis fixed, whate'er of bitterness
There is in death, to bear it; nor shalt
  thou,
O sister, me unhonored longer see.
Pray, let me rave this raving first." He said,
And from the chariot quickly made a spring
Upon the fields; and through the foes,
  through darts,
He rushes, and his sorrowed sister quits,
And bursts in fleet career the central ranks.
And as when from a mountain's crest a rock
In hurry rushes, by a tempest wrenched,—
Whether a rageful show'r hath washed it
  off, 973
Or stealing age hath loosened it by years,—
Adown the steep the felon mount is borne
With mighty swoop, and on the ground
  it vaults,
Sweeping away with it woods, herds, and
  men :
Among the scattered squadrons Turnus thus
Swoops to the city walls, where reeks full
  much
Of earth with gush of blood, and screech
  the gales 980
With javelins; and he beckons with his
  hand,
And with a lusty voice at once begins :
"Forbear now, Rutulans; and, Latins, ye
Your darts withhold : whatever Fortune is,
Is mine; it fairer is that I alone
On your behalf should expiate the league,
And [this our quarrel] by the sword
  decide."
All in the midst withdrew, and gave him
  room.
But sire Æneas, when was heard the
  name
Of Turnus, quits alike the walls, and quits
The tower-heights, and hurries all delays,
Breaks off all labors, bounding with delight,
And terribly enthunders in his arms : 993
As huge as Athos, or as Eryx huge,
Or huge as father Apennine himself,

---

977. Beaumont and Fletcher employ a similar
illustration with a wholly different design :

"Like a wild overflow, that swoops before him
A golden stack, and with it shakes down bridges,
Cracks the strong hearts of pines, whose cable-
  roots
Held out a thousand storms, a thousand thunders,
And, so made mightier, takes whole villages
Upon his back, and in that heat of pride
Charges strong towns, towers, castles, palaces,
And lays them desolate : so shall thy head,
Thy noble head, bury the lives of thousands,
That must bleed with thee like a sacrifice,
In thy red ruins." *Philaster*, v. 3.

When with his waving holms he roars, and
  joys,
With snowy crest uplifting him to heaven.
Now sooth in eagerness e'en Rutulans,
And Trojans, and Italians, all, their eyes
Turned towards them; likewise those who
  occupied 1000
The walls aloft, and those who battered with
  the ram
The walls below; and from their shoulders
  they
Laid down their arms. Latinus is himself
Astounded at the giant heroes, born
In distant quarters of the universe,
In mutual fight engaging, and [the strife]
Deciding by the sword. Now they, what
  time
The plains lay open with a vacant sward,
In swift advance, with lances hurled from far,
Commence the fray with shields and clank-
  ing bronze. 1010
The earth gives forth a groaning; then
  with swords
Repeated blows do they redouble : chance
And bravery are blent in one. And as,
In vasty Sila, or Taburnus' crest,
What time two bulls with brows confronted
  rush
Upon the hostile frays; in fright have fled

---

999. "Methinks I see Death and the Furies waiting
What we will do, and all the heaven at leisure
For the great spectacle."
  Ben Jonson, *Catiline*, v. 5.

1012. "Each at the head
Levell'd his deadly aim; their fatal hands
No second stroke intend; and such a frown
Each cast at the other, as when two black clouds,
With Heaven's artillery fraught, come rattling on
Over the Caspian, then stand front to front,
Hovering a space, till winds the signal blow
To join their dark encounter in mid air :
So frown'd the mighty combatants, that Hell
Grew darker at their frown, so match'd they stood;
For never but once more was either like
To meet so great a foe." Milton, *P. L.*, b. ii.

"Now waved their fiery swords, and in the air
Made horrid circles; two broad suns their shields
Blazed opposite, while Expectation stood
In horror. From each hand with speed retired,
Where erst was thickest fight, the angelic throng,
And left large field, unsafe within the wind
Of such commotion; such as, to set forth
Great things by small, if, Nature's concord broke,
Among the constellations war were sprung,
Two planets, rushing from aspect malign
Of fiercest opposition, in mid sky
Should combat, and their jarring spheres con-
  found." *Ibid.*, b. vi.

1016, 17. So Shakespeare makes the Severn flee
at the sight of the encounter between Mortimer and
Glendower :

"Three times they breath'd, and three times did
  they drink,
Upon agreement, of swift Severn's flood;

The herdsmen! all the flock stands dumb with fear,
And muse the heifers who shall rule the lawn,
Whom all the droves should follow: 'tween them they
With lusty violence commingle wounds,
And, as they butt, their horns infix, and bathe 1021
Their necks and shoulders with abundant blood;
The pasture all rebellows with their roar.
Not otherwise Æneas, sprung from Troy,
And th' Daunian hero with their bucklers tilt
Together; crash prodigious fills the sky.
Jove's self twain scales with balanced tongue upholds,
And puts therein the diff'rent fates of both:—
Whom may his travail doom, and whither Death
May with his weight incline. Here forward springs 1030
Imagining [he might] unharmed, and high
With his whole body rises Turnus up
Upon his sword uplifted, and he strikes.
The Trojans and the quaking Latins shriek,
And hosts of both are lifted [in suspense].
But broken is the traitor sword, and quits
[The warrior] as he glows amid the stroke:
[The prey of death,] save flight advance for aid.
He flees more swift than Eurus, when he viewed 1039
A hilt unknown, a right hand, too, unarmed.
There is a legend, that, in headlong haste,
What time he mounted for the op'ning frays
His collared steeds, his father's falchion left,
While he is in confusion,—he had seized
His charioteer Metiscus' sword, and long
This fully served him, while their flying backs
The Trojans offered: after that it came
To the Vulcanian armor of a god 1048
The mortal falchion, like the brittle ice,
In all directions shivered with the stroke;

The splinters glisten on the tawny sand.
Therefore does Turnus wildly seek in flight
The [field's] wide distant plains, and hither now,
Then thither, mazy circuits he inweaves:
For in all quarters with compacted ring
The Teucri hemmed him in; and on *this* side
A swamp immense, on *that* high walls, enclose.
Nor less Æneas, though from hamp'ring shaft
At times his knees obstruct him, and decline
The race, pursues, and hotly with his foot
Presses the foot of his affrighted [foe]. 1061
As if at times when lighting on a hart,
Imprisoned by a stream, or by the cord
Of crimson feather hedged, a hunter-dog
With speed and bayings plies him hard but he,
Scared by the ambush and the steepy bank,
Flies and flies back [again] a thousand ways;
But th' active Umbrian, as wide he gapes,
Is closing on him, and now now he gripes,
And, like to one [who's in the] griping [act],
Hath chided with his jaws, and is bemocked
With bootless bite. Then sooth up springs a shout, 1072
And banks and lakes return the echo round,
And all the welkin thunders with the coil.
At once the other, flying, chides at once
All the Rutulians, calling each by name,
And earnestly entreats his well-known sword.
Æneas, on the other hand, threats death,
And ruin prompt, should any one approach,
And frights the tremblers, threat'ning he would raze 1080
Their city; and [though] wounded presses on.
Five circuits they complete in their career,
And trace as many back this side and that:
For neither light or gamesome meeds are sought;
But they for Turnus' life and blood contend.
By chance, devote to Faunus, here had stood
A wilding-olive with its bitter leaves,
To seamen erst a wood to be revered,
Where, rescued from the billows, they were used 1089
To fix their off'rings to Laurentum's god,
And hang aloft their consecrated gear;

"Who then, affrighted with their bloody looks,
Ran fearfully among the trembling reeds,
And hid his crisp head in the hollow bank,
Blood-stained with these valiant combatants."
I Henry IV., l. 3.

1027. Milton imitates this at the end of the 4th book of the *Paradise Lost*.

Murphy introduces a new and pleasing idea:

"Heav'n holds its golden ballance forth, and weighs
Zaphimri's and the Tartar's destiny,
While hov'ring angels tremble round the beam."
The Orphan of China, act iii.

1038. The tutor must fill up the ellipsis in v. 733 as best he may.

1080. "We will assail you like rebounding rocks,
Bandied against the battlements of heaven;
We'll turn thy city into desart plains;
And thy proud spires, that seem to kiss the clouds,
Shall with their gilt tops pave the miry streets."
Heywood, *The Foure Prentices of London*.

Æneas may not have been absolutely unjust, for refusing to allow Turnus to get his own sword; but he lost a good opportunity of earning a character for magnanimity.

But its religious stem had Teucer's sons
With no distinction cleared away, that they
Might hurtle on a naked field. Here stood
The javelin of Æneas; to this spot
His whelming impulse had transported it,
And kept it firmed within th' unyielding
    root.
Leaned Dardanus' descendant [to the toil],
And with his hand was minded to out-wrest
The steel, and with the weapon to pursue
Him, whom he could not capture in the race.
Then sooth, distraught with terror, Turnus
    cries: 1102
"O Faunus, pray have pity, and do thou,
O earth thrice-excellent, hold fast the steel,
If I have ever reverenced your dignities,
Which, on the other hand, the Æneadæ
Have treated as unholy by the war."
He said, and called the succor of the god
To no effectless prayers. For, struggling
    long
And dallying upon th' unyielding stem,
By no exertions had Æneas power
The clutches of the timber to unclinch.
While keen he strains, and presses on, once
    more 1113
Into the charioteer Metiscus' guise
Transshaped, the Daunian goddess forward
    runs,
And to her brother renders back his sword.
At which [her act], that it should be allowed
To the bold Nymph, in wrath drew Venus
    near,
And tore the lance from out the deepsome
    root.
They, lifted high, in armor and in soul
Refreshed,—the one relying on his sword,
The other, stern and stately with his spear,—
Stand face to face in panting Battle's fray.
    Meanwhile the monarch of almighty
        heaven 1124
Addresses Juno, from a golden cloud
Gazing upon the fights: "Where now shall be
An end, O consort? What in fine remains?
Thou knowest of thyself, and dost confess
Thou know'st, Æneas as a hero-god 1130
Is due to heav'n, and by the Destinies
Is wafted to the stars. What plannest thou?
Or with what hope among the icy clouds
Dost linger? Was it seemly that a god
Should be dishonored by a mortal wound?
Or that the sword,—for without thee what
    could
Juturna?—should when reft to Turnus be
Restored, and to the conquered strength
    accrue?
Cease now at last, and by our prayers be
    swayed.
Nor let such grievous anguish prey on thee

In silence, and to me thy gloomy cares 1140
Oft from thy honeyed mouth return. The end
We now have reached. By land or waves
    to vex
The Trojans thou hast had the pow'r; curst
    war
To kindle up; to mar the house; and blend
With woe the nuptials. Further to attempt
Do I forbid thee." Jupiter thus spake;
Thus, on the other hand, with crestfall'n look
[Spake] the Saturnian goddess: "Sooth
    because
That will of thine was known to me, great
    Jove,
Both Turnus and the lands, unwilling I
Have quitted; nor should'st thou behold
    me now 1151
Alone in [this our] skyey seat endure
Things worthy, things unworthy; but with
    flames
Begirt, I in the very line would stand,
And draw the Teucri to the hostile frays.
Juturna, I acknowledge, I induced
To help her wretched brother, and approved
Her making greater ventures for his life;
Yet not that she should javelins [hurl], nor
    bend
A bow: I swear by fountain-head of Styx,
That cannot be appeased, which is assigned
The single object of religious awe 1162
To gods above. And now in sooth I yield,
And loathing quit the fights. Of thee this
    [boon],—
Which by no law of destiny is held,—
I crave for Latium, for the dignity
Of thine: when now by their auspicious
    match
Peace,—be it so!—shall they adjust; when
    now
Laws and alliances they shall unite:
Command not that the soil-born Latins
    change 1170
Their ancient name, nor Trojans should
    become,
And Teucrians be called, or that the men
Their speech should alter, or should change
    their garb.
Let it be Latium; Alban be their kings
For ever; puissant be the Roman race
By prowess of Italia; Troy hath fall'n,
And suffer it t' have fallen with its name."
Smiling on her, [thus speaks] of men and
    things
The author: "Thou the sister art of Jove,

1163. "But prayer against His absolute decree
No more avails than breath against the wind,
Blown stifling back on him that breathes it forth:
Therefore to His great bidding I submit."
                        Milton, *P. L.*, b. xi.

And Saturn's other offspring : thou dost roll
Such mountain waves of anger in thy breast !
But come, and quell a rage conceived in
vain.   1182
I grant what thou dost wish ; and, e'en
     subdued
And willing, I myself resign. Their native
     speech
And customs the Ausonians shall retain :
And as it [now] is, [so] the name shall be :
Only, incorporated in the state,
The Teucrians shall sink. The form and
     rites
Of their religious [worship] I will add,
And make them Latins, of one language all.
The strain, which, blended with Ausonian
     blood,   .   1191
Shall hence arise, above mankind, above
The gods, in piety thou'lt see advance ;
Nor any race thy services alike
Shall solemnise." To these doth Juno bow,
And in delight veered round her mind.
     Meanwhile
She issues from the sky, and quits the
     cloud.
These done, the Sire himself within him-
     self
Revolves another [purpose], and prepares
To part Juturna from her brother's arms.
Twin Fiends are called by name " The
     Furies," whom,   1201
And Tartaran Megæra, dismal Night
At one and at the selfsame birth produced,
And girt about with equal coils of snakes,
And added stormy wings. These at the
     throne
Of Jove, and in their rageful monarch's
     court,
Appear, and sharpen ailing mortals' dread,
If ever fearful death and sicknesses

The king of gods designs, or frights with war
The cities that deserve it. One of these
Jove quick sent down from th' empyrean's
     height,   1211
And ordered her Juturna to oppose,
For a portent. She flies, and to the earth
With sweepy whirl is borne : not otherwise
Than, from the string projected through a
     cloud,   ,
The shaft, which, armed with gall of felon
     bane,
Hath Parthian, Parthian or Cydonian,
     shot,—
A cureless bolt,—flies whizzing and un-
     kenned
Athwart the posting shadows. In such sort
Night's daughter sped her way, and sought
     the lands.   1220
When once she spies the Ilian lines, and
     troops
Of Turnus, dwindled to the sudden form
Of [that] small bird, which sometimes on
     the tombs,
Or lonely gables, sitting in the night,
Late chants, of evil omen, through the
     shades ;—
Into this guise transshaped, 'fore Turnus'
     face
The fiend now swoopeth on, now swoopeth
     off,
Screaming, and with her pinions flops his
     shield.
His limbs strange numbness with affright
     relaxed,
And [stood] his hair on end with dread,
     and voice   1230

> Loose scarfs to fall athwart thy weeds,
> Long palls, drawn hearses, cover'd steeds,
> And plumes of black, that, as they tread,
> Nod o'er the scutcheons of the dead ?"
>   *A Night-Piece on Death.*

1208. Parnell shows that properly "death" is *not* fearful :

> " Now from yon black and funeral yew,
> That bathes the charnel-house with dew
> Methinks I hear a voice begin :
> (Ye ravens, cease your croaking din,
> Ye tolling clocks, no time resound
> O'er the long lake and midnight ground !)
> It sends a peal of hollow groans,
> Thus speaking from among the bones :
> ' When men my scythe and darts supply,
> How great a king of fears am I !
> They view me like the last of things ;
> They make, and then they dread, my stings.
> Fools ! if you less provok'd your fears,
> No more my spectre-form appears.
> Death's but a path that must be trod,
> If man would ever pass to God :
> A port of calms, a state to ease
> From the rough rage of swelling seas.'
>   Why then thy flowing sable stoles,
> Deep pendent cypress, mourning poles,

1228. " The ominous raven often doth he hear,
> Whose croaking him of following horror tells,
> Begetting strange imaginary fear,
> With heavy echoes, like to passing bells :
> The howling dog a doleful part doth bear,
> As though they chim'd his last sad burying knells :
> Under his eave the buzzing screech-owl sings,
> Beating the windows with her fatal wings."
>   Drayton, *Barons' Wars*, v. 43.

1230.   " I am thane of Cawdor :
> If good, why do I yield to that suggestion,
> Whose horrid image doth unfix my hair,
> And make my seated heart knock at my ribs,
> Against the use of nature ?"
>   Shakespeare, *Macbeth*, i. 3.

" I could a tale unfold, whose lightest word
> Would harrow up thy soul, freeze thy young
>   blood,
> Make thy two eyes, like stars, start from their
>   spheres,
> Thy knotted and combined locks to part,
> Like quills upon the fretful porcupine."
>   *Hamlet*, i. 5.

Clave to his jaws. But when afar she knew
The whirring of the Fury and her wings,
Juturna, his unhappy sister, tears
Her streaming tresses, marring with her
    nails
Her features, and her breast with clenchèd
    hands.
" What can thy sister aid thee, Turnus, now?
Or what for heartless me doth now remain?
By what device may I now stay the light
For thee? Can I to such a prodigy
Myself oppose? Now, now, I leave the
    lines.   1240
Affright me not, afraid, ill-omened birds :
Your pinions' strokes I know and deathly
    din ;
Nor 'scape me haught behests of high-
    souled Jove.
These for my maidenhood doth he requite?
For what vouchsafed me everlasting life?
Why are death's circumstances reft away?
Such grievous woes now surely I could end,
And comrade to my wretched brother pass
Among the shades. Immortal I ? Or what
Of my [enjoyments] will to me be sweet
Without thee, O my brother? Oh ! what
    earth   1251
Can yawn sufficiently profound for me,

1232.   " Those baleful unclean birds,
Those lazy owls, who, perch'd near fortune's top,
Sit only watchful with their heavy wings
To cuff down new-fledg'd virtues, that would rise
To nobler heights, and make the grove harmo-
    nious."   Otway, *Venice Preserved*, ii. 2.

1244. Had Juturna been more virtuous, she had
been more powerful. Even Clorin says :
                " Sure I am mortal,
The daughter of a shepherd ; he was mortal,
And she that bore me mortal : prick my hand,
And it will bleed : a fever shakes me, and
The selfsame wind that makes the young lambs
    shrink
Makes me a-cold : my fear says I am mortal.
Yet I have heard, (my mother told it me,
And now I do believe it,) if I keep
My virgin flower uncropt, pure, chaste, and fair,
No goblin, wood-god, fairy, elf, or fiend,
Satyr, or other power that haunts the groves,
Shall hurt my body, or by vain illusion
Draw me to wander after idle fires ;
Or voices calling me in dead of night,
To make me follow, and so tole me on,
Through mire and standing pools to find my ruin."
            J. Fletcher, *The Faithful Shepherdess*, i. 1.

1251.   " Then all is lost !
Why pauses ruin, and suspends the stroke ?
Is it to lengthen out affliction's term,
And feed productive woe ? Where shall the groans
Of innocence deserted find redress ?
Shall I exclaim to Heav'n ? Already Heav'n
It's pity and protection has withdrawn.
Earth, yield me refuge then ; give me to lie
Within thy cheerless bosom ; there put off
Th' uneasy robe of being ; there lay down
The load of my distress."
                Smollett, *The Regicide*, iii. 1.

And sink a goddess to the lowest ghosts?"
She thus much having uttered, veiled her
    head
With sea-green mantle, heaving many a
    groan,
And plunged herself within the deepsome
    flood.
Æneas presses on the other side,
And waves a weapon, vasty, like a tree,
And from a furious bosom thus he speaks :
" What after all is now th' impediment ?
Or wherefore, Turnus, now dost thou recoil ?
'Tis not in running that we have to fight,
'Tis hand to hand with ruthless weapons.
Turn thyself   1263
Into all guises ; muster, too, whate'er
Thou'rt able or by courage or by skill ;
Desire on wings the lofty stars to track,
And, jailed, to hide thee in the womby
    earth."
He, waving to and fro his head, [replies] :
" Thy fiery words, O savage, fright me not ;
Fright me the gods and Jupiter my foe."
Nor utt'ring more, he spies a monster stone,
An ancient stone, a monster, which by
    chance   1272
Was lying on the plain, a land-mark placed,
To settle disputation for the fields.
This scarce would twice six chosen [men]
    support
Upon their neck,—such frames of men as
    now
The earth brings forth. [This], seized with
    hurried hand,
The famous hero launched against the foe,
Uprising higher, and hasting with a run.
But, neither as he runs, himself he knows,
Nor as he walks, nor lifting with his hand,
And wielding the huge stone. His knees
    give way ;   1282
His icy blood has curdled with a chill.
Then e'en the hero's rock, through th'
    empty void
Whirled on, nor all the distance overpassed,

1270.   " Tell it, ye conscious walls ;
Bear it, ye winds, upon your pitying wings ;
Resound it, Fame, with all your hundred tongues.
Oh! hapless youth! all heaven combines against
    you !"
        Smith, *Phædra and Hippolytus*, act iv. end.

1272. Spenser had probably this passage in view,
when describing the last attack of Maleger on
Prince Arthure :
                " Thereby there lay
An huge great stone, which stood upon one end,
And had not bene removed many a day ;
Some land-marke seemd to bee, or signe of sundry
    way :
    *   *   *   *   *
The same he snatcht, and with exceeding sway
Threw at his foe."   *F. Q.*, ii. 11, 35-6.

Nor carried home its blow. And as in dreams,
When faintcy rest hath sealed the eyes at night,
In vain to stretch the eager race we seem
To wish, and in the midst of our attempts
Sink feeble down : availeth not the tongue ;
Suffice not in the frame familiar powers ;
Nor voice [n]or words ensue : to Turnus thus, 1292
By whatsoever might a path he sought,
Success the demon dread denies him. Then
Within his bosom sundry thoughts are whirled.
Upon the Rutulans he casts an eye,
And on the city, and demurs through fear,
And shudders at the swooping of the lance ;
Nor [sees he] whither he may 'scape away,
Nor with what power he may make advance 1300
Against the foe, nor anywhere descries
His chariot, and his sister-charioteer.
Against the waverer his doomful lance
Æneas vibrates, having with his eyes
Marked out the destined spot, and it from far
With all his body['s effort] on him hurls.
From mural engine shot, ne'er stones thus roar,
Nor from the flash burst forth such mighty peals.
In likeness of a sooty whirlwind flies,
Destruction awful bringing on, the spear,
And open lays the borders of his mail,
And farthest circles of his sev'n-fold shield ;
Through his mid thigh it hissing grides.
            Down falls 1313
The giant Turnus, smitten to the earth
With doubled knee. Uprise at once with groan
The Rutuli, and all the mount rebellows round,
And wide the deepsome groves return the cry.
He, lowly and in prayerful form, his eyes
And right hand stretching forward, saith :
" [This] sooth have I deserved, nor deprecate ; 1320
Enjoy thy fortune. If can thee affect
Any concern for an unhappy sire ;
I pray thee,—thou hadst such a father, too,

Anchises,—pity Daunus' eld, and me !
Or, if thou wouldest rather, robbed of light,
My body to my [friends], restore. 'Tis thou
Hast conquered, and the conquered stretch his hands
Have Ausons seen. Lavinia is thy bride ;
Persist no further in thy hate." Grim stood
In arms Æneas, rolling [round] his eyes,
And right hand checked, and still and still the more 1331
The wav'rer had the speech begun to bend;
When on his tow'ring shoulder there appeared
The luckless sash, and with familiar studs
The bawdrick of the youthful Pallas gleamed,
Whom, conquered by a wound, had Turnus felled,
And on his shoulders wore the foeman's badge.
He,—after the memorials of fell woe,
And spoils, he with his eyes drank in, inflamed
By frenzies, and terrific in his wrath :—
" Shalt thou, tricked out in plunder of my [friends],   1341

1290. " I strive to call, my tongue has lost its sound :
Like rooted oaks, my feet benumb'd are bound."
            Gay, *Dione*, iv. 1.

" But as in slumbers, when we fain would run
From our imagin'd fears, our idle feet
Grow to the ground, our struggling voice dies inward :
So now, when I would force myself to cheer you,
My falt'ring tongue can give no glad presage."
            Dryden, *Troilus and Cressida*, v. 1.

1328. " Soft beauty is the gallant soldier's due ;
For you they conquer, and they bleed for you."
            Tickell, *On the Prospect of Peace*.

1329. " *Isabella.* Yet show some pity.
Angelo. I show it most of all, when I show justice ;
For then I pity those I do not know,
Which a dismiss'd offence would often gall,
And do him right, that, answering one foul wrong,
Lives not to act another.
Isabella. Oh ! it is excellent
To have a giant's strength ; but it is tyrannous
To use it like a giant."
    Shakespeare, *Measure for Measure*, ii. 2.

Had the unfortunate Turnus fully known the man with whom he had to deal, he might, perhaps, have addressed him thus :

" When I have number'd
A few sad minutes, thou shalt be reveng'd,
And I shall never trouble thee. If this
Be not enough, extend thy malice further,
And, if thou find'st one man that lov'd me, living,
Will honour this cold body with a grave,
Be cruel, and corrupt his charity."
            Shirley, *The Constant Maid*, v. 3.

1340. " Forbear ! the ashy paleness of my cheek
Is scarletted in ruddy flakes of wrath ;
And like some bearded meteor shall suck up,
With swiftest terror, all those dusky mists,
That overcloud compassion in our breast.
You have roused a sleeping lion, whom no art,
No fawning smoothness shall reclaim, but blood."
            Ford, *Love's Sacrifice*, iv. 1.

1341. " Was't not enough that thou hadst murder'd him,
But thou must triumph in thy guilt, and wear
His bleeding spoils ? Oh ! let me tear them from thee !" Whitehead, *The Roman Father*, v. 1.

Be hence delivered from me?
'Tis Pallas, Pallas, victimiseth thee,

Gustavus Vasa differently:
"Thro' my ranks,
My circling troops, the fell Gustavus rush'd:
'Vengeance!' he cried; and with one eager hand
Griped fast my diadem; his other arm
High rear'd the deathful steel,—suspended yet:
For in his eye, and thro' his varying face,
Conflicting passions fought. He look'd,—he stood
In wrath reluctant;—then, with gentler voice,
'Christina, thou hast conquered! Go,' he cried,
'I yield thee to her virtues.'"
Brooke, *Gustavus Vasa*, v. 4.

What numbers might have said to Æneas:
"Thy narrow soul
Knows not the godlike glory of forgiving:
Nor can thy cold, thy ruthless heart conceive
How large the power, how fix'd the empire is,
Which benefits confer on generous minds.

And taketh vengeance on thy cursèd blood."
This saying, he within his hostile breast
The falchion hotly buries: but his limbs
Are with death-chill relaxed, and with a groan
The life disdainful flies beneath the shades.

Goodness prevails upon the stubborn foes,
And conquers more than ever Cæsar's sword did."
Rowe, *Lady Jane Gray*, act v.

And Æneas himself might have considered—
"That his virtues
Will plead like angels, trumpet-tongued, against
The deep damnation of his taking-off;
And Pity, like a naked new-born babe,
Striding the blast, or heaven's cherubin, hors'd
Upon the sightless couriers of the air,
Shall blow the horrid deed in every eye,
That tears shall drown the wind."
Shakespeare, *Macbeth*, i. 7.

ERRATA.

Page 2. Note, line 43, *for* "*tendenti*" *read* "*tondenti*."
,, 9. ,, ,, 150, ,, "Leneothoe" ,, "Leucothoe."
,, 50. ,, ,, 531, ,, "Antony" ,, "Antonio."
,, 54. Line 714, ,, "in" ,, "with."
,, 60. ,, 349, ,, "airs" ,, "airs?"
,, 80. Note, line 714, *dele* last line.
,, 84. *Dele* Note, line 106.
,, 95. Note, line 792, *for* "792" *read* "790," and *insert* "792" *before* "Ben Jonson."
,, 96. Note, line 820, *for* "792" *read* "790."
,, 168. *Before* quotation from Milton *insert* "967."
,, 173. In second column, last line but one, *read* "meed" *for* "mead."
,, 174. Line 18, *for* the second "as" *read* "while."
,, 177. Line 172, *insert* "do" *before* "I."
,, 202. Note, line 1225, *for* "fort" *read* "port."
,, 221. Line 1022, *for* "they" *read* "thou."
,, 264. ,, 88, *dele* "'s."

www.ingramcontent.com/pod-product-compliance
Lightning Source LLC
Chambersburg PA
CBHW021159230426
43667CB00006B/476